Win32 Perl Programming: The Standard Extensions

Dave Roth

D1399359

MACMILLAN
TECHNICAL
PUBLISHING
U·S·A

Win32 Perl Programming: The Standard Extensions

By David Roth

Published by
Macmillan Technical Publishing
201 West 103rd Street
Indianapolis, IN 46290 USA

FIRST EDITION

Printed in the United States of America

Library of Congress Catalog Card Number: 98-84226

International Standard Book Number: 1-57870-067-1

2001   00   99   98   4   3   2   1

Interpretation of the printing code: The rightmost double-digit number is the year of the book's printing; the rightmost single-digit, the number of the book's printing. For example, the printing code 98-1 shows that the first printing of the book occurred in 1998.

Composed in Palatino and MCPdigital by Macmillan Computer Publishing

Trademark Acknowledgments

Warning and Disclaimer

Publisher
Jim LeValley

Executive Editor
Linda Ratts Engelman

Managing Editor
Patrick Kanouse

Acquisitions Editor
Karen Wachs

Development Editor
Christopher Cleveland

Project Editor
Brad Herriman

Copy Editor
Keith Kline

Indexer
Tim Wright

Aquisitions Coordinator
Jennifer Garrett

Manufacturing Coordinator
Brook Farling

Book Designer
Anne Jones

Cover Designer
Aren Howell

Production Team Supervisor
Tricia Flodder

Proofreader
Megan Wade

Indexer
Tim Wright

Production
Cyndi Davis-Hubler

Feedback Information

At Macmillan Technical Publishing, our goal is to create in-depth technical books of the highest quality and value. Each book is crafted with care and precision, undergoing rigorous development that involves the unique expertise of members from the professional technical community.

Readers' feedback is a natural continuation of this process. If you have any comments regarding how we could improve the quality of this book, or otherwise alter it to better suit your needs, you can contact us at networktech@mcp.com. Please make sure to include the book title and ISBN in your message.

We greatly appreciate your assistance.

About the Author

Dave Roth is a prolific creator of Win32 Perl extensions, including Win32::ODBC and Win32::AdminMisc. As a leader in the Perl community, Dave has been featured at several conferences, including the O'Reilly Perl conference. He is the owner of Roth Consulting, which offers a variety of programming and network administration services, and a contributing writer for the Perl journal. Dave has been programming for over 16 years in various languages from assembler to C++ to LPC and Perl. His code is used to automate system processes at various sites, including the Michigan Department of Natural Resources, Carolina Wholesale Office Machine, and American Collegiate Marketing. Dave helped assemble and administer a state-wide WAN for the state of Michigan and has designed and administered LANs for Michigan State University.

About the Technical Reviewers

Jutta M. Klebe is an Engineer and a Microsoft Certified Professional (MCP) with 13 years of programming and operating system experience. After finishing the polytechnic as a mechanical engineer (Dipl.-Ing. in Germany), she has been working since 1990 as a system administrator. Jutta is responsible for the installation process of Windows NT computers and troubleshooting user problems in a heterogeneous network with UNIX servers, Windows NT servers, and Windows NT Workstations.

In her spare time she administers Webservers and develops internet and intranet applications using technologies like ActiveX/COM, HTML, Perl, C/C++, VB, VBScript, and JavaScript.

Jutta lives with her boyfriend in Hannover, Germany. She also does some biking in her spare time.

Joseph Casadonte (joc@netaxs.com) is an Engineering Manager for Manugistics, Inc. In his spare time he advocates the use of Perl to anyone who will listen, especially for use on Win32 systems (which he dislikes intensely but is forced to use). He also delights in writing Perl scripts to do the most trivial tasks. His Perl for Win32 page is at <http://www.netaxcs.com/~joc/perlwin32.html>.

Dick Hardt is a consummate Digital Age pioneer, an innovator and successful entrepreneur who knows the boundaries and lives to push them. As founder and CTO of ActiveState Tool Corp., Dick brought Perl to the Microsoft windows world. Under his guidance ActiveState has grown into the leading developer of Perl tools for Windows, while he himself has achieved recognition as the foremost authority on Perl in the Win32 environment. ActiveState leads the industry in providing professional tools for Perl developers, and introduced Perl 5 to the Win32 environment. Prior to ActiveState, Dick has developed Windows software since v1.03 and played a key role in the development the first commercial email programs; he also founded the West Coast's first Wezine. Not just content to develop innovative software, Dick is also committed to somehow combining his two other passions, ultimate Frisbee and Vancouver's lively lounge culture scene.

Acknowledgments

Anyone who has written a book can tell you that it takes more than just a writer to make it happen. The support I have received from the folks at Macmillan has been absolutely terrific; especially their patience with me while I learned more about publishing than I ever thought I would. In particular, I extend my thanks to my executive editor, Linda Ratts Engelman, and my development editor, Chris Cleveland. I also would like to thank Joe Casadonte and Jutta Klebe on catching my mistakes and giving me such astute feedback. The two of you are absolutely indispensable. Finally, I would like to express my gratitude toward everyone in the Perl community who has participated in extending this language. It is amazing and has incredible capabilities due, in part, to all of our hard work.

Dedication

This is for Nazli, my wonderful and beautiful wife and best friend. Without her patience and love I would never have been able to finish this project.

Contents at a Glance

Table of Contents

x   Win 32 Perl Programming: The Standard Extensions

Foreword

Welcome.

I have known Dave for several years now. He is the author of one of the more popular Win32 modules. Dave is a good guy. He tells funny jokes. Dave is also a good writer. And Dave loves Perl. He must. He spent a lot of time searching, poking, prodding, discovering and finally explaining how to use Perl to solve real problems on Windows.

If you are new to Perl, this book will show you how Perl can automate your computer systems. If you are familiar with Perl on UNIX, this book will help you tame Microsoft's OS. And if you are an experienced Perl for Win32 hack, this book will guide you through the twisted roads of the popular Win32 extensions.. But keep in mind that this book is a guide. The roads of Perl are constantly changing. But do not fear. With well over a million Perl developers, you have many travelling companions. So enjoy your journey with Perl and have the appropriate amount of fun.

Dick Hardt, CTO

ActiveState Tool Corp.

Introduction

Why This Book?

Microsoft's Win32 platforms (such as Windows 95/98 and NT) have become quite popular. The reasons behind this depend upon how you view the industry. Some believe that Win32 is so common because it is a good operating system. Yet others believe the sole reason for its popularity is due to its presence on practically every new PC being shipped. Regardless of the reason, it is uncontested that indeed more and more people are using the Win32 platform.

Along with this surge of Win32 users comes a surge of Win32 Perl programmers. These coders are unique from most others in the Perl community. They have been long pampered with the Microsoft Windows GUI environment which provides clever and convenient techniques to retrieve information. By using icons, graphics, sounds, and a host of other sense provoking resources, the ability to access programming documentation is effortless and even enjoyable.

The documentation that exists regarding Perl's Win32 extensions, however, is far from convenient. Typically it includes a list of functions, the parameters they accept, and a brief description of what each function does. But for a Perl programmer new to Win32 or to someone new to programming in general, such limited documentation can leave him lost, confused, and frustrated. This becomes self-evident if you peruse the Usenet's Perl forums where newbies post questions that others bemoan about being obvious or in some obscure FAQ.

This book takes aim at this issue and documents not only the Win32 extension's functions but explains what they do, why they do it, and goes into detail explaining what to expect as a result of the function. For many functions there are in depth details that give the reader not only the knowledge of how to use the extension but also when to use them.

Lack of Documentation

Since the Perl Win32 extensions generally are written and put out on the Internet without funding, it goes to reason that there would be a lack of documentation. After all, it takes enough time to create, test, and maintain an extension let alone write comprehensive tutorials. Any documentation that an author provides is just icing on the cake. Having written several extensions myself, I can assure you that it sucks up quite a bit of time maintaining them.

Since an extension is not really useful unless you know how it is used, it is reasonable to feel that documentation is quite important. The problem is that the lack of adequate documentation compounded with the need to study such information creates a knowledge void. This is far more prevalent with the Win32 extensions than it is with Perl in general. You can find a plethora of Web pages rehashing Perl's main pages but almost all of these are based on the non-Win32 specific extensions. This does not help my clients who are looking for documentation. They quite often ask me what the best resources are for learning how to use the Win32 extensions. My reply is that there are four basic avenues to follow:

Learning from the Net

The Internet is a wealth of information on the Win32 extensions. Chapter 1 and Chapter 11 list Internet resources that are very valuable to anyone programming the Win32 extensions. Typically these resources are either very vague and not too helpful or they are very specific and technical but do not explain how one extension works with another.

Learning by Reading the Source Code

Studying an extension's source code is the absolute best way to learn how an extension works. This is where you learn the full details on how a particular extension implements its features and even uncovers undocumented features. It also lets you discover bugs that may explain why a function does not work as advertised. The biggest drawback of this way of learning is that many of the Win32 Perl programmers are either not familiar with C or C++ or they don't understand the Perl extension API. For those who feel comfortable with the C programming languages, Chapter 10 explains the details of a Win32 extension.

Learning by Experimentation

Experimentation is one of the most valuable ways to discover the uses of an extension. By creating test scripts that call extension functions in several different contexts, the treasures hidden within a Win32 extension can all fall into place. This particular style of learning, however, can be time consuming and lead to quite a bit of frustration.

Learning via Books

It is books like this that give the reader insight into the extensions. My book-shelves are filled with reference books ranging from Win32 and C++ to AppleTalk and cryptography. A good reference book is more valuable than gold to a programmer. It can save hours of calling up friends, accessing Web search engines and ripping apart header files. It is the aim of this book to find a spot on your bookshelf with other reference books that you find invaluable.

What You Can Expect from This Book

It seems that most Win32 Perl books that have come out lately try to address so much that the details are lost. It does me no good to have 10 books all lightly covering the same topics; I would rather have 5 books each addressing different topics in detail.

This book does not try to teach Perl nor does it try to explain the Win32 API. Instead it explain Perl's standard Win32 extensions. Everything from Chapter 1 to Appendix C revolves around these extensions: how to use them, when to use them, and how to understand them. Along the way I explain many aspects of the Win32 API, Perl, and other related topics, but focus on the extensions. This book was written to compliment good Perl programming and Win32 API books, not to replace them.

Who Would Benefit from This Book?

This book is not really for the Perl beginner. Someone just starting to learn the intricacies of Perl may find this resource a bit confusing. This is not to say that beginners should avoid it but they should understand that this book assumes at least a rudimentary understanding of Perl. Concepts such as regular expressions, scalar variables, hashes, arrays, modules, extensions, and others are routinely tossed around. If a beginning Perl programmer reads this text without a good resource guide to explain these concepts it will probably be of little use.

Just as a Perl newbie will find this book to be a bit more than he bargained for, so will someone with no Win32 background. This book assumes the user is familiar with Win32 concepts such as domains, user and group accounts, the Registry, primary and backup domain controllers, networking, and Remote Access Services (RAS).

Keep in mind that lacking an understanding of these concepts does not preclude anyone from reading and appreciating this book. It simply means that the reader may need to consult other resources to understand them. Some concepts, however, are described because of the nature of the topic. For example, the topics of COM, OLE, ODBC, and named pipes are directly related to the way particular extensions function. Therefore a rudimentary description of these concepts is provided to facilitate learning how to use their respective extensions.

So there you have it. This book targets intermediate and advanced Perl programmers who have at least a basic understanding of Win32 platforms. These readers can be very generally divided into five categories (for the sake of simplicity and brevity I will address only five):

Win32 Users

Users make up the bulk of the Win32 market. Some are forced to use it at work and others use it at home. Yet others fall into fringe categories, but none the less use the platform. Many of these people will eventually have needs to automate processes for a variety of reasons. Maybe they will want all temporary files deleted from the hard drive upon boot up. Maybe some will want to automatically download a Web page every hour. Who knows what would cause a user to want to learn Perl, but indeed users are learning it.

This book explains how most of the common Perl Win32 extensions work. While relating this information, it also explains many of the fine points that help clarify why a function may perform in a way that may not seem reasonable. Tips and notes also pave the way for any user who is learning either Win32 Perl or the Win32 platform (or both).

Win32 Administrators

Administrators have the greatest reason to benefit from using Perl. Having been a system administrator for WANs with thousands of users, I can say without any doubt that Perl has saved my hide too many times to count.

From simple utilities, such as logon scripts to automatic account creation scripts, Perl is an administrator's most indispensable tool. My colleagues and I have used Perl scripts as a poor man's Systems Management Service (SMS)—allowing me to install, update, and manage administrate thousands of client and server machines across LANs, WANs, internets, and intranets.

Win32 Administrators will find this book particularly important since it covers the most important administration functions. Topics such as user, group, and machine management are covered as well as permissions, sending messages, and file management.

Win32 Programmers

Sure you can program some rather sophisticated applications using C, Pascal, or Visual Basic but for quick prototyping I will bet that Perl would beat most any language hands down. The ability to quickly and effectively slap together a working script for a proof-of-concept project is one of Perl's great abilities. For example, I can write code that connects to an ODBC data source, queries the database, retrieves and processes the results faster using Perl than I can open Microsoft Access and create a query by dragging and dropping icons.

Any programmer will feel at home with Perl by her side. Even if she uses another language, Perl can still be the reliable tool that saves the day. Recently I had to walk through all the headers of one of our C++ projects picking out error messages and their associated error code values. The source tree was 38 megs of source code which equates to quite a few header files. By taking 10 minutes to write a Perl script I was able to process all header files in under 15 minutes (including the time to write the script)!

Programmers will find this book to be a valuable reference. Since Perl's Win32 extensions make copious use of the Win32 API any Win32 programmer will have a better understanding of which extension provides the best interface to achieve a desired goal.

Win32 Webmasters

With all the hype about the Internet, Webmasters have found it necessary to learn how to deal with programming issues such as Active Server Pages (ASP), Complex Gateway Interfaces (CGI), Data Source Names (DSN), user accounts logging on as services, permissions, and a variety of other issues. Of course Win32 Perl is a natural in these regards. This book not only addresses common traps that Webmasters fall into but it explains how to avoid them.

Unix Users

For our Unix brethren who have found it necessary to migrate data or machines to the Win32 world, this book can be a life saver. Perl's Win32 extensions can ease the migration by providing functions which are needed to make a Unix user's pilgrimage into the Win32 landscape a bit more familiar. This book covers topics such as scheduling batch jobs to run (similar to CRON entries), InterProcess Communication (IPC) such as named pipes, shortcuts (a kind of symbolic links), and permissions in addition to user and group management.

How This Book Is Structured

The way that this book is structured is a bit of a departure from other books that cover similar topics. It seems that most of them address Perl's Win32 extensions by name. That is to say each chapter covers a particular extension.

One of the biggest complaints I have received from coders on the Internet relates to not knowing what extension performs which function. Now consider this: If you don't know what extension performs which function, how useful is a book that assumes you know each extension's functionality? If you wanted to create a new user group, would you intuitively know to look up the chapter that covers Win32::NetAdmin? Or if you needed to get a list of the CD-ROM drives on your computer, would you know to flip to the pages that discuss the Win32::AdminMisc extension? Most users who have talked with me about these issues tell me that they would have no idea.

This book addresses this problem by designating each chapter with a programming topic. These chapters cover a topic that a Win32 Perl programmer may find useful from computer administration and automation to accessing database data and interfacing directly with the Win32 API. There are some extensions, however, that are so specific in their functionality that they really only apply to one topic, so they end up getting a chapter all to themselves (such as the chapters on OLE and ODBC).

The chapters break out into the following discussions:

Chapter 1: Why Perl on Your Win32 Machine?

This chapter discusses the history of the Win32 port of Perl. Exactly what extensions are and how they are used. This includes an examination of the differences between methods and functions. A discussion regarding how to handle errors when using Perl's Win32 extensions is also covered.

Chapter 2: Network Administration

Chapter 2 covers the basics of network administration. This includes discussions on how to discover the machines on your network, resolving DNS names, managing shared resources, and managing RAS servers.

Chapter 3: Administration of Machines

Details on managing a computer are discussed with emphasis on user and group accounts, user RAS privileges, INI files, the Registry and Event Logs.

Chapter 4: File Management

This chapter is all about files. Any user who is looking for information on how to manage file attributes and permissions would want to crack open this chapter. Win32 shortucts are also covered, including how to create, manage, update, and assign hotkeys to them. Finally the art of monitoring a directory for changes are explained.

Chapter 5: Automation

The ability to automate programs by using OLE is discussed in Chapter 5. Here you will learn not only what automation is but how it works and how you can use it to get the most out of Windows programs.

Chapter 6: Communication

Chapter 6 covers the details surrounding Win32 communication techniques of message sending and named pipes.

Chapter 7: Data Access

This chapter dedicates itself to accessing databases using the Win32::ODBC extension. What ODBC is and how your script can interact with it are what the you can expect. Since SLQ is the query language of choice for ODBC it, too, is discussed.

Chapter 8: Processes

Process management is covered with a emphasis on process creation. You will learn how to spawn a new process using various techniques.

Chapter 9: Miscellaneous

This chapter covers some of the miscellaneous tidbits that don't seem to find a home in the other chapters. Here a detailed discussion about controlling consoles (a.k.a. Dos boxes), playing sound files (in the .WAV format) and interacting with the Win32 API. Additionally, the miscellaneous functions found in the Win32.pm module (and extension) are discussed.

Chapter 10: Writing Your Own Extension

Whether you are writing an extension or reading the source code for an existing extension, this chapter explains the details that make it all make sense. Explanations of scalar variables, arrays, hashes, and references are provided. For anyone who has tried to read an extension's source code, this chapter describes the entire process.

Chapter 11: Common Mistakes and Troubleshooting

This chapter describes some of the more common problems that a programmer will run into when using Perl's Win32 extensions. This includes not only extension specific problems but also CGI and ASP issues are taken to task.

Appendix A: Win32 Perl Resources

This appendix is a detailed reference which illustrates the all of the functions in the extensions which are covered in this book. Each function's syntax is shows along with a brief description of what it does.

Appendix B: Win32::ODBC specific tables

There have been so many requests for Win32::ODBC constant and function details that I am providing this information in Appendix B. Here you will find a wealth of information regarding what functions ODBC supports and what constants unlock the treasures that await an ODBC user.

Appendix C: Win32 Network Error Numbers and Their Descriptions

With the so many possible Win32 network errors, this appendix provides a programmer a way to help figure out what a network related error really means.

Coding Style

Almost all programmers have a programming style that they use. Perl programmers are no exception. Unfortunately many of the styles used are not designed for clarity. This can be problematic for someone who is either new to the language or who has to read through pages upon pages of source code.

I have heard many coders tell me that they don't prefer my style of coding for a variety of reasons, but then again I have been told that my style is relatively easy to read. Since it is true that what one coder dislikes another coder adores, I think that it is important for you to understand my style.

Proper Perl Coding Style

It has been suggested that my coding style is not a *proper* Perl coding style. This is true. If you were to read the popular Perl coding books you will see an obvious distinction between my style and other styles. Whereas my style may not be a proper Perl style, I have to visit a long held notion that Perl programmers keep sacred to their heart, "There is more than one way to do it!"

Hungarian Notation

Generally speaking I make use of the so-called Hungarian Notation programming style. This is where the name of a variable begins with a prefix that indicates the type of data that the variable represents. For example:

```
$iTotal = 0;
$szName = "my test text string";
```

Here the `$iTotal` variable has a prefix of `"i"` indicating that the variable represents an integer value. The other variable `$szName` would represent a character string (in C parlance the `"sz"` is indicative of a NUL terminated string).

Now all of the hard core Perl readers are thinking, "Sure that is fine for C coding, but this is Perl!" Since Perl variables have the ability to morph themselves into whatever format they need to be in, prefixing the variable with a type indicator is not necessary. This is true. True, that is, until either a) your script becomes so large that it is considered a program or b) other (possibly non-Perl) programmers will have to read and modify your code.

It ends up that for many of my clients this style is absolutely invaluable. Some scripts that I have authored are large and are used in production environments by C++ coders. When they have to modify the Perl code it is helpful to understand what the variable's intention was: a boolean flag, a character string, a floating point number, a reference (a.k.a. a pointer), and so on.

Another part of the Hungarian style is the way case plays a role in a variable. Basically speaking the beginning character of a word is capitalized as in:

```
$iTotalSortedEntries = 33;
```

If you were to not use mixed case that variable would look like:

```
$itotalsortedentries = 33;
```

I find it much easier to read the first example.

Formatting

Throughout this book you will run into different formatting styles. Each style has a meaning that is important to understand.

Non-proportional Typeface

Generally speaking filenames, variable, code segments and the output of a script are listed in a `non-proportional typeface` such as:

File: `c:\temp\MyFile.txt`

Variable: `$CountTotal`

Code segment: `print "Welcome to Perl!\n";`

Output: `The file was unable to open.`

Bold

References to functions or extensions are **bold**:

You can find the **CreateUser()** function in the **Win32::NetAdmin** extension.

Brackets

When listing a prototype for a function, optional parameters are listed in brackets ([]). This means that whatever is in the brackets it not required. Typically you will see a comma in the brackets. This means that if the optional parameter is specified then the comma must also be specified:

`ScheduleList( $Machine [, \%List ] );`

If a reference to a hash (`\%List`) is passed into the **ScheduleList()** function then it must have the comma present as in:

`$Result = Win32::AdminMisc::ScheduleList( '\\\\server', \%List );`

If, however, the optional parameter is not passed in then the comma too is not specified:

`$Result = Win32::AdminMisc::ScheduleList( '\\\server' );`

Last Thoughts

Since starting to write this book in early 1998 there have been a great many things that have happened to the Win32 Perl community. Most notably is that the ActiveState and core distribution versions have merged into one comprehensive source tree and has been branded Perl 5.005.

It has been long speculated that when the merge took place there would be no longer a need to maintain several versions of an extension; one version for the ActiveState build and another for the core distribution. Unfortunately even though one source tree exists there are still two flavors: the object oriented version and the conventional non-object oriented version of Perl. Now this simply means that some versions of Perl use an object-oriented class (`CPerlObj`) for Perl's functionality (by defining a C macro called `PERL_OBJECT`). This is commonly referred to as ActivePerl (named after ActiveState no doubt). The other way to build Perl is the conventional non–object-oriented version. The end result is that Win32 extension authors still have to support both ActivePerl and the regular Perl 5.005. Extensions written for one will not work on the other. This is sad, but true.

There have also been many modifications to existing extensions in addition to an army of new extensions that have hit the community. This is great since it gives more functionality to Win32 Perl. It, however, becomes quite difficult to keep on top of all of them. This book addresses the so-called *standard* Win32 extensions. These are the ones that come with ActiveState's build 316 (as well as other builds) and Gurusamy Sarathy's LibWin32.

The context of this book was written using ActiveState's Perl version 5.003_07, build 316 unless otherwise specified.

By the time you read this there may have been changes to newer versions of the source code of both Perl and it's various extensions. An example is that in chapter 9 where a discussion of several functions from the Win32.pm extension is discussed. At the time of the chapter's writing the Perl 5.005 source code showed that certain functions had been moved out of the extension all together. However as we go to press, it appears that ActivePerl adds the functions back into the extension.

Chapter 1

Why Perl on Your Win32 Machine?

All operating systems have ways of automating procedures and tasks. Usually this is done by collecting a series of commands in a file and having some way of executing these commands. Typically, this is performed by a program called a shell. UNIX users have been fortunate to have a myriad of shells to choose from: the C shell, the Borne shell, and BASH, just to name a few. These shells are rich in function and can perform some complex command processing. You could even consider these shells programming environments. In the Microsoft operating systems, however, there has only been the command processor.

The command processor is the default shell for various versions of Microsoft DOS. This shell had minimal functions for processing batched commands. Administrators were forced to write programs in some language such as C, Pascal, and BASIC to perform the basic tasks they needed. Only the most simple of tasks could be automated using the command processor's batching capabilities.

History of Win32 Perl

Win32 platforms started to ship with a command processor that was modified to perform more complicated functions. These modifications, however, were far from sufficient for most administrators. It wasn't until Microsoft contracted with Dick Hardt's team at Hip Communications to port Perl to the Win32 platform that administrators had any hope of a decent freeware scripting utility. It was mid to late 1995 when the early versions of the Win32-compatible version of Perl started to find its way onto machines across the globe.

Not only did Hip Communications' Win32 Perl provide most of the functionality of the UNIX flavors of Perl, but it also extended itself into the Win32 API. This provided an interface into the Win32-specific world of administration. Now it was possible to not only process Perl scripts, but also to access the computer's Registry, event logs, user databases, and various other features that are found only on Windows 95 and NT.

Since the debut of Win32 Perl, there have been many so-called builds with each one fixing bugs and adding more functionality to its predecessor. Hip Communications continued to develop their version of Perl, build by build. To be sure, there were other versions of Perl that would run on the Win32 platform. Some were ingenious enough to implement things that eluded Hip's port, like the ever sought after **fork**() command (as the MKS port provided).

The Hip port finally gained acceptance by the Perl Porters group. There were technical differences between the original version of Perl and the Win32 version (for example Hip's port used C++ classes to encapsulate Perl's functionality). These differences kept the two versions of Perl (the original "core distribution" and Hip's Win32 Port) from merging together.

Since Hip Communications released the original version of Win32 Perl, much has changed. Hip has changed its name from Hip Communications, Inc. to ActiveWare. Then O'Reilly & Associates teamed with ActiveWare to bring about ActiveStateTool Corp. The Perl Porters group has been working together with Hip (then ActiveWare, then ActiveState) to make the core distribution compile and run on the Win32 platform. This is where we are now.

As of this writing, there are plans to roll the ActiveState version into the core distribution. The folks involved have done a tremendous job of maintaining backward compatibility with the old versions of Win32 Perl and Gurusamy Sarathy has been maintaining the standard library of Win32 extensions (known as the LibWin32 library) for the core distribution, which include all the extensions that ActiveState developed.

For most users, there is very little difference between the ActiveState and core distribution versions of Perl. The differences come into play more when an author writes an extension. Most scripts written on one version will run without modification on the other version. The place where differences really show up are with two pieces of software that ActiveState has created: PerlIS.DLL and PerlScript.

PerlIS.DLL is a clever ISAPI filter that allows an ISAPI server (such as a Web server) to quickly load and run Perl scripts. This filter does not cause the script to run any more quickly than it normally would, but it does speed up the loading of the script. On busy Web servers, this extension can make a noticeable difference in CPU use.

PerlScript is ActiveState's response to scripting languages such as VBScript and JavaScript. PerlScript can be used in an ASP (Active Server Page) page to perform both server- and client-side Perl processing.

Both `PerlIS.DLL` and PerlScript require the ActiveState version of Win32 Perl; however, after the two Win32 Perl versions have been merged, they should work on the core distribution.

Many independents have written additional extensions for the Win32 platform as well. Most of these extensions are specific to the Win32 platform, ranging from an interface into any dynamic link library files (DLLs) to Remote Access Services (RAS) administration functions. All these extensions provide an absolute wealth of functionality for anyone who administrates or even just uses Microsoft's Win32 platforms.

Some of the most valuable extensions are found on CPAN under the Win32 modules section (`http://www.perl.com/CPAN-local/modules/by-module/Win32/`). CPAN is a wonderful place to grab modules. Quite often, however, authors have updated versions of a module or even new extensions (alpha, beta, and release versions) available on their Web sites. Table 1.1 documents some worthwhile Web sites for information on Win32 Perl.

Table 1.1   Online resources for Win32 Perl

Site	URL	Contents
ActiveState's Web site	`http://www.activestate.com`	The ActiveState version of Win32 Perl and its standard extensions.
Perl.com	`http://www.perl.com`	The core distribution version of Perl.
Gurusamy Sarathy's LibWin32 library for the core distribution	`http://www.perl.com/CPAN-local/ports/win32/Standard/x86/`	This is a library of the so-called standard Win32 extensions tweaked so that they work with the core distribution version of Perl.
Aldo "dada" Calpini's Perl Lab	`http://www.divinf.it/dada/perl`	**Win32::GUI** **Win32::API** **Win32::Internet** **Win32::Clipboard** **Win32::Console** **Win32::Sound** **Win32::Shortcut**

continues

Table 1.1   Continued

Site	URL	Contents
Roth Consulting's Perl pages	`http://www.roth.net/ perl/`	**Win32::ODBC** **Win32::AdminMisc** **Win32::Pipe** **Win32::Message** **Win32::Tie::Ini** **Win32::RasAdmin**
Jutta Klebe's Web site	`http://www.bybyte. de/jmk/`	**Win32::PerfLib**
Gone Fishing.org	`http://www. gonefishing.org/ techstuff/`	**Win32::FileSecurity**

Additional information regarding modules and extensions, not to mention Win32 Perl itself, can be found at the following sites:

- **Joe Casadonte's Web site:** `http://www.netaxs.com/~joc/perlwin32.html`

- **Tye McQueen's Web site:** `http://www.metronet.com/~tye/`

- **Philippe Le Berre's Web site:** `http://www.inforoute.cgs.fr/leberre1/`

- **LibWin32 Documentation:** `http://theory.uwinnipeg.ca/CPAN/by-name/ libwin32.html`

- **Matt Sergeant's Database FAQ:** `http://www.geocities.com/SiliconValley/Way/6278/ perl-win32-database.html`

- **ActiveState's Win32 Perl FAQ:** `http://www.activestate.com/support/faqs/win32/`

- **Evangelo Prodromou's Win32 Perl FAQ:** `http://www.endcontsw.com/ people/evangelo/Perl_for_Win32_FAQ.html`

- **Robin's Perl for Win32 Pages:** `http://www.geocities.com/SiliconValley/Park/8312/`

There has been, and will continue to be, a huge influx of Win32 extension development. What is the justification for developing Win32 extensions? The following section defines Win32 extensions and explains why more people are taking advantage of the Perl environment for Win32 tasks.

Defining Win32 Extensions

Perl is a very rich language just by itself. It has networking functions, regular expressions and string, array, and hash manipulation functions. Perl can shell out and run other applications, open files, create pipes, and the list goes on.

One of the most ingenious aspects of Perl, however, is the capability to extend the language.

Perl allows itself to be extended in two ways: modules and extensions. Modules are just Perl code that you may want to use from time to time. If you appreciate and use certain functions (such as centering text on the screen or printing text backward), you could store these functions in a Perl module (a .PM) file. Whenever you have a Perl script that needs these capabilities, your script would just issue the Perl **use** command, as in:

```
use MyModule;
```

or

```
use Win32::AdminMisc;
```

From that point on, the script could use any function stored in the module. Quite simple, really. You need to follow certain rules when creating a module, well actually only two: The module must begin with the following command:

```
package MyModule;
```

Where the MyModule is replaced with the *case-sensitive* name of your module. This command can be followed by any Perl code that will initialize variables and perform any startup procedures that you might want performed.

The second rule is that the end of the main block of code must end with the following command:

```
1;
```

Yep, that is a number one followed by a semicolon. This will result in the module returning a TRUE value (the number 1). This tells the **use MyModule** command that it successfully loaded the module. If, for whatever reason, the module does not initialize correctly, it could return a 0 value (which would cause the **use** command to fail, resulting in the script failure).

Similar to modules are *extensions*. These are libraries of code written in another language (typically C). You can give Perl the capability to perform complex functions that Perl either cannot perform by itself or just would not be practical. If you wanted to have Perl compute PI to the thousandth decimal place, for example, it would be much faster to have a small C program do the work instead of Perl. Likewise, if you needed Perl to talk with a Sybase database server, you would want to write that functionality in C and have Perl access those functions, because Perl inherently does not know anything about Sybase servers.

When you create an extension, you also need to create a module that has the same name. When a Perl script uses the module, it will in turn load the extension as well.

Win32 Extensions Are DLLs

Creating extensions is usually a matter of writing a series of functions and storing them in a library of some sort. In the Win32 world, these extensions are in the form of a dynamic link library (a DLL). Win32 users are most likely familiar with DLLs because both Windows 95 and NT are filled with them. Files like KERNEL32.DLL, MSCRT.DLL, or VBRUN300.DLL are riddled throughout the hard drive. These files are, in the simplest of terms, a library of functions and resources. These functions and resources are available to any program that chooses to use them.

> ### Note
>
> *A DLL can have any mix of functions and resources. A resource can be an icon, a wave sound, a font, a dialog box, a menu bar, or a graphic, just to name a few.*

Imagine that you write a Web browser program. This program must be able to open connections to other computers across a TCP/IP network like the Internet. The code to perform these network activities can take up quite a bit of hard disk space. Assume, for example, that this program is 500KB in size. Of this size, also assume that 50KB is the network code. Now let's say that you write an email program. This program must also use the same 50KB of network code. Then you write an FTP program that accesses computers over the Internet, so it will, like the other two, need the same 50KB piece of network code.

Between these three programs, 150KB of your hard drive is taken up with the same code. This is a big waste of valuable drive space. It would be a great idea if you made a library of only these networking functions. All your programs could then just load the library and call the functions from that library. This way you only take up 50KB of your hard drive with the needed network code. This is the idea behind a DLL. Instead of having all network functions statically linked into each of your programs, they dynamically link to your single library of network code. This is exactly what the WINSOCK.DLL file is.

One of the biggest advantages of using DLLs is that they are discrete libraries of code. This means that a DLL is independent from other libraries or programs. Suppose that some program has a bug in it and the author has to fix it. If the bug is in the DLL, the author needs only to send the fixed version of the DLL to his clients. There is no need to send out the entire program again, because only the DLL was affected. Likewise if a program has a bug in it, only the program needs to be fixed and replaced, not necessarily any of its DLLs. Quite often you will see common DLLs such as VBRUN300.DLL (the Visual Basic

Runtime library version 3.00). These are DLLs that are required for programs written using a particular language (in this case Visual Basic).

Win32 Perl extensions are just DLL files. They contain code that can be called from a script. If you are using the core distribution, you will notice file names such as NetResource.DLL and OLE.DLL. For users of the ActiveState version, the files are called NetResource.pll and OLE.pll, presumably for Perl linked library.

Although ActiveState-based extensions end with .pll, don't be fooled, they are just DLLs that have been renamed. The core distribution and ActiveState versions of extensions, however, cannot be interchanged. That is, an extension built for the core distribution cannot be renamed and used with the ActiveState version of Perl. If you tried this, your Perl script would fail with an error message.

Parse Exceptions

ActiveState releases new builds of Win32 Perl every so often. Each new release corrects problems from previous builds and implements or updates functionality. Occasionally a new build will be released that has changed the way Perl works internally. These changes are invisible in scripts, but will break compatibility with Perl extensions.

Those ActiveState Perl users who have upgraded from one build to another might have run into this problem. You know that this is the case because you will see the dreaded Parse Exception error. This error has been the subject of countless emails and Usenet postings.

Just stated, a Parse Exception error takes place when you are trying to use an extension that was created for a version of Perl that you are not using. If you were using ActiveState's Perl build 310 then upgraded to build 311, for example, you might have seen the error message: Error: Parse Exception. What you would need to do is find a version of the extension that has been compiled with the header files from build 311. Usually the maintainer of an extension will make several builds available for just this reason—one for the core distribution, and a few for different ActiveState builds.

Not every new build causes parse exception errors. The builds that were compatible with each other are indicated in the following list (current as of this writing).

    106–110
    300–306
    307–310
    311–316

If you upgrade from build 306 to 307 or from 308 to 312, you will need to update your extensions.

The good news is that when you upgrade to another build of the ActiveState build, all the standard extensions (including the Win32 extensions) are updated as well. It is all part of the downloaded archive. You need only to update any nonstandard extensions—that is, any extension that does not come with Win32 Perl (for example, **Win32::API**).

> ### Warning
>
> *Make sure that when you unarchive Perl that file names are not altered. Some older versions of PKUNZIP and other de-archiving programs did not know how to handle long file names. This can result in the mangling of some very important files.*
>
> *If you are running into an error when running your scripts that indicates you are unable to find* DYNALOADER.PM *or some other file with a file name greater than eight characters, it might be that when you unarchived Perl, the file* DYNALOADER.PM *was renamed to* DYNALO~1.PM *by a program that did not know how to save a long file name.*
>
> *If you find yourself in this situation, either reinstall Perl using a more modern version of PKUNZIP (such as WINZIP or the like) or manually rename all the files. Because you might not know what the real file names are supposed to be, it is probably best to reinstall with a newer unzip program.*
>
> *More recent versions of Win32 Perl come as a self-extracting and auto-installing executable program. This takes care of all the details for you.*

Using Win32 Extensions

After you have Perl and its Win32 extensions installed, you are all ready to cre-ate Perl scripts that will make your life with Windows a bit easier.

If you have to install an extension, however, things can be a bit confusing. Sometimes when you download an extension you may end up with many files and very vague documentation on how to install the extension. There is really nothing to be concerned about, however. The process is very easy and makes total sense after you have walked through it.

Unless you have downloaded source code for an extension, the process of installing is usually just a matter of copying files to proper locations on your hard drive. If you have downloaded source code, you should probably read Chapter 10, "Writing Your Own Extension." If you have downloaded a binary (already compiled and built) version of the extension, all you need to know is where the files go.

Win32 Extensions and Directory Paths

The first thing you need to be familiar with is the Perl library directory. Perl maintains a directory of library files that are important and necessary for Perl. You may never write a script that uses any of these libraries, but you may well download a script that will. Unlike its UNIX-like relatives, Win32 Perl's directory names are not case sensitive. In other words, a directory that is named Perl could be spelled PERL, PerL, perl, or pErL. This is a feature of Win32, not Perl itself.

The Perl library is stored in a LIB directory just underneath the Perl root. On my NT computer, I have Perl installed in c:\PERL, which is my Perl root. The library is in c:\PERL\LIB. The library contains several files and directories. Two directories are of interest: AUTO and Win32.

The Win32 directory is where most of the Win32 extensions are found. This, of course, is why they are called Win32 extensions. When you specify that you are using **Win32::NetAdmin**, for example, Perl will look in the LIB (library) directory for a Win32 subdirectory. If this subdirectory is located, Perl then looks in this subdirectory for a NetAdmin.pm file. The module's associated DLL file will be sought for in the LIB\AUTO\Win32\NetAdmin directory.

The AUTO directory is the location of the DLL files. This directory contains a Win32 subdirectory (among other subdirectories), which will contain yet more subdirectories that represent the extension's namespace. The **Win32::NetAdmin** extension's DLL file, for example, will be located in perl\lib\AUTO\Win32\NetAdmin\NetAdmin.DLL.

If you were to use the **Win32::Tie::Ini** extension, Perl would look in the LIB\Win32\Tie directory for the Ini.pm. file. The **Win32::Tie::Ini** module loads an extension (the DLL file), so it will look for it in LIB\AUTO\Win32\Tie\Ini\Ini.pll.

In other words, when a module is loaded, Perl will look for it in a path derived by replacing the double colons in the module name with a single backslash. So **Win32::ODBC**'s module path becomes LIB\Win32\ODBC.pm. Extensions work the same way, except they are looked for in the LIB\AUTO directory and the extension name becomes the full directory path with double colons replaced by backslashes and the name of the file is the name of the module file replacing the .PM with .PLL. **Win32::ODBC**'s extension is located at LIB\AUTO\Win32\ODBC\ODBC.PLL.

If you are using the core distribution, there is a slight wrinkle in this. Win32 extensions are distributed in the same way except that module paths start with LIB\SITE and extension file paths start with LIB\AUTO\SITE. In the core distribution of Win32 Perl, the **Win32::Shortcut** module is located in LIB\SITE\ Win32\ Shortcut.pm and the extension file is LIB\SITE\AUTO\Win32\Shortcut\ Shortcut.dll. (Recall that core distribution extensions use the .dll file extension.)

This is a good time to point out that the "standard" Win32 extensions (those that come with the ActiveState version of Win32 Perl) do not come with the core distribution. A separate library needs to be installed for core distribution users. These extensions are not considered to be part of Perl itself (as some other modules and extensions are). Instead, if you install these so-called LibWin32 extensions it will be an option unique to your computer or site. An argument can be made that using these "standard" extensions is not unique because most Win32 Perl users have them, but they are unique to only Win32 machines because UNIX, Macintosh, VMS, and other platforms cannot use them. This is the rationale for using the site subdirectory where all the Win32 specific extensions are stored.

The good news regarding all this Path insanity is that ActiveState has introduced a new utility with their version of Perl 5.005 (also known as ActivePerl). This is the Perl Package Manager (PPM.PL). This clever script automates the entire process of locating, downloading and installing extensions from the Internet, making it rather painless to manage your Perl extensions.

By using this utility you can not only install but check for and update extensions. Additionally the script provides the capability to search for extensions (by author, name, or description), verify and even remove already installed extensions.

The Package Manager can be used for installing most any software package (in addition to Perl extensions). For those who either have or are planning on upgrading to Perl 5.005, this utility should be considered as a serious incentive to use ActiveState's ActivePerl. For more details check out their web site (http://www.activestate.com).

Loading Win32 Extensions

When you are going to make use of a Win32 extension (or any module or extension for that matter), you need to first *use* it in your module. The **use** command will load the extension into memory:

```
use Win32::Pipe;
```

Consult a Perl language reference for a full explanation of the **use** command, such as the de facto standard *Programming Perl* by Larry Wall, Tom Christiansen, and Randal Schwartz (O'Reilly & Associates).

After the **use** command loads the extension, your script is ready to call functions within the extension.

> **Tip**
>
> *Not all the Win32 extensions need to be loaded with a **require** or **use** command. The Win32 extension, the mother of all Win32 extensions, does not require the explicit loading of the **Win32.pm** module. This module is automatically loaded when Perl is launched. You can call any of the Win32 functions, such as **Win32::LoginName**() without ever having to load the Win32 module using a **require** or **use** command.*
>
> *There is some question as to whether this will be supported in the future when both the ActiveState and core distribution versions merge.*

Methods Versus Functions

Some extensions are just collections of functions that perform a task. The **Win32::NetAdmin** extension is a perfect example. You can call this extension's functions, which will perform some task and return a result of some sort. A function call into an extension requires that the full namespace be provided, as in Example 1.1.

Example 1.1   *A function call*

```
use Win32::NetAdmin;
if( Win32::NetAdmin::UsersExist( '', "rothd" ) )
{
  print "Rothd is a user.\n";
}else{
  print "Rothd is not a user.\n";
}
```

Other extensions are collections of functions that must be used together. Along with these functions are variables that must be kept in association with the functions.

An example of this is the **Win32::ODBC** extension. When you use **Win32::ODBC**, you are generally connecting to a database. If you need to connect to two separate databases, you must keep two separate collections of variables. This is accomplished using object-oriented programming (OOP).

The **Win32::ODBC** extension enables you to create an object using the **new** command. This object is a collection of variables and functions that all work together. The new object acts like a reference to a hash, which contain functions known as *methods*. These methods can modify variables that reside only within the object. Such variables are called *members*. An object's methods and members all work together as if they all existed in the same namespace. This means that if a member is created in an object, any method can alter it. Unlike a module or extension's function, which requires calling the full namespace (such as **Win32::ODBC::GetDSN**()), methods and members are referenced using a pointer as if you were de-referencing a key from a hash reference, as in Example 1.2.

Example 1.2   *An object's members and methods*

```
use Win32::ODBC;
$db1 = new Win32::ODBC( "Financal Database " ) ¦¦ die;
$db2 = new Win32::ODBC( "Order Database " ) ¦¦ die;
 # print the $db1 object's 'DSN' member (variable)
print $db1->{'DSN'}, "\n ";
   # Call the $db2 object's 'Connection' method.
print $db2->Connection(), "\n ";
print $db2->{'DSN'}, "\n";
print $db1->Connection(), "\n";
```

Throughout this book, references are made to variables, functions, members, and methods. It is important to note the difference, because calling directly into a method as if it were a function could result in incorrect results if not even a script stopping error.

Some extensions' functions can be called as both functions and methods. Their results usually depend on the context in which they were called.

Most extensions are documented either in a README file that comes with the extension, embedded POD code in the module file, or on a Web page somewhere on the Internet. Such documentation traditionally describes the module or extension's variables, functions, members, and methods.

> *Note*
>
> *POD (Plain Old Documentation) is HTML-like code that many authors embed within a module. This convenience provides users with the documentation as long as they have the module file (like* NetAdmin.pm*). You can download certain scripts that parse out the POD code and convert it to text, HTML, RTF, and various other formats. The script* POD2HTML.PL *is one such script that comes with the core distribution of Perl.*

Error Handling

Generally speaking, when Perl encounters an error it sets the variable $! to both the error number and the textual error message. This allows the script to determine the nature of a Perl-generated error. The variable ($!) usually reports system errors modules, and extensions generally do not touch this variable. Instead they use their own way of error reporting, which makes it difficult for a coder to discover error information because type technique differs from extension to extension.

The Win32 extension defines two very important error functions: the **GetLastError**() and **FormatMessage**().

GetLastError() Function

The **Win32::GetLastError**() function returns an error code for the last error that the Win32 API generates. It is important to keep in mind that the error number returned by this function is a Win32 API error, not a Perl error. The Win32 API will generate some errors of which Perl will not be aware.

Win32 API errors are generated when a task fails that requires the operating system to become involved. When Perl opens a file, for example, it passes the request to the operating system. If the OS cannot open the file, it will generate its own error, which can be retrieved with **Win32::GetLastError**(). The OS then tells Perl that the file could not be opened and Perl registers an error. Example 1.3 demonstrates this.

Example 1.3   *Demonstration of the difference between a Perl error and a Win32 API error*

```
01. use Win32;
02.   # Reset any Perl error
03. $! = 0;
04.   # Purposely generate an error...
05. if( ! getpeername( ThisIsABadPeerName ) )
06. {
07.   $Error = int( $! );  # Get the error number`
08.   $Win32_Error = Win32::GetLastError();
09.   print "Perl error number: $Error\n";
10.   print "Perl error message: $!\n";
11.   print "Win32 error number: $Win32_Error\n";
12.   print "Win32 error message: " . Win32::FormatMessage( $Win32_Error );
13. }
```

Example 1.3 uses the **getpeername**() function because it best illustrates how Perl sees an error but Win32 does not. The two error numbers and error text may differ because they come from different sources.

The following output from Example 1.3 shows how Perl may recognize that an error has taken place even though the Win32 API is unaware of any such error:

```
Perl error number:  9
Perl error message: Bad file descriptor
Win32 error number: 0
Win32 error message: The operation completed successfully.
```

Generally, this means that you should rely on the $! error variable only when the error was generated using standard Perl functions. If an error is generated from an extension, you can generally use the **Win32::GetLastError**() function to discover the nature of the error.

The **Win32::GetLastError**() function takes no parameters and returns a numeric value that represents the previous Win32 API error message that the script generated. You cannot use this function to retrieve Win32 API errors generated by other running scripts, only the currently running one.

FormatMessage() Function

After you have retrieved the Win32 API error number (see Example 1.3), you can request the OS to give you a human-readable version of the error with the **Win32::FormatMessage**() function:

```
$ErrorText = Win32::FormatMessage( $ErrorNum );
```

The only parameter passed in ($ErrorNum) is a numeric value (usually obtained with the **Win32::GetLastError**() function) that represents a Win32 API error number. The function will return a string that is the text-based description of the error message.

It is common to see the function **Win32::GetLastError**() passed in to **Win32::FormatMessage**(), as in Example 1.4. This is a convenient and quick way to obtain the Win32 error text.

Example 1.4 *Subroutine for printing Win32 errors*

```
sub PrintError
{
  print Win32::FormatMessage( Win32::GetLastError() );
}
```

Specific Win32 Extension Error Handling

Unfortunately, you cannot use the **Win32::GetLastError**() function with all the Win32 functions. Some extensions require you to use specific error functions for a variety of reasons. This requirement means that you can use the **Win32::GetLastError**() function when you use these extensions. If your call to a particular extension's function fails, however, you should not use **Win32::GetLastError**() to discover why it failed. Instead, you should use whatever error function that extension provides. You will have to check the documentation for that particular extension to determine how to handle such errors.

To help clarify this issue, it is necessary to understand why this error madness exists. When a Win32 API function (such as retrieving a list of user accounts) fails, two things happen. First the function itself returns an error indicating the nature of the failure. It is up to the extension to manage such knowledge. The second event that takes place is that the Win32 API internally stores the error. When you call **Win32::GetLastError**(), it is this stored error number that is returned. Suppose that some Win32 extension's function discovers that an error occurred and it handles it by making other Win32 API function calls in an attempt to correct the problem. Each time these additional API calls are executed, Win32 may internally store their results. By the time the extension's function returns to your code and you call **Win32::GetLastError**() to determine why the error occurred, you might be retrieving the error information for a totally different function. This is why most extensions provide their own error-retrieval function.

Some Win32 extensions (such as **Win32::EventLog**) attempt to set the Perl error variable $! when it generates an error. It is *not* a good idea to depend on using $! under these circumstances. Although the error variable is set to the correct Win32 API error number, the error text message will be incorrect.

Suppose that a Win32 extension tries to load a file but fails. Then the extension sets the $! variable with the Win32 error number that was generated, which is 3 (the system could not find the path specified). If your script then prints the error text using the $! variable, as in:

```
print "Error: $!\n";
```

Perl would print the error text for error number 3, which is No such process. Perl error numbers are not the same as Win32 error numbers. So if a Win32 extension sets $! based on the results of a Win32 function or with the value of **Win32::GetLastError**(), you should avoid relying on $! to correctly report the error. This is another reason why **Win32::GetLastError**() is so important when using the Win32 extensions.

With so many Win32 extensions, many different ways of interpreting and managing errors exist. Four extensions, however, beg for a bit more attention than their documentation provides. These are the **Win32::NetResource**, **Win32::ODBC**, **Win32::RasAdmin**, and **Win32::WinError** extensions.

Win32::WinError Error Handling

The **Win32::WinError** extension exports several constants that can be used when determining the nature of an error. There is some question as to how useful this extension is because it maps error constants with error numbers but not the other way around. The following code will print the error code for the constant ERROR_LOGIN_WKSTA_RESTRICTION, for example:

```
use Win32::WinError;
print "The error number " . ERROR_LOGIN_WKSTA_RESTRICTION . " represents the
error ERROR_LOGIN_WKSTA_RESTRICTION.\n";
```

The real benefit with this extension is in using it for the sake of testing the result of an error, as follows:

```
use Win32;
use Win32::WinError;
...process some code...
  # Test for an error...
$Error = Win32::GetLastError();
if( ERROR_LOGIN_WKSTA_RESTRICTION == $Error )
{
  ...process the error...
}elsif( ERROR_ACCOUNT_LOCKED_OUT == $Error )
{
  ...process the error...
}
```

This can be handy when used with the **Win32::API** extension.

Win32::ODBC Error Handling

When a **Win32::ODBC** function fails, the only way to discover the error number is by using the **Error()** function. This is implemented as both a function and a method:

```
Win32::ODBC::Error();
$db->Error();
```

This function/method takes no parameters and will return either an array or text string, depending on what the caller's context is.

Notice that this particular call can be either a function (**Win32::ODBC::Error()**) or an object's method (**$db–>Error()**). Example 1.5 shows both uses.

Example 1.5   *Using Win32::ODBC's Error() function and method*

```
use Win32::ODBC;
if( !( $db = new Win32::ODBC( "MyDSN" ) )
{
  print "Unable to connect to the database.\n ";
  print "Error: " . Win32::ODBC::Error();
}
if( $db->Sql( "SELECT * FROM Foo " ) )
{
  print "The query produced an error.\n ";
  print "Error: " . $db->Error();
}
```

In an array context, this will return the elements in Table 1.2. Each of the array's elements represents discrete information regarding the error.

Table 1.2   Array returned by Win32::ODBC::Error()

Index	Name	Description
0	ErrorNum	Error number
1	ErrorText	Text description of the error
2	Conn	Connection number (this is a value that is internally used by the extension)
3	SQLState	The SQLState of the error

In Example 1.6, an error array is returned in which the third element (the SQLState of the error) is compared to a particular value. By returning an array, the script can process each aspect of an error.

Example 1.6   *Extracting information from the error array*

```
01. use Win32::ODBC;
02. $db = new Win32::ODBC( "MyDSN" ) ¦¦ die "Can not connect: " .
Win32::ODBC::Error();
03. if( $db->Sql( "SELECT * FROM Foo " ) )
04. {
05.    @Error = $db->Error();
06.    if( "HYT00" eq $Error[3] )
07.    {
08.        print "The database server took to long to process the query.
           We have timed out.\n";
09.    }else{
10.        print "The query produced an error number $Error[0].\n";
11.        print "The error text is $Error[1].\n";
12.        print "The connection number is $Error[2].\n";
13.        print "The SQLState of the error is $Error[3].\n";
14.    }
15. }
```

Win32::NetResource Error Handling

There are two different functions to retrieve error information from the **Win32::NetResource** extension: **GetError**() and **WNetGetLastError**(). Don't be fooled, however; these functions are not interchangeable. When a **Win32::NetResource** function fails, you can retrieve the error with the following:

```
Win32::NetResource::GetError ( $Error );
```

This function always return a 1 and the error number will be stored into the scalar that is passed into it (in the example here, the $Error variable). If the scalar $Error contains the value of 1208 (this is the same value as the constant ERROR_EXTENDED_ERROR from the **Win32::WinError** extension), you need to get the extended error information. This happens when a particular network provider (for example, Microsoft LANManager or Novell NetWare) other than Win32 has reported an error. Some systems may have third-party network protocol stacks and services. Because the OS does not have any idea what kinds of errors these aftermarket services and stacks may be capable of generating, the Win32 error reporting functions will just return ERROR_EXTENDED_ERROR. You can retrieve the provider-specific error information by using the **WNetGetLastError()** function:

```
Win32::NetResource::WNetGetLastError ( $Error, $Description, $Provider);
```

The values of the three parameters passed into the function are ignored, but they are assigned values. The parameters are set such that $Error will contain the error number, $Description will contain a textual description of the error, and $Provider will contain the name of the network provider that generated the error.

A simple way to collect **Win32::NetResource** error information would be to define a function, as in Example 1.7.

Example 1.7   *Retrieving a Win32::NetResource error*

```
01. use Win32::NetResource;
02. use Win32::WinError;
03.
04. sub NetError
05. {
06.     my( $Error, $Text, $Provider );
07.     $Error = Win32::GetLastError();
08.     if( $Error == ERROR_EXTENDED_ERROR )
09.     {
10.         Win32::NetResource::WNetGetLastError( $Error, $Text, $Provider );
11.         $Result = "Error $Error: $Text (generated by $Provider)";
12.     }else{
13.         $Text = Win32::FormatMessage( $Error );
14.         $Result = "Error $Error: $Text";
15.     }
16.     return $Result;
17. }
```

The **NetError()** subroutine in line 4 will return a string containing a description of the error.

There are three ways to retrieve errors when a **Win32::NetResource** function fails. You can use the following functions:

```
Win32::GetLastError();
Win32::NetResource::GetError( $Error );
Win32::NetResource::WNetGetLastError( $Error, $Text, $Provider );
```

There has been much confusion about which function to use, so here is the scoop: When you execute a **Win32::NetResource** function and it fails, you should use **GetError()**:

```
Win32::NetResource::GetError( $Error );
```

This value that is set in $Error will be the error that was generated by the last **Win32::NetResource** function. Using **Win32::NetResource::GetError()** is quite different from using **Win32::GetLastError()**, in that you must pass a scalar into the **Win32::NetResource::GetError()** function, as in:

```
Win32::NetResource::GetError( $Error )
```

If the function successfully retrieves the error number, the scalar $Error will hold it.

Win32::RasAdmin Error Handling

If a **Win32::RasAdmin** function fails, you can find the error it reported by using either the **Win32::RasAdmin::GetLastError()** or the **Win32::GetLastError()** functions. Because RAS errors are not common to all Win32 platforms, the errors are not recognized by the traditional **Win32::FormatMessage()** function. Instead, you will need to use **Win32::RasAdmin::GetErrorString()** to find the textual message associated with the error number. The good news about this is that the error message will be correctly returned regardless of whether the error is RAS related.

Summary

The history of the various Win32 versions is long and twisted, with many interesting details. With all the changes made to Perl over the past few years to make it successfully run on the Win32 platform, it is a wonder that there are gaps in documentation and a general understanding of the issues surrounding it.

One of the benefits of using Win32 Perl over other scripting utilities (such as batch files) is that the programmer is not limited to what the language is capable of. Perl has long had the capability to extend itself by making use of other languages such as C. By extending, Perl programmers are provided the promise of true Win32 integration.

Each discrete extension that Win32 Perl uses is within itself a library of functionality that some author found a need for. Whereas this distribution of work is good for variety, it has also resulted in many disturbing trends such as the lack of any conformity for important issues like how to retrieve error information.

Now that the basics have been covered, the rest of the standard Win32 extensions are yours for the using. You will find that with each extension, Perl is empowered with vast amounts of capabilities. Even those extensions that support only a mere couple of functions provide a Perl script with untold functionality.

Network administrators will find that Perl is a splendid tool for managing their network, but the extensions and functions described in the next chapter will make all the difference for them.

Chapter 2

Network Administration

We often go about our day without ever thinking about networks. We pick up the phone and call someone next door, across the country, or on the other side of the globe. For those of us who play with networks, we generally think about the net as a compilation of computers all talking to each other; but how often do we really consider the workings of our nets? Most of us don't think about it at all, or at least we try not to think about it.

Unlike most people, administrators have to constantly think about the net. Things like domain controllers, master browsers, shared resources, and dial-in connections are just the things that keep them up at night. Because it can be a nightmare keeping track of all of this, there have been Win32 extensions written to make this easy to handle from Perl.

This chapter examines functions that manage the sharing of resources, resolve DNS names, discover network servers, and manage RAS servers. The Win32 extensions discussed include the following:

- Win32::NetAdmin
- Win32::AdminMisc
- Win32::NetResource
- Win32::RasAdmin

Discovering Servers on the Network

As a good administrator, you should be able to rattle off the names of your network servers without blinking an eye; however, a less fallible way to recall servers on the network would be to use the **Win32::NetAdmin::GetServers()** function. This function, if successful, will populate an array with the names of each computer that matches the criteria that you supply.

Win32 platforms refer to computers by using their names. A name is unique to only one computer on a network, can be up to 15 characters in length, and is not case sensitive. Several of the Win32 extensions have functions that either accept or return a computer name. You need to be aware of two forms of a computer name: a computer name and a proper computer name.

A computer name is just the name of the computer as in, "My computer's name is 'DEVBOX1'." A proper computer name, however, is the computer's name prepended with two backslashes as in \\DEVBOX1.

This distinction is important because some functions handle one form but not the other. The **Win32::NetAdmin::GetServers**() function will return an array of *computer names*, for example, but the function **Win32::NetResource::NetShareGetInfo**() requires that you specify a proper computer name (if you specify a server name at all).

Note

In the Win32 world, computers are grouped together in domains. These are not the same as Internet domains, but more like workgroups. Domains names, like computer names, are not case sensitive and can be up to 15 characters in length. Unlike computer names, however, there is no such thing as a "proper" domain name. So prepending a double backslash in front of a domain name does nothing.

All domains must have what is known as a Primary Domain Controller (PDC) that holds a database of all users and computers who participate in the domain. A PDC will manage all Backup Domain Controllers (BDC) in the domain. The PDC will occasionally update the BDCs with the latest information regarding the domain. This means that if an administrator changes something in a user account on a BDC, the PDC will eventually learn of this change and will then not only update itself but will also update all the other BDCs that exist in the domain.

When a computer or user logs on to a domain, either a PDC or a BDC will perform its authentication. Which machine performs the task depends on how busy they all are and how physically close the domain controller is to the requesting computer (typically a DC will respond if it is in the same subnet before another DC that lives on a different subnet).

Many of the functions in Win32 extensions make reference to what is called a primary domain. When a computer or a user logs on to a domain that domain becomes the primary domain—that is, the default domain. This is also known as the logon domain.

The **GetServers**() function takes four parameters:

```
Win32::NetAdmin::GetServers( $Machine, $Domain, $Flags, \@Array );
```

The first parameter ($Machine) is the name of the computer you want to actually process the function. Usually this is an empty string and the local machine processes the request. It could be, however, any proper computer name on the network (such as \\server1).

The second parameter ($Domain) is just the name of the domain that you are requesting information on. If this is empty, then the primary domain of the machine specified in the first parameter is used.

The third parameter ($Flags) is a value that describes the type of machines you are looking for. You can use several constants in combination by logically OR'ing them together (see Example 2.2). The list of constants and their functionality is as follows:

- **SV_TYPE_AFP**. Servers running the Apple File Protocol
- **SV_TYPE_ALL**. All members of the domain
- **SV_TYPE_BACKUP_BROWSER**. Backup browsers for the domain
- **SV_TYPE_DIALIN_SERVER**. Machines that have RAS services for remote dial-in
- **SV_TYPE_DOMAIN_BAKCTRL**. Backup Domain Controllers
- **SV_TYPE_DOMAIN_CTRL**. Primary Domain Controller
- **SV_TYPE_DOMAIN_ENUM**. List of domains
- **SV_TYPE_DOMAIN_MASTER**. Master browser for the entire domain
- **SV_TYPE_DOMAIN_MEMBER**. LAN Manager 2.x Domain Members
- **SV_TYPE_MASTER_BROWSER**. Master browser (there can be a master browser for each subnet of a domain)
- **SV_TYPE_NOVELL**. Novell Servers
- **SV_TYPE_NT**. Machines running NT (Workstation or Server)
- **SV_TYPE_POTENTIAL_BROWSER**. Machines able and willing to run the browser service
- **SV_TYPE_PRINT**. Machines sharing print queues
- **SV_TYPE_SERVER**. Machines running the server service
- **SV_TYPE_SQLSERVER**. Only MS SQL Servers
- **SV_TYPE_TIMESOURCE**. Machines acting as a time server
- **SV_TYPE_WFW**. Machines running Windows for Workgroups
- **SV_TYPE_WORKSTATION**. Only NT workstations
- **SV_TYPE_XENIX_SERVER**. Xenix servers

You can use a few other constants, but for some reason they were not exported by the **Win32::NetAdmin** module; therefore, you have to use the value rather than the constant name (see Table 2.1). In newer versions (beginning with the core distribution libwin32-0.12), these constants are defined; so you can specify the constant names.

Table 2.1   Undocumented constants (you need to specify the value rather than the constant)

Constant	Value	Meaning
SV_TYPE_SERVER_NT	0x00008000	Machines running Windows NT Server that are not domain controllers.
SV_TYPE_WINDOWS	0x00400000	Machines running Windows 95 or later.
SV_TYPE_LOCAL_LIST_ONLY	0x40000000	Machines that are held by the browser service. This really only has useful meaning on master-browsers.
SV_TYPE_MFPN	0x00004000	Machines running the Microsoft File and Print services for NetWare.

The fourth parameter for **GetServers()** (\@Array) is a reference to an array that will be populated with the machine names that fit the criteria specified in the $Flags parameter.

If the **GetServers()** function is successful, it returns a TRUE value; otherwise, it returns a FALSE value.

Suppose that you want to get a list of all Windows machines in your domain. The code in Example 2.1 would enable you to accomplish this task.

Example 2.1   *Retrieving a list of all the machines in a domain*

```
use Win32::NetAdmin;
if( Win32::NetAdmin::GetServers('', '', SV_TYPE_ALL, \@List) )
{
  print "The machines in this domain are:\n";
  map { $iCount++; print "$iCount) $_\n" } @List;
}else{
  print Win32::FormatMessage( Win32::NetAdmin::GetError() );
}
```

In this case, the flag SV_TYPE_ALL indicates that all machine names in the primary domain will be returned.

Example 2.2 assumes that you want the list of all domain controllers (primary and backup) and machines running Windows 95 (and later) for the SOUTH_PARK domain and you want the machine \\server1 to produce the list.

Example 2.2   *Retrieving a list of all Primary and Backup Domain Controllers in the domain*

```
01. use Win32::NetAdmin;
02. $Flag = SV_TYPE_DOMAIN_BAKCTRL ¦ SV_TYPE_DOMAIN_CTRL ¦ 0x00400000;
03. $Server = "\\\\server1";
04. if( Win32::NetAdmin::GetServers($Server, 'SOUTH_PARK', $Flag, \@List) )
05. {
06.     print "The machines in this domain are:\n";
07.     map { print "$_\n" } @List;
08. }else{
09.     print Win32::FormatMessage( Win32::NetAdmin::GetError() );
10. }
```

Note

*The core distribution's version of **Win32::NetAdmin::GetServers**() can accept a reference to a hash rather than an array for the fourth parameter. The hash is populated by the machine name and comment.*

Tip

In Perl, when you specify a backslash (\\) you need to escape it with another backslash. So if you are specifying a server name that is \\Server, *you will have to use double backslashes such as:*

```
$Server = "\\\\Server";
```

This is why you will see double backslashes everywhere.

Even when using single quotation marks, you need to use double backslashes. This usually causes confusion for most coders because you do not have to typically escape a backslash when using single quotation marks. This is correct, except that the task of specifying a proper computer name is one of those rare times that when Perl sees your double backslash it will think that you are escaping a backslash. Because of this, you must include two "escaped backslashes":

```
$Server = '\\\\Server';
```

Some Win32 extensions enable you to supply a server name using forward slashes (/), which the extension will flip automatically for you.

Each element of the array will contain the name of one computer on the network that matches the criteria specified by the third parameter. The format of the computer is always just the name with no slashes. If you run the code in Example 2.2, the output might resemble something like the following:

```
The machines in this domain are:
1) DEV
2) MAIN2
3) LIVERSAUSAGE
```

Notice how each element is only the name of a machine (there are no prepended backslashes).

You may notice that some functions enable you to specify a machine to perform the work (such as **Win32::NetAdmin::GetServers()**). If you are wondering why anyone would ever want to do this, you are in good company; most coders don't have a clue about this.

Usually it doesn't matter which machine performs the task. Notice how I say usually. In some instances, it is prudent to have another machine do the dirty work.

Assume, for example, that you want to get a list of all the current machines in the ACCOUNTING domain. You can use the following line:

```
Win32::NetAdmin::GetServers('', '', SV_TYPE_WORKSTATION, \@List);
```

This will have my machine figure out who is in my primary domain (ROTH.NET). If I want to discover the computer names for another domain, ACCOUNTING, however, I will have to ask a computer in that domain:

```
Win32::NetAdmin::GetServers('\\\\Kyle', 'ACCOUNTING', SV_TYPE_WORKSTATION,
    \@List);
```

If the primary domain for \\Kyle is ACCOUNTING, I could have left the domain name empty.

Finding Domain Controllers

I am always amazed how often I find code that has been written that assumes a particular circumstance will be true. Someone will hardcode a script to refer to a Primary Domain Controller (PDC), for example. It is possible for a Primary Domain Controller to go down and a Backup Domain Controller (BDC) to automatically step in and act as a temporary PDC, or an administrator can manually promote a BDC to take over the role of the PDC (if this occurs, the PDC steps down and acts as a BDC). Because of this, it is a bad idea to hardcode a PDC's computer name into a script. You should, instead, resolve the name of the domain's PDC using the **GetDomainController()** function:

```
Win32::NetAdmin::GetDomainController($Server, $Domain, $Name);
```

For this function, just like **GetServers()**, you specify the first parameter ($Server) as the name of the machine that will process the request (or use an empty string for the local machine). This parameter must be a proper machine name (the name is prepended with two backslashes). Typically, you will leave this entry as an empty string. If you specify a machine name, however, the function usually will execute more quickly.

The second parameter ($Domain) is the name of an NT domain or a blank string that represents the primary domain of the machine passed in as the first parameter.

The third parameter ($Name) is ignored when the function starts; if the function is successful, however, the name of the server is placed in it. Therefore this value *must* be a scalar variable—you cannot use a constant value.

If **GetDomainController**() is successful, it will return a TRUE value and the variable passed in as the third parameter will be set to the name of the PDC. If the function fails, it will return a FALSE value.

If you want to find the PDC for the primary domain, you could use the script from Example 2.3.

Example 2.3   *Discovering the Primary Domain Controller for a domain*

```
use Win32::NetAdmin;
if( Win32::NetAdmin::GetDomainController("", "", $Machine))
{
    print "The primary domain controller is $Machine\n";
}else{
    print Win32::FormatMessage( Win32::NetAdmin::GetError() );
}
```

Notice how the $Machine name is prepended with backslashes (a proper Win32 machine name), which is different from the result you get when you use the **GetServers**() function.

> **Tip**
>
> *If you think that some of the extensions are a bit odd and not very consistent, you are catching on. Most of the Win32 extensions provide a direct interface to the Win32 API. This is fine for those who know the Win32 API and what to expect; for those Perl programmers who have no knowledge of the idiosyncrasies that make up Win32, however, this will look very odd.*
>
> *A perfect example is how some extension functions will return a machine name (without prepended backslashes) but expect an input parameter to be a proper computer name (having the prepended backslashes). Hopefully future versions of extensions will be more consistent. Ideally they would enable you to specify forward slashes rather than backslashes (keeping with how Win32 Perl enables you to specify either types of slashes in a file path).*

The **GetAnyDomainController**() function takes the same parameters as the **GetDomainController**() function. Instead of returning the Primary Domain Controller, however, **GetAnyDomainController**() will return any domain controller. Usually the machine name returned will be the closest and least busy domain controller on your segment of the network.

Note

*The **Win32::NetAdmin::GetServers**() function returns an array of computer names. Conversely, the **Win32::NetAdmin::GetAnyDomainController**() and **Win32::NetAdmin::GetDomainController**() functions return a proper computer name (with prepended backslashes).*

Resolving DNS Names

Few things in life bring as much joy to a network administrator as being able to resolve DNS names to IP addresses. And, of course, Win32 Perl has many ways to resolve DNS names. You can use the DNS module available from CPAN or the DNS functions such as **gethostip**() and its brethren. Oh, but Win32 Perl did not always have such rich DNS support. Because of this, the **Win32::AdminMisc** module included a few functions that are still available:

```
GetHostAddress( $DNS_Name );
gethostbyname( $DNS_Name );
GetHostName( $IP_Address );
gethostbyaddr( $IP_Address );
```

These four functions all work the same: If you pass in an IP address as the parameter, the DNS name will be looked up; and if you pass in a DNS name as the parameter, the IP address will be looked up. The only reason that there are multiple function names is for those who are accustomed to the other **gethostbyXXX**() functions.

If these functions are successful, they will return either the IP address or domain name (depending on what is passed into the function). If they fail, a 0 value is returned.

If you were to run the following code in Example 2.4, the IP address for www.roth.net would be printed.

Example 2.4   *Resolving a DNS name to an IP address*

```
use Win32::AdminMisc;
if( $IP = Win32::AdminMisc::GetHostAddress( "www.roth.net" ) )
{
  print "The IP address is $IP.\n";
}else{
```

```
    print "Unable to resolve the address.\n";
}
```

If you were to run the code in Example 2.5, however, the DNS name would be printed. Notice that both Example 2.4 and 2.5 use the same function (**Win32::AdminMisc::GetHostAddress**()) even though they are looking for different results.

Example 2.5   *Performing reverse DNS on an IP address*

```
use Win32::AdminMisc;
if( $DNS = Win32::AdminMisc::GetHostAddress( "192.198.1.10" ) )
{
  print "The DNS name is $DNS.\n";
}else{
  print "Unable to resolve the name.\n";
}
```

Now you may be wondering why you would use any of these rather than the built-in functions in Perl. Well, the answer is two-fold.

First, consider the ease of use. If you were to write some Perl code that resolves a DNS name to an IP address, it may look like Example 2.6.

Example 2.6   *Resolving a DNS name to an IP address using Perl's gethostbyname() function*

```
$DNS = "www.roth.net";
if( ($Temp, $Temp, $Temp, $Temp, @List) = gethostbyname($DNS) )
{
    @Quads = unpack('C4', $List[0]);
    $IP = join(".", @Quads);
    print "IP address for $DNS is $IP.\n";
}else{
    print "Failed to lookup $DNS.\n";
}
```

If you were to use the **Win32::AdminMisc** functions it could look like Example 2.7.

Example 2.7   *Resolving a DNS name to an IP address using the Win32::AdminMisc::GetHostAddress() function*

```
use Win32::AdminMisc;
$DNS = "www.roth.net";
if( $IP = Win32::AdminMisc::GetHostAddress( $DNS ) )
{
    print "IP address for $DNS is $IP.\n";
}else{
    print "Failed to lookup $DNS.\n";
}
```

The difference between the Perl built-in function **gethostbyname()** and the **Win32::AdminMisc::GetHostAddress()** function is that the latter takes care of most of the work of unpacking the resulting data structure into a dotted quad address. The Perl **gethostbyname()** function, however, can retrieve multiple addresses for a single DNS name, which can be quite handy if there ever is a need for it. If you are looking for all the IP addresses that may be associated with a particular DNS name (www.microsoft.com has about 20 of them), for example, you would want to use the built-in Perl **gethostbyname()** function, as in Example 2.8.

Example 2.8   *Resolving all IP addresses for a DNS name*

```
$DNS = "www.microsoft.com";
print "Dumping all IP addresses for $DNS:\n";
($Temp1, $Temp2, $Temp3, $Temp4, @List) = gethostbyname( $DNS );
foreach $Temp ( @List )
{
  $IP = join( ".", ( unpack( 'C4', $Temp ) ) );
  printf( "\t%02d) %s\n", ++$iTotal, $IP );
}
```

The second reason for using the **Win32::AdminMisc** functions rather than the built-in Perl DNS resolution functions has to do with caching. The **AdminMisc** module caches the DNS names and IP addresses that it resolves.

Originally the purpose of the **AdminMisc** DNS functions were to perform reverse DNS on IP addresses collected by an HTTP server for a Web statistics program. Caching was implemented to speed up the resolution of DNS names that were frequently looked up.

The **Win32::AdminMisc** DNS functions are not always the best way to go. If you have a need for portability between, let's say, UNIX, Macintosh, and Win32, using the Win32-specific extension will only defeat this point. All the DNS functions that **Win32::AdminMisc** provide can be simulated using Perl's native functions.

The caching of DNS entries can result in an incredible increase in speed for scripts that continuously perform DNS lookups as well as reverse DNS resolutions. You can enable and disable caching with the **DNSCache()** function:

```
Win32::AdminMisc::DNSCache( [ $State ] );
```

The only parameter ($State) is optional. If supplied, it sets the state of caching regardless of whether DNS caching is enabled. This value is either a FALSE (0) or a TRUE (any non-zero) value.

If no parameter is passed in, the function will return the current state of DNS caching. If a parameter is specified, caching will be either activated (by passing in a TRUE value) or disabled (by passing in a FALSE value). By default, when the **Win32::AdminMisc** extension is loaded, caching is active.

The function will return a TRUE or FALSE value indicating the state of DNS caching. This return value reflects the state of caching after the function has been called.

You can determine how many DNS entries have been cached by using the **DNSCacheCount**() function:

```
Win32::AdminMisc::DNSCacheCount()
```

The function will return a value indicating how many DNS names have been cached. This number will not exceed the total number of cache elements (the value returned by **Win32::AdminMisc::DNSCacheSize**()).

Example 2.9 illustrates using the **DNSCacheCount**() function.

Example 2.9   *Discovering the number of the DNS names that have been cached*

```
use Win32::AdminMisc;
$TotalCached = Win32::AdminMisc::DNSCacheCount();
print " $TotalCached DNS entries have been cached.\n";
```

By default, there are 600 cache entries available, but that can be increased or decreased with the **DNSCacheSize**():

```
Win32::AdminMisc::DNSCacheSize( [ $Size ] )
```

The only parameter ($Size) is optional and represents the number of cache elements to allocate.

If a value is passed into the function, the DNS cache will be resized to the specified number of elements. This will reset the cache, resulting in the loss of any DNS names already cached.

This function will return the number of elements that have been allocated for DNS caching. This value indicates the total number of DNS names that can be cached. Example 2.10 demonstrates the use of **DNSCacheSize**().

Example 2.10   *Changing the size of the DNS cache*

```
use Win32::AdminMisc;
$Total = Win32::AdminMisc::DNSCacheSize();
print "Total of $Total elements have been allocated for DNS caching.\n";
$Total = Win32::AdminMisc::DSNCacheSize( 1500 );
print "Now $Total elements have been allocated for DNS caching.\n";
```

Note

It is very important to note that when you change the cache size, all currently cached entries will be lost.

Case Study: Resolving DNS Names and IP Addresses

Suppose that you need to write a script that will look up the DNS names for a list of IP addresses that are in a file. This file could be a list of IP addresses that have connected to your Web server. Assuming that this file contains only one IP address per line, you could use the script in Example 2.11.

Example 2.11   *Resolving DNS names and IP addresses*

```
01. use Win32::AdminMisc;
02. open( FILE, "< iplist.txt" ) || die "Could not open file ($!)\n";
03.     # Set the DNS cache to 3500
04. Win32::AdminMisc::DNSCacheSize( 3500 );
05. while( $Host = <FILE> )
06. {
07.     $Host =~ s/\s//gis;    # Remove any white space
08.     if( $Host =~ /[^\.\d]/ ) # Check if $Host is a DNS name or an IP address
09.     {
10.         $IP = Win32::AdminMisc::GetHostName( $DNS = $Host );
11.     }else{
12.         $DNS = Win32::AdminMisc::GetHostName( $IP = $Host );
13.     }
14.     print "The DNS name for $IP is $DNS.\n";
15. }
16. close( FILE );
```

Assume that you create the text file IPLIST.TXT that contains the following text:

```
www.perl.com
www.activestate.com
204.71.200.75
204.159.111.101
```

When you run the Perl script in Example 2.11, you will get the following output:

```
The DNS name for 208.201.239.48 is www.perl.com.
The DNS name for 199.60.48.4 is www.activestate.com.
The DNS name for 204.71.200.75 is www10.yahoo.com.
The DNS name for 204.159.111.101 is ds2.internic.net.
```

The sheer beauty of this code is that up to 3,500 elements will be cached; so if the IPLIST.TXT file contains duplicate entries, there will be no need for your system to go out and re-query your DNS server.

Shared Network Resources

Part of the wonder that is the network is that you can share with others. This capability to share data and resources gives networks their potential and power. After all, what good would a network be without shared resources; it would be like a highway without on or off ramps, an airplane without an airport, a candidate without an election.

Sharing resources is such a prime function of networks that Win32 Perl has access to almost all the Win32 API's sharing functions. Pretty much any resource (directories and printers, for example) can be shared so that users on the network can connect to and use it.

You have several options when dealing with shared resources; you can create shares, delete shares, change the way resources are shared, connect to shares on remote machines, and disconnect from remote shares. All these functions are possible thanks to the **Win32::NetResource** extension.

Now you may be wondering just what a *share* is. It is just as its namesake describes: a shared resource. If you share your C: drive so that users can access it over the network, you have created a share. Shares have names that are sometimes referred to as a *sharepoint*. This name is very important because when others connect to your computer they need to specify the name of the share to connect to. They do this by specifying a UNC (Universal Naming Convention).

UNCs are like a path to a shared resource. You make a UNC by specifying the proper name of a computer (prepended with double backslashes) followed by a backslash and the name of the shared resource. If I were to try to connect to the UNC \\MAIN2\TempFiles, I would be trying to connect to a shared resource named TempFiles on my computer named \\MAIN2 (it just so happens that I have shared my C:\Temp directory with a name of "TempFiles" on that computer).

> **Tip**
>
> *Just like file names on Win32 platforms, a share name can have spaces. For example:*
>
> > \\MAIN2\Program Files\
>
> *is a valid share name on the machine* \\MAIN2.

Types of Network Resources

Resources come in two different types: a connectable share or a container. Connectable shares are just what the name implies: shares that can be connected to (such as printers and directories) and used by other users and machines. Containers (such as domains), unlike connectable shares, are resources that can hold other containers and or multiple shares (such as networks and domains).

Consider when you share your c:\TEMP directory and name it "TempFiles". This is a connectable share because remote users can connect to it and access the files in the c:\TEMP directory. Containers, however, cannot be connected to but instead are just objects that hold other objects (such as containers and connectable shares). This is not as confusing as it may seem.

Suppose that you double-click on the desktop's Network Neighborhood icon and you see a window that looks like Figure 2.1. There are two icons that represent two separate domains. These icons are containers; they are objects that contain other objects.

Figure 2.1 *An example of container objects (two domain icons).*

If you double-click on the Roth.net domain icon, you will see a set of computers (as in Figure 2.2). These icons each represent another container object.

Figure 2.2 *Another example of container objects (two computer icons).*

By double-clicking on the computer called Frenzy, you will see three shares as illustrated in Figure 2.3. These are connectable shares—that is, they are sharepoints that a user can actually connect to and use from across the network. As you can see, a container can hold connectable shares or containers.

Figure 2.3 *An example of connectable share objects (three shared resources).*

If we were to compare shares to hard drives, we could say that containers are directories (which can hold both files and directories) and connectable shares are files.

Sharing Means Data Structures

Before learning how to deal with shares, you need to understand a few details. Resource sharing with Perl revolves around two data structures: the NETRE-SOURCE and SHARE_INFO hashes.

NETRESOURCE Hash Structure

The NETRESOURCE hash is a data structure used when retrieving information about a shared resource. This data structure is a hash that describes attributes about the resource being shared.

If you request a list of shared resources, you will retrieve an array of NETRESOURCE hashes like that shown in the following output (derived from using the **X** command in the debugger).

```
DB<1> X NetResource
 HASH(0x1018b08)
  'Comment' => 'Okidata OL610e/PS PostScript Printer'
  'DisplayType' => 3
  'LocalName' => undef
  'Provider' => 'Microsoft Windows Network'
  'RemoteName' => '\\\\MAIN2\\PRINTER'
  'Scope' => 2
  'Type' => 2
  'Usage' => 1
```

The keys in a NETRESOURCE structure are as follows:

- Comment

- DisplayType

- LocalName

- Provider

- RemoteName

- Scope

- Type

- Usage

Each of these keys in the NETRESOURCE hash structure is described in more detail in the sections that follow.

The Comment Key

The Comment key of the NETRESOURCE hash structure indicates a comment associated with the particular resource. For the output demonstrated previously, this would be 'Okidata OL610e/PS PostScript Printer'.

The DisplayType Key

The DisplayType key of the NETRESOURCE hash structure indicates how the object (either a connectable share or a container) should be displayed when you are browsing. Consider when you are using the Explorer and you double-click on a computer in the Network Neighborhood. In the output to the list of shared resources, the DisplayType has a value of 3, which corresponds to the RESOURCEDISPLAYTYPE_SHARE constant.

Possible values of this key are as follows:

- **RESOURCEDISPLAYTYPE_DOMAIN.** The object should be displayed as if it is a domain.

- **RESOURCEDISPLAYTYPE_GENERIC.** It does not matter how this specific type is displayed.

- **RESOURCEDISPLAYTYPE_FILE.** The object should be displayed as a file.

- **RESOURCEDISPLAYTYPE_GROUP.** The object should be displayed as a group.

- **RESOURCEDISPLAYTYPE_SERVER.** The object should be displayed as if it is a server.

- **RESOURCEDISPLAYTYPE_SHARE.** The object should be displayed as if it is a connectable share.

- **RESOURCEDISPLAYTYPE_TREE.** The object should be displayed as a tree (a hierarchical structure of some sort).

The LocalName Key

This LocalName key of the NETRESOURCE hash structure refers to a local device if the Scope key is RESOURCE_CONNECTED or RESOURCE_REMEMBERED. Currently the **Win32::NetResource** extension is hardcoded to always specify a scope of RESOURCE_GLOBALNET, however, so this key will always be undefined.

The Provider Key

The Provider key of the NETRESOURCE hash structure tells which network provider handles this resource. Typically this will be Microsoft Windows Network, but it could be a Novell NetWare or other network provider. If the provider is unknown, this string will be empty.

The RemoteName Key

The RemoteName key of the NETRESOURCE hash structure is the name that you use to reference this resource. This is usually a Universal Naming Convention (UNC) or computer name such as \\server1\printer or \\fileserver. In the case that the network resource is a container that you typically cannot directly access (such as a network provider, domain, or a workgroup), the RemoteName key will be the name of the object such as Microsoft Windows Network, Roth_Domain, or Managers_Group.

The Scope Key

The Scope key of the NETRESOURCE hash structure represents which resources you are referring to. The possible values of this key are as follows:

- **RESOURCE_CONNECTED.** All those resources that your machine is currently connected to. If this option is used, the Usage key will be undefined.

- **RESOURCE_GLOBALNET.** All resources on the network (network providers, domains, workgroups, computers, printers, directories, and so on).

- **RESOURCE_REMEMBERED.** Only those resources that are persistent (or remembered) connections—that is, those connections that are automatically reconnected to when you log on to the machine. If this option is used, the Usage key will be undefined.

trick about the Scope key is that it will always be RESOURCE_GLOBALNET (value of 2) because this is the value that is hardcoded into the extension. Refer to the description of the LocalName key for a brief explanation.

The Type Key

The Type key of the NETRESOURCE hash structure refers to the type of resource the share is. The possible values of this key are as follows:

- **RESOURCETYPE_ANY.** The share represents all resources. This is typically used when describing a domain (which is considered a share of multiple resources).

- **RESOURCETYPE_DISK.** The resource is a directory.

- **RESOURCETYPE_PRINT.** The resource is a printer.

- **RESOURCETYPE_UNKNOWN.** The resource type is not known.

The Usage Key

The Usage key of the NETRESOURCE hash structure specifies a bitmask that gives the resource usage. This member is defined only if Scope is RESOURCE_GLOBALNET (which is currently the only scope the extension supports). The possible values of this key are as follows:

- **RESOURCEUSAGE_CONNECTABLE.** This resource type represents a connectable share; you can connect to this resource directly.

- **RESOURCEUSAGE_CONTAINER.** This resource type represents a container resource; it can contain other resources. A domain object is a container, for example, because it can contain computer resources.

Hash Structure

The SHARE_INFO hash is a data structure used when retrieving or setting information about a shared resource. This data structure is a hash that describes the attributes about the resource being shared.

From the Perl debugger, a dump of a SHARE_INFO hash (using the **X** command) may look like the following:

```
DB<1> X ShareInfo
  HASH(0x106e138)
  'current-users' => 0
  'maxusers' => '-1'
  'netname' => 'Printer'
  'passwd' => ''
  'path' => '\\\\MAIN2\\Printer,LocalsplOnly'
  'permissions' => 0
  'remark' => 'Okidata OL610e/PS PostScript Printer'
  'type' => 1
```

Note

Only members of the Administrators or Account Operators local group or those with Communication, Print, or Server operator group membership can successfully run these functions that accept or return the SHARE_INFO *structure.*

The keys in a SHARE_INFO structure are as follows:

- current-users
- maxusers
- netname
- passwd
- path
- permissions
- remark
- type

Each of these keys in the SHARE_INFO hash structure is described in more detail in the sections that follow.

The current-users Key

The current-users key of the SHARE_INFO hash structure refers to the number of users who are currently connected to the resource.

The `maxusers` Key

The `maxusers` key of the `SHARE_INFO` hash structure refers to the number of users who can access the resource simultaneously. If there is no limit imposed, the value will be `'-1'`.

The `netname` Key

The `netname` key of the `SHARE_INFO` hash structure refers to the name of the shared resource. This is the name that the resource was shared as. If a share-point is accessed by using the UNC `\\server1\WordFiles`, for example, the `netname` is "WordFiles".

The `passwd` Key

If the server uses share-level security (as Windows 95 does), the `passwd` key of the `SHARE_INFO` hash structure is the password for the share. This password cannot be longer than eight characters.

If the server uses user-level security (as Windows NT does), this key is ignored.

The `path` Key

The `path` key of the `SHARE_INFO` hash structure refers to the path that the server is sharing. If a server shares the directory `c:\TEMP` with a name of "Temp File", for example, the path would be `c:\TEMP`.

The `permissions` Key

The `permissions` key of the `SHARE_INFO` hash structure contains a value that represents permissions placed on the shared resource. These permissions restrict how connected users can access the resource.

If the server sharing the resources makes use of user-level security, this key is ignored and is assigned a value of `0`. This is the case for Windows NT machines, but not Windows 95. The capability to specify user-level permissions (that is, permissions assigned to users and/or groups) on a share is currently not supported by any of the standard Win32 extensions.

The value of this key is a bitmask comprised of the values outlined in Table 2.2.

Table 2.2   List of constants used with the permissions key in a `SHARED_INFO` hash (you must use the values and not the constant names)

Constant	Value	Description
ACCESS_NONE	(0x00)	No permissions are granted.
ACCESS_READ	(0x01)	Permission to read data from a resource and, by default, to execute the resource.

continues

Table 2.2   Continued

Constant	Value	Description
ACCESS_WRITE	(0x02)	Permission to write data to the resource.
ACCESS_CREATE	(0x04)	Permission to create an instance of the resource (such as a file); data can be written to the resource as the resource is created.
ACCESS_EXEC	(0x08)	Permission to execute the resource.
ACCESS_DELETE	(0x10)	Permission to delete the resource.
ACCESS_ATRIB	(0x20)	Permission to modify the resource's attributes (such as the date and time when a file was last modified).
ACCESS_PERM	(0x40)	Permission to modify the permissions (read, write, create, execute, and delete) assigned to a resource for a user or application.
ACCESS_ALL	(0x7f)	Permission to read, write, create, execute, and delete resources, and to modify their attributes and permissions.

Note

For some reason, the permission constant names were not coded into the **Win32::NetResource** *extension; therefore, you must use the numeric values rather than the constant names.*

If you are creating a SHARED_INFO *hash (*$Info*) and you want to specify the read-only permission, you must use the value* 0x01 *rather than the constant name* ACCESS_READ, *as in:*

```
$Info{'permission'} = 0x01;
```

This may change in future versions of the **Win32::NetResource** *extension.*

If you want to specify a value comprised of several attributes, you need to logically OR (¦) them together. If you want to specify read and write permissions, you use the following:

```
$Permission = 0x01 ¦ 0x02;
```

Conversely if you want to test and see whether a particular permission is set, you logically AND (&) the permission with the attribute. If you have a particular permission, for example, you can test whether it has write permissions by using the following:

```
$CanWrite = ($Permission & 0x02) != 0;
```

The variable $CanWrite will result with either a 0 if the attribute is not present or a 1 if it is present.

The remark Key
The remark key of the SHARE_INFO hash structure refers to the comment that was assigned to the shared resource.

The type Key
The type key of the SHARE_INFO hash structure refers to what type of resource the share is. Possible values of this key are as follows:

- **0x00**. A shared directory

- **0x01**. A shared printer queue

- **0x02**. A shared communication device (such as a modem)

- **0x03**. Interprocess Communication (IPC)

Connecting to Shared Network Resources

If your intention is to make a connection to a network share, you must visit the **AddConnection**() function:

```
Win32::NetResource::AddConnection( \%NetResource, $Password, $Userid,
$Connection);
```

The first parameter (\%NetResource) is a reference to a NETRESOURCE hash.

The second and third parameters ($Password and $Userid) are the password and userid, respectively. The userid can be any valid user name (it does not have to be the current user). If the $Userid parameter is an empty string, the current user's userid will be used.

The fourth parameter ($Connection) determines whether the system should remember this connection. If the value for this parameter is a 1, the connection will be remembered and the next time the user logs on there will be an attempt to connect again (the connection will be persistent). This information will be remembered, however, only if it is successful in connecting to the share and the connection redirects a local device. Deviceless connections (that is, connecting as a UNC and not a drive or printer) will not be remembered.

If the **AddConnection**() function is successful, it returns a TRUE value; otherwise, it returns FALSE.

The code in Example 2.12 enables you to connect your R: drive to \\server1\games and remember the connection; therefore, every time you log on, your R: drive will automatically connect.

Example 2.12   *Connecting to a shared resource*

```
01. use Win32::NetResource;
02. %NetResource = (
03.   LocalName => "R:",
04.   RemoteName => "\\\\main2\\asf"
05. );
06. $User = "";
07. $Password = "";
08. if( Win32::NetResource::AddConnection( \%NetResource, $Password, $User, 1 ) )
09. {
10.   print "Successful!\n";
11. }else{
12.    # See Example 1.6 for the NetError() function
13.   print NetError();
14. }
```

The code in Example 2.12 will connect the R: drive to \\server1\games. Notice that only two fields of the NETRESOURCE hash were used: LocalName and RemoteName. There really is no need to use the other fields. If you wanted to specify a userid and password, you would fill out both the Password and User parameters. Typically these parameters are left as empty strings so that the connection is made using the current user's id and password. The fourth parameter of **AddConnection**() in Example 2.12 is a 1. So if the function successfully connects, the user's profile is updated to reconnect every time the user logs on.

> *Note*
>
> *In Example 2.12, you could have left off the LocalName key from the %NetResource hash. This would have made a deviceless connection. You would have been connected to the shared resource but not through a local drive letter. The only way to access the resource would be through a UNC.*
>
> *The user's profile would have not been updated to remember the connection (because deviceless connections cannot be persistent, whereas regular local devices connected to a share can be).*

Finding Information About Shared Network Resources

When you share many resources, it can be easy to forget the details of a share. This is where **NetShareGetInfo**() comes in handy:

```
Win32::NetResource::NetShareGetInfo( $ShareName, $ShareInfo [, $Machine]);
```

The first parameter ($ShareName) is the name of the sharepoint (like "TempFiles" from the UNC \\server1\TempFiles).

The second parameter ($ShareInfo) is a reference to a hash that will be filled in with a SHARE_INFO structure. *This must be a scalar, not a hash or a hash reference!* If you use a reference to a hash (\%ShareInfo), the resulting hash will be empty. You must use a scalar and de-reference the hash to access the hash's keys, as in Example 2.13.

The third parameter ($Machine) is optional and represents the name of the computer that will perform the lookup. So, if you want to get information about a share on another machine, you would specify the proper machine name (prepended with double backslashes) as the third parameter. If this parameter is an empty string or is left out of the function, the local computer is assumed.

If the **NetShareGetInfo**() function is successful, it returns a TRUE value; otherwise, it returns FALSE.

In Example 2.13, you can see how many users are connected to a particular share by using this function:

Example 2.13   *Retrieving information about a shared resource*

```
01. use Win32::NetResource;
02. $ShareName = "Graphic";
03. $Machine = "";
04. if( Win32::NetResource::NetShareGetInfo( $ShareName, $Info, $Machine ) )
05. {
06.   print "There are $Info->{'current-users'} current connections.\n";
07. }else{
08.   # See Example 1.6 for the NetError() function
09.   print NetError();
10. }
11.if( Win32::NetResource::YaddaYaddaYadda() )
12.{
13.  print "Success!\n";
14.}else{
15.  ... error catching code here (see Chapter 1) ...
16. }
```

Changing Shared Network Resource Attributes

Just as you have the ability to change your mind, you have the ability to change attributes of an existing share. You may want to change the number of concurrent connections a share can have or maybe change the comment field of the share. All this is made possible with a function called **NetShareSetInfo**():

```
Win32::NetResource::NetShareSetInfo( $ShareName, \%ShareInfo, $Param
[, $Machine] );
```

Similar to the **NetShareGetInfo**() function, the first parameter ($ShareName) is the name of the sharepoint. The second parameter (\%ShareInfo), however, is a bit different. This parameter must be a reference to a hash.

The third parameter ($Param) must be a scalar because it will contain a returned value. The value is only used for debugging purposes and is of little use. For more information, refer to the third parameter of the **Win32::NetResource::NetShareAdd**() function.

The fourth parameter ($Machine)is optional and represents the name of the computer that will perform the lookup. So if you want to get information about a share on another machine, you would specify the proper machine name (prepended with double backslashes) as the third parameter. If this parameter is an empty string or is left out of the function, the local computer is assumed.

If the **NetShareSetInfo**()function is successful, it will return a TRUE value; otherwise, it returns FALSE.

There is a trick about using the **NetShareSetInfo**() function. If you don't fill out the SHARE_INFO hash fully (leaving out the 'maxusers' key for example), you run the risk of setting values to null. If you filled out the hash to look like the following, for example:

```
$ShareInfo = {
    'netname' => 'Graphic',
    'passwd' => '',
    'path' => 'C:\\Data\\Graphics',
    'permissions' => 0,
    'remark' => 'Come and get my graphics!',
    'type' => 0;
}
```

no one will be able to connect to your share. Notice that the maxusers key was not specified. When you call **NetShareSetInfo**(), the maxusers parameter will be set to 0 because it was not specified. This setting will cause your shared resource to allow zero users to connect to it at any time. This is not good.

A better solution is to first call **NetShareGetInfo**(), and then change the hash values to your liking, and then call **NetShareSetInfo**(), as shown in Example 2.14.

Example 2.14   *Changing the remark field of a shared resource*

```
01. use Win32::NetResource;
02. $ShareName = "Graphic";
03. $Machine = "";
04. $NewRemark = "This is my new remark!!";
05. if( ! Win32::NetResource::NetShareGetInfo( $ShareName, $Info, $Machine ) )
06. {
07.   print "Unable to retrieve share information.\n";
08.   PrintError();
09.   exit;
10. }
```

```
11. $Info->{remark} = $NewRemark;
12. if( Win32::NetResource::NetShareSetInfo( $ShareName, $Info, $Param,
    $Machine ) )
13. {
14.   print "The Remark has been successfully changed.\n";
15. }else{
16.   print "Unable to set the new remark.\n";
17.     # See Example 1.6 for the NetError() function
18.   print NetError();
19.   exit;
20. }
```

Note

*You must be a member of the Administrators or Server Operators groups to successfully use the **Win32::NetResource::NetShareSetInfo**() function; however, members of the Print Operators group can use the function (but only on shared printer resources).*

Canceling Connections to Shared Network Resources

For some odd reason, someone at Microsoft decided that Win32 applications can connect to a sharepoint but they must cancel the connection instead of disconnecting from the sharepoint. This has caused many programmers headaches because it seems more intuitive if one connects to something he must then later disconnect. This may not be intuitive, but it works. To cancel (or disconnect) from a shared resource, you use the **CancelConnection**() function:

```
Win32::NetResource::CancelConnection( $LocalName, $Flag, $Force );
```

The function takes three parameters. The first, $LocalName, is the local name of the shared resource. If you have connected to \\server1\TempFiles as your R: drive, for example, the local name is R:. If you have mapped your LPT2: port to some printer share, your local name is LPT2:. If you have connected to \\server1\source but have not mapped it to any local device, however, you would use the full UNC as the local name.

The second parameter ($Flag) is a flag that indicates how you want to cancel the connection. If you specify a 0, the connection is terminated. If you specify a 1, however, not only will the connection be canceled but also the user's profile will be updated, canceling any persistent connection to the resource. Use this if you want to prevent Windows from automatically connecting to the share the next time you log on.

The third and last parameter ($Force) specifies whether force should be used. If you specify a value of 1, the connection will be forced to disconnect even if there are open files or applications running from that resource. If a value of 0 is specified and there are open files, the function will fail.

If the **CancelConnection**() function is successful, it returns TRUE; otherwise, it returns FALSE.

Suppose that one day your boss demands that you need to disconnect all of your connections to remote drives as well as remove all persistent connections to them. You can use the code in Example 2.15.

Example 2.15   *Disconnecting your machine from all shared disk resources*

```perl
use Win32::NetResource;
use Win32::AdminMisc;
@RemoteDrives = Win32::AdminMisc::GetDrives( DRIVE_REMOTE );
foreach $Drive ( @RemoteDrives )
{
   $Win32::NetResource::CancelConnection( $Drive, 1, 1 );
}
```

This example makes use of the **Win32::AdminMisc::GetDrives**() function, which returns an array of valid drive root directories that match the specified drive type. For more details, refer to Chapter 3, "Administration of Machines."

Creating Shared Network Resources

Creating a share is as easy as filling out a data structure and calling a function. Just fill out a SHARE_INFO hash (defined in the section "Changing Shared Resource Attributes"), and then submit a reference to that structure to the **Win32::NetResource::NetShareAdd**() function:

```perl
Win32::NetResource::NetShareAdd( $Share_Info_Ref, $Param [, $Machine]);
```

The first parameter ($Share_Info_Ref) passed into **Win32::NetResource::NetShareAdd**() must be a reference to a SHARE_INFO hash, not just a hash. You can use a reference to a hash:

```perl
%Share = (
    'path' => "C:\\Temp",
    'maxusers' => -1,
    'netname' => "TempFiles",
    'remark' => "My Temporary Files",
    'passwd' => "",
    'permissions' => 0,
);
Win32::NetResource::NetShareAdd( \%Share, $Param );
```

Or you can use an anonymous hash:

```perl
$Share = {
    'path' => "C:\\Temp",
    'maxusers' => -1,
    'netname' => "TempFiles",
    'remark' => "My Temporary Files",
```

```
       'passwd' => "",
       'permissions' => 0,
};
Win32::NetResource::NetShareAdd( $Share, $Param );
```

Or even:

```
Win32::NetResource::NetShareAdd( {
       'path' => "C:\\Temp",
       'maxusers' => -1,
       'netname' => "TempFiles",
       'remark' => "My Temporary Files",
       'passwd' => "",
       'permissions' => 0,
}, $Param );
```

Any of the preceding reference methods will work just fine.

The second parameter ($Param) is a scalar that will be assigned an error value. This error value is only of use if the function fails and the error is ERROR_INVALID_PARAMETER (this constant comes from the **Win32::WinError** extension). If both of these conditions are true, the $Param variable is set to be the index of the parameter which caused the failure. The value of $Param is used internally and is of very little use to a Perl program. You should just ignore this parameter.

The third, and optional, parameter ($Machine) is the name of a computer that you want the share to be created on. If you do not include this parameter, the share will be created on the local machine. Leaving off the parameter is the same as specifying an empty string as the machine name. The valid formats for the machine name is either the computer's name (server1) or the proper computer name by prepending two backslashes (\\server1).

If the **NetShareAdd()** function is successful, it returns a TRUE value; otherwise, it returns a FALSE. Example 2.16 demonstrates how to share a directory.

Example 2.16   *Sharing a directory*

```
01. use Win32::NetResource;
02. use Win32::WinError;
03. %Share = (
04.     'path' => "C:\\Temp",
05.     'maxusers' => -1,
06.     'netname' => "TempFiles",
07.     'remark' => "My Pathetic Temporary Files",
08.     'passwd' => "",
09.     'permissions' => 0,
10. );
11. $Machine = "\\\\server1";
12. if( Win32::NetResource::NetShareAdd( \%Share, $Param, $Machine ) )
```

```
13. {
14.     print "Successfully shared $Share{path} as $Share{netname}.\n";
15. }else{
16.     print "Failed to share $Share{path} as $Share{netname}.\n";
17.     Win32::NetResource::GetError( $Error );
18.     if( $Error == ERROR_EXTENDED_ERROR )
19.     {
20.         Win32::NetResource::WNetGetLastError( $Error, $Text, $Provider );
21.         $Text .= " ($Provider)";
22.     }else{
23.         $Text = Win32::FormatMessage( $Error );
24.     }
25.     print "Error $Error: $Text";
26. }
```

Example 2.16 shares a particular directory (C:\TEMP) using a name of "TempFiles" on \\server1. If this is successful, you will be able to connect to \\server1\TempFiles. If unsuccessful, a description of the error will be printed.

Keep in mind that creating a share whose name ends with a dollar sign ($) will render the share invisible. When someone browses for a share to connect to, invisible shares are not displayed. You can always, however, connect directly to an invisible share by specifying the UNC instead of browsing.

Warning

If you make a share invisible by providing a dollar sign ($) at the end of its share name, it will be invisible to other Windows machines. It is important to know, however, that the name is not invisible from everyone. The invisibility feature is supported by Windows, but other applications and operating systems do not necessarily support it. Seagate's BackupExec backup program can discover all shares on a server, for example, as well as the UNIX SMB server called Samba.

Note

*Currently the **Win32::NetResource** extension is not capable of applying account-based permissions on a network share. Users who need to apply permissions can use the Explorer or Server Manager programs that come with Windows NT.*

Removing Shared Network Resources

Now that you are familiar with creating shares, you will need to know how to remove or delete shares. This is not as complicated as creating shares. The function you use is **NetShareDel()**:

```
Win32::NetResource::NetShareDel( $ShareName [, $Machine] );
```

The first parameter, $ShareName, is the name of the share. The **NetShareDel**() function is not case sensitive; so if you want to delete the share \\server1\TempFiles, you can specify a $ShareName of "tempFILES".

The optional second parameter ($Machine), just as in the **NetShareAdd**() function, can be left out, or left as an empty string or a computer name (either just a name or a proper name). This parameter refers to the machine that will run the function. If you wanted to delete the share on another machine, you would specify the proper name of the computer in this parameter.

If the **NetShareDel**() function is successful, it returns a 1; otherwise, it returns a 0. Example 2.17 demonstrates how to remove a share.

Example 2.17   *Removing a shared resource from the network*

```
use Win32::NetResource;
if( Win32::NetResource::NetShareDel( "TempFiles" ) )
{
  print "Could not remove the share.\n";
}
```

Checking on a Shared Network Resource

Suppose that you need to check and make sure that a particular device is being shared. You may want to check that your file server is sharing a particular directory or your print server is sharing a particular printer, for example. You can do this using the **NetShareCheck**() function:

```
Win32::NetResource::NetShareCheck( $Device, $Type [, $Machine] );
```

This function checks to see whether $Device (specified in the first parameter) is being shared. A common example of $Device could be D or C. The device must be in capitals and can only be one character long (everything after the first character is ignored).

If the function is successful, the second parameter, $Type, will be set to a value that the device claims to be.

The third parameter ($Machine) is optional. If supplied, it is a computer name or a proper computer name. If this value is an empty string or if it is not supplied, the local machine will be assumed.

Now that you know how the function is *supposed* to work, take a look at how it *does* work.

The **Win32::NetResources::NetShareCheck**() function is an oddity. It makes use of the Win32 API function **NetShareCheck**(), which Microsoft has not documented well and does not work as advertised. If you try to check on a device that begins with a backslash, for example, the function will always claim that the device is a printer queue, even if the device does not exist! You can test this out for yourself by running the code in Example 2.18.

Example 2.18   *Checking whether a device is shared*

```
01. use Win32::NetResource;
02. $Device = "\\" unless ( $Device = $ARGV[0] );
03. %Values = (
04.   0          => "Disk"  # STYPE_DISKTREE,
05.   1          => "Printer"  # STYPE_PRINTQ,
06.   2          => "Communication Port"  # STYPE_DEVICE,
07.   3          => "IPC"  # STYPE_IPC
08. );
09.
10. if( Win32::NetResource::NetShareCheck( $Device, $Type ) )
11. {
12.   print "The $Key '$Device' is a shared $Values{$Type}.\n";
13. }else{
14.     print "The function failed.\n";
15. }
```

The %Values hash in Example 2.18 contains values that are not mentioned in the **Win32::NetResource** documentation. I got these values from the Win32 API documentation. These values are constants such as STYPE_PRINTQ and STYPE_DISKTREE and are not found in the **Win32::NetResource** extension for some reason (so I am using the values here rather than the constant names).

When you run the code, pass in a device (like a drive, directory, or printer device) as the first parameter. For example, the code

```
perl netcheck.pl C
```

on my machine will print:

```
'C' is a Disk.
```

because my C: drive is shared. (You must specify the drive letter as a capital character—lowercase 'c' will fail.)

Because the function seems to recognize only the first character of the specified device, it is not clear how you can specify a printer, modem, or IPC device.

The only thing you can depend on when using this function is that if *any* directory is shared on a drive and you specify that drive as the device, the

Win32::NetResources::NetShareCheck() function will succeed and the `$Type` parameter will be set to a disk type.

> ### *Warning*
>
> *I would strongly advise against using the*
> ***Win32::NetResource::NetShareCheck() function.***

Determining UNCs for Paths on Remote Drives

If you have a drive letter that has been mapped to a network sharepoint, you can discover what the UNC is for any path on that remote drive. This is done by using the **GetUNCName**() function:

```
Win32::NetResource::GetUNCName( $Unc, $Path );
```

The second parameter, `$Path`, is the path you want to translate into a UNC, such as `R:\Temp`. If the function is successful, the first parameter, `$Unc`, is set to the full UNC of `$Path`.

Assume, for example, that you have your S: drive mapped to `\\server1\Graphics` and you want to know what the full UNC would be to access the file `S:\Perl\Camel.gif`. You could try the code in Example 2.19.

Example 2.19   *Retrieving the UNC name of a shared resource*

```
use Win32::NetResource;
$Path = "S:\\PERL\\CAMEL.GIF";
if( Win32::NetResource::GetUNCName( $Unc, $Path ) )
{
  print "The UNC is $Unc\n";
}
```

The output for Example 2.19 would look like this:

```
The UNC is \\server1\Graphics\PERL\CAMEL.GIF
```

So now you know the next time you want to use `CAMEL.GIF` you can tell your graphic editor to open `\\server1\Graphics\PERL\CAMEL.GIF`. This is handy when a user moves from machine to machine (like a system administrator) and cannot depend on a particular network drive letter.

If the **GetUNCName**() function is successful, it returns a `TRUE` value; otherwise, it returns `FALSE`.

Determining Shared Network Resources

Most people like to discover hidden treasures that lurk out there in cyberspace. Perl coders are no exception to this universal rule. This is one of the impetuses for the **GetSharedResources**() function that will return a list of shared resources that exist on the network. The syntax for this function is as follows:

```
Win32::NetResource::GetSharedResources( \@List, $Type );
```

The first parameter (\@List) is a reference to an array. If the function is successful, this array is populated with NETRESOURCE hashes.

The second parameter ($Type) is the type of resource you are looking for. These types are defined under the Type key description of the NETRESOURCE hash.

If the **GetSharedResources**() function is successful, it returns a 1; otherwise, it returns a 0.

The **GetSharedResources**() function does not clean the array reference you pass into it (the first parameter). This means that if you call the function twice, your result will be the total results of both calls. This will most likely result in duplicate data; and on a big domain, this can be very deadly to a Perl script because it will take up large amounts of memory.

> ### Tip
>
> *It is best if you undefine the array reference before you call the* *GetSharedResources() function; otherwise, the results will be appended* *to the array. This could lead to a dramatically large array!*
>
> *For example, you would want to use code that is similar to this:*
>
> ```
> undef @Resources;
> Win32::NetResource::GetSharedResources( \@Resources,
> RESOURCETYPE_DISK );
> ```

Managing RAS Servers

For those of you who have RAS servers, it is awfully convenient to check on your modems to see who is logged on, which ports are in use, and who is allowed to dial in. These functions, among others, are available from the **Win32::RasAdmin** extension.

Discovering Ports on the Server

When you have that urge to find out which ports on your RAS server are in use, you can sink your teeth into the **GetPorts**() function:

```
Win32::RasAdmin::GetPorts( $Server [, \%Hash] );
```

With this function, the $Server parameter is the proper name of the computer you want to query, as in \\server1.

The optional second parameter (\%Hash) is a reference to a hash. If the function is successful, the hash reference will be filled out with a hash of hashes. The key names of the hash are the names of the communication ports (such as COM1) that are available on the server. Each key has an associated value that is a RASPORT hash consisting of the values described in the list that follows.

- **DeviceType.** A description of the type of device connected to the port such as "Modem" or "ISDN".

- **DeviceName.** The name of the device connected to the port, such as "Hayes 9600".

- **MediaName.** The name of the media used for the connection to the port, such as "rasser" or "PCIMACISDN1".

- **User.** The name of the client who has connected to the port.

- **Computer.** The name of the client's computer who has connected to the port.

- **Domain.** The domain that authenticated the user.

- **Flags.** A bitmask of values, which describes the connection made to the port. Possible values are as follows:

  - **GATEWAY_ACTIVE.** The server is using the NetBIOS gateway allowing NetBIOS commands and messages to be passed to the client.

  - **MESSENGER_PRESENT.** The client is running the NT Messenger service (so it can receive net messages).

  - **PORT_MULTILINKED.** The port is multilinked with other ports, allowing multiple ports to act as one port (increasing bandwidth).

  - **PPP_CLIENT.** The client is connected using the PPP protocol. If this is not set, the client connected using the SMB protocol.

  - **REMOTE_LISTEN.** The NetBIOS gateway is set to RemoteListen.

  - **USER_AUTHENTICATED.** The client connected to this port, and the user has been successfully authenticated.

- **StartTime.** The time when the client connected to the port. This value is the number of seconds since January 1, 1970. Because this is the same as the time format Perl uses, you can use the Perl time functions with this value.

- **Server.** This is a flag that if it is not zero then the server with which the port is associated is an NT Server; otherwise, it is an NT Workstation.

- **PortName.** The name of the port such as COM1:.

If the **GetPorts()** function is successful, it returns the number of ports that were found on the specified server and if the second parameter is supplied, the hash is populated with port information. If no ports were found (or if the server does not support RAS), it returns a 0.

Retrieving Port Information

When you are looking for comprehensive information about a particular port such as what protocols are active on the port and the number of types transmitted, you use the **PortGetInfo()** function. Be prepared because there is quite a wealth of information that this function retrieves:

```
Win32::RasAdmin::PortGetInfo( $Server, $Port, \%Hash );
```

The first parameter ($Server) is a proper RAS server name such as \\rasserver1.

The second parameter ($Port) is the name of the port, such as COM1: or COM32:.

The third parameter (\%Hash) is a reference to a hash. If the function is successful, this hash is filled with a series of keys and subhashes. The same set of keys and values returned from the **GetPorts()** function are filled into this hash in addition to the following items:

- **LineCondition.** The condition or state of the port. The possible values are as follows:

  - **RAS_PORT_NON_OPERATIONAL.** There is a problem on the port that is rendering the port nonoperational. The event log can be used to discover the reason for this failure.

  - **RAS_PORT_DISCONNECTED.** The port is not connected to any clients and is in a disconnected state.

  - **RAS_PORT_CALLING_BACK.** The RAS server is currently calling back the client.

  - **RAS_PORT_LISTENING.** The port is waiting for a connection.

  - **RAS_PORT_AUTHENTICATING.** The server is currently authenticating the client.

- **RAS_PORT_AUTHENTICATED.** The client has been successfully authenticated.

- **RAS_PORT_INITIALIZING.** The device attached to the port (such as a modem) is currently being initialized. After the initialization has completed, the state will change to RAS_PORT_LISTENING.

- **HardwareCondition.** The state of the hardware attached to the port. This is usually a modem. The possible values are as follows:

  - **RAS_MODEM_OPERATIONAL.** The device is functioning correctly and is waiting for incoming calls.

  - **RAS_MODEM_HARDWARE_FAILURE.** The device is not functioning correctly.

- **LineSpeed.** The speed in which the port and computer can communicate. This value is in bits per second.

- **Address.** This is a RASPORTADDRESS hash (refer to Table 2.3).

- **ConnectionStats.** A RASPORTSTATS hash (refer to Table 2.4).

- **PortStats.** A RASPORTSTATS hash (refer to Table 2.4). The hash pertains to the physical communication port, not the single connection on that port.

- **Parameters.** A hash that contains data that is pertinent to the particular media in use on the port.

The **PortGetInfo()** function will return a 1 if successful and a 0 if it failed.

Table 2.3   Description of the RASPORTADDRESS *hash*

Address Subhash Key	**Description**
nbf	This is the client's computer name. This key exists only if the client is successfully using NetBEUI.
ip	This is the client's IP address. This key exists only if the client is successfully using TCP/IP.
ipx	This is the client's IPX address. This key exists only if the client is successfully using IPX.

Table 2.4   Description of the RASPORTSTATS *hash*

ConnectionStats Subhash	**Description Key**
BytesXmited	Total number of bytes transmitted from the port.
BytesRcved	Total number of bytes received by the port.

continues

Table 2.4   Continued

ConnectionStats Subhash	Description Key
FramesXmited	Total number of frames transmitted from the port.
FramesRcved	Total number of frames received by the port.
CrcErr	Total number of CRC errors.
TimeoutErr	Total number of timeout errors.
AlignmentErr	Total number of alignment errors.
HardwareOverrunErr	Total number of hardware overruns. This indicates how many times the client has sent data too quickly for the server to read it.
FramingErr	Total number of framing errors.
BufferOverrunErr	Total number of times that the server's buffer was overrun (data coming in quicker than the server could handle).
BytesXmitedUncompressed	Total number of bytes transmitted that were uncompressed.
BytesRcvedUncompressed	Total number of bytes received that were uncompressed.
BytesXmitedCompressed	Total number of bytes that were transmitted that were compressed.
BytesRcvedCompressed	Total number of bytes received that were compressed.

Retrieving Server Information

If you ever forget how a particular RAS server is configured, you can query it using the **ServerGetInfo()** function:

```
Win32::RasAdmin::ServerGetInfo( $Server, \%Info );
```

The first parameter ($Server) is the proper name of a RAS server (something like \\RASServer1).

The second parameter, (\%Info) is a hash reference. If the **ServerGetInfo()** function is successful, this hash is populated with the following keys:

- **Available.** The number of ports currently available for clients to connect to. This represents the number of ports configured for RAS that are not currently in use.

- **InUse.** The total number of ports currently connected with clients.

- **Version**. This is the version of RAS that the server is using. Possible values are as follows:

  - **RASDOWNLEVEL**. LAN Manager RAS server version 1.0

  - **RASADMIN_35**. Windows NT 3.5 or 3.51 RAS server (or client)

  - **RASADMIN_CURRENT**. Windows NT 4.0 RAS server (or client)

If the **ServerGetInfo()** function is successful, it returns 1; otherwise, it returns 0.

Clearing Port Statistics

If you need to tell a port to reset its statistics, you can use the **ClearStats()** function:

```
Win32::RasAdmin::ClearStats( $Server, $Port );
```

The first parameter ($Server) is the proper name of the RAS server. The second parameter ($Port) is the port name such as COM3:.

If the **ClearStats()** function is successful, it returns 1 and all the port's statistics are reset; otherwise, it returns 0.

Disconnecting Clients

If a user has connected in to your RAS server and you want to disconnect him (as a joke or if he has been wreaking terror and havoc on your network), you can force the port on which he is connected in to disconnect using the **Disconnect()** function:

```
Win32::RasAdmin::Disconnect( $Server, $Port );
```

The first parameter ($Server), like the other RasAdmin functions, is the proper name of the RAS server. The second parameter ($Port) is the name of the port such as COM27:.

If the **Disconnect()** function is successful, it returns a 1 and disconnects the user; otherwise, it returns 0.

Case Study: Disconnecting a Particular Userid from All RAS Connections

So your boss comes running up to you, as he does from time to time, and proclaims that someone has stolen his password and he fears that the hacker is dialing in and accessing files. He wants you to change his password, but you realize that changing the password will not do much if the hacker is already logged on (and authorization has been already granted). What you need to do is quickly go through every RAS server and disconnect any user who is logged

on using your boss's userid. Take a look at Example 2.20; it demonstrates a
simple way to accomplish this task.

Example 2.20   *Disconnecting a particular userid from all RAS connections*

```
01. use Win32::NetAdmin;
02. use Win32::RasAdmin;
03. $Userid = "Boss";
04. if( Win32::NetAdmin::GetServers('', '', SV_TYPE_DIALIN, \@List) )
05. {
06.   print "Searching each server for $Userid...\n";
07.   foreach $Server ( @List )
08.   {
09.     my(%Info);
10.     if( Win32::RasAdmin::GetPorts( $Server, \%Info ) )
11.     {
12.       foreach $Port ( keys( %Info ) )
13.       {
14.         if( $Info{$Port}->{User} =~ /^$Userid/i )
15.         {
16.           if( Win32::RasAdmin::Disconnect( $Server,
                  $Info{$Port}->{PortName} ) )
17.           {
18.             print "$Userid was disconnected from $Server port:
                  $Info{$Port}->{PortName}\n";
19.           }else{
20.             print "Could not disconnect $Userid from $Server port:
                  $Info{$Port}->{PortName}\n";
21.             # RasAdmin handles extended version of network errors.
22.             $Error = Win32::RasAdmin::GetErrorString(
                      Win32::RasAdmin::GetLastError() );
23.             print "Error: $Error\n";
24.           }
25.         }
26.       }
27.     }
28.   }
29. }else{
30.   print "Could not find the RAS machine names.\n";
31.   print Win32::FormatMessage( Win32::NetAdmin::GetError() );
32. }
```

Here we are retrieving the list of RAS servers using
Win32::NetAdmin::GetServers(). We then grab information on all the ports
from each of the servers. If we find that a user is logged on to a port using the
$Userid name, we disconnect him. Pretty cool, eh? Now, if you have hundreds
of RAS servers located throughout the country, you can tell your boss that this
little script will handle it and he can relax. There isn't even a need for over-
time!

Summary: Perl and Win32 Networks

With all the hype around networking on the Win32 platform, it is easy to forget that there is quite a bit of management that needs to be handled. Win32 Perl is there just for such purposes.

The basic necessities to manage a network of computers are available using the common Win32 extensions. From RAS server management to network resource sharing, all these things are possible.

It is possible to use non-Perl utilities to accomplish these same tasks. As someone explained to me via email, however, you cannot guarantee that each computer that you run your Perl script on will have each and every one of the utilities you need. Likewise, it is difficult to depend on the utilities because occasionally a utility will change the way it works from version to version. By using a Perl extension, you can always depend on the extension to exist within your Perl library tree.

Perl can be quite a workhorse that can administer your network, saving you quite a bit of money in professional administrative utilities.

Chapter 3

Administration of Machines

Administrating a network of machines is quite a large task that can be quite difficult no matter how the operating system attempts to simplify its interface. Several disciplines must be mastered to keep the network free from problems. Simple concepts such as user accounts, machine accounts, trusts, shares, permissions, and privileges become quite tedious to manage when you are contending with hundreds or thousands of users and machines.

This is really not so much of an issue for the user who is running Windows 95 at home. This user probably will never deal with a network other than the Internet via a dial-up modem. For this scenario, much of this chapter really will not be of much use other than for those with a curious nature.

This chapter addresses the Win32 Perl extensions administrators can use to manage machines. This ranges from creating user accounts and groups (so that users can log on to a machine) to RAS permissions. Configuring a machine by means of INI files and the Registry is also discussed as well as looking for events in the Event log.

User Account Management

One of the most important elements in a domain is the user account. Without these accounts, no users could log on to the domain, and without users logging on no work would get done. Even if your domain is totally automated and needs no user intervention, you still need some accounts. You always need an Administrator account, for example, so that you can log on and manage the domain. Likewise many services need accounts to log on to the machine or domain for them to run.

Testing for User Account Existence

Before creating a new user account, you should use the **UsersExist()** function to make sure that a user account with the same name that you intend to create does not already exist. The syntax that follows shows the basic format of the **UsersExist**() function:

```
Win32::NetAdmin::UsersExist( $Machine, $User );
```

The first parameter (`$Machine`) is the name of the machine that is to be checked for the account. The machine name must be a proper machine name (prepended with double backslashes). If you are checking on a domain, you will want to specify a Domain Controller (Primary or Backup). If this is an empty string, the local machine is assumed.

The second parameter (`$User`) is the name of the account to be checked.

If the account does exist, the function returns a TRUE value; otherwise, it returns FALSE. Refer to Example 3.1 and Example 3.4 to see the **UsersExist**() function in action.

Creating User Accounts

Creating user accounts is rather straightforward; you use the **Win32::NetAdmin**'s **UserCreate**() function, the syntax for which is as follows:

```
Win32::NetAdmin::UserCreate( $Machine, $User, $Password, $PasswordAge,
$Privileges, $HomeDir, $Comment, $Flags, $LogonScript );
```

If the syntax for **UserCreate**() appears to be overwhelming, don't fret; it's much simpler than you may think. The nine parameters that you need to pass into this function are described in detail in the text that follows.

The first parameter (`$Machine`) is the server. This is just the name of the machine that this new user account will reside in. If you are creating an account in a domain, you need to specify the Primary (or Backup) Domain Controller. If you are adding the user to your "Accounting" domain, for example, you could use the **Win32::NetAdmin::GetDomainController**() function to find the Primary Domain Controller for the domain. You would then use that machine as the server for this function. If this parameter is left blank (""), the account is created on the local machine. You could specify a computer name such as `'\\Workstation'`, which would attempt to create the user account on that particular machine.

The second parameter (`$User`) is the new userid. This is what the user would enter when logging on. This userid is not case sensitive.

Tip

For those who are concerned with network security when passing passwords over a network, it is good to know that passwords are encrypted when performing a logon. These passwords, however, are fairly easy to crack if you have a network protocol analyzer. The techniques to crack

NT passwords are documented on several hacker pages on the World Wide Web.

If you truly want to secure passwords from even network sniffers, you should make sure that all passwords are more than seven characters in length. Passwords having eight or more characters encrypt differently from those of up to seven characters. This is so passwords are backward compatible with Microsoft's LAN Manager.

The third parameter for **UserCreate()** ($Password) is the new password for the user account. Note that after this account has been created you cannot use this function to change the password. The length of the password can be no more than 14 characters.

Note

The 14-character limit is defined by the Win32 API and could change in future versions of Windows. If you are a C programmer, this limit is defined in the LMCONS.H *header file.*

The fourth parameter for **UserCreate()** ($PasswordAge) is supposed to represent the number of seconds since the password was last changed. This parameter is ignored, and there have been questions as to why it is even a part of this function. It is possible that some future version of NT may use it, but as of this writing there is no need for it. This parameter can be any value, but it is probably best to keep it 0 or an empty string.

Note

The Win32 API requires the $PasswordAge *parameter when creating a new user account; however, it is not used and the password age is managed automatically by the operating system. This parameter may be included in the function for backward compatibility issues. Whoever ported the function to Perl most likely did not consider the fact that it was not necessary to include it.*

The fifth parameter for **UserCreate()** ($Privileges) represents privileges that a user may need. A user account can have a few different privileges, but when creating an account, you *must* use the USER_PRIV_USER privilege. Table 3.1 documents the full list of privileges.

Table 3.1   User privileges to be used with the Win32::NetAdmin::CreateUser() function

Privilege	Assignment
USER_PRIV_GUEST	Assigned to guest accounts
USER_PRIV_USER	Assigned to regular user accounts
USER_PRIV_ADMIN	Assigned to administrator accounts

A user account's privilege can be changed by group management (such as adding the user account to the Administrators group). The privileges are hierarchical, so if the JOEL account is in the Domain Admins, Domain Users, and the Domain Guests groups, the privilege that JOEL will hold is USER_PRIV_ADMIN.

The sixth parameter for **UserCreate()** ($HomeDir) is the user's home directory. All NT accounts have a home directory and can either be a local directory such as d:\users\joel or it can be a UNC such as \\server2\home\users\joel. Not everyone makes use of this, but it can be quite handy for users who need to have a location on a file server where they can put their files. This is especially important when a company has several PCs and a user can log on to any one of them, making it a necessity to access personal files from anywhere. (This is sometimes known as *hoteling*—where a user uses a different workstation every day, as is popular in data processing centers.)

The seventh parameter for **UserCreate()** ($Comment) serves as a comment. This comment does not have any practical use other than associating a string with the user account. Usually administrators make use of this to make sense of an account. An account called IUSR_MACHINE could have a comment of "The Web Server Account", for example, which makes more sense to a human than the userid does. This string is practically unlimited in size and can be an empty string ("").

The eighth parameter for **UserCreate()** ($Flags) specifies special flags for the account. These flags consist of account options (such as those shown by the User Manager when displaying a user's properties) and account types. This parameter can be any combination of the options listed in Table 3.2 and any *one* from Table 3.3. These values are all logically OR'ed together.

Table 3.2   User account flags

Flag	Description
UF_ACCOUNTDISABLE	Disable the account. When used with the **Win32::NetAdmin::UserCreate()** function, the account will be created but disabled.
UF_DONT_EXPIRE_PASSWD	The password for the account never expires.
UF_HOMEDIR_REQUIRED	A home directory is required. (This flag is ignored in Windows NT.)
UF_PASSWD_CANT_CHANGE	The user cannot change the password, only administrators and account operators can change it.
UF_PASSWD_NOTREQD	No password is required on this account. This overrides any policy that requires all accounts to have passwords, and passwords to be a particular size.

Flag	Description
UF_LOCKOUT	The account is locked out. This is caused by too many incorrect attempts to log on. This flag cannot be set, but it can be cleared if already set.
UF_SCRIPT	This indicates that the logon script was executed. Usually you would check for this flag on an account if you wanted to know whether the account's logon script was executed the last time the user logged on. For some reason, the Win32 API requires that this flag must be set when creating an account.

Table 3.3. Account types specified by a user and computer account's flags

Account Type	Description
UF_INTERDOMAIN_TRUST_ACCOUNT	Used between domains that indicate a *domain trust*. This type of account is used by a Primary Domain Controller when connecting to another domain. A domain that trusts another domain will have an account of this type that the other domain's PDC will log on using.
UF_NORMAL_ACCOUNT	Used for a *global user account*. This is the type of user account that is typically created.
UF_TEMP_DUPLICATE_ACCOUNT	Indicates a *local user account*. The user can use this account to access the primary domain, but not domains that trust this domain.
UF_SERVER_TRUST_ACCOUNT	Backup Domain Controllers have a computer account of this type. This type of account indicates that this machine is a BDC for the primary domain.
UF_WORKSTATION_TRUST_ACCOUNT	This is the type of account that a server (not a domain controller) or a workstation computer. If a computer logs on to a domain using an account of this type, it is a member of the domain. This is used only with computer accounts.

> **Note**
>
> *When creating a user account, you must specify an account type (typically* UF_NORMAL_ACCOUNT*) and at least the* UF_SCRIPT *option. These two are the minimum flags that must be used; otherwise the* **UserCreate**() *function will fail. You need to logically OR these values together, such as:*
>
> ```
> $Flags = UF_SCRIPT | UF_NORMAL_ACCOUNT;
> ```

The ninth parameter for **UserCreate**() ($LogonScript) is the logon script. This is the path to a program or batch file that will be executed when the user is logging on with this account. Any valid local path or UNC is allowed, as is an empty string (" ").

> **Note**
>
> *Only administrators and account operators can successfully call the* **Win32::NetAdmin::UserCreate**() *function.*

The code in Example 3.1 illustrates the use of the **UserCreate**() function.

Example 3.1   *Creating new user accounts*

```
01. use Win32::NetAdmin;
02. use Win32::AdminMisc;
03. $User = "Joel";
04. $FullName = "Joel Smith";
05. $Domain = "Accounting";
06. %Account = (
07.   password => "\U$User\",
08.   homedir  => "\\\\HomeServer\\Home\\$User",
09.   priv     => USER_PRIV_USER,
10.   flags    => UF_SCRIPT | UF_NORMAL_ACCOUNT,
11.   fullname => $FullName,
12.   comment  => "The account for $FullName",
13.   logon    => "perl \\\\LogonServer\\logon\\Logon.pl",
14. );
15. Win32::NetAdmin::GetDomainController( '', $Domain, $Server );
16. if( ! Win32::NetAdmin::UsersExist( $Server, $User ) )
17. {
18.   if( Win32::NetAdmin::UserCreate( $Server, $User, $Account{password}, 0,
      $Account{priv}, $Account{homedir}, $Account{comment},
      $Account{flags},$Account{logon} ) )
19.   {
20.     Win32::AdminMisc::UserSetMiscAttributes( $Server, $User,
        USER_FULLNAME=>$Account{fullname} );
21.   }
22. }else{
23.   print "The account already exists.\n";
24. }
```

Creating Machine Accounts

It may be interesting to know that when an NT machine is registered as part of a domain, a machine account is created just as a user account is created for a new user. This machine account is not much different from a user account. In fact, the Win32 API uses the same function to create machine accounts that it uses to create user accounts. This means that you can create a machine account by calling **Win32::NetAdmin::UserCreate()**. To do this, you must specify the UF_WORKSTATION_ACCOUNT flag from Table 3.3. This will work for not only workstations but for adding Backup Domain Controllers to a domain as well as adding interdomain trusts by specifying the corresponding account type flag listed in Table 3.3.

Unlike creating a normal user account, you must follow some tricks to create a machine account. The following list describes these tricks:

- The first parameter *must* point to the Primary Domain Controller.

- The account type used in the eighth parameter must be UF_WORKSTATION_TRUST_ACCOUNT (or whatever appropriate value you require for the type of account you are creating).

- The name (the second parameter) must be the computer's name in all uppercase characters, and the last character must be a dollar sign ($). The computer name \\BETTYS-COMPUTER would use the name: "BETTYS-COMPUTER$".

- The name must not be more than 15 characters long. This does not include the trailing dollar sign.

- The password (the third parameter) must be the name of the computer in all lowercase characters (as opposed to the account name) and must *not* include a trailing dollar sign. This password cannot be more than 14 characters. If the computer name contains more than 14 characters, truncate the password at the fourteenth character. To use the preceding example, the password for \\BETTYS-COMPUTER would be "bettys-compute".

- The user calling a script that creates machine accounts needs to have the Administrator privilege on the target computer specified in parameter one.

After a workstation's (or server's, controller's, or domain trust's) account has been created, you need to log the machine on to the domain. The first time the new machine is logged on, it negotiates with the PDC for a new password that will be used every time the new machine logs on. This happens automatically when a machine logs on to a domain in which a new account has been created. The PDC detects that the machine is logging on for the first time and initiates the changes.

After a machine account has been created (either manually by a Perl script or by using any domain administration tool), the account can be managed as if it were a regular user account. The account can be renamed, the password changed (be *very* careful with this, because you cannot tell a machine which password to use—only set it to the original password setting as described in the preceding list), it can be deleted, and the accounts can be listed using Perl functions found in **Win32::NetAdmin** and **Win32::AdminMisc**. If you manage machine accounts, you must follow the rules outlined in the preceding list.

As a side note, only administrators and those users who have been granted the SeMachineAccountPrivilege (also known as "Add Workstations to Domain" in the User Manager) can create and manage machine accounts.

Changing User Account Configuration

After an account has been created, it can be manipulated. The various properties that make up an account can be both queried and set by using the **Win32::NetAdmin** extension's **UserGetAttributes** and **UserSetAttributes** functions:

```
Win32::NetAdmin::UserGetAttributes($Machine, $UserName, $Password,
$PasswordAge, $Privilege, $HomeDir, $Comment, $Flags, $ScriptPath);

Win32::NetAdmin::UserSetAttributes( $Machine, $UserName, $Password,
$PasswordAge, $Privilege, $HomeDir, $Comment, $Flags, $ScriptPath);
```

The first parameter ($Machine) is the machine where you want to retrieve the account information. This should be your Primary Domain Controller, but any domain controller will do. (If you use a Backup Domain Controller, it will just take longer for your other DCs to learn about any updates to the account.) If this string is empty, the local machine is assumed. This string should be formatted as a proper machine name with double backslashes as in \\PrimaryDC.

The second parameter ($UserName) is the name of the user account.

The third parameter ($Password) is the password for the account. This is only used with the **UserSetAttributes**() function. The Win32 API does not support retrieving passwords.

The fourth parameter ($PasswordAge) is the age of the password. This indicates how many seconds since the last time the password has been changed. This value is automatically set by NT and cannot be set, only retrieved.

The fifth parameter ($Privilege) is the privilege that the account has been granted. These can be any one listed value from Table 3.1.

The sixth parameter ($HomeDir) is the home directory for the account. This is any full path or UNC. It can also be an empty string.

The seventh parameter ($Comment) is the comment field for the account. This can be an empty string.

The eighth parameter ($Flags) represents the account's option flags. These flags can consist of any number of flags specified in Table 3.2 and one flag from Table 3.3. If you are setting this, these options are logically OR'ed together. If you are testing for these flags, you need to logically AND this parameter with the constant to test whether the flag is set. (A TRUE result indicates the flag is set.)

The ninth parameter ($ScriptPath) is the full path (either local path or UNC) of the account's logon script. This can be an empty string.

If the functions are successful, they return a TRUE value; otherwise they return a FALSE. The **UserSetAttributes**() will update the account with the information passed into the function. The **UserGetAttributes**() will retrieve the values from the account that the passed in parameters represent, as in Example 3.2.

Example 3.2   *Using **Win32::NetAdmin::UserGetAttributes**()*

```
use Win32::NetAdmin;
use Win32::AdminMisc;
$User = "Joel";
$Domain = "Accounting";
Win32::NetAdmin::GetDomainController( "", $Domain, $Server );
if( Win32::NetAdmin::UserGetAttributes( $Server, $User, $Password,
    $PassAge, $Privilege, $HomeDir, $Comment, $Flags, $ScriptPath ) )
{
  print "The user '$User' has a home directory of '$HomeDir'.\n";
}
```

The **Win32::AdminMisc** extension has identical functions with the exception that there is an added parameter. The third parameter is the account's full name. This is generally the full name of the user whom the account represents.

These functions and their kin in the **Win32::AdminMisc** extension are pretty much made obsolete by two functions in the **Win32::AdminMisc** extension called **UserGetMiscAttributes**() and **UserSetMiscAttributes**(). These two functions retrieve and set several different options, ranging from the necessary and obvious to the obscure and vague:

```
Win32::AdminMisc::UserGetMiscAttributes( $Server, $User, \%Attribs )

Win32::AdminMisc::UserSetMiscAttributes( $Server, $User, $Option=>$Attribute[,
$Option2=>$Attribute2[, ...] ] )
```

Both these functions specify a first parameter ($Server) that is the name of the machine or the domain to retrieve the information. If this is an empty string

(""), the domain currently logged on to is assumed. If a machine is specified, you need to prepend the machine's name with double forward- or backslashes, as in \\ServerA or //ServerB. All the functions in the **Win32::AdminMisc** extension allow for this capability to use either forward- backslashes. Be aware, however, that this is not a practice found in most other extensions.

The second parameter ($User) is the name of the user account.

For **UserGetMiscAttributes**(), the third parameter (\%Attribs) is the last one passed into the function. This parameter is a reference to a hash. If successful, this hash will be populated with the keys described in Table 3.4.

For **UserSetMiscAttributes**(), all parameters starting with $Option=>$Attribute must be specified in pairs. These pairs are formatted as either:

    attribute, value

or

    attribute=>value

The format used is not important (because both of them are equivalent), but the second is preferred because it is easier to see what attribute is associated with which value.

When setting attributes, you need only to specify the attributes that you are changing—unlike the **NetAdmin** and **AdminMisc**'s **UserSetAttributes**(), in which you need to specify all values.

Both functions return a TRUE value if successful, and a FALSE value if they fail.

*Table 3.4   User Account attributes used with **Win32::AdminMisc::UserGetMiscAttributes**() and **Win32::AdminMisc::UserSetMiscAttributes**()*

Attribute	Description
USER_ACCT_EXPIRES	Specifies when the account will expire. This value is stored as the number of seconds elapsed since 00:00:00, January 1, 1970. A value of TIMEQ_FOREVER indicates that the account never expires. Note that this is the same time format that Perl uses, so you can pass this value into Perl's time functions such as **localtime**(). To set the time to expire in one week, you could use: time() + (7 * 24 * 60 * 60).
USER_AUTH_FLAGS	The user's operator privileges. This is a read-only value and cannot be changed using the **Win32::AdminMisc**'s **SetUserMiscAttributes**() function. This value is based on membership in local groups. If the user is a member of the Print Operations group, AF_OP_PRINT is set. If the user is a member of Server Operations, AF_OP_SERVER is set. If

Attribute	Description
	the user is a member of the Account Operations group, AF_OP_ACCOUNTS is set. The value AF_OP_COMM is never set. (It looks like it was designed for future versions of NT.)
USER_BAD_PW_COUNT	Specifies the number of times the user tried to log on to this account using an incorrect password. A value of 0xFFFFFFFF indicates that the value is unknown for some reason. This attribute is read-only and is maintained separately on each Domain Controller in the domain. To get an accurate value, each domain controller in the domain must be queried, and the sum is used.
USER_CODE_PAGE	The code page for the user's language of choice. Windows NT does not use this code page, but it is included for backward compatibility.
USER_COMMENT	The user account comment.
USER_COUNTRY_CODE	The country code for the user's language of choice. Windows NT does not use this country code, but it is included for backward compatibility.
USER_FLAGS	This value consists of several flags that determine features of the user account. Table 3.2 lists these flags. This parameter also describes the type of account being described. Table 3.3 lists a description of account types.
USER_FULL_NAME	The full name of the user.
USER_HOME_DIR	The path of the home directory for the user specified.
USER_HOME_DIR_DRIVE	This specifies the drive letter assigned to the user's home directory. This is used primarily for logon purposes.
USER_LAST_LOGOFF	Specifies when the last logoff occurred. This value is stored as the number of seconds elapsed since 00:00:00, January 1, 1970. A value of zero means that the last logoff time is unknown. This attribute is read-only. This attribute is maintained separately on each Domain Controller in the domain. To get an accurate value, each domain controller in the domain must be queried and the largest value is used.
USER_LAST_LOGON	Specifies when the last logon occurred. This value is stored as the number of seconds elapsed since 00:00:00, January 1, 1970. This attribute is read-only. This attribute is maintained separately on each Domain Controller in the domain. To get an accurate

continues

Table 3.4   Continued

Attribute	Description
	value, each domain controller in the domain must be queried, and the largest value is used.
USER_LOGON_HOURS	Points to a 21-byte (168 bits) bit string that specifies the times during which the user can log on. Each bit represents a unique hour in the week. The first bit (bit 0, word 0) is Sunday, 0:00 to 0:59; the second bit (bit 1, word 0) is Sunday, 1:00 to 1:59; and so on.
USER_LOGON_SERVER	The name of the machine to which logon requests are sent. Machine names are preceded by two back-slashes (\\). When a machine name is represented by an asterisk (*), the logon request can be handled by any logon server. An empty string indicates that requests are sent to the domain controller. This attribute is read-only. For Windows NT Servers, **UserGetMiscAttributes()** will return * for global accounts.
USER_MAX_STORAGE	Specifies the maximum amount of disk space the user can use. Use the value specified by USER_MAXSTORAGE_UNLIMITED to use all available disk space. As of Windows NT 4.0, this is not used; but future versions that support disk quotas may use this.
USER_NAME	Specifies the name of the user account. This is a read-only value and cannot be set by the **UserSetMiscAttributes()** function. If you want to change the user name, you need to use the **Win32::AdminMisc::Rename()** function.
USER_NUM_LOGONS	Counts the number of successful times the user tried to log on to this account. A value of 0xFFFFFFFF indicates that the value is unknown. This attribute is read-only and is maintained separately on each Domain Controller in the domain. To get an accurate value, each domain controller in the domain must be queried, and use the sum of all the values.
USER_PARMS	This is set aside for use by applications. This string can be an empty string, or it can have any number of characters. Microsoft products use this attribute to store user configuration information. Altering this value is not recommended.
USER_PASSWORD	Specifies a one-way encrypted LAN Manager 2.x-compatible password. This is not retrieved due to the Win32 API. It is here for backward compatibility with LAN Manager. For all practical purposes, this

Attribute	Description
	attribute is ignored and can neither be set using the **UserSetMiscAttributes**() function nor retrieved with the **UserGetMiscAttributes**() function.
USER_PASSWORD_AGE	Specifies the number of seconds elapsed since the password was last changed. This value is managed automatically by NT and cannot be set.
USER_PASSWORD_EXPIRED	Determines whether the password of the user has expired. For **UserGetMiscAttributes**(), this attribute will be zero if the password has not expired (and nonzero if it has). For **UserSetMiscAttributes**(), specify nonzero to indicate that the user must change his password at next logon and specify zero to turn off the message indicating that the user must change password at next logon. If this parameter is set to a non-zero value the user will only be able to log on interactively, at which time he will be forced to change passwords. Logging on as a process (non-interactively) will fail.
USER_PRIMARY_GROUP_ID	Specifies the relative ID (RID) of the Primary Global Group for this user. This attribute must be DOMAIN_GROUP_RID_USERS (defined in NTSEAPI.H for you C coders). This attribute must be the RID of a global group in which the user is enrolled. For most Perl scripts, this value is ignored.
USER_PRIV	Consists of one of three values that specify the level of privilege assigned the user account. Refer to Table 3.1 for information on the privileges.
USER_PROFILE	A path to the user's profile. This can be an empty string, a full local path, or a UNC.
USER_SCRIPT_PATH	The path of the user's logon script, .COM, .CMD, .EXE, or .BAT file. Basically any executable program can be placed here. If your machine has mapped the .PL extension to execute PERL.EXE, this value could specify a Perl script (such as LOGON.PL). This value can be an empty string to specify that there is no logon script.
USER_UNITS_PER_WEEK	Specifies the number of equal-length time units into which the week is divided. This attribute uses these time units to compute the length of the bit string in the USER_LOGON_HOURS attribute. This value must be UNITS_PER_WEEK for LAN Manager 2.0. This attribute is read-only. For Windows NT services, the units must be one of the following: SAM_DAYS_PER_WEEK, SAM_HOURS_PER_WEEK, SAM_MINUTES_PER_WEEK.

continues

Table 3.4 Continued

Attribute	Description
USER_WORKSTATIONS	This is a list of workstation and server names from which the user can log on. Up to eight machine names can be listed and must be separated by commas (,). An empty string/value indicates that there is no restriction. To disable logons from all workstations to this account, set the UF_ACCOUNTDISABLE value in the USER_FLAGS attribute.

In Example 3.3, the **UserGetMiscAttributes**() and **UserSetMiscAttributes**() functions are used to enable any account in the "Accounting" global group that has been previously disabled. Notice that the USER_FLAGS attribute is logically AND'ed with the UF_ACCOUNTDISABLE constant to determine whether the account has been disabled. To turn off the account disabled bit, you need to be careful not to alter any other bits. This is done by AND'ing the USER_FLAGS value with the two's complement of the UF_ACCOUNTDISABLE constant. If you are not familiar with two's complement, consider it to be the binary inverse of a number. If I specify ~4 (the two's compliment of four), for example, I am referring to the binary value "11111011" which is the inverse of the binary value for 4: "00000100".

By using the two's complement, you can be sure to turn off only the UF_ACCOUNTDISABLE bit; which is the same as enabling the account.

Example 3.3 *Using AdminMisc's UserGetMiscAttributes() and UserSetMiscAttributes()*

```
01. use Win32::NetAdmin;
02. use Win32::AdminMisc;
03. $Group = "Accounting";
04. if( Win32::NetAdmin::GroupGetMembers( "", $Group, \@Members ) )
05. {
06.   foreach $User ( @Members )
07.   {
08.     my%Attribs;
09.     Win32::AdminMisc::GetUserMiscAttributes( "", $User, \%Attribs );
10.
11.      # Check to see if the account disabled bit is set
12.     if( $Attribs{USER_FLAGS} & UF_ACCOUNTDISABLE )
13.     {
14.        # The account is disabled so re-enable it by ANDing the
15.        # flags attribute
16.        # with the two's compliment of the disable account flag.  This will
17.        # turn off only the UF_ACCOUNTDISABLE bit but leave other bits as
18.        # they are
19.        $Flags = $Attribs{USER_FLAGS} & ~UF_ACCOUNTDISABLE;
20.        Win32::AdminMisc::UserSetMiscAttributes( "", $User,
```

```
21        USER_FLAGS=>$Flags );
22.   }
23.   }
24.   }
```

> **Note**
>
> To set the USER_PASSWORD_EXPIRED *flag, the account's password must be able to expire. See the* UF_DONT_EXPIRE_PASSWD *value under the* USER_FLAGS *attribute for more details. You cannot specify zero to negate the expiration of a password that has already expired.*

Renaming User Accounts

Quite often, there is a need to rename an account. If a user changes his or her name for any reason (such as a marriage), for example, there may be a need to rename the userid. You could just create a new user account, but that would mean having to reconfigure it, copy over the old profile, add the account to any needed groups, reapply permissions on to directories and files ... oh just so much work! It is much easier to just rename the account.

By renaming the account, all configuration information remains the same, as do all file permissions and group memberships. In fact, renaming an account only changes the userid name; everything else is left as it originally was.

The **RenameUser()** function facilitates this need:

```
Win32::AdminMisc::RenameUser( $Machine, $User, $NewName );
```

The first parameter ($Machine) is the name of a machine or domain where the user account resides. If this is an empty string, the current domain logged on to is assumed.

The second parameter ($User) is the name of the user account that will be renamed.

The third parameter ($NewName) is the new name of the userid.

The use of this function requires Administrator or Account Operator privileges. If successful, the function returns a TRUE value; otherwise it returns FALSE. Example 3.4 shows an example of how to use the **RenameUser()** function.

Example 3.4   *Renaming a user account*

```
01. use Win32::NetAdmin;
02. use Win32::AdminMisc;
03. $User = "Joel";
```

continues

Continued

```
04. $NewUser = "Jane";
05. $Domain = "Accounting";
06. Win32::NetAdmin::GetDomainController( '', $Domain, $Server );
07. if( Win32::NetAdmin::UsersExist( $Server, $User ) )
08. {
09.   if( Win32::AdminMisc::RenameUser( $Server, $User, $NewUser ) )
10.   {
11.     print "The account '$User' was renamed to '$NewUser'.\n";
12.   }
13. }else{
14.   print "Could not rename account '$User' because it does not exist.\n";
15. }
```

Managing User Passwords

Passwords are always a problem for any administrator and user. The user must be forced to remember a countless number of passwords, some of which he has no control over. The administrator is always resetting passwords for those users who have forgotten them. There are a few ways to manage this hassle with the Win32 extensions.

The first of the password functions can be run by anyone (no special privileges are required):

```
Win32::AdminMisc::UserCheckPassword( $Machine, $User, $Password );
```

The first parameter ($Machine) is the domain name or a proper machine name where the user account resides. If a domain name is specified, the domain's PDC will be looked up and used. If this is an empty string, the domain currently logged on to is assumed.

The second parameter ($User) is the name of the user account. If this is an empty string, the account that is running the script is assumed.

The third parameter ($Password) is the password for the user account.

If the password for the specified user account is correct, the function returns a TRUE value; otherwise FALSE is returned. It is important to know that this function will check the password by attempting to change the password to a new password (which is the same password). **UserCheckPassword**() does this just as if it were calling **Win32::AdminMisc::UserChangePassword**() but passing in the same value for both the old and new passwords. This can be a problem on some systems if they do not allow reuse of passwords or if the account is not allowed to change passwords.

Several functions actually provide the capability to change the password for an account. The first two are identical to each other:

```
Win32::NetAdmin::UserChangePassword( $Machine/$Domain), $User,
$OldPassword, $NewPassword );

Win32::AdminMisc::UserChangePassword( ($Machine ¦ $Domain), $User,
$OldPassword, $NewPassword );
```

Both functions are identical and either can be used.

In both these functions, the first parameter ($Domain or $Machine) is the domain name or proper machine name where the user account resides. If this is an empty string, the domain currently logged on to is assumed.

The second parameter ($User) is the name of the user account. If this is an empty string, the account that is running the script is assumed.

The third parameter ($OldPassword) is the current password for the user account.

The fourth parameter ($NewPassword) is the new password.

If the password is successfully changed, both of these functions return TRUE; otherwise they return FALSE.

The new password is limited to the policies placed down on user accounts such as limits to the number of characters used, if old passwords can be reused, and whether the account is allowed to change passwords. Anyone can change any account password with these functions, provided that he knows the current password for the account.

Administrators usually have to reset a password for users who have forgotten their passwords. This can be done by using the **SetPassword**() function:

```
Win32::AdminMisc::SetPassword( ($Machine ¦ $Domain), $User, $NewPassword );
```

The first parameter ($Domain or $Machine) is the proper machine name or the domain where the account resides. An empty string indicates the domain currently logged on to.

The second parameter ($User) is the name of the user account whose password will be changed.

The third parameter ($NewPassword) is the new password.

The **SetPassword**() function will work only if the user calling it has administrative rights on the machine or domain which houses the user account. It will return a TRUE if the password was successfully changed; otherwise it returns FALSE. Just like the other password functions, policy restrictions can cause this function to fail.

Removing User Accounts

When an account is no longer needed, it can be removed from the user account database. It is usually a better practice to disable the account rather than delete it. This is because if for whatever reason you need the account later you can reactivate it and its configuration as it was when disabled. When an account is disabled, no one can log on using that account; for all practical purposes, it may as well be deleted. For more details on deleting accounts and their consequences, refer to the following note.

Note

Disabling an account is an alternative to deleting one. When an account is deleted, literally all information related to the account is lost. This includes file ownership and permissions, user privileges, group memberships, Registry permissions, and share accesses to name a few.

Suppose that your manager quits one day and your company hires another one. If you deleted the preceding manager's account, you would have to re-create a new one that would have to be totally reconfigured. If you just disabled the preceding manager's account, he could not log on or access his old data. When the new hire starts, you could just rename the disabled account, change the password, and reactivate the account. This way the new manager has her new account with the exact same privileges and permissions and file ownerships that the preceding manager had.

Disabling an account can be accomplished by setting the UF_ACCOUNTDISABLED *bit on the* USER_FLAGS *attribute. Refer to* **Win32::AdminMisc::UserSetMiscAttributes**() *for more details.*

If the account will no longer be used, it can be deleted with the **UserDelete**() function:

```
Win32::NetAdmin::UserDelete( $Machine, $Account );
```

The first parameter ($Machine) is the proper name of the machine to remove the account from. If the specified machine is a domain controller, the account will be removed from the domain the server represents. If the machine specified is a workstation or a server, the account is deleted from the machine's local account database. If an empty string ("") is passed in, the account is removed from the current domain that the machine is logged on to.

The second parameter ($Account) is the name of the account that is to be removed.

If the account is successfully deleted, the function returns a TRUE value; otherwise FALSE is returned.

Tip

When removing a user account from a domain, it is best to point the first parameter to the Primary Domain Controller for the domain. If the account is removed from a Backup Domain Controller (BDC), the BDC must be synchronized with the Primary Domain Controller (PDC) for the account to truly be removed. From then it must be synchronized from the PDC to the remaining BDCs in the domain. This can take some time unless you force domain resyncing using the Server Manager program. This means that even though you delete an account, someone may log on using it 10 minutes later because he logged on to a domain controller that had not been updated.

When an empty string is specified as the first parameter to the **Win32::NetAdmin::UserDelete**() *function, an attempt will be made to delete the account on the PDC.*

Managing User RAS Attributes

When an administrator needs to manage user accounts and whether they have access to RAS and any of its attributes, it can use the **Win32::RASAdmin** extension's **UserGetInfo**() function:

```
Win32::RASAdmin::UserGetInfo( ($Machine ¦ $Domain), $User, \%Info );
```

The first parameter ($Machine or $Domain) is the proper machine name that you want to get the list of groups from. This can also be a domain name. If you specify a domain name, it will use either the PDC or a BDC (whichever is most readily available) for the specified domain. If this is an empty string, a domain controller for the domain currently logged on to will be used.

The second parameter ($User) is the name of the user account.

The third parameter (\%Info) is a reference to a hash that will be emptied and then populated with RAS attributes.

If **UserGetInfo**() is successful, the hash is populated with values found in Table 3.5 and it returns a TRUE; otherwise it returns FALSE. If the function fails, the hash is emptied.

The user's RAS attributes can be changed using the **UserSetInfo**() function:

```
Win32::RASAdmin::UserSetInfo( ($Machine ¦ $Domain), $User, $Attribute=>$Value[,
$Attribute2=>$Value2] );
```

The first parameter ($Machine or $Domain) is the proper machine name that you want to get the list of groups from. This can also be a domain name. If you specify a domain name, it will use either the PDC or a BDC (whichever is most readily available). If you need to be certain that the list comes from the PDC, you need to pass in the proper name of the PDC. If this is an empty string, a domain controller for the domain currently logged on to will be used.

The second parameter ($User) is the name of the user account.

The third and fourth parameters ($Attribute=>$Value and $Attribute2=>$Value2) are the attribute and attributes value respectively. The list of attributes are found in Table 3.5.

Optional fifth and sixth parameters are just like the third and fourth parameters. These optional parameters enable you to set all attributes with one call to this function.

If **UserSetInfo**() is successful, it returns a TRUE; otherwise, it returns FALSE.

*Table 3.5   User attributes used with both the **UserGetInfo**() and **UserSetInfo**() from **the Win32::RASAdmin extension***

Attribute	Description
Callback	If the callback privilege is set, the RAS server will call the user back using this phone number. There is no limit to the number. It can be a long-distance or local call. Any valid phone number syntax is accepted.
Privilege	A set of flags that describe the privileges that the user has. The list of values are a combination of values from Table 3.6.

Table 3.6   RAS privileges

Privilege	Description
RASPRIV_DialinPrivilege	Sets the account such that the user is allowed to dial in to a RAS server. If an account does not have this flag set, that user cannot log on to a RAS server.
RASPRIV_NoCallback	Specifies that there is no callback phone number. After the user dials in and is authenticated, he is then online.
RASPRIV_AdminSetCallback	Specifies that only the administrator can set the callback phone number. This number can be set using the **Win32::RASAdmin::UserSetInfo**() function.
RASPRIV_CallerSetCallback	Specifies that the user can determine which number the server will use as the callback number. When the user logs on, he will be prompted for a callback phone number.

Group Account Management

Where you have user accounts, you will find groups. Basically speaking, a group is a collection of user accounts. You may want to group all users who have administrative privileges into a group called Admins. Anyone who is a guest could be placed into a Guests group. You could also have groups for Email Users and Accountants. In this respect, an NT group is very similar to a traditional UNIX group.

The beauty about NT groups is that a user can be in multiple groups simultaneously. You could have an accountant who has email access, so her account could be in both the Accountants and Email Users groups.

You need to know about two types of groups: *global* groups and *local* groups.

A global group can contain only user accounts and can be accessed from any machine that participates in the domain. You may put all administrators into your global Domain Admins group, for example. This way all the machines in your domain can see and use this global group. You can configure each workstation to allow the Domain Admins total unrestricted access over it. If one of your administrators leaves, you can just remove his name from the Domain Admins global group so that he does not have access over any of the machines in the domain.

A local group can contain both user accounts and global groups. Unlike global groups, a local group can only be accessed from the workstation that defines the group. You can add the domain's global Domain Admins group into the local Administrators group on each of your workstations so that each machine allows all members of the Domain Admins group administrative access over the machine.

Each group must have a unique name. No two groups can be named the same even though one may be global and the other is local.

> *Note*
>
> *Global and local groups are not the same as global and local user accounts. The terms global and local have different meanings when used for groups than they have when used for user accounts.*
>
> *A full description of these meanings is beyond the scope of this book, but it is important to know the differences that exist between the use of global versus local. A good NT administrator's book is recommended.*

Almost all the group functions that appear in the Win32 extensions come in two flavors: one for local groups and another for global groups. Ideally, this would be hidden from the Perl coder by using one function that determines whether the specified group is local or global; but alas this is not the case. The rationale for having two functions for each type of group comes from the Win32 API, which specifies two variations for every group function. It would appear that the original group management functions were direct interfaces to these Win32 API functions. All this means is that you may need to try both functions to get an accurate answer. If you are testing to see whether a user is a member of a group, for example, you need to first test by checking the local group; if it fails, you then check the global group. Because there is typically no way to determine whether a given group is local or global, you should indeed test for both possibilities.

Creating Groups

You can create groups by using one of two functions:

```
Win32::NetAdmin::GroupCreate( $Machine, $Name, $Comment );
Win32::NetAdmin::LocalGroupCreate( $Machine, $Name, $Comment );
```

Both functions are easy to use. You just pass in the proper machine name, the name of the new group, and a comment. If the call is successful a TRUE value is returned; otherwise a FALSE is returned.

The first parameter ($Machine) can be any valid machine name or an empty string. If it is a valid machine name, the group will be added in that machine if you have permissions to add to it. If an empty string ("") is specified, the group will be created on the local machine. If you are adding a global group from a domain, specify the Primary Domain Controller.

The second parameter ($Name) is the name of the group. It can be any string up to 256 characters, with the exception that it cannot be an empty string.

The third parameter ($Comment) is the group's comment and can be any string up to 256 characters long, including an empty string. Example 3.5 shows how to create a global group.

Example 3.5   *Creating a new group*

```
Use Win32::NetAdmin;
$Machine = "\\\\server1";
if( Win32::NetAdmin::GroupCreate($Machine,
"My Group", "This group is a test") )
{
  print "Successful.";
}else{
  print "Failed: " . Win32::FormatMessage( Win32::GetLastError() );
}
```

Adding Users to a Group

After a group has been created, you need to add users to the group. This is achieved by using the **GroupAddUsers()** function:

```
Win32::NetAdmin::GroupAddUsers( $Machine, $Group, $User[, $User2[, ... ] ] );
Win32::NetAdmin::LocalGroupAddUsers( $Machine, $Group, $User[, $User2
[, ... ] ] );
```

The first parameter ($Machine) is the proper name of the machine that contains the group. If this is an empty string, the local machine is assumed.

The second parameter ($Group) is the name of the group.

The third (and optionally more) parameter ($User) is the name of a valid user account. You can specify multiple user accounts by just tacking them to the end of the function's parameter list. You could just use an array of user accounts for this parameter.

If successful, this function returns a TRUE value; otherwise, it returns FALSE.

Notice that Example 3.6 first tries to retrieve a list of users from the group first. This is done to make sure that the group exists before attempting to add any users. This way you can also determine whether the group is a local or global group.

Example 3.6   *Adding users to a group*

```
01. use Win32::NetAdmin;
02. @Users = (
03.    "Patrick",
04.    "Jonathan",
05.    "William",
06.    "Leonard" );
07. $Domain = "Staff";
08. $Group = "Crew";
09. Win32::NetAdmin::GetDomainController( '', $Domain, $Server );
10.
11.    # Let's check to see if the group exists and if it does then we
12.    # will know what type of group it is.
13. if( Win32::NetAdmin::GroupGetAttributes( $Server, $Group, $Comment ) )
14. {
15.    $Result = Win32::NetAdmin::GroupAddUsers( $Server, $Group, @Users );
16. }else{
17.    if( Win32::NetAdmin::LocalGroupGetAttributes( $Server, $Group,
       $Comment ) )
18.    {
19.      $Result = Win32::NetAdmin::LocalGroupAddUsers( $Server,
         $Group, @Users );
20.    }else{
21.      die "The group $Group does not exist.\n";
22.    }
23. }
24. if( $Result )
25. {
26.    print "Users have been added to the group $Group.\n";
27. }else{
28.    print "Could not add users to the group $Group.\n";
29. }
```

Removing Users from a Group

Removing users from a group is very similar to adding users to a group. To remove users from a group, you can use the global or local form of the **GroupDeleteUsers()** function:

```
Win32::NetAdmin::GroupDeleteUsers( $Machine, $Group, $User[, $User2[, ... ] ] )
Win32::NetAdmin::LocalGroupDeleteUsers( $Machine, $Group, $User[, $User2
[, ... ] ] );
```

The first parameter ($Machine) is the proper name of the machine that contains the group. If this is an empty string, the local machine is assumed.

The second parameter ($Group) is the name of the group.

The third (and optionally more) parameter ($User) is the name of a valid user account. You can specify multiple user accounts by just tacking them to the end of the function's parameter list. You could just use an array of user accounts for this parameter.

If successful, this function returns a TRUE value; otherwise it returns FALSE.

Removing a Group

To remove a group, you need to know what kind of group it is: local or global. Two functions accommodate the removal:

```
Win32::NetAdmin::GroupDelete( $Machine, $Group );
Win32::NetAdmin::LocalGroupDelete( $Machine, $Group );
```

Just like the functions that add a group, the first parameter is a valid machine name (in the form of '\\machine') or an empty string ("") that indicates the local machine. If you are removing a global group from a domain, specify the Primary Domain Controller.

The second parameter is the name of the group to be deleted.

If successful, the group will be removed from the machine and a TRUE value will be returned; otherwise, a FALSE value will be returned.

The code in Example 3.7 defines a subroutine that accepts a machine name and group name. This example also attempts to remove the group regardless of whether it is global or local.

The **GroupDelete()** and **LocalGroupDelete()** functions will return a TRUE value if successful and a FALSE value if they fail.

Example 3.7   *Removing a group name*

```
01. Use Win32::NetAdmin;
02. if( MyDeleteGroup( "\\\\server1", "My Group" ) )
03. {
```

```
04.   print "Successful!\n";
05. }else{
06.   print "Failed: " . Win32::FormatMessage( Win32::GetLastError() );
07. }
08.
09. sub MyDeleteGroup
10. {
11.   my($Machine, $Group) = @_;
12.   my($Result) = 1;
13.   if( ! Win32::NetAdmin::GroupDelete ($Machine, "My Group" ))
14.   {
15.     if( ! Win32::NetAdmin::LocalGroupDelete($Machine, "My Group"))
16.     {
17.       $Result = 0;
18.     }
19.   }
20.   return $Result;
21. }
```

Retrieving Lists of Groups

If you need to discover which groups exist, you can use the **GetGroups()** function:

```
Win32::AdminMisc::GetGroups( $Machine, $GroupType, (\@List ¦ \%List)
[, $Prefix ] );
```

The first parameter ($Machine) is the machine that you want to get the list of groups from. This can also be a domain name. If you specify a domain name it will use either the PDC or a BDC (whichever is most quickly available). If you need to be certain that the list comes from the PDC, you must pass in the name of the PDC. If this is an empty string, a domain controller for the domain currently logged on to will be used.

The second parameter ($GroupType) is the type of group you are looking for. Table 3.7 lists possible values.

*Table 3.7   Group types to be used with **Win32::AdminMisc::GetGroups()***

Group type	Description
GROUP_TYPE_LOCAL	Retrieves the list of local groups
GROUP_TYPE_GLOBAL	Retrieves the list of global groups
GROUP_TYPE_ALL	Retrieves all group names (both local and global)

The third parameter for the **GetGroups()** function (\@List or \%List) is a reference to an array or a hash that will be populated with a list of group names. If a hash is specified, it will be populated with subhashes of group information.

The fourth parameter ($Prefix) is optional. If this is specified, only group names that begin with the same characters as are specified in this parameter are returned. Suppose that you need to collect only the group names that begin with "Test" (your test groups). You would specify "Test" as this parameter. This is convenient if your domain has thousands of groups and you need to access only a few of them.

Because of restrictions of the Win32 API, you can only retrieve the list of local groups if you hold administrative privileges (such as administrators and account operators). Anyone can retrieve the global group list. The **GetGroups()** function will populate the specified array or hash and return a value of TRUE if successful and a value of FALSE if not. Example 3.8 shows the **GetGroups()** function in action.

Example 3.8   *Retrieving the list of group names*

```
01. use Win32::AdminMisc;
02. $Domain = "Accounting";
03. if( Win32::AdminMisc::GetGroups( $Domain, GROUP_TYPE_LOCAL, \@Groups ) )
04. {
05.    DumpGroups( "local groups", @Groups );
06. }
07. if( Win32::AdminMisc::GetGroups( $Domain, GROUP_TYPE_GLOBAL, \@Groups ) )
08. {
09.    DumpGroups( "global groups", @Groups );
10. }
11.
12. sub DumpGroups
13. {
14.    my( $Type, @List ) = @_;
15.    my( $iCount ) = 0;
16.    print "This is the list of $Type:\n";
17.    map { printf( "\t%03d) %s\n", ++$iCount, $_ ); }, @List;
18. }
```

Managing Group Attributes

After a group has been created, you can get/set its comment by using the **GroupGetAttributes()**, **LocalGroupGetAttributes()**, **GroupSetAttributes()**, and **LocalGroupSetAttributes()** functions, the syntax for which is as follows:

```
Win32::NetAdmin::GroupGetAttributes( $Machine, $Group, $Comment );
Win32::NetAdmin::LocalGroupGetAttributes( $Machine, $Group, $Comment );
Win32::NetAdmin::GroupSetAttributes( $Machine, $Group, $Comment );
Win32::NetAdmin::LocalGroupSetAttributes( $Machine, $Group, $Comment );
```

All four of these functions accept the same three parameters.

The first parameter ($Machine) is the name of the machine that defines the group. An empty string indicates the local machine. To access a domain's global group, specify the Primary Domain Controller.

The second parameter ($Group) is the name of the group.

The third parameter ($Comment) is the comment for the group.

The **GroupSetAttributes**() and **LocalGroupSetAttributes**() functions will change the comment of the group, whereas the **GroupGetAttributes**() and **LocalGroupGetAttributes**() functions will retrieve the comment for the specified group and assign it to the third variable.

If the function used is successful, it will return a TRUE value; otherwise it returns a FALSE.

Example 3.9 demonstrates the functions for retrieving the comment for a given group.

Example 3.9 *Retrieving a group's comment*

```
01. use Win32::NetAdmin;
02. $Domain = "Accounting";
03. $Group = "Domain Admins";
04. $GroupFound = 1;
05. Win32::NetAdmin::GetDomainController( '', $Domain, $Server );
06. if( ! Win32::NetAdmin::LocalGetAttributes( $Server, $Group, $Comment ) )
07. {
08.   if( ! Win32::NetAdmin::GetAttributes( $Server, $Group, $Comment ) )
09.   {
10.     $GroupFound = 0;
11   }
12. }
13. if( $GroupFound )
14. {
15.   print "The comment for $Group is: '$Comment'.\n";
16. }else{
17.   print "The group $Group could not be found.\n";
18. }
```

Listing Users in a Group

Quite often, you need to process a list of users who are associated with some group. If you have a group called Email Users, for example, you may need to change their logon scripts. To do this, you would first need to know exactly who is in the Email Users group. This is where the global and local versions of the **GroupGetMembers**() function come into play:

```
GroupGetMembers( $Machine, $GroupName, \@Users );
LocalGroupGetMembers( $Machine, $GroupName, \@Users );
LocalGroupGetMembersWithDomain( $Machine, $GroupName, \@Users );
```

There is no difference between the first two functions other than one only works with global groups and the other with local groups. The third function is available from the core distribution's Win32 library version .12 (libwin32-0.12) and later versions. It retrieves both the domain and the user name or each account in a local group.

The first parameter ($Machine) is the name of the machine that holds the list. If this is an empty string the local machine is assumed.

The second parameter ($GroupName) is the name of the group.

The third parameter is a (\@Users) reference to an array that will be populated with the user accounts that are members of the group. If using the **LocalGroupGetMembersWithDomain**() function, the array will be populated with the members' user names and their domains in the form of 'domain\user-name'.

Both functions will return a TRUE value if successful; otherwise, they will return FALSE.

Example 3.10 uses the **GroupGetMembers**() function to change the logon script for all members in a particular group. Notice that the code tries both versions of the function because it does not know whether the group is a local or global group.

Example 3.10   *Retrieving the members in a group*

```
01. use Win32::NetAdmin;
02. use Win32::AdminMisc;
03. $Group = "Email Users";
04. $Domain = "Accounting";
05. $LogonScript = "perl \\\\ServerA\\Logon\\EmailUsers.pl";
06. Win32::NetAdmin::GetDomainController( '', $Domain, $Server );
07.   # Get the list of group members
08. if( ! Win32::NetAdmin::GetGroupMembers( $Server, $Group, \@UserList ) )
09. {
10.    Win32::NetAdmin::LocalGetGroupMembers( $Server, $Group, \@UserList ) ¦¦
       die "There is no group called '$Group'.\n";
11. }
12. foreach $User ( @UserList )
13. {
14.    if( Win32::AdminMisc::UserSetMiscAttributes( $Server, $User,
       USER_LOGON_SCRIPT=>$LogonScript ) )
15.    {
16.      print "Successfully changed logon script for user '$User'.\n";
17.    }
18. }
```

Verifying User Membership in a Group

Sometimes it is quicker to just test and see whether a particular user is a member of a group as opposed to retrieving the list of members and searching through it. You can use the **GroupIsMember**() function for this:

```
Win32::NetAdmin::GroupIsMember( $Machine, $GroupName, $User );
Win32::NetAdmin::LocalGroupIsMember( $Machine, $GroupName, $User );
```

The first parameter ($Machine) is the proper name of the machine that houses the group. If this is an empty string, the local machine is assumed.

The second parameter ($GroupName) is the name of the group.

The third parameter ($User) is the user account to be checked.

If these functions are successful, they return TRUE; otherwise, they return FALSE.

Machine Management

Administrating a domain of machines can be quite a job. Users are always deleting system files, changing bootup configurations, and reconfiguring software. Something is always happening to keep a team of administrators running from desktop to desktop. Luckily Perl's Win32 extensions have some handy functions that make this administration easier.

Administrators of Win32 machines need to manage INI files and the Registry. Additionally, NT machines need the Event log to be managed. Perl provides the capability to perform such tasks.

Managing INI Files

For many years now, INI files have plagued administrators because they are so easy for any user to change. Because there are no tools in NT or Windows 95 (let alone Win 3.x and DOS) to manage INI files, administrators have been using Perl to do the work.

An INI file is a file that programs use to hold configuration information. Think of INI to stand for INItialization, as in the configuration used to initialize a program. These files follow a particular format, which makes it easy to manage because all INI files follow this format. The file is broken into sections, each having a unique name. Each section can contain several keys that have equated values. Example 3.11 shows an INI file that contains one section called FileManager. (This was taken from a Windows 95 machine's File Manager INI file.) This section has four keys: Path, SearchSpec, Flags, and SavedSearches. You can see that the values for these flags can be either numeric or a character string.

Example 3.11   *Example of an INI file*

```
[FileManager]
Path=C:\TEMP
SearchSpec=*.doc
Flags=260
SavedSearches=0
```

Occasionally, you may need to change the contents of an INI file. A company I worked with had to roll out a version of Microsoft's Internet Explorer that worked with NT version 3.51. This version (3.0) made use of an INI file for its configuration. It had been installed on several hundred computers and the users were using it left and right. A network change was made, and the INI files had to be altered to reflect new proxy settings. A new INI file could have been copied down to everyone's machine during his or her logon script, but that would reset any personalization that the user had made. Instead we made use of the **Win32::AdminMisc** extension's capability to read from and write to INI files, as demonstrated in the following sections.

Reading INI Files
Data can be read from an INI file by using the **ReadINI**() function:

```
Win32::AdminMisc::ReadINI( $File, $Section, $Key );
```

The first parameter ($File) is the path to an INI file. This does not need to be a full path, but it does need to point to a valid INI file. If only the file name is specified (with no path), the file will be looked for in the current directory. If it is not found there, the Windows directory is searched followed by the Windows System directory, and then the environmental variable %PATH% is searched.

The second parameter ($Section) is the name of the section in the INI file. This can be an empty string.

The third parameter ($Key) is the name of a particular key in the specified section. If this parameter is an empty string, the function returns an array of key names.

If the **ReadINI**() function is successful, it returns one of the following:

- The data associated with the key in the specified section from the INI file.
- If the $Key parameter is an empty string, an array is returned containing the names of all keys in the specified section.
- If the $Section parameter is an empty string, an array is returned containing the names of all sections in the file.

Example 3.12 shows this function at work.

Writing INI Files
INI files can be altered by using the **WriteINI**() function:

```
Win32::AdminMisc::WriteINI( $File, $Section, $Key, $Value );
```

The first parameter ($File) is the path to an INI file. This does not need to be a full path, but it does need to point to a valid INI file. If only the file name is specified (with no path), the file will be looked for in the current directory. If it is not found there, the Windows directory is searched, followed by the

Windows System directory, and then the environmental variable %PATH% is searched.

The second parameter ($Section) is the name of the section in the INI file. If this is an empty string, the function removes all sections from the specified INI file.

The third parameter ($Key) is the name of a particular key in the specified section. If this is an empty string, the function removes all keys in the specified section.

The fourth parameter ($Value) is the value that will be associated with the specified key. If this is an empty string, the function removes the specified key.

If the **WriteINI()** function is successful, it returns a TRUE value; otherwise it returns a FALSE. When the function succeeds, the result will be one of the following:

- The value will be associated with the specified key in the specified section in the INI file. This overwrites any value already present.

- If the value parameter is an empty string, that key will be removed from the section.

- If the key parameter is an empty string, all keys in the specified section will be removed.

- If the section parameter is an empty string, all sections in the file will be removed.

Example 3.12 demonstrates both the **ReadINI()** and **WriteINI()** functions.

Example 3.12 *Adding and removing data from an INI file*

```
01. use Win32::AdminMisc;
02. $File = "$ENV{WinDir}\\win.ini";
03. $Section = "Devices";
04. @Keys = Win32::AdminMisc::ReadINI( $File, $Section, "" );
05. foreach $Key ( @Keys )
06. {
07.   $Devices{$Key} = Win32::AdminMisc::ReadINI( $File, $Section, $Key );
08. }
09.   # Remove the entire section...
10. if( Win32::AdminMisc::WriteINI( $File, $Section, "", "" ) )
11. {
12.     # Now add the devices again recreating the section...
13.   foreach $Key ( @Keys )
14.   {
15.     print "Adding '$Key=$Device{Key}' to [$Section]...\n";
```

```
16.    Win32::AdminMisc::WriteINI( $File, $Section, $Key, $Device{$Key} );
17.    }
18. }
```

> **Tip**
>
> *It may be handy to know that **Win32::AdminMisc's** ReadINI() and WriteINI() functions are not case sensitive. Therefore you need not concern your script with matching the case of a section or key name.*
>
> *Additionally, the specified file can use either forward or backslashes. The functions will convert any forward slashes to backslashes before doing its work. This is quite nice if you are using Perl-friendly path names as opposed to DOS paths.*

Tieing an INI File

There is another way to access and manipulate INI files: using the Perl **tie** function. If you are not aware of the **tie** function, it would be best to look it up in a good Perl reference book. This is a very powerful function.

Basically, the **tie** function will associate a variable with a Perl module. Whenever any action is performed on the variable, certain methods in the module are called. When you "tie" a variable to a module, you are adding what is called magic to the variable. This makes the variable magic—which is pretty cool!

Consider this example: Suppose that you have hooked up your house lights to your computer so that you can control them by means of a program. Assume also that you have written a Perl extension that controls the lights, enabling you to control them via Perl scripts. You could add code to your extension so that a hash, let's call it %Lights, is created. Now every time you query the hash, such as print $Lights{porch}, the status of the lights returns. If the porch light is on, $Lights{porch} returns a 1; if it is off, it returns a 0. If you were to set $Lights{porch} to 1, as in $Lights{porch} = 1, the porch light would turn on. Likewise setting it to 0 would turn off the porch light.

This could be done using magic (or tied) hashes. When you tell the hash (%Lights) that it is tied to your module, Perl will call your module to handle such things as querying the hashes values, setting the values, enumerating the keys in the hash, and so on. This is what is referred to as tieing or magic (because the hash appears to act as if it were magical).

The **Win32::Tie::Ini** extension provides magic to any hash that is tied with this extension. The hash will be an interface to an INI file.

To use this extension, you must first load it using the **use** command:

```
use Win32::Tie::Ini;
```

After this has been performed, you can tie a hash to any INI file using Perl's **tie** command:

```
tie( %Hash, "Win32::Tie::Ini", $File );
```

The first parameter (%Hash) is the hash you want to tie.

The second parameter is the name of the module; in this case it must be "Win32::Tie::Ini".

The third parameter ($File) is the name of the INI file. This does not need to be a full path, but it does need to point to a valid INI file. If only the file name is specified (with no path), the file will be looked for in the current directory. If it is not found there, the Windows directory is searched, followed by the windows system directory, and then the environmental variable %PATH% is searched.

If the **tie** function is successful, it returns a reference to the hash. There is no need to save this reference because it just points to the first parameter, the hash.

After that you have successfully tied a hash to an INI file, you can start to read settings. It is important to note that because INI files consist of sections containing keys, the hash will reflect that (in that the hash's key is a section name). The value of a key is a reference to another hash. That other hash will contain the section's keys, which are accessible by means of the hash's keys.

Reading from a Tied INI File

To read the keys from a section, you must first retrieve a reference to the section's hash, such as:

```
$SectionRef = $Hash{devices};
```

Now $SectionRef is a reference to a hash that contains the keys to the section. From this point, you can print out the keys and values of the [Devices] section using the following:

```
foreach $Key ( keys( %$SectionRef ) )
{
  print "$Key=$SectionRef->{$Key}\n";
}
```

Notice that you must de-reference $SectionRef to get to its keys because it is a reference to a hash (not just a hash).

You could, of course, de-reference the hash reference when you first assign it by using the following:

```
%Section = %{ $Hash{devices} };
```

Now you could use the %Section hash as a regular hash:

```
foreach $Key ( keys( %Section ) )
{
  print "$Key=$Section{$Key}\n";
}
```

It is very important to note that by de-referencing the hash reference (as in the second example), you have a *copy* of the INI file's data. Making changes to this new hash will not update the INI file. So, if you were to do this:

```
%Section = %{ $Hash{devices} };
$Section{WinFax} = "This is a test";
```

the WinFax key in the [Devices] section of the INI file will not be changed. This is because you are changing a key's data in the %Section hash. This hash is a copy of the INI data; it is not tied to the INI file at all (as %Hash is).

On the other hand, if you used the hash reference, as in the first example, changes made to it will be saved to the INI file. This is because the hash reference is still tied to the INI file. For more details about this, consult a Perl manual regarding hashes, hash references, and tieing (such as O'Reilly & Associate's *Advanced Perl Programming*).

Writing to a Tied INI File
Writing to the INI file is as easy as setting the value of a hash. Continuing from the preceding section, assume that %Hash is tied to an INI file (the WIN.INI file in particular).

You could set the data for the WinFax key in the [Devices] section by using:

```
$Hash{devices}->{WinFax} = "This is my new test data";
```

It is that easy. You could just as well use:

```
$Section = $Hash{devices};
$Section->{WinFax} = "This is my new test data";
```

Notice that only references are used here. If you use a regular hash, it will be a copy of the data from the hash reference—which is not tied, so any changes will not be saved to the INI file.

Removing Data from a Tied INI File
To remove a key or section in an INI file, all you need to do is use the **delete** command as you normally would:

```
delete $Hash{devices}->{WinFax};
```

This removes the `WinFax` key from the `[Devices]` section of the INI file. Likewise this code:

```
delete $Hash{devices};
```

removes the entire `[Devices]` section from the INI file.

Untieing an INI File

After you finish with the INI file, all you need to do is untie the hash. Then you really are finished! You use Perl's **untie** command for this:

```
untie %Hash;
```

The code in Example 3.13 demonstrates how easy it is to use the **Win32::Tie::Ini** extension to perform the same task as Example 3.12.

Example 3.13   *Using the **Win32::Tie::Ini** extension version of Example 3.12*

```
01. use Win32::Tie::Ini;
02. $File = "$ENV{WinDir}\\win.ini";
03. $Section = "Devices";
04. tie( %Hash, "Win::Tie::Ini", $File ) || die "Could not tie to $File.\n";
05.    # Make a *copy* of the INI files section
06. %Devices = %{ $Hash{$Section} };
07.    # Remove the entire section...
08. delete $Hash{$Section};
09.    # Now add the devices again recreating the section...
10. %{ $Hash{$Section} } = %Devices;
11. untie %Hash;
```

Managing the Registry

Not all configuration information is stored in INI files. Since the Win32 platform has been released, Microsoft has been encouraging programmers to make use of the Registry and not use INI files. There is good reason for this, because the Registry is a central repository of configuration data. This makes it easier for administrators to find configuration data because it is always in a database rather than scattered among hundreds of directories and other files on a hard drive.

> *Note*
>
> *On Windows NT machines, a user's Registry information can be stored as the user's profile on a file server. If the user's account is configured to use a "roaming profile," when the user logs on to a different machine, it loads the profile from the file server. This enables the user to always have access to his personal configurations regardless of which machine he may be logged on to.*

On the other hand, in many cases the Registry becomes so huge with information that it slows the machine down when a program is accessing configuration data from within the Registry. Additionally, it is more difficult to modify the Registry than it is to modify an INI file.

Win32 Perl has a standard Registry extension that provides access to Registry data. This makes administrating these important databases a breeze.

The Registry is a database that consists of keys, subkeys, values, and data. Think of it like a file system. A key is like a directory. Whereas a directory can contain files and other subdirectories, a key can contain values and other subkeys. A value is just a name associated with some type of data, just as a file name is just name associated to data (the data held within the file).

Just like your Win32 machine can have multiple drives, the Registry has multiple root keys. These roots define what kind of data is held underneath them. To illustrate this, imagine that you have only system files on your C: drive, only data files on your D: drive, and only applications on your E: drive. These roots will come into play in the section on opening keys.

The **Win32::Registry** extension automatically creates Win32::Registry objects that point to the Registry's root keys (or hives). Table 3.8 lists these objects.

*Table 3.8   Predefined **Win32::Registry** objects that reflect the Win32 Registry root keys*

Registry object	Description
$HKEY_LOCAL_MACHINE	Points to the hive that contains configuration information about the computer. This includes device drivers and service configurations.
$HKEY_CURRENT_USER	Points to the current user's hive. This hive is not available when accessing a Registry remotely.
$HKEY_CLASSES_ROOT	This is the root key for all OLE/COM-related class information. This includes MIME types and file associations. This root is a link to HKEY_LOCAL_MACHINE\ Software\Classes. This is important to know because this root key is unavailable when connecting a Registry remotely.
$HKEY_USERS	This is the root key for all user hives.
$HKEY_PERFORMANCE_DATA	This is the root key for all performance data. The Win32 does not have a separate API to gather performance data; instead it uses the Registry API (the **RegQueryValueEx**() function in particular) to retrieve performance data. The Registry API maps requests using

Registry object	Description
	this root key to the actual performance data counters and registers.
$HKEY_CURRENT_CONFIG	Points to the current configuration in the Registry.
$HKEY_DYN_DAT	This root key is the Windows 95/98 equivalent to NT's HKEY_PERFORMANCE_DATA.

A *hive* is any key and all its values and subkeys. Typically a hive will represent a tree of keys and subkeys related to something. A user's personal configuration on an NT machine is stored as part of the user's profile, for example. When the user logs on to a machine, it will load up that user's hive into the Registry and point the HKEY_CURRENT_USER root key to it. If a user's profile does not exist, a new one is created based on the default profile. This way you always know that the current user's configuration information is available via that root key. A hive is basically any collection of keys, subkeys, and values.

Hives can be loaded into and unloaded from the Registry. An administrator may need to modify a particular user's Registry settings, for example. The administrator could log on to a machine using the user's ID and password (presuming that he knew it or reset it). This would cause the user's personal hive to be loaded into the Registry and linked to the HKEY_CURRENT_USER root. The administrator could then proceed to edit the HKEY_CURRENT_USER's contents. When the administrator logs off, the hive is unloaded from the Registry. This could be quite a burden if the administrator had to change several users' configurations.

The alternative to this tedious approach is to manually load the user's hive into the Registry of some machine. When a hive is manually loaded, a temporary key name is specified and created, such as Joel's Hive. If the hive loaded successfully, the administrator can edit the contents of the root key Joel's Hive. When finished, the hive is just unloaded. This technique allows a Perl script to systematically load, modify, and unload any number of hives quickly and without human interaction.

Note

*The authors of the **Win32::Registry** extension included some pretty useful Registry functions. For some unknown reason, however, they did not provide access to all these methods through its module. This means that to use these functions you have to access the extension's functions directly as functions, not as methods. Each function will be discussed when appropriate.*

Opening a Registry Key

When accessing data in the Registry, you need to open a key, just like you would open a directory using the **opendir**() function. After the key has been opened, you can manipulate the values and data within the key. To open a key, use the **Open**() method:

```
$RegistryObject->Open( $Path, $Key )
```

Notice that **Open**() is a method of a **Win32::Registry** object. The first time you are opening a Registry key, you should use one of the root key objects (which are predefined by the extension) listed later in Table 3.9.

The first parameter (`$Path`) passed into the method is the path to the key that is to be opened. The path is relative to the object that is calling the method. If you want to open `HKEY_LOCAL_MACHINE\Software\ActiveState`, for example, you would specify a path of `Software\ActiveState` and the method is called from the `$HKEY_LOCAL_MACHINE` object.

The second parameter (`$Key`) is a scalar that will become a Registry object. You will use this later to call other methods.

If successful, the **Open**() method returns a TRUE value and a new Registry object is created and the scalar specified as the second parameter is set to the new object. If the method fails, it returns a FALSE. The method may fail because the key does not exist or because you do not have permissions to open the key.

Now that a key is opened, you can enumerate subkeys and values as well as retrieve and set data. Refer to Example 3.14.

Example 3.14   *Opening a Registry key*

```
use Win32::Registry;
if( $HKEY_LOCAL_MACHINE->Open( "Software\\ActiveState", $Key ) )
{
  ...process registry key...
  $Key ->Close();
}else{
  print "Could not open the key.  It may not exist.\n";
}
```

Creating a Registry Key

Just like opening a key, you can create a key using the **Create**() method. Creating a key will not only create the key, but it will open it just like the **Open**() method. If the key already exists, the key is opened and the method is successful.

```
$RegistryObject->Create( $Path, $Key );
```

The first parameter passed into the **Create**() method (`$Path`) is the path to the key that is to be created. The path is relative to the object that is calling the

method. If you want to create
`HKEY_LOCAL_MACHINE\Software\ActiveState\Perl5`,
for example, you would specify a path of `Software\ActiveState\Perl5` and the
method is called from the `$HKEY_LOCAL_MACHINE` object.

The second parameter (`$$Key`) is a scalar that will become a Registry object.
You will use this later to call other methods.

If successful, the **Create()** method returns a TRUE value and the specified key is
created as well as a new Registry object is created and the scalar specified as
the second parameter is set to the new object. If the **Create()** method fails, it
returns a FALSE. The **Create()** method may fail because the key was unable to
be created or opened due to permissions. Example 3.15 demonstrates this
method.

Example 3.15   *Creating a Registry key*

```
01. use Win32::Registry;
02. if( $HKEY_LOCAL_MACHINE->Create( "Software\\ActiveState\\Perl5", $Key ) )
03. {
04.     # We come here if the key was successfully created
05.     # or if the key already existed and the Create() method
06.     # successfully opened the key.
07.     ...process registry key...
08.     $Key->Close();
09. }else{
10.   print "Could not create the key.  It may not exist.\n";
11. }
```

Connecting to a Registry

Because administrators occasionally have to manipulate the Registry on remote
machines, the Win32 API defines a function that will connect to a remote
Registry. This is done with the **Connect()** method:

```
$RegistryObject->Connect( $Machine, $Root );
```

The first parameter (`$Machine`) is the name of a machine. This needs to be a
proper machine name in the format of `\\MachineName`.

The second parameter (`$Root`) is a scalar variable that will be set to a new
Registry object. You will use this later to call other methods.

The **Connect()** method is called from one of the predefined root keys listed in
Table 3.8. If successful, the scalar variable passed into the second parameter
will be a Registry object that represents the root key on the remote machine
that was used to call the method. The return value, if successful, is TRUE; otherwise it is FALSE.

Assume that you use this method from the $HKEY_LOCAL_MACHINE object:

```
$HKEY_LOCAL_MACHINE->Connect( "\\\\ServerA", $ServerRoot );
```

The result is that you will have a new Registry object that represents the HKEY_LOCAL_MACHINE root key on the machine \\ServerA that $ServerRoot represents. Anywhere you need to access something from the HKEY_LOCAL_MACHINE key on the remote machine (\\ServerA), you would just use $ServerRoot. Example 3.16 demonstrates this.

Note

*Some versions of **Win32::Registry** did not expose the **Connect()** function, so it was up to the author to hack the REGISTRY.PM file and add one. This can be done by adding the following code to the REGISTRY.PM file:*

```perl
sub Connect
{
  my $self = shift;
  if( $#_ != 1 ){
     die 'usage: Connect( $Machine, $KeyRef )';
  }
  ($Machine) = @_;
  local( $Result, $SubHandle );
  $Result = Win32::Registry::RegConnectRegistry( $Machine,
              $self->{handle}, $SubHandle);
  $_[1] = _new( $SubHandle );
  if( !$[1] ){
    return 0;
  }
  return $Result;
}
```

Example 3.16 *Processing Registry entries on all BDCs in a domain*

```perl
01. use Win32::Registry;
02. use Win32::NetAdmin;
03. $Domain = "Accounting";
04. Win32::NetAdmin::GetServers( '', $Domain, SV_TYPE_DOMAIN_BAKCTRL, \@BDCs );
05. foreach $Machine ( @BDCs )
06. {
07.   if( $HKEY_LOCAL_MACHINE->Connect( $Machine, $Root ) )
08.   {
09.       # We have a connection to the BDC...
10.     if( $Root->Open( "Software\\ActiveState", $Key ) )
11.     {
12.       ...process registry key...
13.       $Key->Close();
14.     }
```

```
15.     $Root->Close();
16.   }
17. }
```

Managing Registry Keys

Registry keys can contain values and subkeys. The values have data associated
with them. The names of these elements can be a bit confusing because their
relatives in INI files use similar names but have different meanings. In an INI
file, for example, a key is the equivalent of a Registry value. Likewise, an INI
file has keys associated with values, but the Registry has values associated with
data. This seems pretty screwy, but it is not too difficult to get used to.

> **Tip**
>
> *The Registry functions are not case sensitive with respect to key and
> value names. When specifying either a key or a value name, you can mix
> case if you like. To open a key, for example, the following two statements
> are considered valid and the same:*
>
> ```
> $HKEY_CURRENT_USER->Open( "Software\\Microsoft", $Key);
> $HKEY_CURRENT_USER->Open( "SOFwarE\\mICROsofT", $Key);
> ```

Any **Win32::Registry** object can be used to open a key, not just the predefined
root keys. This means that a **Win32::Registry** object created by successful calls
to the **Open()** or **Create()** methods can be used to open subkeys. In Example
3.17, the "HKEY_LOCAL_MACHINE\Software\ActiveState\Perl5" key is opened
twice. The first time it is opened as a subkey from the $Key object, and the sec-
ond time it's opened by using a root key object. This illustrates that it really
does not matter how you open the keys; either method will work.

Example 3.17   *Opening subkeys*

```
01. use Win32::Registry;
02. if( $HKEY_LOCAL_MACHINE->Open( "Software\\ActiveState", $Key ) )
03. {
04.     # Open a subkey using a previously created registry object
05.     if( $Key->Open( "Perl5", $SubKey ) )
06.     {
07.       ...process registry subkey...
08.       $SubKey->Close();
09.     }
10.     # Open the same subkey using a root key object
11.     if( $HKEY_LOCAL_MACHINE->Open( "Software\\ActiveState\\Perl5",
        $SubKey ) )
12.     {
13.       ...process registry subkey...
14.       $SubKey->Close();
15.     }
16.     $Key->Close();
17. }else{
18.     print "Could not open the key.  It may not exist.\n";
19. }
```

Generally, if you are processing keys by recursively calling a function, it is easier to pass a new Registry object into the recursive function, as in Example 3.18.

Example 3.18   *Processing keys using recursive functions*

```
01. use Win32::Registry;
02. if( $HKEY_LOCAL_MACHINE->Open( "Software\\ActiveState", $Key ) )
03. {
04.     # Dump all value names and sub keys...
05.     ProcessKey( $Key );
06.     $Key->Close();
07. }
08.
09. sub ProcessKey
10. {
11.     my( $Key ) = $_;
12.     my( $SubKeyName, $SubKey, @KeyList);
13.     mY( $Value, %ValueList );
14.
15.     # Dump the key's values...
16.
17.     $Key->GetValues( %Values );
18.     foreach $Value ( sort( keys( %ValueList ) ) )
19.     {
20.       print "$Value=$ValueList{$Value}[2]\n";
21.     }
22.     # Process all subkeys
23.     $Key->GetKeys( \@KeyList );
24.     foreach $SubKeyName ( sort( @KeyList ) )
25.     {
26.       if( $Key->Open( $SubKeyName, $SubKey ) )
27.       {
28.         print "Processing key: $SubKeyName:\n";
29.         ProcessKey( $SubKey );
30.         $SubKey->Close();
31.       }
32.     }
```

Querying Registry Keys

You can retrieve information about a key such as how many subkeys and how many values it contains by using the **QueryKey()** method:

```
$RegistryObject->QueryKey( $KeyClass, $NumOfKeys, $NumOfValues );
```

The first parameter ($KeyClass) is a scalar variable that will be set to the class of the key. This class is vaguely defined in the Microsoft SDK, but it seems to be inherited from previous versions of Windows when a Registry key could have only one value (or more accurately one data item associated with the key). In the Win32 world, this is equivalent to the default value for a key—the data which is assigned to a value with no name. (The name is an empty string.)

The second parameter ($NumOfKeys) is a scalar variable that will be set to the number of subkeys contained in the key that the $RegistryObject represents.

The third parameter ($NumOfValues) is a scalar variable that will be set to the number of values that the key has.

The **QueryKey()** method is handy to determine how many subkeys and values a key has; but other than that, it is really not of much value, as illustrated in Example 3.19.

If the **QueryKey()** method is successful, it returns a TRUE; otherwise it returns FALSE.

Example 3.19   *Querying a Registry key*

```
01. use Win32::Registry;
02. $KeyName = "Software\\Microsoft\\NetDDE\\DDE Shares\\CHAT\$";
03. if( $HKEY_LOCAL_MACHINE->Open( $KeyName, $Key ) )
04. {
05.   if( $Key->QueryKey( $MyClass, $NumOfKeys, $NumOfValues ) )
06.   {
07.     print "The '$KeyName' key contains $NumOfKeys subkeys and
          $NumOfValues values.\n";
08.   }
09.   $Key->Close();
10. }
```

Retrieving Subkey Names
For the sake of enumerating, you can retrieve a list of subkeys that are in a particular key. This can be done with the **GetKeys()** method:

```
$RegistryObject->GetKeys( \@SubKeys );
```

The only parameter is a reference to an array that will be populated with the names of each subkey.

If the method is successful, it will return a TRUE value and the array will be filled with subkey names. Otherwise the method returns a FALSE. Example 3.18 makes use of this method.

Removing Registry Keys
A key can be removed, or deleted, from the Registry. Care should be used when deleting keys because you can easily delete a key with several subkeys. Consider that if you delete the HKEY_CURRENT_USER\Software key, all software configuration for the user will be lost. Likewise, deleting HKEY_LOCAL_MACHINE\System will remove the configuration for Windows; all system drivers and such will be lost.

Deleting a key is done using the **DeleteKey()** method:

```
$RegistryObject->DeleteKey( $KeyName );
```

The only parameter passed in ($KeyName) is the name of the key. This is a path to a name relative to the $RegistryObject.

If the key was successfully deleted, **DeleteKey**() returns TRUE; otherwise, it returns FALSE.

Example 3.20 illustrates the **DeleteKey**() method.

> ### Warning
>
> *Opening a key does not prevent it from being deleted. If you open the* HKEY_LOCAL_MACHINE\Software\Microsoft *key, for example, you can still delete the* HKEY_LOCAL_MACHINE\Software *key (which will remove all sub-keys, including the Microsoft key you opened).*

Example 3.20   *Deleting a key*

```
use Win32::Registry;
if( $HKEY_LOCAL_MACHINE->Open( "Software", $Key ) )
{
  $Key->DeleteKey( "ActiveState\\Perl5" );
  $Key->Close();
}
```

Retrieving Registry Key Value Data

Any key can have any number of values. Each value has data associated with it. This data can either be a number, binary, or text data. To retrieve the data a value is associated with, you can use the **QueryValue**() method:

```
$RegistryObject->QueryValue( $SubKeyName, $Value );
```

The first parameter ($SubKeyName) is the name of a subkey that will be queried.

The second parameter ($Value) will be set with the data associated with the default value for the specified key.

Chances are that **QueryValue**() is not what you think it is. If you want to query a value in a key, this will not do it for you. Let me explain.

This method calls the Win32 API's **RegGetValue**() function, which was introduced in Windows 3.1. Back in Windows 3.1, there was no concept of a key having multiple values. Actually there was no difference between a value and a key. This function exists only for backward compatibility with Windows 3.1. Because Win32 Perl has never existed in the Windows 3.1 environment, however, there is some question as to why the **QueryValue**() function was ever exposed by the **Win32::Registry** extension.

The **QueryValue**() method retrieves the default data value from the key specified. This is of little value to most programmers because they normally will need to retrieve data for a named value (as opposed to the unnamed values).

The **QueryValueEx()** method enables you to retrieve data for a value name of
`""` (an empty string)—this is the exact same as using the **QueryValue()** method.
Because of this, you should consider **QueryValue()** to be obsolete and of little
use. Instead, use **QueryValueEx()**.

A much better way of querying a value's data is using the **QueryValueEx()**
method:

```
$RegistryObject->QueryValueEx( $ValueName, $DataType, $Data );
```

The first parameter (`$ValueName`) is the name of the value to be retrieved. This
can be an empty string.

The second parameter (`$DataType`) is a scalar variable that will be set to contain
the data type. Table 3.9 lists the data types.

The third parameter (`$Data`) is a scalar variable that will be set to contain the
data of the value.

If the **QueryValueEx()** method call is successful, it will return a TRUE value and
the second parameter and third parameter's variables are set to contain their
respective information. Otherwise, the method returns FALSE.

In some builds of both ActiveState and core distribution versions of this extension, **QueryValueEx()** was not exported by the extension's module. If you run
into this, you can call the extension's function directly by using the following:

```
Win32::Registry::RegQueryValueEx( $RegistryObject->{handle}, $ValueName,
    $Reserved, $DataType, $Data );
```

Notice that this is not called as an object's method but instead as an extension's function. The first parameter is the Registry's handle from the Registry
object. This is just the "handle" key from the Registry object.

The second parameter (`$ValueName`) is the name of the value.

The third parameter (`$Reserved`) is a reserved setting that directly translates to a
reserved setting in the Win32 API function. Always specify a zero (`0`).

The fourth parameter (`$DataType`) is a scalar variable that will be set to contain
the data type. Table 3.9 lists the data types.

The fifth parameter (`$Data`) is a scalar variable that will be set to contain the
data of the value.

Just like the method version of this function, if **RegQueryValueEx()** is successful, it will return a TRUE value and the second parameter and third parameter's
variables are set to contain their respective information. Otherwise, the method
returns FALSE.

Setting Registry Key Values

To create a value in a key, you use the **SetValue()** method:

```
$RegistryObject->SetValue( $KeyName, $Type, $Data );
```

The first parameter ($KeyName) is the name of a key that will be created.

The second parameter ($Type) is the type of data the value will hold and *must* be REG_SZ (refer to Table 3.9).

The third parameter ($$Data) is the data to be associated with the value name.

The **SetValue()** method will create a subkey with the name specified by the first parameter. This new key will contain one value that will have no name and its data will be set to the data passed in as the third parameter. If successful, **SetValueEx()** returns a TRUE value; otherwise, it returns a FALSE.

The **SetValue()** method reflects the same problem as the **QueryValue()** method. In most cases, a programmer will want to set a value in a key (not create a new key with a non-named value). You should consider **SetValue()** as obsolete and of little value. Instead use **SetValueEx()**:

```
$RegistryObject->SetValueEx( $ValueName, $Reserved, $DataType, $Data );
```

The first parameter ($ValueName) is the name of the value. If this value does not exist, it will be created.

The second parameter ($Reserved), oddly enough, is not used. You should always pass a zero (0) as this parameter. The Win32 API requires this parameter. Because it is always 0, however, I do not know why the authors of the extension decided to expose it in the Perl interface.

The third parameter ($DataType) is the data format that will be stored. Refer to Table 3.9 for a list of data types.

The fourth parameter ($Data) is the actual data to be stored.

If a call to the **SetValueEx()** method is successful, the key's specified value will be set with the specified data. A TRUE value will also be returned. If it fails, FALSE is returned. The code in Example 3.21 shows how to use the **SetValueEx()** method.

Example 3.21   *Modifying a value's data*

```
01. use Win32::Registry;
02. $KeyName = "Software\\Microsoft\\Office\\8.0\\Word\\Options";
03. $ValueName = "AutoSave-Path";
04. if( $HKEY_CURRENT_USER->Open( $KeyName, $Key ) )
05. {
06.   if( $Key->QueryValueEx( $ValueName, $DataType, $Data ) )
07.   {
08.     if( ( REG_SZ == $DataType ) || ( REG_EXPAND_SZ == $DataType ) )
```

```
09.   {
10.       # If we were autosaving to the C: drive change it
11.       # to the D: drive.
12.       $Data  =~ s/^c:/d:/i;
13.       $Key->SetValueEx( $ValueName, 0, $DataType, $Data );
14.   }
15. }
16. }
```

Table 3.9   Registry data types

Registry data type	Description
REG_SZ	A typical character string.
REG_EXPAND_SZ	A character string that has embedded environmental variables that need to be expanded.
REG_MULTI_SZ	An array of null terminated strings. The end of the list is terminated by a null character (so there should be two null characters at the very end of the list).
REG_BINARY	Any form of binary data. This could be of any length.
REG_DWORD	A 32-bit number.
REG_DWORD_LITTLE_ENDIAN	A 32-bit number in little endian format (where the most significant byte of the word is the high-order word). Typically this is the same as REG_DWORD. This type is used on Intel processors.
REG_DWORD_BIG_ENDIAN	A 32-bit number in big endian format (where the most significant byte of the word is the low-order word). Motorola processors make use of this format.
REG_LINK	A symbolic link in the Registry. This is the data type used to map root keys such as HKEY_CURRENT_USER to another key within the Registry.
REG_NONE	No defined value.
REG_RESOURCE_LIST	A device driver resource list.

Listing Registry Key Values

To get a list of values from an opened key, you can use the **GetValues()** method:

```
$RegistryObject->GetValues( \%ValueList );
```

The only parameter passed in this method is a reference to a hash.

If the method is successful, it will return a TRUE value and populate the hash; otherwise, it returns FALSE.

When the **GetValues()** method completes successfully, the hash is populated with keys that represent the names of the values in the key. Each of the hash's keys is associated with an array consisting of the three elements listed in Table 3.10. Notice that element 0 of the array is identical to the hash's key name. Example 3.18 demonstrates this method.

Table 3.10   The array returned by GetValues()

Array Element	Description
Element 0	The name of the value.
Element 1	The data type of the value's data. Refer to the list of data types in Table 3.9.
Element 2	The value's data.

Removing Registry Key Values

You can delete a value just as you can delete a key. This is done by using the **DeleteValue()** method:

```
$RegistryObject->DeleteValue( $ValueName );
```

The only parameter specified in this method is the name of the value to be deleted.

If **DeleteValue()** is successful, it will return a TRUE; otherwise it returns a FALSE value.

Managing Registry Hives

You can save any key (and its values and subkeys) to a file. This file is considered to be a hive that can be loaded into a Registry.

Saving a Hive

Saving a Registry hive is an easy way to migrate Registry modifications across several machines. By saving a hive to a file, a script can later either load the hive or replace an existing key with the saved hive. This way you could configure a program, save the hive that contains the program's configuration values to a file, and then use that file on other Registry. Descriptions about how to load hives and replace keys with hives follow this section.

To save a hive (a key with all its values and subkeys), you use the **Save()** method:

```
$RegistryObject->Save( $File );
```

The only parameter passed in **Save()** is the name of a file that will be created.

If successful, the **Save()** method will save the key and all its values and subkeys to a binary file that will be marked as a hidden, read-only system file. If the file already exists, the method will fail.

The resulting file is considered to be a hive. Example 3.22 demonstrates saving a Registry hive.

Example 3.22   *Saving a Registry hive*

```
use Win32::Registry;
$HiveFile = "c:\\temp\\Software.key";
if( $HKEY_LOCAL_MACHINE->Open( "Software", $Key ) )
{
  $Key->Save( $File );
  $Key->Close();
}
```

> **Note**
>
> *It is very important to note that all methods and functions in the* **Win32::Registry** *extension that make use of files (such as* **Save()** *and* **Load()***) assume that the file's path is relative to the machine housing the Registry. This means that if you are connected to a remote Registry and load a hive from* `c:\temp\hive.reg`, *the file must be on the remote machine's* `c:\temp` *directory.*
>
> *Additionally, the Microsoft Win32 documentation specifies that Registry files created with any file extension on a FAT-formatted drive will fail to load. This does not seem to be the case in Windows 95, but your mileage may vary.*

Loading a Hive

After a hive has been saved to a file, it can be loaded into a Registry where it can be edited. This is what the **Load()** method is all about:

```
$RegistryObject->Load( $KeyName, $File );
```

The first parameter (`$KeyName`) is the name of the key that will represent the hive. This name must not already exist. You cannot load a hive over an existing key; if you try, the method will fail.

The second parameter (`$File`) is the path to a saved hive file.

The `$RegistryObject` that calls this method must be one of either `$HKEY_LOCAL_MACHINE` or `$HKEY_USERS`. It cannot be any non-root key that you have opened.

> **Note**
>
> *The* **Load()** *method can only be called from a true root key such as* `HKEY_LOCAL_MACHINE` *and* `HKEY_USERS`. *Other root keys such as*

continues

Continued

> HKEY_CURRENT_USER *are not truly root keys because they are just links to other non-root keys.*
>
> *The root* HKEY_CURRENT_CONFIG *is really just a link to* HKEY_LOCAL_MACHINE\System\CurrentControlSet\ Hardware Profiles\Current, *for example. Because* HKEY_CURRENT_CONFIG *is not a true root key, the method cannot be called from it.*

If the **Load()** method is successful the hive will have been loaded and can be accessed by opening the key name specified as the first parameter to this method. The **Load()** method will return a TRUE if successful; otherwise, it returns a FALSE. Refer to Example 3.23 to see the **Load()** method in action.

Warning

Registry key names can consist of any character except the backslash (\) because the backslash is used to delimit keys in a Registry path. If you try to create a key containing a backslash in the Registry Editor, it will fail and give you an error message. The **Win32::Registry** *extension, however, enables you to create key names with a backslash.*

It is in your best interest to not create keys with backslashes because you may not be able to open the key to either modify or remove it.

Unloading a Hive

If you have a recent version of the **Win32::Registry** extension that has a method for unloading a hive, you can use the **UnLoad()** method:

```
$RegistryObject->UnLoad( $KeyName );
```

The only parameter is the name of the key that you had previously loaded a hive with.

This function and method will return a TRUE if it successfully unloaded the hive; otherwise, a FALSE is returned.

When the hive is unloaded, it is saved so that any changes made to the hive (any keys have been renamed, deleted, or added, or any values or data changed) will be saved to the hive's file. Refer to Example 3.23 to see how to unload a Registry hive.

You can only unload hives from one of the root keys. Specifying the handle of any key other than a root key (or in calling the method from any object other than a root object) will result in the function failing.

The **UnLoad()** method is not exported in all versions of the **Win32::Registry** extension. Hopefully, this will change in future versions of the module. In the meantime, you can unload any hive by using the **RegUnLoadKey()** function:

```
Win32::Registry::RegUnLoadKey( $Handle, $KeyName )
```

The first parameter ($Handle) is the handle to a root Registry key such as HKEY_LOCAL_MACHINE. The handle is a numeric value held in the Registry object's "handle" member. You can access this as $HKEY_LOCAL_MACHINE->{handle}, assuming that you are looking for the local machine's root handle.

The second parameter ($KeyName) is the name of the key which you had previously loaded a hive with.

Example 3.23   *Loading and unloading Registry hives*

```
01. use Win32::Registry;
02. $HiveFile = "c:\\temp\\joel.key";
03. $KeyName = "Joels Hive";
04.    # Load the hive into this registry.
05. $HKEY_LOCAL_MACHINE->Load( $KeyName, $HiveFile ) ||
       die "Can not load the hive";
06. if( $HKEY_LOCAL_MACHINE->Open( "Software", $Key ) )
07. {
08.    ...process key...
09.    $Key->Close();
10. }
11.    # Remove the hive from this registry (saving the contents).
12. $HKEY_LOCAL_MACHINE->UnLoad( $KeyName );
```

Restoring Registry Keys

Two functions in the **Win32::Registry** extension are wonderfully valuable, but they are just not exposed by the extension's module. Because of this, you must access them as functions. Just like the other such functions, the extension may change in future releases to provide methods to access these functions.

The first of these functions, **RegRestoreKey()**, restores a key with another key that was saved to a file (refer to the "Saving a Hive" section to learn how to save a key to a file). This function takes the Registry key values and subkeys from a given file and overwrites any currently existing keys. This is great if you want to make backups of important Registry keys and later restore them. The syntax for the **RegRestoreKey()** function is as follows:

```
Win32::Registry::RegRestoreKey( $Handle, $File[, $Flag ] );
```

The first parameter ($Handle) is a handle to an opened key. You can use any key that has been opened (by using either the **Open()** or **Create()** methods). Access the handle by referring to the "handle" member of the key's object as in:

```
$Key->{handle}
```

The second parameter ($File) is the name of a file that has had a previously saved key.

The third parameter ($Flag) is optional and specifies the volatility flag. This flag can either be 0 or REG_WHOLE_HIVE_VOLATILE. If REG_WHOLE_HIVE_VOLATILE is specified, the hive will be active until the next time the machine is rebooted. After reboot, the key will resort back to its original state. This flag can be specified only on keys that exist under HKEY_USERS or HKEY_LOCAL_MACHINE roots. The default for this parameter is 0.

If successful, the key will be replaced by the contents of the hive file and the function will return TRUE. FALSE is returned on failure.

If a key is restored, all its original values and subkeys are lost and replaced with the contents of the specified file.

The other function that restores a key but also provides a backup for the previous key is the **RegReplaceKey()** function:

```
Win32::Registry::RegReplaceKey( $Handle, $KeyName, $File, $BackupFile )
```

The first parameter ($Handle) is a handle to an opened key. You can use any key that has been opened (by using either the **Open()** or **Create()** methods). Access the handle by referring to the "handle" member of the key's object as in:

```
$Key->{handle}
```

The second parameter ($KeyName) is the name of the key to be replaced.

The third parameter ($File) is the name of a file that has had a previously saved key. The contents of this file will replace the specified key.

The fourth parameter ($BackupFile) is the name of a file that will be created. A backup of the key will be stored into this file before it is replaced.

If the **RegReplaceKey()** function is successful, it will return TRUE, a backup file will have been created containing the original key (its values and subkeys), and the key will have been replaced by the contents of the file specified in the third parameter. If the **RegReplaceKey()** function fails, it will return FALSE.

Closing an Open Registry Key
After you have finished with a key that you have opened, you need to close it using the **Close()** method:

```
$RegistryObject->Close();
```

If successful, **Close()** returns a TRUE and the Registry object no longer exists. Any further method calls using this object will fail. If the method fails, it returns a FALSE value.

Managing the Event Log

The Windows NT operating system contains a mechanism to track events and messages generated by the operating system, applications, services, and drivers. This is similar to the UNIX SYSLOG daemon. The mechanism is known as the Event log and it can be a powerful tool (if not the only tool) to capture important messages that can predict network failures, non-working devices, and other such information.

Win32 Perl can access the database of messages that comprises the Event log by using the **Win32::EventLog** extension.

Opening the Event Log

Before performing any actions on the Event log, you need to open the Event log. The function used to open the log will result in a new **Win32::EventLog** object that will be used to perform all other methods.

To open the Event log, you can use the **Open()** method:

```
Win32::EventLog::Open( $Object, $Source [, $Machine ] );
```

The first parameter ($Object) is a scalar variable that will be set to the newly created Event log object. This object will be used to call other methods.

The second parameter ($Source) is the source name. This is a string that will be used to identify the origin of any events that may be stored in the log. This is usually some string that is meaningful to whichever user will be looking at the logs. By default, there are three sources on a Win32 machine: Application, Security, and System. A script could, however, create its very own source such as "Perl Database Manager" or "Joel's funky event source". This could be an empty string.

The third parameter ($Machine) is optional and represents a computer whose Event log to which this object will be connected. Any methods that the created **Win32::EventLog** object performs will be done on this machine's Event log. The default for this is the local machine. This is just the computer name (not the proper name with prepended backslashes).

If successful, a TRUE is returned and a new **Win32::EventLog** object is created representing the Event log on the specified machine. If this fails, **Open()** returns a FALSE value.

In newer builds of the **Win32::EventLog** extension, another function exists for creating the object: Perl **new** command:

```
$Object = new Win32::EventLog( $Source[, $Machine ] );
```

All the parameters are the same as the **Open()** function except that the $Object scalar is moved out of the parameter list.

Counting Events

Because the Event log is a database of messages, you can query the database to determine what the latest message number is by using the **GetNumber**() method:

```
$EventlogObject->GetNumber( $Number );
```

The only parameter is a scalar variable that will be set to the number of records (or events) in the Event log database.

If the **GetNumber**() method is successful, it returns TRUE and the scalar variable passed into the method is set to the number of records in the database. The method returns FALSE if it fails.

Similar to the **GetNumber**() method is the **GetOldest**() method, which will return the record number of the oldest event in the database:

```
$EventlogObject->GetOldest( $Record );
```

The only parameter passed in is a scalar variable that will be set to the record number that is the oldest record in the Event log database.

If this is successful it returns TRUE and sets the scalar variable to the record number of the oldest record in the database. Failure is indicated by a FALSE return value.

Reading Event Messages

Reading messages from the Event log is fairly straightforward. You just use the **Read**() method:

```
$EventlogObject->Read( $Flags, $Record, $Event );
```

The first parameter ($Flags) refers to the flags that indicate how the read process is handled. This can be a combination of values from Table 3.13 logically OR'ed together.

The second parameter ($Record) is the record number from the database that you want to read. This number is ignored unless the EVENTLOG_SEEK_READ flag is specified in the first parameter.

The third parameter ($Event) is a reference to a hash. This should be in the form of a scalar ($Event) as opposed to a hash (\%Event) reference because some older versions of this extension did not correctly work with hash references.

If the method is successful the hash is filled with the structure defined in Table 3.11 and a TRUE value is returned. Otherwise FALSE is returned. Example 3.24 shows how the **Read**() method is used.

Example 3.24   *Printing all system errors over the past week*

```
01. use Win32::EventLog;
02. $SecPerWeek = 7 * 24 * 60 * 60;
03. $Now = time();
04. $WeekAgo = $Now - $SecPerWeek;
05. $Event = new Win32::EventLog( "System", "" ) ||
       die "Unable to open event log.\n";
06. if( $Event->GetNumber( $Num ) )
07. {
08.    $Flag = EVENTLOG_BACKWARDS_READ | EVENTLOG_SEEK_READ;
09.    do
10.    {
11.      if( $Event->Read( $Flag, $Num, \%Hash ) )
12.      {
13.        if( $Hash{EventType} == EVENTLOG_ERROR_TYPE ) )
14.        {
15.          print "$Hash{Source} on $Hash{Computer} indicated an error".
             "at". localtime( $Hash{TimeGenerated} ) . ".\n";
16.        }
17.      }else{
18.        undef %Hash;
19.      }
20.      # This will cause the next reading of the registry to move to the
21.      # next record automatically.
22.      $Num = 0;
23.    } while( $WeekAgo < $Hash{TimeGenerated} );
24.    Win32::EventLog::CloseEventLog( $Event->{handle} );
25. }
```

Table 3.11   *The Event log record hash*

Hash Key	Description
Source	The source of the event message. This is normally the name of the application or device that generates the event. This name is mapped to an application or DLL file that contains information on how to format the event message.
Computer	The name of the computer that generated the event.
Length	The number of bytes of data associated with the event. This data is found in the "Data" key.
Data	Binary data of any length that is associated with the message. The length of this data is found in the "Length" key. Usually, this is some sort of data that is reported when an application generates an error. For most practical purposes, this key is ignored.
Category	This represents a category of the event. This is usually a number that is defined by the source that generated the event. You would need to know what this number

continues

Table 3.11   Continued

Hash Key	Description
	represents to the particular source for it to be of any use.
RecordNumber	The record number in the Event log database of the event.
TimeGenerated	The time that the event was generated. This number is represented as the number of seconds since January 1, 1970. You can use this number as if it were generated from Perl's **time**() function.
Timewritten	The time that the event was physically written to the database. This value is managed by the operating system and cannot be written by a Perl script. This number is represented as the number of seconds since January 1, 1970. You can use this number as if it were generated from Perl's **time**() function.
EventID	The ID number of the event. This number is specific to the source that generated the event. This ID number's meaning changes from source to source.
EventType	This represents the type of event. The different event types are listed in Table 3.12.
ClosingRecordNumber	This is reserved by the Win32 API and currently has no meaning. Ignore this key.
Strings	The different data strings used to format the event's message. These strings can be passed in as an anonymous array.

Table 3.12   Event log event types

Event Type	Description
EVENTLOG_ERROR_TYPE	The event was an error.
EVENTLOG_WARNING_TYPE	The event was a warning.
EVENTLOG_INFORMATION_TYPE	The event was used to inform that some event took place.
EVENTLOG_AUDIT_SUCCESS	The event was a successful audit. This occurs if an administrator has specified an object to be audited (such as a file, directory, or Registry key), and a user successfully accessed the object.
EVENTLOG_AUDIT_FAILURE	The event was a failed audit. This occurs if an administrator has specified an object to be audited (such as a file, directory, or Registry key), and a user unsuccessfully accessed the object.

Table 3.13   Event log reading flags

Flag	Description
EVENTLOG_FORWARDS_READ	The events are read from the database forward in chronological order.
EVENTLOG_BACKWARDS_READ	The events are read from the database backward in chronological order.
EVENTLOG_SEEK_READ	Reads the specified record number.
EVENTLOG_SEQUENTIAL_READ	Reads the next record in the database.

Writing to the Event Log

You can create your own entries into the Event log. This can be used when automated scripts run and errors occur. This is done with the **Report()** method:

```
$EventlogObject->Report( \%Event );
```

The only parameter is a reference to an event hash, as described in Table 3.11.

If the method is successful, an entry is added to the Event log database consisting of the data contained in the hash whose reference was passed into the method. A TRUE value is also returned. A FALSE value is returned if the method fails.

Clearing the Event Log

The Event log database can become quite large. Because of this, you may want to clear the database using the **Clear()** method:

```
$EventlogObject->Clear( $File );
```

The only parameter passed in is a file name.

Before the Event log is cleared, it will be backed up into the file specified. If this is successful, the **Clear()** method will return TRUE; otherwise it returns FALSE.

> *Note*
>
> *When you clear the Event log, it is automatically closed. Because of this, the Event log object that called the **Clear()** method is no longer valid and should be discarded.*

Backing Up the Event Log

Just as the **Clear()** method will create a backup log file of the Event log, so does the **BackupEventLog()** function. The only difference is that it does not empty the Event log. This function is so very useful that I do not understand why it was not exposed to the Event log object by means of a method. Instead you must access it directly by means of a function call:

```
Win32::EventLog::BackupEventLog( $Handle, $File );
```

The first parameter ($Handle) is a handle to an open Event log. You can specify the "handle" member of the Event log object for this parameter.

The second parameter ($File) is the name of the backup file that will be created.

If the **BackupEventLog()** function is successful, the Event log has been backed up to the file and the function returns TRUE. FALSE is returned to indicate a failure.

Closing the Event Log

For some very odd reason, the authors of the **Win32::EventLog** extension failed to expose the function that closes an opened database. It is good practice to always close any opened Event log files using the **CloseEventLog()** function:

```
Win32::EventLog::CloseEventLog( $Handle );
```

The only parameter accepted is a handle to an open Event log. You can specify the "handle" member of the Event log object for this parameter.

If the Event log is successfully closed, it returns TRUE; otherwise, it returns FALSE. Refer back to the code in Example 3.24 to see how the **CloseEventLog()** function is used.

Summary

Administrators using the Win32 extensions should consider themselves lucky to have such a war chest of valuable functions to assist them in their daily chores of running a network of users and machines.

The Win32 extensions provide a wide range of functionality to manage accounts. Not only user but also machine accounts can be managed. This is not limited to the general adding and removing of accounts, but also includes renaming, disabling, and changing passwords, as well as modifying the current state of an account.

As if account management weren't enough, the Win32 extensions also provide access to group management. Creating, modifying, and removing both local and global groups are supported. With these functions, users can be added to, enumerated, and removed from groups. Additionally, you can also check a user's membership in a group.

User accounts and groups are not the only things that need management. Administrators need to also manage machines. The Win32 extensions provide access into the Event logs to both query events as well as add them. Win32 Perl extensions also contain a set of functions that provides access into the Registry, enabling administrators to modify or restore components.

Chapter 4

File Management

Win32 does a remarkable job of providing access to data. It provides copious amounts of information regarding its data sources such as disk files. These files are incredibly important for storing user data, as well as for supporting the operating system.

This chapter focuses on managing files and directories on a machine. It covers file attributes, advanced file information, permissions, shortcuts, and monitoring directories for changes.

Files contain not only data, but they can also contain meta information that describes the file itself (such as whether it has been altered, whether it is a system file, its author, and its version number). This meta information, or *attributes*, is important for an administrator to track (for example, version numbers of executable and DLL files). This chapter explains how to access and manage this information.

Shortcuts are convenient to use but tedious to manage. If a directory name changes or data is moved from one server to another, many shortcuts may need to be updated. Doing this manually on all machines on a network can take quite a bit of time and patience. Descriptions on how to create and modify these shortcuts are covered later on in this chapter.

Files and directories on NTFS partitions can have permissions placed on them. This is what grants or denies a user the ability to access files. For servers in a secure environment, managing this is not only important but it is necessary, especially when automation scripts are written that must create a directory tree and apply permissions to it. These issues are covered in detail.

Finally, the chapter covers the concept of directory monitoring. Watching a directory for changes that occur is useful for daemon services that need to know when a file size or directory name has changed.

File Attributes

If you have ever played around with files, you know that all files and directories in the Win32 world have the four basic common file attributes listed in Table 4.1 (inherited from the DOS world).

Table 4.1   Common file attributes

Attribute	Description
ARCHIVE	The ARCHIVE attribute is set any time that the file's contents change. Backup programs that back up only files with the ARCHIVE flag set use this.
HIDDEN	A file with the HIDDEN attribute set does not appear in directory listings.
READONLY	The operating system does not allow files with the READONLY flag set to change.
SYSTEM	The SYSTEM attribute specifies that a file is a system file. System files require special handling by the operating system. The main two files that make up the core of DOS, for example, are IO.SYS and MSDOS.SYS (presuming that we are talking about Microsoft's DOS, that is). These files have the system flags set so that DOS knows to handle these important files with special care. Typically, system files are rendered as invisible, so they do not appear in normal directory listings.

What Are the File Attributes?

Win32 Perl has a standard extension known as **Win32::File** that allows for only two functions: retrieving and setting file attributes.

These two functions are fast and cover more attributes than the DOS box's **attrib** command. Whereas the **attrib** command recognizes the attributes in Table 4.1, the **Win32::File** extension recognizes the attributes listed Table 4.1 as well as those attributes listed in Table 4.2.

*Table 4.2   Additional file attributes recognized by the **Win32::File** extension*

Attribute	Description
COMPRESSED	The file has been compressed by the operating system to conserve disk space. This does not apply to files that have been compressed by means other than the operating system (such as archiving programs like zip.exe).
DIRECTORY	This attribute distinguishes a file from a directory. It will only be set if the path is a directory.
NORMAL	When this attribute is set, all *common* attributes are cleared (ARCHIVE, HIDDEN, READONLY, and SYSTEM).

Some other attributes are of equal importance; for some reason, however, both are undocumented and their constant names are not recognized by the extension. You can still test and set them, but you must use the value of the constant as opposed to the constant's name. Table 4.3 lists these values.

*Table 4.3   File attributes not recognized by the **Win32::File** extension*

Attribute	Hexadecimal Value	Description
OFFLINE	0x1000	The file's data is currently not available. This can occur when the operating system has moved the data to offline storage (as when a floppy disk has been removed).
TEMPORARY	0x0100	The file was created as a temporary file and is most likely going to be destroyed by the application that created it.

Now that you know what attributes are available, it is time to see what limitations there are when using these attributes.

Not all attributes can be set. The DIRECTORY and the COMPRESSED attributes are read-only. They cannot be set by the **Win32::File** extension. You would have to run the DOS box's **compact** command or use the Explorer program to compress a file or directory. This will set the COMPRESSED bit. Using the same means can clear the bit as well. Refer to the **compact** command for directions.

The DIRECTORY bit is set only on directories. It would not make sense to set the DIRECTORY bit on a file. After all, a file is not a directory no matter what you do to it (unless, of course, you delete the file and create a directory by the same name).

You need to be aware that the NORMAL attribute is the most unique of the attributes. When you set the NORMAL attribute, all the attributes are removed (except DIRECTORY and COMPRESSED). You can use this to reset the state of a file or directory.

Retrieving File Attributes

When you need to check the attributes on a file or directory you should use the **GetAttributes**() function:

```
Win32::File::GetAttributes( $Path, $Attributes );
```

The first parameter ($Path) is the path to the file or directory that you want the attributes for. This can be a full path, a relative path, or a UNC. If the path is a directory it does not matter if it ends with a backslash or not.

The second parameter ($Attributes) will receive, if successful, the attributes in a bitmap format. To test for particular attributes, you can logically AND the resulting value of this parameter with one of the constants, as line 5 of Example 4.1. If the **GetAttributes**() function is successful, it returns a 1; otherwise it returns nothing.

Example 4.1   *Checking for the READONLY attribute*

```
01. use Win32::File;
02. $File = "c:/temp/test.txt";
03. if( Win32::File::GetAttributes( $File, $Attrib ) )
04. {
05.   if( $Attrib & READONLY )
06.   {
07.     print "$File is read only.\n";
08.   }else{
09.     print "$File is NOT read only.\n";
10.   }
11. }else{
12.   print "Error: " . Win32::FormatMessage( Win32::GetLastError() ) . "\n";
13. }
```

Setting File Attributes

Setting the attributes of a file or a directory is rather easy when you use the **SetAttributes**() function:

```
Win32::File::SetAttributes( $Path, $Attributes );
```

The first parameter ($Path) is the path to a file or a directory. This can be either a relative path, a full path, or a UNC.

The second parameter ($Attributes) is a bitmask of file attributes. You can logically OR the attribute constants together to specify a combination of attributes to set, as in line 4 of Example 4.2. If the **SetAttributes**() function is successful, it returns a 1; otherwise nothing is returned.

Example 4.2   *Setting the READONLY and HIDDEN attributes*

```
use Win32::File;
$File = "c:/temp/test.txt";
$Attrib = READONLY | HIDDEN;
if( Win32::File::SetAttributes( $File, $Attrib ) )
{
  print "$File is now READONLY and HIDDEN.\n";
}else{
  print "Error: " . Win32::FormatMessage( Win32::GetLastError() ) . "\n";
}
```

Note that the DIRECTORY *and* COMPRESSED *attributes are read-only, that is, you can retrieve them with* **Win32::File::GetFileAttributes()**, *but you cannot set them with* **Win32::File::SetFileAttributes()**. *To set the* COMPRESSED *bit on a file or directory, you can use the* **compact** *command from a DOS box. You can not set the* DIRECTORY *bit on a file nor can you clear the bit on a directory.*

Case Study: Retrieving File Attributes with the DOS attrib Command

The DOS **attrib** command is used to read and set the common file attributes on files and directories. From Perl, you can shell out and run the **attrib** command using Perl's backtick, but this results in rather large memory and time penalties, as illustrated in Example 4.3.

Example 4.3 *Retrieving file attributes with the DOS **attrib** command*

```
01. $Time = time();
02. @List = <c:/temp/*.*>;
03. foreach $File ( @List )
04. {
05.    %Attributes = GetAttributes( $File );
06.    $Count++;
07.    print "$File has the following attributes:\n";
08.
09.       # Print each attribute for the file
10.    foreach $Key ( sort( keys( %Attributes ) ) )
11.    {
12.       print "\t\u$Key\n" if ( $Attributes{$Key} );
13.    }
14. }
15. $Time2 = time();
16. %Time = ComputeTime( $Time2 - $Time );
17. print "\nTotal files: $Count\n";
18. printf( "Total time: %02d:%02d:%02d\n", $Time{hour}, $Time{min},
       $Time{sec} );
19.
20. sub GetAttributes
21. {
22.    my( $File ) = @_;
23.    my( @Output, @Attribs, %Hash );
24.       # Here we shell out using backticks. This is a big performance hit!!
25.    @Output = `attrib $File`;
26.    (@Attribs) = ( $Output[0] =~ /^(.)  (.)(.)(.)(.)/);
27.    %Hash = (
28.       'archive'   => ( $Attribs[0] eq "A" ),
```

continues

Continued

```
29.      'system'    => ( $Attribs[1] eq "S" ),
30.      'hidden'    => ( $Attribs[2] eq "H" ),
31.      'read-only' => ( $Attribs[3] eq "R" )
32.    );
33.    return %Hash;
34. }
35.
36. sub ComputeTime
37. {
38.    my($Temp) = @_;
39.    my(%Time);
40.    $Time{hour} = int( $Temp / 3600 );
41.    $Temp = $Temp % 3600;
42.    $Time{min} = int( $Temp / 60 );
43.    $Time{sec} = int( $Temp % 60 );
44.    return %Time;
45. }
```

As you can see by the code in Example 4.3, your script will suffer due to the time it takes to shell out and process the **attrib** command for each and every file processed. Thanks to the wonders of Win32 Perl, there is a much better way of doing this: the **Win32::File** extension.

To demonstrate the speed increase realized when using the **Win32::File** extension, take a look at Example 4.4, which is the same script as Example 4.3 with the exception of using **Win32::File::GetFileAttributes**() instead of shelling out to the **attrib** command.

I ran both scripts on my machine, which has 152 files in the c:\TEMP directory. The code in Example 4.3 took a total of 38 seconds to complete. The code in Example 4.4 took only 9 seconds. If you look at the code carefully, you will notice that the 9 seconds includes the overhead of loading and initializing the **Win32::File** extension.

Example 4.4   *Retrieving file attributes with the **Win32::File** extension*

```
01. $Time = time();
02. use Win32::File;
03. @List = <c:/temp/*.*>;
04. foreach $File ( @List )
05. {
06. %Attributes = GetAttributes( $File );
07. $Count++;
08. print "$File has the following attributes:\n";
09. foreach $Key ( sort( keys( %Attributes ) ) )
10. {
11. print "\t\u$Key\n" if ( $Attributes{$Key} );
12. }
13. }
14. $Time2 = time();
15. %Time = ComputeTime( $Time2 - $Time );
```

```
16. print "\nTotal files: $Count\n";
17. printf( "Total time: %02d:%02d:%02d\n", $Time{hour}, $Time{min},
      $Time{sec} );
18.
19. sub GetAttributes
20. {
21.   my( $File ) = @_;
22.   my( @Output, @Attribs, %Hash );
23.   if( Win32::File::GetAttributes( $File, $Attrib ) )
24.   {
25.     %Hash = (
26.       'archive'    => $Attrib & ARCHIVE,
27.       'system'     => $Attrib & SYSTEM,
28.       'hidden'     => $Attrib & HIDDEN,
29.       'read-only'  => $Attrib & READONLY,
30.       'directory'  => $Attrib & DIRECTORY,
31.       'compressed' => $Attrib & COMPRESSED,
32.       'temporary'  => $Attrib & 0x0100,
33.       'offline'    => $Attrib & 0x1000
34.     );
35.   }
36.   return %Hash;
37. }
38.
39. sub ComputeTime
40. {
41.   my($Temp) = @_;
42.   my(%Time);
43.   $Time{hour} = int( $Temp / 3600 );
44.   $Temp = $Temp % 3600;
45.   $Time{min} = int( $Temp / 60 );
46.   $Time{sec} = int( $Temp % 60 );
47.   return %Time;
48. }
```

File Information

In addition to the file attributes that describe the state of a file, such as READONLY and HIDDEN, the Win32 platform allows files to have additional information embedded within the file. This information ranges from the company who created the file to the original name of the file.

This information is stored as a resource within the file; therefore it is only available on files that can have embedded file information resources, such as executable files and DLLs.

You can view this information from the Property window by right-clicking on the file in Explorer, selecting Properties, and then selecting the Version tab (if it exists). The file information will be displayed as in Figure 4.1.

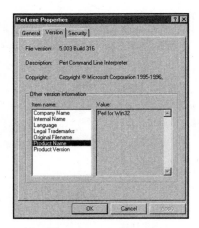

Figure 4.1   *Explorer's view of a file's version information.*

Unlike the attributes discussed in the "File Attributes" section, this file information is not required; therefore it is not found in all .EXE and .DLL files. On files that do have such information, the **Win32::AdminMisc** extension can retrieve this data.

Retrieving File Information

To retrieve a file's information fields, you must first load the **Win32::AdminMisc** extension. After doing this, you can use the **GetFileInfo()** function:

```
Win32::AdminMisc::GetFileInfo ( $Path, \%Info );
```

The first parameter ($Path) is the path to a file. This file needs to be a file with an embedded file information resource such as an executable or DLL. This path can be a local file or a UNC.

The second parameter (\%Info) is a reference to a hash. This will be populated with version information if it is available. Table 4.4 lists the keys of the hash.

*Table 4.4   Information returned by the **Win32::AdminMisc::GetFileInfo()** function*

Hash Key	Description
CompanyName	The name of the company credited with the file's creation.
FileVersion	Version of the file.
InternalName	The name the file is referred to as. The developer usually uses this.

Hash Key	Description
LegalCopyright	Any copyright notice.
OriginalFilename	The original name of the file. This is handy if the file was accidentally renamed.
ProductName	Name of the product.
ProductVersion	Version of the product.
LangID	The language ID of the file in hexadecimal notation. For example, the ID 0x0409 represents US English and 0x0407 represents German.
Language	The language as a string such as, "English (United States)".

If the **Win32::AdminMisc::GetFileInfo**() function is successful, it will populate the hash reference passed in as the second parameter and return a 1; otherwise it returns a 0.

> ### Tip
>
> The **Win32::AdminMisc::GetFileInfo**() function accepts paths with both backslashes and slashes as in Example 4.5. This can be convenient when porting scripts because UNIX paths use slashes as directory delimiters.

Example 4.5   *Using the **Win32::AdminMisc::GetFileInfo**() function*

```
01. use Win32::AdminMisc;
02. $Path = "$ENV{SYSTEMROOT}/notepad.exe";
03. if( Win32::AdminMisc::GetFileInfo( $Path, \%Info ) )
04. {
05.   foreach $Key ( sort( keys( %Info ) ) )
06.   {
07.     print "\t$Key: $Info{$Key}\n";
08.   }
09. }else{
10.   print "Error: " . Win32::FormatMessage( Win32::GetLastError() );
11. }
```

Shortcuts

With the introduction of Windows NT 4.0 and Windows 95 the concept of a *shortcut* was brought to the Win32 platform. A shortcut is a type of alias for a file or directory. You can use a collection of shortcuts that point to your favorite directories and files. These files could be commonly used programs or documents you read or edit often. Creating these shortcuts in a particular directory makes a convenient way of jumping to your commonly used programs, files, and directories—this is what Microsoft Office products do when they create the Favorites directory.

A shortcut is like a link in the UNIX world, except that it is not processed by the OS directly; instead, it is processed by an application (try accessing a shortcut using an older Windows program—it will think that it is an actual file and not a link to another file or directory).

These links are handy from a graphical interface point of view. In an open dialog box, selecting a shortcut will either open the file or change to the directory that the shortcut points to.

Shortcuts are special binary files that have an .LNK extension, and their iconic representations on the Desktop or in the Explorer have a little white box filled with a curving arrow in the lower left of its icon (see Figure 4.2). There are different types of shortcuts (such as Dial-Up Networking and Printer shortcuts), but the **Win32::Shortcut** extension addresses file, program, and directory shortcuts.

Figure 4.2 *A shortcut representing Eudora Pro.*

Shortcuts consist of a collection of properties, which are documented in Table 4.5.

Table 4.5 Shortcut properties

Property	Description
Arguments	The arguments passed into the application. This is used when the shortcut points to an application (not a file or directory).
Description	This is a general description. Currently it does not benefit a user. (You cannot view this description from the Explorer program.) This can be handy if you need to place a description of the shortcut's use for later reference.
File	This is the full path to the shortcut file. You should name this file with an .LNK extension (as in C:\TEMP\MYFILE.LNK). UNCs are allowed.

Property	Description
Hotkey	This is a bitmask that represents a combination of keyboard keys (such as Control+Alt+E). This combination of keys will activate the shortcut.
IconLocation	A full path to a resource containing icons. Typically this is a file containing icon resources such as a program, DLL, or an icon file (such as PERL.ICO). UNCs are allowed.
IconNumber	This is the icon number found in the file pointed to by the IconLocation property.
Path	The full path to the object the shortcut will link to. This is usually either a program, a file, or a directory. UNCs are allowed.
ShortPath	This is a read-only property (you cannot change it). This property is the 8.3 version of the Path property. If you change the Path property this will not change until you save and reload the shortcut.
ShowCmd	With this property, you can specify how the shortcut will display itself if launched from the Desktop or the Explorer program. Table 4.6 shows the options for this property.
WorkingDirectory	This is the working directory for the application specified in the Path property. If the Path is not an application, but a file or a directory, this property is ignored.

Table 4.6   Options for the ShowCmd property

Option	Description
SW_SHOWNORMAL	Display the result of the shortcut in a normal window.
SW_SHOWMINNOACTIVE	The result of the shortcut is minimized, but the currently active window remains active.
SW_SHOWMAXIMIZED	The result of the shortcut is maximized.

Note

The Win32 API defines additional SW_SHOW constants to those listed in Table 4.6. If you specify their values, however, the shortcut will replace the value with SW_SHOWNORMAL.

Explaining the Hotkey Property

The Hotkey property requires a little bit of explaining—first in technical speak, and then in English. The Hotkey value is derived from a 16-bit word (2 bytes). The most significant byte is the bitmask of the modifier keys and the least significant byte is the virtual key code.

Okay, now for the explanation in English. If you look at the value in hexadecimal, you will notice 2 bytes. If the value of the Hotkey property is 1840 (decimal), for example, you can convert it to hexadecimal using the Perl **sprintf()** function as in Example 4.6.

Example 4.6　*Converting a decimal value to hexadecimal*

```
$Hex = sprintf( "0x%04x", 1840 );
```

If you print out $Hex, you will get "0x0730". This shows that the decimal value 1840 is composed of 2 bytes: the first (most significant byte) is 0x07 and the second (least significant byte) is 0x30.

The first byte (0x07) represents a bitmask of the modifier keys in Table 4.7.

Table 4.7　Modifier key codes for the Hotkey property

Modifier Key	Hexadecimal Value
Shift Key	0x01
Control Key	0x02
Alt Key	0x04

You can determine which modifier keys are used by using the subroutine **GetModifier()** defined in Example 4.7.

Example 4.7　*Decoding the modifier keys*

```
01. $Hotkey = 1840;
02. ( $KeyCode, $Modifier ) = unpack( "cc", pack( "S", $Hotkey ) );
03.
04. %ModifierKeys = GetModifier( $Modifier );
05. print "The modifier keys are\n";
06. foreach $Key ( keys( %ModifierKeys ) )
07. {
08.   print "\t$Key\n" if ( $ModifierKeys{$Key} );
09. }
10.
11. sub GetModifier
12. {
13.   my( $Value ) = @_;
14.   my( %Hash ) = (
15.     Alt     =>  ($Value & 0x04)? 1:0,
16.     Control =>  ($Value & 0x02)? 1:0,
17.     Shift   =>  ($Value & 0x01)? 1:0,
18.   );
19.   return %Hash;
20. }
```

The code in Example 4.7 prints out the modifier keys for the bitmask of 0x07. Line 2 uses a trick to programmatically discover the modifier and the keycode values. By packing the Hotkey property into a single unsigned short integer and then unpacking the values of the first and second bytes individually, we have broken the numeric value of $HotKey into the two separate values we need. An explanation of how this actually works is beyond the scope of this book and is left as an exercise for the reader. Likewise, this trick may need to be modified to work on non-Intel platforms and is assuming that an unsigned short is 16 bits.

Notice that lines 15–17 test the bitmask for the modifier keys. If the test determines that the modifier key is used, a value of 1 is assigned to the particular key; otherwise 0 is assigned.

The second byte (0x30) is a *virtual key code*. This value corresponds to a key on the keyboard. This is the key that you press (in addition to the modifiers) to activate the shortcut. Table 4.8 provides the list of virtual key code values.

Table 4.8   Key codes for the Hotkey *property*

Keyboard Key	Hexadecimal Value
Backspace	0x08
Tab	0x09
Clear	0x0C
Enter	0x0D
Shift	0x10
Control	0x11
Alt	0x12
Pause	0x13
Caps Lock	0x14
Escape	0x1B
Spacebar	0x20
PageUp	0x21
PageDown	0x22
End	0x23
Home	0x24
Left Arrow	0x25
Up Arrow	0x26
Right Arrow	0x27
Down Arrow	0x28
Print Screen	0x2C
Insert	0x2D
Delete	0x2E
Help	0x2F

continues

Table 4.8   Continued

Keyboard Key	Hexadecimal Value
0	0x30
1	0x31
2	0x32
3	0x33
4	0x34
5	0x35
6	0x36
7	0x37
8	0x38
9	0x39
A	0x41
B	0x42
C	0x43
D	0x44
E	0x45
F	0x46
G	0x47
H	0x48
I	0x49
J	0x4A
K	0x4B
L	0x4C
M	0x4D
N	0x4E
O	0x4F
P	0x50
Q	0x51
R	0x52
S	0x53
T	0x54
U	0x55
V	0x56
W	0x57
X	0x58
Y	0x59
Z	0x5A
Left Windows key	0x5B

Keyboard Key	Hexadecimal Value
Right Windows key	0x5C
Applications key	0x5D
Numeric keypad 0	0x60
Numeric keypad 1	0x61
Numeric keypad 2	0x62
Numeric keypad 3	0x63
Numeric keypad 4	0x64
Numeric keypad 5	0x65
Numeric keypad 6	0x66
Numeric keypad 7	0x67
Numeric keypad 8	0x68
Numeric keypad 9	0x69
Numeric Keypad *	0x6A
Numeric keypad +	0x6B
Numeric keypad Enter	0x6C
Numeric keypad –	0x6D
Numeric keypad Num Lock	0x6E
Numeric keypad /	0x6F
F1	0x70
F2	0x71
F3	0x72
F4	0x73
F5	0x74
F6	0x75
F7	0x76
F8	0x77
F9	0x78
F10	0x79
F11	0x7A
F12	0x7B
Num Lock	0x90
Scroll Lock	0x91

Creating a Hotkey

The section "Explaining the Hotkey property" discussed how to interpret the Hotkey value. This section explains how to create a value that you can use to assign a hotkey.

Creating a Hotkey value is considerably easy. First look through Table 4.8 and pick out the value of the key you want to use. Suppose that you want to use the PageUp key, which has a value of 0x21:

```
$KeyCode = 0x21;
```

Next, pick the modifier keys you want to use. For purposes in this example, you will use the Alt+Control keys, whose values are 0x04 and 0x02, respectively.

You need to logically OR the modifier keys together to get the modifier bitmask:

```
$Modifier = 0x02 | 0x04;
```

Now you need to create the Hotkey value. Use the reverse of the trick used on line 2 of Example 4.7.

```
$Value = pack( "s", pack( "cc", $Hotkey, $Modifier ) );
```

That is it! The variable $Value now contains the value of 1569, which you will assign to the Hotkey property of your shortcut.

Note

On the Win32 platform, virtual key codes are not exactly the same as ASCII codes. It would be impossible to make keyboard codes match ASCII codes because a keyboard does not know the difference between the lowercase a and the uppercase A. The keyboard knows only that the key that represents the letter A has been pressed. If the operating system sees that the Shift key has been pressed at the same time as the A key, it knows that the capital letter A was intended.

What a virtual key code really represents is the numeric value that the keyboard sends to the computer telling which key was pressed. Table 4.8 lists these values.

The numeric keypad can generate different codes, however, depending on whether the Num Lock is active. The keypad's 7 key will generate either 0x24 if the Num Lock is not active, for example, and a 0x67 if it is.

Creating a Shortcut

Creating a shortcut is quite easy and is accomplished by first creating a shortcut object:

```
$Shortcut = new Win32::Shortcut( [$Path] );
```

The only parameter ($Path) is optional. If a path to an already created shortcut file is passed in as the first parameter, the shortcut that the path points to is loaded. If there isn't a valid shortcut file, the $Path parameter is ignored.

If no parameter is passed in (or if the path passed in is not a valid shortcut path) an empty shortcut is created. You will have to set the properties of the shortcut (described later in this section); otherwise it will not be functional.

If the function succeeds, a shortcut object is returned; otherwise undef is returned. Example 4.8 shows how to create a shortcut object.

> *Note*
>
> *Creating a shortcut object does not commit the shortcut to disk. You must save the shortcut by calling the **Save**() method (see the section titled "Saving the Shortcut").*

Example 4.8   *Creating a shortcut object*

```
use Win32::Shortcut;
$File = "c:\\winnt\\profiles\\administrator\\desktop\\iexplorer.lnk";
if( -e $File )
{
   $Shortcut = new Win32::Shortcut( $File ) ||
      die "Could not create a
shortcut object\n";
   print "The shortcut points to $Shortcut->{'Path'}\n";
}
```

Modifying the Shortcut's Properties

After you have a shortcut object (refer to the "Creating a Shortcut" section), you can directly modify the shortcut properties. There are two methods to do this: modifying the members of the shortcut object (see Table 4.5) or using the **Set**() method:

```
$ Shortcut Set( $Path, $Arguments, $WorkingDirectory, $Description, $Showcmd,
$Hotkey, $IconLocation, $IconNumber );
```

The **Set**() method requires all the parameters to be passed in; otherwise, what ever parameters are left off will default to 0 or an empty string (depending on the context of the property).

The **Set**() method will always return a 1, even if not enough parameters are passed in. Therefore, do not reply on error checking to determine whether you supplied enough parameters.

The parameters passed in are as follows (in order):

1. The Path property

2. The Arguments property

3. The WorkingDirectory property

4. The `ShowCmd` property

5. The `Hotkey` property

6. The `IconLocation` property

7. The `IconNumber` property

Refer to Table 4.5 for descriptions of these properties.

The alternative to the **Set**() method would be to directly modify the properties. This can be done by modifying the property keys within the object (refer to Table 4.5), as shown in Example 4.9.

Example 4.9   *Modifying property keys within an object*

```
01. use Win32::Shortcut;
02. $Shortcut = new Win32::Shortcut();
03. $File = "c:\\winnt\\profiles\\administrator\\desktop\\iexplorer.lnk";
04. if( $Shortcut->Load( $File ) )
05. {
06. $Shortcut->{'Description'} = "My new description";
07. $Shortcut->{'WorkingDirectory'} = "c:\\temp";
08. $Shortcut->Save();
09. $Shortcut->Close();
10. }
```

Modifying and Retrieving Properties

There is an alternative to the procedures described in the "Modifying the Shortcut's Properties" section. The **Win32::Shortcut** extension defines a set of methods for both retrieving and setting the properties. The methods are as follows:

```
$Shortcut->Path( [$Value] );
$Shortcut->WorkingDirectory( [$Value] );
$Shortcut->Arguments( [$Value] );
$Shortcut->Description( [$Value] );
$Shortcut->ShowCmd( [$Value] );
$Shortcut->Hotkey( [$Value] );
$Shortcut->IconLocation( [$Value] );
$Shortcut->IconNumber( [$Value] );
```

Each of these methods can accept an optional parameter. If the parameter is passed in, the property is set to the value of the parameter.

All the methods return their respective property values. Example 4.10 shows the use of the **Path**() method to both retrieve and set the `Path` property.

Example 4.10   *Using the property methods to alter a shortcut's path*

```
use Win32::Shortcut;
$File = "c:\\winnt\\profiles\\administrator\\desktop\\Graphics.lnk";
$Shortcut = new Win32::Shortcut( $File ) ¦¦ die
  "Unable to create a
shortcut object.";
$Location = $Shortcut->Path();
$Location =~ s/c:/d:/;
$Shortcut->Path( $Location );
$Shortcut->Save();
$Shortcut->Close();
```

Loading a Shortcut

After you have created a shortcut object, you can load it with shortcut data
using the **Load**() method:

```
$Shortcut->Load( $File );
```

The first parameter is a path to a shortcut file. The path can be relative (to the
current directory), a full path, or a UNC. The file specified must be a valid
shortcut file.

If the **Load**() method is successful, the shortcut object will be filled with the
properties from the shortcut file $File and a 1 will be returned; otherwise undef
is returned.

Resolving Invalid Paths

If there comes a time when the target of a shortcut (the Path property) changes,
the shortcut will need to be updated. This can be done by either changing the
Path property and saving the shortcut or by using the **Resolve**() method:

```
$Shortcut->Resolve( [$Flag] );
```

There will be an attempt to resolve the Path property of the shortcut by verify-
ing that it points to a valid path.

By default the method works silently; however, if a 2 is passed in as $Flag, a
GUI dialog box will be invoked enabling the user to specify 2 new path if
Win32 cannot resolve the path.

If the method is successful, the resolved path will be returned and the Path
property will have been updated; otherwise, an undef will be returned.

Saving the Shortcut

If the shortcut object has been modified, you need to commit your changes to
the hard drive by calling the **Save**() method:

```
$Shortcut->Save( [$File] );
```

The first parameter ($File) is optional, but if supplied will save the shortcut to $File. The value passed in can be a relative path (relative the current directory), a full path, or a UNC.

If the file was saved successfully, the method returns a 1; otherwise it returns undef.

> **Warning**
>
> *No errors generate when creating or saving a shortcut over another file! You should make sure that whatever file you are saving the shortcut as is not some file you need.*

Finishing with a Shortcut

After you have finished with your shortcut, you should use the **Close**() method:

```
$Shortcut->Close();
```

This method is not required, but is good programming style. When this method is invoked, the shortcut object is closed and can no longer access its methods (including **Load**()). The **Close**() method always returns a 1.

> **Note**
>
> *When the **Close**() method is called, the object is closed without saving the shortcut. Make sure you commit any changes by calling the **Save**() method before calling **Close**().*

Case Study: Modifying Shortcut Properties

I recently added a hard drive to my machine and moved over many data directories to the new disk. Because of this move, my shortcuts had to be altered. Because I have so many of them, however, I decided to use the script in Example 4.11.

The code scans every shortcut in all directories of my user's profile for a path that begins with D:\DATA and replaces that path with F:\DATA. It then prints how many shortcuts were scanned and how many were altered.

I have been able to use this script as the basis for many shortcut modifications. It is rather a handy piece of code.

Example 4.11   *Altering all shortcuts to point to a new path*

```
01. use Win32::Shortcut;
02.
```

```
03. $Dir = "$ENV{'SystemRoot'}\\profiles\\roth";
04. %Path = (
05.   old => "D:\\DATA",
06.   new => "F:\\DATA"
07. );
08.   #   Let's escape our backslashes in the %Path hash since
09.   #   we will be using the values in a regex.
$Path{old}=~s/(\\.\$})/\\$1/g;
10.
11.   #
12.   #   The meat of the script
13.   #
14. $Shortcut = new Win32::Shortcut ||
  die "Unable to create a
    shortcut object.";
15. ProcessDir($Dir);
16. $Shortcut->Close();
17.
18. print "Total shortcuts checked: $Total{checked}\n";
19. print "Total shortcuts changed: $Total{changed}\n";
20.
21.   #
22.   #   ProcessDir() walks through a directory processing shortcuts
23.   #   and recursively calling ProcessDir() for other directories
24.   #
25. sub ProcessDir
26. {
27.   my( $Dir ) = @_;
28.   my( @Dirs, @List, $File );
29.   print "\nDIR: $Dir\n";
30.   if( opendir( DIR, $Dir ) )
31.   {
32.     @List = readdir( DIR );
33.     closedir( DIR );
34.     foreach $File ( @List )
35.     {
36.       next if ( $File eq "." || $File eq ".." );
37.       push( @Dirs, $File ) if ( -d "$Dir\\$File" );
38.       ProcessShortcut( "$Dir\\$File" ) if ( $File =~ /\.lnk$/i );
39.     }
40.     foreach $File ( @Dirs )
41.     {
42.       ProcessDir( "$Dir\\$File" );
43.     }
44.   }
45. }
46.
47.   #
48.   #   ProcessShortcut() processes the shortcut file. If it has a path
49.   #   pointing to the old path, change it to the new path.
50.   #
51. sub ProcessShortcut
52. {
```

continues

Continued

```
53.    my( $File ) = @_;
54.    my( $Path, $Name );
55.    $Total{checked}++;
56.    if( $Shortcut->Load( $File ) )
57.    {
58.      ( $Name ) = ( $File =~ /([^\\]*)\.lnk$/i );
59.      print "\t$Name\n";
60.      $Path = $Shortcut->Path();
61.      if( $Path =~ s/^$Path{old}/$Path{new}/i )
62.      {
63.        $Shortcut->Path( $Path );
64.        $Shortcut->Save();
65.        $Total{changed}++;
66.        print " ***\t\t^^^ Changed ^^^\n";
67.      }
68.    }
69. }
```

File Streams

There is an interesting thing about files on an NTFS partition: file streams. Files on an NTFS formatted drive are not the same as files on a FAT or HPFS partition. NTFS files consist of what are known as streams. Typically a file is comprised of one stream. The stream is the collection of data that you think of as the file's data. For example:

```
open( FILE, "> test.txt" ) || die "Error: $!";
print FILE "This is a cool test\n";
close( FILE );
open( FILE, "< test.txt" ) || die "Error: $!";
print <FILE>;
close( FILE );
```

This will just write to a file, and then print out its content; however, if you then run this code:

```
open( FILE, "> test.txt:stream2" ) || die "Error: $!";
print FILE "Holy cow, how can this be?\n";
close( FILE );
open( FILE, "< test.txt:stream2" ) || die "Error: $!";
print <FILE>;
close( FILE );
```

You will see different output.

If you think there is nothing nifty about this, that we have created two separate files, then think again. Look at the directory listing and you will see only one file: text.txt.

Rename this file to testfile.txt *and run this code:*

```
open( FILE, "< testfile.txt:stream2" ) |¦ die "Error: $!";
print <FILE>;
close( FILE );
```

The point of this exercise is that a file can have multiple data streams. If you move the file, the streams move as well because, as far as NTFS is concerned, all these data streams are just attributes (like the READONLY *and* HIDDEN *flags) associated to a file. As a matter of fact, data in any NTFS file is considered to be an attribute (even if the data is hundreds of megabytes in size).*

Macintosh users should feel at home with this concept because Macintosh files have always had two streams: the data and resource forks.

File Permissions

The Windows NT operating systems support the NTFS file format, which allows, among other things, for permissions to be placed on files and directories. Permissions are rules that determine which user can access the file or directory as well as how the user can access it.

The scope of permissions and how they work is a very broad topic that itself could be the focus a book. This section just covers the basics so that using the **Win32::FileSecurity** extension will make sense.

Warning

You need to be warned that messing around with permissions on files and directories can be incredibly dangerous! If you make a simple mistake, it could render the file or directory inaccessible and you would have to have your administrator take ownership of the file and reapply permissions.

Access Control Lists

Each file and directory on an NTFS partition has an associated list of which users and groups are allowed access. This is known as an Access Control List (ACL). ACLs are really tables that relate a user or group to a permission. Table 4.9 shows an example of this relationship.

Table 4.9   Example of the account-to-permission releationship in an ACL

User Account	Permission
Administrator	Full Permissions
Guest	No Access
Rothd	Change
Operator	Read, Write
Users	Read

Many different permissions can be applied to a file, as indicated in the list in Table 4.10.

Table 4.10   List of permission constants

Permission Constant	Description
DELETE	Ability to remove the file.
READ_CONTROL	Ability to read the control information.
WRITE_DAC	Ability to write the discretionary Access Control List. This grants permission to modify permissions on the file.
WRITE_OWNER	Ability to edit the owner of the file.
SYNCHRONIZE	This is the right for the file to become signaled from a synchronization object such as a mutex or semaphore or a file notification.
STANDARD_RIGHTS_READ	Read permission for directories.
STANDARD_RIGHTS_WRITE	Write permission for directories.
STANDARD_RIGHTS_EXECUTE	Execute permission for directories. (This allows someone to open a directory.)
STANDARD_RIGHTS_ALL	Full permissions for a directory.
GENERIC_READ	Basic read access.
GENERIC_WRITE	Basic write access.
GENERIC_EXECUTE	Basic execute access.
GENERIC_ALL	All basic access rights (read, write, execute, delete).
R	Read access.
READ	Read access.
C	Change (modify) access.
CHANGE	Change (modify) access.
F	Full access. This grants read, write, delete, change permission, and change owner access.
FULL	Full access. This grants read, write, delete, change permission, and change owner access.

> **Note**
>
> *The capability to manage and alter file permissions is based all on whether you have the permission to do so. Basically this means that you need the "change permissions" permission. This is the same as the* WRITE_DAC *permission.*
>
> *If a file grants a user the* WRITE_DAC *or* FULL *permissions, the user has the right to modify permissions.*
>
> *This is what happens when you grant the administrator* FULL *permissions on a file, for example.*

The Win32::FileSecurity Extension

Considering how complicated file security can be, the **Win32::FileSecurity** extension is remarkably easy to learn and use. It provides a basic interface to retrieve, set, and decode permissions.

To use the extension, you must, as with all extensions, **use** it:

```
use Win32::FileSecurity;
```

Using Constants

Early on in the development of the **Win32::FileSecurity** extension, constants were resolved in an unconventional manner. This changed with the advent of the core distribution's libwin32 version 0.10. The rest of this section on constants refers to the version of the extension that comes with ActiveState's build 316 and libwin32 before version 0.10.

The **Win32::FileSecurity** extension did not export the constants from the extension's module into the main namespace. This means that you cannot just use a constant by specifying its name. For example:

```
$Mask = STANDARD_RIGHTS_READ ¦ STANDARD_RIGHTS_WRITE;
```

will not work. You must specify the constant by its full namespace; and to make matters even odder, you must specify the constant as a function, as in:

```
$Mask = Win32::FileSecurity::STANDARD_RIGHTS_READ() ¦
Win32::FileSecurity::STANDARD_RIGHTS_WRITE();
```

The reason for this is that the constants are supported by the extension, but the module does not export the list of constant names. Because the names are not exported into the main namespace, Perl does not know what the constant is or how to resolve it. When you attempt to call a function in the **Win32::FileSecurity** extension that has the name of a constant, this forces Perl to attempt to resolve the function's name. By doing this, the constant's value is resolved instead.

After a constant has been resolved, the value is cached and you can later refer to the constant by its full namespace name and not a function, as in Example 4.12.

Example 4.12   *Accessing a **Win32::FileSecurity** constant*

```
use Win32::FileSecurity;
$Mask = Win32::FileSecurity::READ();
if( $Mask & READ )
{
   print "The mask contains the read permission\n";
}
```

An alternative is to use the **Win32::FileSecurity::constant**() function:

```
$Value = Win32::FileSecurity::constant( $Permission, $Value );
```

The first parameter ($Permission) is a string representation of a constant such as "ADD". Refer to Table 4.10 for a list of constants.

The second parameter ($Value) can be anything, but it must be passed in.

If the **Win32::FileSecurity::constant**() function is successful, the value of the constant is returned; otherwise, a 0 is returned. This can be quite a problem because it is impossible to determine whether a constant's value is 0 or whether there is no such constant.

The Security Hash

The **Win32::FileSecurity** extension utilizes a security hash. This hash consists of keys named after a user or group account name. The values associated with a key is the permission mask (see "The Win32::FileSecurity Mask" section). Example 4.13 demonstrates a security hash dump. Notice that the keys are legitimate user or group names and the values are numeric masks that can be decoded using the **EnumerateRights**() function (refer to the section, "Decoding a Permission Mask").

Example 4.13   *A dump of a security hash*

```
%Perms = (
    'BUILTIN\\Administrators' => 2032127
    'rothd' => 1245631
    'CREATOR OWNER' => 2032127
    'Everyone' => 1245631
    'NT AUTHORITY\\SYSTEM' => 2032127
)
```

The Win32::FileSecurity Mask

When dealing with permissions, you will come across the concept of a mask. A permission mask is a bitmask of permission values all logically OR'ed together.

When you set permissions, you need to assign a mask to a user or group account. You can create a hash by either OR'ing the constant values together (see the section "Using Constants" for details about using constants in this extension) or you can use the **Win32::FileSecurity::MakeMask()** function:

```
$Mask = Win32::FileSecurity::MakeMask( $Permission [, $Permission [, ... ] ] );
```

Any number of permission strings can be passed into the **MakeMask()** function. The permissions passed in are the string versions of those listed in Table 4.10.

Note

When using the MakeMask() function, it is very important to pass in the names of the constants as strings. To create a mask of READ *and* DELETE *access, you would use:*

```
$Mask = Win32::FileSecurity::MakeMask( "READ", "DELETE" );
```

In older versions of the extension, you could specify only the constant name, but this will not work in the newer versions.

Newer versions export the constant names, so passing in just the name of the constant will result in the numeric values being passed in. This indeed would not work well.

Retrieving File Permissions

When you need to retrieve the permissions from a file or directory, you can use the **Win32::FileSecurity::Get()** function:

```
Win32::FileSecurity::Get( $Path, \%Perms );
```

The first parameter ($Path) is the path to the object for which you want security information. This can be either a relative path, a full path, or a UNC.

The second parameter (\%Perms) is a reference to a hash. If the function is successful, this hash will be populated with keys that represent the user or group account. The values of the keys will be the permission mask for that account.

If the **Get()** function is successful, it will return a 1; otherwise it returns a 0.

Decoding a Permission Mask

After you have retrieved the permission hash using the **Get()** function, you can decode the mask by using the **Win32::FileSecurity::EnumerateRights()** function:

```
Win32::FileSecurity::EnumerateRights( $Mask, \@Permissions );
```

The first parameter ($Mask) is the bitmask that was either created with the **MakeMask()** function or retrieved by the **Get()** function.

The second parameter (\@Permissions) is a reference to an array. Strings representing the permissions that make up the mask will populate this array. These strings can be used to feed into the **MakeMask()** function. If the function is successful, it will return a 1; otherwise it returns a 0. Example 4.14 demonstrates the **EnumerateRights()** function.

Example 4.14   *Displaying account permissions on a file*

```
01. use Win32::FileSecurity;
02.
03. $Path = $ARGV[0];
04. if( Win32::FileSecurity::Get( $Path, \%Perms ) )
05. {
06.   print "Permissions for $Path:\n";
07.   foreach $Account (sort( keys( %Perms ) ) )
08.   {
09.     print "\t$Account:\n";
10.     if( Win32::FileSecurity::EnumerateRights( $Perms{$Account}, \@List ) )
11.     {
12.       map { print "\t\t$_\n";} ( @List );
13.     }else{
14.       print "\t\tNone\n";
15.     }
16.   }
17. }else{
18.   print "Error accessing permissions for '$Path':\n";
19.   print Win32::FormatMessage( Win32::GetLastError() );
20. }
```

Applying Masks to Directories or Files

When you have a mask that you want to apply to a directory or file, you use the **Win32::FileSecurity::Set()** function:

```
Win32::FileSecurity::Set( $Path, \%Permissions );
```

The first parameter ($Path) is a path to a file or directory. This parameter can be a UNC.

The second parameter (\%Permissions) is a reference to a security hash (refer to Example 4.13).

If the **Set()** function is successful, the permissions are placed on the file or directory and returns a 1; otherwise 0 is returned.

Case Study: Directory Security

I have occasionally opened my server up to guests for various reasons. Because of this, I have had to secure particular directories from alterations by the anonymous users. The script listed in Example 4.15 removes all write permissions for the Guest account and Guests group from the files in the c:\TEMP directory.

Example 4.15 *Removing write permissions for a user on all files in a directory*

```
01. use Win32::FileSecurity;
02. $Dir = "c:/temp";
03. $User = "Guest";
04. print "Removing the WRITE permissions for $User in directory:\n";
05. print "$Dir\n";
06. while( $Path = glob( "$Dir/*.*" ) )
07. {
08.    next if (-d $Path);
09.    $Total{files}++;
10.    ( $File ) = ( $Path =~ /([^\\\/]*)$/ );
11.    print "\t$Total{files}) $File...";
12.      # Get the permissions of the file
13.    if( Win32::FileSecurity::Get( $Path, \%Perms ) )
14.    {
15.      foreach $Account ( keys( %Perms ) )
16.      {
17.          # If we have found the user then modify the permissions
18.        $Changes = ModifyPerms( \$Perms{$Account} )
             if( $Account =~ /$User$/i );
19.      }
20.      if( $Changes )
21.      {
22.          # If changes have been made then apply the new permissions
23.        if( Win32::FileSecurity::Set( $Path, \%Perms ) )
24.        {
25.          print "\t\tSuccessful.\n";
26.          $Total{success}++;
27.        }else{
28.          print "\t\tUnable to set the new permissions for $Path.\n";
29.          Error();
30.        }
31.      }else{
32.        print "\t\tno changes were made.\n";
33.      }
34.
35.    }else{
36.      print "Unable to get the permissions for $Path.\n";
37.      Error();
38.    }
39. }
40. print "\nTotal files: $Total{files}\n";
```

continues

Continued

```
41. print "Total changes: $Total{success}\n";
42.
43. sub ModifyPerms
44. {
45.   my( $Mask ) = @_;
46.   my( @List, $Remove );
47.     # Decode the permission mask.
48.   if( Win32::FileSecurity::EnumerateRights( $$Mask, \@List ))
49.   {
50.     for( $Temp = $#List; $Temp >= 0; $Temp— )
51.     {
52.         # If the following permissions exist then pop them
53.         # out of the permission array.
54.       if( $List[ $Temp ] eq "WRITE" ||
55.           $List[ $Temp ] eq "STANDARD_RIGHTS_WRITE" ||
56.           $List[ $Temp ] eq "GENERIC_WRITE" ||
57.           $List[ $Temp ] eq "ADD" ||
58.           $List[ $Temp ] eq "CHANGE" )
59.       {
60.         splice( @List, $Temp, 1 );
61.         $Remove++;
62.       }
63.     }
64.       #   Recreate the permission mask.
65.     $$Mask = Win32::FileSecurity::MakeMask( @List );
66.   }else{
67.     print "\t\tNo permissions for $Account were found.\n";
68.   }
69.   return $Remove;
70. }
71.
72. sub Error
73. {
74.   my( $Path ) = @_;
75.   print Win32::FormatMessage( Win32::GetLastError() );
76. }
```

Line 13 retrieves a hash containing accounts and permission masks for a file using the **Get**() function. The hash is scrutinized for a specified account. (In this example, the GUEST account is targeted.) For each of them, the permission bitmask is passed into a **ModifyPerms**() subroutine. This routine walks through the hash and picks apart the permission bitmask using the **EnumerateRights**() function, removing any permission that would allow writing. If any changes are made, they are applied to the file using the **Set**() function in line 23.

Monitoring Directory Changes

Changes to a directory can be a nightmare for administrators who need to know exactly what a directory contains. Suppose, for example, that you have users who need to add and remove files from an FTP server's public directory tree. If each directory in the FTP site contains an index file enumerating which files are available or if there are HTML pages on your Web server that provide links to each file in the directory, they need to be updated whenever someone changes the contents of the FTP directory tree.

There are a few ways to manage this:

1. You could force all users to go through you or your staff when they add or remove files so that your staff could update these pages manually.

2. You could have a process scheduled every night to go out and update the pages.

3. You could use a CGI script or an ASP page to scan each of the directories to dynamically create the pages.

All three of these have some pretty massive drawbacks. The first suggestion could cause a time bottleneck and put quite a bit of strain on your staff. The second suggestion would give a large time resolution of updated files. If someone copies a file out to the directory tree for a client, it would not be listed until the next day. The third is the quickest and least stressful, but it would be processor intensive if you have a large number of users hitting the pages.

There is an alternative: the **Win32::ChangeNotify** extension. This extension (and its identical twin **Win32::ChangeNotification**—they are identical except in name) does nothing but monitor a directory for changes. You can use this to detect a change that triggers a Perl script to run. This would be an ideal solution.

First you must, of course, load the **Win32::ChangeNotify** extension:

```
use Win32::ChangeNotify;
```

There is another extension called **Win32::ChangeNotification**, which is the exact same as **Win32::ChangeNotify**. Evidently someone decided the latter is easier to type, so it was renamed. You can use either one, just make sure that you do not mix namespaces by using one extension but calling a function from the other. Additionally you may not have both in your Win32 Perl installation; so check for the one you do have.

Before you can monitor a directory, you need to first create a change notification object. This is accomplished by using the **FindFirst**() method:

```
Win32::ChangeNotify::FindFirst( $Object, $Path, $SubTree, $Flags )
```

The first parameter ($Object) is a scalar variable that, if the function succeeds, will be set to point to a **Win32::ChangeNotify** object.

The second parameter ($Path) is the directory that is to be monitored. This can be either a full path or a UNC. Both forward and backslashes are supported as directory delimiters. This path must not end in a slash (or backslash); otherwise it will fail. The only relative path that appears to work is the single dot current directory (".").

The third parameter ($SubTree) is a Boolean value that indicates whether only the specified directory is monitored or whether the directory and all its subdirectories are monitored as well. A TRUE value (1) indicates that all subdirectories are also monitored.

The fourth parameter ($Flags) represents flags that govern what is monitored. This can be any combination of values from Table 4.11 logically OR'ed together.

Table 4.11   Change notification flags

Flag	Description
FILE_NOTIFY_CHANGE_ATTRIBUTES	Monitors all file and directory attributes, alerting when any change.
FILE_NOTIFY_CHANGE_DIR_NAME	Monitors all directory names, alerting when a one changes.
FILE_NOTIFY_CHANGE_FILE_NAME	Monitors all file names, alerting when one changes.
FILE_NOTIFY_CHANGE_LAST_WRITE	Monitors the "last write" time stamps (the time the file or directory was last written to or modified) on all files and directories, alerting when any of them change.
FILE_NOTIFY_CHANGE_SECURITY	Monitors the security permissions on all files and directories, alerting when any change.
FILE_NOTIFY_CHANGE_SIZE	Monitors the size of a file or directory, alerting when any change. This will detect new files and directories that are added. Oddly enough, however, it will not alert if a file is deleted.

The name of the **FindFirst**() function is a bit misleading because it sounds like you are looking for the first object in a series of objects. Think of this function as if it were called **new**(). Basically all that it does is create a new change notification object used for monitoring.

If the **FindFirst**() function is successful, the scalar variable passed in as the first parameter is set with a reference to a new change notification object and returns TRUE. Otherwise it fails and returns undef. Example 4.16 shows how this function is used.

Example 4.16   *Monitoring a directory (and subdirectories) for attribute or size changes*

```
01. use Win32::ChangeNotify;
02. $Path = "c:\\temp";
03.   # create a change notification object
04. Win32::ChangeNotify::FindFirst( $Monitor, $Path, 1,
      FILE_NOTIFY_CHANGE_ATTRIBUTES | FILE_NOTIFY_CHANGE_SIZE) || die
      "Unable to create a change notification object. Error:" .
      Win32::FormatMessage( Win32::GetLastError() ) . "\n";
05. print "Preparing to monitor $Path...\n";
06. while( $Monitor->FindNext() )
07. {
08.   print "Monitoring...\n";
09.   $Monitor->Wait( INFINITE );
10.   print "\tWOW! There was a change to $Path!!!\n";
11. }
12. $Monitor->Close();
```

After a monitoring object has been created, you need to indicate that you are monitoring it. This is done with the **FindNext()** method:

```
$NotifyObject->FindNext();
```

If **FindNext()** is successful, it returns TRUE; otherwise if returns undef.

FindNext() takes no parameters and will start the process of monitoring. This method itself is not enough to provide a Perl script with the capability to know when a change has occurred. After monitoring is active, the script must wait for a change. This is done with a call to the **Wait()** method:

```
$NotifyObject->Wait( $Timeout );
```

The $Timeout parameter is the number of milliseconds to use as a timeout value. That is to say that this method will wait for up to the specified number of milliseconds. A value of 0 will just immediately timeout, and a value of INFINITE will never timeout. In the latter case, the only way for the method to return is if the specified change occurs.

The **Wait()** method will wait for the type of change to occur that was specified when the change notification object was created. If either a change or the time-out value is breached, the method returns.

Wait() will return a FALSE (0) value if a change has been detected; otherwise (if the method times out), it returns a TRUE value (not 0 and not undef).

When a call to the **Wait()** method returns, you can check the return value to determine whether it returned because of a timeout or because of the sought-after change occurred. Either way, the script can continue monitoring by again call-ing **FindNext()**, which resets the monitoring and then wait by calling **Wait()**.

After the monitoring has been completed, the change notification object needs to be destroyed and removed from memory. This is done by using the **Close()** method:

```
$NotifyObject->Close();
```

This will always return a TRUE value.

It is important to understand how this entire process works. After a change notification object has been created, any change is queued up. When you call **FindNext()**, it will clear the current state (if a change had already been detected by the **Wait()** method, it is cleared) and advance the queue—literally finding the next change. A call to **Wait()** will then check the queue. If it finds a change in the queue, it will return; otherwise it will wait for a change to enter the queue and return (or return due to a timeout).

This may seem a bit awkward, but it is important because when your script returns from the **Wait()** method it will probably have to process some data. If during this time another change takes place, it will be queued up. The call to **FindNext()** will reset the state and allow **Wait()** to discover the next queued change. This prevents your script from missing a change because it was busy processing something.

The queue is only one element in length; so if 50 changes occur while your script is processing, it will only queue one of them. Really, that is all your script needs. There is no point in being told that 50 changes occurred because it will have to process the entire directory at once anyway.

It is interesting to know that if **Wait()** returns because of a timeout it can be called again. If it returns because it detected a change, however, the state must be cleared with a call to **FindNext()** before **Wait()** will detect any new change; any attempt to call it again without first calling **FindNext()** will return with a value indicating a change has occurred even if no such change took place. The point here is that if **Wait()** returns a 0 value (indicating a change has been detected), you *must* reset the current state by calling **FindNext()**.

If you need to clear the current state and any change that may be queued up, you can call **FindNext()** twice. By doing so, you reset the current state and advance the queue. Doing so twice will, in effect, clear the current state as well as the queue.

Example 4.17 is a good example on how change notification could be used. It accepts a directory path as a command line parameter.

*Some versions of **Win32::ChangeNotify** (and
Win32::ChangeNotification) did not export the INFINITE constant.
Because this is one of the most commonly used constants from this extension, it would be wise to manually add it to the list of exported constants
from the CHANGENOTIFY.PM file.*

You could always use the constant's value instead, which is 0xFFFFFFFF.

Example 4.17   *Report any size changes to a particular directory*

```
01. use Win32::ChangeNotify;
02. $Path = "c:/" unless ( $Path = $ARGV[0] );
03.   # Remove any trailing slashes
04. $Path =~s/[\\\/]*$//;
05. $IncludeSubDirs = 1;
06. $Flags = FILE_NOTIFY_CHANGE_FILE_NAME | FILE_NOTIFY_CHANGE_SIZE;
07.   # This is the index of a value returned by the stat() function.
08. $STAT_FILE_SIZE = 7;
09. print "Setting up to monitor '$Path'...\n";
10. Win32::ChangeNotify::FindFirst( $Monitor, $Path, $IncludeSubDirs,
        $Flags ) ||
            die "Could not create a notification object. Error:", Error(),
            "\n";
11. $FileList = ScanDir( $Path );
12. while( $Monitor->FindNext() )
13. {
14.    print "\nMonitoring '$Path' ", ( $IncludeSubDirs )? "(and sub
       directories)":"", "...\n";
15.    $Monitor->Wait( INFINITE );
16.    ( $FileList, $Changes ) = DetectChanges( $FileList, $Path );
17.    print "  -Changes detected at " . localtime() . "\n";
18.    $iCount = 0;
19.    foreach $File ( sort( keys( %$Changes ) ) )
20.    {
21.       $Count++;
22.       print "    $Count) $File $Changes->{$File}.\n";
23.    }
24.    print "   - No noticeable changes occured.\n";
25. }
26. $Monitor->Close();
27.
28. sub DetectChanges
29. {
30.    my( $OldList, $Path ) = @_;
31.    my( $NewList ) = ScanDir( $Path );
32.    my( $Changes, $File );
33.    foreach $File ( sort( keys( %$OldList ) ) )
34.    {
35.       $Delta = $NewList->{$File} - $OldList->{$File};
36.       if( $Delta )
```

continues

Continued

```perl
37.      {
38.        if( ! -e $File )
39.        {
40.          $Changes->{$File} = "has been removed";
41.        }
42.        elsif( $Delta < 0 )
43.        {
44.          $Delta = abs( $Delta );
45.          $Changes->{$File} = "has been reduced by $Delta bytes";
46.        }
47.        else
48.        {
49.          $Changes->{$File} = "has grown by $Delta bytes";
50.        }
51.      }
52.    }
53.    foreach $File ( sort( keys( %$NewList ) ) )
54.    {
55.      if( ! defined $OldList->{$File} )
56.      {
57.        $Changes->{$File} = "has been added";
58.      }
59.    }
60.    return( $NewList, $Changes );
61. }
62.    # Generate a hash of files and their sizes
63. sub ScanDir
64. {
65.    my( $Path, $List ) = @_;
66.    my( @Entries, $Temp );
67.    $Path =~ s/\\/\//g;
68.    if( opendir( DIR, $Path ) )
69.    {
70.      @Entries = readdir( DIR );
71.      closedir( DIR );
72.    }
73.    foreach $Temp ( sort( @Entries ) )
74.    {
75.      next if( $Temp eq "." || $Temp eq ".." );
76.      $Dir = "$Path/$Temp";
77.      if( -d $Dir )
78.      {
79.        ScanDir( $Dir, $List ) if( $IncludeSubDirs );
80.      }
81.      else
82.      {
83.        $List->{$Dir} = FileSize( $Dir );
84.      }
85.    }
86.    return( $List );
87. }
88.    # Return the size of a file
89. sub FileSize
```

```
90. {
91.   my( $Path ) = @_;
92.   return( ( stat( $Path ) )[$STAT_FILE_SIZE] );
93. }
94.
95. sub Error
96. {
97.   return( Win32::FormatMessage( Win32::GetLastError() ) );
98. }
```

Summary

Files can contain a wealth of information that we take for granted. Not only does the data contained within the file have significant value, but so does the file itself. The file's attributes tell much about the state of a file. In addition, file information such as the original name of the file can be of great interest to anyone (especially administrators).

The Win32 Perl extensions provide functions that empower administrators to manage files and directories by giving access to the attributes of both. In addition, with file systems that provide extended attributes, file and directory attributes are available to a Perl script as well.

File attributes are taken for granted by most users. Users generally don't care whether a read-only bit is set or whether the archive bit has been turned off—just as long as everything works. When an administrator needs to set a configuration file as read-only or check whether a file is compressed, however, he appreciates the **Win32::File** extension.

It is not often that a user needs to know the version number of a particular .DLL file. Administrators do need to know this, however, to keep a machine in sync with others. Using the **Win32::AdminMisc** extension opens the door to accessing a plethora of file information.

Shortcuts are being used more and more by users, and they too have to be managed. These files can be managed by using the **Win32::Shortcut** Win32 Perl extension. Managing these shortcuts is one of the problems that impact administrators, but most don't known about it until it becomes a need.

For the most part, file permissions can make or break a well-managed machine. After all, if a user cannot access a file when he needs to, you (as an administrator) look like you have failed. If a user can access sensitive information when he should not be able to, you have a security breach. The **Win32::FileSecurity** extension is the tool to use when you need to manage the permissions of files and directories.

Chapter 5

Automation

One of the most useful elements that all Win32 machines share is the capability to embed and automate data and programs. Microsoft has accomplished this by implementing the complex technology known as Object Linking and Embedding (OLE). Just as it is strikingly similar to the UNIX-based CORBA, it is also just as powerful. Therefore, many users have learned to take advantage of OLE in such a way that it is no longer considered to be a separate technology, but instead it is assumed to be an imperative part of the operating system.

This chapter describes how a Perl script can make use of OLE by using the **Win32::OLE** extension.

Understanding OLE

In early versions of 16-bit Windows (such as 3.1), Microsoft introduced a new concept they called Object Linking and Embedding (OLE). The idea behind this new technology was that you could embed an object within another object. If you were sending an email message using Microsoft Mail, for example, you could paste a copy of a Word document into it. This was very cool because the receiver could just double-click on the attached document (which was displayed as an icon), which would tell your word processor to load the document automatically. If the word processor was not already running, it would be first launched and would then load the document. Linking objects with other objects was a great idea, but OLE itself was quite limited. Originally OLE used DDE (Dynamic Data Exchange) as the protocol to communicate between programs.

A few years later OLE 2.0 was released. This replaced DDE with COM (discussed later in the section titled "COM") as the communication mechanism. OLE 2.0 also supported enhancements that finally made it easy and a pleasure to use. OLE 2.0 provided the capability to edit embedded data within a document. OLE enables a user to paste an Excel spreadsheet into a Word document, for example, but editing the spreadsheet with OLE 1.0 would cause Excel to run and load the spreadsheet. The user would then have to switch to

Excel, edit the spreadsheet, save the changes, and then quit Excel. OLE 2.0, on the other hand, fostered a sense of integration. To edit the embedded spreadsheet, the user just placed the cursor into the spreadsheet that appeared in the Word document. At that point, OLE 2.0 merged Word's menu and toolbars with Excel's menu and toolbars. This way a user could edit the Excel spreadsheet from within the Word program. The capability to activate one program's functionality from within another was called *in place activation.*

OLE 2.0 also brought about a new concept called *automation.* This is where one program can tell another application what to do. Imagine a user who needs to send a letter to everyone in a database of names and addresses. He could perform a query on his database, and then use automation to load his word processor, create a form letter inserting the names and addresses retrieved from the database, and then tell the word processor to print out the letters.

Before going into the explanation of how Perl can use OLE, it may be of use to explain exactly what OLE is and how it works. There are many terms to define and acronyms to explain so that OLE makes any sense, especially because the industry has been using the terms OLE, COM, and ActiveX synonymously. So first, familiarize yourself with some basic terms.

OLE

Object Linking and Embedding (OLE) is the overall technology that allows one process to control or talk to another process. An OLE transaction consists of a client process, a server process, and a communication protocol in which the processes use to talk with each other.

COM

The Component Object Model (COM) is a protocol used to communicate between processes involved in an OLE transaction. This protocol replaced DDE as the communication method of choice with the introduction of OLE 2.0. All Win32 processes that make use of OLE use COM to transfer data and send instructions to each other. (Win32 still supports DDE for other reasons, but not with OLE.)

When a program wants to talk to another program, it must follow the rules of conduct prescribed in the COM protocol. Consider COM to be the "rules of the road" for programs to chat with each other. By following these rules, each program knows what to expect from another program while using COM to talk with each other. For all practical purposes, a Perl programmer needs only to know that there exists a thing called COM and it is related to OLE. The actual OLE programs (such as Excel and Word) take care of the rest.

ActiveX

An ActiveX component is just a COM-based server (described later in the section titled "How OLE Works") that follows certain rules that all ActiveX components must follow. These rules allow the component to be embedded in other applications such as HTML pages and Web browsers. As of this writing, most ActiveX components are not supported by Win32 Perl because they use certain Win32 features (such as OLE events and asynchronous calls) that Perl cannot yet handle. This will most likely change in the future.

How OLE Works

When a program wants to talk to another program, it can use OLE (or more accurately COM) to strike up a conversation. The program (or process) that starts the conversation is called a *controller* because it is beginning the process of controlling the other application. Any program or process that a controller talks to is known as a COM *server* because it will be serving the controller. Programs that act as servers come in two flavors: in-process and out-of-process servers.

Simply stated, an in-process server (also known as an *inproc server*) is just a DLL file that the controller process loads into memory and uses. It is called an in-process server because a DLL file is always loaded into the same process (or memory) space as the application loading it. An example could be a fax printer driver. If your application wanted to send a fax, all it would have to do is load the fax printer driver's DLL and make calls into the DLL directly.

An out-of-process server (sometimes called a *local server application*) is a separate executable program run when the controller begins a conversation with it. After the local server application is running, the controller process talks to it using the COM protocol. An example of this could be some program such as Microsoft Excel. When Excel is loaded as a local server application, it literally is started up as if a user had double-clicked on its icon. Some applications will run but hide its main window so that users are unaware that it had started.

If DCOM (Distributed COM) is installed, the out-of-process server could be on another machine and communication is done over a network. This is cool because the server application will physically run on another computer. If this was the case, the out-of-process server would be called a *remote server application*.

For the most part, knowing whether a COM server is in-process or out-of-process is not very important to the average Perl coder. Either way Perl interacts with the COM servers the same way.

Using OLE in Perl

Suppose that you want to place data in an Excel spreadsheet. You would want to first create an Excel COM object. Of course, this process is called Automation and COM is just the communication protocol. The fine folks in Microsoft's marketing department are pushing COM to be the acronym du jour, however, and hence you need to create an Excel COM object. You then interact with the object, and after you are finished with it you just destroy it. Now, isn't that simple? The trick here is knowing what to do with the COM object. Generally speaking you can examine it, alter it, and tell it to do things.

COM Objects

To explain exactly what a COM object is, we must first go off on a tangent and talk about something that may be a little bit easier to understand: those wonderful ATMs (Automated Teller Machines). For you to use an ATM, you need to first go to your bank and get your ATM card. Once armed with this piece of plastic, you can not only query the bank's database and get the balance of your accounts, but you can also tell the bank to perform transactions such as deposit, withdraw, or transfer money from account to account.

COM objects are similar to the ATM card; each COM object has a particular set of values known as *properties* (such as your balance) and functions that are called *methods*, which perform a task (such as deposit and withdraw). After you have a COM object, you can check its properties to query the state of the object, change properties altering the object's state, or tell the object to perform some function. Examples of properties could be the font of a particular spreadsheet cell or the file name of a document. Examples of methods could be **Open()**, **Print()**, or **Quit()**.

Identifying COM Objects

Okay, suppose that you decide that you want to write code that interacts with a COM object. You now need to determine what *type* of COM object you are going to interact with. If you have two versions of Word (version 6.0 and Office 97) installed on your machine, for example, you need to make sure that you are interacting with the correct version. Likewise you will need to know how to interact with Excel rather than Word.

Every COM object is based on a *class*. A class is like a blueprint that describes how an object will behave. This class is just like an object-oriented Perl class or a C++ class. An OLE-aware program typically consists of several classes. Excel consists of the classes described in Table 5.1, for example (there are others, but these are the common ones):

Table 5.1   Basic types of classes found in Excel 5.0

Class	Functionality
Application class	Describes the program and how it runs.
Workbook class	Describes how a workbook functions.
Worksheet class	Describes how a worksheet functions.
Graph class	Describes how a graph functions.

Excel defines each of these classes and exposes them so that a controller application (like your Perl script) can request any of them to be instantiated into COM objects that you can interact with.

Some classes rely on others. If you just want to create a new Excel worksheet, for example, you could request a worksheet object. To have a worksheet, however, Excel must first be started and a new workbook be created—often (but not always), this is done automatically by the server application. The resulting COM object would only represent the worksheet, even though both Excel and a workbook have also been created.

GUIDs

Each OLE class has a *GUID* (Global Unique Identifier—pronounced "goo-id" and rhymes with "grid") that no other class shares. These are those funky looking strings found throughout the Registry. All GUIDs follow a specific format that looks like the one that follows (which represents the Excel 5.0 application):

```
{00020841-0000-0000-C000-000000000046}
```

It is important to understand GUIDs are hard coded and do not change. A GUID for a class on Joel's computer will be identical to the one for the same class on Jane's computer. All computers that have MS Access 1.0 installed will have the same GUID. If you have MS Access 2.0 installed, you will have a different GUID. If you have both versions installed, you will have both GUIDs in your Registry. The point here is that you can depend on a particular GUID to always represent a particular program.

> Note
>
> *When a programmer writes an OLE-aware application, she needs to create a GUID for it. Typically she will run Microsoft's* GUIDGEN.EXE *application, which generates shiny new GUIDs.*
>
> *Because of the mathematical probability involved with the creation of GUIDs, it is unlikely that any two GUIDs will ever be the same. For all practical purposes, it is so unlikely that it is considered not possible. This, of course, assumes that you use the Microsoft approved GUID-generating algorithm that is a part of the OLE API (which* GUIDGEN.EXE *indeed does use).*

A GUID is often referred to as a CLSID (CLaSs IDentifier), an AppID (Application ID), an IID (Interface ID), or a UUID (Universally Unique ID).

Class Names

Class names are implemented because a GUID is quite long and difficult for humans to understand and remember. A class name is just a common name used to reference the GUID.

When you use OLE, you can specify either the GUID "{73FDDC80-AEA9-101A-98A7-00AA00374959}" or you could instead use the class name "Wordpad.Document.1." They both refer to the same OLE class, but one makes it obviously easier for humans to understand the program it represents.

Perl and OLE

Win32 Perl has had the capability to handle OLE transactions by means of the original OLE.PM module. For the most part, this module is quickly becoming obsolete and replaced with the **Win32::OLE** extension by Gurusamy Sarathy and Jan Dubois. Where the fundamentals between the two are the same, the implementations are somewhat different and in some cases the original OLE.PM is just not designed to handle what **Win32::OLE** can.

For the most part, this chapter describes **Win32::OLE**—even though the extension is not compatible with the ActiveState versions before 5.005.

> ### Tip
> If you have scripts that make use of the OLE.PM module, you should consider migrating to the **Win32::OLE** extension. It provides much more flexibility and is less prone to runtime errors and breaking.

Creating COM Objects

When a Perl script needs to interact with an application using COM, the script is considered to be a controlling process. The Perl script needs to first access a COM object. It is important to understand that the Perl script does not create the COM object, instead the OLE server (that is, the OLE application the script is to interact with—this is sometimes called a COM server) creates the object on the Perl script's behalf. After that object has been created, the Perl script can interact with it.

Basically your Perl script needs to obtain a COM object from an OLE server. There are several different ways to do this because there are several different ways to obtain the object. You can either request an OLE server to create the object, you can try to find an existing object, or you can try to load a persistent object (typically this is stored as a file somewhere).

*Many users of **Win32::OLE** (and the original OLE.PM) module think that the module creates the COM object. To understand COM, you must understand that the Perl script never creates a COM object; it requests that the object be created. This distinction is very important.*

If the Perl script could create a COM object, it would be considered a COM server application, which it is not. Because the Perl script is just a controller application, it can only request that server applications create a COM object.

Technically speaking, a COM server application must support what is known as the OleFactory, which is a "factory" that manufactures COM objects. When a Perl script (or any controller application) requests a COM object to be created, the server application uses its OleFactory, to create the COM object and then hands it to the controlling application. After the object has been created, the Perl script can interact with it.

Creating a New COM Object

For a Perl script to interact with a COM object, it must first create a **Win32::OLE** object, which in turn requests the OLE server application to create a COM object. This is what the **new**() method is used for. By using this method, you are requesting the server application to create a new COM object for your use. There are two ways to use **new**(); the first listed is the more conventional way, but they both work:

```
$Object = new Win32::OLE( $ClassID [, $DestroyCommand ] );
$Object = Win32::OLE->new( $ClassID [, $DestroyCommand ] );
```

The first parameter ($ClassID) is a text string that represents a registered class ID. This is either the OLE server application's GUID or one of its class names. This parameter could also be a reference to an array of two elements the first being a computer name (such as "\\ServerA" or "www.blah.com") and the second element consisting of the string representing the class ID (either a GUID or a class name). By specifying an array reference, you are telling the **Win32::OLE** extension that you want to use DCOM (Distributed COM). If your local machine and the remote address you specify both have DCOM installed, an attempt to access a remote COM object will take place.

The second parameter ($DestroyCommand) is optional and is either a string or a code reference. It represents either a method of the COM object or a subroutine that your script defines, which will be called when the Perl **Win32::OLE** object is destroyed. Unfortunately some COM objects do not automatically unload from memory when they are destroyed. This means that when a Perl script terminates, some COM objects may remain floating around in memory. (This is a big problem with out-of-process server objects—you may end up with many copies of a server application remaining in memory.) To avoid this, a **Win32::OLE** object will call whatever method is specified as the second para- meter when it is destroyed. Typically you specify the method to quit the OLE application. For an Excel object, you would want to specify "Quit" so that the **Quit**() method will be called when the **Win32::OLE** object is destroyed.

If the $DestroyCommand parameter is a reference to a code segment, that code is called when the **Win32::OLE** object is destroyed. The **Win32::OLE** object (which is being destroyed) is the only parameter passed into the specified code segment. The routine can use this to interact with the COM object.

If the **Win32::OLE** object is successfully created, a **Win32::OLE** Perl object is returned; otherwise, undef is returned.

When specifying the class ID (the first parameter), you can use either a GUID or a class name. If you specify a class name, Win32 will just look up the class's GUID from the class database (located in the HKEY_LOCAL_CLASSES hive in the Registry). The main reason for using a class name is that it is easier for humans (in particular a programmer) to recognize.

Warning

*Keep in mind that the use of the **new**() method will request that a new COM object be created. This can have substantial memory and proces- sor overhead. If you were to request an Excel COM object by using the **new**() method, for example, Win32 would have to start an instance of Excel.*

*If a script requests several Excel COM objects using the **new**() method, you could quite quickly run out of memory and see a radical performance hit. This would not be a wise choice for a CGI script.*

*Typically COM objects created using the **new**() method are not visible on the screen. Regardless, they are indeed running and taking up memory. Line 14 in Example 5.1 sets the Visible property to 1 so that you can see that indeed an instance of Excel is running. If you were to run this code five times simultaneously, you would see that five instances of Excel are started.*

If it is possible that several instances of a COM object will be necessary, it would be wiser to request the first one using the **new**() method and the remain- ing ones using the **GetActiveObject**() method instead, as in Example 5.1.

Example 5.1   *Creating and interacting with a COM object*

```
01. use Win32::OLE;
02.   # Set some variables
03. $Class = "Excel.Application";
04. $File = "c:\\temp\\MyTest.xls";
05.   # If the file exists already then delete it
06. unlink( $File ) if (-e $File);
07.   # If you can use an already running copy of Excel
08. $Excel = Win32::OLE->GetActiveObject( $Class );
09. if( ! $Excel )
10. {
11.   $Excel = new Win32::OLE( $Class, \&QuitApp )
                 ¦¦ die "Could not create an OLE '$Class' object";
12. }
13.   # Show the Excel object so we can see it
14. $Excel->{Visible} = 1;
15. $Excel->{SheetsInNewWorkbook} = 1;
16.   # Add (or create) a new workbook
17. $Workbook = $Excel->Workbooks->Add();
18.   # Select the first worksheet in the workbook
19. $Worksheet = $Workbook->Worksheets(1);
20. $Worksheet->{Name} = "My Test Worksheet";
21.   # Change the contents of a "range" of cells (actually only one cell)
22. $Range = $Worksheet->Range("A1");
23. $Range->{Value} = "Hey, this is a test!";
24.   # Save the workbook
25. $Workbook->SaveAs( $File );
26.
27. sub QuitApp
28. {
29.   my( $ComObject ) = @_;
30.   print "Quitting " . $ComObject->{Name} . "\n";
31.   $ComObject->Quit();
32. }
```

In Example 5.1 a class name is used ("Excel.Application") to create the
COM object. The server application's GUID ("{00020841-0000-0000-C000-
000000000046}") could be used instead. Also notice that a destroy method is
specified (as a reference to a code segment). The reason is that if the COM
object is created on our behalf (by the **new**() method in line 11), the code is
responsible for making sure that the COM object is terminated when it is finished. Most COM objects are thoughtful enough to know when they are no
longer needed and terminate themselves. Microsoft Office 97 is, evidently, not
one of them, so we must make sure that Excel's **Quit**() method is called. When
the $Excel object is destroyed (even in the event that the script terminates early
from, for example, pressing Ctrl+Break), the **Win32::OLE** object will call the
Perl subroutine specified as the second parameter of the **new**() method (line
11). In this example when the **Win32::OLE** object is destroyed, the object will
call the **QuitExcel**() subroutine and pass in a reference to the Perl object being
destroyed. The routine will explicitly call the COM object's **Quit**() method.

If you changed line 11 of Example 5.1 to:

```
$Excel = new Win32::OLE( [ "www.blah.com", $Class ], \&QuitExcel ) ¦¦ die
"Could not create an OLE '$Class' object";
```

Win32::OLE would use DCOM to request the COM object from the computer
www.blah.com. This means that, if successful, the Excel server application would
be running on the remote machine (www.blah.com) rather than your local computer. This can be very handy if you have a powerful application server that
can handle the load of several instances of an application running. It can also
be a devastating prank if you target a coworker's computer who is not aware
of what you are doing.

Using DCOM for delegating power servers to handle many instances of Excel
or MS Access, for example, can be quite inviting. You may have a Web server
that receives several simultaneous hits on CGI scripts or ASP pages that request
COM objects, for example. By using DCOM, you can keep your Web server
from bogging down under the load of COM object requests. Keep in mind,
however, that this would come at a cost of bogging down other machines
(which you would have running the COM server applications) and increasing
network traffic.

Creating a COM object is quite often necessary, but it can be more practical
(regarding both memory and processor usage) to use existing objects. This is
why the **GetActiveObject()**method exists.

> ### Note
>
> *Numerous articles and books have been written that suggest using the*
> *CreateObject() method. Whereas this will work the same as the **new()***
> *method, it is only provided for backward compatibility with previous ver-*
> *sions such as the older* OLE.PM *module.*
>
> *It is highly recommended that you use the **new()** method rather than*
> *CreateObject(). There is no guarantee that CreateObject() will be sup-*
> *ported in future releases.*

Accessing an Existing COM Object

An alternative to **new()** is the **GetActiveObject()** method. Whereas **new()** will
request that a COM object be created, **GetActiveObject()** will return a reference to an object that already exists:

```
$Object = Win32::OLE->GetActiveObject( $ClassID );
```

The only parameter ($ClassID) is a string representing the class ID. This ID can
either be a GUID or a class name. Unlike the **new()** function, you cannot supply an anonymous array for this parameter. Evidentially, DCOM is not supported by the **GetActiveObject()** function.

The function returns a **Win32::OLE** object that represents the specified type of COM object only if such an object already exists in memory. Otherwise the function fails and returns undef.

Note that unlike the **new()** method, **GetActiveObject()** will neither start the server application nor create an instance of the specified COM object. It is a good idea to first use this method in a script. If it fails, use the **new()** function. This way if Excel is already running your script, for example, it will not force another instance of Excel to run. This will save on memory and processor usage.

Line 8 in Example 5.1 demonstrates the use of the **GetActiveObject()** function. If the function fails to find a COM object, the code will call the **new()** function and request that a COM object be created.

Accessing a Persistent COM Object

Yet another way to obtain a COM object is to request one based on a persistent object. A *persistent object* is considered a COM object that has been saved, typically as a file on a hard drive. If you are editing a Microsoft Word document and save it as C:\FILES\MFILE.DOC, for example, this file is considered to be a persistent object because when you load it back into Word it is in the same state as it was when you saved it. You could consider the document to be kind of a snapshot of the word processor the last time you saved the document. If you consider the document to be an object (which COM does), you could say that the file represents a saved state of the object. This is known as a persistent object; however, most folks think of them as simple Word, Excel, or some other application document files.

The **Win32::OLE** extension enables you to access persistent COM objects, such as a file, by using the **GetObject()** function:

```
$Object = Win32::OLE->GetObject( $Path );
```

The only parameter ($Path) is the path to a persistent object (like a .DOC or .XLS file). Like some Win32 extensions that enable you to use slashes (/) in a path, you must use backslashes (\) in this parameter. This path can be a relative, full, or UNC path.

This path can contain an optional named subcomponent by appending an exclamation point (!) and the name of the object to the path. Suppose that you need to obtain an object that represents a particular worksheet called "Totals" in a workbook, you can specify the path to the workbook file concatenated with "!Totals". The path passed into the **GetObject()** method would look like the following:

```
$Worksheet = Win32::OLE->GetObject( "c:\\temp\\test.xls!Totals" );
```

The resulting object would reflect the workbook's specified subcomponent (the "Totals" worksheet).

This is how it is *supposed* to work; however, just as in life, things don't always work as advertised. The preceding example will fail when used with Excel 97 (and possibly other versions). This appears to be a bug in the application.

If the **GetObject()** method is successful, it returns a **Win32::OLE** object that represents a COM object based on the specified path; otherwise, it fails and returns undef. Example 5.2 demonstrates the **GetObject()** method.

This example attempts to discover the title, subject, and author of all Word documents in a given directory. If line 11 cannot obtain a COM object-based return, the script continues on to the next file. Otherwise the COM object is queried for its type and compared with the type that a Word document would report ("_Document"). If indeed the query is successful and the COM object is a Word document, Title, Subject, and Author properties are queried and printed.

Example 5.2   *Using GetObject() to generate a summary of all .DOC files*

```
01. use Win32::OLE;
02. $Dir = "c:\\temp";
03. $FileSpec = "*.doc";
04. foreach $File ( glob( "$Dir/$FileSpec" ) )
05. {
06.   ProcessFile( $File );
07. }
08. sub ProcessFile
09. {
10.   my( $File ) = @_;
11.   my( $Doc ) = Win32::OLE->GetObject( $File ) || return;
12.   return if( "_Document" ne Win32::OLE->QueryObjectType( $Doc ) );
13.   if( $Doc )
14.   {
15.     print "$File:\n";
16.     print "\tTitle: " . $Doc->BuiltInDocumentProperties( "Title" )->{Value}
        . "\n";
17.     print "\tSubject: " . $Doc->BuiltInDocumentProperties(
        "Subject" )->{Value} . "\n";
18.     print "\tAuthor: " . $Doc->BuiltInDocumentProperties(
        "Author" )->{Value} . "\n";
19.     print "\n";
20.   }
21. }
```

Tip

*You may be wondering how Win32 can possibly know what class ID to use when using **Win32::OLE->GetObject()**. After all, you supply only a path to a file, you are not supplying the name of the class. The operating system will try four steps to determine which class ID to use:*

*1. When **Win32::OLE**'s **GetObject**() method asks the OS for a COM object based on a file name, it will first look through the current list of objects in memory. If an object already exists representing the specified file, the OS returns that COM object.*

*2. If there are no currently instantiated objects based on the file, the OS next tries to read the class ID from the file. This can occur only if the file is a structured storage file. These types of files are created by programs such as MS Office 97 where each file can have a title, subject, author, and other similar information in addition to the files class ID. The DocFile Viewer application (*DFVIEW.EXE*) that comes with Microsoft's development programs (such as Visual C++) enable you to peruse the contents of such files.*

3. If the class ID is not yet discovered, the OS resorts to walking the keys found in the Registry hive:

```
HKEY_CLASSES_ROOT\FileType
```

The interesting thing about these keys is that their name is a class ID. The way that the OS determines the class ID that matches the specified file is by systematically opening each of the key's subkeys. A subkey will hold a data value containing four comma-separated fields such as:

```
0,2,FFFF,DBA5
```

The format for this data is:

```
POSITION, BYTES, MASK, RESULT
```

The OS will then open the specified file and load the number of bytes specified by BYTES *from the location specified by* POSITION. *Next, the loaded data will be logically AND'ed with the value of* MASK. *If the resulting data is the same as* RESULT, *the OS assumes that the file matches this class ID.*

4. If the previous steps were inconclusive, the OS will walk through all the Registry keys that represent file extensions looking for one that matches the extension of the specified file. When one matches, the class name is extracted from the key's data value and the class ID is looked up based on that class name.

*If all these steps fail, the OS gives up and **Win32::OLE–>GetObject**() will fail.*

Retrieving the COM Object Type

After you have a COM object, you may need to discover what type of COM object it is. You can use the **QueryObjectType()** for this:

```
Win32::OLE->QueryObjectType( $Object );
```

The only parameter ($Object) is a **Win32::OLE** object. This can be obtained by calls to **new()**, **GetActiveObject()**, **GetObject()**, or some COM object's internal method.

The value returned is based on the context of the call. If the method is called in a scalar context, the class name is returned. If the method is called in an array context, the returned value is an array consisting of the type library (described later) and a class name.

If the **QueryObjectType()** method is successful, it returns type information for the COM object; otherwise, it fails and returns undef.

The returning class name is defined by the COM object itself, so there is no way to accurately predict what an object's type may be. It is best to experiment with different COM objects to know what strings they will return.

The script in Example 5.3 accepts an input parameter that is some document file. The script tries to create a COM object based on the file (such as a Word document or an Excel workbook) and prints the type of the object.

Example 5.3   *Determining a COM object's class name*
```
use Win32::OLE;
$File = $ARGV[0];
if( $Object = Win32::OLE->GetObject( $File ) )
{
  $Type = Win32::OLE->QueryObjectType( $Object );
  print "The object type for $File is '$Type'.\n";
}
```

Example 5.4 is the same as Example 5.3 except that it also prints out the object's type library.

Example 5.4   *Determining both a COM object's type library and class name*
```
use Win32::OLE;
$File = $ARGV[0];
if( $Object = Win32::OLE->GetObject( $File ) )
{
  @TypeInfo = Win32::OLE->QueryObjectType( $Object );
  print "The object type for $File is '$TypeInfo[1]'\n";
  print "The type library is: '$TypeInfo[0]'.\n";
}
```

Interacting with COM Objects

After you have successfully obtained a COM object, your Perl script can begin having fun. You need to familiarize yourself with just a few concepts before all this will make sense; these are COM objects and COM collections.

COM Objects

When you create a **Win32::COM** object, you are creating Perl object that represents a COM object. The COM object can contain properties and methods. By interacting with the properties and methods, you can change the state of the object and command the object to perform tasks.

If you have never dealt with COM objects before, think about starting MS Word. After you have Word running, you can consider the program's main window to be a Word Application object. You can interact with it by pressing toolbar buttons and selecting menu items. You select the menu's File, Open command. It enables you to specify a file to open, and after the file is loaded, you now have a document window. You can consider that window to be a document object.

This object enables you to edit text, format, print, and save. These would be some of the document object's methods. You could tell the document that it is read-only, to be saved as a text file, or that the left margin is at one inch. These are considered to be properties of the document, or the document object's properties.

Basically this is what a COM object is. Almost everything is an object—applications, documents, paragraphs. Even a font is an object because it represents a bunch of properties such as the font type, size, attributes (like bold and italics). One COM object is a bit different, however. This would be the collection object.

COM Collections

At times you need to select many objects that are the same type. MS Word may have five documents open, for example. If you wanted to save and close all of them quickly, you could either select a document object, tell it to save and close, and then move on to the next document object, repeating this pattern until all the documents are closed. If you have 100 open documents, however, this could take quite some time. You could, instead, request a *collection* of document objects. A collection is a special COM object that represents many of a particular type of object. If you could obtain a COM document collection object that represented all 100 of the open documents, you could tell the object to save and quit in one mighty stroke.

Collection objects are obtained by calling certain methods. If you have a Word COM object, for example, you could call the **Documents**() method:

```
$AllDocuments = $Word->Documents();
```

This would return a COM collection object representing all the documents that Word has opened. Collection objects, like other objects, have properties and methods. One property most all collections have is the Count property, which indicates how many objects the collection represents. One method that most collection objects have is the **Add**() method. This method will create a COM object based on the type that the collection represents. If you were to use the following code, for example:

```
$Doc = $Word->Documents()->Add();
```

You would be requesting a new Word document object.

Collection objects can make a job not only easier but faster. Consider Example 5.5 and Example 5.6.

Example 5.5 *Using a collection object*

```
01. use Win32::OLE;
02. $Class = "Word.Application";
03. $Word = Win32::OLE->GetActiveObject( $Class )
       ¦¦ die "Could not find a $Class object.\n";
04. # Save and quit all documents
05  $Docs = $Word->Documents()
       ¦¦ die "Unable to get the documents collection\n";
06. $Docs->Save();
07. $Docs->Quit();
```

Example 5.6 *An alternative to using collection objects*

```
01. use Win32::OLE;
02. $Class = "Word.Application";
03. $Word = Win32::OLE->GetActiveObject( $Class )
       ¦¦ die "Could not find a $Class object.\n";
04.    # Find How many documents are open
05. $iTotal = $Word->Documents()->{Count};
06.    # For each document save and quit
07. while( $iTotal— )
08. {
09.    $Doc = $Word->Documents( $iTotal );
10.    $Doc->Save();
11.    $Doc->Quit();
12. }
```

Example 5.5 shows one way to get around using collections; Example 5.6 does the same thing. Lines 5 through 7 in Example 5.5 obtain the documents collection whose **Save**() and **Quite**() methods are called. Because it does not loop for each document, the overall effect is much faster than the equivalent lines 5 through 12 of Example 5.6. The former example is as fast as it takes the server application to save and quit the documents as opposed to the latter example obtaining a COM object for each document and then saving and quitting that specific object.

> **Tip**
>
> *Most methods that are plural (as in **Documents**(), **Worksheets**(), and **Paragraphs**()) return COM collection objects. For example, the code:*
>
> ```
> $AllDocs = $Word->Documents();
> ```
>
> *returns a COM collection object that represents all the open documents. The following code will save and close all the open documents:*
>
> ```
> $AllDocs = $Word->Documents();
> $AllDocs->Save();
> $AllDocs->Close();
> ```
>
> *These pluralized methods usually will return one COM object if you pass in an object identifier. If you call the **Documents**() method passing in a number, for example, it will return a single COM document object represented by the passed-in value. The following code segment will return the first open Word document:*
>
> ```
> $Doc = $Word->Documents( 1 );
> ```
>
> *These methods typically enable you to pass in a string to use as an identifier. The string represents the name of the object you seek:*
>
> ```
> $Doc = $Word->Documents( "Test.doc" );
> ```

> **Tip**
>
> *When accessing objects from a collection object is important to know that the objects are numbered starting with the number 1. An Excel workbook object has a method called **Worksheets**() which returns a collection object of Worksheets. To obtain the first worksheet you would call **Worksheets(1)** and not **Worksheets(0)**. This is important because an attempt to obtain a COM object calling **Worksheets(0)** will fail.*

Using COM Objects and Collections

Suppose that you have a document that has 10 paragraphs. In Word, each paragraph is an object. You could say that the document has a collection of 10 paragraph objects. Just as the Word application object can contain a collection of different documents (if you have opened up many documents), so can a document object contain a collection of paragraph objects. If you were to select half of the paragraphs and change the font size, you would be changing the property of a collection of paragraph objects. This is the same as if you selected half of the paragraphs in your document using your mouse and then, while the paragraphs are highlighted, you change the font size. We, as humans, say that you are just changing the font size for a bunch of paragraphs, but a program would say that it is altering the font-size property on a collection of paragraph objects. This is what Example 5.7 illustrates.

Example 5.7 *Using collections to alter many objects simultaneously*

```
1. use Win32::OLE;
2. $File = "c:\\temp\\test.doc";
3. $Doc = Win32::OLE->GetObject( $File );
4. $Count = int( $Doc->Paragraphs()->{Count} / 2 );
5. $StartingParagraph = $Doc->Paragraphs(1)->{Range}->{Start};
6. $EndingParagraph =    $Doc->Paragraphs($Count)->{Range}->{End};
7. $Collection = $Doc->Range(
      {
           Start => $StartingParagraph, End => $EndingParagraph
      } );
8. $Collection->{Font}->{Size} = 20;
9. $Doc->Save();
10. $Doc->Close();
```

Line 4 of Example 5.7 determines how many paragraphs exist by referring to the Count property from the collection of paragraph objects. You see, the **Paragraphs()** method returns a collection of all the paragraph objects. This collection represents all paragraphs in the document. It contains properties and methods just as a regular object does. In line 4, the Count property is used to determine the total number of paragraph objects represented by the collection.

Line 7 calls the **Range()** method from the document. The range is between the beginning of paragraph 1 (the paragraph 1 object is returned by a call to **Paragraphs(1)**—line 5) and the end of the middle paragraph. The **Range()** method will return the collection of characters between the specified points. Notice that we are using named parameters (described in the next section) in the call of the **Range()** method.

Line 8 treats the collection as if it were any other object (such as a character or paragraph object), changing the Size property in the **Font** object (the value of the Font property is a **Font** object).

COM Object Methods

A COM object usually has methods that provide some sort of functionality. You cannot call methods for one type of object from another Excel workbook containing worksheets, for example. The workbook object will have a **Save()** method, but the worksheet will not. Because worksheets are not individually saved, it makes no sense for a worksheet object to be saved. Workbooks, on the other hand, can be saved, which will save all the workbook's worksheets. After a Perl script makes changes to a worksheet and it is time to save the changes, a workbook object must be used to call **Save()**. If line 6 of Example 5.8 were changed to:

```
$Worksheet->Save()
```

The script would fail because worksheet objects do not have a **Save()** method.

Example 5.8   *Calling the Save() method from the correct COM object*

```
use Win32::OLE;
$File = "c:\\temp\\test.xls";
$Workbook = Win32::OLE->GetObject( $File ) ¦¦ die "Could not load $File.\n";
$Worksheet = $Workbook->Worksheets(1);
$Worksheet->Range("A1")->{Value} = "My Unique Change.";
$Workbook->Save();
```

When you call a method and pass in parameters they are *positional parameters* by default. This means that the parameters depend on their position to indicate their meaning. For example, if a method assumes that the first parameter passed in is a file name and the second parameter is the file type then this order must be respected otherwise the method will most likely fail.

Some methods have a parameter order that needs to be respected but some of the parameters may be optional. This poses quite a dilemma. Take the **SaveAs()** method in Word. All of its parameters are optional but there is an order to these optional parameters. The **SaveAs()** method's first parameter is a file path and the second is the file format but both of them are optional. If you need to specify the third parameter (password) but do not want to specify the first (file path) or the second parameter (file format) then you have a problem since parameter order must be respected—how do you specify the third parameter without specifying the first two? This is accomplished by using undef. In this case you would use undef for the first two parameters as in:

```
$Doc->SaveAs( undef, undef, "NewPassword" );
```

Some methods allow the use of *named parameters*. These are parameters that are associated with a name. When using named parameters you must first pass in any required positional parameters, then you can pass in a hash reference with key/value pairs. These pairs constitute the names and values of the named parameters. It is important to note that some positional parameters may be required before any named parameters are specified. Suppose that some method requires two parameters and a bunch of optional named parameters. You would first specify the positional parameters then the hash array of named parameters:

```
$Object->Method( $RequiredParam1, $RequiredParam2, { Named1=>$NameParam1,
Named2=>$NameParam2 } );
```

For example, a Word document's **SaveAs**() method allows you to supply optional parameters such as file format, file name, and a password. Example 5.9 shows this in action.

Example 5.9   *Using named parameters in a method call*

```
use Win32::OLE;
use Win32::OLE::Const 'Microsoft Word';
$File = "c:\\temp\\Test.doc";
$NewFile = "c:\\temp\\Test.rtf";
$Doc = Win32::OLE->GetObject( $File );
$Doc->{Parent}->{Options}->{SavePropertiesPrompt} = 0;
$Doc->SaveAs( {Filename   => $NewFile,
               FileFormat => wdFormatRTF,
               Password   => $Password } );
```

Example 5.9 was designed to work with Word 97, so line 6 may not be applicable on older versions of Word. (This line prevents Word from requesting you to enter document information before the save occurs.)

Any number of named parameters can be in a method call, but they must all reflect some real meaning. Supplying named parameters that are not recognized by the method may cause the method to fail.

Under certain circumstances, it may not be possible to access a method or property because of its spelling. Consider a non-English language version of Win32 that uses dialectic marks such as the umlaut (as in ö), a ç character, or a ñ character. These types of nonstandard ASCII characters are not supported by Perl. Therefore it is very difficult to access a method whose name consists of such characters. For this reason, the **Invoke**() method has been exposed for a Perl script:

```
$Object->Invoke( $Method [, @Parameters ] );
```

The first parameter ($Method) is a string that represents either a method or property.

The second parameter (@Parameters) is actually a list of parameters, as many as are needed for the specified method. If the first parameter represents a property, this method will only return the property's value—it will not set the property. Therefore, only the first parameter is required when dealing with a property.

Just like any other COM object method, you can supply a reference to a hash (or an anonymous hash) to specify named parameters. See the section that discusses named parameters in this chapter for more information.

Example 5.10 makes use of the **Invoke**() method. Notice how line 8 not only accesses the **Documents**() method, but also the Name property by using **Invoke**() from the collection object returned by the **Documents**() method.

Example 5.10   *Using the Invoke() method*

```
use Win32::OLE;
$Word = Win32::OLE->GetActiveObject( "Word.Application" )
  ¦¦ die "Word is not running.\n";
$Total = $Word->Invoke( "Documents" )->{Count};
print "There are currently $Total open documents.\n";
while( $Total )
{
  printf( "%02d) %s\n", ++$iCount,
            $Word->Invoke( "Documents", $iCount )->Invoke( "Name" ) );
  $Total--;
}
```

Tip

When you do not pass any parameters into a object's method, you do not need to specify parenthesis even when chaining methods together. For example, the following code:

```
$Word->Documents()->Save();
```

is the same as:

```
$Word->Documents->Save;
```

This can cause confusion because it may look like Documents *and* Save *are properties. For the sake of sanity it is wise to always use the first format.*

Object Properties

Properties are simple variables that describe the state of the object. If you have a Word document object, for example, it would have a "Name" property that represents the name of the document. Additionally it will have a "FullPath" property that describes the location where the file resides (either as a local file or a UNC).

Properties can be protected—that is, they are read-only. Usually properties that reflect a condition of the object are read-only because changing the value would not change the condition. Word has several protected properties that describe how many characters, words, and paragraphs exist in a document object, for example.

A COM object's property is accessed as if it were a hash key in the object. A Word document's name, for example can be discovered by this:

```
$DocumentName = $WordObject->{Name};
```

Setting a property value is as you would expect for any hash reference:

```
$WordObject->{Name} = "blah.doc";
```

Interestingly enough some properties are writeable, but they are overwritten by other actions. You can change a Word document object's Name property, for example, but when you save the document the Name property is changed back to its preceding value. (The correct way to change the name is to call the **SaveAs**() method.)

Tip

Win32::OLE does not require your Perl scripts to respect a COM object's properties and methods case—that is, they are not case sensitive. The following two calls are identical:

```
$Object->SaveAs( $File );
$Object->saveas( $File );
```

And the following property accesses are identical:

```
$Object->{Value} = 1;
$Object->{vALuE} = 1;
```

Additionally if a method call does not have any parameters passed in, the parenthesis can be left off. Therefore the following are identical:

```
$Object->Document()->{Value};
$Object->Document->{Value};
```

Because different programmers have different styles, it can be quite confusing whether the next line is accessing a method or a property (because it could be either):

```
$Object->Count;
```

To make your code understandable by other programmers, you may want to follow these conventions:

- *Use the case that any documentation suggests. MS Word's documentation, for example, indicates that the **SaveAs**() method has a capital S and A. You should respect this case.*

- *All methods should always use parentheses even if no parameters are passed in.*

- *All properties should be enclosed in braces, just as if it were a hash key.*

Some property values are really COM objects. An Excel worksheet contains a property called Parent, for example. The value of this property is a COM object, which represents the workbook in which the worksheet resides (the worksheet's parent object). Likewise that workbook object has a Parent property, which is a COM object that represents the Excel application. Example 5.11 illustrates this by creating a simple Word document and using its Parent property to access the document object's parent object (which happens to be the Word application).

Example 5.11   *Accessing COM objects from within COM objects*

```
use Win32::OLE;
$Doc = new Win32::OLE( "Word.Document" );
print "Document name is " . $Doc->{Name} . "\n";
print "Application name is " . $Doc->{Parent}->{Name} . "\n";
```

If you are accessing a property, you do not necessarily need to enclose it in braces. For example:

```
print $Object->Parent->Name;
```

is the same as

```
print $Object->{Parent}->{Name};
```

If a **Win32::OLE** cannot resolve a method, it will try to access it as a property. This is good to know because many programmers write code using this feature, which could mislead you to believe that Parent is a method and not a property.

Just like any Perl function, you can chain function calls and properties together. Example 5.12 illustrates how to do this.

Example 5.12   *Chaining methods and properties*

```
01. use Win32::OLE;
02. $File = "c:\\temp\\test.xls";
03. $Workbook = Win32::OLE->GetObject( $File )
       || die "Could not load $File.\n";
04.   # Get the total number of worksheets in this workbook
05. $iTotal = $Workbook->Worksheets()->{Count};
06.   # For each worksheet autofit each column
07. while( $iTotal )
08. {
09.   $Workbook->Worksheets(1)->Columns()->AutoFit();
10.   $iTotal--;
11. }
12. $Workbook->Save();
13. $Workbook->{Parent}->Quit();
```

Line 5 accesses the Count property for a collection that is returned by the **Worksheets**() method. This line could have been broken into two parts:

```
$Collection = $Workbook->Worksheets();
$iTotal = $Collection->{Count};
```

By chaining the method call and property access together, it is done in one line and prevents the mess of adding additional variables (in this case, the $Collection variable).

A better example of this is line 9. This line first calls the $Workbook object's **Worksheets**() method, which returns a worksheet COM object that represents the first worksheet in the workbook. (This is tricky because when you close the first workbook, the second workbook becomes the first. This is why you always specify workbook number 1.)

Then the **Columns**() method is called from within the worksheet object. Because no particular column is specified, it returns a collection of all the columns. This collection is yet another COM object (known as a Columns collection). Finally the **AutoFit**() method is called from within the Columns collection object. The overall effect of all this is that all the columns in the specified worksheet are autofitted. (The columns are sized so that you can see their contents.) If you broke this out, it could take several lines, but there is no need because you can chain the properties and methods together.

Note

One of the most discouraging aspects of programming Perl scripts that access COM objects is that there are no standards for properties and methods. That is, if you are trying to automate Excel and Photoshop, the two could have radically different property names and methods. Additionally, methods that are named the same could take different parameters.

If you start an Excel COM object and want to print the name of the application, for example, you could use:

```
print $Object->{Name};
```

But Photoshop would require:

```
print $Object->{FullName};
```

*This can be quite confusing for someone who is just learning how to interact with a particular object. Some objects must use an **Open**() method, for example, where others may employ **Load**().*

*The point here is that it would be futile to make a script that attempts to treat every object the same. It would be best to use the **Win32::OLE–>QueryObjectType**() method to determine what kind of object you have and interact with it accordingly.*

Destroying COM Objects

After you have finished using a **Win32::OLE** object, it needs to be destroyed. Destruction is accomplished by either letting the object fall out of scope or by forcing it to destroy itself. Falling out of scope is quite easy; when the function, code block, or script terminates, the object is destroyed. Forcing the object to destroy itself requires that you call the object's **DESTROY()** method:

```
$Object->DESTROY();
```

This method takes no parameters and causes the object to terminate. Generally speaking, this method is used internally by the object itself and not by a Perl script.

It is possible that a script could run for hours but only needs to create a COM object for just a few minutes. Assuming that for some reason you need to release the object, you could call the **DESTROY()** method.

OLE Errors

The **Win32::OLE** extension supplies a method to query any error that the preceding action on a COM object may have produced. Every interaction with a COM object (a call into a method or a query or setting of a property) will set the error state even if no error was generated. Therefore you must always query the error state before any other interaction with any COM object.

The error state is obtained with a call into the **LastError()** method:

```
Win32::OLE->LastError();
```

The **LastError()** method will return a value based on context. If the method is called in a numeric context, the returned value is the reported error number. If the method is called in a string context, the return value is the error text message.

This method always returns the current error state that was last generated by a **Win32::OLE** object.

Miscellaneous OLE Items

A few additional **Win32::OLE** surprises await your use. These are the lesser-known elements, but can be very powerful in your programming arsenal. Some of these things are taken from Visual Basic, but they do come in very handy in Perl scripts.

The in() Method

When you have a COM collection object, you really have a special object that, for all practical purposes, is similar to a Perl array. The problem is that the object you are working with is a **Win32::OLE** object, not an array.

If you were to obtain a collection object (of open workbooks) from Excel, you may want to print the name of each workbook. The problem is that you cannot access the collection object as if it were an array, so you have to walk through a loop accessing each workbook name one at a time as in Example 5.13.

Example 5.13   *Accessing items in a collection—the hard way*

```
use Win32::OLE;
$Excel = Win32::OLE->GetActiveObject( "Excel.Application" )
  ¦¦ die "Excel is not running.\n";
$Workbooks = $Excel->Workbooks();
$iCount = $Workbooks->{Count};
while( $iCount )
{
  print "Workbook $iCount: $Workbooks->Item($iCount)->{Name}\n";
  $iCount--;
}
```

This is where the **in()** method comes in. This method will return an array of every element in the collection:

```
@Array = in( $Object );
```

The only parameter passed in is the **Win32::OLE** object, which represents a COM collection object.

The array will consist of the value of the default property of the object, which is usually COM objects (or more precisely **Win32::OLE** objects).

If the **in()** method is successful, it will return an array of values or **Win32::OLE** objects; otherwise if it fails, it will return nothing. Example 5.14 shows how simple it is to use the **in()** method.

Example 5.14   *Accessing items in a collection—the easy way using the in() method*

```
use Win32::OLE 'in';
$Excel = Win32::OLE->GetActiveObject( "Excel.Application" )
  ¦¦ die "Excel is not running.\n";
map{ print "Workbook: $_->{Name}\n"; } ( in( $Excel->Workbooks() ) );
```

It is very important to know that the **in()** method is not exported by default therefore you must purposely specify that you want **in()** exported when you load the **Win32::OLE** extension. You do this by specifying the string "in" with the **use** command:

```
use Win32::OLE 'in';
```

This will import the **in**() method into your main namespace and you can use **in**() as if it was a normal Perl function. If you do not import it then you must access it as if it was a method of **Win32::OLE** as in Example 5.14.

Example 5.15   *Using in() without importing it*

```
use Win32::OLE;
$Excel = Win32::OLE->GetActiveObject( "Excel.Application" )
  ¦¦ die "Excel is not running.\n";
map{ print "Workbook: $_->{Name}\n"; } ( Win32::OLE->in(
$Excel->Workbooks() ) );
```

The valof() Method

When dealing with **Win32::OLE** objects, things can get tricky because the object is really a reference to a blessed Perl object. If you assign the value of a **Win32::OLE** object to a variable you are really only assigning a reference to an object. Think about it this way: A friend comes to you holding a helium balloon. You ask to hold it, so she ties another string to the balloon and hands the free end of that string to you. Now you are both holding a string that connects to the same balloon.

This is what happens when you run the code in Example 5.16. You have two variables, $PointToDoc and $PointToDoc2. They are both pointers to the same **Win32::OLE** object. Line 7 causes the object to be destroyed, so by the time line 8 is executed the object that $PointToDoc2 points to no longer exists. Therefore the code will not be able to determine what kind of object it was.

Just like the balloon analogy, if the balloon is popped by a pin, it does not matter that two people were holding its strings ($PointToDoc and $PointToDoc2) because the balloon (the COM object) no longer exists!

Example 5.16   *Copying a Win32::OLE object*

```
use Win32::OLE;
$File = "c:\\temp\\test.doc";
$PointToDoc = Win32::OLE->GetObject( $File )
  ¦¦ die "Could not open $File.\n";
$PointToDoc2 = $PointToDoc;
print "The name of the document is $PointToDoc->{Name}.\n";
print "The name of the document is $PointToDoc2->{Name}.\n";
$PointToDoc->DESTROY();
print "Type of object is: " .
   Win32::OLE->QueryObjectType( $PointToDoc2 ) . "\n";
```

The **valof**() method will return the "default" value of an object. This way you can obtain the value of an object rather than a reference to it:

```
$Value = valof( $Object );
```

The only parameter is a **Win32::OLE** object. This must be an object or a collection; it cannot be a property.

If successful, the **valof**() method will return the default value for the object; otherwise, it fails and returns `undef`.

The default value for a given object is defined by the object itself. Sometimes it is obvious, like for a Word document the default value is the name of the document. You could just as easily access the `Name` property, but different objects have different default values.

This is typically used when you need to access a default value of an object and you have no idea what that object will be and hence you cannot just access a given property.

The code in Example 5.17 demonstrates the difference between the "`value of`" a **Win32::OLE** object and the actual object itself.

Example 5.17   *Using the valof() method*

```
use Win32::OLE 'valof';
$Object = Win32::OLE->GetObject( $ARGV[0] ) ¦¦ die "Could not open
$ARGV[0].\n";
$RefToObject= $Object;
$ValueOfObject = valof( $Object );
print "The pointer to the COM object is: $RefToObject.\n";
print "The default value of the COM object is: $ValueOfObject.\n";
```

The variable `$PointerToObject` is an exact copy of `$Object`. If `$Object` is the string on the balloon, `$PointerToObject` is the second string tied to the balloon. This would make `$ValueOfObject`, let's say the writing on the balloon (like "Eat at Joe's"), the *default value* of the object (in this analogy, the balloon).

Just as with the **in**() method, **valof**() is not exported by default, so you have to explicitly tell **Win32::OLE** to export it by passing in the string "`valof`" while loading the extension (refer to line 1 of Example 5.17).

The with() Method

One of the most powerful of the miscellaneous methods that **Win32::OLE** has is the **with**() method. This method was inspired from Visual Basic where there is a good need for it. In Perl the same need arises. Basically it makes tedious tasks a bit easier. If you have an object that you need to set several properties for, it could take several lines of code to do it. Take, for example, a font object. This type of object can contain a font name, size, color, and whether it is bold, italic, or underlined. If you were to write code to set all these values, it would look like Example 5.18.

Example 5.18   *Altering properties manually*

```
01. use Win32::OLE;
02. $Sheet = Win32::OLE->GetObject( "c:\\temp\\test.xls!Sheet1" )
    ¦¦ die "Could not open the workbook.\n";
03. $Cells = $Sheet->Range{"A1:C5");
```

```
04. $Cells->{Font}->{Name} = "Courier New";
05. $Cells->{Font}->{Size} = 20;
06. $Cells->{Font}->{ColorIndex} = 6;
07. $Cells->{Font}->{Bold} = 1;
08. $Cells->{Font}->{Italic} = 0;
09. $Sheet->{Parent}->Save();
10. $Sheet->{Parent}->Close();
```

The code in Example 5.18 is not only messy, but it makes many more calls into the object than it needs to, slowing down your script. You could replace this by using one call to the **with**() method:

```
with( $Object, Property1=>Value1 [, Property2=>Value2 [, ... ] ] );
```

The first parameter is a **Win32::OLE** object.

The second parameter is really a list of key/value pairs. These pairs are the same as you would use when defining a hash. The key is the object's property name, and the value is the value you want to set the property to. You can have any number of these key/value pairs.

If the **with**() method is successful, all the listed object's properties will have been set to their corresponding values. This method does not return any value.

This method is not exported by default, so your script will have to explicitly export it by passing in the value "with" when loading the extension. Notice how this is illustrated in line 1 of Example 5.19.

Example 5.19 requires an explanation for line 9. Excel 5.0, 7.0, and maybe 8.0, have a bug that requires you must make the workbook visible before saving. This is identified by Microsoft's knowledge base article Q111247. Line 9 sets the worksheets parent's (the workbook) Visible property to 1 (TRUE—sets the object to be visible).

Example 5.19   *Altering properties using the **with**() method*

```
01. use Win32::OLE 'with';
02. $Sheet = Win32::OLE->GetObject( "c:\\temp\\test.xls!Sheet1" )
       ¦¦ die "Could not open the workbook.\n";
03. with( $Cells = $Sheet->Range("A1:C5")->{Font},
04.    Name       => "Courier New",
05.    Size       => 20,
06.    ColorIndex => 6,
07.    Bold       => 1,
08.    Italic     => 0);
09. $Sheet->{Parent}->{Visible} = 1;
10. $Sheet->{Parent}->Save();
11. $Sheet->{Parent}->Close();
```

For an example of a more administrative nature, refer to Example 5.20. This code will connect to an IIS Web server (either to "LocalHost" or one specified as the first parameter in the command line) and add a new virtual directory to the root (the default) Web site on that server.

Example 5.20   *Creating a virtual directory in the default IIS Web site*

```
01.    # Details on IIS COM objects are found in the SDK
02.    # which comes with the IIS 4.0 server.
03.    # This will create a new "virtual" subdirectory
04.    # for the specified web site "Root"
05. use Win32::OLE;
06. $Server = "LocalHost" unless ( $Server = $ARGV[0] );
07. %WebSite = (
08.        name  =>  "Root",
09.        vdir  =>  "PerlTest",
10.        path  =>  "c:\\temp"
11. );
12.
13. %Class =(
14.    service =>  "IIS://$Server/w3svc",
15.    server  =>  "IIsWebServer",
16.    vdir    =>  "IIsWebVirtualDir",
17.    dir     =>  "IIsWebDirectory"
18. );
19.
20.    # Get an IIS COM object for the local machine
21. $Object = $Class{service};
22. $WebService = Win32::OLE->GetObject( $Object ) || Error( $Object );
23.
24.    # Get a web server object
25. $Object = $Class{server};
26. $WebServer = $WebService->GetObject( $Object, 1 ) || Error( $Object );
27. if( $WebServer->Class() ne $Object )
28. {
29.    Error( $Object );
30. }
31.    # Get a virtual web site (the default specified site).
32. $Object = $Class{vdir};
33. $VRoot = $WebServer->GetObject( $Object, $WebSite{name} ) || Error( $Object );
34.
35.    # Create a new virtual directory in the site
36. $Object = $Class{vdir};
37. $VDir = $VRoot->Create( $Object, $WebSite{vdir} ) || Error( $Object );
38.
39.    # Set the new directory path and enable users to read its files
40. $VDir->{AccessRead} = 1;
41. $VDir->{Path} = $WebSite{path};
42.
43.    # Commit our changes
44. $VDir->SetInfo();
45.
46. sub Error
47. {
48.    my( $Object ) = @_;
49.    print "Unable to create a '$Object' object.\nError: $!\n";
50.    exit();
51. }
```

Variants

You need to know one last thing about using **Win32::OLE:** *variants.* The way that **Win32::OLE** actually works is by passing every COM object interaction (either accessing a method or querying or setting a property) through a single method known as **Dispatch().** This method is the only way in which a Perl **Win32::OLE** object ever actually communicates with a COM object. The reasons for this are rather technical and just a tad beyond the scope of this book. Suffice it to say that every interaction made with a COM object ends up calling the **Dispatch()** method.

The **Dispatch()** method is similar to the **Invoke()** method in that the method or property name is passed in along with any parameters. It is these parameters that we are interested in right now. You see, if you pass a string into a COM object's method, the string must be converted from a Perl string into a string the OLE can understand (a Unicode, length-prefixed, null-terminated string). Likewise if the method returns a string, it must be converted from an OLE-approved Unicode string into a Perl string.

Now keeping in mind that this type of data transformation must take place, how could OLE possibly know that we are passing in a string and not binary data or an integer for that matter? Additionally, how would Perl know that the method is returning a string and not binary data or an array of floating-point numbers? It is because of this exact reason that the *variant* data type was created.

Simply stated, a variant is a data structure designed to accommodate almost any type of variable (strings, Nulls, integers, real numbers, dates, Booleans, and so on). When any program (Perl, Visual Basic, C++, whatever) wants to pass data into a COM object using the COM object's **Invoke()** method (what is technically known as the IDispatch interface's **Invoke()** method), it must fill out a variant data structure for each parameter that is to be passed in. When the results of the method are received, the data must be extracted out of the data structure as well.

Win32::OLE does a remarkably wonderful job at handling this for you automatically. It correctly maps your input and output data to variants invisibly. There are, however, some times when you need to help the extension out a bit. Suppose, for example, that you have a variable, $Cost, that represents the cost of some product. Assume also that $Cost has a value of 35. When your script passes in $Cost as a parameter to a COM object's method, **Win32::OLE** will most likely convert it into an integer form of a variant. This is a problem if the method expects to receive a floating point value of 35.00.

To get around this problem, you could create a floating-point (a real data type) variant and pass it in rather than the value of your variable. This means that the **Win32::OLE** extension will not have to convert that particular parameter because it is already in a variant form.

Creating and manipulating variants is accomplished by using the **Win32::OLE::Variant** extension. This comes with the **Win32::OLE** extension. Therefore if you have OLE capability, you most likely have this extension as well. As with any extension, you must first **use** it before you can make use of any of its functions and methods:

```
use Win32::OLE::Variant;
```

Creating a variant is done with the **Variant()** function:

```
$Var = Variant( $Type, $Value );
```

The first parameter ($Type) is the type of variant that you are creating. This can be any one of the constants defined in Table 5.3. This parameter may also be logically OR'ed with either or both of the values in Table 5.2.

Table 5.2   Variant data type flags

Flag	Description
VT_ARRAY	This flag indicates that the variant represents an array of values.
VT_BYREF	This flag indicates that the variant data type is a pointer to the actual data. In other words, the value held in the variant is a reference pointer to the data.

Table 5.3   The variant data types

Data Type	Description
VT_BOOL	A simple Boolean value.
VT_BSTR	A length-prefixed, null-terminated Unicode string. This is the only type of string that COM objects understand.
VT_CY	A 64-bit currency data type.
VT_DATE	A date data type (internally stored as a double).
VT_DISPATCH	An IDispatch interface. Consider this to be the same as a **Win32::OLE** object.
VT_EMPTY	This data type has no meaning other than void of any value. This is not the same as Perl's undef (to OLE undef is VT_ERROR).
VT_ERROR	An OLE HRESULT value. This is what OLE and COM use to indicate results (like success or error values).
VT_I2	A signed short (2 bytes) integer.

Data Type	Description
VT_I4	A signed long (4 bytes) integer.
VT_R4	A float (4 bytes).
VT_R8	A double (8 bytes).
VT_UI1	An unsigned character (1 byte)—not Unicode.
VT_UNKNOWN	An IUknown interface. This is similar to VT_DISPATCH except that there is no Perl equivalent. This is used internally.
VT_VARIANT	A reference to another variant.

The second parameter of the **Variant()** function ($Value) is the value that the variant will represent.

If the function succeeds, it returns a **Win32::OLE::Variant** object; otherwise, it fails and returns undef.

This function is scarcely ever used because almost all variant conversions are handled automatically. But for those who either have a specific need or want to play around with it, Example 5.21 demonstrates its use.

Example 5.21   *Using a variant*

```
use Win32::OLE;
use Win32::OLE::Variant;
$Sheet = Win32::OLE->GetObject( "c:\\temp\\test.xls!Sheet1" )
¦¦ die "Could not open the workbook.\n";
$Cells = $Sheet->Range{"A1"};
$Var = Variant( VT_BSTR, "Oh what a happy day" );
$Cells->{Value} = $Var;
```

You may have been thinking about this whole variant thing and wondered how arrays are handled. Arrays are interesting because, of course, they cannot be defined as a discrete parameter—they are a list of parameters. Arrays are converted into the OLE data type known as a SAFEARRAY. This is simply an array of variants. All of the elements within an array are first converted into variants then the resulting list of variants are converted into a SAFEARRAY. Finally a new variant is created of the data type VT_VARIANT ¦ VT_BYREF ¦ VT_ARRAY.

You must note that multidimensional Perl arrays are converted into an array of equal elements. In other words, if you have an array consisting of two anonymous arrays (one with two elements and the other with three elements) the array will be converted into a 2 by 3 array. That is to say it will consist of two arrays each with three elements. Any elements that had to be added to satisfy this transformation will consist of the VT_EMPTY data type.

This array handling is what makes it possible to submit multidimensional arrays. Example 5.22 demonstrates how arrays are handled for both passing into an object and retrieving from an object.

Example 5.22   *Using arrays*

```
use Win32::OLE;
$Sheet = Win32::OLE->GetObject( "c:\\temp\\test.xls!Sheet1" )
  || die "Could not open the workbook.\n";
$Sheet->Range("A1:C2")->{Value} = [
  [ qw( A1 B1 C1 ) ],
  [ qw( A2 B2 C2 ) ]
];
$array_ref = $Sheet->Range("A1:C2")->{Value};
foreach $row_ref ( @{$array_ref} )
{
print join(",", @{$row_ref} ), "\n";
}
```

or

```
use Win32::OLE;
$Sheet = Win32::OLE->GetObject( "c:\\temp\\test.xls!Sheet1" )
  || die "Could not open the workbook.\n";
$Sheet->Range("A1:C2")->{Value} = [
  [ qw( A1 B1 C1 ) ],
  [ qw( A2 B2 C2 ) ]
];
($Row1, $Row2) = @{$Sheet->Range("A1:C2")->{Value}};
print join(",", @{$Row1}), "\n";
print join(",", @{$Row2}), "\n";
```

Type Libraries

The purpose of OLE is to allow an application to interact with another application even though they are made by different programmers. This allows Outlook to interact with Photoshop and a fax printer driver to interact with your list of fax numbers held in Eudora. None of these programs were written with any other in mind, so none of them know how to interact with any of them. This is what OLE was designed to fix.

To make these programs work, they must be able to learn about each other's properties' and methods' prototypes. That is, if one program is going to use the **Open**() method on a COM object, it will need to learn what types of parameters the method takes. OLE applications create libraries of technical information that any other program can access. These libraries define the types of properties and methods (in addition to tons of other information) that exist in a particular class. The repositories of information are known as *type libraries*.

Typically type libraries are those funny .TLB files that you find all over your hard disk. These are binary files that contain the information needed by an application to know how to handle a particular COM object.

Type library information does not have to be in a .TLB file, however. In can be embedded in a .DLL, .OCX, or even an .EXE file. They are also not required, so some OLE applications just do not have any type libraries.

Constants

Just when you think that you understand OLE and how to use it, a new twist reveals itself. When you program using the **Win32::OLE** extension, you will most likely run into the problem of needing to use constants. Look at line 168 of Example 5.24 in the case study at the end of the chapter, where it sets a range of cells' horizontal alignment to xlCenter. That constant equates to some value that even the Excel documentation does not describe. (It only tells you to use the constant.) Unless you somehow discover the value, you will need to reference the xlCenter constant by name. This is where the problem comes in: Perl does not define the xlCenter constant; however, type libraries do.

Constants and their values are among all the information held within a type library. You can load the constants from a type library by using the **Win32::OLE::Const** module:

```
use Win32::OLE::Const $TypeLibrary [, $VerMajor [, $VerMinor
[, $Language ] ] ];
```

You can specify four parameters when loading the module (although it is not necessary to pass in any).

The first parameter ($TypeLibrary) is a string to a type library. This is the name of a type library, as in "Microsoft Word 8.0 Object Library". You can specify regular expression wildcards to make it easier to match a library. This parameter is passed in to a regular expression as /^$name/, so you could specify a type library name of ".*Basic" to load the constants for "Visual Basic for Applications". If multiple versions of the same type library are registered, the most recent version (the latest version) will be used.

The second parameter ($VerMajor) is optional and represents the major version number. This would be a 5 for the Windows Media Player 5.2. By specifying this parameter, the constants from the type library will be loaded *only* if a library is found whose major version number matches this parameter.

The third parameter ($VerMinor)is optional and is used only if a value is passed in for the second parameter. (If undef is passed in as $VerMajor, this parameter is ignored.) This value represents the lowest minor number that is acceptable. By specifying a 5 for the second parameter and a 2 for this parameter, for example, a type library will be loaded only if it is version 5 and has at least a minor number of 2 (such as 5.2 or 5.3). Type libraries with a version of 5.1 or 6.0 will not be loaded.

The optional fourth parameter ($Language) represents a language ID. If this is specified, a library is loaded only if it has a matching language ID. You would want to use this if, for example, you need to load the constants for the Turkish language. To make use of this parameter, you will need to use the **Win32::OLE::NLS** module. A description of this is beyond the scope of this chapter. If you need to use this, you should study the documentation embedded in the NLS.PM module.

If successful, the module will load and the user's namespace will be populated with the constants from the specified type library. If unsuccessful, the module will load but no constants will be loaded. Example 5.24 demonstrates how the module is used in this way.

If you need to access constants but will not know the name of the type library until runtime, you could use the **Load**() method:

```
$Hash = Win32::OLE::Const->Load( ( $TypeLibrary ¦ $Object ) [, $VerMajor
[, $VerMinor [, $Language ] ] ] );
```

The parameters are identical to those specified with the **use** command to load the module, with one exception. The first parameter can be either a string describing a type library or it can be an Perl **Win32::OLE** object.

The **Load**() method will return a reference to a hash containing the type libraries constants and values if successful. If the method fails, it returns undef. Example 5.23 illustrates how this method is used.

Example 5.23   *Loading constants at runtime*

```
01. use Win32::OLE;
02. use Win32::OLE::Const;
03. if( $Object = Win32::OLE->GetObject( $ARGV[0] ) )
04. {
05.    $Const = Win32::OLE::Const->Load( $Object );
06.    print "Constants for ";
07.    print Win32::OLE->QueryObjectType( $Object );
08.    print ":\n";
09.    foreach $Constant ( sort( keys( %$Const ) ) )
10.    {
11.       $iCount++;
12.       print "$iCount) $Constant = '$Const->{$Constant}'\n";
13.    }
14. }
```

Warnings

There is a variable that can be set to handle warnings and errors relating to a COM object and Perl's interaction with it. The **$Win32::OLE::Warn** variable can be set to one of four values listed in Table 5.4. Setting this variable will affect the way that Perl contends with OLE errors.

Table 5.4   Values for the $Win32::OLE::Warn variable

Value	Description
0	Errors are ignored. Any interaction with a COM object that causes an error will return undef. Use the **Win32::OLE–>LastError**() method to determine the error.
1	A warning message is displayed (the **Carp::carp**() function is called) only if the $^W variable is set (as is done with the -w switch). This is the default value.
2	A warning message is displayed (by means of the **Carp::carp**() function). Unlike the 1 value, the warning message is displayed regardless of the setting of $^W.
3	An error message is displayed and the script terminates (by calling the **Carp::croak**() function).

OLE and COM Object Documentation

One of the greatest dilemmas that face OLE programmers is the nuisance of documentation. In order to know how a script can interact with a COM object, documentation on the object model of the OLE class is necessary. This can be difficult to find because most users do not need this information.

The best places to start looking for OLE information (in particular the object model of a given class) are the help files. Microsoft has done a good job of publishing the object model for their major application such as Office 97 in their help files. To find this documentation you need to go to the help file and look up the Visual Basic for Applications section.

For all practical purposes **Win32::OLE** can make use of OLE related Visual Basic documentation (help files, books, magazines, and so forth). Such information describes the different objects, methods, properties, and constants.

If you are looking for sources of documentation you can find much in Software Development Kits (SDKs). For example Microsoft's NetShow, ADSI, and IIS SDK's come with help files that not only describe the object models but also give code examples. The code samples are fantastic to study and port to Perl.

There is one place to go for documentation that is usually overlooked: type libraries. Most all OLE applications come with type libraries either embedded within their executable, .DLL, or .OCX files or as a separate .TBL file. The problem is that this data is binary and difficult to read so you would need a type library browser. It just so happens that Microsoft has one called "OLE View" (VC/C++ 6.0) or "OLE COM Viewer" (VC/C++ 5.0). It comes with the developer environments (such as Visual C++, Visual Basic, or InterDev). You can also get a copy of it by downloading the Microsoft Platform SDK Tools however this is a large download (around 12.3MB).

A type library browser will describe the different classes, methods, properties, enumerations, constants, properties, and other information. These descriptions are very descriptive indeed and include method parameter types and return values. As an added bonus, most type libraries have help strings that explain what a method, property, or constant is and how it is used. And to think that all of this information is right on your hard drive just not able for you to easily get to.

Case Study: Daily Administrative Network Reports

For many administrators who have a large server farm, it becomes difficult tracking each and every NT server. Ideally, the administrator would come in in the morning and run the event viewer program. She would then connect to each server in her domain and look through the logs for any errors. But this is ideal and in the real world this is simply an unacceptable use of time.

A Perl script could be scheduled to run every morning (let's say an hour before the administrator comes in) that would scan the Net for all servers then connect to each one's event log. It could then query for all errors that have occurred over the past 24 hours and dump them to an Excel spreadsheet.

Now all the administrator needs to do is come in every morning and check the administrators workbook for the daily list of errors. This is a much quicker solution.

Example 5.24 accomplishes this by using **Win32::OLE** to interact with Excel. It must load the workbook or create it if it does not already exist. The script creates a new worksheet and labels it with the current date. If one already exists with the same date then the new sheet is given a name with the date followed by a number such as "98.10.31 #2". The new worksheet is then populated with only errors and warnings from the event logs on different servers.

Example 5.24   *Using **Win32::OLE** to populate a spreadsheet with server errors*

```
001. use Win32::OLE qw( with );
002. use Win32::OLE::Variant;
003. use Win32::EventLog;
004. use Win32::NetAdmin;
```

```
005. use Win32::OLE::Const 'Microsoft Excel';
006.
007. $DateFormat = "DDD mmm dd, yyyy -- hh:mm:ss";
008. $Class = "Excel.Application";
009. $Domain = "MyDomain";
010.
011. @EVENT_SOURCES = ( "System", "Application" );
012. $EVENT_TYPE = EVENTLOG_ERROR_TYPE ¦ EVENTLOG_WARNING_TYPE;
013.
014. $Dir = "c:\\temp";
015. $FileName = "AdminReport.xls";
016. $File = "$Dir\\$FileName";
017.
018. $SecPerDay = 24 * 60 * 60;
019. $Now = time();
020. $TimeLimit = $Now - ( $SecPerDay * 7);
021.
022. $Excel = GetApplication( $Class ) ¦¦ Error( "Could not start $Class" );
023. $Book = GetWorkbook( $Excel ) ¦¦ Error( "Could not obtain a workbook" );
024. $Sheet = GetWorksheet( $Book ) ¦¦ Error( "Could not obtain a worksheet" );
025.
026. print "Fetching list of servers...\n";
027. Win32::NetAdmin::GetServers( '', $Domain, SV_TYPE_DOMAIN_CTRL ¦
                                SV_TYPE_DOMAIN_BAKCTRL , \@Servers );
028.
029. $Row = 3;
030. foreach $Machine ( sort( @Servers ) )
031. {
032.   print "Processing $Machine.\n";
033.   $Sheet->Range( "A" . ++$Row )->{Value} = $Machine;
034.   $Sheet->Range( "A$Row" )->{Font}->{Bold} = 1;
035.
036.   map{ ProcessLog( $Machine, $_, $EVENT_TYPE ); } ( @EVENT_SOURCES );
037.
038.   $Row++;
039. }
040.
041. ShutDownSheet( $Sheet );
042.
043. print "Finished\n";
044.
045.
046. sub ProcessLog
047. {
048.   my ( $Machine, $Source, $Type )= @_;
049.   my $Flag, $Num, %Hash;
050.
051.   my $Event = new Win32::EventLog( $Source, $Machine ) ¦¦
052.     sub
053.     {
054.       $Sheet->Range( "B" . ++$Row )->{value} = "Unable to connect.";
055.       return;
056.     };
```

continues

Continued

```perl
057.    if( $Event->GetNumber( $Num ) )
058.    {
059.      $Flag = EVENTLOG_BACKWARDS_READ | EVENTLOG_SEQUENTIAL_READ;
060.      do
061.      {
062.        if( $Event->Read( $Flag, $Num, \%Hash ) )
063.        {
064.          if( $Hash{EventType} & $Type )
065.          {
066.            my ( $EventType, $Color, $Time );
067.
068.            if( $Hash{EventType} == EVENTLOG_ERROR_TYPE )
069.            {
070.              $EventType = "Error";
071.              $Color = 3;      # Red
072.            }
073.            elsif( $Hash{EventType} == EVENTLOG_WARNING_TYPE )
074.            {
075.              $EventType = "Warning";
076.              $Color = 53;     # Red-Orange
077.            }
078.            elsif( $Hash{EventType} == EVENTLOG_INFORMATION_TYPE )
079.            {
080.              $EventType = "Information";
081.              $Color = 1;      # Black
082.            }
083.            $Row++;
084.              # Format the time so that we can create a date based variant
085.            $Time = "" . localtime( $Hash{TimeGenerated} );
086.            $Time =~ s/^.*?\s+(.*?)\s+(.*?)\s+(.*?)\s+(.*)/$1 $2 $4 $3/;
087.            $Sheet->Range( "B$Row:G$Row" )->{Value} = [
                 "$Source: $EventType",
                 $Hash{Source},
                 ($Hash{Event}) ?Hash{Event}:"None",
                 ($Hash{User}) ? $Hash{User}:"N/A",
                 $Hash{Computer},
                 new Win32::OLE::Variant( VT_DATE, $Time )
                 ];
088.            $Sheet->Range( "B$Row" )->{Font}->{ColorIndex} = $Color;
089.          }
090.        }
091.        else
092.        {
093.          undef %Hash;
094.        }
095.        # This will cause the next reading of the registry to move to the
096.        # next record automatically.
097.        $Num = 0;
098.      } while( $TimeLimit < $Hash{TimeGenerated} );
099.      Win32::EventLog::CloseEventLog( $Event->{handle} );
100.    }
101. }
```

```
102.
103. sub GetApplication
104. {
105.   my( $Class ) = @_;
106.   my( $Application );
107.
108.   $Application = Win32::OLE->GetActiveObject( $Class );
109.   if( Win32::OLE->QueryObjectType( $Application )
          ne "Excel_Application" )
110.   {
111.     $Application = new Win32::OLE( $Class , "Quit" );
112.   }
113.   $Application->{Visible} = 1 if( $Application );
114.
115.   return( $Application );
116. }
117.
118. sub GetWorkbook
119. {
120.   my( $Application ) = @_;
121.   my( $Book, $Temp );
122.
123.   if( ! ( $Book = $Application->Workbooks( $FileName ) ) )
124.   {
125.     if( ! ( $Book = $Application->Workbooks->Open( $File ) ) )
126.     {
127.       $Temp = $Application->{SheetsInNewWorkbook};
128.       $Application->{SheetsInNewWorkbook} = 1;
129.
130.       $Book = $Application->Workbooks->Add();
131.       $Book->SaveAs( $File );
132.
133.       $Application->{SheetsInNewWorkbook} = $Temp;
134.       $UseSheetNumber = 1;
135.     }
136.   }
137.   return( $Book );
138. }
139.
140. sub GetWorksheet
141. {
142.   my( $Book ) = @_;
143.   my( $Sheet );
144.   if( $UseSheetNumber )
145.   {
146.     $Sheet = $Book->Worksheets( $UseSheetNumber );
147.   }
148.   else
149.   {
150.     $Sheet = $Book->Worksheets()->Add();
151.   }
152.   SetupWorksheet( $Sheet );
153.   return( $Sheet );
154. }
```

continues

Continued

```
155.
156. sub SetupWorksheet
157. {
158.   my( $Sheet ) = @_;
159.   my( $Range );
160.   my( $Date, $Name, $iCount, @Date );
161.   @Date = localtime();
162.   $Date = sprintf( "%04d.%02d.%02d", $Date[5] + 1900,
          $Date[4] + 1, $Date[3] );
163.   $Name = $Date;
164.   $iCount = 1;
165.   while( $Sheet->{Parent}->Worksheets( $Name ) )
166.   {
167.     $Name = "$Date #" . ++$iCount;
168.   }
169.
170.   $Sheet->{Name} = $Name;
171.   $Range = $Sheet->Range( "A1" );
172.   $Range->{Value} = "Server Error Logs for the morning of $Date";
173.   $Range->{Font}->{Size}=24;
174.   $Range->{Font}->{ColorIndex} = 6;     # Yellow
175.   $Sheet->Rows("1:1")->{Interior}->{ColorIndex} = 5;   # Blue
176.   $Range = $Sheet->Range("A3:G3");
177.   $Range->{Value} = [ "Server", "Type", "Source", "Event",
          "User", "Computer", "Time" ];
178.   with( $Range->{Font},
179.         Bold   => 1,
180.         Italic => 1,
181.         Size   => 16
182.      );
183.   $Range->{HorizontalAlignment} => xlCenter;
184.   $Range->Columns()->AutoFit();
185.   with( $Sheet->Columns( "G" ),
186.      NumberFormat => $DateFormat,
187.      HorizontalAlignment => xlCenter
188.   );
189. }
190.
191. sub ShutDownSheet
192. {
193.   my( $Sheet ) = @_;
194.   $Sheet->Columns( "B:G" )->AutoFit();
195.   $Sheet->{Parent}->Save();
196.   $Sheet->{Parent}->Close();
197. }
198.
199. sub Error
200. {
201.   my( $Error ) = @_;
202.   print "$Error\n";
203.   exit();
204. }
```

Notice that line 7 decides the date format that will be used in the worksheets. This works well for English systems but may need to change based on your locale. For example those in Germany may want to change this to "ttt mmm tt, jjjj -- hh:mm:ss".

Line 1 loads the **Win32::OLE** requesting that the **with** method be exposed. Line 2 loads support for OLE variants and line 5 will load the **Win32::OLE::Const** module exporting all of the constants related to Microsoft Excel.

Lines 22 through 24 Call the functions **GetApplication()**, **GetWorkbook()**, and **GetWorksheet()**. These functions are defined by the script itself.

The **GetApplication()** attempts to obtain a COM object of the specified class with a call to **Win32::OLE–>GetActiveObject()** (line 108). If the object was either not obtained or the wrong type of COM object was obtained (for some odd reason) then a new COM object is requested with a call to the **new()** method on line 111. Line 113 sets the appliaction's main window to be visible so the user can see what is happening.

The **GetWorkbook()** function attempts to load the administration report spreadsheet. This occurs on line 123 with a call to the application's **Workbooks($FileName)** method. Notice that the name of the file is passed in, not the full path to the file. This is because this line attempts to find the workbook in the list of currently open workbooks. The **Workbooks()** method will search the collection of open workbooks for one with a name that is passed in. This name is not a path but just the file name.

If the workbook is not currently open then line 123 will fail and line 125 is given a chance to run. This line attempts to open the workbook specified by $File. If this fails then line 128 sets the applications SheetsInNewWorkbook property to 1. This tells Excel that any new workbook that is created will only have one spreadsheet. Then line 130 creates the new workbook with a call to the **Add()** method and line 131 saves this new workbook using the path $File. If a workbook is created using **Add()** then a global variable $UseSheetNumber is set to 1 for use in the call to **GetWorksheet()**.

The **GetWorksheet()** function will either request the particular worksheet specified by the global variable $UseSheetNumber (line 146) or create a new workseet (line 150). Either way the **SetupWorksheet()** function is then called that formats the worksheet.

Lines 161 through 168 figure out what to name the worksheet. Each worksheet is given a name based on the current date. The name follows the universal date format (like 1998.10.31). This is created in line 162. However, if the program is run more than once a day it will already have a worksheet with the current date as its name.

To avoid name collisions lines 164 through 168 will query the workbook to see if a worksheet exists with the given name. If one does exist then $iCount is increased and the name is changed to reflect the date and the new count, such as 1998.10.31 #2.

The script will loop between lines 165 and 168 until the call into $Sheet->{Parent}->Worksheets($Name) does not return anything. If the worksheet exists then the method call will return a COM object representing the specified name. This indicats that the worksheet exists.

Line 170 changes the name of the current worksheet. Then lines 171 through 188 format the worksheet setting the appropriate font attributes, cell alignments, number formats, and colors.

The actual engine of the program is between lines 27 and 39. Line 27 retrieves a list of all of the domains and Primary and backup domain controllers that are currently online. For each machine the **ProcessLog**() funtion is called. This function connects to the machines event log (line 51). All event log entries are read in backward seqential order (starting with the most recent entry) and are processed until the first entry is retrieved that is not more recent than $TimeLimit—which is defined as the one day before the current time (line 20 defines it as the current time minus 24 hours).

Line 87 uses an anonymous array to store values into multiple cells of the spreadsheet.

Summary

While OLE applications have become quite important building the COM-based infrastructure for Win32 Perl has been empowered with the capability to tap into this pool of resources—OLE, COM, or whatever you want to call the technology quickly becoming *the* interface for managing a Windows machine (in particular NT boxes). Future versions of NT will include the Active Directory Services Interface (ADSI) that gives full administration management capabilities by using COM.

Perl's **Win32::OLE** extension and its related modules not only give access to OLE-enabled applications but also make COM interaction very easy by automatically handling variant creation and disassembly as well as dispatch marshalling. It is quite literally as easy to use COM objects in Perl as it is in Visual Basic. Actually to some degree, it is easier.

The biggest problem with the **Win32::OLE** extension is that it is difficult to find documentation for different object models. Without such documentation, a COM object is like a black box; you can see it, but you do not know what it does or how to use it. For the most part, this dilemma is resolved by vigilant research looking for SDK help files and help files from applications. Additionally, books and articles written about Visual Basic can give wide insight into how to interact with COM objects.

Win32::OLE may well be the most important and impressive extension in the Win32 Perl arsenal. With patience and study, this extension can empower your code to interact with almost any OLE application, which includes almost any Win32-specific function.

Chapter 6

Communication

To me one of the coolest things a programmer can do is to use a computer to communicate. Talking is what computers do best and they do it constantly. Whether it is between the video card and the microprocessor, a program with another program, or one computer to another, this need to transfer information is commonplace.

Perl gives a script access to various communication interfaces such as sockets, anonymous pipes, file handles, and directory handles to name a few. Native Perl does not, however, make use of Win32 communication needs such as sending network messages and using Win32 named pipes. This is where Win32 extensions, once again, come to the rescue.

This chapter covers the following extensions:

- **Win32::Message**
- **Win32::Pipe**

These extensions provide the capability to send messages across the network and transfer data over named pipes from process to process and machine to machine.

Sending Messages

The Win32 networking environment is based mostly on Microsoft's LAN Manager. This environment is based on the NetBEUI protocol, which is an extended version of the NetBIOS protocol. This protocol is fairly useful and quite efficient under typical LAN-based networks.

One of the features of NetBEUI is that each computer on the network has a unique name that identifies the machine from other machines. This means that for one computer to talk to another computer it would have to know the name of the machine. When a computer connects to the network, it makes an announcement that it exists and it wants to use a particular name. If any computer already uses that name, it is up to the computer with that existing name to inform the newcomer that the name is already taken. At that point the computer will refuse to connect to the network. This process is known as *name registration.*

A computer can register two different types of names: a *unique name* that can be registered by only one computer, and a *group name* that several computers can register.

When a computer wants to talk to another, it will send out a request onto the network looking for the target computer. The request includes the MAC address of the computer wanting to talk. This request is broadcast to every computer on the network. If the target computer hears this request, it will respond directly to the calling computer by using the MAC address found in the request. This response informs the calling computer of the destination computer's MAC address. After this name resolution has occurred, both computers know each other's MAC addresses and can talk directly to each other without having to send out broadcasts to every other computer on the network.

> *Note*
>
> *A Media Access Code (MAC) address is a unique 12-digit code that no other network card in the world shares. Network vendors work together to guarantee that this code is indeed unique for each network card produced.*
>
> *All network cards have a hard-coded MAC address, so it is not necessary to configure one. For some cards (such as IBM's Token Ring cards), however, an administrator can specify a different MAC address. This is sometimes known as a locally administered address.*

When you send a message to a group of computers, the message is sent as a broadcast. When a computer hears the broadcast and if that computer has registered a group name that matches the name in the broadcast, the computer will process the message. All other computers in the network will ignore the message.

When a computer registers a group name on the network, it is in essence proclaiming that it belongs to a particular group of computers. Windows for Workgroups took advantage of group names and used them to create workgroups. Later, when Windows NT was released, group names were used to represent domains.

Similar to unique computer and group names are user names. A user name is registered on a machine representing the user who has logged on. As you may expect, a machine that runs services that require a user account to log on (such as a Web server or fax server) makes an attempt to register the user name on the network. As with all user names, however, if one exists already on the network, the attempt fails and no additional attempts are made. This is why if you log on to Workstation A and then log on to Workstation B without first logging off of Workstation A, network messages sent to your user name will go to Workstation A.

The **Win32::Message** extension gives Perl the capability of managing these names and sending messages. To receive sent messages on Windows 95, Windows 98, and Windows for Workgroups, the `WINPOPUP.EXE` program must be running. Windows NT requires that the messaging network service be installed and started; the NetBIOS interface must be installed, as well.

> ### Note
>
> The **Win32::Message** *extension does not work on Windows 95 machines. This is because the messaging API that this extension uses does not exist on Windows 95. Until Windows 95 supports the API, this extension is only supported from NT machines. However, any Windows machine (NT, Win95, Win98, and Windows for Workgroups) can receive messages sent by means of this extension.*

It is important to note the difference between a computer name and a user name. When a user logs on to a Windows NT, Windows 95, Windows 98, or Windows for Workgroups machine, the user's userid is registered as a user name. This allows someone to send a message to that user, but this does not allow someone to access shared resources using the user name. If the administrator logs on to an NT machine that happens to be sharing its CD-ROM as `\\machine\cdrom`, for example, you could not access that share as `\\administrator\cdrom` because there is a difference between a user and computer name. You could, however, send a message to `administrator` or `machine`.

Microsoft allows a network name to be up to 15 characters long. When the name is registered on the network, it will be 16 characters long regardless of how many characters you specified. This is because the sixteenth character is special and indicates the type of name being represented. If you register a user name of `JOEL`, the actual name registered on the network is:

```
JOEL_____<0x00>
```

Notice that the four letter name `JOEL` is padded with NULL characters (here they are shown as _____) so that it is 15 characters long. Then the value `<0x00>` is placed in the sixteenth position. This value identifies this name as a unique user or computer name. Table 6.1 and Table 6.2 illustrate the list of possible values with their meanings.

Typically, when the operating system loads a unique network name is registered identifying the machine. Depending on which services are running on the machine, however, other network names are registered as well. They will use the same name, but the sixteenth byte will change reflecting the service. There may be a name registered indicating the computer's name, another indicating that the machine is a domain master browser, another name indicating that NetDDE is running, and yet another showing that the machine is a RAS client. All in all, there could be five or more network names registered—all with the same name, differing only in the value of the sixteenth byte. Refer to Table 6.1 and Table 6.2 for more information regarding the values of the sixteenth byte.

When registering a network name, you cannot specify the value of the sixteenth byte unless you do some fancy Win32 API stuff. A service that runs and needs to register a special sixteenth byte value must use special API calls to do it. When a user adds a network name, he is only adding a unique (non-group) name—equivalent to a user or computer name.

> **Tip**
>
> To see what various names are registered on your machine, you can run the NBTSTAT.EXE command using the -n or -s flags:
>
> ```
> nbtstat -n
>
> nbtstat -S
> ```

Table 6.1   Unique NetBIOS name values

Sixteenth Byte Value	Description
0x00	Workstation service name. This is also known as a computer name.
0x03	Messenger service name. A name with this character is used by the messager service to send network messages. This value is appended to user and computer names.
0x06	RAS server service. Servers running the RAS service will have a network name with this value.
0x1B	Domain master browser name. A name with this value Primary Domain Controller.
0x1F	NetDDE service. If a machine has NetDDE running, a computer name will be registered with this value.
0x20	Server service. A machine that runs the Server service (which allows other machines to access its files) will register a network name with this value.
0x21	RAS client. Any RAS clients will register a network name with this value.

Sixteenth Byte Value	Description
0xBE	Network monitor agent. Any machine running a network monitoring agent software (collecting network traffic statistics) will register a network name with this value.
0xBF	Network monitor. Machines running network monitoring (network sniffer) software will register a name with this value.

Table 6.2   Group NetBIOS name values

Sixteenth Byte Value	Description
0x1C	A domain group.
0x1D	A master browser group name.
0x1E	A normal group name.
0x20	An administration group.
MSBROWSE	This is a special case. No value is placed specifically in the sixteenth byte, but instead the _MSBROWSE_ is appended to a domain name. This is broadcast on a subnet announcing the domain to any master browser that may be listening.

Note

*All the functions in the **Win32::Message** extension can be performed on remote machines. To do this, however, the script must be running from an account with administrative privileges.*

Registering Names on the Network

To register a user name on the network, you can use the **Win32::Message::NameAdd()** function:

```
Win32::Message::NameAdd( $Machine, $Name );
```

The first parameter ($Machine) is the name of the machine you are adding the specified name to. The computer name can be prepended with double backslashes or double forward slashes as in "\\Server" or "//Server". Using an empty string rather than a computer name results in registering the name of the computer running the script.

The second parameter ($Name) is the name you are adding. The name can consist of any (even non-printing) characters with the exception of a NUL (a character with a value of 0), which would terminate the string. The string can be up to 15 characters long. Even though NetBIOS/NetBEUI names can be 16 characters in length, Microsoft reserves the last character to identify the type of name (a user, machine, domain, workgroup, or some other type of name).

If the name is successfully added, the function will return a TRUE value; otherwise, it returns FALSE.

In Example 6.1, a new network name is added to the local computer. Notice that the new name not only has a space and a single quotation mark, but it also has the character 0xFF in the twelfth character. There is no significance to the character 0xFF in the twelfth position other than to illustrate that it can be done.

Example 6.1   *Adding a network name to a computer*

```
use Win32::Message;
$Name = "Joel's Home\xFF";
if( Win32::Message::NameAdd( '', $Name ) )
{
  print "Successfully added the name '$Name'.\n";
}
```

Listing Registered Machine Names

Because you can add names to your machine, it is only a matter of practicality that you should be able to discover what names your machine has registered. You can discover this information with **Win32::Message::NameEnum()**:

```
Win32::Message::NameEnum( $Machine );
```

The only parameter ($Machine) is the name of the machine from which you want to generate the list. This computer name can be prepended with either forward slashes or backslashes. If this parameter is an empty string, the computer running the script is used.

The **NameEnum()** function will return an array of computer and user names that the machine has registered on the network. There is no way to discern which is a user name or a computer name.

Example 6.2 shows how you can use **NameEnum()** to get a list of computer names from both your local computer as well as a remote machine.

Example 6.2   *Discovering a computer's registered network names*

```
01. use Win32::Message;
02. $Server = "FileServer";
03. @List = Win32::Message::NameEnum( "" );
04. DumpNames( "Local machine", @List );
05. @List = Win32::Message::NameEnum( $Server );
06. DumpNames( $Server, @List );
07.
08. sub DumpNames
09. {
10.   my( $Server, @List ) = @_;
11.   print "Registered names for:\n";
```

```
12.    map { print "\t$$_\n" } @List;
13. }
```

Removing Names from a Machine

Along with adding and listing network names, the **Win32::Message** extension supports the capability to remove names that you have added from a machine. The **Win32::Message NameDel**() function removes a name on either your local machine or a remote machine:

```
Win32::Message::NameDel( $Machine, $Name );
```

The first parameter ($Machine) is the name of the machine you want to remove a user name from. If this parameter is an empty string, the local machine will be used. The machine name can be prepended with double forward or backslashes if desired (but these are not required).

The second parameter ($Name) is the name to be removed. This name is not case sensitive and can support any character except a NUL value, just like the **NameAdd**() function.

If the function is successful, the return value is TRUE and the specified machine will de-register the user name from the network. This will allow other computers to successfully register the name. The specified machine will no longer respond to messages sent to the user name that has been removed.

The **NameDel**() function will remove *only* user names that you have already added from the specified computer. Any attempt to remove a non-user name (such as computer names, group names, and so forth) will result in the function failing.

Example 6.3 demonstrates adding a new user name to a machine. If the name is successfully registered on the network, it is removed. The last part of the code attempts to remove the registered computer name. This should fail; otherwise, you may have found a bug in the OS!

Example 6.3 *Removing user names from a machine*

```
01. use Win32;
02. use Win32::Message;
03.   # Get this machine's computer name
04. $Computer = Win32::NodeName();
05. $NewName = "Joel's Home";
06. if( Win32::Message::NameAdd( $Computer, $NewName ) )
07. {
08.    print "Successfully added the name '$NewName'.\n";
09.    if( Win32::Message::NameDel( $Computer, $NewName ) )
10.    {
11.      print "Successfully removed the name '$NewName'.\n";
12.    }
```

continues

Continued

```
13.   else
14.   {
15.     print "Unable to remove the name '$NewName'.\n";
16.   }
17. }
18. else
19. {
20.   print "Unable to add the name '$NewName'.\n";
21. }
22.
23. if( Win32::Message::NameDel( $Server, $Server ) )
24. {
25.   print "Successfully removed the name '$Server'.\n";
26.   print "This should never, EVER happen!\n";
27. }
28. else
29. {
30.   print "Unable to remove the name '$Server'.\n";
31.   print "This is expected and what should occur.\n";
32. }
33.
```

Sending Messages Between Machines

User names are very useful when you need to send messages to and from a computer. A message can be sent to a specific user, a computer, or a group. When a message is received on an NT machine, a window appears displaying the message along with who sent it and when it was sent. A Windows 95 or Windows for Workgroups machine will display the message only if the WIN-POPUP.EXE program is running. If you have ever printed to a network printer and received a message informing you that the print job was successfully printed, you have witnessed the wonder of sending messages.

To send a message, you can use the **Win32::Message::Send**() function:

```
Win32::Message::Send( $Machine, $Receiver, $Sender, $Message);
```

The first parameter ($Machine) is the name of a computer that will send the message. This can be any computer name, but you must have the required permissions to force the remote machine to send the message. If this parameter is an empty string, the local machine will send the message. This is handy if an administrator needs to send a message from a server but he is on another machine.

The second parameter ($Receiver) is the name of the receiver. This can be a computer name or a user name and can have prepended forward or back-slashes (but these are not required).

The third parameter ($Sender) is a bit of an oddity. It *should* be an empty string, but it does not have to be. If you supply anything other than the machine that sends the message (whatever is passed in as the first parameter), however, the function will fail and the message will not be sent. This limitation is imposed by the operating system, supposedly to prevent someone from sending a message claiming to be from another source (*spoofing*). The reason why you can specify anything for this parameter is so that if future versions of Win32 support specifying any receiver, the **Send**() function will support it. Unfortunately, the current versions of the Win32 platform do not yet support such a feature.

The fourth parameter ($Message) is the message to be sent. This can be a message (either text or binary) of any size. There is no imposed limit; however, a receiver may have a size limit. Windows for Workgroups and Windows 95, for example, both use the WINPOPUP.EXE application to send and receive messages. This application may have a limit to how many characters can be displayed. Windows NT, however, does not seem to have a limit for receiving messages.

If the function is successful, the message is sent to the receiver and the return value is TRUE. If the function fails, the return value is FALSE.

If the **Send**() function returns a TRUE, the message has been sent, but there is no guarantee that the message was successfully received by the recipient. There is no way to know for sure whether the message went through.

> ### Tip
>
> *You can send a message to all users on a computer, domain, or workgroup by specifying the name and appending an asterisk (*). For example if you use:*
>
> ```
> Win32::Message::Send('', 'ACCOUNTING*', '', 'The file server is
> going down at 10:00');
> ```
>
> *everyone in the* ACCOUNTING *domain (or workgroup) will receive the message. Likewise, if you specify a computer name appended with an asterisk, the message will be sent to every user on that machine. This is handy if you are using a multiuser version of NT, such as Cytrix's WinFrame, which allows multiple users to be logged on at the same time.*

Example 6.4 shows how you can send a message to all Windows NT Servers in a specified domain. This example makes use of the **Win32::NetAdmin::GetServers**() function, which is described in Chapter 2, "Network Administration."

Example 6.4   *Sending a message to all NT machines in a domain*

```
01. use Win32::Message;
02. use Win32::NetAdmin;
03. $Message = "Don't forget to log off of your machine tonight.
      We are updating everyone's profiles and you need to be logged off.";
04. if( Win32::NetAdmin::GetServers( '', '', SV_TYPE_SERVER_NT, \@List ) )
05. {
06.   foreach $Machine ( @List )
07.   {
08.     Win32::Message::Send( '', $Machine, '', $Message );
09.   }
10. }
```

Named Pipes

Another form of Interprocess Communication (IPC) is the named pipe. Really there is not much difference between name pipes and anonymous pipes other than a named pipe has a name associated with the client end, which allows other processes to connect to it. The Win32 ports of Perl do not provide native support for named pipes; this is why the **Win32::Pipe** extension was written.

> *Note*
>
> *Win32 pipes are not the same as named pipes from other operating systems. A named pipe created on a Win32 machine may not necessarily allow for non-Win32 pipe access. Don't be surprised if a script you write that creates a Win32 named pipe does not interoperate with a client running on a UNIX machine.*

In the Win32 world, the named pipe's name is shared among server processes. This means that if you create two named pipes using the same name, what really happens is that the first script creates the named pipe and the second script *thinks* that it created a pipe but it really is using the pipe already created.

After a pipe is created, the server process creates an *instance* of the pipe using the **Connect()** method. An instance of a named pipe is a particular connection between a client process and a server process. Think of a named pipe as a help desk. There are several "help desk engineers" (server processes) waiting for phone calls from confused users. When a user (the client process) calls the help desk phone number, a connection will be made to only one engineer. Even though each frustrated user is calling the same phone number (the named pipe), the user (client) is connected to a particular engineer (server). This telephone connection is an instance of the phone call (similar to an instance of the named pipe). This means that you can have multiple server processes all waiting for connections on the same named pipe. The Win32 OS will decide which call was waiting first for a connection and will arbitrate all connections.

There are no limits to the number of instances that can exist of a named pipe as well as there is no limit to how many different named pipes can exist on a machine.

> **Tip**
>
> *When creating a named pipe, you are not limited to any namespaces. This means that you can create a named pipe that looks like the following instances:*
>
> ```
> \\ServerName\pipe\MyPipe
> \\ServerName\pipe\Stats\Logons
> \\ServerName\pipe\Stats\Logoffs
> ```
>
> *Notice in the last two examples the named pipe resides in what appears to be a directory called* Stats. *The rules for naming named pipes are the same as those that govern naming files.*
>
> *The pipe names are just literally names of pipes. Even though the examples show a* Stats *directory, no such directory really exists on any hard drive. Additionally no* Stats *directory ever had to be created.*

The Client/Server Paradigm and Named Pipes

Just like an anonymous pipe, the named pipe works by using a client/server model. That is, a server creates the pipe and listens to one end. A client then attaches and either talks or listens on the other end of the pipe. From the client's point of view, the pipe can act just like a file handle. As a matter in fact, a client can access a named pipe by opening the pipe as if it were a file using the **open**() function as shown in Example 6.5.

Example 6.5   *A process connecting to a named pipe as a client*

```
01. use Win32;
02.
03. $User = Win32::LoginName();
04. $Node = Win32::NodeName();
05. $Time = localtime();
06.
07. $PipeName = "\\\\server\\pipe\\Logs";
08. open( FILE, "> $PipeName" ) ||
    die "Unable to open the pipe due to error
    $!.\n"
09.
10. print FILE "User $User on machine $Node logged on at $Time.\n";
11. close( FILE );
```

The client process does not need to know anything specific about the named pipe or how the named pipe was created; all it needs to do is open a file and treat it as if it were indeed a file. Example 6.5 accesses a named pipe called `"\\server\pipe\Logs"`. For the sake of this example, assume that some process has created the pipe and is waiting for some other process to write data to it. When the process hears incoming data, it will save the data to a log file. The example shows how a client makes a connection to this named pipe. Notice how the connection is made by using the **open()** function as if it were opening a regular file. As far as the script is concerned, the named pipe is exactly that, a regular file.

> **Tip**
>
> *When you create a server or client-side pipe using **Win32::Pipe**, it is automatically in binary mode. No character interpretation occurs during these pipe transmissions.*
>
> *If you open a client side of a named pipe using the Perl **open()** function, however, you may want to use the **binmode()** function to make sure that all data transferred in and out of the pipe is in binary mode.*

Types of Named Pipe States

In the Win32 world, two different types, or states, of named pipes exist: byte and message. If a named pipe is set to the *byte* state, data is sent through the pipe as a stream of bytes. Data is sent one byte at a time and received as a stream of bytes. This is similar in nature to streams that you might expect when you open a file. The byte state is used to send large amounts of data or data that is unpredictable in size, such as when you are sending data files.

In the *message* state of a named pipe, all data is sent over the pipe in discrete-sized messages. If you want to send more data than fits into the message size, you must send multiple messages. Messages are useful when a client must send a packet of information that is formatted and in a predictable size—for example, if you need to send a data structure or a simple message. The size of a message is determined by the buffer size of the named pipe.

> **Note**
>
> *When dealing with named pipes, the terms mode and state are thrown around quite interchangeably. This is not by design, but by circumstance.*
>
> *The Win32 API makes references to states as well as modes representing the same thing. In some cases, there may be a constant such as `PIPE_READMODE_BYTE`, which represents the read state of a named pipe. The fact that the word `MODE` is part of the constant would lead one to*

believe that it represents a mode and not a state. That would, however, be an incorrect belief.

Keep in mind that when you see the terms mode or state, you should consider them to be the same.

After a pipe has been created, the state of the pipe cannot be changed. A process can, however, change the way that the data is read from the pipe. There is a difference between the state of a pipe and the read state of a process's connection to a pipe. The former has already been discussed, but the latter refers to how the process will read data from the pipe.

If a pipe is in the message state, a client process can set the read state of its end of the pipe to either the byte or the message state by using the **State**() method. Only pipes created in the message state allow for this. Pipes created in the byte state can be read only as byte pipes.

A few methods allow for quick and efficient transactions between a client and server, but they require that the read state of the pipe be in the message state.

Note

*All named pipes are of the blocking type. This means that when a named pipe is waiting for a process to connect to the other end of the pipe (the process is listening) or data is being either sent or received over the pipe, all Perl processing waits. The **Win32::Pipe** extension does not take advantage of non-blocking async-named pipe capabilities.*

Creating Named Pipes

A process creates a named pipe object with the **new**() function:

```
$pipe = new Win32::Pipe( $Name[, Timeout[, $State ] ] );
```

The first parameter ($Name) is the name of the pipe. This name will be accessed using a full UNC where the share name is "pipe" and the pipe's name is appended to the end of the UNC as if it were a file name. If a name of "LogFiles" were passed in as the pipe's name, for example, a client would connect to it as "\\server\pipe\LogFiles". The name can consist of any characters that can make up a valid Win32 file name—any character except for:

```
:<>"\/¦
```

The second parameter ($Timeout) is optional and represents the timeout in milliseconds. This value specifies how long the pipe will wait for a client to connect before giving up. Table 6.3 describes constants that you can use for this parameter.

Table 6.3   Named pipe timeout values

Value	Description
NMP_USE_DEFAULT_WAIT	The operating system's default timeout value.
NMP_NOWAIT	Do not wait at all. If the function cannot be processed immediately, just give up.
NMP_WAIT_FOREVER	This will wait forever.

The optional third parameter for the **new**() function ($state) is both the read and write states of the named pipe. This value can be a combination of a single value from Table 6.4 logically OR'ed with a single value from Table 6.5. If nothing is specified, the PIPE_TYPE_BYTE and PIPE_READMODE_BYTE are used.

Table 6.4   Pipe read states that can be specified during a named pipe's creation

Pipe State	Description
PIPE_READMODE_BYTE	The named pipe will be created in byte read mode. This will read data from the pipe as a stream of bytes just as one would read from a file. This is usually used when data is expected from the pipe (such as sending binary file data).
PIPE_READMODE_MESSAGE	The named pipe will be created in message read mode. This will read data from the pipe in discrete messages of a fixed size. A typical application of this would be if the process expects announcements or commands from another process.

Table 6.5   Pipe write states that can be specified during a named pipe's creation

Pipe state	Description
PIPE_TYPE_BYTE	The named pipe will be created in byte mode, which means that data is sent across the pipe as a stream of bytes. This stream can be of any size in length.
PIPE_TYPE_MESSAGE	The named pipe will be created in message mode, sending data across the pipe as messages of a fixed and predictable size.

If the pipe was successfully created, the return value is a **Win32::Pipe** object; otherwise, undef is returned.

In Example 6.6, a named pipe is created called "My Test Pipe". It has a time-out value of 10,000 milliseconds (10 seconds) and is a message type of pipe, so the process will read data from the pipe in the message mode.

Example 6.6 *Creating a named pipe*

```
use Win32::Pipe;
$pipe = new Win32::Pipe( "My Test Pipe", 10000,
PIPE_READMODE_MESSAGE | PIPE_TYPE_MESSAGE ) || die;
```

Connecting to Named Pipes

A client process can connect to a named pipe in two different ways: by creating a named pipe connection object or by just opening the named pipe using the **open**() function described in Example 6.5.

By creating a client-end **Win32::Pipe** object, however, you can control many aspects of the pipe itself; these aspects are discussed in the "Changing Named Pipe States" section.

To connect to a named pipe using a **Win32::Pipe** object, you create a client end (that is, you connect to an already existing pipe) by using the **new**() command:

```
$pipe = new Win32::Pipe( $Name[, Timeout[, $State ] ] );
```

The first parameter ($Name) is the full UNC of the named pipe, such as \\server\pipe\LogFiles. The UNC will always begin with the machine name and a share name of pipe.

The second parameter ($Timeout) is optional and represents the timeout in milliseconds. This value specifies how long the pipe will wait for a client to connect before giving up. Table 6.3 describes constants that you can use for this parameter.

The optional third parameter ($State) for the **new**() command is the read state of the pipe. Unlike the third parameter used when creating a named pipe, this parameter is only the read state of the pipe. (Because the pipe has already been created, the pipe's state has already been determined.) This can be any single value previously documented in Table 6.4

Even though the operation for opening the named pipe is carried out the same way a server process creates a named pipe, when the **Win32::Pipe** extension sees that a full UNC has been specified as the first parameter, the pipe object created will be a client end.

> *Tip*
>
> *When a client process connects to a named pipe that is on the same computer, a period (.) can be used rather than a computer name in the UNC. The following two UNCs are the same, for example, if the client is located on the machine called* `FileServer`*:*
>
> ```
> \\FileServer\pipe\LogFiles
> \\.\pipe\LogFiles
> ```
>
> *When a script is accessing a named pipe located on the same machine, the use of the period in lieu of the machine name is much faster because the OS will not have to go through the network stack.*
>
> *On the other hand, it may be detrimental because it renders the script useless if it is run from another machine.*

A client process can also connect to a named pipe using Perl's **open**() function, as in Example 6.5. This is much easier, but limits the functionality of the client to only reading and writing data. Using the **open**() function this way enables you to specify read-only, write-only, or read/write access on the named pipe just as if a regular file were being opened.

Listening for Clients

When a server process creates a named pipe, it must then wait for a client to connect. After the connection is made, processing can continue and data can be sent and received over the pipe. The server process will listen for a connection by using the **Connect**() method:

```
$pipe->Connect();
```

The script will wait on this method until either a client connects to the pipe or the timeout value specified when the pipe was created is exceeded.

The function returns a TRUE if a client is connected to the other end of the pipe; otherwise, a FALSE is returned.

> *Note*
>
> *A client would never need to call the **Connect**() method. Only the server process uses this method because a client opening the client end of a named pipe has already connected to it.*

Sending Data Across Named Pipes

After a named pipe instance has been initiated and the server and client processes are connected, data can flow across the pipe. The **Win32::Pipe** extension creates full-duplex pipes so that both the server and client can both send and receive data.

When a process wants to send data across the pipe, there are a few different ways of doing this by using either the **Transact**(), or **Write**() methods. The most obvious choice is to use the **Write**() method:

```
$pipe->Write( $Data )
```

The $Data parameter refers to the data to be sent.

The method **Write**() writes the data to the named pipe and returns a value of TRUE if it successfully sent the data; otherwise, it returns FALSE.

Both Example 6.10 and Example 6.11 illustrate the use of the **Write**() method.

Note

> *It is possible when a process uses the **Write**() method to send data, but the other process may be delayed in reading the data.*
>
> *The method will return when the data was successfully sent to the other end of the pipe. That does not mean that the other process has read the data, however. The data may have been stored in a buffer waiting to be read.*

Another way of sending data is by using the **Transact**() method. This will not only send data to the other end of the pipe, but it will wait for a reply and return whatever is received. There is no difference between this and calling **Write**() followed by the **Read**() methods other than convenience and speed. **Transact**() is a bit faster than the **Write**()/**Read**() combination (some sources benchmark it at 10% faster). The **Transact**() method, however, can *only* be run on a pipe created in the message state and the read mode is message:

```
$pipe->Transact( $SendData, $ReadData );
```

The first parameter ($SendData) is the data you are sending to the other process.

The second parameter ($ReadData) will receive the data that is sent back to the process over the pipe.

The **Transact**() method will wait up to the timeout value specified when the **Win32::Pipe** object was created. The return value is the data received from the pipe.

The **Transact**() method can be used by either client or server process; however, because a server process typically receives data, processes it, and then sends the results back to the client, a server process usually has no need to use this method.

The method will send all the data you pass into the method over the named pipe. This means that the message size is the size of the data you submit. When reading, it will read all the data received in one call. This means that the receive buffer must be able to hold all the received data.

In Example 6.9, the **Transact**() method is used to submit a message to the server process. The method then returns after receiving a message from the server process. Notice that when the client end of the pipe is connected, the read state of the pipe is set to PIPE_READMODE_MESSAGE, which is required for the **Transact**() method to work.

Another, and more typical, way of receiving data from a named pipe is by means of the **Read**() method:

```
$pipe->Read();
```

The **Read**() method will wait until data has been read before returning. The return value is the data that was read from the pipe.

An example of the **Read**() method is found in Example 6.10, which is the equivalent to the code found in Example 6.8 and Example 6.9. Because the **Read**() method does not require any specific read mode, no optional parameters are passed in during the connection to the client end of the pipe.

The **Read**() method waits until it receives data from the pipe. If there is no data waiting in the pipe's buffer, the **Read**() method waits until either the data is received or the other end of the pipe is disconnected (or closed). This can cause a problem if you need to check for any data that may be sitting in the pipe. If there is no such data, your script will sit waiting, possibly for a long, long time.

To avoid this time lag, your script can peek ahead and see whether there is anything in the pipe by using the **Peek**() method:

```
$pipe->Peek( $Size );
```

The $Size parameter is the maximum number of bytes to return.

If the **Peek**() method is successful, it returns up to $Size bytes of data; otherwise, undef will be returned if there is either nothing waiting in the pipe or if an error occurred.

> **Note**
>
> *It is important to note that **Peek**() will not remove any data from the pipe; so if **Peek**() returns any data, you may want to actually retrieve the data from the pipe using the **Read**() method. The data returned by **Peek**() is the same data that will be returned by a call to **Read**()— except that **Read**() will return all the data, whereas **Peek**() will only return up to the specified number of bytes.*

The **Peek**() method is very useful when you must monitor several pipes for processing. This method can be used to check each pipe for data without waiting on the pipe, as in Example 6.7.

Example 6.7   *Monitoring pipes for processing using the **Peek**() method*

```
01. use Win32::Pipe;
02. $pipe = new Win32::Pipe( "My Test Pipe",
                        NMP_WAIT_FOREVER,
                        PIPE_TYPE_MESSAGE ¦ PIPE_READMODE_MESSAGE ) ¦¦
                        die;
03.
04. $pipe2 = new Win32::Pipe( "My Test Pipe",
                        NMP_WAIT_FOREVER,
                        PIPE_TYPE_MESSAGE ¦ PIPE_READMODE_MESSAGE ) ¦¦
                        die;
05. $bFlag = 1;
06. $pipe->Connect();
07. $pipe2->Connect();
08. while( $bFlag )
09. {
10.    $bFlag = Process( $pipe ) if( $pipe->Peek( 100 ) );
11.    $bFlag = Process( $pipe ) if( $pipe->Peek( 100 ) );
12. }
13. $pipe2->Close();
14. $pipe->Close();
15.
16. sub Process
17. {
18.    my( $pipe ) = @_;
19.    my( $Data ) = $pipe->Read();
20.    if( $Data =~ /^quit/i )
21.    {
22.      return 0;
23.    }
24.    print "Recieved: $Data\n";
25.    return 1;
26. }
27.
```

Example 6.8 *A client for accessing the server from Example 6.7*

```
01. open( FILE, "+< \\\\.\\pipe\\My Test Pipe" ) ||
        die "Could not connect: $!\n";
02.
03.     # Turn on autoflush — the same as removing file buffering.
04. select( FILE );
05. $| = 1;
06. select( STDOUT );
07.
08. $Message = "This is my test message.\n";
09. print FILE $Message;
10. $Input = <FILE>;
11. print $Input;
12. close( FILE );
```

Example 6.9 *A **Win32::Pipe**-based client for accessing the server from Example 6.7 using the **Transact**() method*

```
01. use Win32::Pipe;
02. $pipe = new Win32::Pipe( "//./pipe/My Test Pipe",
                    NMP_WAIT_FOREVER,
                    PIPE_READMODE_MESSAGE ) || die;
03. $Message = "This is my test message.";
04. $pipe->Transact( $Message, $Input );
05. print $Input;
06. $pipe->Close();
```

Example 6.10 *Another **Win32::Pipe**-based client for accessing the server from Example 6.7*

```
use Win32::Pipe;
$pipe = new Win32::Pipe( "//./pipe/My Test Pipe" ) || die;
$Message = "This is my test message.";
$pipe->Write( $Message );
$Input = $pipe->Read();
print $Input;
$pipe->Close();
```

Disconnecting a Named Pipe from a Client

The purpose of a server process creating a named pipe is to allow client processes to connect to it. If a client successfully connects and performs whatever transactions are needed, the server process will consider the session with the client finished. At this point, the server will need to disconnect from the client.

Disconnecting means that the server process kicks the client off of the named pipe. After this is done, the server can neither read from nor write to the pipe because there is no client on the other end. The server will want to call the **Connect**() method, which will wait for another client to connect to the pipe.

Many users of named pipes think that the server process should close the pipe. This indeed would effectively disconnect the client process from the pipe, but it would also literally close the pipe so that the server no longer has access to it. So long as the server process needs to use the pipe, it should not be closed; instead, it should be disconnected:

```
$pipe->Disconnect( [$Purge] );
```

The only parameter is optional. If it is non-zero, all data will be flushed from the pipe before it is disconnected. The method call will wait until the flush is completed before returning. If, for any reason, the flush takes a long time (maybe the client process is taking its time reading the data), the script will wait until all data has been flushed before continuing.

If the function is successful, the client process is disconnected from the named pipe and the method returns TRUE; otherwise, FALSE is returned.

It is interesting to note that a client process can call **Disconnect**(), but it should not. If a client process calls it, the process's connection to the named pipe is closed, but the Perl named pipe object remains active.

Example 6.11 demonstrates, among other things, the **Disconnect**() method. This example is a server process that creates a new named pipe and waits for clients to connect to it. A client will write some data to the pipe, which this example will read and print out. Notice that in line 40 the server process calls the **Disconnect**() method, which forces the client process to close its connection to the pipe. At this point, the pipe has only the server process on one end and the other end is not connected to anything. The script then loops back to line 11 and waits for another client to connect.

Example 6.11   *A server process that logs user submissions*

```
01. use Win32::Pipe;
02.
03. $LogFile = "users.log";
04.
05. open( LOG, "> $LogFile" ) || die "Could not open $LogFile: $!.\n";
06. select( LOG );
07. $| = 1;
08. select( STDOUT );
09.
10. $pipe = new Win32::Pipe( "My Test Pipe",
                NMP_WAIT_FOREVER,
                PIPE_TYPE_MESSAGE | PIPE_READMODE_MESSAGE )
                || die;
11. while( $pipe->Connect() )
12. {
13.   $In = $pipe->Read();
14.   if( ! $In )
15.   {
```

continues

Continued

```
16.    #  We received no data...something is wrong so
17.    #  give up and wait for another connection
18.    #  This happens when the client terminates its
19.    #  connection without telling us.
20.    next;
21.    }
22.    $LastUser = $User;
23.    $LastTime = $Time;
24.    @Info = $pipe->GetInfo();
25.    $User = $Info[2];
26.
27.    $Time = time();
28.    print LOG "$User:$Time:$In\n";
29.
30.    $Count++;
31.
32.    print "$Count) $User at " . localtime( $Time ) . "\n";
33.
34.    $Message = "You are user number $Count.";
35.    if( $Count > 1 )
36.    {
37.      $Message .= "  \tThe previous user was $LastUser at " .
             localtime( $LastTime );
38.    }
39.    $pipe->Write( $Message . "\n" );
40.    $pipe->Disconnect();
41. }
42.
43. END
44. {
45.    $pipe->Close();
46.    close( LOG );
47..}
48.
```

Closing Named Pipes

After a pipe has been used and is no longer needed, it must be closed, just like a regular file. All pipes need to be closed when no longer needed, whether it is a server end or a client end of the named pipe. The **Close()** method performs this action:

```
$pipe->Close();
```

After the pipe is closed, the pipe object is no longer valid and any attempt to use its methods will fail.

Changing Named Pipe States

If a named pipe was created as a message type pipe (not a byte type), both the server and client ends of the pipe can be set the read mode to make the pipe appear as if it is a message or byte type of pipe. This is typically used before any calls to the **Transact()** method are made, because that method will only work on pipes whose read mode is of the message type. The method to change the read mode of a pipe is the **State()** method:

```
$pipe->State( [$ReadMode] );
```

The optional [$ReadMode] parameter specifies which read mode is desired.

The **State()** method will return the current state that the read mode is in. If a parameter was passed in, the return value reflects any the new state of the pipe. If no parameters are passed in, the method retrieves only the current state. If a parameter is passed in, an attempt to change to that state is made.

The only way to know whether the method was successful is to check the return value. The value will be the same as the desired state.

Retrieving Named Pipe Information

Information pertaining to the named pipe can be of value to a script. Through the **GetInfo()** method, you can obtain information that details the user who is connected to the other end of the pipe and how many instances of the named pipe exist, for example:

```
$pipe->GetInfo();
```

The **GetInfo()** method returns an array that consists of five elements. Table 6.6 lists these elements.

*Table 6.6   Array elements returned from the **GetInfo()** method*

Element	Description
Element 0	State of the pipe. This value actually contains other data that is not of any use to Perl (such as whether the named pipe uses non-blocking async IO that is not implemented in this extension). To determine the state (or mode) of the pipe, logically AND element 0 with PIPE_TYPE_MESSAGE. If the result of the logical AND is 0, the mode of the pipe is PIPE_TYPE_BYTE.
Element 1	Number of instances. This number reflects how many instances of the named pipe currently exist in the OS.
Element 2	The client userid. This is the userid of the process connected to the client end of the pipe.
Element 3	This indicates how many bytes of data that the OS collects before actually sending the data over the pipe to the other end. The data will be sent if either the OS has collected this number of bytes or any amount of data has been waiting for at least the number of milliseconds indicated in element 4.
Element 4	This indicates how much time the OS waits before sending any data across the pipe in milliseconds. The data will be sent if either the OS has waited this long or if there are at least the number of bytes waiting to be sent, as indicated in element 3.

Checking and Resizing a Named Pipe Buffer

When a named pipe is created, a buffer is allocated that can accept incoming data. If a server process creates a named pipe, it has a buffer (as does a client who just connects to an existing named pipe). You can check the size of the buffer with the **BufferSize()** method:

```
$pipe->BufferSize();
```

The returned value is the size of the pipe's buffer.

If you want to change the buffer size, you can use the **ResizeBuffer()** method:

```
$pipe->ResizeBuffer( $Size );
```

The only parameter ($Size) is the size, in bytes, of the new buffer. Any existing buffer, and its data, will be destroyed before the new buffer is allocated.

Both methods return the size of the current buffer, or the new buffer in the case of **ResizeBuffer()**.

Establishing Connectionless Access to a Named Pipe

The **Win32::Pipe** extension has support for non connection-based client access to a named pipe. If all you need to do is send some data over an existing named pipe and receive the server's reply, there is no need for the overhead associated with actually opening a client connection to the pipe. Instead, you can use the **CallNamedPipe()** function:

```
Win32::Pipe::CallNamedPipe( $Name, $Data, $ReadBuffer );
```

The first parameter ($Name) is the name of the named pipe. This is a full UNC that can use either forward slashes or backslashes. If the server end of the named pipe is on the same computer as the client end, you can use a period (.) as the computer name, as in \\.\pipe\My Test.

The second parameter ($Data) is the data to be sent to the server end of the pipe.

The third parameter ($ReadBuffer) is a buffer that will be filled with the data received from the server.

If the **CallNamedPipe()** function is successful, it returns a TRUE; otherwise, it returns a FALSE value.

The **CallNamedPipe()** function is a quick and easy way to perform a simple transaction across a named pipe. It requires that the named pipe be of a message type (created using the PIPE_TYPE_MESSAGE option), however. It will make a connection to the named pipe and, if successfully connected, send $Data, and then read from the pipe and put the retrieved data into $ReadBuffer. Example 6.12 shows how **CallNamedPipe()** can be used to make a powerful but very small script.

Example 6.12   *Using the CallNamedPipe() function*

```
use Win32::Pipe;
if( Win32::Pipe::CallNamedPipe( "//server/pipe/My Test", "Test", $Buffer ) )
{
  print "$Buffer\n";
}
```

Setting and Retrieving Named Pipe Win32 File Handles

The **Win32::Pipe** extension abstracts Win32 named pipes from Perl so that they are a bit easier to handle without having to contend with the details of Win32 file handles. If you are willing to deal with Win32 file handles, however, a new world of possibilities opens up.

You can retrieve the named pipe's Win32 file handle from the pipe object using the **GetHandle()** method:

```
$pipe->GetHandle();
```

The value returned is a Win32 file handle. This value can be used in other functions that accept Win32 file handles, such as **Win32::AdminMisc::CreateProcess()**. That particular function enables you to specify a Win32 file handle for the new process' STDIN or STDOUT.

Another related function will either set or retrieve a standard handle. In a Win32 console application, the STDIN, STDOUT, and STDOUT handles can be retrieved or set using the **StdHandle()** method:

```
$pipe->StdHandle( $Type[, $Handle ] );
```

The first parameter ($Type) is the type of standard handle. This is one of the following values:

- **STD_INPUT_HANDLE.** The standard input handle.

- **STD_OUTPUT_HANDLE.** The standard output handle.

- **STD_ERROR_HANDLE.** The standard error handle.

The second optional parameter ($Handle) is the Win32 file handle that is to be set as the standard file handle specified, as parameter 1.

The return value is the Win32 file handle for the specific standard handle. If you are setting the handle, the new value of the handle is returned.

> ### Tip
>
> The **Win32::AdminMisc::CreateProcessAsUser()** *function enables you to create a process that maps the standard file handles to valid Win32 file handles. This is remarkably cool because you can open a named pipe and map it to either* STDIN, STDOUT, *or* STDERROR. *All you need to do is pass the return value from* $pipe->GetHandle() *into the function. There is a catch, however: If you specify one standard file handle, you must specify all three of the standard handles (a Microsoft-imposed requirement). This is where the **StdHandle()** method comes in.*
>
> *You can make calls to **StdHandle()** and get the Win32 file handle for each standard handle you want to pass into the **CreateProcessAsUser()** function.*

Summary

Messaging and named pipes are simple and easy ways to pass data from one machine to another. The named pipes in particular provide a wonderful way of transferring data in full-duplex between not only processes but machines as well. Because both messages and named pipes work independently from network protocols, you are not limited to using them only on TCP/IP networks, as sockets are so limited.

A named pipe can transfer any text or binary data. This can be data obtained or created by a script, read from a file, or queried from a database. One of my original uses of the named pipe extension was to interface a series of Microsoft Access and FoxPro ODBC databases on one machine with a Web server on another machine.

Chapter 7

Data Access

For most administrators, their jobs take their Perl programming into realms of maintaining user accounts and managing servers. More and more administrators are finding it important to write scripts that interact with databases, however, whether for Web-based Common Gateway Interface (CGI) scripts or for querying administrative databases for reports.

Many Perl modules and extensions support databases such as the variations of xDBM_File and libraries for SQL Server, Sybase, Oracle, MySQL, Dbase, and various others. A couple of Win32-specific extensions, however, marry the Win32 platform with generic database services such as ODBC. This chapter provides an overview on using the **Win32::ODBC** extension.

What Is ODBC?

All databases have their own unique way of doing things. When a programmer wants to access database services from within his code, he has to learn how to use that particular database. Really this is not so difficult because most of the major database vendors document their systems and provide libraries that a coder can link to. This is all fine and good as long as you always use one particular database. The moment you need to access a different type of database, however, not only will you have to learn an entire set of commands and procedures, but you will also need to change your scripts so that they can interface with this new database. Usually this means a total rewrite of the code.

Now imagine that you want to write a database application that would work with any database that your client may have. A perfect example is that you want to write a shopping cart CGI script for the Web. Because you do not know which database your client may have implemented, you would have to write several variations of the same script to handle all the possible databases. If this is not more than you want to contend with, just imagine what it would be like to support all those scripts. Testing them would be just as horrific because you would have to install each and every database system.

Wouldn't it be nice if all databases conformed to just one standard so that if you programmed your scripts to utilize it, then one script would work across all database systems? This is where ODBC (Open DataBase Connectivity) comes in.

ODBC is an initiative that the database industry has come to accept as the standard interface. Now many people believe that ODBC is a Microsoft product, but they are incorrect in believing so. Microsoft did champion the API and was one of the first companies to have working implementations of it. The actual interface standard was designed, however, by a consortium of organizations such as X/Open SQL Access Group, ANSI, ISO, and several vendors such as IBM, Novell, Oracle, Sybase, Digital, and Lotus among others.

The standard was designed to be a platform-independent specification, and it has been implemented on the Win32, UNIX, Macintosh, and OS/2 platforms just to name a few. ODBC has become so widely accepted that some vendors like IBM, Informix, and Watcom have designed their database products' native programming interface based on ODBC.

ODBC Models

When a program uses ODBC, it just makes calls into functions defined by the ODBC API. When a Perl script makes a call in to the ODBC API, it is typically calling in to a piece of software known as the ODBC Manager. This manager is a dynamic link library (DLL) that decides how to handle the call. Sometimes the Manager will perform some task, such as listing all available Data Source Names (DSNs), and return to the calling script. Other times the ODBC Manager will have to load a specific ODBC driver and request that driver (usually another DLL) to perform the task, such as connecting to the database and executing a query. Each level of software that the ODBC Manager has to pass through to accomplish a task is known as a tier.

ODBC has different tiered models that describe how the basic infrastructure works. Each model is premised on how many tiers exist between the ODBC Manager and the actual database. There could, in theory, be an unlimited number of tiers, but the impracticality of administrating and configuring so many tiers renders only three common models: the one-, two-, and three-tier models.

One-Tier Model

The one-tier model consists of only one step (or tier). The client application talks to the ODBC Manager, which asks the ODBC driver to perform the task. (This is the first tier.) The driver opens the database file.

This is a very simple model in which the ODBC driver performs the work of database lookup and manipulation itself. Examples of single-tier ODBC drivers include Microsoft's Access, FoxPro, and Excel ODBC drivers.

Two-Tier Model

Just like the one-tier model, the client application talks to the ODBC Manager, which talks to the ODBC driver. (This is the first tier.) Then the ODBC driver will talk to another process (usually on another machine via a network), which will perform the actual database lookup and manipulation. (This is the second tier.) Examples of this are IBM's DB2 and MS's SQL Server.

Three-Tier Model

Just like the first two models, in the three-tier model the client application talks to the ODBC Manager that talks to the ODBC driver (tier one). The ODBC driver then talks to another process (usually running on another machine) which acts as a gateway (tier two) and relays the request to the database process (tier three) which can be a database server or a mainframe such as Microsoft's SNA server.

These different tiers are not so important to the programmer as they are to the administrator who needs to configure machines with ODBC installed. However, understanding the basic infrastructure helps in making decisions such as how to retrieve data from the driver so that network traffic is held to a minimum, as discussed later in the section titled "Fetching a Rowset."

Data Source Names

To truly separate the client application from the database, there are Data Source Names (DSNs). DSNs are sets of information that describe to the ODBC Manager what ODBC driver to use, how the driver should connect to the database, what userid is needed to log on to the database, and so forth. This information is collectively referred to by using a simple name, a Data Source Name. I may set up a DSN that tells the ODBC Manager that I will be using a Microsoft SQL Server on computer \\DBServer, for example, and that it will be accessed via named pipes using a userid of 'JoeUser'. All this information I will call "Data."

When writing an application, I will just make an ODBC connection to the DSN called "Data" and ODBC will take care of the rest of the work. My application needs only to know that I connect to "Data," and that is it. I can later move the database to an Oracle server, and all I need to do is change the ODBC driver (and, of course, configure it) that the "Data" DSN uses. The actual Perl script never needs to be altered. This is the beauty of ODBC.

ODBC is an application programming interface (API), not a language. This means that when you are using ODBC you are using a set of functions that have been predefined by the groups who created the ODBC specification. The ODBC specification also defines what kinds of errors can occur and what constants exist. So ODBC is just a set of rules and functions.

Now, when you use ODBC you need to interact somehow with the database. ODBC provides a set of rules and functions on how to *access* the database but not how to *retrieve data* from the database. To do this you need to learn about a data querying language known as SQL.

SQL

The language that ODBC uses to request the database engine to perform some task is called SQL (pronounced SEE-kwel), an acronym for Structured Query Language. SQL was designed by IBM and was later standardized as a formal database query language. This is the language that ODBC uses to interact with a database. A full discussion on SQL is beyond the scope of this book, but this chapter covers the general concepts that most people use.

Before discussing how to use SQL, first you need to understand some very simple but basic SQL concepts such as delimiters and wildcards.

Note

SQL is not case sensitive, so preserving case is not imperative; however, conventionally, SQL keywords are all in caps. So, if you were to issue a query like this:

```
SELECT * FROM Foo
```

it would yield the same results as this:

```
SelECt * froM Foo
```

Delimiters

When you need to specify a separation of things, you use a delimiter. Typically, a delimiter is an object (such as a character) that symbolizes a logical separation. We all know about these, but some may not know them by name. When you refer to a path such as `c:\perl\lib\win32\odbc.pm`, for example, the backslashes (\) delimit the directory names with the last backslash delimiting the file name. The colon (:) delimits the drive letter from the directory names. In other words, each backslash indicates a new directory; backslashes separate directory names or they *delimit* the directory names.

Many coders will delimit things to make them easier to handle. You may want to save a log file of time, status, and the name of the user who ran a script, for example. You could separate them by colons so that later you can parse them out. If you have saved to a file the line `joel:896469382:success`, when you read it back you can parse it out using Example 7.1.

Example 7.1 *Parsing data using delimiters*

```
open( FILE, "< test.dat" ) || die "Failed to open: ($!)";
while( <FILE> )
{
  my( @List ) = split( ":", $_ );
  print "User=$List[0]\nDate=" . localtime($List[1]) . "\nStatus=$List[2]\n";
}
close( FILE );
```

When it comes to SQL, delimiters are quite important. SQL uses delimiters to identify *literals*. A literal is just a value that you provide. If you are storing a user's name of 'Frankie' into a database, for example, 'Frankie' is a literal. Perl would refer to it as a value (as in, "you assigned the value 'Frankie' to the variable $UserName"). In the SQL query in Example 7.3, the number 937 and the string 'Noam Chomsky' are both considered literals.

When you delimit a literal, you must understand that there are actually two separate delimiters: one for the beginning (known as the *literal prefix*), and one for the end of the literal (the *literal suffix*). If that isn't enough to remember, consider this: Each data type has its own set of delimiters! Therefore you use different delimiters when specifying a numeric literal, time literal, text literal, currency literal, and the list goes on.

The good news is that it is not too difficult to discover the delimiters that a particular ODBC driver expects you to use. By using the **GetTypeInfo()** method, you can discover what delimiters, if any, are required by your ODBC driver for a particular data type (as in Example 7.2 and Example 7.3). For more on how to use this method, refer to the "Retrieving Data Type Information" section.

Example 7.2 *Determining literal delimiters*

```
01. # This assumes that $db is a valid Win32::ODBC object.
02. $String = "Your data";
03. $DataType = $db->SQL_CHAR;
04. if( $db->GetTypeInfo( $DataType ) )
05. {
06.   if( $db->FetchRow())
07.   {
08.     %Type = $db->DataHash();
09.   }
10. }
11. $Field = "$Type{LITERAL_PREFIX}$String$Type{LITERAL_SUFFIX}";
```

The even better news is that most databases follow a simple rule of thumb: Text literals are delimited by single quotation marks (both the prefix and suffix), and all other literals are delimited by null strings (in other words, they do not require delimiters). So you can usually specify a SQL query such as the one in Example 7.3 where the text literal is delimited by single quotation marks and the numeric literal has null or empty string delimiters (nothing delimiting it).

Example 7.3   *Delimiting a text literal in SQL*
```
SELECT * FROM Foo WHERE Name = 'Noam Chomsky' AND ID > 937
```

The use of delimiters when specifying literals can cause problems when you need to use a delimiter in the literal itself. If the prefix and suffix delimiters for a test literal is the single quotation mark ('), for example, it causes a problem when the literal text has a single quotation mark or apostrophe within itself. The problem is that because the text literal has an apostrophe (a single quotation mark) it looks to the database engine as if you are delimiting only a part of your literal, leading the database engine to consider the remaining part of the literal as a valid SQL keyword. This usually leads to a SQL error. In Example 7.4, the text literal is `'Zoka's Coffee Shop'`, and the SQL statement is this:

```
SELECT * FROM Foo WHERE Company like 'Zoka's Coffee Shop'
```

Notice the three text delimiters, one of which is meant to be the apostrophe in "`Zoka's`". This will be parsed out so that the database will think you are looking for a company name of "`Zoka`", and that you are using a SQL keyword of "`s Coffee Shop`", and then starting another text literal without. This will result in an error.

Example 7.4   *Specifying a text literal with a character that is a delimiter. (This would cause a SQL error.)*
```
$CompanyName = "Zoka's Coffee Shop";
$Sql = "SELECT * FROM Foo WHERE Company like '$CompanyName' ";
```

The way around this is to escape the apostrophe. This is performed by prepending the apostrophe with an escape character. There is no difference between this and how Perl uses the backslash escape character when printing a new line ("\n") or some other special character. The SQL escape character is the single quotation mark. "But wait a moment," you may be thinking, "the single quotation mark is typically a text literal delimiter!" Well, although that is true, if SQL finds a single quotation mark in between delimiters and the single quotation mark is followed by a valid escapable character, SQL will consider it indeed to be an escape character.

What this means is that when you are using a single quotation mark in your text literals, you must escape it with another single quotation mark. The most practical way of doing this is to search through your strings and replace all single quotation marks with two single quotation marks (*not* a double quotation mark—there is a big difference) as in Example 7.5.

Example 7.5   *How to replace single quotation marks with escaped single quotation marks*

```
$TextLiteral =~ s/'/''/g;
```

If you wanted to correct the code in Example 7.4, you could add a function that performs the replacement for you, as in Example 7.6.

Example 7.6   *Escaping apostrophes*

```
$CompanyName = Escape( "Zoka's Coffee Shop" );
$Sql = "SELECT * FROM Foo WHERE Company = '$CompanyName' ";

sub Escape
{
  my( $String ) = @_;
  $String =~ s/'/''/g;
  return $String;
}
```

> *Tip*
>
> *Not all ODBC drivers use single quotation marks to delimit text literals. Some may use other characters, and some may go as far as to use different delimiters for the beginning and ending of a literal.*
>
> *The way you find out which characters to use is by calling the **GetTypeInfo()** method, which is discussed in the "Retrieving Data Type Information" section.*

Wildcards

SQL allows for wildcards when you are querying text literals. The two common wildcards are as follows:

- **Underscore (_).** Matches any one character.
- **Percent sign (%).** Matches any number (zero or more) of characters.

These wildcards are used only with the LIKE predicate (discussed later in this chapter in the section titled "SELECT Statement"). For now you need to be aware that wildcards are supported by most databases (but not all). You can use the **GetInfo()** method to determine whether your ODBC driver supports wildcards (see Example 7.7).

If you need to specify a percent sign or an underscore in your text literal and not have it interpreted as a wildcard, you will have to escape it first, just like you have to escape apostrophes. The difference between escaping apostrophes and escaping wildcards is twofold:

- Not all ODBC drivers support escaping wildcards (believe it or not).
- Usually, the escape character is the backslash (\), but you can change it to be something else.

The first of the differences is pretty much self-explanatory; not all ODBC drivers allow support for escaping wildcards. You can check whether your ODBC driver supports wildcard and escapable wildcards by using the **GetInfo()** method, as in Example 7.7.

Example 7.7   *Determining the wildcard escape character*

```
# This assumes that $db is a valid Win32::ODBC object.
if( "Y" eq $db->GetInfo( $db->SQL_LIKE_ESCAPE_CLAUSE ) )
{
   $EscapeChar = $db->GetInfo( $db->SQL_SEARCH_PATTERN_ESCAPE );
   print "Escaping wildcards is supported.\n";
   print "The wildcard escape character is: $EscapeChar\n";
}
```

If your ODBC driver supports the use of escaped wildcards, you can set the escape character to be whatever you want it to be (you don't have to settle for what the ODBC driver uses by default) by using a *LIKE predicate escape character sequence*. This process is described later in the chapter in the section on escape clauses.

Quoted Identifiers

At times, you may need to use special characters in a query. Assume, for example, that you have a table name that has a space in its name, such as "Accounts Receivable." If you were to use the table name in a SQL query, the parser would think you are identifying two separate tables: Accounts and Receivable. This is because the space is a special character in SQL. Ideally you would rename your table to "Accounts_Receivable" or something else that does not have such special characters. Because this is not an ideal world all the time, ODBC provides a way around this called the *identifier quote character*.

Most databases use a double quotation mark (") as the identifier quote character, but because some do not, you may want to query your ODBC driver to discover which character you should use. This is done using the **GetInfo()** method, which is discussed later in the "Managing ODBC Options" section.

When you need to use special characters in an identifier, surround the identifier with the identifier quote character. Example 7.8 shows a SQL query making use of the identifier quote characters for the table name "Accounts Receivable."

Example 7.8   *Using identifier quote characters*

```
SELECT * FROM "Accounts Receivable"
```

SQL Grammar

When you construct a SQL statement, you are using a standardized language that has been around for a while. There are dozens of good books available that explore SQL and can provide insight on how to optimize your queries and take full advantage of SQL's powerful features. This section is just provided for the sake of completeness because SQL is the language that ODBC uses.

When you use SQL, you construct what is called a *statement*. A statement is a type of command that can have many details. If you want to get all the rows from a database table that meets some criteria (such as a value of 25 in the Age column), for example, you use a SELECT statement.

SELECT **Statement**

A SELECT statement retrieves a set of data rows and columns (known as a *dataset*) from the database. It is quite simple to use. The basic structure of a SELECT statement is

```
SELECT [ALL ¦ DISTINCT] columnname [, columnname] …
FROM tablename
[WHERE condition]
[ORDER BY columnname [ASC¦DESC] [, columnname [ASC¦DESC]] …]
```

where:

columnname is the name of a column in the table.
tablename is the name of a table in the database.
condition is a condition that determines whether to include a row.

A SELECT statement will retrieve a dataset consisting of the specified columns from the specified table. If an asterisk (*) is specified rather than a column list, all columns are retrieved.

Every row in the table that meets the criteria of the WHERE clause will be included in the dataset. If no WHERE clause is specified, all rows will be included in the dataset.

The rows in the dataset will be sorted by the column names listed in the order listed if you specify an ORDER BY clause. If you use ORDER BY LastName, FirstName, the resulting dataset will be sorted in ascending order (the default) first by LastName and then by FirstName.

For each column specified, you can use the ASC or DESC keyword to indicate sorting the column by ascending or descending order, respectively. If neither keyword is specified, the column will be sorted however the previous column was. If no keyword is specified for the entire ORDER BY clause, ASC will be assumed.

It is interesting to note that instead of specifying a column name for the ORDER BY clause, you can refer to a column number (for example, ORDER BY 5 ASC, LastName DESC, 4, 3).

Example 7.9 retrieves a dataset consisting of all the fields (the asterisk indicates all fields) from all the records contained in the table called 'Foo'.

Example 7.9   *Simple SELECT query*
```
SELECT * FROM Foo
```

The WHERE predicate specifies a search condition. Only rows that meet the criteria set by the WHERE clause are retrieved as part of the dataset. WHERE clauses consist of conditional statements that equate to either true or false such as "Age > 21". Table 7.1 lists the valid conditions.

Table 7.1   Valid conditional predicates

Operator	Description
X = Y	X is equal to Y.
X > Y	X is greater than Y.
X < Y	X is less than Y.
X >= Y	X is greater or equal to Y.
X <= Y	X is less than or equal to Y.
X <> Y	X is not equal to Y
X [NOT] BETWEEN Y AND Z	X is between the values of Y and Z. If the NOT keyword is used, X is *not* between the values Y and Z.
X [NOT] LIKE 'Y'	X is the same as Y (when comparing text data types). If the NOT keyword is used, X is *not* the same as Y. The Y value can consist of a text literal with wildcards. This comparison is only needed when using wildcards; otherwise, it is more efficient to use =.
EXISTS (subquery)	This will be true for every row returned from a subquery (another SELECT statement).
X IS [NOT] NULL	The column X is NULL. If the NOT keyword is used, column X is *not* NULL.
X [NOT] IN (Y, Z, ...)	The value X is found in the list of (Y, Z, ...). If the NOT keyword is used then the value X is *not* found in the list (Y, Z, ...). The list (Y, Z, ...) could be another SELECT subquery.

Operator	Description
X <operator> {ALL¦ANY} (subquery)	A subquery (another SELECT statement) is {ALL¦ANY} operator> (subquery)performed and the rows from the resulting dataset are compared to the value X using an operator, which could be any in this list. If the ALL keyword is used then all rows from the subquery must match the condition set by the operator. If the ANY keyword is used, any row that matches the condition set by the operator will return a true value.

Usually, the conditional statement includes the name of a column. When a column is referred to, you are referring to the value in the column. In Example 7.10, a search condition of Age > 21 is used. Every row that has a value of greater than 21 in the Age column will satisfy the condition; therefore it will be returned in the dataset.

Example 7.10   *Specifying a WHERE clause*

```
SELECT *
FROM Foo
WHERE Age > 21
```

Example 7.11 makes use of the WHERE predicate to indicate a condition of the search. The query will retrieve a dataset consisting of the Firstname, Lastname, and City fields in the Users table only if the user's first name begins with the letter 'C' (the '%' is a wildcard that indicates that you don't care what comes after the 'C'—refer to the section on wildcards). The dataset will then be sorted by Lastname (by default the order will be ascending).

Example 7.11   *Complex SELECT query*

```
SELECT Firstname, Lastname, City
FROM Users
WHERE Firstname like 'C%'
ORDER BY Lastname
```

Multiple conditions can be used in a WHERE clause by using Boolean conjunctions such as AND and OR. Example 7.12 will return a dataset with rows whose Age column have values of greater than 21 *and* LastName column begins with either the letters 'C' or 'R'.

Example 7.12   *Using multiple conditions in a SELECT statement*

```
SELECT *
FROM Foo
WHERE Age > 21 AND
      (LastName like 'C%' OR LastName like 'R%')
```

For another SELECT statement consider Example 7.13. This query will return a dataset consisting of all fields only if the City field is 'Seattle' and the Zip code is not equal to 98103. The list will then be sorted in descending order (starting with Z's and ending with A's) by last name.

Example 7.13   *SELECT statement with sorting and a condition*

```
SELECT *
FROM Users
WHERE City like 'Seattle' AND Zip <> 98103
ORDER BY Lastname DESC
```

INSERT **Statement**

An INSERT statement adds a row to a table in a database. The structure of an INSERT statement is as follows:

```
INSERT INTO tablename
    [(columnname1[, columnname2] ... )]
VALUES (value1[, value2] ... )
```

where:

> tablename is the name of a table in the database.
> columnname is the name of the column to receive a value.
> value is the value to be placed into the column.

The INSERT statement is used when you need to add a record to a table. The trick here is that when you specify a list of column names, you must list the values for those columns in the same order as the columns.

The list of column names is optional and if left out, the first value specified will be stored into the first column, the second value will be stored into the second column, and so on.

Example 7.14 adds a row into the table Foo assigns the value 'Dave' to the Name column, 'Seattle' to the City column, and 98103 to the Zip column.

Example 7.14   *A simple INSERT statement*

```
INSERT INTO Foo
(Name, City, Zip)
VALUES ('Dave', 'Seattle', 98103)
```

Just to demonstrate how you can use the INSERT statement without providing any column names, look at Example 7.15.

Example 7.15   *Using the INSERT statement without any column names*

```
INSERT INTO Foo
VALUES ('Zoka''s Coffee Shop', 'Double Late', 2.20)
```

This example assumes that the first and second columns are text data types and the third is either a floating type or a currency type (notice that the example escapes the apostrophe in the first value).

> *It is rather important to understand that although the SQL language is fairly standardized, not all data sources implement it in the same way. To MS SQL Server, the* INTO *keyword for an* INSERT *statement is optional, for example; however, MS Access requires it.*
>
> *It is most practical to never use data source-specific shortcuts or leave out optional keywords unless you are sure that your script will always be used with a particular data source.*

UPDATE Statement

Not only can you select and insert data into a table, but you can also change the values in a given row of a table. The capability to *update* a row is tremendously powerful and is performed using an UPDATE statement. The statement's syntax is similar to that of the INSERT statement:

```
UPDATE tablename
SET columnname1=value1
    [, columnname2=value2]
    ...
[WHERE condition]
```

where:

tablename is the name of a table in the database.

columnname is the name of the column to receive a value.

value is the value to the column should be set to.

condition is a search condition as defined in the SELECT statement section.

This statement can be used to modify the existing rows of data. Example 7.16 uses an UPDATE statement to change the Department column for all rows in the Users table. If a row's Department column contains the value Personnel it is changed to the more politically correct Human Resources.

Example 7.16   *Using the UPDATE statement*

```
UPDATE Users
SET Department = 'Human Resources'
WHERE Department = 'Personnel'
```

DELETE Statement

To remove a row from a table is not difficult at all. This is done with a DELETE statement:

```
DELETE [FROM] tablename
[WHERE condition]
```

where:

> tablename is the name of a table in the database from which rows will be deleted.
>
> condition is a search condition as defined in the SELECT statement section.

The first FROM keyword is optional—some data sources may require it. The tablename (following the optional first FROM keyword) is the table that will be affected by the statement.

If search condition specified is TRUE for a row, the row is deleted from tablename. In Example 7.17, all rows from the table Students will be deleted as long as the row has a value greater than 4 in the Year column and the SchoolName column contains the value Michigan State University.

If no search condition is specified, *all* rows from tablename are deleted as in Example 7.18.

Example 7.17   *Using the DELETE statement*

```
DELETE FROM Students
WHERE Year > 4 AND
      SchoolName = "Michigan State University"
```

Example 7.18   *Deleting all rows in a table*

```
DELETE FROM Students
```

Escape Sequences

Each and every data source has its own way of dealing with specific data types. The DATE data type format for Oracle 6 is "Aug 20, 1997", for example, but IBM's DB2 is "1997-08-20". This becomes quite a problem when creating a SQL statement where you have no idea what the actual database engine will be.

Because ODBC attempts to abstract the particulars of different databases, the ODBC standard has adopted a technique to contend with this problem. This technique is called an *escape sequence*. When an ODBC driver finds an escape clause in a SQL statement, it converts it to whatever format it needs to be to suit the particular database the statement will be sent to.

Date and Times

The escape clause for a date is {d 'yyyy-mm-dd'}. So to create an ODBC SQL statement that will be properly interpreted by all databases, you could use the following:

```
SELECT * FROM Foo WHERE Date = {d '1997-08-20'}
```

The time/date-based escape sequences are as follows:

- **Date:** {d 'yyyy-mm-dd'}

- **Time:** {t 'hh:mm:ss'}

- **Timestamp:** {ts 'yyyy-mm-dd hh:mm:ss'}

Outer Joins

If you need to use an outer join, you can use the outer join escape sequence:

```
{oj outer_join}
```

where the *outer join* consists of:

```
tablename {LEFT | RIGHT | FULL} OUTER JOIN{tablename | outer_join} ON
search_condition
```

In Example 7.19, the outer join specifies all the fields from every record of the Machine table and every record from the Users table in which the field MachineName (from the Users table) matches Name (from the Machine table) as long as the field Processor (from the Machine table) is greater than 487.

Example 7.19   *An outer join escape clause*

```
SELECT *
FROM {oj Machine LEFT OUTER JOIN Users ON Machine.Name = Users.MachineName}
WHERE Machine.Processor > 486
```

Because this query uses an outer join as an escape sequence, you can be guaranteed that it will work on any ODBC driver that supports outer joins. Even if the particular driver uses a nonstandard syntax for outer joins, the ODBC driver will convert the escape sequence into the correct syntax before executing it.

Before you actually make use of an outer join, you may want to check to make sure that your ODBC driver supports them. Example 7.20 shows a simple line that will check for outer join support. If the variable $CanUseOuterJoins is 1, outer joins are supported.

Example 7.20   *Discovering whether an ODBC driver supports outer joins*

```
# This assumes that $db is a valid Win32::ODBC object.
$CanUseOuterJoins = $db->GetInfo( $db->SQL_OJ_CAPABILITIES ) &
$db->SQL_OJ_FULL;
```

Scalar Functions

Scalar functions such as time and date, character, and numeric functions can be implemented by means of escape sequences:

```
{fn function}
```

where `function` is a scalar function supported by the ODBC driver. Example 7.21 compares the `Date` column (which is of a `timestamp` data type) with the current date.

Example 7.21   *A SQL statement that uses a scalar function*

```
SELECT *
FROM Foo
WHERE Date = {fn curdate()}
```

For a full list of scalar functions, refer to Appendix B. Before using a scalar function, you should see whether it is supported by the ODBC driver. You can use Example 7.22 to discover this. If the variable `$IsSupported` is 1, the **curdate()** scalar function is supported. The value returned from GetInfo($db->SQL_TIMEDATE_FUNCTIONS) is a bitmask for all the supported time and date functions.

Example 7.22   *Checking whether the ODBC driver supports the **curdate()** function*

```
$IsSupported  = $db->GetInfo($db->SQL_TIMEDATE_FUNCTIONS) &
$db->SQL_FN_TD_CURDATE;
```

Stored Procedures

Stored procedures can be called by means of escape sequences. The syntax is as follows:

```
{[?=]call procedure_name[([parameter][,parameter]...)]}
```

If a return value is expected, you need to specify the preceding ?=, as in the following:

```
{? = call MyFunction('value')}
```

Otherwise, a call can be constructed like this:

```
{call MyFunction('value')}
```

> *Note*
>
> **Win32::ODBC** *does not support parameter binding, so using the '?' as a "passed in" parameter to a stored procedure is not supported and will probably result in an error.*

The only exception to this is the return value of a stored procedure. For example if a SQL statement was submitted like this:

```
{? = call MyStoredProc( 'value1', value2 ) }
```

The value returned by the procedure would be stored in a dataset containing one row. Future versions of this extension will support parameter binding.

LIKE Predicate Escape Character

Even though it is not common to do so (because you can always use the default escape character), you can change the character used to escape a wildcard by using the LIKE predicate escape character sequence:

```
{escape 'character')
```

where 'character' is any valid SQL character.

Example 7.23 demonstrates this.

Example 7.23   *Specifying an escape character*
```
SELECT *
FROM Foo
WHERE Discount LIKE '28#%' {escape '#'}
```

This example will return all columns from the table Foo that have "28%" in the Discount column. Notice that by specifying the LIKE predicate escape character sequence, the pound character (#) is used to escape the wildcard. This way, the wildcard is deemed a regular character and not interpreted as a wildcard. Because the resulting condition will not include any wildcards, the condition could have been this:

```
WHERE Discount = '28%'
```

This particular example demonstrates the use of the LIKE predicate escape clause, however, so we are using the LIKE predicate.

Usually, this escape sequence is not necessary because the default escape character is the backslash (\) and the same SQL statement could have been this:

```
SELECT *
FROM Foo
WHERE Discount LIKE '28\%'
```

How to Use Win32::ODBC

The **Win32::ODBC** extension attempts to make connecting to an ODBC data source as easy as possible. In doing this, it hides many details from the user. This is either a good or bad thing, depending on your point of view. Nonetheless, the extension is designed to be as flexible as the ODBC API is without requiring the user to learn the API itself. Of course, to utilize the more exotic ODBC features a good book on ODBC is recommended; otherwise you will drive yourself insane with all the constants, functions, and terminology!

When an application wants to connect to an ODBC data source, it must create the following items, in order:

1. An ODBC environment

2. An ODBC connection to the data source

3. A statement handle

Because all database interaction uses a statement handle, all three steps must be performed, in order, before any database interaction can occur. It is possible to have multiple statement handles per connection. This is how there can be many queries simultaneously.

Win32::ODBC attempts to simplify this process. When you create a new **Win32::ODBC** object, all interaction with the data source goes through this object. If you need to connect to many data sources at once, you just create many **Win32::ODBC** objects. For those users who need to create multiple queries to one data source (the equivalent of having multiple statement handles), the capability to *clone* an object has been implemented. Cloned objects share the same ODBC connection but have separate statement handles.

The use of **Win32::ODBC** is very straightforward in most instances; there are basically five steps:

1. Connecting to the database

2. Submitting a query

3. Processing the results

4. Retrieving the data

5. Closing the database

Because **Win32::ODBC** is a Perl extension, it must be loaded by means of the **use** command. Typically this is placed in the beginning of your script, as in Example 7.24.

Example 7.24 *Loading the ODBC extension*

```
use Win32::ODBC;
```

Connecting to the Database

After your Perl application loads the **Win32::ODBC** extension, it needs to initiate a conversation with a database. This is performed by creating an ODBC connection object using the **new** command:

```
$db = new Win32::ODBC( $DSN [, $Option1, $Option2, ... ] );
```

The first parameter ($DSN) is the data source name. This parameter can be either a DSN or a DSN string. This is described later in this section.

The optional additional parameters are connection options that can also be set by using the **SetConnectOption()** method, which is discussed in the "Connection Options" section. Some options, however, must be set before the actual connection is made to the ODBC driver and database. Therefore, you can specify them in the **new** command.

Example 7.25 assumes a few things: It assumes that you have already created a DSN called "My DSN", and that it is configured correctly. The example also assumes that the current user has permissions to access the DSN. This is not so much a problem for Windows 95 users as it is for Windows NT users.

Example 7.25 *Connecting to DSN*

```
$db = new Win32::ODBC( "MyDSN" );
```

If all went well, you will have an object, $db, which you will use later. Otherwise something went wrong, and the attempt to connect to the database failed. If something indeed did go wrong, the object will be empty. A simple test, as in Example 7.26, can be used to determine success or failure in connecting to the database. If the connection fails, the script will die printing out the error. Error processing is discussed later in the chapter in the section titled, strangely enough, "Error Processing."

Example 7.26 *Testing if a connection to a database succeeded*

```
if(! $db)
{
   die "Error connecting: " . Win32::ODBC::Error() . "\n";
}
```

You can override your DSN configuration by specifying particular configuration elements in the DSN name when creating a new ODBC connection object. To do this, your DSN name must consist of driver-specific keywords and their new values in the following form:

```
keyword=value;
```

You can specify as many keywords as you like and in any order you like, but the "DSN" keyword must be included (and should be the first one). This keyword indicates which DSN you are using and the other keyword/value pairs that will override the DSN's configuration.

Table 7.2 provides a list of standard keywords. A data source may allow additional keywords (for example, MS Access defines the keyword DBQ to represent the path to the database file) to be used.

Table 7.2   Standard DSN keywords

Keyword	Description
DSN	The value would be the name of an existing DSN.
FILEDSN	The value would be the name of a file-based DSN. Such files end with the .DSN extension. *This is only available with ODBC 3.0 or higher.*
DRIVER	A description of the ODBC driver that is to be used. This value can be obtained by using the **Win32::ODBC::Drivers**() function.
UID	The value represents a user ID (or user name) that will be sent to the data source.
PWD	The value represents a password that will be sent to the data source.
SAVEFILE	The value is a name of a file-based DSN that the DSN string will be saved as. *This is only available with ODBC 3.0 or higher.*

> **Note**
>
> *If ODBC 3.0 or higher is being used, there are two keywords that cannot be used together. They are DSN and FILEDSN. If they both appear in a connection string, only the first one is used.*
>
> *Additionally ODBC 3.0 allows for a DSNless connection string in which no DSN or FILEDSN keyword is used. A DRIVER keyword must be defined, however, in addition to any other keywords necessary to complete the connection.*

Suppose a DSN exists called "OZ" that points to an Access database. If you want to use that DSN but specify a userid to log on to the database as (in Access, a keyword of UID) and password (keyword of PWD), you could use the line:

```
$db = new Win32::ODBC( "DSN=OZ;UID=dorothy;PWD=noplacelikehome" );
```

A connection would be made to the "OZ" DSN, overriding the default userid and password would be difficult.

Other than the practical limitations of memory, you have no real limit as to how many database connections you can have. Although some tricks can help speed things up, you should conserve on memory use and make the most of an ODBC connection (but more on that later).

After you have your ODBC object(s), you are ready to begin querying your database.

Tip

*The **Win32::ODBC** extension's functions also map to another namespace called **ODBC**. It is not necessary to always use the full **Win32::ODBC** namespace when calling functions or constants. For example, the following two function calls are the same:*

```
@Error = Win32::ODBC::Error();
@Error = ODBC::Error();
```

Likewise, when you create a new ODBC object, you can use either of the following:

```
$db = new Win32::ODBC( "MyDSN" );
$db = new ODBC( "MyDSN" );
```

*Anywhere that you may need to use the full namespace of the extension, you instead use the abbreviated version: **ODBC**.*

Submitting the Query

Now that you have an ODBC connection object, you can begin to interact with your database. You need to submit a SQL query of some sort. This is where you use the **Sql**() method:

```
$db->Sql( $SqlStatement );
```

The first and only parameter is a SQL statement. This can be any valid SQL statement.

The **Sql**() method will return a nonzero integer corresponding to a SQL error number if it is unsuccessful.

Note

*It is very important to note that the **Sql**() method is the only method that returns a non-zero integer upon failure.*

---

continues

Continued

> *The reason for this is to keep backward compatible with the original version of **Win32::ODBC**, then called **NT::ODBC**, which was written by Dan DeMaggio.*
>
> *Originally, **NT::ODBC** used the return value of the **sql()** method (then the method was all lowercase) to indicate the error number. This technique of error checking has been made obsolete with the introduction of the **Error()** method. For the sake of backward compatibility, however, the return values have not changed.*

Suppose you have a database called oz with a table called Characters. The table consists of the fields (also known as columns) in Table 7.3.

Table 7.3   The table called Characters in a fictitious database called OZ

Field Name	Data Type
Name	char(20)
Origin	char(20)
Goal	char(30)

Suppose also that you want to query the database and find out who is in oz. Example 7.27 will connect to the database and submit the query.

Example 7.27   *Submitting the SQL query*

```
01. use Win32::ODBC;
02. if( ! $db = new Win32::ODBC( "OZ" ) )
03. {
04.   die "Error connecting: " . Win32::ODBC::Error() . "\n";
05. }
06. if( $db->Sql( "SELECT * FROM Characters" ) )
07. {
08.   print "Error submitting SQL statement: " . $db->Error() . "\n";
09. }
10. else
11. {
12.   ... process data ...
13. }
```

The SQL statement "SELECT * FROM Characters" in line 6 will, if successful, return a dataset containing all fields from all rows of the database. By passing this statement into the **Sql()** method, you are requesting the database to perform this query.

If the **Sql()** method returns a nonzero result, there was an error and the error is printed. If the query was successful (a return value of zero), you will need to move onward and process the results.

Processing the Results

After you have a dataset that has been prepared by a SQL statement, you are ready to process the data. The way this is achieved is by moving, row by row, through the dataset and extracting the data from columns in each row.

The first thing you must do is tell the ODBC connection that you want to move to the next available row. Because you just performed the query, you are not even looking at a row yet; therefore, you need to move to the next available row, which in this case will be the first row. The method used to move from row to row is **FetchRow()**:

```
( $Reult, @RowResults ) = $db->FetchRow( [$Row[, $Mode]] );
```

Before explaining the optional parameters, it is important to understand that the parameters are usually not used. They refer to the extended capabilities the ODBC function **SQLExtendedFetch()**. This is explained later in the section titled "Advanced Features of **Win32::ODBC**."

The first optional parameter ($Row) is the row number that you want to move to. For more details refer to the aforementioned section on advanced **Win32::ODBC** features.

The second optional parameter ($Mode) is the mode in which the cursor will be moved. If this parameter is not specified, SQL_FETCH_RELATIVE mode is assumed. For more details, refer to the aforementioned section on advanced **Win32::ODBC** features.

The **FetchRow()** method will return a one value if it successfully moved to the next row. If it returns a zero, it usually means that no more data is left (that is, you have reached the end of your dataset) or that an error has occurred.

Another value is returned, but is typically not of any use unless you use the advanced features of **FetchRow()**. For more information, refer to the section titled "Advanced Row Fetching" later in the chapter.

Example 7.28 shows a typical usage of the **FetchRow()** method. The loop continues to execute as long as you can advance to the next row. After the last row has been obtained, **$db->FetchRow()** returns a FALSE value that causes the loop to terminate.

Example 7.28 *Fetching rows*

```
while( $db->FetchRow() )
{
    ...process data...
}
```

> **Note**
>
> *As of version 970208, the **FetchRow**() makes use of the*
> ***SQLExtendedFetch**() ODBC function. Unfortunately not all ODBC dri-*
> *vers support this and therefore fail when **FetchRow**() is called.*
>
> *If this happens, you can either use another ODBC driver, such as a newer*
> *version or from another vendor, or you can use an older version of*
> ***Win32::ODBC**. Versions of the extension before 970208 use the regular*
> ***SQLFetch**() ODBC function.*
>
> *Future releases of **Win32::ODBC** will support both fetch methods and*
> *use whichever the ODBC driver supports.*

Retrieving the Data

After a row has been fetched, the data will need to be retrieved from it. There
are two methods for doing this: the **Data**() method and the **DataHash**()
method.

The **Data**() method returns an array of values:

```
@Data = $db->Data( [$ColumnName1[, $ColumnName2 ... ]] );
```

A list of parameters can be passed in. Each parameter is a column name of
which you are retrieving data.

The **Data**() method returns an array of values corresponding, in order, to the
column names that were passed into the method. If nothing is passed into the
method, all column values are returned in the order that they appear in the
row. Example 7.29 shows how the **Data**() method can be used.

Example 7.29   *Using the **Data**() method*

```
if( $db->FetchRow() )
{
  @Data = $db->Data( "LastName", "FirstName" );
  print "First name is $Data[1]\n";
  print "Last name is $Data[0]\n";
}
```

Notice how the first element in the @Data array ($Data[0]) is the value of the
first column name specified. The order of the column names passed in determines the order they are stored in the array.

The second and more practical way to retrieve data is to use the **DataHash**()
method. The **DataHash**() method is the preferred method when retrieving data
because it associates the column name with the column's data. The **DataHash**()
method returns either an undef if the method failed or a hash with column
names as keys and the hash's values consisting of the column's data:

```
%Data = $db->DataHash( [$ColumnName1[, $ColumnName2 ... ]] );
```

A list of parameters can be passed in. Each parameter is a column name of which you are retrieving data. If no parameters are passed in, the data for all columns will be retrieved.

If you were to query the table previously described in Table 7.3 using the code in Example 7.30, you may get output that looks like this:

```
1) Dorothy is from Kansas and wants to go home.
2) The Scarecrow is from Oz and wants a brain.
3) The Wicked Witch is from The West and wants the ruby slippers.
```

This output would continue until all rows have been processed.

Example 7.30   *Extracting data using the **DataHash**() method*

```
01. use Win32::ODBC;
02. if( ! $db = new Win32::ODBC( "OZ" ) )
03. {
04.   die "Error connecting: " . Win32::ODBC::Error() . "\n";
05. }
06. if( ! $db->Sql( "SELECT * FROM Characters" ) )
07. {
08.   while( $db->FetchRow() )
09.   {
10.
11.     my(%Data) = $db->DataHash();
12.     $iRow++;
13.     print "$iRow) $Data{Name} is from $Data{Origin} and ",
        "wants $Data{Goal}.\n";
14.   }
15. }
16. $db->Close();
```

Tip

*When using the **DataHash**() method, it is best that you* undef *the hash used to hold the data before the method call. Because the **DataHash**() method is typically called from within a while loop that fetches a row and retrieves data, it is possible that the hash may retain values from a previous call to **DataHash**().*

Closing the Connection

Up to now, you have opened the database, submitted a query, retrieved and processed the results. Now you need to finish by closing the database. The proper way to perform this is by calling the **Close**() method. This method tells the ODBC Manager to properly shut down the ODBC connection. The ODBC Manager will, in turn, tell the driver to clean up after itself (removing temporary files, closing network connections, flushing buffers, and so on) and the

ODBC connection object will be destroyed so that it cannot be used any longer. The syntax for the **Close**() method is this:

```
$db->Close();
```

The **Close**() method has no return value.

Example 7.30 in the preceding section shows a full working example of how you may use the **Win32::ODBC** module, including the **Close**() method.

The Win32::ODBC API

Win32::ODBC supports a rich set of features, most of which are never used (yet still exist). Some of these require knowledge of ODBC that is beyond the scope of this book. You can find several books that do discuss this topic.

Constants

For almost every method and function in **Win32::ODBC**, a set of constants are needed. These constants represent a numeric value that may change as the ODBC API changes over time, so it is important that you use the constant names and not the values they represent.

One of the most questioned aspects of the **Win32::ODBC** extension is how to make use of the constants. Only a small group of constants are actually exported from the ODBC module, so to use most of the constants you need to specify a namespace such as:

```
Win32::ODBC::SQL_COLUMN_TABLE_NAME
```

Or, if you have an ODBC connection object, you can access the constant value as if it were a member of the object, as in:

```
$db->SQL_DATA_SOURCE_NAME
```

Because **Win32::ODBC** creates a synonymous **ODBC** namespace and maps it to **Win32::ODBC**, you could use:

```
ODBC::SQL_CURSOR_COMMIT_BEHAVIOR
```

Notice that the preceding example just uses the **ODBC** namespace rather than the **Win32::ODBC** namespace. Both are valid, but the latter is a bit shorter.

The reason why all constants are not exported into the main namespace is because the **ODBC** API defines more than 650 constants, each of which is important to have. The decision was made to not export all the constants because it would bloat memory use and clutter the main namespace with an entire list of constants that will most likely not be used.

You could always edit the ODBC.pm file and export constants that you would like to export; but then again, it is not so difficult to just make use of one of the formats listed earlier.

Catalog Functions

The **ODBC** API supports metadata functions such as cataloging. **Win32::ODBC** supports access to such information with two methods:

```
$db->Catalog( $Qualifier, $Owner, $Name, $Type );
$db->TableList( $Qualifier, $Owner, $Name, $Type );
```

Both of these are really the same method, so they can be used interchangeably. The only difference is in how the results are obtained.

The first parameter ($Qualifier) represents the source the database will use. In Access, for example, the $Qualifier would be the database file (such as c:\data\mydatabase.mdb); whereas in MS SQL Server, it would be the database name.

The second parameter ($Owner) is the owner of the table. Some database engines can put security on tables either granting or denying access to particular users. This value would indicate a particular owner of a table—that is to say, the user who either created the table or to whom the table has been given.

The third parameter ($Name) is the name of the table.

The fourth parameter ($Type) is the table type. This can be any number of database-specific types or one of the following values:

- TABLE

- VIEW

- SYSTEM TABLE

- GLOBAL TEMPORARY

- LOCAL TEMPORARY

- ALIAS

- SYNONYM

A call to the **Catalog()** or **TableList()** method can include search wildcards for any of the parameters. Passing in "USER%" for the third parameter will result in retrieving all the tables with names that begin with USER.

The difference between these two methods is that the **Catalog()** method returns a result set that you need to process with **FetchRow()** and **Data()** or **DataHash()**. On the other hand, **TableList()** returns an array of table names that meet the criteria you specified.

Basically, **TableList**() is a quick way of getting a list of tables, and **Catalog**() is a way of getting much more information.

If the **Catalog**() method is successful, it returns a TRUE and results in a dataset with four columns: TABLE_QUALIFIER, TABLE_OWNER, TABLE_NAME, TABLE_TYPE, and REMARKS. There may also be additional columns that are specific to the data source. Each row will represent a different table. You can use the normal **FetchRow**() and **DataHash**() methods to retrieve this data. If the method fails, a FALSE is returned.

Note

*The resulting dataset generated by a call to the **Catalog**() method will result in a different result set if ODBC 3.0 or higher is used. In this case,* TABLE_QUALIFIER *becomes* TABLE_CAT *and* TABLE_OWNER *becomes* TABLE_SCHEM.

This is due to a change in the ODBC specification for version 3.0.

If the **TableList**() method is successful, it will return an array of table names.

If all parameters are empty strings except the fourth parameter (table type), which is only a percent sign (%), the resulting dataset will contain all valid table types. You can use this when you need to discover which table types a data source can use.

If the $Owner parameter is a single percent sign and the qualifier and name parameters are empty strings, the resulting dataset will contain the list of valid owners that the data source recognizes.

If the $Qualifier is only a percent sign and the $Owner and $Name parameters are empty strings, the resulting dataset will contain a list of valid qualifiers. Example 7.31 describes how you can use both of these methods.

Example 7.31   *Using the TableList() and Catalog() methods*

```
01. use Win32::ODBC;
02. $db = new ODBC("MyDSN" ) || die "Error connecting: " . ODBC::Error();
03. $TableType = "'TABLE','VIEW','SYSTEM TABLE'," .
                 "'GLOBAL TEMPORARY','LOCAL TEMPORARY'," .
                 "'ALIAS','SYNONYM'";
04. @Tables = $db->TableList();
05. print "List of tables:\n";
06. map {$iCount++; print "$iCount) $_\n";} @Tables;
07.
08. if( $db->Catalog( "", "", "%", $TableType ) )
09. {
10.   while( $db->FetchRow() )
11.   {
12.     undef %Data;
```

```
13.      %Data = $db->DataHash();
14.      print "$Data{TABLE_NAME}\t$Data{TABLE_TYPE}\n";
15.   }
16. }
17. $db->Close();
18.
```

Managing Columns

Each column (or field—whichever way you prefer to say it) can be of a different data type. One column may be a text data type (for a user's name, for example) and another may be a numeric data type representing a user's age.

At times, a programmer may need to learn about a column—things such as what data type the column is, whether he can conduct a search on that column, or whether the column is read-only. If the programmer created the database table, chances are that he already knows this information; if the table came second-hand, the programmer may not know such information. This is where the **ColAttributes**() method comes into play:

```
$db->ColAttributes( $Attribute, [ @ColumnNames ]);
```

The first parameter ($Attribute) is the attribute, a numeric value representing attributes of a column. Appendix B contains a list of valid constants that can be used.

Additional parameters may be included—specifically, the names of columns you want to query. If no column names are specified, all column names will be queried.

The output of the **ColAttributes**() method is a hash consisting of column names as keys and the attribute for the column as the key's value.

The code in Example 7.32 will print out all the data types in a tabled called "Foo" from the DSN called "MyDSN". In line 14, the column's data type's are retrieved with a call to the **ColAttributes**() method. The resulting hash is passed into a subroutine, **DumpAttribs**(), which prints out each column's data type.

Example 7.32   *Printing out a table's column data types*

```
01. use Win32::ODBC;
02.
03. $DSN = "MyDSN";
04. $Table = "Foo";
05. $db = new ODBC($DSN) || die "Error connecting: " . ODBC::Error();
06.
07. if( ! $db->Sql("SELECT * FROM $Table") )
08. {
09.   if( $db->FetchRow() )
10.   {
```

continues

Continued

```
11.      @Fields = $db->FieldNames();
12.      foreach $Field (@Fields)
13.      {
14.        %Attrib = $db->ColAttributes( $db->SQL_COLUMN_TYPE_NAME, $Field);
15.        DumpAttribs( %Attrib );
16.      }
17.    }
18.    else
19.    {
20.      print "Fetch error: " . $db->Error();
21.    }
22. }
23. else
24. {
25.   print "SQL Error: " . $db->Error();
26. }
27.
28. sub DumpAttribs
29. {
30.   my( %Attributes ) = @_;
31.   my( $ColumnName );
32.   foreach $ColumnName (sort (keys ( %Attributes ) ) )
33.   {
34.     print "\t$ColumnName = $Attributes{$ColumnName}\n";
35.   }
36. }
```

Data Source Names

Most administrators will create and manage a Data Source Name (DSN) by using the nifty GUI interface such as the ODBC Administrator program or the Control Panel ODBC applet. Both of these (actually they are the same application) do a tremendous job at managing DSNs. Be aware, however, that at times you may need to programmatically manage DSNs. An administrator may want to write a Web-based CGI script enabling the management of DSNs, for example. **Win32::ODBC** uses the **ConfigDSN()** function to do just this:

```
Win32::ODBC::ConfigDSN( $Action, $Driver, $Attribute1 [, $Attribute2, ...] );
```

The first parameter ($Action) is the action specifier. The value of this parameter will determine what action will be taken. The valid actions and their values are as follows:

- **ODBC_ADD_DSN.** (0x01) Adds a new DSN.

- **ODBC_MODIFY_DSN.** (0x02) Modifies an existing DSN.

- **ODBC_REMOVE_DSN.** (0x03) Removes an existing DSN.

- **ODBC_ADD_SYS_DSN.** (0x04) Adds a new System DSN.

- **ODBC_MODIFY_SYS_DSN.** (0x05) Modifies an existing System DSN.

- **ODBC_REMOVE_SYS_DSN.** (0x06) Removes an existing System DSN.

In some versions of **Win32::ODBC,** the system DSN constants are not exported so their values can be used instead.

The second parameter ($Driver) is the ODBC driver name which will be used. The driver must be one of the ODBC drivers that are installed on the computer. You can retrieve a list of available drivers by using either the **DataSources()** or the **Drivers()** function.

The remaining parameters are the list of attributes. These may differ from one ODBC driver to the next, and it is up to the programmer to know which attributes must be used for a particular DSN. Each attribute is constructed in the following format:

```
"AttributeName=AttributeValue"
```

These examples were taken from a DSN using the Microsoft Access ODBC driver:

```
"DSN=MyDSN"
"UID=Cow"
"PWD=Moo"
"Description=My little bitty Data Source"
```

The "DSN" attribute is one that *all* ODBC drivers share. This attribute must be in the list of attributes you provide; otherwise, ODBC will not know what to call your DSN or, in the case of modifying and removing, which DSN you alter. It is wise to always include the "DSN" attribute as the first attribute in your list.

When you are adding or removing, you need only to specify the "DSN" attribute; others are not necessary. In the case of adding, any other attribute can be added later by modifying the DSN.

Modifying DSNs

When you are modifying, you must include the "DSN" attribute so that ODBC will know which DSN you are modifying. Any additional attributes can either be added to the DSN or replace any attributes that already exist with the same name.

Some ODBC drivers require you to specify additional attributes (in addition to the "DSN" attribute) when using **ConfigDSN().** When adding a new DSN that uses the Microsoft Access driver, for example, you must include the following database qualifier attribute:

```
"DBQ=C:\\SomeDir\\MyDatabase.mdb"
```

In Example 7.33, the **ConfigDSN()** function is used three times. The first time (line 10), **ConfigDSN()**creates a new DSN. The second time (line 18)

ConfigDSN() modifies the new DSN by adding the password (PWD) attribute and changing the user (UID) attribute. The third call to the ConfigDSN() function (line 22) removes the DSN that was just created. This code is obviously not very useful because it creates and then removes a DSN, but it shows how to use the ConfigDSN() function.

Example 7.33   *Adding and modifying a DSN*

```
01. use Win32::ODBC;
02.
03. $DSN = "My DSN Name";
04. $User = "administrator";
05. $Password = "adminpassword";
06. $Dir = "C:\\Database";
07. $DBase = "mydata.mdb";
08. $Driver = "Microsoft Access Driver (*.mdb)";
09.
10. if( Win32::ODBC::ConfigDSN( ODBC_ADD_DSN,
11.                              $Driver,
12.                              "DSN=$DSN",
13.                              "Description=A Test DSN",
14.                              "DBQ=$Dir\\$DBase",
15.                              "DEFAULTDIR=$Dir",
16.                              "UID=" ) )
17. {
18.    Win32::ODBC::ConfigDSN( ODBC_MODIFY_DSN,
19.                            $Driver,
20.                            "UID=$User",
21.                            "PWD=$Password");
22.    Win32::ODBC::ConfigDSN( ODBC_REMOVE_DSN,
23.                            $Driver,
24.                            "DSN=$DSN" );
25. }
```

Line 8 assigns the $Driver variable with the name of the ODBC driver to be used. This value should come from a value obtained with a call to **Win32::ODBC::Drivers()**. The reason for this is because this value could change based on localization. A German version of ODBC, for example, would require line 8 to be:

```
$Driver = "Microsoft Access Treiber (*.mdb)";
```

The value returned by the **Drivers()** function is obtained from the ODBC driver directly, so the value will be correct for the locale.

The **ConfigDSN()** function returns a TRUE if it is successful; otherwise, it returns a FALSE.

> **Tip**
>
> *If you do not know what attributes to use in a call to **ConfigDSN**(), you can always cheat! You just use the ODBC administrator program or the Control Panel's ODBC applet and create a temporary DSN.*
>
> *After you have completed this, you need to run the Registry Editor (*regedit.exe *or* regedt32.exe*). If you created a system DSN, open this key:*
>
> ```
> HKEY_LOCAL_MACHINE\Software\ODBC\Your_DSN_Name
> ```
>
> *If you created a user DSN, open this key:*
>
> ```
> HKEY_CURRENT_USER\Software\ODBC\Your_DSN_Name
> ```
>
> *The value names under these keys are the attributes that you specify in the **ConfigDSN**() function.*

After a DSN has been created, you may want to review how it is configured. This is done by using **GetDSN**():

```
Win32::ODBC::GetDSN( $DSN ); $db->GetDSN();
```

GetDSN() is implemented as both a function and a method. When called as a function, you must pass in a parameter that is the name of a DSN whose configuration will be retrieved.

When used as a method, nothing is passed in to **GetDSN**(). The DSN that the ODBC connection object represents will be retrieved.

A hash is returned consisting of keys that are the DSN's attribute keyword. Each key's associated value is the DSN's attribute value. These key/value pairs are the same as those used in the **ConfigDSN**() function.

It is possible to retrieve a list of available DSNs by using the **DataSources**() function:

```
Win32::ODBC::DataSources();
```

DataSources() returns a hash consisting of data source names as keys and ODBC drivers as values. The ODBC drivers represented in the hash's values are in a descriptive format that is used as the second parameter in a call to **ConfigDSN**().

Example 7.34 illustrates how to retrieve the list of available DSNs and how to use **ConfigDSN**() to remove these DSNs.

Example 7.34   *Removing all DSNs*

```
01. use Win32::ODBC;
02.
```

continues

Continued

```
03. if( %DSNList = Win32::ODBC::DataSources() )
04. {
05.   foreach $Name ( keys( %DSNList ) )
06.   {
07.   print "$Name = '$DSNList{$Name}'\n";
08.     if( ! Win32::ODBC::ConfigDSN( ODBC_REMOVE_DSN,
                                      $DSNList{$Name},
                                      "DSN=$Name" ) )
09.     {
10.       #  If we were unable to remove the
11.       #  DSN maybe it is a system DSN...
12.       Win32::ODBC::ConfigDSN( ODBC_REMOVE_SYS_DSN,
                                  $DSNList{$Name},
                                  "DSN=$Name" );
13.     }
14.   }
15. }
```

Notice how Example 7.34 uses the names and drivers that make up the hash returned by the **DataSources**() function. These values are used as the DSN name and driver in the calls to **ConfigDSN**().

Returning Available ODBC Drivers

Drivers() is yet another DSN-related function:

```
Win32::ODBC::Drivers();
```

This function returns a hash consisting of available ODBC drivers and any attributes related to the driver. Note that these attributes are not necessarily the same as the ones you provide in **ConfigDSN**().

The returned hash consists of keys that represent the ODBC driver name (in descriptive format), and the key's associated value contains a list of ODBC driver attributes separated by semicolons (;) such as this:

```
"Attribute1=Value1;Attribute2=Value2;..."
```

These attributes are really not that useful for the common programmer, but may be of use if you are programming ODBC drivers or if you need to make sure that a particular driver is configured correctly.

> ### Note
>
> *The attributes returned by the **Drivers**() function (which are the ODBC driver's configuration attributes) are not the same type of attributes used in the **ConfigDSN**() attributes (which are an ODBC driver's DSN attributes).*

Case Study: Changing the Database Paths for All MS Access DSNs

Jane's boss came running into her office and told her that the junior administrator did something really devastating to one of her Web servers. Somehow, he has managed to corrupt the D: drive, the one where all the Access database files were kept.

Jane realized that she could not take the server down to reinstall a drive until the weekend. She also began kicking herself for not having already installed the RAID subsystem.

To correct the problem, she had someone restore the database files from a tape backup on to the server's E: drive. She figured that all she had to do was change the ODBC DSNs to point to their respective databases on the E: drive rather than the D: drive. No problem...until she realized that there were hundreds of DSNs!

So, Jane sat down and wrote the Perl script in Example 7.35.

Example 7.35   *Changing the database paths for all MS Access DSNs*

```
01. use Win32::ODBC;
02. $OldDrive = "d:";
03. $NewDrive = "e:";
04.  # We are looking for Access databases
05. $Driver = GetDriver( ".mdb" ) || Error( "finding the ODBC driver" );
06.
07. %DSNList = Win32::ODBC::DataSources() ||
            Error( "retrieving list of DSNs" );
08. foreach $DSN ( keys( %DSNList ) )
09. {
10.    next if( $DSNList{$DSN} ne $Driver );
11.    my( %Config ) = Win32::ODBC::GetDSN( $DSN );
12.    if( $Config{DBQ} =~ s/^$OldDrive/$NewDrive/i )
13.    {
14.      if( ! Win32::ODBC::ConfigDSN( ODBC_MODIFY_DSN,
15.                               $Driver,
16.                               "DSN=$DSN",
17.                               "DBQ=$Config{DBQ}" ) )
18.      {
19.        # If the previous attempt to modify the DSN
20.        # failed then try again but using a system DSN.
21.        Win32::ODBC::ConfigDSN( ODBC_MODIFY_SYS_DSN,
22.                               $Driver,
23.                               "DSN=$DSN",
24.                               "DBQ=$Config{DBQ}" );
25.      }
26.    }
27. }
```

continues

Continued

```
28.
29. sub Error
30. {
31.   my( $Reason ) = @_;
32.   die "Error $Reason: " . Win32::ODBC::Error() . "\n";
33. }
34.
35. sub GetDriver
36. {
37.   my( $Extension ) = @_;
38.   my( %Sources, $Driver, $Description );
39.   Extension =~ s/([\.\\\$])/\\$1/gs;
40.   if( %Sources = Win32::ODBC::Drivers() )
41.   {
42.     foreach $Driver ( keys( %Sources ) )
43.     {
44.       if( $Sources{$Driver} =~ /FileExtns=[^;]*$Extension/i )
45.       {
46.         $Description = $Driver;
47.         last;
48.       }
49.     }
50.   }
51.   return $Description;
52. }
```

The script in Example 7.35 first seeks the driver description for the ODBC driver that recognizes databases with an .mdb extension. This is performed by calling a subroutine **GetDriver()** on line 5. The subroutine makes a call to **Win32::ODBC::Drivers()** to get a list of all installed drivers, and then tests them looking for one which has a keyword FileExtns that matches the specified file extension (lines 40–50). Notice that line 39 prepends any period, backslash, and dollar sign with an escaping backslash. This is so that when the $Extension variable is used in the regular expression (line 44), the characters are not interpreted.

After the script has the driver description, it retrieves a list of available DSNs (line 7) and compares their drivers with the target one.

If the drivers match, the DSN's configuration is obtained (line 11) and the database file is compared to see whether the database is on the old D: drive. If so, the drive is changed to E:. The DSN is then modified to use the new path by first modifying it as a user DSN (line 14); if that fails, it then tries it as a system DSN (line 21).

By running this, Jane could quickly fix all the DSNs on her server in just a few minutes and with no errors. If she had manually altered the DSNs through a graphical ODBC administrator program, it would have taken much longer and would have been prone to mistakes. Jane also added a task to her calendar reminding her to install the server's RAID subsystem.

Miscellaneous Functions

The ODBC API has a multitude of functions, many of which the **Win32::ODBC** extension exposes to a Perl script. A typical user will never use most of these, but for those who are migrating data or need to perform complex queries and cursor manipulation, among other tasks, these functions are required. This section discusses these functions and methods.

It is possible, for instance, to retrieve an array of column names using the **FieldNames()** method, although this is not the most useful feature because it only reports column names and nothing else. The syntax for the **FieldNames()** method is as follows:

```
@List = $db->FieldNames();
```

The returned array consists of the column names of the result set. There is no guarantee to the order in which the names are listed.

Managing ODBC Connections

Connections to data sources quite often have attributes that govern the nature of the connection. If a connection to a data source occurs over a network, for example, it may allow the network packet size to be changed. Likewise logon timeout values, ODBC tracing, and transaction autocommit modes are considered to be connection attributes.

These attributes can be modified and examined by two **Win32::ODBC** methods: GetConnectOption() and SetConnectOption():

```
$db->GetConnectOption( $Option );
$db->SetConnectOption( $Option, $Value );
```

For both methods, the first parameter ($Option) is the connection option as defined by the ODBC API. Appendix B contains a list of connect options.

The second parameter in the **SetConnectOption()** ($Value) indicates the value to set for the specified option.

The return value for **GetConnectOption()** is the value for the specified option.

> ### Warning
> *Be careful with this, because **GetConnectOption()** does not report any value to indicate an error—if the method fails, it will still return some value that may be invalid.*

The return value for **SetConnectOption()** is either TRUE if the option was successfully set or FALSE if the method failed to set the option.

In Example 7.36, the ODBC tracing state is queried in line 4. (Tracing is where all ODBC API calls are copied into a text file so that you can later see what your ODBC driver was doing.) If ODBC tracing is already active, the current trace file is retrieved (in line 12) and is printed. Otherwise the trace file is set (line 6) and tracing is turned on (line 7).

Example 7.36   *Using the **GetConnectOptions()** and **SetConnectOptions()** methods*

```
01. use Win32::ODBC;
02. $db = new Win32::ODBC( "MyDSN" ) || die "Error: " . Win32::ODBC::Error();
03. $TraceFile = "C:\\TEMP\\TRACE.SQL";
04. if($db->GetConnectOption( $db->SQL_OPT_TRACE ) == $db->SQL_OPT_TRACE_OFF )
05. {
06.   $db->SetConnectOption( $db->SQL_OPT_TRACEFILE, $TraceFile );
07.   $db->SetConnectOption( $db->SQL_OPT_TRACE, $db->SQL_OPT_TRACE_ON );
08.   print "ODBC tracing is now active.\n";
09. }
10. else
11. {
12.   $TraceFile = $db->GetConnectOption( $db->SQL_OPT_TRACEFILE );
13.    print "Tracing is already active.\n";
14. }
15. print "The ODBC tracefile is '$TraceFile'.\n";
16.
17. ...continue with your code...
18. $db->Close();
```

> *Note*
>
> *The ODBC API specifies so many options that are quite useful (and in some cases necessary) for a user but are just far beyond the scope of this book. Appendix B lists most of these options and includes a brief description of them. Some of these descriptions are quite technical so that ODBC programmers can understand their impact.*
>
> *For those who need more information on the ODBC options and their values or for those who are just curious, it is highly recommended to consult a good book on the ODBC API. A couple of recommended books are Microsoft's "ODBC SDK and Programmer Reference" and Kyle Geiger's "Inside ODBC."*

Managing ODBC Statement Options

Just as an ODBC connection has attributes that can be queried and modified, so can an ODBC statement. When a script creates a **Win32::ODBC** object, it has both connection and statement handles. This means that you can not only manage the connection attributes, but you can also manage statement attributes such as the cursor type, query timeout, and the maximum number of rows in a dataset from a SELECT query. These statement attributes are managed by the **GetStmtOption()** and **SetStmtOption()** methods:

```
$db->GetStmtOption( $Option );
$db->SetStmtOption( $Option, $Value );
```

The first parameter is the statement option as defined by the ODBC API. Appendix B contains a list of these statement options.

The second parameter in **SetStmtOption()** indicates the value to set for the specified option.

The return value for **GetStmtOption()** is the value for the specified option.

> **Warning**
>
> *Be careful with this, because **GetStmtOption()** does not report any value to indicate an error—if the method fails, it will still return some value that may be invalid.*

The return value for **SetStmtOption()** is either TRUE if the option was successfully set or FALSE if the method failed to set the option.

In Example 7.37, the SQL_ROWSET_SIZE statement option is set to 100. This will retrieve a rowset of no more than 100 rows every time **FetchRow()** is called. Because the rowset size is greater than 1, the actual row processed after the **FetchRow()** will increase by 100. This is why we are using the **GetStmtOption()** with the SQL_ROW_NUMBER option to determine the current row number.

Example 7.37 *Using the GetStmtOption() and SetStmtOption() methods*

```
01. use Win32::ODBC;
02. $db = new Win32::ODBC( "MyDSN" ) ¦¦ die "Error: " . Win32::ODBC::Error();
03. if( ! $db->Sql( "SELECT * FROM Foo" ) )
04. {
05.    $db->SetStmtOption( $db->SQL_ROWSET_SIZE, 100 );
06.    while( $db->FetchRow( 1, SQL_FETCH_NEXT ) )
07.    {
08.      my( %Data ) = $db->DataHash();
09.      ...process data...
10.      if( $Row = $db->GetStmtOption( $db->SQL_ROW_NUMBER ) )
11.      {
12.        print "Processed row $Row.\n";
13.      }
14.      else
15.      {
16.        print "Unable to determine row number.\n";
17.      }
18.    }
19. }
20. $db->Close();
```

Obtaining General ODBC Information

There is one addition method that will retrieve information pertaining to the ODBC driver: **GetInfo()**. The information retrieved by **GetInfo()** is read-only and cannot be set.

```
$db->GetInfo( $Option );
```

The only parameter (`$Option`) is a value that represents the particular information that is desired. Appendix B provides a list of values.

Example 7.38 shows how **GetInfo()** can be used to determine whether the data source is read-only.

Example 7.38   *Using the **GetInfo()** method*

```
01. use Win32::ODBC;
02. $db = new Win32::ODBC( "MyDSN" ) || die "Error: " . Win32::ODBC::Error();
03. if( ! $db->Sql( "SELECT * FROM Foo" ) )
04. {
05.   $Result = $db->GetInfo( $db->SQL_DATA_SOURCE_READ_ONLY );
06.   if( $Result =~ /y/i )
07.   {
08.     print "OOOPS! This data source is read only!\n";
09.     $db->Close();
10.     exit;
11.   }
12.   ...process data...
13. }
14. $db->Close();
```

Checking for ODBC Function Support

Not all ODBC drivers support all ODBC functions. This can cause problems for script writers. To check whether a connection supports a particular ODBC function, you can use the **GetFunctions()** method:

```
%Functions = $db->GetFunctions( [$Function1[, $Function2, ...]]);
```

The optional parameters are constants that represent ODBC functions such as `SQL_API_SQLTRANSACT` (which represents the ODBC API function **SQLTransact()**). There can be any number of functions passed in as parameters. If no parameters are passed in, all functions are checked.

A hash is returned consisting of keys that represent an ODBC API function, and the key's value is either a TRUE or FALSE. If parameters were passed into the method, the resulting hash consists of only the keys that represent the parameters passed in.

In Example 7.39, the **GetFunctions()** method is used to learn whether the ODBC driver supports transaction handling by means of the ODBC API's **SQLTransactions()** function. If it does, the Perl script can call **$db->Transaction()**.

Example 7.39   *Using the GetFunctions() method*

```
use Win32::ODBC;
$db = new Win32::ODBC( "MyDSN" ) ¦¦ die "Error: " . Win32::ODBC::Error();
%Functions = $db->GetFunctions();
if( $Functions{$db->SQL_API_SQLTRANSACT} )
{
    print "Hey, this ODBC driver supports the SQLTransact() function!\n";
}
```

Limits on Column Size

When a query returns a result set, a buffer must be created for each column. Generally **Win32::ODBC** can determine the size of the buffer based on the column data type. Some data types, however, do not describe the size of their data (such as the memo data type found in MS Access). In these cases, **Win32::ODBC** allocates a buffer of a predetermined size. This size is the maximum size that a buffer can be. This limit, however, can be both queried and changed with the **GetMaxBufSize()** and **SetMaxBufSize()** methods:

```
$db->GetMaxBufSize();
$db->SetMaxBufSize( $Size );
```

The **SetMaxBufSize()** method takes one parameter ($Size), which represents the size in bytes that the limit of a buffer can be. Both functions return the number of bytes that the current buffer size is limited to.

Retrieving Data Type Information

Because each database has its own way of handling data, it can become quite difficult to know how to manage a particular data type. One database may require all text literals to be enclosed by single quotation marks, whereas another database may require double quotation marks. Yet the MONEY data type may require a prefix of some character such as the dollar sign ($) but nothing to terminate the literal value. Because a script using ODBC must be able to interact with any kind of database, it is important to be able to query the database to learn this information. This is where **GetTypeInfo()** comes in:

```
$db->GetTypeInfo( $DataType );
```

The first, and only, parameter is a data type. This value can be any one of the following data types:

SQL_ALL_TYPES	SQL_TYPE_DATE
SQL_CHAR	SQL_TYPE_TIME
SQL_VARCHAR	SQL_TYPE_TIMESTAMP
SQL_LONGVARCHAR	SQL_INTERVAL_MONTH
SQL_DECIMAL	SQL_INTERVAL_YEAR
SQL_NUMERIC	SQL_INTERVAL_YEAR_TO_MONTH
SQL_SMALLINT	SQL_INTERVAL_DAY
SQL_INTEGER	SQL_INTERVAL_HOUR
SQL_REAL	SQL_INTERVAL_MINUTE

SQL_FLOAT	SQL_INTERVAL_SECOND
SQL_DOUBLE	SQL_INTERVAL_DAY_TO_HOUR
SQL_BIT	SQL_INTERVAL_DAY_TO_MINUTE
SQL_BIGINT	SQL_INTERVAL_DAY_TO_SECOND
SQL_BINARY	SQL_INTERVAL_HOUR_TO_MINUTE
SQL_VARBINARY	SQL_INTERVAL_HOUR_TO_SECOND
SQL_LONGVARBINARY	SQL_INTERVAL_MINUTE_TO_SECOND

If successful, the **GetTypeInfo**() method returns TRUE and a dataset that describes the data type passed is returned; otherwise, the method returns FALSE.

Any resulting dataset will contain one row representing the specified data type. Use the **FetchRow**() and **DataHash**() methods to walk through the resulting dataset. Table 7.4 describes the columns of the dataset. If SQL_ALL_TYPES is specified as the data type, the dataset will contain a row for every data type that the data source is aware of.

Example 7.40 illustrates the use of the **GetTypeInfo**() method. Line 8 assigns the value SQL_ALL_TYPES to the variable $Type. This could be any valid data type constant from the preceding list. Notice the hack to obtain that value; referring to it as a method from the $db. This is necessary because the data type constants are not exported from the ODBC.PM file (unless you edit ODBC.PM and add the constants to the EXPORT list).

Table 7.4　Dataset returned by the **GetTypeInfo()** *method*

Column Name	Description
TYPE_NAME	Data source dependent name (such as MONEY). This is a text value.
DATA_TYPE	The SQL equivalent data type. This is an integer value.
COLUMN_SIZE	The maximum column size (in bytes) the data source supports for the data type.
LITERAL_PREFIX	The string used to prefix literal value. On most data sources, for example, a char data type would specify a single quotation mark (').
LITERAL_SUFFIX	The string used to terminate a literal value. On most data sources, for example, a char data type would specify a single quotation mark (').
CREATE_PARAMS	A comma-separated list of keywords required when specifying this data type (as described by the TYPE_NAME column). The order of these keywords is the order to specify. The DECIMAL data type, for example, would return "precision, scale". This indicates that when you specify a DECIMAL data type (as when creating a table), you must supply precision and scale values.

Constant	Description
NULLABLE	Whether the data type can be NULL. Possible values are SQL_NO_NULLS SQL_NULLABLE SQL_NULLABLE_UNKNOWN
CASE_SENSITIVE	Whether the data type is case sensitive. Possible values are SQL_TRUE SQL_FALSE
SEARCHABLE	This value illustrates how the data type is used in a WHERE clause.
UNSIGNED_ATTRIBUTE	Whether the data type is unsigned. Possible values: SQL_TRUE SQL_FALSE NULL (if not applicable, such as for a char type)
FIXED_PREC_SCALE	Whether the data type has a predefined fixed precision and scale such as MONEY. Possible values: SQL_TRUE SQL_FALSE.
AUTO_UNIQUE_VALUE	Whether the data type is auto-incrementing (such as a counter). Possible values: SQL_TRUE SQL_FALSE NULL (if this is not applicable, or if the data type is a character).
LOCAL_TYPE_NAME	A localized (based on language such as English or German) version of the data type's name.
MINIMUM_SCALE	The minimum scale of the data type, or NULL if it's not applicable.
MAXIMUM_SCALE	The maximum scale of the data type, or NULL if it's not applicable.

Example 7.40   *Determining how an SQL literal is handled using GetTypeInfo()*

```
01. use Win32::ODBC;
02. $DSN = "My DSN" unless $DSN = $ARGV[0];
03. if( ! ( $db = new Win32::ODBC( $DSN ) ) )
04. {
05.    print "Error: Could not connect to \"$DSN\".\n" . Win32::ODBC::Error();
06.    exit;
07. }
08. $Type = $db->SQL_ALL_TYPES;
09. if( $db->GetTypeInfo( $Type )
10. {
11.    my %Data;
12.    if( $db->FetchRow() )
13.    {
```

continues

Continued

```
14.     my (%Data) = $db->DataHash();
15.     print "$Data{TYPE_NAME} data is referred to as: " .
                "$Data{LITERAL_PREFIX}data$Data{LITERAL_SUFFIX}\n";
16.   }else{
17.     $Data{TYPE_NAME} = "---not supported---";
18.   }
19. }else{
20.   print "Can't retrieve type information: " . $db->Error() . "\n";
21. }
```

Processing More Results

If supported by your ODBC driver, you can submit multiple queries in one call to **Sql()**. If the query is successful, you would fetch and process the data from the first SQL statement and then call the **MoreResults()** method and repeat the process of fetching and processing the data:

```
$db->MoreResults();
```

The return value is either TRUE, indicating that another result set is pending, or FALSE, indicating that no more result sets are available. Example 7.41 demonstrates using **MoreResults()**.

Example 7.41   *Processing multiple result sets with MoreResults()*

```
01. use Win32::ODBC;
02. $db = new Win32::ODBC( "MyDSN" ) ¦¦ die "Error: " . Win32::ODBC::Error();
03. $Query = "SELECT * FROM Foo SELECT * FROM Bar";
04. if( ! $db->Sql( $Query ) )
05. {
06.   do
07.   {
08.     while( $db->FetchRow() )
09.     {
10.       my( %Data ) = $db->DataHash();
11.       ...process data...
12.     }
13.   } while ( $db->MoreResults );
14. }
15. $db->Close();
```

ODBC Transaction Processing

By default, most ODBC drivers are in *autocommit mode*. This means that when you perform an INSERT, UPDATE, DELETE, or some other query that modifies the database's data, the changes are made immediately; they are automatically *committed*. For some situations, however, this is unacceptable. Consider a CGI-based shopping cart script. Suppose this script will submit an order by adding information to a table in a database. Then it updates another table which describes the particular customer (the time he placed the order, what that order number was, and so forth). This is a case where autocommit mode can be a problem. Suppose that for some odd reason the second update fails. The script will tell the user that the order failed, but the first update has already been submitted, so the order is now queued to be processed.

This situation can be avoided by setting autocommit mode to off. When autocommit is off, you can submit as many modifications to the database as you want without having the modifications actually committed until you explicitly tell it to do so with the **Transact**() method:

```
$db->Transact( $Type )
```

The only parameter ($Type) is the type of transaction. This can be either of the following listed values:

- **SQL_COMMIT**. All modifications are committed and saved to the database.

- **SQL_ROLLBACK**. All modifications are ignored and the database remains as it was before any modifications were made to it.

The **Transact**() method will return a TRUE if the transaction was successful and a FALSE if it failed.

> **Note**
>
> *Not all ODBC drivers support the **Transact**() method. You can use the **GetFunctions**() method to check whether your driver does support it.*

Before using the **Transact**() method, you need to make sure that the autocommit mode is turned off. Example 7.42 describes how to turn autocommit off as well as how to use **Transact**().

Example 7.42 *Using the **Transact**() method*

```
01. use Win32::ODBC;
02. $db = new Win32::ODBC( "MyDSN" ) || die "Error: " . Win32::ODBC::Error();
03.
04. $db->SetConnectOption( $db->SQL_AUTOCOMMIT, $db->SQL_AUTOCOMMIT_OFF );
05. $Query = "INSERT INTO Foo (Name, Age) VALUES ('Joe', 31 )";
06. if( ! $db->Sql( $Query ) )
07. {
08.    ...process something that sets $bSuccess...
09.
10.    if( $bSuccess == 1 )
11.    {
12.       $db->Transact( $db->SQL_COMMIT );
13.    }
14.    else
15.    {
```

continues

Continued

```
16.      $db->Transact( $db->SQL_ROLLBACK );
17.   }
18. }
19. $db->Close();
```

Row Counts

Some SQL statements (UPDATE, INSERT, DELETE, and sometimes SELECT) return a value that represents the number of rows that were affected by the statement. Not all drivers support this. If it is supported, however, you can obtain this number with the **RowCount**() method:

```
$db->RowCount();
```

The return value is either the number of rows affected or -1 if the number of affected rows are not available. The -1 value can be a result of an ODBC driver that does not support this function (such as the Access driver).

Advanced Features of Win32::ODBC

So far, this chapter has discussed the simplest usage of the **Win32::ODBC** extension. This is how most scripts use it, however, **Win32::ODBC** provides access to most of the ODBC 2.0 API. This means that if you are familiar with ODBC you can control your interactions with databases using some pretty powerful features, including fetching rowsets, cursor control, and error processing.

Fetching a Rowset

Suppose that you submit a query to a SQL Server. This query will return 10,000 rows and you need to process each row. Every time you use the **FetchRow**() method, a command will be sent to the server requesting the next row. Depending on the network traffic, this can be quite a slow process because your ODBC driver must make 10,000 network requests and the SQL Server must respond with data 10,000 times. Add on top of this all the data required to package this network data up (such as TCP/IP headers and such) and you end up with quite a bit of network traffic. To top it all off, each time you fetch the next row your script must wait until the request has made it back from the server. All this can cause inefficient and slow response times.

If you could convince the ODBC driver to always collect 1,000 rows from the server each time a **FetchRow**() was called, the driver would only have to call to the server 10 times to request data.

This is where the concept of a rowset comes in. When you fetch rows, the ODBC driver really fetches what is known as a *rowset*. A rowset is just a collection of rows. By default a rowset consists of one row. Typically this configuration suffices, but it can be changed.

You can change the number of rows that make up a rowset by calling the **SetConnectOption**() method specifying the SQL_ROWSET_SIZE option. Once done, the advanced options of the **FetchRow**() method can be used to obtain a desired rowset. Then by just resetting the rowset size to 1, a regular call to **FetchRow**() will retrieve one row at a time. Refer to the next section, "Advanced Row Fetching," as well as Example 7.44 for more details.

Advanced Row Fetching

Although the **FetchRow**() method was described earlier, you need to revisit it now. A few parameters that can be passed into it need some explaining:

```
( $Result[, @RowResults] ) = $db->FetchRow( [$Row [, $Type]] );
```

If no parameters are passed in, the method will act as was described in the section titled "Processing the Results."

The first parameter ($Row) is a numeric value that indicates a row number.

The second value ($Type) indicates the mode in which the row number (the first parameter) will be used. The following list shows possible values for this parameter. If this parameter is not specified, the default value of SQL_FETCH_RELATIVE will be used.

- **SQL_FETCH_NEXT**. Fetch the next rowset (typically this is just one row) in the dataset. This will disregard the row value passed into **FetchRow**(). If this is the first **FetchRow**() to be called, this is the equivalent to SQL_FETCH_FIRST.

- **SQL_FETCH_FIRST**. Fetch the first rowset in the dataset.

- **SQL_FETCH_LAST**. Fetch the last rowset in the dataset.

- **SQL_FETCH_PRIOR**. Fetch the previous rowset in the dataset. If the cursor is positioned beyond the dataset's last row, this is equivalent to SQL_FETCH_LAST.

- **SQL_FETCH_ABSOLUTE**. Fetch the rowset that begins at the specified row number in the dataset. If the row number is 0, the cursor is positioned before the start of the result set (before physical row number 1).

- **SQL_FETCH_RELATIVE**. Fetch to rowset beginning with the specified row number in relation to the beginning of the current rowset. If row is 0, the current rowset will not change (instead, it will be updated).

- **SQL_FETCH_BOOKMARK**. This is not supported, but is included for completeness.

The **FetchRow()** method will move the rowset to the new position based on the row and mode parameter.

There are two return values for the **FetchRow()** method. The first indicates whether the fetch was successful. It will return a TRUE if successful; otherwise, it returns FALSE—unless, however, optional parameters are passed into the method. If this is the case, the first return value will be SQL_ROW_SUCCESS if successful; otherwise, it will be some other value.

The second return value is only returned if optional parameters are passed into the method. This second return value is an array of values. The array consists of a return value for each row fetched in the rowset. By default ODBC drivers use a value of 1 for the rowset size so the **FetchRow()** will only return one value (because it only fetches one row). If you change the rowset to greater than one, however, your return value array will reflect the number of rows in your rowset.

Each value in the returned array corresponds with one of the values in the following list:

- **SQL_ROW_SUCCESS**. The row was successfully fetched.

- **SQL_ROW_UPDATED**. The row has been updated since the last time it was retrieved from the data source.

- **SQL_ROW_DELETED**. The row has been deleted since the last time it was retrieved from the data source.

- **SQL_ROW_ADDED**. The row has been added since the last time it was retrieved from the data source.

- **SQL_ROW_ERROR**. The row was unable to be retrieved.

Note that it is possible to set your cursor to a type that will reflect alterations made to the data. Suppose, for example, that you are retrieving all the rows from a data source with "SELECT * FROM FOO". Your script then begins to retrieve rows one at a time. While your script is fetching row 100, another program has deleted row 195 from the database. When you get to row 195, your ODBC driver will try to fetch it even though it has been deleted. This is because when you execute your query the driver receives a list of row numbers which it will fetch. Because row number 195 was included in this list, the driver will try to fetch it when requested to, regardless of whether it has since been deleted. The driver will report the fact that it has been deleted by returning a value of SQL_ROW_DELETED in the return array.

For the following example, assume that the rowset size was set to ten so that every time you perform a **FetchRow()**, ten rows are actually fetched. When you fetch the rowset starting at 190, **FetchRow**() will return a ten-element array that will consist of the values shown in Example 7.43.

Example 7.43   *The returned row result array from **FetchRow**() indicating that the fifth row has been deleted*

```
01. $RowResults[0] == SQL_ROW_SUCCESS;
02. $RowResults[1] == SQL_ROW_SUCCESS;
03. $RowResults[2] == SQL_ROW_SUCCESS;
04. $RowResults[3] == SQL_ROW_SUCCESS;
05. $RowResults[4] == SQL_ROW_SUCCESS;
06. $RowResults[5] == SQL_ROW_DELETED;
07. $RowResults[6] == SQL_ROW_SUCCESS;
08. $RowResults[7] == SQL_ROW_SUCCESS;
09. $RowResults[8] == SQL_ROW_SUCCESS;
10. $RowResults[9] == SQL_ROW_SUCCESS;
```

Example 7.44 demonstrates how you can use the extended features of **FetchRow**() to jump ahead several rows in a result set.

Example 7.44   *Advanced and simple example of **FetchRow**()*

```
01. use Win32::ODBC;
02. $db = new Win32::ODBC( "MyDsn" ) ¦¦ die "Error: " . Win32::ODBC::Error();
03.
04.   # Prevent the cursor from closing automatically
05. $db->SetStmtCloseType( SQL_DONT_CLOSE );
06.
07.   # Change our cursor type to static (assuming the driver supports it)
08. $db->SetStmtOption( $db->SQL_CURSOR_TYPE, $db->SQL_CURSOR_STATIC );
09.
10. if( ! $db->Sql( "SELECT * FROM Foo" ) )
11. {
12.   if( ( $db->FetchRow( 9000, SQL_FETCH_ABSOLUTE ))[0] ==
            $db->SQL_ROW_SUCCESS )
13.   {
14.     do
15.     {
17.       my( %Data )= $db->DataHash();
18.       print "User: $Data{Name}\n";
19.     } while( $db->FetchRow() );
20.   }
21. }
22. $db->Close();
```

The operation in Example 7.44 can save one quite a bit of both time and network bandwidth (if the ODBC driver is talking to a network database server) because the first **FetchRow**() (line 12) will position the cursor to point at row 9,000 right away. The alternative would be to walk through the database one row at a time until it got to the nine thousandth row.

At this point, the column's data will be retrieved and printed for the rest of the remaining rows by using the simple **FetchRow**() method.

Managing Cursors

Those familiar with SQL will be happy to know that cursors are supported. If you have no idea what a cursor is, you probably don't need to be concerned about them. Cursors are beyond the scope of this book, so very little time will be spent on this topic. Several ODBC functions pertain to their use, however, and these are described in this section.

Basically, the cursor is an indicator that points to the current row in a given rowset. This is just like a cursor on a DOS window; it shows you where your current position in the DOS window is. The ODBC cursor just shows you where the current row is from which you will be retrieving data.

Win32::ODBC, by default, resets the state of all cursors automatically for you whenever you use the **Sql**() or any other method that returns rows of data (such as **GetTypeInfo**() and any of the cataloging functions). Whenever these methods are used, the current cursor is dropped—that is to say, it is destroyed and forgotten.

This automatic dropping can be a problem when you need to keep a cursor open or if you have named a cursor and need to retain its name. This handling of the cursor can be overridden by changing the statement close type with the following method:

```
$db->SetStmtCloseType( $CloseType[, $Connection ] );
```

The first parameter ($CloseType) is one of the close types documented in the following list.

- **SQL_CLOSE**. The current statement will not be destroyed, only the cursor. For all practical reasons, this is the same as SQL_DROP.

- **SQL_DROP**. The current statement is destroyed as well as the cursor.

- **SQL_DONT_CLOSE**. This will prevent the cursor from being destroyed anytime new data is to be processed.

- **SQL_UNBIND**. All bound columns buffers are unbound. This is of no use and is only included for completeness.

- **SQL_RESET_PARAMS**. All bound parameters are removed from their bindings. Because **Win32::ODBC** does not yet support parameter binding, this is of no use and is only included for completeness.

The optional second parameter ($Connection) is the connection number for an existing ODBC connection object. If this is empty, the current object is used. This is the object whose close type will be set.

The **SetStmtCloseType**() method will return a text string, indicating which close type is set on the object.

Yet another method that will enable you to retrieve the current close type on a connection object is as follows:

```
$db->GetStmtCloseType( [$Connection] );
```

The optional first parameter ($Connection) is an ODBC connection object number that indicates which object will be queried. If nothing is passed in, the current object is assumed.

Just like the **SetStmtCloseType**() method, **GetStmtCloseType**() will return a text string indicating which of the five values documented in the list for **SetStmtCloseType**() is the close type.

A connection's cursor can be dropped by force if you need to. This can be very handy if you have previously set its close type to SQL_DONT_CLOSE:

```
$db->DropCursor( [$CloseType] );
```

The first optional parameter ($CloseType) indicates how the cursor is to be dropped. Valid values are the same as documented for **SetStmtCloseType**(), with the exception of SQL_DONT_CLOSE; this value is not allowed. If no value is specified, SQL_DROP is assumed.

Note that this will not only drop the cursor, but also the current statement and any outstanding and pending result sets for the connection object.

All cursors that are created are given a name either by the programmer or by the ODBC driver. This name can be useful in queries and other SQL statements that allow you to use the cursor name such as "UPDATE table ... WHERE CURRENT OF cursor_name." To retrieve the cursor name, you use the **GetCursorName**() method:

```
$db->GetCursorName();
```

The method will return a text string that is the name of the cursor. If no cursor is defined, the method returns an undef.

If you want, you can name the cursor yourself. This may be necessary for stored procedures that require particular cursor names to be set:

```
$db->SetCursorName( $Name );
```

The first and only parameter ($Name) is the name of the cursor. Each ODBC driver defines the maximum length of it's cursor names but the ODBC API recommends not exceeding 18 characters in length.

If the cursor's name is successfully set, the method returns a TRUE; otherwise, it returns a FALSE.

> ### Note
>
> *A cursor's name will be lost when the cursor is reset or dropped. For this reason it is important that you set the statement close type to* SQL_DONT_CLOSE *before you set the cursor name. Otherwise, the moment the SQL query is generated the cursor will be destroyed and the name will be lost.* **Win32::ODBC** *closes cursors before executing SQL statements unless the close type is set to* SQL_DONT_CLOSE. *You can always force the cursor to be dropped with the* **DropCursor()** *method.*

Cloning ODBC Connections

ODBC connection objects do not share anything with each other. For example if you create two objects ($db1 and $db2), even from the same database, the two objects cannot communicate with each other. If $db1 has created a dataset with a named cursor $db2 can not access $db1's data. There is a way, however, for $db1 to talk with $db2, using cloning. When you *clone* a Win32::ODBC object you are creating a duplicate object. This cloned object talks with the same data source and for all practical matters is the same as the original object. Because these objects are separate and discrete from each other they can run separate queries and process results as if they were two totally separate connections.

The wonderful nature of cloned objects is that they can talk with each other. If one object issues a query that produces a dataset, the other object can use that dataset for its own query. Cloned objects are created using the **new** command:

```
new Win32::ODBC( $Object );
```

If you pass in another **Win32::ODBC** connection object rather than a DSN name, the object will be cloned—that is, another object will be created which shares the same connection to the database. In technical terms, the objects will share the same environment and connection handles although their statement handles will be unique.

This is used mostly in conjunction with cursor operations.

Error Processing

An ODBC error is an error generated by either the ODBC Manager or an ODBC driver. This is a number that refers to an error that occurred internally to ODBC. In practice this error is really only useful if you have an ODBC API manual or information on error numbers for a particular ODBC driver. The SQL state, however, is a standardized string that describes a condition that all ODBC drivers adhere to.

Retrieving Errors

Win32::ODBC tracks ODBC errors in two ways. The first way is that the module itself will always track the last ODBC error that occurred. The second way is that a particular ODBC connection object will track its own errors. You retrieve the error information by calling **Error()** either as an object method or as a module function:

```
Win32::ODBC::Error();
$db->Error();
```

If used as a module function (the first example), it will report the last error that the ODBC module had generated regardless of which connection was responsible for the error. If used as an object's method (the second example), however, the last error that the particular object generated will be reported.

When retrieving error information with the **Error()** method (or function), the results could be in one of two formats, depending upon the context of the assignment: as an array or as a text string in a scalar context.

Array Context

If a call were made to **Error()** in an array context:

```
@Errors = $db->Error();
```

the returning array, @Errors, would consist of the following elements:

```
( $ErrorNumber, $Tagged Text, $Connection Number, $SQL State)
```

Table 7.5 lists a description for each element.

Scalar Context

If a call were made to **Error()** in a scalar context:

```
$Error = $db->Error();
```

the result would resemble the following string:

```
"[Error Number] [Connection Number] [Tagged Text]"
```

Table 7.5 lists descriptions for these elements.

*Table 7.5   Fields returned by the **Error**() function and method*

Field	Description
Error Number	The actual error number as reported by ODBC (not too useful unless you have an ODBC API manual). This number may be specific to an ODBC driver, so it could have one meaning to an Oracle driver but another meaning to a Sybase driver. When an error occurs, there is always an ODBC-specific error number. This is different from the SQL State because it identifies an error that ODBC generated. This error is not an ISO standard, but instead it is an ODBC-specific error.
Tagged Text	The text description of the error. Either the ODBC Manager or the ODBC driver report this. This text is in a tagged format—that is, it identifies both the vendor and the component that generated the error. For example, the error text "[Microsoft][ODBC Microsoft Access 2.0 Driver] Unable to open database file" identifies that the Microsoft ODBC Access driver reported an error "Unable to open database file." The first tag is the vendor, and the second tag is the ODBC component that generated the error. Another example:[Microsoft][ODBC Manager] The data could not be retrieved because the database server is offline illustrates that the Microsoft ODBC Manager reported the error that the server is unavailable.
Connection Number	The number of the ODBC connection that generated the error. If there was no connection number, the number is left as an undef. Each **Win32::ODBC** object has an associated unique connection number. You can discover an ODBC connection object's connection number by calling the **Connection**() method.
SQLState	The SQL state of the error. This value complies with the ISO SQL-92 standard; hence a programmer can rely on it to represent a particular error condition regardless of which ODBC driver generated the error. It would be a good idea to invest in a book on ODBC so that the SQL state will make sense.

The SQL State

The current SQL state can be retrieved by using the **SQLState()** method:

```
$db->SQLState();
```

The value returned constitutes the last SQL state of the particular ODBC connection object. Because the SQL state represents the state of the connection and it is not driver specific (as the error number is), it is the same for all ODBC drivers. Any good book on the ODBC API will list all possible SQL state codes.

Summary

Interacting with databases is not a very difficult thing to do, but having to interact with several, potentially different, databases can cause nightmares because of a lack of conformity across them. The expectation of writing a Perl script to recognize all different types of databases is just too high to be realistic.

The ODBC API is commonly found on Win32 machines and it addresses this issue of database conformity. By using ODBC, a programmer can create huge scripts that will work with any database and can be easily transported from machine to machine.

The **Win32::ODBC** extension has provided thousands of CGI, administrative, and other types of scripts with access to ODBC. This extension provides a relatively thin layer of abstraction from the ODBC API that is ideal for anyone who is prototyping an application in Perl that will be programmed in C or C++ to access the ODBC API. Any coder who is familiar with the ODBC API will feel at home using this extension.

If a programmer is not familiar with ODBC, the extension hides most of the tedious work required so that the coder can focus on manipulating data and not worry about how to retrieve it.

You can also access ODBC data sources in other ways such as using the Perl DataBase Interface (DBI) which has a basic ODBC driver. Considering that the DBI ODBC extension exists on both Win32 and UNIX platforms, it is ideal for cross-platform scripts. Additionally the **Win32::OLE** extension (refer to Chapter 5) provides access into Microsoft's ActiveX Database Objects (ADO) and other COM-based ODBC implementations.

Chapter 8

Processes

Perl scripts are quite powerful and can do pretty much anything you need them to; at times, however, you need a separate application to process data or some other task for you—something that may be impractical or impossible for Perl to do itself. Perl supplies basic functions that will create such new processes. These functions were inherited from the UNIX world. These are quite powerful and helpful, but the Win32 platforms provide options for process creation that are not supported by the standard Perl process creation function.

This chapter investigates what is involved in creating a new process that makes use of the Win32 way of doing things. This chapter also looks at how to manage a process's priority, suspend state, and destruction.

In addition, this chapter looks at the difference between Perl file handles and Win32 handles. This is important to understand because some of the process creation functions have options that involve these handles.

The Win32 extensions used in this chapter include **Win32::AdminMisc** and **Win32::Process**.

The STD Handles

Perl makes use of what are known as the standard file handles: STDIN, STDOUT, and STDERR. Perl opens these file handles automatically when a script is started. When a script starts, for example, unless otherwise specified all output from a **print** command is automatically routed to STDOUT (standard output device). The following command:

```
print "Hello.\n";
```

is really the same as:

```
print STDOUT "Hello.\n";
```

If you do not specify a file handle to print to, STDOUT will be used. STDOUT is a special file handle, which by default, sends data to the standard output device–typically, the screen. The STDIN (standard input device) defaults to the keyboard, and STDERR (standard error device) defaults to the screen, just like STDOUT.

Perl is very good at enabling you to redirect these standard file handles to other file handles, files, sockets, and pipes. The Win32 API uses a different type of handle, however, one that can be inherited.

Handle Inheritance

The concept of handle inheritance warrants some explanation. When you open a file, bind to a socket, create a named pipe, connect to a remote Registry, or do anything in which you receive some sort of identifying object, your process has been given a handle. Simply stated, a handle is a number that represents something. When you open a file, for instance, the operating system returns to you a number. Any time you want to read from or write to that file, you must tell the operating system what that number is. In Perl, this number is hidden so that everything is a little easier for the programmer. From the debugger, you can dump the contents of your Perl file handle as demonstrated in Example 8.1. Notice that line 11 shows that the file handle DATA has a fileno (or file number) of 3. This number represents the open file.

Example 8.1   *Discovering a file's handle in the debugger*

```
01. C:\Perl\test>perl -d test.pl
02. Stack dump during die enabled outside of evals.
03.
04. Loading DB routines from perl5db.pl patch level 0.95
05. Emacs support available.
06. Enter h or `h h' for help.
07. main::(test.pl:2): open( DATA, "> stuff.txt" );
08.   DB<1> n
09. main::(test.pl:3): print DATA "Hello!\n";
10.   DB<1> X DATA
11. FileHandle(DATA) => fileno(3)
```

Processes can inherit Win32 handles. Notice that I am specifying Win32 handles and not Perl file handles; this is very important. When you create a new process you can tell the new process to inherit the handles that you have acquired in the current process (any open sockets, files, pipes, and so forth). If the new process you create is a Perl script, however, don't expect to be able to access those opened sockets and files you inherited. This is because a Perl file handle differs from a Win32 handle. You see, to open a file, Perl creates a file handle by asking the C language's runtime library to open the file. The C library, in turn, asks the operating system to open it. The Win32 API will return a handle (just a number that the OS associates with the open file), and the C library will store the handle into some data structure that it creates. A pointer to this structure will be returned to Perl, which puts this pointer into yet another structure. Perl will then associate a Perl file handle, one that the programmer specifies, with this structure.

Okay, so this is a bit technical, but the point is that a Win32 handle is not the same as a Perl file handle. Although a process can inherit Win32 handles, it does not help a Perl script much if it opens a file in one process and attempts to access the open file in another process because only the Win32 file handle (and not the Perl file handle) was inherited. The next section addresses this problem.

When managing Win32 processes, occasions arise when a Win32 file handle needs to be specified. Because this file handle is not the same as a Perl file handle, you need a way to obtain a Win32 file handle.

Retrieving Win32 Standard Handles

The **Win32::AdminMisc** extension provides the capability to discover the Win32 file handle for all three of the standard file handles that are opened by default. You can retrieve the Win32 standard handles by utilizing the **Win32::AdminMisc::GetStdHandle**() function:

```
$Handle = Win32::AdminMisc::GetStdHandle( $HandleName );
```

The first parameter ($HandleName) can be one of the following constants:

- **STD_INPUT_HANDLE.** The standard input handle (STDIN).

- **STD_OUTPUT_HANDLE.** The standard output handle (STDOUT).

- **STD_ERROR_HANDLE.** The standard error handle (STDERR).

If the **GetStdHandle**() function is successful, it returns a number that represents the Win32 handle. This value can be of importance for functions such as **Win32::AdminMisc::CreateProcessAsUser**(). If the **GetStdHandle**() function is not successful, it returns a 0.

Process Management

The Microsoft Visual C++ documentation defines a process as "an executing instance of an application. For example, when you double-click the Notepad icon, you start a process that runs Notepad." Processes have long been a necessity to Perl programmers, and the language reflects this by providing several commands that enable you to create processes:

- **System command.** system("program.exe");

- **Open command using piped output.** open(PROGRAM, "program.exe |");

- **Open command using piped input.** open(PROGRAM, "| program.exe");

- **Backticks.** @Output = `program.exe`;

Each of these commands enables you to launch a program. The problem with these, however, is that the new process cannot be controlled. If you run the code in Example 8.2, for instance, the Notepad program will start but the Perl script will not complete until you quit the Notepad program. The script will wait until the Notepad process terminates. This temporary pause means that your script will not be able to continue running while the new Notepad process ran. This can be more than just an inconvenience.

Example 8.2   *Creating a new process using the* **system**() *command*

```
$Program = "notepad.exe";
print "Running $Program...\n";
system( $Program );
print "Finished.\n";
```

This lack of simultaneity can be corrected by using the **start** command that is built in to the Windows NT and Windows 95 command processor. Using the **start** command creates the new process independently from the Perl script that spawned it. This means that the script can continue running and even end regardless of the state of the newly created process. Running the code in Example 8.3 will print `Running notepad.exe...` followed by `Finished.` and terminate. The Notepad program will start up in the meantime. You will notice that the Perl script is not tied in any way to the Notepad program, so when one ends it does not affect the other.

Example 8.3   *Starting an independently running process with the* **system**() *function*

```
$Program = "notepad.exe";
print "Running $Program...\n";
system( "start $Program" );
print "Finished.\n";
```

Creating a Process with Win32::Spawn()

Using the **start** command is the equivalent of using the **Win32::Spawn**() function. You can use either, but the **Spawn**() function will be just a little bit more efficient because it does not have to shell out to a command processor just to run each time. In addition to efficiency, the **Win32::Spawn**() function will return the process ID (PID) of the newly created process. This can be important if you want to later manage the new process. The syntax for the **Win32::Spawn**() function is as follows:

```
Win32::Spawn( $Program, $CommandLine, $PID );
```

The first parameter ($Program) is the path to the executable file that you are going to run. This can be a relative path, a full path, or a UNC. The full name of the executable, however, must be provided; you must use "notepad.exe" instead of simply using "notepad".

The second parameter ($CommandLine) is the command-line version of the program. This is a bit odd, but this must be a string that contains whatever you would enter on a command line to execute the process including both the program and any switches or command-line options. If you wanted to load a readme.txt file with Notepad, you would specify the path to notepad.exe as the first parameter and the second parameter would be "notepad readme.txt". The first part of this string does not *have* to be the program you run (for technical reasons beyond the scope of this book), but it should pertain to the environment of the new process. You could use "MyFootHurts readme.txt" as the second parameter, and it would work just as well. This is unusual but alas it is the way it is.

The third parameter ($PID) is set to the process ID of the process.

If the process is successfully created, a 1 will be returned; otherwise, a 0 is returned.

Example 8.4 illustrates proper implementation of the **Win32::Spawn**() method.

Example 8.4   *Creating a new process with **Win32::Spawn()***

```
01. use Win32;
02. $App = "notepad.exe";
03. $Cmd = "notepad readme.txt";
04. if( Win32::Spawn( $App, $Cmd, $Pid ) )
05. {
06.   print "$Cmd was created with the process ID $Pid.\n";
07. }
08. else
09. {
10.   print "Could not start $Cmd.\n";
11.   print "Error: " . Win32::FormatMessage( Win32::GetLastError() );
12. }
```

"This is all fine and good," you may be thinking, "but what if I need to control the new process?" Well, that is where Perl falls short. In the UNIX world, you could run ps to find the process ID of a process and then call a kill to terminate it. Likewise you could run the nice utility to change the priority that the process runs under, but this does not help us Win32 users. Sure, similar utilities are available such as tlist.exe and kill.exe, but you cannot guarantee (unlike our UNIX counterparts) that each machine on which you run your script will have these nonstandard utilities. This is where the **Win32::Process** extension comes in.

With the **Win32::Process** extension, you create a blessed **Win32::Process** object that contains several methods as described in the sections that follow.

When you create a new **Win32::Process** object, you are actually creating a new process that is a running program, as if you called the **system()** function. The real difference is that with the object you can manage the new process.

Creating a Controllable Process

Suppose that you wanted to create a new Notepad process. You could use the **Win32::Process::Create()** function:

```
Win32::Process::Create( $Process, $Program, $CommandLine, $Inherit, $Flags,
$Directory );
```

The first parameter ($Process) holds the process object that is created (if the creation is successful, that is). Note that whatever this parameter contains upon entry into the function is ignored.

The second parameter ($Program) is the path to the executable file that you are going to run. This is the same as the first parameter to the **Win32::Spawn()** function.

The third parameter ($CommandLine) performs the same role as the second parameter of the **Win32::Spawn()** function.

The fourth parameter ($Inherit) is a boolean value that specifies whether to inherit handles from the currently running process. A 1 means to inherit handles, and a 0 means to not inherit handles. This makes more sense if you read the section titled "Handle Inheritance."

The fifth and most exciting parameter ($Flags) describes how the new process should be created and how fast it should run. This parameter is created by logically OR'ing the constants found in Table 8.1 and *only one* priority constant from Table 8.2. The default creation flag action (if no constants from Table 8.1 are specified) will be to use the same console as the current process for input and output. The default priority class is normal.

Table 8.1   Process creation flag constants

Constant	Description
DEBUG_PROCESS	This tells the new process (and any child processes that it creates) that the process that is creating the new process (known as the debugger process) is debugging it. Anytime certain events take place in the new process or any of its children (known

Constant	Description
	as debuggees), the debugger process will be notified. This debugging has to do with Win32 programs and is not in any way related to the Perl debugger. Most Perl coders will never have a need to use this flag.
DEBUG_ONLY_THIS_PROCESS	Same as DEBUG_PROCESS except that only the new process is in the debug state. Child processes of the new process are not in the debug state. Like the DEBUG_PROCESS flag, most Perl coders will never have a need to use this flag.
CREATE_SUSPENDED	The new process is created, but does not run until it is told to do so with the **Resume**() method. This is very handy for synchronizing events. See the section titled "Suspending a Process" for more details.
DETACHED_PROCESS	If the process being created is a console application (that is, a program that uses a DOS-like window for output), it will be created without any console window. You would want to use this if the application does not need either input or output.
CREATE_NEW_CONSOLE	If the process being created is a console application, a new console window will be created. This new window will be used for input and output.
CREATE_NEW_PROCESS_GROUP	The new process will start a new process group. All processes in a process group will receive notification of certain events such as a Ctrl+C or Ctrl+Break. Now, before you get excited about this, you must know that to take advantage of this option you must access the Win32 API **GenerateConsoleCtrlEvent**() function. You can find this in the **Win32::Console** and **Win32::API** extensions.
CREATE_DEFAULT_ERROR_MODE	The new process is to use the default error mode. A discussion of a process's error mode is beyond the scope of this book, but if you are aware of what it is and how to use it, this flag will cause the new process to not inherit the current process's error mode.

continues

Table 8.1   Continued

Constant	Description
CREATE_SEPARATE_WOW_VDM	If the new process is a 16-bit Windows application (a program written for Windows 3.x), a separate virtual DOS machine will be used.
CREATE_UNICODE_ENVIRONMENT	Chances are that you will never have a need to use this, but if you used it, the new process would use Unicode characters for its environment variables.

Table 8.2   Process priority constants

Constant	Description
IDLE_PRIORITY_CLASS	The process runs only when the computer has nothing else to do—that is, when the system is idle.
NORMAL_PRIORITY_CLASS	The process runs as if it were a normal process.
HIGH_PRIORITY_CLASS	The process is given much more CPU time than other processes. This makes the process more responsive, but all other processes will suffer by slowing down. You should probably avoid using this.
REALTIME_PRIORITY_CLASS	The process is given as much CPU time as the operating system will allow. This makes all other processes slow down to a crawl. You should not use this unless you know what you are doing and have a real need for it.

Finally, the sixth parameter of the **Win32::Process::Create**() function ($Directory) specifies which directory the new process will use as its default directory.

You can see that this is much more complicated than the **Win32::Spawn**() function, but it gives you much more control. Example 8.5 demonstrates the **Create**() function.

Example 8.5   *Using the **Win32::Process::Create**() function*

```
01. use Win32::Process;
02.
03. $App = "c:\\windows\\notepad.exe";
04. $Cmd = "notepad readme.txt";
05. $bInherit = 1;
06. $Flags = CREATE_NEW_PROCESS;
07. $Dir = ".";
```

```
08. $Result = Win32::Process::Create( $Process,
09.                                    $App,
10.                                    $Cmd,
11.                                    $bInherit,
12.                                    $Flags,
13.                                    $Dir);
14. if( $Result )
15. {
16.   print "$Cmd has been created with a process ID of $Result.\n";
17. }else{
18.   print "Unable to start $Cmd.\n";
19.   print "Error: " . Win32::FormatMessage( Win32::GetLastError() );
20. }
```

Note

Security and the New Process. *It is interesting to note that the*
***Win32::Process::Create*()** *function will create a process by passing in*
NULL pointers for the process and thread security attributes. This means
that the process will be created with what is known as a default security
descriptor, which means that anyone can access, kill, and change the pri-
ority of the process—that is, there is no security placed on the process.

Killing a Process

If there is a need to terminate a process that you have created with
Win32::Process::Create(), you can use the **Kill**() method:

```
$Process->Kill();
```

This assumes that you have created a **Win32::Process** object called $Process.

The **Kill**() method makes use of the Win32 API's **TerminateProcess**() function,
which has a reputation of being pretty rough. When you force a termination
this way, the process is terminated but any DLLs that have been loaded are not
notified before they shut down. This prevents any last minute cleanup such as
writing data to files or removing any temporary files that may have been created. Generally speaking, you don't want to use this unless you have to (see
Example 8.6).

Example 8.6 *Killing a process*

```
01. use Win32::Process;
02.
03. $App = "c:\\perl\\bin\\perl.exe";
04. $Cmd = "perl c:\\perl\\test\\myscript.pl";
05. $bInherit = 1;
06. $Flags = CREATE_NEW_PROCESS;
07. $Dir = "c:\\perl\\test";
08. $Result = Win32::Process::Create( $Process,
09.                                    $App,
```

```
10.                              $Cmd,
11.                              $bInherit,
12.                              $Flags,
13.                              $Dir);
14. if( $Result )
15. {
16.   print "$Cmd has been created with a process ID of $Result.\n";
17.   print "Now killing the process...\n";
18.   $Process->Kill();
19.   print "Process has been killed!\n";
20. }else{
21.   print "The process $Cmd was not created!\n";
22.   print "Error: " . Win32::FormatMessage( Win32::GetLastError());
23. }
```

Suspending a Process

When you have created a process with **Win32::Process::Create**(), you may want to temporarily stop the process, or pause it. This is handy when you need to synchronize processes or if the process is some daemon like a Web server that needs to be temporarily paused. Suspending a process is performed with the **Suspend**() method:

```
$PrevTotal = $Process->Suspend();
```

What really happens when you use **Suspend**() is that the process's primary thread is put into a suspended state—that is, the thread is not given any CPU time. This results in the process just sitting there and not doing anything.

> ### Note
>
> *A thread is a dedication of CPU time to run a process. If you have multiple threads, you are requesting the CPU to not only multitask your process with other processes, but also multitask functions within your process as well. Having multiple threads in a process is similar to having multiple processes on an operating system. All Win32 applications have at least one thread, the so-called primary thread. This thread is the first (and for many applications the only) thread that is created.*

A process can be suspended multiple times. Each time it is suspended, an internal suspension counter is incremented by one. This can occur up to a limit that the Win32 kernel defines, which happens to be 127 (as of this writing, but with Windows 98 and NT 5.0 being released this may change). If you try to suspend a process more than 127 times, an error will occur. The return value of the **Suspend**() method is the total number of times the process has been suspended *before* the method was called. This means that when you use **Suspend**() it may return a 0; but this does not mean an error, it just means that previous to the method's call, the process had been suspended 0 times; it was not suspended. If you create a process with the CREATE_SUSPENDED flag, the process will be created and put into a suspended state automatically. This, of course, will increase the internal suspension counter to 1.

Because the suspension is performed by placing the primary thread of a process into a suspended state, it is possible that the process started other threads before you could call the **Suspend**() method. (This would not be the case if you created the process with the CREATE_SUSPENDED flag.) Therefore if you try to suspend some application, such as Microsoft Word, that uses multiple threads, don't be surprised if the application continues to run (or at least parts of it continue to run).

If the **Suspend**() method fails, it returns a -1 to indicate an error.

Example 8.7 demonstrates the use of the **Suspend**() method. In this case, a Web server process is created. Lines 18–28 cause the script to sleep for one minute and then check the number of network connections made to (and from) the machine. If the number is greater than 100 (actually 96 because NETSTAT.EXE outputs 4 lines of non-connection information), the Web server is suspended for two minutes—long enough for the connections to time out.

This example is not very practical, but it does illustrate how the **Suspend**() (and **Resume**()) method works.

Resuming a Suspended Process

When a process has been suspended—that is, the internal suspension counter is greater than 0—the only way to take it out of its suspended state is to use the **Resume**() method:

```
$PrevTotal = $Process->Resume();
```

By calling this method, you are going to decrement the internal suspension counter for the primary thread of your process. When this internal counter becomes 0, your process will continue to run where it left off. If you have called the **Suspend**() method five times, you must call the **Resume**() method five times before the process resumes execution (the exception is if you created the process with the CREATE_SUSPENDED flag, which means you would have to call **Resume**() six times).

Resume() will return the *previous* number of suspensions before the method was invoked. Therefore if it returns a 1, you know that the process is no longer suspended. If there is an error, it will return -1.

It is possible for another application to suspend your process without your knowledge. Therefore calling **Resume**() may not cause the process to leave the suspended state. If your script needs to indeed resume a suspended process, it is best to call **Resume**() until the return value is 1. This indicates that the previous

suspend call to the process was 1, so your **Resume()** call decremented the suspension state to 0. Line 26 of Example 8.7 illustrates calling **Resume()** until it
returns a value that is not greater than 1.

Example 8.7   *Suspending and resuming a process*

```
01. use Win32::Process;
02.
03. $App = "c:\\webserver\\webserver.exe";
04. $Cmd = "webserver 192.168.1.10";
05. $bInherit = 1;
06. $Flags = CREATE_NEW_PROCESS;
07. $Dir = ".";
08. $Result = Win32::Process::Create( $Process,
09.                                   $App,
10.                                   $Cmd,
11.                                   $bInherit,
12.                                   $Flags,
13.                                   $Dir);
14. if( $Result )
15. {
16.   print "$Cmd has been created with a process ID of $Result.\n";
17.   $Continue = 100;
18.   while( $Continue-- )
19.   {
20.     sleep( 60 );
21.     my @Output = `netstat`;
22.     if( scalar @Output > 100 )
23.     {
24.       $Process->Suspend();
25.       sleep( 2 * 60 );
26.       while( $Process->Resume() > 1 ){};
27.     }
28.   }
29.   $Process->Kill();
30. }else{
31.   print "Unable to start $Cmd.\n";
32.   print "Error: " . Win32::FormatMessage( Win32::GetLastError() );
33. }
```

Waiting for a Process to End

At times, you will want to start a process and then wait until the process is
over before continuing your Perl script. This is why the **Wait()** method exists:

```
$Process->Wait( $TimeOut );
```

The first parameter ($TimeOut) is a timeout value. This value is in milliseconds
and represents the length of time in which your script is willing to wait for the
process to terminate. If it does not terminate by the determined time, your
script continues processing regardless of whether the process has terminated. If

this parameter is the constant INFINITE, your script will wait forever, or until you power off your machine.

The **Wait**() method returns a 1 if the process has terminated while you were waiting; otherwise, it returns a 0, meaning that the process is still running but the **Wait**() method has exhausted the timeout value.

Process Priority

Because Win32 is a multitasking platform, the CPU (or CPUs if you have a multiprocessor box) runs one process for a specific duration of time and then moves on to run the next process. This continues until the CPU has spent a bit of time running each process, at which time it then repeats this pattern from the beginning of the process list. This way each process runs just as much as the others, giving the illusion that the processes are all running simultaneously. At least this is what you generally believe is happening.

In Win32, each process has a priority classification. This classification tells the operating system how responsive the process is, therefore clarifying how much attention to give it. Typically speaking, most processes are given a normal priority. Some processes may not need that much attention, however, so they can have a lower priority and require less attention from the CPU. A Web server needs to respond to incoming requests, for example, so it needs a fairly responsive class (like NORMAL_PRIORITY_CLASS or maybe even HIGH_PRIORITY_CLASS). A screen saver needs to only monitor whether the user input has input anything before it kicks in. With such monitoring, there is no need for the screen saver to be very responsive; therefore it could have the IDLE_PRIORITY_CLASS class.

Priorities are divided into four classes, as shown in Table 8.3. After a process is set to a priority class, this generally tells you how responsive the process is. All new processes created without any specified priority class default to NORMAL_PRIORITY_CLASS with one exception: If a process that has a priority class of IDLE_PRIORITY_CLASS creates a child process, that child will also be of IDLE_PRIORITY_CLASS.

Table 8.3   List of priority classes a process can have

Priority class	Description
IDLE_PRIORITY_CLASS	The process is given CPU time only when the system is idle—that is, nothing else is really going on. Even when you have several applications running, there is still idle CPU time.
NORMAL_PRIORITY_CLASS	This is the class that a process becomes by default (if no other priority is specified in

continues

Table 8.3   Continued

Priority class	Description
	the creation flags with a call to **Win32::Process::Create**(). When you run an application by double-clicking its icon, this is the class it runs under.
HIGH_PRIORITY_CLASS	A process with this priority class is much more responsive than the idle or normal classes. Any process running under this priority causes the other processes to noticeably slow down. Use this sparingly.
REALTIME_PRIORITY_CLASS	This is a special class that takes up so much CPU attention that it can cause some problems, such as rendering other processes from finishing I/O in a timely manner (hence the potential for data loss). This class was designed for tasks that are very short in duration and that need to not be interrupted during their execution. A user needs to have a special privilege (Increase Scheduling Priority) to set this priority class; typically administrators have this.

Getting a Process's Priority

Retrieving the current priority class of a process is fairly simple, you use the **GetPriorityClass**() method of your **Win32::Process** object:

```
$Process->GetPriorityClass( $Priority );
```

The variable you pass in will be set to the actual priority class that the process runs under. This value will reflect one of the constants in Table 8.3. There is a trick, however, to obtaining the value. The value is returned as a packed character—that is, it is converted from the C long variable type to a Perl string. Example 8.8 shows how to unpack the value. In the core distribution's LibWin32 library and in the new release, this return value is already unpacked.

The **GetPriorityClass**() method will return a 1 if it successfully retrieved the priority class; otherwise, it will return a 0 to indicate that it failed.

Example 8.8 shows how the **GetPriorityClass**() method is used. Notice that line 37 needs to exist only if you are not using LibWin32 or Perl 5.005. Lines 22 and 26 both call a subroutine called **GetPriority**(), which in turn calls **GetPrioritClass**()in line 34 and returns the priority class name. The process's priority is also changed in line 24.

Example 8.8 *Determining the priority class for a process*

```
01. use Win32::Process;
02. %Class = (
03.    Win32::Process::IDLE_PRIORITY_CLASS     => "IDLE",
04.    Win32::Process::NORMAL_PRIORITY_CLASS   => "NORMAL",
05.    Win32::Process::HIGH_PRIORITY_CLASS     => "HIGH",
06.    Win32::Process::REALTIME_PRIORITY_CLASS => "REALTIME"
07. );
08. $App = "c:\\windows\\notepad.exe";
09. $Cmd = "notepad readme.txt";
10. $bInherit = 1;
11. $Flags = CREATE_NEW_PROCESS;
12. $Dir = ".";
13. $Result = Win32::Process::Create( $Process,
14.                                   $App,
15.                                   $Cmd,
16.                                   $bInherit,
17.                                   $Flags,
18.                                   $Dir);
19. if( $Result )
20. {
21.    print "$Cmd has been created with a priority of ";
22.    print GetPriority( $Process ), "\n";
23.    print "Changing priority to IDLE_PRIORITY_CLASS...\n";
24.    $Process->SetPriorityClass( IDLE_PRIORITY_CLASS );
25.    print "Now process has a priority of ";
26.    print GetPriority( $Process ), "\n";
27. }
28.
29. sub GetPriority
30. {
31.    my( $Proc ) = @_;
32.    my $PriorityClass = "Unknown";
33.    my $Prority;
34.    if( $Proc->GetPriorityClass( $Priority ) )
35.    {
36.        # Next line not needed with libwin32 or Perl 5.005
37.        $Priority = unpack( "c", $Priority );
38.        $PriorityClass = $Class{$Priority};
39.    }
40.    return( $PriorityClass );
41. }
```

Setting a Process's Priority

Just as you can retrieve a process's priority, you can also set it using the
SetPriorityClass() method:

```
$Process->SetPriorityClass( $Priority );
```

The parameter you pass in ($Priority) is one of the constants listed in
Table 8.3.

If the **SetPriorityClass()** method is successful, it returns a 1; otherwise, it returns 0 to indicate a failure.

Refer to Example 8.8 and its explanation in the "Getting a Process's Priority" section.

Creating a Process as Another User

There is yet another way to create a process: creating one as another user. The **Win32::AdminMisc** extension has a function that does just that, **CreateProcessAsUser()**. This will run an application using the security credentials of another user providing the process with the security clearance granted to the specified user. This is how many services such as Microsoft's Internet Information Service (IIS) provide user-specific permissions.

There are a few prerequisites to use this function:

- The user account that calls this function must have the following privileges (these can be assigned to a user in the User Manager program):
  SE_ASSIGNPRIMARYTOKEN_NAME (Replace a process level token)
  SE_INCREASE_QUOTA_NAME (Increase quotas)

- A call to **Win32::AdminMisc::LogonAsUser()** (which is covered in Chapter 9) must precede this function (otherwise the new process will be created using the current user).

- It can only be run on Windows NT because only NT supports impersonation and creating processes while impersonating another user.

> *Note*
>
> *If you are using Microsoft's Internet Information Server (IIS) 4.0, you will notice that the service uses an account such as IUSER_<computername> (where <computername> is your computer's network name) to anonymously access Web pages. This means that when a user tries to read a Web page without specifying a userid and password, the Web server service will log on as IUSER_<computername> and access the Web page. If the Web page requested is a CGI script, the script will run under the IUSER_<computername> account. (Refer to Chapter 9 for more information on logging on as another user or impersonation.)*
>
> *If a user supplies a valid userid and password when accessing a CGI script, the Web service will first log on as the user. If the logon is successful, it will create the CGI script using the same method that CreateProcessAsUser() uses.*

You can choose an entire host of options if you want to enhance the process:

```
Win32::AdminMisc::CreateProcessAsUser( $Application [, $DefaultDirectory] [,
%Config ] );
```

The first parameter ($Application) is the application (and any parameters that need to be passed into it) that you want to run. If you wanted to run Notepad and have it load a file, for example, you could pass in the string "Notepad.exe c:\\temp\\readme.txt".

Note

The second and third parameters are optional. You can specify either one or both. It does not matter which one you use; but if you use both, the order is important.

The second, optional, parameter ($DefaultDirectory) is the default directory that the application will use.

The third, optional, parameter (%Config) is a hash of configuration information. Notice that this is not a reference to a hash but a hash itself. This means that you could, instead, replace the hash with a series of hash-like associations such as this:

```
"Xsize" => 200, "Ysize" =>50, ...
```

The configuration hash can contain keys and values listed in Table 8.4.

Table 8.4   The keys and values of the %Config *hash when using* **Win32::AdminMisc::CreateProcessAsUser()**

Key/Value	Description
Title	The title of the process's window. This is what will be displayed in the title bar. This applies only to console-based applications.
Desktop	A virtual desktop. Don't include this in your %Config hash unless you know what you are doing; otherwise, the process will attempt to be created in a "virtual" desktop. The default is "winsta0\default".
X	The X coordinate of the upper-left corner of the process's window (in pixels).
Y	The Y coordinate of the upper-left corner of the process's window (in pixels).
Xsize	The width of the process's window (in pixels).
Ysize	The height of the process's window (in pixels).

continues

Table 8.4   Continued

Key/Value	Description
Xbuffer	Number of chars wide the buffer should be. This only applies to console-based applications.
Ybuffer	Number of chars high the buffer should be. This only applies to console-based applications.
Fill	The color to fill the window. This only applies to console-based applications. Table 8.6 lists possible values. These values can be logically OR'ed together.
Priority	The priority to run the process under. It can use one of the constants defined in Table 8.3.
Flags	Flags specifying process startup options. The list of possible values are defined in Table 8.1 and can be logically OR'ed together.
ShowWindow	State of the process's window during startup. Table 8.5 lists possible values.
StdInput, StdOutput, StdError	Specifies which handle to use for standard STDIN, STDOUT, and STDERR. If one of these is specified, *all* must be specified. You can use **Win32::AdminMisc::GetStdHandle()** to retrieve the current Win32 standard handles. Refer to the section titled "The STD Handles."
Inherit	Specifies to inherit Win32 file handles.
Directory	Specifies a default directory. This is the same attribute as the $DefaultDirectory. You can use this instead of passing a string in as the second parameter to **CreateProcessAsUser()**.

Table 8.5 lists the window state constants as specified by the ShowWindow key. Some of these are listed for the sake of Win32 API completeness, but do not have any intrinsic value with current extension functions.

Table 8.5   List of window state constants

Constant	Description
SW_HIDE	The process is created but never shown because the window is hidden.
SW_MAXIMIZE	The process starts with its initial window maximized.
SW_MINIMIZE	The process starts with its initial window minimized.
SW_RESTORE	The process starts with its initial window in the state that it was designed to be.
SW_SHOW	When the process is created, it is shown—that is, made visible. This was provided for completeness with the Win32 API and does not have any value with the **CreateProcessAsUser()** function, because an application, when started, is typically visible to begin with.
SW_SHOWDEFAULT	Not applicable for the **CreateProcessAsUser()**function.
SW_SHOWMAXIMIZED	Same as SW_MAXIMIZE.
SW_SHOWMINIMIZED	Same as SW_MINIMIZE.
SW_SHOWMINNOACTIVE	The created process is created in the minimized state, and the focus is not taken away from other processes.
SW_SHOWNOACTIVATE	The process is created, but it should not take the focus away from other processes.
SW_SHOWNORMAL	The process is displayed in the normal state.

The values in Table 8.6, as specified by the Fill key, can be logically OR'ed together to make a composite color. For example, BACKGROUND_RED ¦ BACKGROUND_BLUE ¦ BACKGROUND_GREEN ¦ FOREGROUND_BLUE ¦ FOREGROUND_INTENSITY will result in a white background (red and green and blue) with bright-blue characters (foreground).

Table 8.6   Console application color constants

Constant	Description
BACKGROUND_RED	The color of the background will have a red component.
BACKGROUND_BLUE	The color of the background will have a blue component.
BACKGROUND_GREEN	The color of the background will have a green component.
BACKGROUND_INTENSITY	The background will be intensified (bright).
FOREGROUND_RED	The foreground text will have a red component.

continues

Table 8.6   Continued

Constant	Description
FOREGROUND_GREEN	The foreground text will have a green component.
FOREGROUND_BLUE	The foreground text will have a blue component.
FOREGROUND_INTENSITY	The foreground text will be intensified (bright).

Note

*Any process you run that requires use of the impersonated user's personal Registry settings will not function correctly. This is because the Win32 **LogonAsUser**() function that provides impersonation does not load the impersonated user's profile and Registry hive. If you need to access program settings and such you should have your script load the Registry after you successfully impersonate the user. You can use the **Win32::Registry** extension to do this.*

Case Study: Running Applications as Another User

Suppose that you are an administrator and you sometimes have to log on to your machine as another user to test for security permissions and such. You can log off of your workstation and log on as that user, but this would require you to close all your applications. Assume for the sake of argument that your work habits are like mine, so you have 50 or so windows open all running different, seemingly important, processes. This makes logging off a bit undesirable.

You decide to let Win32 Perl help you out of this dilemma, so you use a Perl script that will impersonate the user and run a program as that user. The script in Example 8.9 provides this functionality.

Example 8.9   *Running an application as another user*

```
01. use Win32::AdminMisc;
02.
03. if( $#ARGV < 0 )
04. {
05.   die "Not enough arguments";
06. }
07.
08. ($Domain) = ( $ARGV[0] =~ /(.*?)\\.*?$/ );
09. ($User) = ( $ARGV[0] =~ /([^\\]*?)$/ );
10. $Password = $ARGV[1];
11. $Process = $ARGV[2];
12.
13. if( ! $ARGV[1] )
14. {
```

```
15.   print "Enter Password:";
16.   $Password = <STDIN>;
17.   chop $Password;
18. }
19.
20. print "\nStarting \"$Process\" as $User in the \U\"$Domain\"\
    E domain...\n\n";
21.
22. if( Win32::AdminMisc::LogonAsUser($Domain,
                                      $User,
                                      $Password,
                                      LOGON32_LOGON_INTERACTIVE ) )
23. {
24.   $LogonUser = Win32::AdminMisc::GetLogonName();
25.   print "Successfully logged on as $LogonUser.\n";
26.   print "\nLaunching $Process...\n";
27.   $Result = Win32::AdminMisc::CreateProcessAsUser(
28.              $Process,
29.              "Flags" => CREATE_NEW_CONSOLE,
30.              "XSize" => 640,
31.              "YSize" => 400,
32.              "X" => 200,
33.              "Y" => 175,
34.              "XBuffer" => 80,
35.              "YBuffer" => 175,
36.              "Show" => SW_MINIMIZE,
37.              "Title" => "Title: $User" . "'s $Process program",
38.              "Fill" => BACKGROUND_BLUE |
39.                        FOREGROUND_RED |
40.                        FOREGROUND_BLUE |
41.                        FOREGROUND_INTENSITY |
42.                        FOREGROUND_GREEN,
43.                 );
44.   if( $Result )
45.   {
46.     print "Successful! The new processes PID is $Result.\n";
47.   }else{
48.     print "Failed.\n\tError: ", Error(), "\n";
49.   }
50. }else{
51.   print "Failed to logon.\n\tError: ", Error(), "\n";
52. }
53.
54. sub Error
55. {
56.   return Win32::FormatMessage( Win32::GetLastError() );
57. }
```

To use the script in Example 8.9, my account has to be granted the following privileges (their Win32 API equivalent names are also shown in parenthesis):

- The assign primary token privilege (SE_ASSIGNPRIMARYTOKEN_NAME)

- The increase quotas privilege (SE_INCREASE_QUOTA_NAME)

I may typically run this command as

```
perl runas.pl mydomain\JOEL JOELSPASSWORD "cmd"
```

or

```
perl runas.pl JOEL JOELSPASSWORD "cmd"
```

Notice that in the first example the domain is specified and in the second one no domain is specified (so it defaults to the primary domain). These examples will attempt to log on as JOEL with the password JOELSPASSWORD. If the logon is successful then an attempt is made to run the CMD application. If all goes well, a DOS box will appear that has the security privileges of the user JOEL. You can access files that only that user account is allowed.

Summary

Win32 processes can be quite simple to create as with the **Win32::Spawn()** function or as complex as **Win32::AdminMisc::CreateProcessAsUser()**. As these functions become more complex, so do their features and capabilities. It is important to note that although each of the process-creating functions do practically the same thing, they provide radically different features.

The **Win32::Spawn()** function enables you to create a new process quickly and without much fuss. After the process is created, however, you cannot do much with it.

The **Win32::Process::Create()** function enables you to create a new process, but it takes a bit more understanding of how Win32 operates. The benefit, however, is that you can control the new process by using the various **Win32::Process** package's methods.

The **Win32::AdminMisc::CreateProcessAsUser()** function can be very easy to use or very complex to use, depending on what you want it to be. The benefit of this, of course, is that it runs processes as another user (quite beneficial at times).

Chapter 9

Console, Sound, and Administrative Win32 Extensions

This chapter covers a few commonly used extensions that have remarkable practicality for an administrator. This chapter covers functionality from the following extensions:

- **Win32::Console**
- **Win32::Sound**
- **Win32::API**
- **Win32**
- **Win32::AdminMisc**

Consoles

Win32 platforms support the concept of a *console*. Every Win32 Perl programmer is familiar with consoles; he just may not be aware of his familiarity. A console is a chunk of memory that Win32 reserves (called a console buffer) that is bound to a window that displays the contents of the buffer. A program can fill this chunk of memory with characters (and specify the color of the characters). An application binds a console buffer to the console that you see as the output text window of the program. When Perl executes a print command and you see the results on your screen, you are really seeing the output being sent to a console buffer and displayed by the console window. Consoles are created by requesting the Win32 OS to allocate one. Any application can request a console to be allocated for it, even GUI-based Windows applications (imagine something like MS Word with a DOS-like console window).

When an application allocates (creates) a console, three buffers are automatically created: one for STDIN, one for STDOUT, and one for STDERR. The buffer associated with STDOUT is displayed by default. In the case of a DOS box or console-based application (like perl.exe), a console is automatically allocated, so there is no need for it to request Win32 to allocate the console.

An application (even a console-based one) can destroy its console and reallocate one later. No real benefit accrues by doing this, but it indeed can be done. An application can only have one console associated with it; so if it attempts to allocate more than one console, all requests after the first will fail.

This may sound just like a DOS box because every DOS box has a console and a console buffer associated with it. This means that when you run a Perl program and a window appears for input and output, Win32 has automatically created a console buffer and bound input and output from the Perl script to it.

> **Note**
>
> *It is important to know that an application can have any number of console buffers, but only one of them can be displayed at any given time. Additionally you can change which buffer is displayed at any time. Displaying a different console buffer, however, does not change which buffer is considered to be the standard output device. This means that if you create a buffer and display it, all your print statements that are dumped to* STDOUT *will go to the original buffer and not to the currently displayed buffer.*

In these days of GUI environments, the Win32 console does not get much attention, but it can be remarkably powerful. To output data to a console is much easier than creating and managing GUI-based windows. Quick development of software can benefit from the **Win32::Console** extension.

All processes can have any number of console buffers associated with them, but only one can be displayed at any given time. This enables you to allocate several consoles to store information and display whichever one is needed at a specific time. You could write a server application that accepts incoming named pipes or sockets, for example. If a message comes in from a computer belonging to upper management, it could be stored in the management buffer. User messages could be stored in the user buffer. Messages from the system (like computer error messages) could be stored in the system buffer. Your server process could enable you to switch between each of these consoles to be displayed.

> **Tip**
>
> *Win32 defines two separate constants that represent the standard input and output devices:*
>
> ```
> CONIN$
> CONOUT$
> ```
>
> *These can both be used when opening a file. For example:*
>
> ```
> open( INPUT, "< CONIN\$" ) || die;
> $In = <INPUT>;
> print "You typed '$In'\n";
> close( INPUT );
> ```
>
> *I cannot think of a reason why you would want to use these instead of using* STDIN *and* STDOUT, *but nonetheless, they exist.*

Creating and Destroying a Console

If a Perl script needs to create a console, it can call the **Alloc()** function:

```
Win32::Console::Alloc();
```

The function takes no parameters, and if successful it will allocate a console that can then display a console buffer. Generally speaking, a Perl script will never have a need to call this method because starting Perl itself automatically creates a console.

The **Alloc()** function will fail if the process already has a console allocated—a process can have only one console attached to it. If the method succeeds, it returns a TRUE value (non-zero) and returns FALSE (actually undef) if it fails.

> **Tip**
>
> *When you create a process with the* DETACHED_PROCESS *flag (see Chapter 8, "Processes"), it is created without any console allocated. If the process is a Perl script, it will have no way to output data to the screen. If it needs to have a console, you can always create one with the **Alloc()** method. If a script uses this, however, it should destroy the console with the **Free()** method before it terminates.*

If a console has been allocated (or created), it can be destroyed (or freed) using the **Free()** function:

```
Win32::Console::Free();
```

The **Free()** function takes no parameters and will destroy the console attached to the process. A script can then re-allocate a new console if need be.

Most Perl programs will never use this or the **Alloc**() method. But if one does, it can expect that a non-zero TRUE value will be returned on success in addition to destroying the console. A FALSE value (undef) is returned on error.

Both **Alloc**() and **Free**() can be run as methods of a console object, but it is not advised. Consoles are not related to buffers, but instead buffers are related to consoles. It is important to make this distinction between a buffer and console. The console is just the window that displays the contents of a console buffer. By destroying the console (the window), you are not destroying any of your buffers (except the STDIN/STDOUT/STDERR created automatically by the console).

Alloc() and **Free**() can be very handy if you are writing a Perl script that will run as a service that needs to display information. Services generally do not have consoles allocated for them by default. Example 9.1 illustrates how a script may allocate a console and free it as well.

It is interesting to note that console buffers exist after you **Free**() your console and then **Alloc**() another one. It seems that they are not dependable, however. (It appears as if buffers start to overlap each other.) It is best to close all your buffers when you **Free**() your console and re-create them if you **Alloc**() another console. Example 9.1 shows in line 12 that the buffer is **undef**'ed. This causes Perl to call the buffer object's **DESTROY**() method, which, in turn, causes the buffer to be freed. In this example, line 12 is not needed because the $Buffer object will fall out of scope (at the end of the script), and hence be automatically **undef**'ed.

Example 9.1   *Creating and destroying consoles*

```
01. use Win32::Console;
02.
03.   # Create a console buffer
04. $Buffer = new Win32::Console();
05.
06.   # This will fail if a console already exists.
07. Win32::Console::Alloc();
08. $Buffer->Write( "This is being displayed in the console window!\n" );
09.
10.   # Destroy any allocated console.
11. Win32::Console::Free();
12. undef $Buffer;
```

Creating Console Buffers

Creating consoles is fairly easy; you make a new **Win32::Console** object two separate ways:

```
$Console = new Win32::Console( $Handle );
$Console = new Win32::Console( [ $AccessMode [, $ShareMode ] ] );
```

In the first form, the only parameter is one of the handles listed in Table 9.1. This is used to create an object that can be used to gather input or output to the current input and output devices.

Table 9.1   The standard device handles

Handle	Description
STD_OUTPUT_HANDLE	The standard output device (typically the screen).
STD_ERROR_HANDLE	The standard error device (typically the screen).
STD_INPUT_HANDLE	The standard input device (typically the keyboard).

The second form requires two separate parameters. The first parameter ($AccessMode) specifies the access mode for the console, and is optional. This mode determines how the console will be used, whether for input or output or both. This parameter can be a combination of the constants listed in Table 9.2. These constants can be logically OR'ed together. If nothing is specified for this parameter, the default value of GENERIC_READ | GENERIC_WRITE will be used.

Table 9.2   Console access mode constants

Constant	Description
GENERIC_READ	Provides read access to the console. This allows you to read data from the console.
GENERIC_WRITE	Provides write access to the console. This allows you to write data to the console.

The second parameter ($ShareMode) is optional and specifies the share mode of the console. This determines how your buffer can be accessed by other processes and Win32 file operations. Table 9.3 lists the constants that can be used. These constants can be logically OR'ed together.

Table 9.3   Console share mode constants

Constant	Description
FILE_SHARE_READ	Other processes can access the buffer for the purpose of reading data.
FILE_SHARE_WRITE	Other processes can access the buffer for the purpose of writing data to it.

Normally sharing is not an issue with Perl scripts because they do not have access to the Win32 functions that would allow them to access such buffers from other processes. It is possible, however, that you could write a non-Perl application or a Perl extension that accesses these buffers. If this parameter is not supplied, it defaults to use FILE_SHARE_READ | FILE_SHARE_WRITE.

The **Console**() function is used to create either a new console buffer (the second form of the function) or to return the console buffer for a standard device (the first form of the function). Example 9.2 shows how these buffers can be allocated and used. Just as in Example 9.1, the last two lines (15 and 16) are not necessary; they are only there to illustrate a proper way of closing the buffers. Because the end of the script causes the $Buffer and $Out objects to fall out of scope, they are automatically **undef**'ed.

Example 9.2   *Creating and manipulating console buffers*

```
01. use Win32::Console;
02. $Out = new Win32::Console( STD_OUTPUT_HANDLE ) || die;
03. $Buffer = new Win32::Console() || die;
04. $Buffer->Write( "This is my nifty display buffer\n" );
05. $Buffer->Display();
06. $Buffer->Write( "We will count to 10 then go back to the original
    display.\n" );
07. for $Temp ( 1 .. 10 )
08. {
09.   $Buffer->Write( "$Temp\n" );
10. }
11. $Buffer->Write( "Hit the enter key to continue...\n" );
12. $In = <STDIN>;
13. $Out->Display();
14. print "Welcome back to the original display!\n";
15. undef $Buffer;
16. undef $Out;
```

Notice that in Example 9.2, line 3 creates a console buffer object for a new buffer ($Buffer) and line 2 creates a console buffer object for the standard output device ($Out). The only reason for making the $Out object is so that we can display it in the end of the script. Otherwise, there would be no way to display the standard output buffer.

If the new Win32::Console() call is successful, it returns a Perl object that represents the particular console buffer. If the function fails, it returns a FALSE value (undef to be exact). When a buffer is no longer needed, it is best to destroy it with the **undef** command so that it is removed from memory:

```
undef $Buffer;
```

Alternatively, you can use the **_CloseHandle**() method to force the buffer to be purged from memory without undefining the variable:

```
$Buffer->_CloseHandle();
```

This method takes no parameters, and it is undocumented; but this is what is called during a DESTROY call on the object (which occurs when you **undef** the object). It is best that you use **undef**; but if you want to experiment, the

_CloseHandle() does exist. Keep in mind that because it is undocumented, it may change in some future version of the extension.

Displaying a Console Buffer

Suppose you have created a dozen console buffers and you have been writing things into them but you still only see the STDOUT in your console window. What good are these buffers? Well here comes the fun part: You can tell the console window to display whichever buffer you want by using the **Display**() method:

```
$Buffer->Display();
```

The **Display**() method takes no parameters and will return a TRUE value (non-zero) if it successfully switches to the new buffer; otherwise, it will return FALSE (undef).

> **Tip**
>
> *You will want to know about a little trick when using this method. After you have displayed a buffer, the console will continue displaying that buffer until told otherwise. There is no automatic way to switch back to the STDOUT buffer. So, before you use **Display**(), you will probably want to create a console object based on the STD_OUTPUT_HANDLE constant (refer back to Example 9.2).*

Writing to a Console Buffer

After a console buffer has either been allocated or obtained (in the case of the standard input/output/error handles), text can be written to it. It is important to remember that STDOUT is really just a console buffer. When you print something to STDOUT, it is being printed to the STDOUT console buffer. Example 9.3 shows three different ways to perform the same function: printing to STDOUT. This example is a bit extreme because there is quite a bit of overhead just to print to STDOUT by means of writing directly to its console buffer, but it demonstrates how it can be accomplished.

Example 9.3 *Various methods of printing to STDOUT*

```
use Win32::Console;
print "This is attempt 1 to print to STDOUT.\n";
print STDOUT "This is attempt 2 to print to STDOUT.\n";
$Out = new Win32::Console( STD_OUTPUT_HANDLE );
if( $Out )
{
  $Out->Write( "This is attempt 3 to print to STDOUT.\n" );
  Undef $Out;
}
```

Clearing a Console Buffer

Before learning about writing data, you need to understand how to clear a buffer first. If a buffer has become cluttered, you can clear the contents of it by using the **Cls()** method:

```
$Buffer->Cls( [ $ColorAttribute ] );
```

The only parameter ($ColorAttribute) is optional, and it specifies the color with which to fill the buffer. This value can be any combination of values documented later in the chapter in Table 9.8 (or one foreground and background color variable from Table 9.9). This combination of values is logically OR'ed together. The net effect of calling the **Cls()** method with a color attribute parameter is to clear the buffer and change the color of it at the same time.

If no parameter is passed into the method, the value of the $main::ATTR_NORMAL variable will be used. By default the extension defines this variable as gray text on a black background.

If the **Cls()** method is successful, it fills the buffer with the space character (and thus "clears" the buffer) and each character's color attribute will be set to either $ATTR_NORMAL or whatever is passed in to the method. If the method fails, undef is returned.

Writing to a Console Buffer with Write()

Writing to a console buffer is performed by using the **Write()** method:

```
$Buffer->Write( $Data );
```

The only parameter is any text string to be written to the console buffer. You could specify this as binary data if you like, but because it is to be dumped into a text-based console buffer it will result in the appropriate ASCII characters being displayed. This poses a problem for character data you need to write that are ANSI-based (such as accented characters or umlauts). In situations such as these, you need to convert the ANSI character to a corresponding OEM character.

If the **Write()** method is successful, it will return the number of characters that were written into the buffer; otherwise, it will return undef.

The text will start to be displayed at the location of the buffer's cursor. You can change the cursor's position prior to using the **Write()** method.

The text will be printed using the color attributes associated with the buffer. Refer to the **Attr()** method for more information regarding this. Refer back to Example 9.3 for a demonstration of the **Write()** method.

Writing to a Console Buffer with WriteChar()

Another way to write data to a buffer is to do so by specifying which X and Y location to start writing at. You use the **WriteChar()** method for this:

```
$Buffer->WriteChar( $Data, $X, $Y );
```

The first parameter ($Data) is the text data to write into the buffer. This can be data that was returned from the **ReadChar()** method.

The second and third parameters ($X and $Y) are the X and Y coordinates, respectively, of the character location where you want the data to begin writing.

The **WriteChar()** method is not quite what you may believe it to be. The data is written to the buffer without using any of the color attributes associated with the buffer. In other words, whatever text colors exist that your data will over-write will remain after the **WriteChar()** method has completed. If you want to also change the colors, you must execute the **WriteAttr()** method.

If the **WriteChar()** method is successful, it returns the number of characters written; otherwise, it returns undef. Refer to Example 9.6 in the next section for a demonstration of the **WriteChar()** method.

Applying Colors to a Console Buffer with WriteAttr()

Because the **WriteChar()** method does not write color attributes for each char-acter, another method performs that task; it is **WriteAttr()**:

```
$Buffer->WriteAttr( $Data, $X, $Y );
```

The first parameter ($Data) is a string of color attributes, one attribute per character, that will be written. If you supply a string of three color attributes, only three characters will be colored. Each color attribute consists of any com-bination of constants documented later in the chapter in Table 9.8 (or any foreground and background variable combination from Table 9.9) logically OR'ed together. The resulting value must be a binary value, not an interpreted value. This means that when you create the string, you must convert each resulting color value into a discrete character. You can do this by using either the Perl **chr()** or **pack()** functions as demonstrated in Example 9.4 and Example 9.5. Even though both examples use different techniques, they are equivalent.

The second and third parameters for **WriteAttr()** ($X and $Y) are the X and Y coordinates, respectively, where the data will begin to be written in the buffer. This is relative to position 0,0 being in the upper-left corner of the buffer.

Example 9.4 *Creating a data string for the **WriteAttr()** method using chr()*

```
$Data = chr( $FG_YELLOW | $BK_BLUE );
```

Example 9.5 *Creating a data string for the **WriteAttr**() method using pack()*
```
$Data = pack( "c", ( $FG_YELLOW | $BK_BLUE ));
```

If the **WriteAttr**() method is successful, it will write the color data into the buffer at the specified coordinates and then return the number of attributes that are written. If it fails, **WriteAttr**() will return undef.

Example 9.6 demonstrates the use of the **WriteAttr**() method. Lines 14 and 37 read character and attribute data from the first buffer. (These read methods are covered later in the section titled "Reading from a Console Buffer.") Line 17 uses the **WriteChar**() method to write the character data to the new buffer. Line 40 writes the color attributes to the new buffer using the **WriteAttr**() method.

Example 9.6 *Copying character and color data from one buffer to another using **WriteChar**() and **WriteAttr**()*
```
01. use Win32::Console;
02. $Buf1 = new Win32::Console();
03. $Buf2 = new Win32::Console();
04. $StdOut = new Win32::Console( STD_OUTPUT_HANDLE );
05.   # Set the colors for Buffer 1
06. $Buf1->Attr( $FG_YELLOW | $BG_BLUE );
07.   # Clear both buffers
08. $Buf1->Cls();
09. $Buf2->Cls( $FG_WHITE | $BG_GREEN );
10.   # Write a bunch of stuff to buffer 1
11. $Buf1->Write( join('', ( (a..z) x 100 ) ) );
12.
13.   # Read a rectangle of data from Buffer 1
14. if( $Data = $Buf1->ReadChar( 100, 0, 0 ) )
15. {
16.   print "Read the character data now writing it to the other buffer...";
17.   if( ! $Buf2->WriteChar( $Data, 10, 20 ) )
18.   {
19.     print "Failure!\n";
20.   }
21.   else
22.   {
23.     print "Success!\n";
24.   }
25. }
26. else
27. {
28.     print "Reading data failed.\n";
29. }
30.   # Display the original buffer
31. Display( $Buf1 );
32.   # Display the buffer with the character data from buffer 1
33. Display( $Buf2 );
34.   # Display STDOUT
35. $StdOut->Display();
36.   # Now let's copy the color attributes…
```

```
37. if( $Data = $Buf1->ReadAttr( 100, 0, 0 ) )
38. {
39.   print "Read the character data now writing it to the other buffer...";
40.   if( ! $Buf2->WriteAttr( $Data, 10, 20 ) )
41.   {
42.     print "Failure!\n";
43.   }
44.   else
45.   {
46.     print "Success!\n";
47.   }
48. }
49. else
50. {
51.     print "Reading data failed.\n";
52. }
53. # Display the original buffer
54. Display( $Buf1 );
55.   # Display the buffer with the character data from buffer 1
56. Display( $Buf2 );
57.   # Display STDOUT
58. $StdOut->Display();
59.
60. sub Display
61. {
62.   my( $Buffer ) = @_;
63.   $Buffer->Display();
64.   $Buffer->Write( "\nHit ENTER to continue...\n" );
65.   $In = <STDIN>;
66. }
```

Writing Blocks of Data to a Console Buffer

Another way to write data to a buffer is by specifying a rectangle of character and color data. The method that does this is **WriteRect()**:

```
@Result = $Buffer->WriteRect( $Rect, $Left, $Top, $Right, $Bottom );
```

The parameters for the **WriteRect()** method are as follows:

- $Rect is binary data that is the result of a call to the **ReadRect()** method.

- $Left is the column number of the left side of the rectangle.

- $Top is the row number of the top of the rectangle.

- $Right is the column number of the right side of the rectangle.

- $Bottom is the row number of the bottom of the rectangle.

If the **WriteRect()** method is successful, the data overwrites whatever is in the area that the rectangle covers and an array is returned representing the coordinates of the rectangle that was written. See Table 9.4 for details on the returned array. If the method fails, undef is returned.

*Table 9.4   The array returned from the **WriteRect()** method*

Array Element	Description
$Result[0]	The column number of the left side of the rectangle.
$Result[1]	The row number of the top of the rectangle.
$Result[2]	The column number of the right side of the rectangle.
$Result[3]	The row number of the bottom of the rectangle.

Example 9.7 demonstrates use of the **WriteRect()** method.

Example 9.7   *Copying a block from one buffer to another using **WriteRect()***

```
01. use Win32::Console;
02. @Rect = ( 5, 3, 60, 20 );
03. $Buf1 = new Win32::Console();
04. $Buf2 = new Win32::Console();
05. $StdOut = new Win32::Console( STD_OUTPUT_HANDLE );
06.    # Set the colors for Buffer 1
07. $Buf1->Attr( $FG_YELLOW | $BG_BLUE );
08.    # Clear both buffers
09. $Buf1->Cls();
10. $Buf2->Cls( $FG_WHITE | $BG_GREEN );
11.    # Write a bunch of stuff to buffer 1
12. $Buf1->Write( join('', ( (a..z) x 100 ) ) );
13.    # Read a rectangle of data from Buffer 1
14. if( $Rect = $Buf1->ReadRect( @Rect ) )
15. {
16.   print "Read the data now writing it to the other buffer...";
17.   if( ! $Buf2->WriteRect( $Rect, @Rect ) )
18.   {
19.     print "Failure!\n";
20.   }
21.   else
22.   {
23.     print "Success!\n";
24.   }
25. }
26. else
27. {
28.     print "Reading rectangle failed.\n";
29. }
30.    # Display the original buffer
31. $Buf1->Display();
32. $Buf1->Write( "\n\nHit ENTER to continue..." );
33. $In = <STDIN>;
34.    # Display the buffer with the copy of the rectangle from buffer 1
35. $Buf2->Display();
36. $Buf2->Write( "\n\nHit ENTER to continue..." );
37. $In = <STDIN>;
```

Scrolling Blocks of Data Around in a Console Buffer

You can use one final method to write data to a buffer. Actually it moves data from one point in a buffer to another point within the same buffer. This is the **Scroll**() method:

```
$Buffer->Scroll( $Left, $Top, $Right, $Bottom, $Col, $Row, $Char, $Attribute
[, $ClipLeft, $ClipTop, $ClipRight, $ClipBottom ] );
```

The parameters for the **Scroll**() method are as follows:

- $Left is the column number of the left side of the rectangle.

- $Top is the row number of the top of the rectangle.

- $Right is the column number of the right side of the rectangle.

- $Bottom is the row number of the bottom of the rectangle.

- $Col and $Row are the X (column) and Y (row) coordinates (respectively) where the upper-left corner of the rectangle defined by the first four parameters will be moved to.

- $Char is the character that will be used to fill the space that has been moved. This value *must* be an integer, not a character or character string. Do not use some value like "A" or 'A'; instead use a value like that returned by unpack("c", "A").

- $Attribute is the color attribute of the character that will be used to fill the space that has been moved.

- $ClipLeft, $ClipTop, $ClipRight, and $ClipBottom are the left, top, right, and bottom row and column values (respectively) that define a clipping region.

If the **Scroll**() method is successful, it returns a non-zero (TRUE) value and moves the contents of the defined rectangle to its new upper-left coordinates defined by the fifth and sixth parameters. The space left empty after the move will be filled with the character and color defined by the seventh and eighth parameters. If the **Scroll**() method fails, it returns undef.

Specifying a clipping rectangle (parameters 9 through 12) will prevent any of the moved rectangle from moving outside the boundaries specified by the clipping rectangle. This protects the contents of the buffer outside of the clipping rectangle from being overwritten. Example 9.8 demonstrates use of the **Scroll**() method.

It is interesting to note that line 14 uses **Scroll**() to move a block of data from one location to another within the buffer without clipping. The first parameter is an array of four values (the position of the block to be moved). Also notice that "fill character" is the result of an **unpack**() function.

Line 27 is practically the same as line 14 except that a clipping window is specified (the last four parameters) by an array of four values. If the any part of the block of data that is moved (or scrolled) falls out of the clipping window, that data is discarded. This is very practical if you need to make sure that any size of block is moved into a smaller window without overwriting the window border.

Example 9.8   *Using the **Scroll**() method both with and without a clipping region*

```
01. use Win32::Console;
02. $FillChar = " ";
03. $FillColor = $FG_YELLOW ¦ $BG_BLACK;
04. @Rect = ( 5, 5, 30, 30 );
05. @Rect2 = ( 2, 2, 50, 20 );
06. @Clip = ( 0, 0, 40, 10);
07.    # Create our console buffers
08. $StdOut = new Win32::Console( STD_OUTPUT_HANDLE );
09. $Buf1 = new Win32::Console();
10. $Buf1->Display();
11.    # Fill the buffer with nonsense...
12. FillBuffer( $Buf1 );
13.    # Scroll a part of the buffer without clipping...
14. if( $Buf1->Scroll( @Rect, 20, 20, unpack("c", $FillChar), $FillColor ) )
15. {
16.   Write( $Buf1, "Successfully scrolled!" );
17. }
18. else
19. {
20.   Write( $Buf1, "Scroll failed.\n" );
21. }
22. Write( $Buf1, "Hey, hit ENTER to scroll again with clipping!" );
23. $In = <STDIN>;
24.    # Fill the buffer again...
25. FillBuffer( $Buf1 );
26.    # Now let's scroll again but this time specifying clipping...
27. if( $Buf1->Scroll( @Rect2, 5, 3, unpack("c", $FillChar),
        $FillColor, @Clip ) )
28. {
29.   Write( $Buf1, "Successfully scrolled!" );
30. }
31. else
32. {
33.   Write( $Buf1, "Scroll failed." );
34. }
```

```
35. Write( $Buf1, "Hey, hit ENTER to end.\n" );
36. $In = <STDIN>;
37.
38. sub FillBuffer
39. {
40.   my( $Buffer ) = @_;
41.     #clear and set the buffer's color
42.   $Buffer->Attr( $FG_YELLOW | $BG_BLUE );
43.   $Buffer->Cls();
44.     # Fill the buffer full of just nonsense stuff
45.   foreach $Temp ( 1..20 )
46.   {
47.     $Buffer->Write( "..-" x 35 . "\n" );
48.     $Buffer->Write( "~=" x 35 . "\n" );
49.   }
50. }
51.
52. sub Write
53. {
54.   my( $Buffer, $String ) = @_;
55    my $Color = chr( $FG_WHITE | $BG_BLUE ) x length( $String );
56.   $Buffer->Write("\n\n");
57.   my( $x, $y ) = $Buffer->Cursor();
58.   $Buffer->WriteChar( $String, $x, $y );
59.   $Buffer->WriteAttr( $Color, $x, $y );
60. }
```

Note

A bug in the CONSOLE.PM *file caused the **Scroll**() method to use a clipping rectangle of (0,0,0,0) when a clipping rectangle is not supplied. There are two ways around this: Either always specify a clipping rectangle (this can be an obnoxiously large size like (0,0,1000,1000) to ensure that there is no clipping), or patch the* CONSOLE.PM *file. The latter is easy to do by adding one line and altering another.*

To alter the CONSOLE.PM *file, you need to locate the **Scroll** subroutine. Add the following line just before the first* return *statement:*

```
my( @Clip ) = ( $left2, $tip2, $right2, $bottom2 ) if defined $left2;
```

The next alteration is that you need to replace the last four parameters passed into the _ScrollConsoleScreenBuffer() *function with* @Clip.

This would make the function look like this:

```
return _ScrollConsoleScreenBuffer($self->{'handle'}, $left1, $top1,
    $right1, $bottom1, $col, $row, $char, $attr, @Clip );
```

This fix is applicable to version: 0.03 (07 Apr 1997). It is possible that this has been fixed by the time this book goes to press.

Reading from a Console Buffer

Just as you can write to a console buffer, you can read from a buffer. You can read characters, the color attributes, or a rectangle of both. The **ReadChar()** method will read a number of characters from the buffer:

```
$Data = $Buffer->ReadChar( $Number, $X, $Y );
```

The first parameter ($Number) is the number of characters to read. This must be a positive integer.

The second and third parameters ($X and $Y) are the column (the X coordinate) and the row (the Y coordinate), respectively, that indicate where to begin reading within the buffer.

If the **ReadChar()** method is successful, it returns a string of character data; otherwise, it returns undef.

Retrieving Color Data from a Console Buffer

A related method does practically the same thing as **ReadChar()** except it reads the color attributes rather than the character data. This is the **ReadAttr()** method:

```
$Data = $Buffer->ReadAttr( $Number, $X, $Y );
```

The first parameter ($Number) is the number of characters to read. This must be a positive integer.

The second and third parameters ($X and $Y) are the column (the X coordinate) and the row (the Y coordinate), respectively, that indicate where to begin reading within the buffer.

The results of the **ReadAttr()** method (if it is successful) can be applied using the **WriteAttr()** method.

If the **ReadAttr()** is successful, it returns a string of character data; otherwise, it returns undef.

Reading Blocks of Data from a Console Buffer

The last of the reading methods will read a rectangular area of both character and color data. This is the **ReadRect()** method:

```
$Data = $Buffer->ReadRect( $Left, $Top, $Right, $Bottom );
```

The parameters for the **ReadRect()** method are defined as follows:

- $Left is the column number of the left side of the rectangle.
- $Top is the row number of the top of the rectangle.

- $Right is the column number of the right side of the rectangle.

- $Bottom is the row number of the bottom of the rectangle.

If the **ReadRect()** method is successful, the character and color data that represent the area of the rectangle is returned in a binary format. This can be used in conjunction with the **WriteRect()** method. If the method fails, undef is returned.

Reading User Input from a Console Buffer

Another method reads data from a buffer, but this only works from a console buffer object created by specifying the STD_INPUT_HANDLE constant as the only parameter to the **new** function. Such a console object can be used to execute the **InputChar()** method:

```
$Data = $InputBuffer->InputChar( $Number );
```

The first parameter ($Number) is a numeric integer value that represents the total number of characters to read.

The **InputChar()** method returns the characters that have been read. The method does not return until $Number of characters have been read. If the **InputChar()** method fails, it returns undef. Example 9.9 demonstrates how **InputChar()** is used.

Example 9.9   *Using the InputChar() method*

```
01. use Win32::Console;
02. $StdIn = new Win32::Console( STD_INPUT_HANDLE );
03. print "Hit the Q key to Quit .\n";
04. $Data = $StdIn->InputChar( 1 );
05. if( "\U$Data "eq"Q")
06. {
07.   print "Quitting...\n";
08.   exit;
09. }
10. print "Continuing...\n";
11. ...add your code...
```

Console Properties

General attribute information can be obtained regarding the console window by using the **Info()** method. This method can only be called from a non-input control buffer:

```
@Attributes = $Buffer->Info();
```

The method takes no parameters and returns an array of values described in Table 9.5. If the **Info()** method is successful, an array is returned; otherwise, undef is returned.

Table 9.5   Array elements returned by the **Info**() *method*

Array Element	Description
$Attributes[0]	The number of columns in the current console buffer.
$Attributes[1]	The number of rows in the current console buffer.
$Attributes[2]	The column where the cursor is located in the current console buffer.
$Attributes[3]	The row where the cursor is located in the current console buffer.
$Attributes[4]	The color attribute that will be used to write data in the current console buffer.
$Attributes[5]	The column number of the current buffer displayed as the left side of the current console window.
$Attributes[6]	The row number of the current buffer displayed as the top line of the current console window.
$Attributes[7]	The column number of the current buffer displayed as the right side of the current console window.
$Attributes[8]	The row number of the current buffer displayed as the last line of the current console window.
$Attributes[9]	The maximum number of columns that the current console window can display. This value depends on the current buffer size, font, and other such values.
$Attributes[10]	The maximum number of rows that the current console window can display. This value depends on the current buffer size, font, and other such values.

Finding the Size of a Console Window

To discover what the largest possible console window size is, use the
MaxWindow() method:

```
($MaxCol, $MaxRow) = $Buffer->MaxWindow();
```

The **MaxWindow**() method returns the largest possible size that the console
window could be based on the console window's font size and the resolution of
the video card.

If the **MaxWindow**() method is successful, it returns an array consisting of the
highest number of columns and rows possible for a console window. If
MaxWindow() fails, it returns undef.

Setting I/O Modes for Console Windows

A console window can have particular modes set for input and output. These
modes can be set using the **Mode**() method:

```
$Buffer->Mode( [ $Mode ] );
```

The first parameter ($Mode) is optional and can consist of any combination of the constants listed in Table 9.6. These constants can be logically OR'ed together.

Table 9.6   Console window modes

Mode	Description
ENABLE_ECHO_INPUT	Input is echoed to the current console buffer. This mode can be used only if the ENABLE_LINE_INPUT mode is also enabled.
ENABLE_LINE_INPUT	This will accept input only after a carriage return is supplied. If this flag is not set, input can be read one character at a time. Refer to the **InputChar**() method.
ENABLE_MOUSE_INPUT	If the mouse pointer is within the borders of the console window and the window has the keyboard focus, mouse events generated by mouse movement and button presses are placed in the input buffer. To use this you need to first disable Quick Edit mode in the Console Properties dialog box.
ENABLE_PROCESSED_INPUT	Ctrl+C is processed by the system and is not placed in the input buffer. This means that the Perl script will not be able to see the Ctrl+C event. Other control keys are also processed by the system and are not placed into the input buffer. If the ENABLE_LINE_INPUT mode is also enabled, backspace, carriage return, and linefeed characters are handled by the operating system and not placed into the input buffer.
ENABLE_PROCESSED_OUTPUT	Characters written to the console buffer using the **Write**() method are examined for ASCII control sequences and the correct action is performed. Backspace, tab, bell, carriage return, and linefeed characters are processed.
ENABLE_WINDOW_INPUT	User interactions that change the size of the console screen buffer are reported in the console's input buffer. Information about these events can be read from the input buffer.
ENABLE_WRAP_AT_EOL_OUTPUT	When writing to the buffer, the cursor moves to the beginning of the next row when it reaches the end of the current row. This causes the rows displayed in the console window to scroll up automatically when the cursor advances beyond the last row in the window. It also causes the contents of the screen buffer to scroll up (discarding the top row of the screen buffer) when the cursor advances beyond the last row in the screen buffer. If this mode is disabled, the last character in the row is overwritten with any subsequent characters.

The **Mode**() method returns the current mode of the console window (and displayed console buffer). If the method fails, it returns undef.

Reading and Setting Titles for Console Windows
The title of the console window can be both read and set using the **Title**() method:

```
$Buffer->Title( [$Title] );
```

The only parameter ($Title) is optional and can be any text string. There is no limit to the length of the string.

The method returns the current title of the console window. The title is associated with the console window and not with any console buffer. If the **Title**() method fails, it returns undef.

Example 9.10 shows a convenient way of changing the title when buffers are displayed. The idea behind this is that you may want to change the title every time you display the buffer.

Example 9.10   *Setting the console window's title*

```
01. use Win32::Console;
02.   # Create buffers
03. $Buf1 = new Win32::Console();
04. $Buf2 = new Win32::Console();
05.   # Hack up the console object and add a "title" key
06.   # so we can use it later
07. $Buf1->{title} = "This is Buffer 1";
08. $Buf2->{title} = "This is Buffer 2";
09.   # Display buffer 1
10. Display( $Buf1 );
11. $Buf1->Write( "Blah blah blah blah.\nHit enter to continue.\n" );
12    $In = <STDIN>;
13.   # Display buffer 2
14. Display( $Buf2 );
15. $Buf2->Write( "More blah blah blah blah.\nHit enter to continue.\n" );
16. $In = <STDIN>;
17. sub Display
18. {
19.   my( $Buffer ) = @_;
20.   $Buffer->Display();
21.     # Set the console title to reflect which buffer is displayed
22.   $Buffer->Title( $Buffer->{title} );
23. }
```

Querying and Setting a Console Window Size
The size of the console window can be both queried and set by using the **Window**() method:

```
@Window = $Buffer->Window( [ $PositionFlag, $Left, $Top, $Right, $Bottom ] );
```

All the parameters are optional; but if one is supplied, all five of them must be supplied.

The parameters for the **Window**() method are defined as follows:

- $PositionFlag is the position flag. This flag represents whether the coordinates specified are relative to the current console window or absolute. A value of 0 means the coordinates are relative and a 1 indicates the coordinates are absolute.

- $Left is the column number of the left side of the window.

- $Top is the row number of the top of the window.

- $Right is the column number of the right side of the window.

- $Bottom is the row number of the bottom of the window.

Passing parameters into **Window**(), the method triggers an attempt to reset the console window size. If the coordinates are within the possible size (refer to the **MaxWindow**() method), the window will be set. If you have multiple buffers, the console window will change only when that buffer is displayed. A buffer must have the GENERIC_WRITE access mode set to change the console window size. Refer to the **new** function.

The **Window**() method returns a TRUE (non-zero) value if it successfully sets the window size. If no parameters are passed in to **Window**(), an array is returned describing the console window (as illustrated in Table 9.7). If the method fails, it returns undef.

*Table 9.7   The array returned from the **Window**() method*

Array Element	Description
$Window [0]	The column number of the left side of the rectangle.
$Window [1]	The row number of the top of the rectangle.
$Window [2]	The column number of the right side of the rectangle.
$Window [3]	The row number of the bottom of the rectangle.

Attributes of a Console Buffer

A console buffer is more than just a chunk of memory used to store text. It has specific size and color attributes that can be set and queried as detailed in the sections that follow.

Determining and Setting Console Buffer's Color

The **Attr**() method determines the current color of the console buffer:

```
$Buffer->Attr( [ $Color ] );
```

The only parameter ($Color) is optional and consists of two components: a background and foreground color. Any combination of background and foreground variable listed in Table 9.8 (or any combination of variables from Table 9.9) can be logically OR'ed together to make up the value of this parameter.

The constants in Table 9.8 can be logically OR'ed in any combination. If you want to have bright cyan (blue and green) on a black background, for example, you can specify BACKGROUND_BLACK ¦ FOREGROUND_GREEN ¦ FOREGROUND_BLUE ¦ FOREGROUND_INTENSITY.

Table 9.8   Color constants that can be used with a console buffer

Constant	Description
BACKGROUND_BLUE	Screen color is blue.
BACKGROUND_GREEN	Screen color is green.
BACKGROUND_RED	Screen color is red.
BACKGROUND_INTENSITY	Screen color is intensified (bright).
FOREGROUND_BLUE	Text color is blue.
FOREGROUND_GREEN	Text color is green.
FOREGROUND_RED	Text color is red.
FOREGROUND_INTENSITY	Text color is intensified (bright).

The variables in Table 9.9 are defined by the **Win32::Console** extension and represent colors based on the constants listed in Table 9.8.

Table 9.9   Premixed color values that can be used with a console buffer

Value	Description
$FG_BLACK	Text is black.
$FG_BLUE	Text is blue.
$FG_LIGHTBLUE	Text is light blue.
$FG_RED	Text is red.
$FG_LIGHTRED	Text is light red.
$FG_GREEN	Text is green.
$FG_LIGHTGREEN	Text is light green.
$FG_MAGENTA	Text is magenta.
$FG_LIGHTMAGENTA	Text is light magenta.
$FG_CYAN	Text is cyan.
$FG_LIGHTCYAN	Text is light cyan.
$FG_BROWN	Text is brown.
$FG_GRAY	Text is gray.
$FG_WHITE	Text is white.
$BG_BLACK	Screen color is black.

$BG_BLUE	Screen color is blue.
$BG_LIGHTBLUE	Screen color is light blue.
$BG_RED	Screen color is red.
$BG_LIGHTRED	Screen color is light red.
$BG_GREEN	Screen color is green.
$BG_LIGHTGREEN	Screen color is light green.
$BG_MAGENTA	Screen color is magenta.
$BG_LIGHTMAGENTA	Screen color is light magenta.
$BG_CYAN	Screen color is cyan.
$BG_LIGHTCYAN	Screen color is light cyan.
$BG_BROWN	Screen color is brown.
$BG_GRAY	Screen color is gray.
$BG_WHITE	Screen color is white.

The **Attr**() method returns the current attribute value. If the method sets the attribute, the returning value is the new attribute.

In Example 9.11, the color of the STDOUT console buffer is changed to cyan text on a blue background (line 5). Later, the buffer is set back to its original color (line 8). Therefore characters printed after that point are as they were when the script started to run. Notice that the code writes to the buffer using both the **Write**() method (line 6) and **print** (line 9). This is to illustrate how the buffer is modified so that no matter how data is written to the console buffer it is affected by the buffer's color attribute. The last line (10) is not needed (because the console buffer $Out will fall out of scope as the script ends), but is included to show the proper way to destroy a console buffer.

Example 9.11 *Modifying the color of a console buffer*

```
01. use Win32::Console;
02. $Out = new Win32::Console( STD_OUTPUT_HANDLE ) ¦¦ die;
03. print "We are now going to change the color of the text...\n";
04. $Attribute = $Out->Attr();
05. $Out->Attr( $FG_CYAN ¦ $BG_BLUE );
06. $Out->Write( "Wow! Check out this color\n" );
07. print "Yes, this color is cool!\n");
08. $Out->Attr( $Attribute );
09. print "Welcome back to the original color!\n";
10. undef $Out;
```

Querying and Setting a Console Buffer's Cursor Position

In addition to setting buffer colors, you can also query and set the current position of the buffer's cursor using the **Cursor**() method:

```
@Cursor = $Buffer->Cursor( [$X, $Y [, $Size, $Visible] ] );
```

This method takes four optional parameters. If any of the parameters are specified, all four must be supplied. The parameters for the **Cursor()** method are defined as follows:

- $X and $Y are optional parameters and represent the X and Y position (respectively) of where the cursor is to be moved to in the buffer. Position 0,0 is the upper-left corner of the buffer. If these parameters have a value of -1, they are ignored—this is used if you want to set the size and visibility of the cursor without setting the cursor's location.

- The $Size parameter represents the size of the cursor. This value is a bit odd, but blame it on the Win32 API. The value specified is an integer between 1 and 100, which specifies the percentage of the character cell that is filled to indicate the location of the cursor. A typical value is 50 (50% of the character cell is filled). If you do not know what to use for this value, just specify 50.

- The $Visible parameter represents whether the cursor is visible. A value of 1 shows the cursor, and 0 hides it.

The returned array reflects the current state of the cursor after any changes have been made by the method.

If successful, the **Cursor()** method returns a four-element array that reflects the current state of the cursor. Table 9.10 describes the values of the array. If the method fails, a FALSE value (undef) is returned.

*Table 9.10   The elements of the array returned by the **Cursor()** method*

Array Element	Description
$Cursor[0]	The X position of the cursor.
$Cursor[1]	The Y position of the cursor.
$Cursor[2]	The size of the cursor. This value is between 1 and 100, which represents the percentage of the character cell that is filled to indicate the location of the cursor.
$Cursor[3]	The visibility of the cursor. (This value is either TRUE or FALSE.)

Resizing Console Buffers

The size of a console buffer can be modified using the **Size()** method:

```
@Size = $Buffer->Size( [$X, $Y] );
```

The two parameters ($X and $Y) are optional.

The first parameter ($X) specifies the new number of columns the buffer will be set to. If this parameter has a value of -1, the buffer's number of columns will not change.

The second parameter ($Y) specifies the new number of rows the buffer will be set to. If this parameter has a value of -1, the buffer's number of rows will not change.

If the two parameters are specified, the buffer's size is altered. The size of the buffer cannot be made smaller than the size of the console window. If either of the parameters passed in have a value of –1, that parameter is not altered. If the values (-1, 255) are passed in, only the number of rows are changed to 255.

If no values are specified, no changes are made (only the current size is returned).

The **Size()** method returns an array consisting of the number of columns and rows that currently represent the size of the buffer. Resizing does not clear the buffer. The only exception to this is when a buffer is made smaller. In this case, data in the columns and rows that are removed is lost.

If the **Size()** method is successful, it returns an array of values. If parameters are passed in, the buffer is resized. If the method fails, it returns undef.

The code in Example 9.12 illustrates how to both retrieve the size of the buffer and resize it.

Example 9.12 *Resizing a console buffer*

```
use Win32::Console;
$Buffer = new Win32::Console();
   # Get the current size of the buffer
($X, $Y) = $Buffer->Size();
print "The buffer size is $X columns by $Y rows.\n";
   # Resize only the number of rows.  Give a huge amount!
($X, $Y) = $Buffer->Size( -1, 1000 );
print "The new buffer size is $X columns by $Y rows.\n";
```

Filling Console Buffers with Characters

A buffer can be filled with a particular character by using the **FillChar()** method:

```
$Buffer->FillChar( $Char, $Number, $X, $Y );
```

The parameters for the **FillChar()** method are defined as follows:

- The $Char parameter is a character that is to be written to the buffer. This is an actual character such as "A". If a string with more than one character is specified, only the first one will be used.

- The $Number parameter specifies how many characters will be written to the buffer.

- The $X and $Y parameters represent the row and column (respectively) that determine the location in the buffer where the writing of the character specified in the first parameter will begin.

If the **FillChar()** method is successful, it returns the number of characters written to the buffer; otherwise, it returns undef. Refer to Example 9.13 for an example on using the **FillChar()** method.

Filling Console Buffers with Color

Just as a buffer can be filled with a character, it can be filled with a color as well. The **FillAttr()** method handles this:

```
$Buffer->FillAttr( $Color, $Number, $X, $Y );
```

The parameters for the **FillAttr()** method are defined as follows:

- The $Color parameter is the color value that is to be written to the buffer. Any combination of background and foreground color variables, listed previously in Table 9.9 (or any combination of variables from Table 9.8) can be logically OR'ed together to make up the value of this parameter.

- The $Number parameter specifies how many colors will be written to the buffer.

- The $X and $Y parameters represent the row and column (respectively) that determine the location in the buffer where the writing of the character specified in the first parameter will begin.

If the **FillAttr()** method is successful, it returns the number of colors written to the buffer; otherwise, it returns undef. Example 9.13 illustrates the use of both the **FillChar()** and **FillAttr()** methods.

Example 9.13   *Filling a console buffer with characters and colors*

```
use Win32::Console;
$Buffer = new Win32::Console();
$Buffer->FillChar( ".", 300, 0, 0 );
$Buffer->FillAttr( $FG_YELLOW ¦ $BG_BLUE, 300, 0, 0 );
$Buffer->Display();
$Buffer->Write( "\nHit ENTER to end this.\n" );
$In = <STDIN>;
```

Sound

One of the exciting things that Win32 platforms can handle is the capability to play back sound files, known as .WAV (wave) files. The .WAV format is the standard audio format that Win32 understands. Win32 machines typically have several .WAV files that come with the operating system.

The **Win32::Sound** extension facilitates the capability to play back these .WAV sounds. This can greatly enhance a Perl script by signaling when an event takes place.

Types of Sounds

The following three types of sounds can be played:

- **System Beeps.** A system beep is the default beep-like sound that Windows will utter when it does not know what else to do. This is a very simple and quick beep sound. This can be played using the **Play()** function and specifying a system event called "DefaultBeep".

- **System Events.** A system event is a sound associated with a particular event. When Windows starts, for example, it attempts to play the "Start Windows" sound. These sounds are configurable by means of the Sounds Control Panel applet.

  The sounds can be configured (and new names added) by means of the Registry. The names and associated paths to wave files are located in the HKEY_CURRENT_USER\AppEvents\Schemes\Apps\.Default Registry key. The current state of the extension supports only the names specified in this Registry key. Other sounds can be configured, but only those under this key are accessible from the extension.

- **Wave Files.** A path to a .WAV file can be specified. The path can either be relative to the current directory or a full path. The name of the file can either be a full name such as Welcome.WAV or just the file name without the file extension, such as Welcome. If no extension is specified, .WAV will be assumed.

Playing Sounds

You can play a sound using the **Play()** function:

```
Win32::Sound::Play( [ $Sound [, $Flag ] ] );
```

The first optional parameter ($Sound) indicates which sound to play. This can be a full or relative path to a .WAV file or it can be the name of a system event.

The second optional parameter ($Flag) is a flag consisting of any of the constants listed in Table 9.11. These constants can be logically OR'ed together. If nothing is specified for this parameter, no flags will be used by default.

Table 9.11   Sound-playing flags

Constant	Description
SND_ASYNC	The sound is played asynchronously. That is, the function returns immediately and the Perl script continues to process while the sound continues to play. If this flag is not specified, the sound plays synchronously and the function will not return until the sound has finished playing.
SND_LOOP	The sound will play repeatedly until it is purposely stopped. If this flag is specified, SND_ASYNC should also be specified; otherwise, the sound will continue to play and the Perl script will not return from the play function.
SND_NODEFAULT	Typically, a default beep is played when the specified sound is not able to play (that is, the sound file or the sound name is not found). This flag will prevent this beep from playing.
SND_NOSTOP	When this flag is specified, calling the **Play()** function while another sound is playing will cause the function to fail without interrupting the current sound.

If no parameters are passed in to **Play()**, any currently playing sound will be stopped regardless of the SND_NOSTOP flag.

The **Play()** function returns a TRUE value if it is successful. The only time this function does not return a TRUE value is when it cannot play the specified sound and there is no defined default sound. Example 9.14 shows how to use the **Win32::Sound::Play()** function.

Example 9.14   *Using the **Win32::Sound** extension to play a* .WAV *file*

```
01. use Win32::Sound;
02. $File = "c:\\winnt\\media\\The Microsoft Sound.wav";
03. @Events = (
04.   "MenuPopup",
05.   "SystemDefault",
06.   "SystemAsterisk",
07.   "SystemExclamation",
08.   "SystemExit",
09.   "SystemHand",
10.   "SystemQuestion",
11.   "SystemStart"
12. );
13. Win32::Sound::Play( $File );
14. foreach $Sound ( @Events )
15. {
16.   print "Playing $Sound...\n";
17.   Win32::Sound::Play( $Sound, SND_NODEFAULT ¦ SND_LOOP ¦ SND_ASYNC );
18.   sleep( 3 );
19.   Win32::Sound::Stop();
20. }
```

Stopping Sounds from Playing

When a sound is played with the SND_ASYNC flag, it will play while the Perl script continues to process. The script can tell the sound to stop playing by calling the **Stop**() function:

```
Win32::Sound::Stop();
```

Any currently playing sound will stop playing. This function always returns a TRUE value. The **Stop**() function is demonstrated in the previous section in Example 9.14.

Win32 API

Almost all the Win32-specific extensions make use of some Win32 API function calls. Many of these extensions exist only because Perl does not have any native way of calling these functions. This is where the **Win32::API** extension comes into play.

This extension provides a facility to make calls into the Win32 API. Specifically, the extension allows a Perl script to make any call into any dynamic link library (DLL). These DLLs are not limited to only Win32-specific libraries; any DLL can be used.

> ### Warning
>
> *A word of warning regarding the **Win32::API** extension: It is not for non-programmers! This extension gives full, unlimited access to any DLL that a user can find. This can easily cause damage to your computer by corrupting data files, Registry, and hard drives; and other damage is possible. Before experimenting with DLL functions, you should seek documentation on how to use it.*

This section covers the use of the **Win32::API** extension. A description on how DLLs work, what functions are available from various DLLs, and other topics such as what a void pointer, string pointer, and NULL pointer are goes far beyond the scope of this book. You can find many sources for information such as the Microsoft Developer Network (MSDN), C or C++ compiler's documentation, any good C Win32 programming book, and the Web.

Calling Functions from a DLL

When you want to call a function from a DLL, you need to load the DLL and import the function. You can do this by creating a new API object:

```
$Api = new Win32::API( $Dll, $FunctionName, $InputPrototype, $ReturnType );
```

The parameters for this function call are as follows:

- The $Dll parameter is the name of the DLL file. This can be either a relative file name or a full path. The name of the file does not need to include the .DLL extension. If no path is specified, the system will look for the file in the current directory, the Windows and Windows system directories, and then the path will be checked for the file.

- The $FunctionName parameter is the name of the function to be used. This is a case-sensitive parameter.

- The $InputPrototype parameter is an input prototype for the function. This value is an anonymous array. The elements of the array can consist of any of the constant values in Table 9.12.

- The $ReturnType parameter is the output value prototype. This value is a single constant listed in Table 9.12.

Table 9.12　Data type constants

Constant	Description
I	A short number such as an int or short.
N	A long number. This is the equivalent of long.
P	A pointer. This can be a pointer to a character string, a Unicode string, a void pointer, a structure pointer, etc

Take, for example, the **GetTickCount()** function in the Kernel32.dll library, which takes no parameters but returns a DWORD. Its C prototype is this:

```
DWORD GetTickCount(VOID)
```

Because **GetTickCount()** has no input parameters (it is void), the third parameter will be an empty anonymous array: [ ]. The function does return a DWORD, which is a 32-bit number, the same as long; therefore the fourth parameter will be an N (representing a long number). To create a Win32::API object for this function would be:

```
$Api=new Win32::API("kerne32.dLL", "GetTickCount", [],N);
```

Another example is the kernel32.dll's **GetSystemDirectory()** function. Its C prototype is this:

```
UINT GetSystemDirectory( LPTSTR pszBuffer, UINT iSizeOfBuffer )
```

To construct the third parameter for the **new** command, you need to analyze the input parameters to this function. The first input parameter is a pointer to a string, so you will use a P value. It is followed by an unsigned integer (a 16-bit int), so an I data type will suffice. The resulting anonymous array that will be used will be [P, I]. The return value of the function is a UINT, which is represented (as already seen) by a short (16-bit integer); therefore you will specify an I value.

This means that the API object will be created using the following:

```
$ApiObject = new Win32::API( "kernel32", "GetSystemDirectory", [ P, I ], I );
```

The result of this function will either be a new **Win32::API** object or it will be undef.

After the **Win32::API** object has been created, you can actually call the function by using the **Call()** method:

```
$ApiObject->Call( $Input1, $Input2, $Input3 ...);
```

The input parameters are defined by the function prototype. The method returns the result from the function.

Using Win32::API

Now that the mechanics have been discussed, we should walk through a few examples for this to make any sense. You will have to use several tricks to make use of the functions. Some of these may not be obvious.

In the example cited earlier that would call the **GetSystemDirectory()** Win32 function, the result was a Win32 API object. Before the **Call()** method can be executed, there must be some preparations first. The API function expects the first pointer to point to a character string and the second parameter (the UINT) is the number of bytes that have been allocated for the pointer. Because the pointer must point to allocated memory, memory must first be allocated. This is accomplished by creating a string of characters with the following:

```
$String = "\x00" x 1024;
```

This will allocate a string of 1024 bytes. It is a good idea to fill the string with NUL characters \x00 because any API function that expects an incoming string will expect it to be terminated with a NUL character.

Now that a 1KB string has been allocated, the **Call()** method can be called:

```
$Result = $ApiObject->Call( $String, length( $String ) );
```

Notice that the string that was allocated is passed in as the pointer value (as specified by the P constant), and the second value is the size of the allocated buffer (which will be interpreted as an integer value because the I constant defined it). The result was defined as a long data type (the N constant). When the method call returns, the returned value is converted into a normal Perl-based integer value. In this case, it represents how many characters were stored into the allocated buffer.

The resulting path stored in the buffer will be a proper C-based NUL terminated string, so there is a need to extract everything up to the first NUL character:

```
($Dir) = ( $String =~ /(.*?)\x00/ );
```

That is it! Example 9.15 shows the code in its entirety.

Example 9.15   *Using **Win32::API** to retrieve the system directory*

```
use Win32::API;
$ApiObject = new Win32::API( "kernel32", "GetSystemDirectory", [ P, I ], I );
$String = "\x00" x 1024;
$Result = $ApiObject->Call( $String, length( $String ) );
($Dir) = ( $String =~ /(.*?)\x00/ );
print "The system directory is '$Dir'\n";
```

Using Structures with Win32::API

To demonstrate another, more complex, example consider the **GetVersionEx()**
Win32 API function. This returns information regarding the Windows version
numbers. This example is interesting because it deals with a data structure.

The **GetVersionEx()** prototype function is as follows:

```
BOOL GetVersionEx( OSVERSIONINFO *pOSVersion );
```

The return type BOOL can be held in an int, so the constant I will be used. The
input parameter is a pointer to a data structure (P). Hence the input parameter
anonymous array will be [P].

Considering this, the API object will be created using this:

```
$ApiObject = new Win32::API( "kernel32", "GetVersionEx", [P], I );
```

To continue, you need to allocate memory to hold the data structure. The
structure is prototyped as follows:

```
typedef struct _OSVERSIONINFO
{
  DWORD dwOSVersionInfoSize;
  DWORD dwMajorVersion;
  DWORD dwMinorVersion;
  DWORD dwBuildNumber;
  DWORD dwPlatformId;
  TCHAR szCSDVersion[ 128 ];
} OSVERSIONINFO;
```

Because a DWORD is the equivalent to a 32-bit long data type, you will use the
long instead. The TCHAR data type is either a character or a Unicode character,
depending on how the extension was compiled. If the extension was compiled
enabling Unicode, the 128-element TCHAR array will be 256 bytes long (because
a Unicode character is 16 bits wide). Before allocating the memory, you need to
determine whether you are using Unicode. This can be done using the
IsUnicode() function:

```
Win32::API::IsUnicode();
```

The function returns a TRUE value if the extension was compiled to always use Unicode; otherwise, it returns FALSE.

Therefore to create the data structure, you could use the following:

```
# Determine how large a character is
$CharSize = 1 + Win32::API::IsUnicode();
$Struct = pack( "L5c*",  ( (0) x 5 ), ( (0) x ( $CharSize * 128 ) ) );
$StructSize = length( $Struct );
$Struct = pack( "L5c*",  $StructSize, ( (0) x 4 ), ( (0) x ( $CharSize * 128 )
) );
```

This is a bit of a hack, but the memory structure requires that the first DWORD (dwOSVersionInfoSize) is set to have the size of the memory structure. So by packing it once, you can then get the length of the structure so you can repack it with this value.

Now that the structure has been created, submit it into the API function:

```
$Result = $ApiObject->Call( $Struct );
```

This particular function returns a 0 if it failed; if it successfully filled out the structure, it returns a non-zero value. If the function returned a non-zero value, you need to unpack the structure into variables:

```
( $StructSize, $Ver{major}, $Ver{minor}, $Ver{build}, $Ver{platform},
$Ver{servicepack} ) = unpack( "L5a*", $Struct );
```

The last thing that must be done is to rip out any NUL characters that are left in the $Ver{servicepack} variable:

```
$Ver{servicepack} =~ s/\x00//g;
```

To see the code in its entirety, refer to Example 9.16.

Example 9.16   *Retrieving the Windows version information using* **Win32::API**

```
01. use Win32::API;
02. $ApiObject = new Win32::API( "kernel32", "GetVersionEx", [P], I );
03.   # Find how many bytes we need for the char string—based on whether
04.   # we are dealing with Unicode or not
05. $CharSize = 1 + Win32::API::IsUnicode();
06. $Struct = pack( "L5c*",  ( (0) x 5 ), ( (0) x ( $CharSize * 128 ) ) );
07. $StructSize = length( $Struct );
08. $Struct = pack( "L5c*",  $StructSize,
                             ( (0) x 4 ),
                             ( (0) x ( $CharSize * 128 ) ) );
09. if( $Result = $ApiObject->Call( $Struct ) )
10. {
11.   ( $StructSize, $Ver{major}, $Ver{minor},
        $Ver{build}, $Ver{platform},
        $Ver{servicepack} ) = unpack( "L5a*", $Struct );
12.   $Ver{servicepack} =~ s/\x00//g;
```

continues

Continued

```
13.   print "This is Windows $Ver{major}.$Ver{minor} " .
            "build $Ver{build} $Ver{servicepack}\n";
14. }
15. else
16. {
17.   print "The call to GetVersionEx() failed.\n";
18. }
```

Common Routines

Because many Win32 functions require allocating memory blocks of a specific size and handling Unicode strings, it is handy to have some functions around that facilitate such needs. Example 9.17 lists some of these routines. These functions include the following:

- **Alloc($Size)**. This function returns an allocated string of the specified size. The string is filled with NUL characters.

- **AnsiToUnicode($String)**. This function returns a Unicode version of the passed-in ANSI string.

- **UnicodeToAnsi($String)**. This function returns an ANSI version of the passed-in Unicode string.

Example 9.17 *Commonly used routines*

```
01. sub Alloc
02. {
03.   my( $Size ) = @_;
04.   my( $Pointer ) = "\x00" x $Size;
05.   return $Pointer;
06. }
07.
08. sub AnsiToUnicode
09. {
10.   my( $Unicode ) = $@_;
11.   $Unicode =~ s/(.)/$1\x00/gis;
12.   return $Unicode;
13. }
14.
15. sub UnicodeToAnsi
16. {
17.   my( $Ansi ) = @_;
18.   $Ansi =~ s/(.)\x00/$1/gis;
19.   return $Ansi;
20. }
```

Impersonating a User

Sometimes a script needs to log on as a different user—what is known as *impersonation*. Consider a Web CGI script that enables a user to modify her user account information (such as her full name) or make modifications to her home directory. The script could accept the user's userid and password as input parameters and attempt to log on as that user. If successful, the script could have access to files and directories to which only she has permission. Services use this feature quite often, such as Web servers and Telnet daemons.

The **Win32::AdminMisc** extension provides an impersonation function called **LogonAsUser()**:

```
Win32::AdminMisc::LogonAsUser( $Domain, $User, $Password[, $LogonType ] );
```

The parameters for the **LogonAsUser()** function are defined as follows:

- $Domain is the name of the domain where the user account exists. If this parameter is an empty string (" "), the current domain is assumed.

- $User is the name of the user account that is to be impersonated.

- $Password is the password for the user account specified in the second parameter.

- $LogonType is optional and represents the type of logon to be attempted. This can be any value from Table 9.13.

*Table 9.13   The logon types used with **Win32::AdminMisc::LogonAsUser()***

Logon Type	Description
LOGON32_LOGON_INTERACTIVE	This type caches logon information.
LOGON32_LOGON_BATCH	This logon type is similar to the LOGON32_LOGON_NETWORK type except that it can be used in conjunction with **CreateProcessAsUser()**.
LOGON32_LOGON_SERVICE	This is the logon type used by services. For this type to be used, the impersonated account must have the privilege to log on as a service.
LOGON32_LOGON_NETWORK	This logon type is designed for quick authentication. It is quite limited because the **CreateProcessAsUser()** function is not supported using this impersonation logon type. This logon type is not recommended.

The **LogonAsUser()** function requires the script calling the function to have the following privileges:

- SE_TCB_NAME. Act as part of the operating system.

- SE_CHANGE_NOTIFY_NAME. Bypass traverse checking. (This privilege needs to be granted unless the account the script runs under is either the local system or is a member of the Administrators group.)

- SE_ASSIGNPRIMARYTOKEN_NAME. Replace a process level token.

> **Tip**
>
> *A bug that crept into the **Win32::AdminMisc** extension causes **LogonAsUser**() to incorrectly return a 1 even if the logon was unsuccessful. A simple way to verify that the impersonation was successful is to check the logon name immediately after the call to **LogonAsUser**():*
>
> ```
> Win32::AdminMisc::LogonAsUser( $Domain, $User, $Password );
> $UserName = Win32::AdminMisc::GetLogonName();
> print "Failed to logon" if( "\L$User" ne "\L$UserName" );
> ```

After you have successfully logged on as another user, you may need to check who you are logged on as. The **Win32::AdminMisc::GetLogonName**() does just this. Unlike the **Win32::LoginName**() function, **GetLogonName**() correctly reports the logon name of an impersonated user:

```
Win32::AdminMisc::GetLogonName();
```

The function takes no parameters and returns the name of the current user. If the logged on user is impersonated, this function returns the impersonated user name.

After a script has impersonated a user, it will eventually want to stop impersonation. To stop impersonating another user, you use the **LogoffAsUser**():

```
Win32::AdminMisc::LogoffAsUser();
```

This function always returns a TRUE value. Example 9.18 demonstrates how to impersonate a user.

Example 9.18 *Impersonating a user*

```
01. use Win32::AdminMisc;
02. my( $Domain, $User, $Password ) = @ARGV;
03. Win32::AdminMisc::LogonAsUser( $Domain, $User, Password );
04. $Name = Win32::AdminMisc::GetLogonName();
05. if( "\L$User" ne "\L$Name" )
06. {
07.    print "The logon failed.\n";
08. }else{
09.    print "Successfully logged on as $Name\n";
10.    Win32::AdminMisc::LogoffAsUser();
11. }
```

Miscellaneous Win32 Functions

Many miscellaneous functions come with the standard **Win32** extension. These functions include some important and quite often overlooked necessities.

This extension is interesting because functions from this extension could be called without ever having to explicitly load the **Win32** extension—the extension was built in to Win32 Perl. This means that you could call a function directly without ever loading the **Win32** module as in Example 9.19. In this example, line 1 is not necessary. This is a bad Practice, however, because it is not supported in Perl version 5.005.

Example 9.19. *Using functions from the **Win32** module*

```
use Win32;
$User = Win32::LoginName();
$Machine = Win32::NodeName();
$Domain = Win32::DomainName();
print "Your user name is $User\n";
print "Your machine name is $Machine\n";
print "Your domain name is $Domain\n";
```

Discovering Build and Version Numbers

The version (or to be more precise the build number) of Perl can be obtained with a call to **PerlVersion()**:

```
Win32::PerlVersion();
```

The build number is returned by a call to this function. A call to this function using ActiveState's Win32 Perl 5.003_07 Build 316 results in the returned text string "Build 316", for example.

> **Note**
>
> The **PerlVersion()** function has been depreciated in Perl 5.005 and no longer exists. Scripts that make a call into **Win32::PerlVersion()** using Perl 5.005 will fail.

Retrieving OS Version Information

You can retrieve information regarding the operating system's version by using the **GetOSVersion()** function:

```
@Version = Win32::GetOSVersion();
```

An array is returned consisting of the values listed in Table 9.14.

*Table 9.14   Array elements returned from **Win32::GetOSVersion()***

Element	Description
$Version[0]	The Win32 Service Pack number. This is also known as the Corrective Service Disk (CSD) number. This is a string value similar to "Service Pack 3". If no service packs have been applied, this value is an empty string.
$Version[1]	Major version number. If you are running NT 4.0, this value would be 4.

continues

Table 9.14   Continued

Element	Description
$Version[2]	Minor version number. If you are running NT 4.0 or 3.51, this value would be either 0 or 51, respectively.
$Version[3]	Build number. This is the Win32 build number.
$Version[4]	Platform ID. This value describes the type of Win32 operating system running on the machine. Possible values are: 0 (Win32s) 1 (Win32 as in 95 or 98) 2 (Win NT)

Retrieving Win32 Machine Type Information

Two functions describe the type of Win32 machine that the script is running on, be it Windows NT or Windows 95:

```
Win32::IsWinNT();

Win32::IsWin95();
```

Both functions return a TRUE if their respective type of machine is represented; otherwise, a 0 is returned. Example 9.20 demonstrates how to use the **IsWinNT()** and **IsWin95()** functions.

Example 9.20   *Using the **Win32::IsWinXX()** functions*

```
use Win32;
print "This is a Windows NT machine.\n" if( Win32::IsWinNT() );
print "This is a Windows 95 machine.\n" if( Win32::IsWin95() );
```

Retrieving Microprocessor Information

An undocumented function returns the type of microprocessor used by the computer. This function is **GetChipName()**:

```
Win32::GetChipName();
```

The return value is the type of the machine's microprocessor, such as "486" or "586". (On a Pentium II NT box, this function returns "586".)

This function should only be considered useful and accurate on a Windows 95 machine because it relies on data that Microsoft's Developer Network suggests should not be used for Windows NT machines (and is provided with NT for backward compatibility with Windows 95). This does not reflect multiprocessor environments. Additionally, this function has been depreciated in Perl 5.005 and is not available in that version.

For more accurate processor information, use the **GetProcessorInfo()** function in the **Win32::AdminMisc extension.**

Discovering Various Names

The **Win32** extension provides functions to discover the name of the current user, the computer name, and the current domain name:

```
Win32::LoginName();
Win32::NodeName();
Win32::DomainName();
```

Each of these will return their respective names or the string "<Unknown>" if the name could not be determined for some reason. Refer back to Example 9.19 to see the use of these functions.

Discovering the File System of a Drive

Different drives can be formatted using different file systems. A Windows NT machine may have one drive formatted as FAT, for example, another as NTFS, and yet another as HPFS (although NT's support for HPFS has been dropped). To help determine the format, there is the **FsType()** function:

```
Win32::FsType();
```

This function takes no parameters and will return a text string representing the file system (such as "FAT", "NTFS", or "HPFS"). There is a catch here, however. The drive that is reported is the current drive based on the current working directory. To check different drives, you must change the current working directory first (refer to the section titled "Discovering the Current Working Directory"). Additionally, because UNCs cannot be set as current working directories (by using the **Win32** extension), a script cannot discover a file system type for a UNC.

In Perl 5.005, this function has been changed to return either a text string or an array, depending on the return value's context. The array consists of the elements in Table 9.15.

*Table 9.15   Array elements returned from Perl 5.005's **Win32::FsType() function***

Array Element	Description
Element 0	String representing the text of the file system type (such as "FAT" or "NTFS").
Element 1	A numeric value representing different flags that the volume (or drive) have set.
Element 2	A numeric value representing the maximum number of characters that can be used in a file or directory name.

Example 9.21 shows a typical use of the **Win32::FsType()** function. Notice that line 5 attempts to change the current directory using an undocumented **Win32** extension function **SetCwd()**, which is covered in the section titled "Discovering the Current Working Directory."

Example 9.21   *Discovering a drive's file system type*

```
use Win32;
$NewDrive = "c:\\";
($Drive, $Path) = ( Win32::GetCwd() =~ /(\d:).*)/ );
print "The file system for $Drive is " . Win32::FsType() . "\n";
if( Win32::SetCwd( $NewDrive ) )
{
  ($Drive, $Path) = ( Win32::GetCwd() =~ /(\d:).*)/ );
  print "The file system for $Drive is " . Win32::FsType() . "\n";
}
```

Tip

*The **Win32::AdminMisc::GetVolumeInfo()** function effectively does the same thing as the Perl 5.005 version of **Win32::FsType()**. The only real difference is that with the **GetVolumeInfo()** function, any drive (or UNC) can be specified.*

Example 9.22 is similar to Example 9.21 except that it takes advantage of the additional information returned by the function when using Perl 5.005.

Example 9.22   *Discovering a drive's file system type with Perl 5.005*

```
01. use Win32;
02. $NewDrive = "c:\\";
03. ($Drive, $Path) = ( Win32::GetCwd() =~ /(\d:).*)/ );
04. @Volume = Win32::FsType();
05. print "The file system for $Drive is $Volume[0].\n";
06. print "The largest file name can be $Volume[2] characters long.\n";
07. if( Win32::SetCwd( $NewDrive ) )
08. {
09.   @Volume = Win32::FsType();
10.   print "The file system for $Drive is $Volume[0].\n";
11.   print "The largest file name can be $Volume[2] characters long.\n";
12. }
```

Discovering the Current Working Directory

Every executable that runs on a Win32 machine can have a current working directory. (It is also possible that an executable can have no working directory, but I digress.) Perl is no exception. If there is a need to discover what the current working directory is, use the **GetCwd()** function:

```
Win32::GetCwd();
```

This returns a text string that represents the current working directory. This will be in the format similar to "c:\Program Files\MyDirectory". Refer back to Example 9.21 for a demonstration of how to properly use the **GetCwd()** function.

Changing the Current Working Directory

Just as you can retrieve the current directory, you can also change it using the undocumented **SetCwd()** function:

```
Win32::SetCwd( $Path );
```

The only parameter that it takes is a string representing the path that is to become the current working directory. This path can be a relative or full path, but it cannot be a UNC.

If the function is successful, it returns a TRUE (1) value and the working directory is set to the new path; otherwise the function fails and returns undef. Refer back to Example 9.22 for a demonstration of how to properly use the **SetCwd()** function.

Discovering the Next Available Drive

Sometimes it is important to learn what the next available drive letter is. This represents a drive that is not mapped to a network share and has no CD-ROM, floppy disk drive, or hard drive attached to it. By determining the next available drive, you can figure out which drives do exist on your system. This information can be obtained by the **GetNextAvailDrive()** function:

```
Win32::GetNextAvailDrive();
```

This function returns the first free drive letter not in use. The returned value is a string that represents the drive's root path such as D:\ and M:\.

The most serious drawback of this function is that it looks at each drive starting a A:\ and working to Z:\. It reports back the first drive letter without any attached device. Because many machines have only one floppy disk drive, this means that the first available drive is B:\; therefore this function will typically return B:\ on most machines. This issue is addressed in Perl version 5.005, in which the function examines only drives C:\ through Z:\.

The **Win32::AdminMisc** extension has a series of similar functions that not only report the drive letters in use but also what type of device the drive letter represents (a CD-ROM, floppy disk drive, hard drive, network share). Refer to Chapter 3, "Administration of Machines," for more information.

Shutting Down a Machine

If your user account has been granted the appropriate privileges, your script can force a Win32 machine to shut down using the **InitiateSystemShutdown()** function:

```
Win32::InitiateSystemShutdown( $Machine, $Message, $Count, $Force, $Reboot );
```

The parameters for the **InitiateSystemShutdown**() function are defined as follows:

- $Machine is the name of a machine that is to shut down. If this parameter is an empty string (""), the local machine will be affected.

- $Message is a text string message that will be displayed on the screen of the computer specified in the first parameter. Typically this is something informing the user that the machine is going to shut down so all files should be saved.

- $Count is a numeric value that represents the amount of time (in seconds) before the shut down process begins—a type of countdown. When a shutdown is initiated, the message specified as the second parameter displays on the screen and the number of seconds before shut down display. This countdown will start at the time specified as the third parameter. An administrator will usually specify some amount of time, such as five minutes, giving a user enough time to properly finish saving files or finish and send email messages.

- $Force is a flag indicating whether the machine should force a shutdown. If a system shutdown is forced, applications will not be given a chance to save open files—they are just shut down. This forceful shutdown will occur if the fourth parameter is a non-zero value. Otherwise, each application will ask the user to save open files during the shutdown process.

- $Reboot is a flag that indicates whether to reboot the machine. If the value is non-zero, the machine will shut down followed by a reboot.

The **InitiateSystemShutdown**() function returns TRUE (1) if the specified computer will initiate the shutdown process; otherwise, the computer will not shut down and the function returns FALSE (0).

For the **Win32::InitiateSystemShutdown**() function to be successful, the user who calls the function must have the privilege SE_SHUTDOWN_NAME ("Force A Shutdown From A Remote System") enabled on the computer to be shut down.

If the $Count value (the third parameter) is zero (0), no message will be displayed on the specified computer and the shutdown will begin immediately—without any chance to abort the shutdown.

Aborting System Shutdown

At any time during the countdown process (before shutdown actually begins), the shutdown can be aborted using the **Win32::AbortShutdown**() function:

```
Win32::AbortSystemShutdown( $Machine );
```

The only parameter ($Machine) specifies which computer is to abort a shutdown. If the parameter is an empty string (""), the local machine is specified.

This function will return TRUE (1) if the function is successful. The function is considered successful if it submits the request to abort a shutdown and the specified machine accepts the request. Even if the specified machine is not shutting down but the abort request was successfully sent, the function is considered successful. Otherwise the function fails and returns FALSE (0).

Just as with **Win32::InitiateSystemShutdown**(), the SE_SHUTDOWN_NAME privilege ("Force A Shutdown From A Remote System") must be enabled on the specified machine for the user who calls the **Win32::AbortShutdown**() function.

If a user initiates a system shutdown by means of pressing Ctrl+Alt+Del and specifying "shutdown", the operating system will initiate the shutdown with a countdown of zero; therefore this type of shutdown cannot be aborted using this function.

> *Note*
>
> *Both the **Win32::InitiateSystemShutdown**() and **Win32::AbortShutdown**() have been moved out of the Win32 extension in Perl 5.005. The source code suggests that it will be moved to other extensions, but does not indicate which ones.*

Exiting Windows Instead of System Shutdown

There is an alternative to the **Win32::InitiateSystemShutdown**() function that provides for more options, although it only works on the local machine. This is the **Win32::AdminMisc::ExitWindows**() function:

```
Win32::AdminMisc::ExitWindows( $ExitType );
```

The only parameter ($ExitType) is a flag that specifies exactly how Windows will exit. This can be any value from Table 9.16. This value can also be logically OR'ed with EWX_FORCE, which will cause applications to quit without saving any open files. This is a harsh way of shutting down, but could be necessary if an unattended shutdown or logoff is required.

Table 9.16 Various Exit Types for the **Win32::AdminMisc::ExitWindows**() *function*

EWX_LOGOFF	Log the user off. Applications will be informed, so the user may be prompted to save files.
EWX_POWEROFF	Force the system to shut down and power off. The system must support poweroff. On Windows NT, the user account calling the function must have the SE_SHUTDOWN_NAME privilege.
EWX_REBOOT	Shut down the system and reboot the computer. On Windows NT, the user account calling the function must have the SE_SHUTDOWN_NAME privilege.

continues

Table 9.16   Continued

EWX_SHUTDOWN	Shut down the system, but don't reboot. On Windows NT, the user account calling the function must have the SE_SHUTDOWN_NAME privilege.

If the **Win32::AdminMisc::ExitWindows()** function is successful, it returns a TRUE value and begins its exiting process; otherwise, it fails and returns FALSE.

Resolving User SIDs

At first glance, one would think that the following two functions belong in Chapter 3 where user accounts are discussed. These functions are the **Win32::LookupAccountName()** and **Win32::LookupAccountSID()** functions. Chapter 3, however, refers to managing groups and accounts; whereas these functions do not manage anything. As a matter of fact, I find it difficult to determine exactly where they belong because they are more related to topics beyond the scope of this book (probably more suited to a discussion about Windows NT security). These functions either look up a security identifier (SID) for an account, or look up an account for a given SID. You will find it useful to understand exactly what a SID and an account mean.

An account is just a group of information that relates to a given user such as user name, password, privileges, and so forth. Accounts, however, are not only limited to users. Every machine registered as a member of a domain has an account. So does every local and global user group. Additionally every Primary Domain Controller (PDC) of a trusted domain has an account.

A SID is a binary data structure that NT's local security authority (or LSA— the heart of Windows NT security) maintains for each account. When an administrator sets permissions on a file or directory, he selects a user or group and grants it a particular type of permission. Every account has only one SID, and every SID is mapped to only one account.

For all practical purposes, a SID will not be of any use to a Perl script for several reasons. The most glaring reason is that you can't do anything with a SID. Because a SID is an internal Win32 data structure, it does not do much good to expose it to Perl. To quote from Ralph Davis' *Win32 Network Programming*, "[SIDs are] intended to be an opaque data type, which applications are not supposed to access directly." (Ralph Davis, *Win32 Network Programming*, Addison Wesley Developers Press, page 599) Because SIDs are mapped to accounts, it is much easier to specify a user's account or group name instead of managing a large binary data structure.

Now that SIDs have been briefly explained, it is time to examine the **LookupAccountName()** function:

```
Win32::LookupAccountName( $Machine, $Account, $Domain, $Sid, $Type );
```

The parameters for the **LookupAccountName**() function are defined as follows:

- $Machine is the name of the computer that is to perform the user account lookup. If this parameter is an empty string (" "), it assumes to use the local machine. This value can a machine name like SERVER_A or it can be a proper computer name such as \\SERVER_A.

- $Account is the name of the account to be looked up. This can be a user name, a group name, a trusted domain name, or a computer name (computer and Domain name must end with a dollar sign).

- $Domain is an output parameter, so it must be a scalar variable and will be set by the function; therefore it can be any value when calling the function (as long as it is a scalar variable and not a constant). If the function is successful, this scalar is set with the name of the domain in which the account belongs to.

- $Sid is an output parameter, so it must be a scalar variable. This variable will be set to the value of the account's SID.

- $Type is an output parameter, so it must be a scalar variable. This variable will be set to a value that represents the type of SID that this account represents. The value that this variable is set to can be any one of the values listed in Table 9.17.

Table 9.17   Different SID and account types

Value	Account Type
0x01	User account. The account (and SID) represents a typical user account.
0x02	Group account. The account (and SID) represents a global group.
0x03	Domain account. The account (and SID) represents a domain account. This is also known as a domain trust account that is used by one domain to log on to another domain. Examples are ACCOUNTING, REDMOND, and MY_DOMAIN.
0x04	An alias account. This is just the formal Win32 description for a local group account. Examples are ADMINISTRATORS, USERS, and GUESTS.
0x05	Well-known name account. These are those accounts that you always see but can never modify such as SYSTEM, EVERYONE, CREATOR OWNER.
0X06	Deleted account. This represents an account that has been deleted.
0x07	Invalid account. The account has become corrupt or somehow invalid.
0x08	Unknown. The system is unable to determine any information regarding the SID or account.

If the **LookupAccountName**() function is successful, it will map an account name from the specified machine to its domain name, SID, and type, and return a TRUE value. Otherwise, it returns FALSE.

After you have a SID, you can figure out which account it represents by using the **LookupAccountSID()** function:

```
Win32::LookupAccountSID( $Machine, $Sid, $Account, $Domain, $Type );
```

The parameters for the **LookupAccountSID()** function are defined as follows:

- $Machine is the name of the computer that is to perform the user account lookup. If this parameter is an empty string ("”), the **LookupAccountSID()** function assumes the local machine is performing the lookup. This value can be a machine name like SERVER_A or it can be a proper computer name like \\SERVER_A.

- $Sid is an account's SID. This is typically obtained using the **Win32::LookupAccountName()** function.

- $Account is an output parameter, so it must be a scalar variable. This is the name of the account that the $Sid represents.

- $Domain is an output parameter, so it must be a scalar and will be set by the function; therefore it can be any value when calling the function (as long as it is a scalar variable and not a constant). If the function is successful, this scalar is set with the name of the domain in which the account was found.

- $Type is an output parameter, so it must be a scalar variable. This variable will be set to a value that represents the type of account that the SID represents. The value that this variable is set to can be any one of the values previously listed in Table 9.17.

If the **LookupAccountSID()** function is successful, it maps a SID from the specified machine to its account name, domain name, and type and returns a TRUE value. Otherwise, it returns FALSE.

> *Note*
>
> *In Perl 5.005, the two functions **Win32::LookupAccountName()** and **LookupAccountSid()** have been removed from the **Win32** extension. They may find their way into another extension, but that is yet to be determined as of this writing.*

It is important to note that for both the **LookupAccountName()** and **LookupAccountSID()** functions, the $Sid is a binary data structure that by itself is of no use. This structure is usually something like 400 bytes long and does not provide any information that is easily discernable. Only those who have a specific need for this data will find it useful. Example 9.23 demonstrates a very simplistic use of **LookupAccountName()** and **LookupAccountSID()**.

Example 9.23 *Using Win32::LookupAccountName() and Win32::LookupAccountSid()*

```
01. use Win32;
02. @AccountTypes = ( 'a user',
                      'a global group',
                      'a domain',
                      'a local group',
                      'a well-known',
                      'a deleted',
                      'an invalid',
                      'an Unknown' );
03. @Accounts = ( 'system', 'creator owner', 'guest', 'administator' );
04. foreach $Name sort( @Accounts )
05. {
06.   if( Win32::LookupAccountName( '', $Name, $Sid, $Domain, $Type ) )
07.   {
08.     print "$Name is $AccountTypes[$Type] account.\n";
09.     push( @Sids, $Sid );
10.   }
11. }
12. foreach $Sid ( @Sids )
13. {
14. if( Win32::LookupAccountSid( '', $Sid, $Name, $Domain, $Type ) )
15.   {
16.     print "$Name is $AccountTypes[$Type] account.\n";
17.     push( @Sids, $Sid );
18.   }
19. }
```

Summary

This chapter covered some of the more obscure extensions that have functions of significance. These functions are not well understood. For those programmers who need to use them, however, they are indispensable.

The **Win32::Console** extension provides a script with the capability to manage console applications. This is quite handy when an administrator wants an application that requires user input but does not need the overhead of a GUI interface. Additionally, it is very handy for a service or CGI script to kick open a console and output information to it.

The **Win32::Sound** extension provides a coder with rudimentary sound capabilities. Most of the scripts I write to act as services use this extension to play back .WAV files, which tell me what event is occurring. A most valuable tool!

Considering that most of the Win32 Perl users are not familiar with creating their own proprietary extensions, the **Win32::API** extension is a godsend. Providing the capability to access most of the Win32 API functions, a script can access those functions that a public extension has yet to address.

Finally, the miscellaneous functions found in the **Win32** extension are often overlooked, but are a treasure chest of capability.

Perl's wide range of Win32 extensions makes it a remarkable scripting tool. Even the vast number of extensions cannot cover all programmers' needs, however. This is where Perl's capability to extend itself comes in. Chapter 10, "Writing Your Own Extension," discusses how you can create your own extension to solve those problems that no other extension solves.

Chapter **10**

Writing Your Own Extension

Everything has limits, and Perl is no exception. Although it is true that Perl has a very rich function set, there are things that it just cannot do.

If you need to do some task very quickly, for example, Perl may not be able to run fast enough for your needs. Or you may not be able to control your machine in a particular way with Perl. This is why extensions are written.

Because so many extensions have been written, most people never need to write their own extension; instead, you can use one that someone else made—usually people will upload their extensions to CPAN (the Comprehensive Perl Achieve Network) where you can get them whenever you need (http://www.cpan.org/).

Sometimes, however, even the extraordinary CPAN does not have what you need. This is the time you need to start to consider making your own extension. It may sound quite daunting, but it really isn't.

This chapter describes the basics behind the inner workings of Perl and how to apply that knowledge to create your very own Perl extension. For those who do not intend to write extensions, this chapter is useful in understanding how existing extensions work. Many bugs have been caught not by C++ programmers but by Perl hacks who were just looking over an extension's source code.

This chapter requires at least a little knowledge of C or C++; otherwise, you may be scratching your head in confusion. Likewise this chapter is only a brief introduction into creating extensions. It is meant for a coder who needs to extend Perl quickly and is by no means the definitive guide to making extensions. For that I refer you to either the Perl man pages (http://www.aisd.com/technology/perl/man/) or some other sources such as the excellent work *Advanced Perl Programming* by Sriram Srinivasan (O'Reilly & Associates).

What Is an Extension?

Perl has the capability to load external libraries of functions used to augment Perl's built-in functions. Different operating systems use different methods, but the Win32 platform uses DLLs (dynamic linked libraries) or, as the ActiveState version of Win32 Perl prefers, PLLs (Perl linked libraries).

These DLLs do not differ from the other DLLs you have on your system, such as KERNEL32.DLL, MSVCRT20.DLL, or VBRUN300.DLL. They are basically a collection of functions compiled and stored in one file. Really this is the same thing as a Perl module because it too is a collection of functions all stored in one file. The difference between a Perl extension and a Perl module is that the module contains functions written in Perl and the extension contains functions written in another language, typically C or C++. Additionally, extensions rely on modules to load the extension into Perl.

Because an extension is written in C (from this point on, I will assume you are using C/C++ to write the extension), it is capable of anything that C is capable of doing—and that is an awful lot!

Think about all the available programs written in C, such as administration utilities, word processors, and games. The capabilities of these C-based applications are quite extensive; your extension can be also. An extension can make calls into the Win32 API or load up other libraries. An example of this could be that an extension could load a faxing library and generate a fax that could be sent out over a fax/modem. Likewise you could write an extension that makes a connection to an Internet FTP site that then downloads a file. Although you can do the same thing using Perl functions, you may prefer an extension because of the speed increase an extension gives and/or source code protection issues. Everything covered in this book is either an extension or related to a Win32 Perl extension.

> ### Note
>
> *API is an acronym for application programming interface. APIs are everywhere and necessary for programmers. An API is the set of rules that a programmer must use to interact with some software. If you want to have Windows open a file, for example, you would use the* **OpenFile()** *function (if you open a file using C's* **fopen()** *it will, in turn, call* **OpenFile()**). *To successfully use* **OpenFile()**, *you must pass in certain values in a particular order. Therefore you must know the syntax and rules for calling the function. Likewise to understand the return value (usually which determines whether the function was successful), you need a list of return codes. This information is part of the Win32 API. If it were not for APIs, nobody would know how to tell Windows to open a file. It*

may seem obvious that APIs need to be publicly available, but there was a time when some companies, such as IBM, would not publish their APIs. This way they could charge a fee to those who wanted to use them. Even today some APIs are not easily obtained, such as Windows NT's LSA API (the Local Security Authority API, which is the set of functions that manipulate very low-level security).

What Is a DLL?

In the Win32 world, a DLL is just a collection of functions. Such a collection of functions is not necessarily simple, however. A DLL can be as simple as a single function or it can be as complex as being a self-contained program. All Win32 Perl extensions are DLLs, so it is important to understand how they work. They are discussed in detail later in the section titled "The **DllMain()** function."

How to Write a Perl Extension

Before understanding how to create an extension, you need to familiarize yourself with a couple of rather important topics, the first of which is how Perl handles variables.

The Guts of Perl Variables

A Perl scalar variable is really a memory structure known as an SV (scalar variable). When your script creates a new scalar variable, a memory structure is allocated and the value is assigned to it. If you ever access the value in a different context (such as accessing an integer as a string), the SV will convert itself to the context value. If you create a variable assigning it the value 10, for example, SV is created containing the integer value 10. If you then try to print out the value, the SV will have to convert the integer 10 into the text string "10". At that point, the SV will store the text string; therefore it will then have two values: 10 and "10". If you later try to add .5 to the variable, the SV will have to convert the value of 10 to a floating point of 10.0. This new value will also be stored so that there are three values associated with the value: an integer, a string, and a floating-point number.

It is important to note that when a string representation of a value is stored in an SV structure, it is stored not as a character string—as a C programmer might expect—but as a byte array. Both the number of bytes (or characters—the length of the string) as well as the data is stored in the structure. This is important because a Perl string (unlike a C char string) can have NUL characters (characters with a value of 0) within them. You can use a scalar variable to represent a text string (like "Hello world!") or binary data (like a GIF file or any other binary data). In C and C++, a character string is NUL-terminated, meaning that the end of the string is represented by a 0 value. A Perl string does not work this way. It works in a fashion more like Pascal where there is a string of bytes and a numeric value that tells how many bytes long the string is. Taking this into consideration, it may be inaccurate to refer to Perl strings. They are more like byte arrays, a collection of bytes that can be of any value.

Because a Perl string, also known as a PV (pointer variable), can be binary data, it is possible to place a C structure into a string. This is essentially what the Perl **pack**() function does. It is rather easy for an extension to pack a C structure (or multiple structures) into a PV and return it back to Perl where it can be **unpacked**()'ed. Example 10.23 illustrates this.

Therefore every time you create a Perl scalar variable, you are really allocating an SV memory structure.

Creating SVs

It is rather easy to create an SV. All you need to do is figure out which kind of SV to create. When you first create the SV, it must know which type of value it is being assigned. Table 10.1 lists the different SV value types.

Table 10.1   Different SV value types

Value Type	Description
PV	A string such as "Hello World". PV stands for pointer value. This can also be used to represent binary byte arrays and C structures.
IV	An integer value. This is a number large enough to hold a pointer. Typically this means that it is 32 bits long; depending on your machine, however, it could be 32 or 64 bits long.
NV	This is equivalent to a double value.
RV	A reference to another SV.

An SV is created by using the **newSVxx**() macros defined in the Perl header files (discussed later in the section titled "Beginning Your Extension"). The **newSVxx**() macros include the following:

```
SV* newSViv( IV lValue )
SV* newSVnv( double dValue)
SV* newSVsv( SV* pSV )
SV* newSVpv( char* szString, int iLength )
```

The result of each of these macros is a new SV pointer; otherwise if the macro failed for some reason, the return value is NULL.

These macros are defined as follows:

- **newSViv()**. Create an integer-based SV with the value passed into the macro. Notice that the IV data type is 32 bits (or 64 bits on a 64-bit machine) in length, longer than an int.

- **newSVnv()**. Accepts a double value.

- **newSVsv()**. Accepts a pointer to another SV. This will really just make a clone or copy of the existing SV passed into it

- **newSVpv()**. Requires a little bit of explaining. The first parameter passed into it (char* szString) is a pointer to an array of bytes. Notice that I specify an array of bytes, not characters. This is because this array is not necessarily a character string; it could be a data buffer. Perl does not expect that this string will be null terminated as a proper C string is.

  The second parameter to **newSVpv()** (int iLength) is the length of the array that the first parameter points to. This length should *not* include any terminating null. It is common to use the result of C's **strlen()** function as the value for the second parameter because it returns only the number of characters in the string and does not include the terminating null character. If this parameter is 0 or the constant na, the macro will calculate the length of the string using **strlen()**.

In Example 10.1, several SVs are created.

Example 10.1   *Creating several different SVs*

```
01. long lValue = 3287663;
02. double dValue = 3.141592;
03. char *pszValue = "This is a test string.";
04. char *pBuffer = {1, 0, 53, 255, 0, 32};
05. int iLength = 6;
06. SV *pSV[5];
07. pSV[0] = newSViv( lValue );
08. pSV[1] = newSVnv( dValue );
09. pSV[2] = newSVpv( pszValue, na );
10. pSV[3] = newSVpv( pBuffer, iLength );
11. pSV[4] = newSVsv( (SV*) pSV[1] );
```

Notice that the first **newSVpv()** in line 9 specifies na as the length. This tells the macro to use **strlen()** to figure out how long the string is. The second **newSVpv()** in line 10, however, specifies the exact length of the string because it contains data with embedded NUL characters. The last line makes a copy of the second SV that was created.

Determining the SV Type

If you are unsure which type an SV is, you can query it to discover the kind of data it holds. Using the **SVTYPE**() macro will do this:

```
enum SVTYPE( SV* pSV )
```

The parameter passed into the macro (pSV) is a pointer to an SV.

The **SVTYPE**() macro will return an enumerated value that represents a type of value. The enumerated types are defined in the header files discussed later in the section titled "Beginning Your Extension." This macro is the equivalent of using Perl's **ref**() function. The return value is one of the types listed in Table 10.2.

Table 10.2   Values returned from the SVTYPE() macro

Value	Description
SVt_IV	Integer
SVT_NV	Double
SVt_PV	String
SVt_PVAV	Array
SVt_PVHV	Hash
SVt_PVCV	A code segment that represents a Perl sub-routine. This is the equivalent of the value of \&MySubRoutine(). Use of this type in an extension is beyond the scope of this book
SVt_PVGV	A glob. This type represents a namespace. This is equivalent to Perl's *variable name feature. Use of this type in an extension is beyond the scope of this book
SVt_PVMG	A magical or blessed SV. This is a special SV that has "magical" powers. Either it acts as a Perl object or as a "smart" variable such as $!, which returns either an error number or error text string depending on the context used. Use of this type in an extension is beyond the scope of this book

When you stumble upon an SV and don't know what type of data it represents, you can use the **SVTYPE**() macro to determine how to handle it, as in Example 10.2. Note that line 17 is using **printf**() to print the string data obtained in line 16. This works fine if the SV contains only text data; but because an SV can contain binary data, including NUL characters, **printf**() may not be the best way to print its contents.

Example 10.2   *Dumping the contents of an SV*

```
01. void DumpSV( SV* pSV )
02. {
03.   switch( SVTYPE( pSV ) )
04.   {
05.     case SVt_IV:
06.         printf( "The SV is an integer with a value of %d.\n",
                    (long) SvIV( pSV ) );
07.         break;
08.
09.     case SVt_NV:
10.         printf( "The SV is an floating point with a value of %f.\n",
                    (double) SvNV( pSV ) );
11.         break;
12.
13.     case SVt_PV:
14.       {
15.         int iLength;
16.         char *pszString = SvPV( pSV, &iLength );
17.         printf( "The SV is an string with a length of %d and "
                    "a value of '%s'.\n",
                    iLength,
                    pszString );
18.       }
19.         break;
20.
21.     case default:
22.         printf( "Unable to determine the SV's type.\n" );
23.   }
24.   return;
25. }
```

Verifying an SV Type

When you have an SV, you can guarantee that the SV is of a particular type by using the **SvxOK**() macros:

```
int SvIOK( SV* pSV )
int SvNOK( SV* pSV )
int SvPOK( SV* pSV )
int SvROK( SV* pSV )
int SvOK( SV* pSV )
int SvTRUE( SV* pSV )
```

The only parameter that all these macros accept is a pointer to an SV structure.

Each macro will return a 1 if the specified SV contains a value of the specified type and a 0 if it does not. Table 10.3 explains which macro checks for what type of value.

Table 10.3 The SvxOK() macros and what they check

Macro	Functionality
SvIOK()	Checks for an integer value.
SvNOK()	Checks for a double value.
SvPOK()	Checks for a string value.
SvROK()	Checks for a reference value. References are discussed in the section titled "References."
SvOK()	Checks that any value is present. If no value is present (as in undef), FALSE is returned.
SvTRUE()	Checks that the value is TRUE—that is, it does not equate to 0 or undef.

Extracting Values from SVs

After you have an SV, you can discover the value it holds by using the **SvxV()** macros:

```
IV SvIV( SV* pSV )
double SvNV( SV* pSV )
char* SvPV( SV* pSV, int* iLength )
SV* SvRV( SV* pSV )
```

All these macros take only one parameter, which is a pointer to an SV. The exception to this is the **SvPV()** macro, which also requires a pointer to an integer to be passed in as a second parameter. If **SvPV()** is successful, it will return a char pointer to the SVs character string. Additionally the integer whose address is passed in as the second parameter is set to the length of the string.

If you use one of these macros on an SV of a different type, the SV will convert its value to the correct type. If an SV contains an integer but you use **SvPV()** on it, for example, the SV will create an internal character string version of the integer value and return a pointer to that string.

If one of these macros cannot convert the SV's data type to the specified type, the macro returns 0. If an SV contains the string "Hello world!", for example, the **SvIV()** macro will return 0 because there is no appropriate way to convert the text string into an integer. If the string were "321", it could be converted into the integer value 321; so the **SvIV()** macro would return the value 321.

The **SvIV()** macro will return the integer value from the specified SV.

The **SvNV()** macro will return the double value from the SV.

SvPV() will return a pointer to the character string held in the SV. The integer that the second parameter points to will be set to the length of the string.

The **SvRV**() macro will return a pointer to an SV that the reference passed in points to. It is important that any pointer passed into this macro actually be a reference to an SV and not an SV pointer. Use the **SVTYPE**() or **SvROK**() macros to ensure that you truly have a reference. References are explained later in the section titled "References."

Setting SV Values

When you need to set the value of an SV, you can use the **sv_setxv**() macros:

```
sv_setiv( SV* pSV, int iValue)
sv_setnv( SV* pSV, double dValue)
sv_setpv( SV* pSV, char* pszString )
sv_setpvn SV* pSV, char* pszString, int iLength )
sv_setsv( SV* pDestinationSV, SV* pSourceSV )
```

All these macros take a first parameter, which is a pointer to the SV whose value will be set. The macros are defined as follows:

- **sv_setiv**(). Sets the specified SV with the specified integer value.

- **sv_setnv**(). Sets the specified SV with the specified double value.

- **sv_setpv**(). Copies the string pointed to by the second parameter into the SV. The string must be a NUL-terminated string.

- **sv_setpvn**(). The same as **sv_setpv**() except that it accepts a third parameter, which specifies how long the string is (in bytes). This enables you to specify a string of data that has embedded NUL characters.

- **sv_setsv**(). Copies the source SV that is passed in as the second parameter to the destination SV that is passed in as the first parameter. The resulting destination SV (the first parameter) will be an identical copy of the source SV (the second parameter).

> *Note*
>
> Both the *sv_setpv*() and *sv_setpvn*() macros make copies of the strings passed into them. The memory whose pointer is passed into the macros can later be freed without any impact to the SV.

The sample code in Example 10.3 shows how to set SV values. Notice that the SV is created as an integer-based IV (line 1). Line 2 then changes the value of the SV. Finally, line 3 sets yet another value, but this time it will also translate the SV from an integer-based to a string-based SV. The point here is that an SV can change from type to type on-the-fly.

Example 10.3 *Setting the value of an SV*

```
SV* pSV = newSViv( 4567 );
set_iv( pSV, 1234567 );
set_pv( pSV, "Hello Joe!" );
```

Concatenating Strings

In addition to setting string values on SVs with **sv_setpv()** and **sv_setpvn()**, you can concatenate byte arrays (or strings) using the **sv_catpvx()** macros:

```
sv_catpv( SV* pSV, char* pszString )
sv_catpvn( SV* pSV, char* pData, int iLength )
```

Both macros take an SV pointer as their first parameter and take a pointer to a string for the second parameter. The string in **sv_catpv()** *must* be a NUL-terminated string. Example 10.4 describes how to concatenate two strings.

sv_catpvn() takes a third parameter, which is the length of the string. Its data (second parameter) can be any byte array. (It does not have to be a NUL-terminated string.)

Example 10.4 illustrates the use of **sv_catpvn()** to concatenate byte arrays.

Example 10.4 *Concatenating strings*

```
char pszString1 = "This is a ";
char pszString2 = "concatenation test!";
SV* pSV = newSVpv( pszString1 );
sv_catpvn( pSV, pszString2 );
printf( "%s", SvPV( pSV ) );
```

The XS function **ExtensionGetFileSizes()** searches for all files that match the specified criteria. For each file found, a memory structure is filled out that holds the file's name and size. Line 4 in Example 10.4 concatenates this structure into a PV using **sv_catpvn()**. The Perl script that calls the **Win32::Test::GetFileSizes()** extension in this example will need to use **unpack()** to access the structures. Example 10.5 shows how to unpack the data structures returned by a call to the example **GetFileSizes()** function.

Example 10.5 *Unpacking concatenated data structures from the extension in Example 10.4*

```
use Win32::Test;
$Count = Win32::Test::GetFileSizes( "c:\\temp\\*.*", $Data );
%List = ( unpack( "A256l" x $Count, $Data ) );
```

Reference Counts

When an SV is created, it contains a reference counter that is set to 1. This counter indicates how many other structures, such as references (RVs are covered in the next section "References"), point to this memory structure. If you create a reference that points to an SV, for example, the SV's reference counter increases by one. If you later attempt to delete the SV, the reference count decreases by one. Only when the reference count is 0 is it actually purged from memory.

This prevents some very bad situations, such as an RV that points to an SV that has been deleted. Any attempt to dereference the RV under this circumstance could be quite catastrophic because the reference is pointing to memory that is no longer a valid SV; it could be pointing to anything! Bad, very, very bad.

A reference count can manually be increased or decreased, but you are strongly discouraged from doing so unless you know what you are doing. If you need to force an SV to de-allocate itself from memory, you could decrease the reference count until it is 0 (at which time Perl will automatically de-allocate the memory structure). Likewise if you want to guarantee that an SV is not allocated, you could manually increase the reference count. The **svREFCNT_xxx()** macros manage reference counts:

```
svREFCNT_inc( SV* pSV )
svREFCNT_dec( SV* pSV )
```

The macros will either increase or decrease the reference count of the SV passed in to it. If the reference count is decreased to 0, the SV is purged from memory.

References

A special type of SV is known as a reference. References are the same as the Perl reference $Ref in Example 10.6.

Example 10.6   *Using a reference*
```
$Dozen = 12;
$Ref = \$Dozen;
print "There are $$Ref in a dozen.";
```

Running that code will print out the string "There are 12 in a dozen." When you create a Perl reference, a new SV is created and marked as a reference. This SV will point to another SV structure.

When the variable $Dozen is assigned its value, an SV structure is allocated in memory. Then when the script creates the variable $Ref, Perl allocates yet another SV structure. Because this second SV is going to be assigned the reference to the $Dozen variable (that is, what \$Dozen represents), Perl will set a flag in $Ref's SV structure that indicates that it is a reference to another SV. Then Perl will set a pointer in $Ref's SV structure to point to $Dozen's SV.

To write the equivalent of Example 10.6 in C, you would make an int and assign it the value 12. Then you make an integer pointer and you assign it the address of your first integer. You then print out your string as in Example 10.7

Example 10.7   *C equivalent of Example 10.6*

```
int iDozen;
int *piRef;
iDozen = 12;
piRef = &iDozen;
printf( "There are %d in a dozen.", *piRef );
```

This may sound rather vague and complicated, but it isn't. Consider that for every scalar variable you make in Perl, you are creating an SV somewhere in memory. If you create a reference variable, you are still creating an SV, but no scalar value will be stored in it. Instead, a pointer to another SV will be stored. This allows Perl to dereference the SV and find the original SV structure that has the value printed in Example 10.6.

To create a reference in an extension, you can use the **newRV()** macros:

```
SV* newRV( SV* )
SV* newRV_inc( SV* )
SV* newRV_noinc( SV* )
```

All these methods return a pointer to an SV structure. This SV structure will, in turn, point to another SV. Normally when you create a reference, the SV you are referring to will increase its reference counter by one. All these macros except **newRV_noinc()** will do this. Actually **newRV()** and **newRV_inc()** perform the same function; there is no difference between the two macros. Generally speaking, **newRV_noinc()** is not used except for some specific reason to not increase the reference count. Most all references will increase the reference count.

All the **newRV()** macros accept an SV pointer, which is what the new reference will point to as illustrated in Example 10.8. This example is not as clear as if we were doing this using straight C (rather than using Perl SVs) as in Example 10.8. This is because to illustrate how RVs are used, we need to create an RV and then immediately dereference it. This defeats creating an RV altogether, but it does illustrate how one is created and dereferenced. Line 4 creates the reference to pSV. Line 6 then dereferences pRefSV. Note that after line 6 pDerefedSV is equal to pSV. Finally, line 8 extracts the integer value from the SV and prints it out in line 9.

Example 10.8   *Creating a reference to an SV*

```
    // First create an SV to hold the integer 12...
SV* pSV = newSViv( 12 );
    // Now create a reference SV (an RV) which points to pSV...
SV* pRefSV = newRV( pSV );
    // Now we must dereference the reference to get the original SV...
SV* pDerefedSV = SV( pRefSV );
    // Last we get the integer value from the dereferenced SV...
int iDozen = SvIV( pDerefedSV );
printf( "There are %d in a dozen.", iDozen );
```

> **Warning**
>
> *The lifetime of an SV is defined by its reference count. As long as the count is greater than 0, the SV is alive. Because of this, it is really important that SVs not be created on the stack—unless your code is aware that stack-based variables are only available in the scope of a given code block. Consider this code:*
>
> ```
> SV *MyBadFunction()
> {
>   SV svBad;
>   SV *pReference = new_RV( &svBad );
>   return( pReference );
> }
> ```
>
> *The problem here is that the SV svBad is an automatic variable (created on the stack). The function returns a reference to svBad; when the function returns, however, svBad is automatically destroyed. The returned reference does not know that svBad has been destroyed, however. Any attempt to dereference the returned SV pointer will most likely cause a fault.*

The SV Lifespan

When the reference count of an SV is decremented to 0, the SV is automatically destroyed and purged from memory. This defines the lifespan of an SV. If you create an SV, it remains in memory until you either manually remove it or decrease its reference count to 0 (in which case Perl will remove it). This can be a problem if you need to create an SV that you return to Perl from some function. Suppose, for example, that you write a function that adds two numbers together and creates an SV to hold the result. If you want to pass this SV back to Perl so that your script can use it, you may run into a slight problem. What if no variable catches your return result?

In this example, assume that your Perl script calls your function like this:

```
$Result = AddNumbers( 1, 2 );
```

The **AddNumbers**() function will add 1 and 2 together, and will then create an SV that holds the result. The SV is then passed back to Perl so that $Result will use it. When the SV is created, the reference count is 1. When the SV is assigned to $Result, the reference count will increase to 2. Later if $Result is destroyed, the reference count is reduced back to 1, but because it is not 0 it is not purged from memory. This means that you may have SVs hanging around with reference counts of 1 that are just taking up memory. This is not a good thing.

What you can do is tag the SV as *mortal*. When an SV is mortal, Perl will keep track of it and when it leaves the Perl script's current scope, its reference count will automatically be decreased. If you tag the SV created in the **AddNumbers()** function as mortal, its reference count will decrease by one after it leaves the **AddNumbers()** function (the scope in which it was created). If some variable, such as $Result, links to it, the reference count is increased to 1 again and it is not destroyed. When $Result is destroyed, however, the reference count goes to 0, and hence the SV is also destroyed.

Mortality just guarantees that an SV that has been created will be destroyed if it is no longer used.

To indicate mortality, you can use one of the **mortal** macros:

```
SV* sv_newmortal()
SV* sv_2mortal( SV* pSV )
SV* sv_mortalcopy( SV* pSV )
```

These macros are defined as follows:

- **sv_newmortal()**. Creates a new SV tagged as mortal. You can use this SV as you would any other, but at the end of the current scope it will be destroyed.

- **sv_2mortal()**. Marks an existing SV passed into the macro as mortal.

- **sv_mortalcopy()**. Creates a copy of the SV passed in and marks that new SV as mortal.

All the **mortal** macros return a pointer to a new SV that has been marked as mortal. The exception to this is **sv_2mortal()**, which does not create a new SV but just marks the SV passed in as mortal and returns a pointer to it.

If an SV has been marked as mortal, you can manually increase its reference count by one to essentially remove its mortality. This means that when the SV leaves the current Perl scope, its reference count is decremented (but from 2 to 1). Because the count does not reach 0, it is not purged from memory.

Perl and Arrays

When you deal with an array, you are playing with a special type of SV known as an AV (array variable). Simply stated, an AV is a structure that contains a list of pointers to other SV-like structures. These other structures can be other SV-related structures such as scalars (SV), arrays (AV), hashes (HV), and references (RV).

Creating AVs

To create a new array, you use the **newAV()** macro:

```
AV* newAV()
```

A pointer to the AV structure is returned.

An alternative to **newAV()** is the **av_make()** macro. This will create an array and populate it, assuming that you already have an array of SV pointers:

```
AV* av_make( int iNumber, SV** pSVList )
```

The first parameter (int iNumber) is the number of elements that will be placed into the array.

The second parameter (SV** pSVList) is a pointer to an array of SV pointers.

This will return a pointer to the newly created AV as depicted in Example 10.9.

Example 10.9   *Creating AVs*

```
01. AV* pAV1 = newAV();
02. AV* pAV2 = NULL;
03. SV* ppSV[ 10 ];
04. int iTemp;
05. for( iTemp = 0; iTemp < 10; iTemp++ )
06. {
07.   ppSV[ iTemp ] = newSViv( iTemp );
08. }
09. pAV2 = av_make( 10, ppSV );
10. printf( "There are %d elements in pAV2.\n", av_len( pAV2 ) );
```

After you have an AV, you can query it to find out how many elements it contains using the **av_len()** macro:

```
long av_len( AV* pAV )
```

The **av_len()** macro takes a pointer to an AV and returns the number of elements that the AV contains.

Array Management

When you have an AV, you can add elements to and remove elements from it by using the **av** series of macros. The first of these macros is **av_clear()**, which will clear out the contents of the array:

```
av_clear( AV* pAV )
```

The only parameter is a pointer to the AV. When this macro is used, the reference count for every element in the array will be decremented by one. After this decrement, each element is replaced with the undef value. The overall effect is that the array is cleared—that is, no more values are left in the array. The array, however, remains the same size.

There is no return value.

Similar to **av_clear**() is the **av_undef**() macro, which will not only decrement each element's reference count but it will also decrement the array's reference count.

```
av_undef( AV* pAV )
```

This macro does not return any value. As with any SV, if an element's reference count is decremented to 0, it is de-allocated from memory automatically. Similarly if the array's reference count is decremented to 0, it is freed up from memory.

If your code just wants to remove all entries from the array, it would want to use **av_clear**(); but if it needs to destroy an array, it needs to call **av_undef**().

You can put elements into an array as well as remove them from the array. This is where the **av_push**() and **av_pop**() macros come in:

```
av_push( AV* pAV, SV* pSV )
SV* av_pop( AV* pAV )
```

The first parameter for both of these macros (AV* pAV) is a pointer to the AV.

The **av_push**() accepts one additional parameter (SV* pSV), which is a pointer to an SV that is to be pushed on to the end of the array. After this has been done, the number of elements in the array increases by one and the SV pointer passed in becomes the last element in the array. This macro does not return any value.

The **av_pop**() macro will return a pointer to the SV that has been popped off of the array. The SV pointer returned points to the SV that was the last element of the array. After the macro is called, the second to last element becomes the last element, and hence the number of array elements decreases by one.

The reference count of the SV removed from the array by the **av_pop**() macro is *not* altered by the pop action. This is important because if your code calls **av_pop**() but ignores its return value, the popped SV will not be destroyed (because its reference count is not altered). Let's say that your code pops off 100 stack elements, but it ignores the return value. Unless somehow the SVs popped off of the array are destroyed, they will be sitting around taking up memory. Example 10.10 shows two functions that pop all elements off of an array. The first one, **RemoveElementsBad**(), pops off all elements from the array, but ignores them. **RemoveElementsGood**() marks each SV popped off the array as mortal. This guarantees that the SV will be destroyed by Perl.

Example 10.10   *Popping elements from an array*

```
01. void RemoveElementsBad( AV* pAV )
02. {
03.    int iCount = av_len( pAV );
04.    while( iCount--)
05.    {
06.       av_pop( pAV );
07.    }
08. }
09.
10. void RemoveElementsGood( AV* pAV )
11. {
12.    int iCount = sv_len( pAV );
13.    while( iCount--)
14.    {
15.       sv_2mortal( av_pop( pAV ) );
16.    }
17. }
```

Two additional macros perform similar functions to **av_push()** and **av_pop()**; these are called **av_unshift()** and **av_shift()**:

```
av_unshift( AV* pAV, long lNumber )
SV* av_shift( AV* pAV )
```

Both macros accept a first parameter (pAV), which is a pointer to the AV to be processed.

The **av_unshift()** accepts a second parameter (lNumber), which is the number of elements to put the front of the array starting at element 0. Each element added to the array contains the undef value. This macro is handy if you want to grow the array size without having to add SVs.

The **av_shift()** is just like **av_pop()** except that the first element is removed from the array. The return value is a pointer to the element that has been removed from the array. The array is decremented by one. Just like **av_pop()**, the removed SV's reference count is not altered.

Only two more macros allow for array management. These are the **av_fetch()** and **av_store()** macros:

```
SV** av_store( AV* pAV, long lIndex, SV* pSV )
SV** av_fetch( AV* pAV, long lIndex, long lValue )
```

Both macros accept three parameters. The first (AV* pAV) is a pointer to an AV that will be processed.

The second parameter (long lIndex) is the index number of the element to be either stored or retrieved.

For the **av_store()** macro the third parameter (SV* pSV) is a pointer to an SV that is to be stored into the element specified in parameter two.

The **av_fetch**() macro accepts a third value; if it is a non-zero value, the specified array element will be replaced with undef. This is equivalent to calling **av_fetch**() followed by **av_store**() in which you are storing an empty SV in the same array element. Whereas this is not a common practice, it can be useful if you are just removing an element from an array.

Both **av_store**() and **av_fetch**() return a pointer to the SV that is the element of the array specified by the second parameter. Example 10.11 shows how these macros can be used.

Example 10.11   *Manipulating array elements*

```
01. void DumpArray( AV *pAV );
02.
03. SV* pSV;
04. SV* pSV2;
05. AV* pAV = newAV();
06. int iTemp;
07.
08. //  Add ten elements to the array
09. for( iTemp = 0; iTemp < 10; iTemp++ )
10. {
11.    pSV = newSViv( iTemp );
12.    av_push( pAV, pSV );
13. }
14.
15. // pAV now contains: [(front) 9, 8, 7, 6, 5, 4, 3, 2, 1, 0 (end)]
16. printf( "The array contains:\n" );
17. DumpArray( pAV );
18.
19. // Remove the first array element (9)
20. pSV = av_pop( pAV );
21.
22. // pSV now == 9
23. // pAV now contains: [8, 7, 6, 5, 4, 3, 2, 1, 0]
24.
25. //  Take the last element and move it to the first element
26. pSV2 = av_shift( pAV );
27.
28. // pSV2 now == 0
29. // pAV now contains: [8, 7, 6, 5, 4, 3, 2, 1]
30. av_push( pAV, pSV2 );
31.
32. // pAV now contains: [0, 8, 7, 6, 5, 4, 3, 2, 1]
33. // Add an empty element to the end of the array
34. av_unshift( pAV, 1 );
35.
36. // pAV now contains: [0, 8, 7, 6, 5, 4, 3, 2, 1, undef]
37. //  Store the previously removed element at the end
38. iTemp = (int) av_len( pAV );
```

```
39.
40. //  Decrease the index by one since the array is zero based
41. //  (the first element starts at position 0)
42. printf( "The array is now:\n" );
43. DumpArray( pAV );
44.
45. void DumpArray( pAV )
46. {
47.    int iCount = av_len( pAV );
48.    int iTemp;
49.    for( iTemp = 0; iTemp < iCount; iTemp++ )
50.    {
51.      SV **pSVTemp = av_fetch( pAV, iCount );
52.      printf( "\tElement %d: '%s'\n", iTemp, SvPV( *pSVTemp ) );
53.    }
54. }
```

Hash Variables

Perl provides the capability to create arrays with associated keys—that is, each element in the array has a name associated with it. This way it is not necessary to keep track of which element number contains what data inside an array. Instead you always refer to the array's element by name, not number. This is called an *associated array*, commonly known as a *hash*.

Creating Hashes

A hash is created by using the **newHV()** macro:

```
HV* newHV()
```

The macro will create a new hash and return a pointer to it. Unlike arrays, this is the only macro that can create a hash.

Storing Hash Values

After you have a hash, you can store values into it using the **hv_store()** macro:

```
SV** hv_store( HV* pHV, char* pszKey, long lKeyLength, SV* pValue, long lHash )
```

The first parameter (HV* pHV) is a pointer to the hash structure you are storing the value into.

The second parameter (char* pszKey) is a character string (or a byte array) that represents the key the value will be associated with.

The third parameter (long lKeyLength) is the length of the string passed in as the second parameter. You *must* pass in a value here because the macro will not figure it out for you.

The fourth parameter (SV* pValue) is a pointer to an SV that you are storing.

The fifth, and last, parameter (long lHash) is the hash to use. If you pass in a 0, the macro will create a hash for you. You should pass in 0 unless you really know what you are doing.

If the **hv_store**() macro is successful, it returns a pointer to a pointer to the SV. A pointer to the SV is stored into the hash. This is important to understand because if the SV is destroyed, the hash entry points to an invalid SV.

Retrieving Hash Values

To retrieve a value from a hash, you use the **hv_fetch**() macro:

```
SV** hv_fetch( HV* pHV, char* pszKey, long lKeyLength, long lVal )
```

The parameters for the **hv_fetch**() macro are defined as follows:

- HV* pHV is a pointer to the HV.

- char* pszKey is a pointer to a character string that is the key.

- long lKeyLength is the length of the key string that is passed in as the second parameter. You need to specify this because the macro will not figure it out for you.

- long lVal is used internally and you should always specify a 0 for this value.

If the **hv_fetch**() macro is successful, it returns a pointer to a pointer to an SV. If the macro fails, it returns NULL.

Because the return value is a double pointer, you must make sure that you dereference the pointer before using it as in Example 10.12.

Example 10.12   *Fetching a key's value from a hash*

```
01. //...assuming that pHV is an existing hash...
02. SV** ppSV = NULL;
03. char* pszKey = "name";
04. ppSV = hv_fetch( pHV, pszKey, strlen( pszKey ), 0 );
05. if( NULL != ppSV )
06. {
07.   SV* pSV = *ppSV;
08.   char* pszValue = SvPV( pSV, na );
09.   printf( "The value of the %s key is: %s.\n", pszKey, pszValue );
10. }
```

Verifying Key Existence in a Hash

To check whether a key exists in a hash, you can use the **hv_exists**() macro:

```
hv_exists( HV* pHV, char* pszKey, long lKeyLength )
```

The parameters for the **hv_exists**() macro are defined as follows:

- `HV* pHV` is a pointer to the hash.

- `char* pszKey` is a pointer to a string that is the key name.

- `long lKeyLength` is the length of the key specified in the second parameter.

If the key exists, the **hv_exists**() macro will return a TRUE; otherwise, it returns a FALSE.

Deleting Keys from a Hash

To delete a key from a hash, you use the **hv_delete**() macro:

```
SV *hv_delete( HV* pHV, char* pszKey, long lKeyLength, long lFlag)
```

The parameters for the **hv_delete**() macro are defined as follows:

- `HV* pHV` is a pointer to the hash.

- `char* pszKey` is a pointer to a string that is the key name.

- `long lKeyLength` is the length of the key specified in the second parameter.

- `long lFlag` is a flag. If this flag is set to G_DISCARD, the key will be deleted and nothing is returned. Otherwise the key is deleted, but a mortal copy of the SV that the key pointed to is created and returned.

Removing Data from a Hash

Two other macros exist to remove data from a hash: the **hv_clear**() and **hv_undef**() macros:

```
hv_clear( HV* pHV )
hv_undef( HV* pHV )
```

Both of these macros require a pointer to a hash to be passed in.

The **hv_clear**() will clear out all the entries in the hash, but the hash will remain. The reference count for each SV that the hash's elements point to is decremented. Then each element in the hash is removed. This does not explicitly destroy the SV in each element. (If their count becomes zero, however, Perl destroys them automatically.) Just as with **av_clear**(), the elements are removed, but the hash itself remains (its reference count is not touched). After the **hv_clear**() macro is called, the hash is empty.

The **hv_undef**() will, like **hv_clear**(), clear out all the entries, but it will also destroy the hash. This causes all elements' reference counts to be decremented. Note that this will not explicitly destroy any of the SVs. (If their reference counts become zero, however, Perl then destroys them.) Unlike **hv_clear**(), **hv_undef**() decrements the hash's reference count. If the reference count becomes zero, the hash is destroyed.

Walking Through a Hash

Walking through a hash is not as simple as one would like, but it really is not too difficult either. Basically if you need to enumerate each key in a hash, you must follow these steps:

1. Prepare the hash for a walkthrough using the **hv_iterinit**() macro.

2. Locate the first element by calling the **hv_iternext**() macro. The first time this macro is called, it will point to the first element in the hash.

3. Retrieve both the current element's key and value with **hv_iterkey**() and **hv_iterval**() macros, respectively.

4. Repeat steps 2 and 3 until either all elements have been exhausted or until the desired element has been found.

An alternative to steps 2 and 3 is to call the **hv_iternextsv**() macro.

To start a hash walkthrough, you need to first prepare the hash to be iterated with the **hv_iterinit**() macro:

```
long hv_iterinit( HV* pHV )
```

The **hv_iterinit**() macro takes in one parameter, which is a pointer to a hash. The macro will prepare the HV to be iterated. It also returns the number of keys that are in the hash.

After the hash has been prepared for iteration, you need to use the **hv_iternext**() macro:

```
HE* hv_iternext( HV* pHV )
```

The only parameter is a pointer to the hash you are iterating.

The **hv_iternext**() macro will return a pointer to a data structure known as an HE (a hash element). This is a pointer to a link in a linked list that the HV uses to store its keys and values. This pointer is used in other macros.

Now that you have iterated and have an HE pointer, you can use it to retrieve both the key and value of the hash's element using the **hv_iterkey**() and **hv_iterval**() macros:

```
char* hv_iterkey( HE* pHE, long* lKeyLength )
SV* hv_iterval( HV* pHV, HE* pHE )
```

The **hv_iterkey**() macro accepts the HE pointer returned from the **hv_iternext**() macro as a first parameter.

The second parameter of **hv_iterkey**() (lKeyLength) is a pointer to a long. The length of the key name will be set into this long. The macro returns a pointer to a character string, which is the name of the key.

The **hv_iterval**() macro accepts a pointer to the hash as the first parameter and the HE pointer that is returned by the **hv_internext**() macro as the second parameter.

The **hv_iterval**() macro will return a pointer to the SV that holds the value associated with the particular element in the hash.

Now that you have retrieved both the key and values of the iterated hash element, you can call **hv_iternext**() again to move on to the next element in the hash.

Just for the sake of convenience, you can use the **hv_iternextsv**() macro. This macro iterates the next element in the hash and retrieves the key and value at the same time:

```
SV* hv_iternextsv( HV* pHV, char** ppszKey, long* lKeyLength )
```

The parameters for the **hv_iternextsv**() macro are defined as follows:

- pHV is a pointer to the hash you are iterating.

- ppszKey is a pointer to a pointer to the element's key name.

- long* lKeyLength is a pointer to a long that will be stored with the length of the key name.

The **hv_iternextsv**() macro will advance to the next element in the hash, and will then return a pointer to the key's value's SV.

> ### Warning
>
> *When walking through a hash, it is safe to delete the current element using hv_delete(), but it is not safe to store anything in the hash (using hv_store()). The reason behind this is that when you store elements in a hash, the hash may need to reorganize its internal hash. This would break the capability to continue walking through the hash.*
>
> *If hv_store() was called, your code would have to call hv_iterinit() and start the walkthrough all over.*

Example 10.13 illustrates all the iteration macros. The example creates two functions—**DumpHash**() and **DumpHash2**(). The former uses the **hv_iternext**() technique, and the latter uses **hv_iternextsv**(). Notice that in both functions pSVValue points to the element's value SV. In lines 13 and 28, the **SvPV**() macro is used to convert the SV to a character string. This makes it easier to print out because we then do not have to be concerned with whether the value is an IV, NV, or PV.

Example 10.13   *Iterating a hash*

```
01. void DumpHash( HV *pHV )
02. {
03.   HE *pHE = NULL;
04.   long lElements = hv_iterinit( pHV );
05.   printf( "Dumping %d elements:\n", lElements );
06.   printf( "\tKey\tValue\n\t--\t-----\n" );
07.
08.   while( NULL != ( pHE = hv_iternext( pHV ) ) )
09.   {
10.     long lKeyLength;
11.     char *pszKey = hv_iterkey( pHE, &lKeyLength );
12.     SV *pSVValue = hv_iterval( pHV, pHE );
13.     printf( "\t'%s'\t'%s'\n", pszKey, SvPV( pSVValue, na ) );
14. }
15.
16. void DumpHash2( HV *pHV )
17. {
18.   long lKeyLength;
19.   char *pszKey = NULL;
20.   SV *pSVValue = NULL;
21.
22.   long lElements = hv_iterinit( pHV );
23.   printf( "Dumping %d elements:\n", lElements );
24.   printf( "\tKey\tValue\n\t--\t-----\n" );
25.
26.   while( NULL != ( pSVValue = hv_iternextsv( pHV, &pszKey, &lKeyLength ) ) )
27.   {
28.       printf( "\t'%s'\t'%s'\n", pszKey, SvPV( pSVValue, na ) );
29.   }
30. }
```

Beginning Your Extension

The overview of an extension is quite simple. It consists of the following elements:

- Any required headers including the necessary Perl headers

- Any required non-Perl functions

- Any Perl functions; those which require the use of the **XS**() macro

- The Perl bootstrap function

- Optionally, the Windows **DllMain**() function

The very first thing you should do in your extension source file is to include the headers. Some Perl headers are required and need to be included. In Example 10.13, line 13 declares that the lines 13–21 are to be compiled as regular C and not as C++ (by using extern "C"). Otherwise, you will see some pretty nasty function name mangling, which can be the cause of many frustrated debugging sessions. This is only necessary if you are using C++ with either the ActiveState headers or the headers for Perl 5.005 *and* PERL_OBJECT is defined.

With both the ActiveState and 5.005 versions of Perl, you can make use of the CPerl class. This requires C++ to compile and it provides many nifty capabilities. Basically this class abstracts the Perl interpreter into an object. All the Perl functions are mapped to methods of the object. In version 5.005, the CPerl class has been renamed to CPerlObj (but they are effectively the same).

> **Tip**
>
> *If you are compiling the extension using the ActiveState headers, you need to define the following three macros:*
>
> ```
> MSWIN32
> EMBED
> PERL_OBJECT
> ```
>
> *Without these macros defined (they can be empty, but need to be defined), the build process will fail. In my extensions, I test for the definition of* PERL_OBJECT. *If it is not defined, I assume that I am using the core distribution's headers; otherwise, I assume that I am using ActiveState's.*
>
> *I usually define these macros in the MSVC project settings dialog box. This way they are not hard coded in my files anywhere and I can create different configurations with or without these macros, enabling me to create configurations that compile using the core distribution's headers or the ActiveState headers.*

To use the CPerl/CPerlObj class, a macro called PERL_OBJECT must be defined. The macro can be empty, but it needs to be defined. This can be defined in the build settings of a Microsoft Visual C++ project, or it can be hard wired into the source files.

It is very important to understand that an extension compiled with PERL_OBJECT will not work with Perl that was not compiled with the macro defined and vice versa.

Notice that in Example 10.14 there are some checks for Borland and Microsoft compilers. This has been borrowed from Gurusamy's code; he was the first to point this out to me and I use it religiously now.

Example 10.14 *Including the required Perl headers*

```
01. #ifdef __BORLANDC__
02.        // wchar_t is in tchar.h but unavailable unless UNICODE is defined
03.    typedef wchar_t wctype_t;
04. #endif
05.
06. #include <windows.h>
07.        //  Gurusamy's right, Borland compilers need this here!
08. #include <stdio.h>
09.        //  Gurusamy's right, MS compilers need this here!
10. #include <math.h>
11.
12. #if defined(__cplusplus)  && !defined(PERL_OBJECT)
13.    extern "C" {
14. #endif
15.
16. #include "EXTERN.h"
17. #include "perl.h"
18. #include "Xsub.h"
19.
20. #if defined(__cplusplus)  && !defined(PERL_OBJECT)
21.    }
22. #endif
```

Writing Extension Functions

When you start writing the C/C++ functions that you want to be able to access from within Perl, you need to use the **XS()** macro:

```
XS( FunctionName )
```

The **XS()** macro declares the function as a Perl function. The parameter passed in will be the function name that will be mapped in the bootstrap function (refer to the section titled "The Bootstrap Function").

Really this is quite easy to do. Whenever you are creating a function that will be called directly from a Perl script, you just declare the function using the **XS()** macro. This will guarantee that the function can communicate with Perl.

After you have declared your function, you need to set up the Perl variables that are needed by many of Perl's macros. This is accomplished using the **dXSARGS** macro:

```
dXSARGS
```

That is it, nothing more. This will set up your Perl stacks and create the sp (stack pointer) variable in addition to a series of other things. Basically the **dXSARGS** macro is what declares everything your function needs to get values passed into the function from Perl and set variables to be passed back to Perl. **dXSARGS** also initializes some variables that are used by Perl's macros and can be used by your function.

The Stack

Perl makes use of several stacks, but one stack requires a bit of explanation. When a Perl script calls an extension function, any values passed into the function are placed on a stack. The extension's function is given access to this stack, which it can use for both input and output between the extensions function and Perl. This stack is just an array of SV pointers. Each pointer represents a passed-in parameter. This is stack is the equivalent to a Perl subroutine's @_ array.

When a function calls the **dXSARGS** macro, the function is given access to the stack and a variable called items is created. The items variable contains a value indicating how many parameters were passed into the function (just like argc).

Retrieving Values Passed into the Function

To retrieve the passed in parameters from the stack, you can use the **ST()** macro:

```
SV* ST( int iElement )
```

The **ST()** macro accepts an integer that identifies which element off of the stack you are requesting. The return value is a pointer to an SV.

Make sure that you do not specify an element that is greater than or equal to items, because items is the total number of elements on the stack and the stack is a zero-based array. This means that if items is 1 (indicating only one value on the stack), the one parameter is in element 0 of the stack. This would be accessed with **ST(0)**. Because there is no second value, a call to **ST(1)** would be a bad idea.

After an SV pointer has been retrieved from the stack, its value can be retrieved using one of the value extraction macros described in the section titled "Extracting Values from SVs."

Returning Values

After the function is ready to end and return to Perl, it can place return values on to the stack so that Perl can retrieve them. The same stack that stored the input parameters will be used for the return values.

When assigning values back to the stack, it is best to tag them as mortal. This way if the value is ignored, on the function's return to Perl the SV will die and be purged from memory (for an explanation of this refer to the section titled "The Lifespan of an SV").

To assign return values back to the stack, you use the same **ST**() macro that you used to extract the values from the stack. It takes the following format:

```
ST( iStackElement ) = pSV;
```

iStackElement is the stack element number, and pSV is a pointer to an SV. This will just assign the specified SV pointer to the specified stack element.

Refer to Example 10.14 for an illustration of using the **ST**() macro.

After you have prepared the stack with your return values, you need to tell Perl how many values you have stored on the stack using the **XSRETURN**() macro:

```
XSRETURN( long lValue )
```

The parameter passed into the macro indicates how many values are stored on the stack. If the value 4 is passed in to this macro, Perl will pop off the first four elements from the stack when the function returns. The calling script can retrieve these values:

```
($Value1, $Value2, $Value3, $Value4) = Win32::Test::MyFunction();
```

If you have only one or no values to return, you may as well use the **XSRETURN_xxx**() macros:

```
XSRETURN_NO
XSRETURN_YES
XSRETURN_UNDEF
XSRETURN_EMPTY
XSRETURN_IV( long lValue )
XSRETURN_NV( double dValue )
XSRETURN_PV( char* pszValue )
```

These macros set the stack with the specified value and report the correct **XSRETURN**() value. Your code does not need to call either **ST**() or **XSRETURN**() if you use one of these macros; however, it works if you have *only* one or no values to return.

The **XSRETURN_xxx**() macros will return one value back to Perl. The value returned depends on the macro used. Table 10.4 lists the returned values.

Note that the **XSRETURN_PV**() macro accepts only a character string and does not accept a length. This means that the macro requires that the string passed in be a NUL-terminated string.

Table 10.4   Return value types

Return value	Description
XSRETURN_NO	Returns a FALSE value (0).
XSRETURN_YES	Returns a TRUE value (non-zero).
XSRETURN_UNDEF	Returns an undef.
XSRETURN_EMPTY	Returns nothing. This is the same as XSRETURN(0).
XSRETURN_IV()	Returns the long value that is passed in.
XSRETURN_NV()	Returns the double value that is passed in.
XSRETURN_PV()	Returns the string that is passed in. This string must be a NUL-terminated string.

The **XSRETURN_xxx**() macros work by creating a mortal SV and putting it as the first element of the stack. It then uses the **XSRETURN(1)** macro, indicating that Perl can expect one value on the stack.

Example 10.15 sets two return values on the stack and returns, informing Perl to expect two return values. Notice that line 4 creates a new string-based SV, and then line 5 first marks the SV as mortal and stores it in the stack (as the first element—element 0). Line 6 creates a new SV, which is a floating-point number, marks it as mortal, and then stores it as the second element in the stack.

Example 10.15   *Returning two values from a function*

```
XS( MyFunction )
{
  dXSARGS;
  SV* pSV = newSVpv( "My test string!", na );
  ST( 0 ) = sv_2mortal( pSV );
  ST( 1 ) = sv_2mortal( newSVnv( (double) 6.02 ) );
  XSRETURN( 2 );
}
```

Both of the returned SVs were marked as mortal so that they would die after the function returns back to Perl. If the calling Perl scripts assign these return values to variables upon return of the function, their reference counts are increased from 0 to 1. This will prevent them from being automatically destroyed by Perl. If the script discards these values (does not assign the return values to any variable), however, they will indeed be destroyed.

Example 10.16 demonstrates using the **ST()** macro to obtain values passed into the function from the calling Perl script. Notice that line 4 checks the items variable (which was initialized with the **dXSARGS** macro) to see whether two values were indeed passed in. Line 9 adds the integer values of both passed-in

SVs, and then line 10 uses the **XSRETURN_IV()** macro to tell Perl that it is returning one long value. If the two parameters are not passed in to the function, line 14 tells Perl to return an undef.

Example 10.16 *Returning one value from a function*

```
01. XS( MyFunction2 )
02. {
03.     dXSARGS;
04.     if( 2 == items )
05.     {
06.         long lSum;
07.         SV* pSV1 = ST( 0 );
08.         SV* pSV2 = ST( 1 );
09.         lSum = SvIV( pSV1 ) + SvIV( pSV2 );
10.         XSRETURN_IV( lSum );
11.     }
12.     else
13.     {
14.         XSRETURN_UNDEF;
15.     }
16. }
```

The Perl script that calls this can expect two return values:

```
($Text, $AvagadrosNum) = Win32::Test::MyFunction();
```

Modifying Input Parameters

You may notice that some extensions change input variables. You may see a Perl script call some function such as this, for example:

```
if( Win32::Test::MyFunction( $Value1, $Value2, $Sum ) )
{
    print "The sum of $Value1 and $Value2 is $Sum.\n";
}
```

When the function is called, it may add the first two values passed in and store the sum in the third parameter. This is actually a very easy thing to do.

In your extension's function, all you need to do is retrieve the SV for the particular called parameter. In the preceding example, you want to set the value of the third parameter so that you need to get the SV for the third parameters using the **ST(3)** macro.

When the function is entered, the stack has three SV pointers on it. You want to modify the value of the third one. Therefore you grab the SV pointer to it with this:

```
SV *pSV = ST(3)
```

This gives you an SV pointer to the Perl script's $Sum variable. When you set the value of this SV pointer, you are directly setting the value of $Sum. However, when you later use:

```
ST(3) = pSV;
```

you are just replacing the contents of the third element of the stack.

Simply stated, there is a difference between replacing the value of a stack element and replacing the value of an SV that happens to be pointed to by a stack element. Example 10.17 illustrates this.

Example 10.17   *Changing the value of an input parameter*

```
01. XS( MyFunction )
02. {
03.    dXSARGS;
04.    long lValue1, lValue2, lSum;
05.
06.    if( items != 3 )
07.    {
08.      XSRETURN_NO;
09.    }
10.    lValue1 = SvIV( ST( 0 ) );
11.    lValue2 = SvIV( ST( 1 ) );
12.    lSum = lValue1 + lValue2;
13.
14.    // Get the third parameter's SV
15.    pSV = ST( 3 );
16.      // Now pSV points to the SV that was passed in as the
17.      // 3rd parameter.
18.
19.    // Set the new value of the SV we got.  This will literally change
20.    // the contents of the Perl script's $Sum variable.
21.    sv_setiv( pSV, (long) lSum );
22.
23.    // Return a TRUE (non zero) value to indicate that the
24.    // function was successful.
25.    XSRETURN_YES;
26. }
```

Calling Other Functions

Calling other functions from within a function that Perl calls directly may need some explaining. Normally you would just call another function, such as a Win32 API call or a library function of some sort. If your function will make use of Perl macros, however, you need to treat it like an extension function.

Suppose that your extension's function will call another function that processes some variable. If it needs to access any Perl macros, it must use the **dXSARGS** macro (just like your extension function). This will set up the Perl stack and items variable as well. Now, that was not so difficult.

The difficulty with this is that the way you prototype your function depends on which version of Win32 Perl you are using. If you are building this extension for the core distribution, you have no more work to do. If you are using the ActiveState version, however, you have to consider the CPerl object.

You see, when the ActiveState version of Perl calls into an extension's function one of the parameters that is passed in is a pointer to the C++ Perl object. This object is an instance of the CPerl class (in Perl 5.005 it has been renamed to CPerlObj), which all macros will make use of. Generally, this is no problem and is invisible. However, when you call into another function you need to pass in a pointer to that CPerl object; otherwise, the macros used in that function will just fail (actually it will not compile).

If you are certain that your extension won't be called in a multithreaded state, you could make a global pointer:

```
CPerl *pPerl;
```

and set it to the pPerl that was passed in to your function, as in Example 10.17. This works wonderfully until you try to use the extension with ActiveState's PerlIS.dll ISAPI application. This application gives quick Perl processing to Microsoft's IIS Web server. Because the extension works in a multithreaded environment, it is quite possible that your extension could be loaded in a multithreaded environment. Consider an example in which your Web server calls a CGI that uses your extension. If you set a global CPerl pointer as in Example 10.18, it is possible that while this script is running, another instance of it will be started. When your extension's function is called, the global is reset to the new CPerl object. If this occurs while your first script is accessing a function that relies on the global pPerl, you have a problem.

For more information on multithreading issues, refer to the section titled "Multithreading in an Extension."

Example 10.18 *Using a global* CPerl *pointer*

```
01.   // Define the global CPerl object
02. CPerl *pPerl = NULL;
03.
04. XS( MyFunction)
05. {
06.   dXSARGS;
07.     // Set the global CPerl object (::pPerl) with
08.     // the local CPerl object (pPerl).
09.   ::pPerl = pPerl;
10.   SV* pSV = ST( 0 );
11.     // Now call the other function
12.   MyOtherFunction( pSV );
13. }
14.
15. void MyOtherFunction( SV* pSV )
```

```
16. {
17.     // Now with the global CPerl object set all of the
18.     // Perl macros which rely on pPerl will simply use
19.     // the global pPerl.
20.   dXSARGS;
21.   ...process pSV...
22. }
```

One way around this is to prototype all your functions that will use Perl macros to accept a first parameter as a CPerl object pointer. I defined a couple of macros to do this. By using these macros, I can just redefine them if I use the core distribution's headers (because the core distribution does not recognize CPerl).

You can define the macros from Example 10.18 in your header files. Whenever you need to create a function that makes any use of Perl macros, you can prototype it as follows:

```
void MyFunction( PERL_ONLY_ARG_PROTO );
void MyFunction2( PERL_ARG_PROTO char *pszString );
```

Notice that the first prototype takes only one parameter. Because of this, it uses the **PERL_ONLY_ARG_PROTO** macro. This macro defines that only one parameter is passed in and it is a CPerl object. The second prototype takes more than one parameter, so it is using the **PERL_ARG_PROTO** macro.

Both prototypes return nothing, and they both accept a CPerl object if you compile them using the ActiveState headers; otherwise, the macros do not expand to anything when using the core distribution.

Example 10.19 *Establishing compatibility between the core distribution and ActiveState versions of Perl*

```
01. //  If PERL_OBJECT is defined we are using ActiveState's headers
02.   #ifdef PERL_OBJECT
03.   #define PERL_ARG_PROTO CPerl *pPerl,
04.   #define PERL_ONLY_ARG_PROTO CPerl *pPerl
05.   #define PERL_ARG pPerl,
06.   #define PERL_ONLY_ARG pPerl
07. #else // Must be using core distribution
08.   #define PERL_ARG_PROTO
09.   #define PERL_ONLY_ARG_PROTO
10.   #define PERL_ARG
11.   #define PERL_ONLY_ARG
12. #endif
```

In Example 10.19, the **PERL_ONLY_ARG_PROTO** and **PERL_ARG_PROTO** macros are used, and thus provide a full extension that could be compiled using either ActiveState or core distribution headers.

The Bootstrap Function

One of the things that Perl does after loading the extension is to run the bootstrap function. The DynaLoader loads the DLL, and then looks for an
exported function called **boot_ExtensionName**, where **ExtensionName** is the
full name of the extension, replacing colon (:) characters with underscores.
Therefore, the **Win32::Test**'s bootstrap function will be called
boot_Win32__Test.

When the bootstrap function is called, this is the extension's opportunity to
make an association with a C function and a Perl subroutine. In other words,
the bootstrap function will bind your C function to a Perl subroutine name so
that Perl can make calls into your C code. This is done with the **newXS()**
macro:

```
newXS( char *pszPerlName, XSSubroutine, char *pszFileName )
```

The first parameter (`pszPerlName`) is the full Perl function name. If our extension has a function name called **MyFunction()**, for example, this parameter
would be **Win32::Test::MyFunction**.

The second parameter (`XSSubroutine`) is the name of the C function that was
declared with the **XS()** macro. If the **MyFunction()** function was declared as
XS(MyFunction), this parameter would be `MyFunction` (notice there are no quotation marks around this).

The third parameter (`pszFileName`) is a file name string. This is used for debugging purposes and is typically declared as `__FILE__`, which is a compiler's macro
for the currently compiling file.

You would have one **newXS()** macro for every function that is to be accessible
from Perl.

The end of the bootstrap function needs to return a TRUE value back to the
DynaLoader so that it knows that the extension was successfully loaded. This
is commonly performed by using the **XSRETURN_YES** macro. Example 10.20
shows this.

Example 10.20   *The bootstrap function*

```
XS( boot_Win32__Test )
{
  dXSARGS;
  char *pszFile = __FILE__;

  newXS( "Win32::Test::MyFunction", MyFunction, pszFile );

  XSRETURN_YES;
}
```

The .def File

When creating a DLL file (as all Win32 Perl extensions are), you need to declare a definition (.def) file. This definition file will describe what the library is called and what functions to export. An in-depth explanation of the .def file is beyond the scope of this book. You may want to consult some Win32 programming manuals, however, such as *Win32 Programming*, by Brent Rector and Joseph Newcomer (Addison Wesley Developers Press) and *Win32 Network Programming*, by Ralph Davis (Addison Wesley Developers Press).

When creating a Perl extension, only two things really need to be included in the .def file: the **LIBRARY** and **EXPORTS** statements.

The **LIBRARY** statement declares the name of this particular DLL. Typically this is the name of your extension, not the full namespace. If you are creating the **Win32::Test** extension, the library name is "Test".

The **EXPORTS** statement just informs the linker what function is to be exported. Only one function really must be exported, the boot function. The name of the bootstrap function is described in the section titled "The Bootstrap Function."

After the .def file is created, it must be added to the C project so that when the extension is compiled and linked, the .def file will be included in the process.

The DllMain() function

When a process loads a DLL, Windows will look for a function known as **DllMain**(). If the DLL has such a function, it is called. Likewise when a process unloads a DLL (such as when the process is terminating), Windows, again, calls the **DllMain**() function.

> **Note**
>
> *All DLLs have a **DllMain**() function. If the programmer did not program one, the compiler created one that does nothing.*

If a DLL has been loaded into a running program and a thread is created, once again Windows will call the **DllMain**(), this time notifying it that a new thread has been created. Likewise, when a thread is terminated, Windows will call **DllMain**() notifying it of the terminating thread.

For many extensions, **DllMain**() is not an issue; most extensions appear to not make use of it. However, you may want to consider taking advantage of it for several reasons. These advantages are reviewed later during the detailed discussion of **DllMain**().

To be more accurate, Windows does not call **DllMain**(); instead it calls the C runtime library. The function that Windows *really* calls is **_DllMainCRTStartup**(). This initializes the DLL's C runtime environment (declaring standard file handles, initializing static and global variables, and so on), and eventually calls the **DllMain**() function.

When the **DllMain**() function is called, it is passed in three parameters:

```
BOOL WINAPI DllMain( HINSTANCE hInsance, DWORD dwReason, LPVOID pReserved )
```

The first parameter is the instance of the DLL. This is important because many Win32 API calls require the instance. The **DllMain**() function is your extension's chance to save the DLL's instance. You may want to save it to a global variable.

The second parameter is a DWORD that indicates the reason the function was called. Typically your code will react differently depending on what the reason was for being called. Table 10.5 lists the possible values for dwReason.

The third parameter is an LPVOID, which is reserved and should be ignored.

Table 10.5   Possible values for dwReason *in the* **DllMain**() *function*

Value	Description
DLL_PROCESS_ATTACH	The DLL is being loaded for the first time by a process.
DLL_THREAD_ATTACH	The process just started a new thread.
DLL_THREAD_DETACH	The process just terminated a thread.
DLL_PROCESS_DETACH	The process is unloading the DLL.

The **DllMain**() function returns a Boolean value. If TRUE is returned, Windows will consider the function successful and continue processing as normal. If the function returns FALSE, Windows will report that the DLL was unable to be loaded. This means that your extension will have failed to load and Perl will report this.

Basically, your **DllMain**() function should always return TRUE unless there is some compelling reason not to. If the DLL depends on another resource (such as a database or network connection) that is not available, for example, it may be prudent to return FALSE because the DLL will be unable to perform its job correctly.

Example 10.21 demonstrates a very simple **DllMain**() function. In this example, line 9 stores the DLL's instance handle in ghInstance. This will be handy if later the extension needs to specify the instance—if it needs to load icon or dialog resources for example. Line 15 increments a thread counter, gdwThreads. The only reason we do this is so that the extension knows how many threads are active at any given time.

Example 10.21   *A simple DllMain() function*

```
01. HINSTANCE ghInstance = NULL;
02. DWORD gdwThreads = 0;
03. BOOL WINAPI DllMain( HINSTANCE hInstance, DWORD dwReason, LPVOID
    lpReserved )
04. {
05.   BOOL bResult = TRUE;
06.   switch( dwReason )
07.   {
08.     case DLL_PROCESS_ATTACH:
09.       ghInstance = hInstance;
10.       //  ...check for needed resources. If they are not
11.       //  ...available set bResult = FALSE
12.       break;
13.     case DLL_THREAD_ATTACH:
14.       // Let's keep track of the number of threads — for kicks
15.       gdwThreads++;
16.       break;
17.     case DLL_THREAD_DETACH:
18.       gdwThreads — ;
19.       break;
20.     case DLL_PROCESS_DETACH:
21.       break;
22.   }
23.   return( bResult );
24. }
```

Multithreading in an Extension

Currently threading is not fully supported by Perl. There is some experimental threading support, but it is just that: experimental. The PerlIS.dll extension, however, runs as an ISAPI application that is multithreaded. This means any extension you write that may be used with PerlIS.dll needs to be multithread aware. For the most part, your code should not use global variables that may need to change for every thread. Many extensions use a global DWORD to hold the last generated Win32 error, for example, something like gdwLastError.

If a Web server is using PerlIS.dll and it runs two scripts using the same extension at the same time, they may run into memory-contention issues. Suppose the first script generates an error and saves the error code into gdwLastError. Before it has a chance to report the error, however, the second script generates a different error. This new error's value is also stored in gdwLastError, essentially overwriting the first script's error code. When the first script reports its error, it will really be reporting the second script's error instead.

To make matters worse, extensions built using PERL_OBJECT (such as the ActiveState builds) require a special object called pPerl (which is a CPerl pointer or a CPerlObj pointer if you are using Perl 5.005 with PERL_OBJECT support). All Perl-related functions are mapped as methods of this object. So a call to **croak**() is compiled as pPerl->croak(). For a function to call another function, it needs to somehow pass the pPerl object. Some extensions have done this by using a global pPerl pointer as in Example 10.22. This works just fine until you have two or more threads overwriting the gpPerl variable. This can cause some pretty funky crashes.

Example 10.22   *A non-multithread friendly way of handling* pPerl

```
01. CPerl *gpPerl;
02.
03. XS_MyFunction()
04. {
05.    // pPerl is automatically defined in XS functions
06.    gpPerl = pPerl;
07.    MyFunction2();
08. }
09.
10. void MyFunction2()
11. {
12.    CPerl *pPerl = gpPerl;
13.    ...some code goes here...
14.    return;
15. }
```

There are several ways to handle multithreading issues, but the most practical advice is to avoid the use of global variables. Instead, either pass in a needed value (such as for pPerl) explicitly as in Example 10.23 or use *thread local storage*.

Example 10.23   *A multithread-friendly way of handling* pPerl

```
01. XS(MyFunction)
02. {
03.    dXSARGS;
04.    // pPerl is automatically defined in XS functions
05.    MyFunction2( pPerl );
06. }
07.
08. void MyFunction2( Cperl *pPerl )
09. {
10.     // ...some code goes here that uses Perl macros so
11.     // ...it needs pPerl
12.    return;
13. }
```

Thread Local Storage
Each thread in a process has its own stack but share the same heap as the other threads. This means that automatic variables declared on the stack are not shared among threads, but memory allocated on the heap using functions

such as **new**() and **malloc**() are easily accessible by other threads. Additionally, because global variables are stored in the heap, they too are accessible by all threads.

What would be ideal would be the capability for a thread to have its own set of data that is not accessible by other threads. Automatic variables are perfect for this except that they are destroyed when they fall out of scope, such as when a function returns. This brings us to the concept of *thread local storage* (TLS).

Win32 allows each thread to save information (in the form of a void pointer) that is unique to the thread. Whenever the thread needs that information, it can retrieve it. This is called thread local storage (or as I read it, "local thread storage"). Upon request, Win32 creates thread local storage *slots*, which are basically void pointers. Each slot is like an element in an array—there is an index number associated with it. If you request two TLS slots, Win32 will allocate two entries large enough to hold void pointers and return the index numbers to these slots.

Think of TLS as a banking system. Each customer (or thread) gets a savings and checking account. Each account (a TLS slot) has its own account number (or TLS slot index) such as 1 for savings and 2 for checking. When a customer goes to the bank to check her balances, she first provides her customer number (or thread ID) so that the teller knows which accounts to look at. Then she specifies which account number she intends to inquire about.

Just as the bank provides an account number for each account a customer has, Win32 hands out a TLS slot index number for each variable that a thread needs to save. When the thread wants to retrieve data it stored in one of these slots, it queries the specified slot's TLS index number (just as the customer specifies the account number). Because the index number is shared by all threads, you can store the slot's index number in a global variable that all threads can access. This is akin to telling your DLL that all threads are to store some particular value (for example, the last generated error) in slot X.

What is really happening is that Win32 allocates an array of void pointers for each thread. When your code allocates a new TLS slot, it returns an index to one element in the array. Every time a thread stores or retrieves data using that TLS slot, Win32 just looks to the array that has been allocated for that particular thread. The slot index number informs Win32 which element in the array to access.

Example 10.24 demonstrates the use of thread local storage. Detailed information regarding functions within the example follow.

Example 10.24 *Using thread local storage*

```
01.   // Add Perl Headers here
02.   // Create the global TLS index variables
03. DWORD gdwPerlIndex = 0;
04. DWORD gdwErrorIndex = 0;
05. HINSTANCE ghInstance = NULL;
06.
07.   // Declare our function prototypes...
08. DWORD GetError();
09. void SetError( DWORD dwError );
10. CPerl *GetPerl();
11. void SetPerl( CPerl *pPerl );
12. void MyFunction();
13.
14. DWORD GetError()
15. {
16.   return( (DWORD) TlsGetValue( gdwErrorIndex ) );
17. }
18. void SetError( DWORD dwError )
19. {
20.   TlsSetValue( gdwErrorIndex, (LPVOID) dwError );
21. }
22. CPerl *GetPerl()
23. {
24.   return( (CPerl*) TlsGetValue( gdwPerlIndex ) );
25. }
26. void SetPerl( CPerl *pPerl )
27. {
28.   TlsSetValue( gdwPerlIndex, (LPVOID) pPerl );
29. }
30.
31. XS(GetLastError)
32. {
33.   dXSARGS;
34.   DWORD dwError = GetError();
35.   ST( 0 ) = sv_newmortal();
36.   sv_setiv( ST( 0 ), (IV) dwError );
37.   XSRETURN( 1 );
38. }
39.
40. void MyFunction()
41. {
42.   CPerl *pPerl = GetPerl();
43.   dXSARGS;
44.     // ...now that you have a pPerl object
45.     // ...you can call Perl macros and such.
46.   return;
47. }
48.
49. BOOL WINAPI DllMain( HINSTANCE hInstance,
50.                      DWORD dwReason,
51.                      LPVOID lpReserved )
```

```
52. {
53.    BOOL bResult = TRUE;
54.    switch( dwReason )
55.    {
56.      case DLL_PROCESS_ATTACH:
57.        ghInstance = hInstance;
58.          // Allocate a TLS for the pPerl object...
59.        gdwPerlIndex = TlsAlloc();
60.          // Allocate a TLS for the last error...
61.        gdwErrorIndex = TlsAlloc();
62.          // ...check for needed resources. If they are not
63.          // ...available set bResult = FALSE
64.        if( FALSE == bResult )
65.        {
66.            // If something went wrong and we are returning FALSE
67.            // then we need to free up the TLS indexes!
68.            TlsFree( gdwErrorIndex );
69.            TlsFree( gdwPerlIndex );
70.        }
71.        break;
72.
73.      case DLL_THREAD_ATTACH:
74.        break;
75.
76.      case DLL_THREAD_DETACH:
77.        // If any memory has been allocated for this thread then
78.        // now is the time to free it!
79.        break;
80.
81.      case DLL_PROCESS_DETACH:
82.        TlsFree( gdwErrorIndex );
83.        TlsFree( gdwPerlIndex );
84.        break;
85.    }
86.    return( bResult );
87. }
```

To use TLS, your DLL must call **TlsAlloc()** for each value it intends to store when the process attaches to it. The DWORD returned by **TlsAlloc()** is the slot index number used by other TLS functions to identify the particular variable that has been stored. The prototype for **TlsAlloc()** is:

```
DWORD TlsAlloc()
```

This function takes no parameters and it creates a TLS slot. The slot's index number is returned as a DWORD.

If the **TlsAlloc()** function is successful, it allocates TLS slot and returns the index number.

Example 10.24 stores two variables for every thread: a CPerl pointer and a DWORD representing the last error Win32 generated. The global indexes are defined in lines 3 and 4. Lines 59 and 61 call **TlsAlloc()** for each variable that will be stored. This allocates a TLS slot that can fit a void pointer.

After a TLS index has been created, your extension can store values in each slot by calling the **TlsSetValue()** function:

```
BOOL TlsSetValue( DWORD dwIndex, LPVOID pVoid )
```

The first parameter is a DWORD, which is the index value returned by **TlsAlloc()**. This index number refers to a TLS slot that the value of the second parameter will be stored into.

The second parameter is a value that has the size of a void pointer (typically 32 bits, but this can change from processor to processor). For most values that are not void pointers, you will need to type cast them to either (LPVOID) or (void*).

If the value was successfully set into the specified TLS index slot, the function returns TRUE; otherwise it returns FALSE and no value is stored.

Example 10.24 creates two functions to set the Perl object and the error number: **SetPerl()** and **SetError()**. These functions set the value passed into them into their corresponding TLS slot.

After a value has been stored in a TLS slot, it can be retrieved by using **TlsGetValue()**:

```
LPVOID TlsGetValue( DWORD dwIndex )
```

The only parameter is a DWORD, which represents the TLS slot index. This is the same index used to store the value in a call to **TlsSetValue()** and is returned by a call to **TlsAlloc()**.

If the **TlsGetValue()** function succeeds, it returns the value stored in the specified TLS slot. That return value can be any value including zero, so there is no way to determine whether the function failed.

Example 10.24 also defines two functions to retrieve specific values from TLS storage: **GetPerl()** and **GetError()**.

After an application or DLL no longer requires TLS storage, a call to **TlsFree()** must be called for every TLS slot that was created:

```
BOOL TlsFree( DWORD dwIndex )
```

The only parameter is the index number of a TLS slot that is to be freed.

If the **TlsFree()** function succeeds, it returns TRUE; otherwise, it fails and returns FALSE. Really the only time this function will fail is if the specified index has not already been allocated with a call to **TlsAlloc()**.

After the **TlsFree()** function has been called for a TLS slot index, that slot is no longer valid for *any* thread. Other slots that have been allocated are still usable; only those specified in a call to **TlsFree()** are no longer valid.

Also in Example 10.24, lines 68 and 69 call **TlsFree()** for each TLS slot allocated in. Notice that this occurs when **DllMain()** has been called with dwReason set for DLL_PROCESS_DETACH. This is because Windows is telling the DLL that the process is about to unload it and therefore it had better free up all resources that it had already allocated.

A Practical Example

Now that most of the necessities have been covered, it is time to go about creating an example. I used Microsoft's Visual C++ 5.0, so you may need to make changes to your specific environment where necessary.

The first thing you need to do is create the files listed in Example 10.25, Example 10.26, Example 10.27, and Example 10.28:

- Example 10.24 is a Perl script that demonstrates how to call the extension.
- Example 10.25 is a Perl module required to load the extension.
- Example 10.26 is the actual extension itself.
- Example 10.27 is the DLL definition (.def) file.

The next step is to create a new Win32 DLL project (don't use any MFC classes). In MSVC 5.0, creating a new project automatically creates a new workspace for the project. Add the two files test.cpp (Example 10.27) and test.def (Example 10.28) to the project.

Now you need to define a couple of macros. You can hard code them into the test.cpp file, but that would limit the ability of others to use the file. You may want to define it in the project's compiler options. Set the options so that it defines the **MSWIN32** macro.

This will turn on Perl's Win32 options. Another macro needs to be defined only if you are doing the following:

- Using the ActiveState build, or
- Using build 5.005 and you want to use the CPerlObj class.

This is necessary if your extensions will be running on Web servers using the ISAPI application PerlIS.dll or interacting with ActiveState's various builds.

(Hint: all of ActiveState's builds use these classes.) If this is the case, define the macro:

```
PERL_OBJECT
```

From this point, set the project's include path to include the Perl header files (obtained from www.activestate.com, www.perl.com, or www.cpan.org).

If you are using the 5.004 core distribution, you will also need to inform the linker where the perl.lib file is so that it can link to the Perl library.

The next step is to compile and link!

Assuming that everything went well, you will have a resulting test.dll file (or whatever you named it). For the sake of this example, you need to make a directory for the .dll file. The directory name is the name of the extension. Because this extension is **Win32::Test**, the .dll file will be copied into a directory called Win32\Test. This path must be placed in the library's AUTO directory:

```
perl\lib\AUTO
```

Perl 5.005 and the 5.004 core distribution, use alternate directories for the Win32 extensions. The actual paths have changed from build to build, so your path may differ; however, the general method is to start with a site directory such as:

```
perl\lib\site\AUTO
```

or

```
perl\site\AUTO
```

Create the Win32\Test directory in the AUTO directory. Then copy the test.dll file into the directory. An example of the command line to copy the file into the appropriate directory is:

```
xcopy test.dll c:\perl\site\auto\win32\test\*.*
```

The **xcopy** command will create the directories if needed.

Next you need to copy the Perl module into the correct module directory. The path is the same as where you copied the .dll file except that it is not in the AUTO directory. An example of a command to copy the Perl module is:

```
xcopy test.pm c:\perl\site\win32\*.*
```

Now you are ready to run the Perl script test.pl.

That is all there is to it!

Example 10.25   *A Perl script* (test.pl) *using the* **Win32::Test** *extension*

```
01.    # First load our new module which in turn will load
02.    # our extension.
```

```
03. use Win32::Test;
04.
05.    # Call the AddNumbers() function...
06. $Sum = Win32::Test::AddNumbers( 500, 42102 );
07.
08.    # Now let's try the GetFileSizes() function...
09. if( $Count = Win32::Test::GetFileSizes( 'c:\temp\*.*', $Data ) )
10. {
11.      # Unpack the array of data structures that was passed back to
12.      # us from the extension's GetFileSizes() function. We must
13.      # use the unpack template of "A256l" because the extension's
14.      # FileStruct data structure consisted of:
15.      #  {
16.      #    char szName[256];
17.      #    long lSize;
18.      #  }
19.      # So we must unpack first the 256 characters followed by a long
20.      # variable hence the unpack template of "A256l".
21.      # Note that we will use "A256l" x $Count because we need to unpack
22.      # for each file that was found. Since the extension concatenated
23.      # all of the data structures together it is the same as one long
24.      # array of structures.
25.      # The output is fed directly into a hash (%Files) because a
26.      # hash is an array with the format of
27.      # ( key, value, key2, value2, ...). We will be unpacking the data
28.      # in the format of ( file, size, file2, size2, ... ). This makes
29.      # for a perfect hash with file names as the key and sizes as value.
30.    %Files = unpack( "A256l" x $Count, $Data );
31.    foreach $FileName ( keys( %Files ) )
32.    {
33.       print "The file '$FileName' is $Files{$FileName} bytes.\n";
34.    }
35. }
```

Example 10.26 *The Perl module (test.pm) for the **Win32::Test** extension*

```
01.    # We must declare the name of this package (or module)
02. package Win32::Test;
03.
04.    # Load the DynaLoader module so that
05.    # we can dynamically load our extension
06.    # If we need to export constant values and such
07.    # we will need to use the Exporter but for this
08.    # test we don't need it.
09. require DynaLoader;
10.
11.    # We must add DynaLoader to the
12.    # ISA array. This is ISA as in "is a" not as in the
13.    # PC bus architecture (as opposed to PCI). The
14.    # ISA array tells that we are inheriting functions
15.    # and such from the specified module. We need to
16.    # specify DynaLoader so that we can use its
```

continues

Continued

```
17.    # bootstrap function later.
18. @ISA= qw( DynaLoader );
19.
20.    # Call the bootstrap function in our extension.
21.    # This will register all the exported functions
22.    # from our extension with Perl so that we can
23.    # later call them.
24. bootstrap Win32::Test;
25.
26.    # As silly as this last line looks it is imperative
27.    # that it exists. By returning a 1 value we are reporting
28.    # to Perl that the module has loaded alright
29. 1;
```

Example 10.27 *The Win32::Test extension (test.c or test.cpp, depending on whether you compile with C or C++)*

```
001. #ifdef __BORLANDC__
002.   typedef wchar_t wctype_t; /* in tchar.h, but unavailable unless _UNICODE */
003. #endif
004.   //  WIN32_LEAN_AND_MEAN is a Microsoft Windows macro which
005.   //  is needed. This will prevent most of the Window specific
006.   //  stuff that we simply don't need
007. #define WIN32_LEAN_AND_MEAN
008. #include <windows.h>
009.   //  Gurusamy's right, Borland compilers need this here!
010. #include <stdio.h>
011.   //  Gurusamy's right, MS compilers need this here!
012. #include <math.h>
013. #if defined(__cplusplus)  && !defined(PERL_OBJECT)
014.   extern "C" {
015. #endif
016. #include "EXTERN.h"
017. #include "perl.h"
018. #include "Xsub.h"
019. #if defined(__cplusplus)  && !defined(PERL_OBJECT)
020.   }
021. #endif
022.
023.   // Declare some global variables
024. HINSTANCE ghInstance = NULL;
025. DWORD gdwThreads = 0;
026.
027.   //  If this is defined we are using ActiveState's headers
028. #ifdef PERL_OBJECT
029.   // If you are using PERL_OBJECT with Perl 5.005 then
030.   // uncomment the next line. 5.005 changed the class from
031.   // CPerl to CPerlObj...
032.   // #define CPerl CPerlObj
033.   #define PERL_ARG_PROTO CPerl *pPerl,
034.   #define PERL_ONLY_ARG_PROTO CPerl *pPerl
```

```
035.    #define PERL_ARG pPerl,
036.    #define PERL_ONLY_ARG pPerl
037.  #else
038.      // We get here if PERL_OBJECT is not defined such
039.      // as the core distribution of 5.004 and version
040.      // 5.005 without PERL_OBJECT support
041.    #define PERL_ARG_PROTO
042.    #define PERL_ONLY_ARG_PROTO
043.    #define PERL_ARG
044.    #define PERL_ONLY_ARG
045.  #endif
046.
047.    // Prototype our non Perl callable function
048.  long ExtractLongFromSV( PERL_ARG_PROTO SV* pSV );
049.
050.  XS( ExtensionAddNumbers )
051.  {
052.    dXSARGS;
053.    long lNum1;
054.    long lNum2;
055.    long lSum;
056.    SV* pSV;
057.
058.    if( items != 2 )
059.    {
060.      // If 2 parameters were not passed in then complain about it
061.      // and print the syntax
062.      croak( "Usage: $Sum=Win32::Test::AddNumbers( $First, $Second )" );
063.    }
064.    // Get the first SV passed in and extract the value from it
065.    pSV = ST( 0 );
066.    lNum1 = ExtractLongFromSV( PERL_ARG pSV );
067.
068.    // Get the second SV passed in and extract the value from it
069.    pSV = ST( 1 );
070.    lNum2 = ExtractLongFromSV( PERL_ARG pSV );
071.
072.    lSum = lNum1 + lNum2;
073.
074.    // Create a new SV with the sum
075.    pSV = newSViv( lSum );
076.
077.    // Tag the SV as mortal so that it will die after this function
078.    // has finished.
079.    // Set the return value into the first position on the stack
080.    ST( 0 ) = sv_2mortal( pSV );
081.
082.    // Inform Perl that we have 1 value on the stack and let's get
083.    // back to our Perl script.
084.    XSRETURN( 1 );
085.  }
086.
```

continues

Continued

```
087.    // Our simple function to retrieve the IV (long) value from an SV
088. long ExtractLongFromSV( PERL_ARG_PROTO SV* pSV )
089. {
090.    dXSARGS;
091.    long lValue = 0;
092.       // Check that the SV contains an integer and if so
093.       // extract it.
094.    if( SvIOK( pSV ) )
095.    {
096.      lValue = SvIV( pSV );
097.    }
098.    return( lValue );
099. }
100.       // Define a structure to hold a file name and size
101. typedef struct
102. {
103.    char m_szPath[256];
104.    DWORD m_dwSize;
105. } FileStruct;
106.
107. XS( ExtensionGetFileSizes )
108. {
109.    dXSARGS;
110.    FileStruct File;
111.    WIN32_FIND_DATA fileFind;
112.    HANDLE hSearch;
113.    SV *pSV = newSVpv( "", 0 );
114.    char *pszPath = NULL;
115.    int iTotal = 0;
116.    BOOL bContinue = TRUE;
117.
118.    if( 2 != items )
119.    {
120.      croak( "Usage: $Count=Win32::Test::GetFileSizes( $Path, $Data )" );
121.    }
122.       // Get the path to search. This is the first parameter passed into
123.       // the function so it is the SV returned by ST(0)
124.    pszPath = SvPV( ST( 0 ), na );
125.
126.       // Now start searching the path using the Win32 file
127.       // search functions
128.    hSearch = FindFirstFile( pszPath, &fileFind );
129.    if( INVALID_HANDLE_VALUE != hSearch )
130.    {
131.      while( bContinue )
132.      {
133.          // Is the file that was found not a directory then
134.          // process it.
135.        if( ! ( fileFind.dwFileAttributes & FILE_ATTRIBUTE_DIRECTORY ) )
136.          {
```

```
137.            // Fill out our data structure
138.            ZeroMemory( File.m_szPath, sizeof( File.m_szPath ) );
139.            strncpy( File.m_szPath, fileFind.cFileName, sizeof( File.m_szPath
        ➥) - 1 );
140.            File.m_dwSize = fileFind.nFileSizeLow;
141.              // Concatenate the data structure to an SV
142.            sv_catpvn( pSV, (char*) &File, sizeof( File ) );
143.            iTotal++;
144.          }
145.        bContinue = FindNextFile( hSearch, &fileFind );
146.      }
147.      FindClose( hSearch );
148.    }
149.    else
150.    {
151.      pSV = &sv_undef;
152.    }
153.      // Create a mortal SV with the integer value iTotal
154.      // then set it to the first element on the stack
155.      // (element 0).
156.    ST( 0 ) = sv_2mortal( newSViv( iTotal ) );
157.      // Take the SV passed in as the second parameter (which is
158.      // element 1 on the stack) and set its SV to point to
159.      // our pSV which contains all of the binary data structures
160.      // we created for each of the files found. This does not
161.      // do anything to the stack but instead sets the value of
162.      // the SV which was passed into this function on the stack.
163.    sv_setsv( ST( 1 ), pSV );
164.      // Return to Perl informing the script that we are returning
165.      // with only one value (element 0 on the stack).
166.    XSRETURN( 1 );
167. }
168.
169.  // Now define the bootstrap. This is the only exported
170.  // function. Your Perl module will call into this function
171.  // which will register all XS() functions. Once this is done
172.  // a Perl script (or your Perl module) can call any of the
173.  // exported XS() functions directly.
174.  // The name of this bootstrap is tied to the namespace of your
175.  // extension. In this case boot_Win32__Test represents the
176.  // namespace Win32::Test
177. XS( boot_Win32__Test )
178. {
179.    dXSARGS;
180.    char *pszFile = __FILE__;
181.    newXS( "Win32::Test::GetFileSizes", ExtensionGetFileSizes, pszFile );
182.    newXS( "Win32::Test::AddNumbers", ExtensionAddNumbers, __FILE__ );
183.
184.    ST( 0 ) = &sv_yes;
185.    XSRETURN( 1 );
186. }
187.
```

continues

Continued

```
188. BOOL WINAPI DllMain( HINSTANCE hInstance,
189.                       DWORD dwReason,
190.                       LPVOID lpReserved )
191. {
192.   BOOL bResult = TRUE;
193.   switch( dwReason )
194.   {
195.     case DLL_PROCESS_ATTACH:
196.       ghInstance = hInstance;
197.       break;
198.     case DLL_THREAD_ATTACH:
199.       // Let's keep track of the number of threads—for kicks
200.       gdwThreads++;
201.       break;
202.      case DLL_THREAD_DETACH:
203.       gdwThreads--;
204.       break;
205.     case DLL_PROCESS_DETACH:
206.       break;
207.   }
208.   return( bResult );
209. }
```

Example 10.28 *The **Win32::Test** .def file (`test.def`)*

```
LIBRARY Test
EXPORTS
     boot_Win32__Test
```

Summary

The folks who designed and wrote Perl should be congratulated for their work. They have designed a forward-thinking language that is totally extendable.

The capability to extend a language is not only a practicality, but a must. Of course no one language can include everything that is needed. To be sure, Perl does a fine job at doing almost anything a programmer needs. But when it comes to needing something it does not support, you can extend it rather easily.

You must consider several pitfalls when creating extensions, but with a bit of thought none of them are insurmountable. Judging from the wide range of extensions available, it seems that this indeed is the case.

Chapter 11

Common Mistakes and Troubleshooting

This chapter investigates the common traps and pitfalls that plague Win32 Perl users, in particular when using the Win32 extensions.

All programmers have to look out for certain perils and pitfalls inherent to a programming language. Perl is no exception to this phenomenon. With Win32 Perl being in a state of constant change, it is only inevitable that there will be problems.

Volumes could be written regarding all the possible issues, caveats, and exceptions that a Win32 Perl programmer must consider when coding. Instead, this chapter covers some of the more common problems that have hit the newsgroups and email listservers. The chances are that most coders have stumbled upon some if not all of these issues at one time or another. Hopefully this brief overview provides enough to help shine the light on at least some problems that you may be facing.

General Win32-Specific Mistakes

One of the most obvious differences between the UNIX and Win32 platforms is that of file paths. Any UNIX user can tell you that there is only one root with many subdirectories. All hard drives, network shares, floppy drives, or any other external media storage device is mounted as a subdirectory under the root. Because Perl was originally designed to work under the UNIX platform, this is what Perl expects.

The Win32 world, however, uses drive letters to designate a storage device. This, of course, limits the number of possible drives to 26 (A: through Z:). This does not include network shares that are not mapped to a drive letter.

Another difference between the two platforms is that UNIX uses a forward slash (/) to delimit directories, whereas Win32 (and DOS for that matter) uses the backslash (\).

These little subtleties can make all the difference when using Perl on a Win32 machine—especially when porting UNIX scripts to a Windows box.

The most common problems that Win32 Perl users face relate to the following:

- File paths
- File permissions

File Paths

UNIX variants and Win32 systems vary in the way that files and paths are structured. UNIX, generally, makes use of the slash character (/) to delimit a path, as in /usr/bin/perl.

Win32 operating systems, however, use the backslash to delimit path and file names. Additionally, Win32 uses a drive letter that identifies a partition on a hard drive. This characteristic has been inherited from the older days when Windows was based on DOS (even though Windows 95 is still based on DOS). An example of a Win32 path is c:\perl\bin\perl.exe.

Win32 Perl can handle either style when referring to file and directory paths. The code in Example 11.1, for example, works exactly the same as in Example 11.2.

Example 11.1   *Using UNIX style paths*

```
open( FILE, "< /temp/misc.txt" );
@Data = <FILE>;
close( FILE );
```

Example 11.2   *Using Win32 style paths*

```
open( FILE, "< \\temp\\misc.txt" );
@Data = <FILE>;
close( FILE );
```

Many Win32 Perl coders routinely use the slash rather than the backslash when writing paths because it is easier to both write and read. Consider creating a string that represents the file c:\TEMP\MISC.TXT. To make a Perl string, you will have to either use single quotation marks, as in the following:

```
$File = 'c:\temp\misc.txt';
```

Or, you would have to escape the backslashes with another backslash, like this:

```
$File = "c:\\temp\\misc.txt";
```

If you were to use the backslash (regardless of the use of single or double quotation marks), you would be doomed to stay on a Win32 machine. You would run into errors if you tried to run the script on a UNIX box.

The ability to use forward or backslashes makes Win32 Perl rather powerful because this means that you can run scripts developed for UNIX machines on a Win32 box; however, when Win32 extensions come into play, this consistency breaks apart.

Because delimiters can be expressed as either a slash (/) or backslash (\), one may be encouraged to use slashes when referring to something like a proper computer name. To do this could generate a runtime error or just never resolve a computer name because most extensions do not convert slashes into backslashes.

Consider the **Win32::NetAdmin::UserGetAttributes**() function, for example. If you pass in a server name of \\server, it will function correctly; but if you pass in //server, it will fail to locate the proper network server. It is important to note which extensions do and do not allow the slash to replace the backslash delimiter. If you have an error in which a machine name is not recognized, it may be due to this problem.

One additional caveat that pertains to backslashes must be pointed out. When you specify a proper computer name such as \\ServerA using single quotation marks, Perl will interpret the prepended backslashes as a single escaped backslash. So, calling a function like

```
Win32::NetAdmin::GetUsers( '\\ServerA', FILTER_NORMAL_ACCOUNT, \@UserList );
```

will fail because after Perl has processed the parameters the extension would see the first parameter as \ServerA. Notice how the two backslashes were interpreted as an escaped backslash, resulting in only one backslash. This is a "gotcha" that has claimed the lives of many scripts.

Permissions

Normally, when someone creates a Perl script, he has permissions to access Perl and its various library files. It is easy to forget that other user accounts may not have permission on all the files needed to successfully run the script.

Suppose that an administrator has written a script that opens a Registry key. Assume also that this is executed as a logon script for each user during logon. If the user does not have read permissions on the **Win32::Registry** extension file (REGISTRY.PLL or REGISTRY.DLL), the script will break with a runtime error because it could not load the extension.

Suppose that another user logs on and the script runs. This user has full access on all files in the Perl directory, so he loads the **Win32::Registry** extension, unlike the preceding user. This user does not have read access on the Registry key that will be opened, however. This time the script will run, but it will not be able to access the Registry key (it will fail to open the key).

Both of these problems occur because permissions were not set for a given user. The author never encountered these problems because he had the required permissions. It is quite important to consider permission issues, especially when writing scripts that will run under different environments or under different user accounts.

CGI Script Problems

Now that the media has hyped the World Wide Web, CGI scripting has become a full-time job for some folks. Perl is a wonderful language to write CGI scripts because of its excellent text management, socket, and file capabilities. Using Perl for CGI scripts on a Win32 Web server, however, brings along with it an entire armada of problems.

The most common Win32 Perl CGI-related problems can be boiled down to just a few topics:

- Using **PerlIS.dll**. This is ActiveState's ISAPI application that can run Perl scripts with more efficiency than perl.exe. When using this, you need to handle scripts a little bit differently than if you were just using perl.exe.

- **Security issues.** Permissions and security settings of a Web server can cause your scripts to behave erratically.

- **Network communications.** When running Perl scripts as a CGI script, some network communications are impaired.

- **PerlScript.** The Windows host scripting language version of Perl. Writing PerlScript code takes some special considerations that are not normally needed.

PerlIS.dll

The ActiveState version of Win32 Perl supports an ISAPI application called PerlIS.dll. The filter will only run on Web servers that support ISAPI applications. Installing PerlIS.dll on a machine running a Web server that supports ISAPI applications provides fast Perl script loading. This curious piece of software speeds up CGI script loading because after the application is loaded it remains in memory until the Web server process terminates. This eliminates Perl's process load time—the time it takes for the system to load and execute the perl.exe program (loading perl.exe, locating, and then loading its needed DLL files). Chances are that you won't really notice speed improvements unless you are running many scripts at the same time. It is important to note that the PerlIS.dll will not make your Perl scripts run any faster; however, they will *begin* to execute more quickly.

Consider a Web server that takes one second to load and run `perl.exe`. This time includes locating and loading all needed .dll files (such as `Perl.dll`, `Perl300.dll`, `PerlCRT.dll`, or any extension .dll files). If your Web server receives a request to run a Perl-based CGI script, it will take one second to load Perl; then it must compile the script, and then execution begins. Suppose that 10 requests come in at the same time for a Perl-based CGI script. Collectively it would take at least 10 seconds for Perl to load for all the requests. Because the 10 requests occur at the same time; however, there will be a bit of additional time overhead because you will have all 10 processes attempting to start simultaneously. On slower machines, this could stretch from 10 to 20 seconds or even longer.

Using `PerlIS.dll` radically reduces this time burden because no new processes must be started. A thread is obtained from a pool of waiting threads, which takes practically no time overhead. Because all DLL files are already loaded, the entire load time is minimized to the time it takes to load the Perl script itself. Web servers that receive many hits on Perl-based CGI scripts can indeed see dramatic speed improvements. Servers with few Perl script requests, however, will probably not see much improvement.

> **Note**
>
> *As of this writing, the* `PerlIS.dll` *is only supported using ActiveState's version of Win32 Perl. This may change in the future as both the ActiveState and core distributions merge together.*

In Web servers such as Microsoft's Internet Information Server (IIS), different file extensions can be mapped to different executables. Many administrators associate CGI scripts that have a .pl extension to run `perl.exe` and scripts with extensions of .cgi (or something similar) to run using `PerlIS.dll`. This gives the Webmaster flexibility to use either method for Perl script execution. When installing the `PerlIS.dll`, however, ActiveState suggests using the .plx suffix with `PerlIS.dll`. Really, it does not matter which extension you use with which process—the choice is totally up to the Webmaster. It may be wise, however, to avoid the .pl extension because any hacker can identify that you are using Perl. This could be an invitation for a hacker who is familiar with Perl.

Default Directories

When you run a script executed by the `PerlIS.dll` ISAPI application, the script may not know what a current directory is. This is an odd concept to have to contend with because Win32 supports a current directory, as does Perl. Any script that has been written assuming that a current directory exists may fail. Example 11.3 works when run from a command line or when run as a CGI script using `perl.exe`, but could fail if run from a Web server using `PerlIS.dll`.

Example 11.3   *Using the current directory fails under* PerlIS.dll

```
$| = 1;
print "Content-type: text/html\n\n";
open( FILE, "< ./data.txt" ) || die "Could not open the file ($!).\n";
print join( "<br>", <FILE> );
close( FILE );
```

This limitation is due to how ISAPI Web servers handle this situation (such as IIS 3.0). PerlIS.dll does not impose it. Some Web servers have corrected this and provide a current directory even for PerlIS.dll-based scripts. If you are using IIS 4.0 and are experiencing this particular problem, you may be able to correct it by changing the CreateCGIWithNewConsole setting to 1 in the MetaBase. This setting will enable a CGI script to make use of current and default directories, as well as use backticks and the **system**() function to spawn processes. Example 11.4 demonstrates a simple Perl script that sets the MetaBase's CreateCGIWithNewConsole setting to 1. This example uses the **Win32::OLE** extension, so it will only work with either the core distribution's libwin32 or with Perl 5.005. If you have ActiveState pre-5.005 build on your Web server (such as Build 316) and you have DCOM installed on another machine with Perl 5.005, you can run the script from that other machine. In this case, you will have to specify which Web server to modify.

> *Tip*
>
> *IIS 4.0 uses a data repository for storing its settings called the MetaBase. This is the* METABASE.BIN *file usually located in the* C:\WINNT\SYSTEM32\INETSRV *directory. It is not commonly known why this method of storing settings information was used instead of the Registry. Regardless, there are a few ways to change settings in the MetaBase, one of which is a MetaBase editor (similar to the Registry editor* REGEDIT.EXE *and* REGEDT32.EXE*) that comes with the IIS 4.0 Resource Kit. Alternatively, you can change values in the MetaBase using a utility called cscript and a Visual Basic script that come with IIS 4.0. The script is in the* \winnt\system32\inetsrv\adminsamples *directory and will enable you to modify MetaBase settings. To set the* CreateCGIWithNewConsole *setting to 1 you can use:*
>
> > cscript adsutil.vbs SET w3svc/CreateCGIWithNewConsole "1"
>
> *You can use the Perl script in Example 11.4 to set this property as well.*

Example 11.4   *Setting the* CreateCGIWithNewConsole *property for an IIS Web server*

```
01. use Win32::OLE;
02.    # Pass in a server name (or address) as the first parameter
03.    # into the script otherwise assume to use the local host.
```

```
04. $Server = "LocalHost" unless ( $Server = $ARGV[0] );
05.    # Get a web server object
06. $Object = "IIS://$Server/w3svc";
07. $WebServer = Win32::OLE->GetObject( $Object, 1 )
       ¦¦ die "Can not talk to $object";
08.    # Set the property
09. $WebServer->{CreateCGIWithNewConsole} = 1;
10. $WebServer->SetInfo();
```

To avoid this problem, a Perl script must use full path names when referencing files and directories. This makes it difficult to move scripts from one server to another because a Web server's CGI script directory may be in a physically different location from another server.

Some Web servers provide an environmental variable in the CGI environment that contains the value of the current directory for the running script. A script can make use of this to get around the lack of a current directory, as illustrated in Example 11.5. Example 11.5 uses the environmental variable PATH_TRANS-LATED, which IIS provides and is the full path to the script file.

The PerlIS.dll extension defines an environmental variable PERLXS. This allows any script to check and see whether it is running under this extension.

Example 11.5 *Using environmental variables to determine the current directory*

```
01. $¦ = 1;
02. print "Content-type: text/html\n\n";
03.
04.    # We will dump this file from the current directory
05. $File = "page.htm";
06.
07. if( $Dir = $ENV{'PATH_TRANSLATED'} )
08. {
09.      # The environmental variable exists so we can strip off the
10.      # file name and we now have our directory path.
11.      $Dir =~ s/(\\[^\\]*?)$//;
12.      print "<br>Using env var: dir='$Dir'<p>\n";
13. }
14. else
15. {
16.      # If the environmental variable does not exist assume this is
17.      # not using PerlIS.dll and we can use a current directory.
18.      print "br>Not using env var!<p>\n";
19.      $Dir = ".";
20. }
21. open( FILE, "< $Dir/$File" ) ¦¦ die "Could not open '$File' ($!).\n";
22. print join("<br>", <FILE> );
23. close( FILE );
```

Threads

The PerlIS.dll ISAPI application works by assigning a thread for each script that is executed. Generally, this approach is fine and makes for efficient management. Some Win32 extensions are not thread safe, however. This is not always a problem, but it can become one. Thread issues do not arise when running from a command line, so it is difficult to find them when debugging your scripts. Instead, they usually come up when you are running multiple instances of a script at the same time, such as in a production environment (typically online for the world to see).

The problem arises when an extension is not written to be thread aware. This just means that the author of the extension made assumptions that only one script would be accessing memory and data at a time. The **Win32::NetAdmin** extension, for example, records any error that it generates into an internal variable called lastError. If a script calls a **Win32::NetAdmin** function that fails, it needs to call the **Win32::NetAdmin::GetError()** function to retrieve the contents of the lastError variable (which is the Win32 error that the function returned). The extension's lastError variable, however, is global in scope. This is not thread friendly.

Consider two scripts (Script A and Script B). Script A calls the **Win32::NetAdmin::GetUsers()** function to get the list of users. This function fails (because the specified server is offline, for example) and sets the lastError variable to 53 ("The network path was not found."). The script now has to figure out whether the function failed and if it did, the script calls the **Win32::NetAdmin::GetError()** function to find out what the error number was. While Script A is figuring out whether the function failed, Script B makes a call into another **NetAdmin** function (checking whether a user is a member of a group), which is successful. This causes lastError to be set to the result indicating that the last function was successful (a value of 0). By now, Script A has concluded that its attempt to get a list of users failed, so it will call the **GetError()** function. The result, however, will be the result of Script B's last call (the successful one).

This is known as a race condition, where two processes fight for one resource. When the PerlIS.dll application is loaded, all scripts it runs are executed using a different thread but they all share the same memory. For those not familiar with threads, DLLs, and C coding, think of this as a problem of writing a big Perl script that uses a global variable that each function changes. If one function changes the global variable, another function may not know that the variable was changed, so it assumes all is fine.

Perl was not designed to be thread safe, and hence many of its extensions do not bother to worry about such issues. Now that the PerlIS.dll application has become quite popular and future versions of Perl will support threading, Perl extensions have had to change how they manage these issues. Consider a Web site where several administrators use CGI scripts to manage user accounts. If they are running these scripts at the same time, several threads could be overwriting the lastError variable. There would most likely be several conflicts.

A solution to this problem is to either guarantee that the scripts run one at a time by using a semaphore or some other mechanism, or to configure the Web server to only run sensitive scripts by using perl.exe rather than perlIS.dll. When threading finally does come to Perl, it is inevitable that the authors of extensions will eventually rewrite their software to be thread safe.

Exactly what is meant by "thread safe" is difficult to explain because there are numerous implications. A couple of issues that relate, however, include the addressing of a process' memory space and the startup code of a DLL.

When an application runs, it is given a chunk of memory that the process can do with as it wants. Anything that exists in the memory space, the process can use. When a DLL is loaded, it is put into the memory of the process that loaded it. At this point, the process accesses the DLL's functions and variables as if they were part of the program. If a function in the DLL starts a new thread that the calling program is unaware of, however, problems can arise. If this thread alters some variable, for example, the calling program may be totally unaware of this and expect the variable to be something else. If the program were "aware" of the possibility that a thread may alter this variable, it would never make assumptions about a variable's state.

Another "thread awareness" issue has to do with when a DLL is loaded. Every time a Win32 DLL is loaded, a function called **DllMain()** is called automatically. When this function is called (by the system), the DLL will know that it is being loaded and should initialize itself. The **DllMain()** function is also called when a new thread is started, when a thread terminates, and when the DLL is unloaded from memory. A thread-safe extension would use this function to know when a thread is started and mark certain variables as related to the thread. An example of this as a problem was the **Win32::ODBC** extension. Before it was rewritten to be thread safe, problems occurred when running it under PerlIS.dll on a Web server. PerlIS.dll uses a different thread to run each Perl script. If two scripts were running at the same time, which accessed ODBC databases, the **Win32::ODBC** extension would overwrite certain global variables. This caused script errors and even crashes in some cases. Now that the extension is thread safe, each thread has its own set of variables that it, and only it, uses.

Security

Security is always an issue with CGI scripts, but the most blaring and obvious security risk is to have a physical copy of perl.exe in a CGI directory. I cannot emphasize enough how dangerous this is—so don't do it!

If some hacker discovers that you have a Perl executable in your CGI directory (or somewhere else in your Web tree), all he has to do is submit some command like this:

```
http://www.blah.com/cgi-bin/perl?-e+"`kill.exe+*`"
```

If your server has the kill.exe somewhere in its path, your server will crash in moments. Or maybe the hacker could submit something like this:

```
http://www.blah.com/cgi-bin/perl?-e+"unlink(glob('*'))"
```

That could erase all the files in your cgi-bin directory. Of course, depending on how your other security settings are set up, this may or may not be a problem. It is quite clear, however, that placing the Perl executable anywhere in your Web tree is just an unnecessary security risk. Even if you have all sorts of security set, chances are that a hacker could still submit the following:

```
http://www.blah.com/cgi-bin/perl?-d+"map{open(FILE,$_);while(read(FILE,
$data,2048)){print+$data;}close(FILE)}glob('*')"
```

This will dump the contents of all files in your cgi-bin directory. If you have sensitive data or scripts that would show where data is stored, this indeed could be a security breach.

CGI Script Permissions

It is important to recognize that each process that runs on a Windows NT machine is granted what is known as a *security token*. The actual process and implications of this are beyond the scope of this book, but suffice enough to say that this token is like an identification card. When a process tries to do something that is considered to be restricted (such as opening a file, loading a Registry hive, or modifying a user account), the operating system checks the ID card (the security token) of the process to see whether it is allowed to perform the task. If the OS determines that the process does not have the correct credentials (or permissions), the process is denied the capability to do what it wants to do.

Every process has one of these security tokens attached to it, even services. When a user logs on, the system assigns a security token to the user. When the user then starts a program, the program is given a duplicate of the user's security token. This is where processes get these tokens. When a user runs a Perl script from a command line, the Perl process receives a duplicate of the user's security token. This is very important to understand because when a service starts, the same thing occurs.

When you install a service, you must tell the service when to start (never start, start only when told to do so, or start automatically whenever the system boots up). You can either tell the service to start as a part of the "system" or as a user (in which case, you supply the user account and password). If configured to start as the system, the service is given a default system security token. Otherwise, it will try to log on as the specified user and will be given a duplicate of the user's security token.

Most Web servers run as a service, so they are assigned a security token from either the system or from a specified user account. Suppose that a Web server runs under an account name of something like IUSR_TEST. Assume also, that an administrator logs on to the Web server and runs a Perl script from a command line. The script runs exactly as expected. The administrator then tries running the same script from a Web browser and it fails. The problem most likely is that the administrator has privileges identified in his security token that are needed, but which the Web server does not have.

The solution to this predicament is to grant the required permissions and privileges to the account that the Web server will run under. The things to consider when determining why a script fails when run under a different account (such as by a Web server) are file permissions; Registry key permissions; and privileges to administrate accounts and other resources such as network shares, printers, and communication devices.

> **Tip**
>
> *Sometimes, determining which privileges and permissions are causing problems can be quite difficult because of the many possibilities. One of the quickest ways to help narrow down a cause of contention is to use auditing.*
>
> *From the User Manager program, an administrator can enable system auditing such as logon attempts. The Registry, files, and directories can also be audited. Auditing is enabled by the same dialog box that enables you to change permissions on these same resources.*
>
> *After auditing has been enabled, the Event Viewer's security log will show all the audit tracking information. Be forewarned, however, if auditing is enabled on busy servers, the event log can fill up quite quickly.*

Network Communications

A problem that occurs when running a Perl script as either a CGI script or as an ASP page (when using PerlScript) is accessing network resources. One would assume that if the Web server account has permissions to access a network resource (like a printer, a net share, and so forth), the script could just access the resource. If the Web server has read access on the file:

`\\ServerA\Data\products.dat`

(assuming that this file is tab-delimited containing product names, prices, and Web links), the script in Example 11.6 should work.

Example 11.6   *Simple CGI script accessing a network resource*

```
01. $| = 1;
02. $File = "\\\\ServerA\\Data\\products.dat";
03. print "Content-type: text/html\n\n";
04. print "<HTML><HEAD><TITLE>Product List</TITLE></HEAD><BODY>\n";
05. if( open( FILE, "< $File" ) )
06. {
07.   @Data = <FILE>;
08.   close( FILE );
09.   print "<UL>\n";
10.   foreach $Item ( @Data )
11.   {
12.     chop $Item;
13.     ($Item, $Price, $Href) = split('\t', $Item);
14.     print "<LI><a href=\"$Href\">$Item</a> (\$$Price)</LI>\n";
15.   }
16.   print "</UL>\n";
17. }
18. else
19. {
20.   print "<H1>Can not open $File: $!</H1>";
21. }
22. print "</BODY></HTML>\n";
```

Don't be surprised, however, if Example 11.6 doesn't work. For some reason, Microsoft's Web servers (IIS 3.0 and 4.0) both seem to have a problem that, under certain circumstances, fails to open the file (regardless of permission and privilege settings). I have yet to find an adequate answer to explain why this happens. Unless there has been a patch to the Web server itself that corrects this problem, there does not seem to be a fix. Just be aware that this may be a problem if you choose to write CGI scripts that access files on remote machines. An occasional quick check on Microsoft's Web site for a hot fix may be in order if you stumble upon this problem.

PerlScript

The PerlScript does not understand the concept of a current directory. Because of this, your CGI scripts *must* specify full paths and not relative ones. Refer to the section on PerlIS.dll for a more thorough explanation.

Printing

When you run a CGI script using either PerlIS.dll or perl.exe, you can print to STDOUT and that is sent directly to the client (such as a Web browser).

PerlScript, however, is not quite so understanding.

In PerlScript, an object called $Response has specific capabilities. How to use this object (and its brethren such as $Server and $Session) is beyond the scope of this book, but it does have one method worth examining here. This is the **Write**() method.

When your script would normally print to STDOUT, you just need to pass the outputted data to the $Response->Write() method, as in Example 11.7. Notice that instead of printing the scalar $HTML, we are sending it as a parameter into $Response->Write().

Example 11.7 *Printing in a PerlScript*

```
$HTML = "<HTML><HEAD><TITLE>My Test</TITLE></HEAD><BODY>";
$HTML .= "<H1>This is my Test!!!</H1>";
$HTML .= "</BODY></HTML>";
$Response->Write( $HTML );
```

Win32::NetAdmin

If an error occurs during a function call, using the **GetError**() may return an incorrect value if running in a multithreaded environment such as using the PerlIS.dll ISAPI application or using PerlScript. The reason for this is that the last error is held in a single variable. If an error occurs, the error number is stored in the variable. It is possible that between the time you call a function and the time you call **GetError**(), another script could have been run (a CGI script on a Web server, for example) that would change the value of the LastError variable. The **Win32::NetAdmin** extension is not thread friendly. For more information about this, refer to the "Threads" section in this chapter.

Win32::Registry

Many users have had problems with loading Registry keys, which requires backup and restore privileges. The ActiveState (builds up to and including 316) of the **Win32::Registry** extension does not enable the privilege to the user running the script. This means that the script must do it. An extension called **Win32::Procctrl** does exactly this.

To save keys, you must enable the SeBackupPrivilege privilege. To load keys, you must enable the SeRestorePrivilege privilege using the following:

```
Win32::Procctrl::SetPrivilege( "SeBackupPrivilege", 1 );
Win32::Procctrl::SetPrivilege( "SeRestorePrivilege", 1 );
```

It appears that **Load**() (illustrated in Example 11.8) requires that both privileges be enabled, so it is probably a good idea to always enable both of them.

Evidently, this is not a problem for the core distribution's libwin32 (since version 1.0) or for Perl 5.005.

Example 11.8   *Loading and unloading Registry hives*

```
01. use Win32::Registry;
02. use Win32::Procctrl;
03.
04. $Key = "TempHive";
05. $File = "c:\\temp\\key.dat";
06.    # Give the backup privilege...
07. Win32::Procctrl::SetPrivilege("SeBackupPrivilege", 1)
       || die "Could not grant the Backup privilege (" .
          Win32::Procctrl::GetLastError() . ")\n";
08.    # Give the restore privilege...
09. Win32::Procctrl::SetPrivilege("SeRestorePrivilege", 1 )
       || die "Could not grant the Restore privilege (" .
          Win32::Procctrl::GetLastError() . ")\n";
10.
11. $HKEY_USERS->Load( $Key, $File )
       || die "Could not load $File into the key $Key: " .
          Win32::GetLastError() . "\n";
12.
13. ...process your code...
14.
15. $HKEY_USERS->Unload( $Key )
       || die "Could not unload the key $Key: " .
          Win32::GetLastError() . "\n";
```

> **Note**
>
> *According to the Microsoft Win32 SDK, when loading a Registry hive or restoring a Registry key from a file, the file cannot have a file extension if it resides on a drive formatted as FAT. Files residing on NTFS and HPFS formatted drives can include a file extension. It is a mystery as to why Microsoft made it this way.*

Saving and Loading Keys to a Remote Registry

When you connect to a remote Registry and either save a key to a file or load a key from a file, it is important to note that the path to the file that is specified is relative to the computer on which the Registry lives. Suppose, for example, that a script connects to \\ServerA and tries to load a key from c:\temp\key.dat using the following command:

```
$Remote_HKEY_LOCAL_MACHINE->Load( "TestKey", "c:\\temp\\key.dat" );
```

The file that will be loaded is in \\ServerA's c:\temp directory. If the file exists on the machine running the script but not on \\ServerA, the function will fail. The same is true for the **Save()** method—the file will be saved on \\ServerA.

Win32::ODBC

The **Win32::ODBC** extension requires that 32-bit ODBC (version 2.5 or later) be installed on your machine. This is very important and evidently not so obvious to some users. ODBC may or may not be installed on your machine, depending on which applications are installed. Usually installing something like Microsoft's Office suite will install a compatible version. If you need to install ODBC, you can obtain it from `http://www.microsoft.com/odbc/`. It is easy to get sidetracked at Microsoft's ODBC Web page because they also promote other services such as ADO, OLEDB, RDO, Universal Database Services, and others. It is important to note that most of these services rely on ODBC and are not replacements for it.

To determine whether you have ODBC installed on your machine, you can go to the Windows Control Panel and look for an ODBC applet. If there is none, you do not have ODBC installed; however, it is possible to have it installed but no Control Panel applet—if you accidentally deleted the applet from your `system32` directory. If this is the case, you better reinstall it anyway.

After you have ODBC installed, you need to install ODBC drivers. Generally, you need an ODBC driver for each type of database you will be accessing. If you need access to an Oracle database, for example, you need an Oracle ODBC driver but not the SQL Server driver (unless, of course, you also need to access a SQL Server database). Some drivers can handle multiple types of databases like the MS Access driver that manages Access, FoxPro, Excel, and text files. These each appear as different ODBC drivers in the Control Panel applet, but they all use the same `.DLL` files.

Several third-party ODBC driver companies produce high-performance drivers that can (usually) speed up queries on a database more than the standard driver that comes with a database. These companies also provide drivers for other platforms such as the Macintosh and UNIX.

Permissions

One common problem that usually appears on Web servers is incorrect permissions. When an administrator writes a script using **Win32::ODBC**, he may find that the script that works when he tests it fails when accessing it as a CGI script or when other users access the script. This is typically due to inadequate permissions.

A user who runs a script using **Win32::ODBC** must have (at least) read permissions on the ODBC Manager and ODBC driver files. These are usually held in the `C:\WINNT\SYSTEM32` directory. Additionally, permissions must be granted on the actual database itself. Sometimes this is not a practical matter, for example, when dealing with a database server such as Oracle or SQL Server. These types of databases typically require the database administrator to apply permissions on the database system as opposed to permissions placed on files (as in the case of FoxPro and Paradox databases).

Some ODBC drivers also require read and write permissions on certain directories and files. The Access ODBC driver, for example, needs write access on the temporary directory (usually `C:\TEMP`) so that it can create, access, and delete temporary files. Additionally, it needs write access to the directory in which the database file resides. This is because the driver will create and manage an `.LDB` file that contains information regarding who is currently accessing the database file. This caveat makes it difficult to interact with Access database files on CD-ROMs.

Win32::OLE

One of the most notable things I have discovered with the **Win32::OLE** extension is the way methods return values (or, I should say, do not return values). This deserves some clarification.

Most all Perl functions return some sort of value to indicate either success or failure. **Win32::OLE** is one of those rare exceptions. Now this really is not the extension's fault because there is no way for the extension to know what the return value would represent. If a COM object's method did not return any value, how would the **Win32::OLE** extension possibly know that the method is supposed to not return any value? For this reason, the extension is playing it smart by not making assumptions.

Suppose that I am playing around with MS Word and I create a document object. My code wants to save the document, so it calls:

```
$Result = $Doc->Save();
```

After the line is executed, the `$Result` variable will be empty regardless of whether the **Save()** method was successful. This is because the **Save()** method does not return any value to my Perl script. So how am I to know whether the save actually worked? By using the **LastError()** method.

I can always query the **Win32::OLE–>LastError()** method to discover whether my last interaction with a COM object was successful or whether an error occurred. If the method returns a `0`, there is no error. If it returns some error message, I know there was a problem. Based on this, I should rewrite my code that saves the Word document:

```
$Doc->Save();
if( $Error = Win32::OLE->LastError() )
{
  print "An error occurred while saving document: $Doc->{Name}\n";
  print "$Error\n";
}
```

Summary

With all that Win32 Perl is capable of doing, it is difficult to find reasons to be dissatisfied with it. It would be wonderful to write a script that just works as you would expect it to, but we live in an imperfect world where we have to consider all possibilities lest we find that our scripts fail when we need them the most.

All sorts of Win32 Perl resources are available on the Internet. Many of these provide tips for troubleshooting as well as the latest details on bug fixes. Some of the more common ones include the following:

- **ActiveState Tool Corp. (`http://www.activestate.com/`).** This is the ActiveState Web site. Here you can find most of the updated information regarding Win32 Perl (aka ActivePerl). This is also the place to go to subscribe to the many Win32 Perl List servers such as

  - Win32-Admin (administrative issues)

  - Win32-Database (database issues)

  - Win32-Users (general usage issues)

  - Win32-Web (Web issues such as CGI scripts)

  You can also search the online database of messages for each group.

- **The Official Perl Home Page (`http://www.perl.com/`).** The "official" Perl Web site. Here is where you can find articles, announcements, links, and other neat-o things including the source for Perl 5.005.

- **CPAN (the Comprehensive Perl Archive Network) (`http://www.cpan.org/`).** Long heralded as *the* place to find Perl-related modules, extensions, and scripts. This archive is mirrored all over the Internet, and most mirrors are kept well up-to-date. If you are looking for a script or extension that performs a particular task, try looking here first.

- **Joe Casadonte's Perl for Win32 page** (`http://www.netaxs.com/~joc/perlwin32.html`). This is a collection of links, scripts, extensions, tutorials, utilities, programs, and the list goes on. From here you can also hop on to the Perl Web ring. This site is a must for anyone from a novice to a full-fledged guru.

- **Jutta Klebe's Perl page** (`http://www.bybyte.de/jmk/`). Jutta's site explains her **Win32::PerfLib** extension with details, examples, and links to other related sites. You can also find her binaries here.

- **Dada's Perl Lab** (`http://www.divinf.it/dada/perl/`). This is Aldo Calpini's Perl page. He has documented most of his extensions rather well at this site. You can also find binaries for these extensions as well as information regarding future versions and new extensions.

- **Roth Consulting's Perl Page** (`http://www.roth.net/perl/`). This has links to the **Win32::AdminMisc** and **Win32::ODBC** FAQs.

- **Philippe Leberre's Perl Pages** (`http://www.inforoute.capway.com/leberre1/`). Philippe Le Berre's Perl Web site. Here you can find some really good breakdowns of some of the common extensions. This is a good source for information; however, it is generally technical in detail, so beginners may be a bit awestruck.

- **Robin's Perl for Win32 Page** (`http://www.geocities.com/SiliconValley/Park/8312/`). This resource contains links, explanations, and some sample scripts to help get you started with Win32 extension fundamentals.

- **Matt's Perl Pages** (`http://www.fastnetltd.ndirect.co.uk/Perl/`). This site is produced by Matt Sergeant and is chock full of interesting details and tidbits.

- **The Perl Journal** (`http://www.tpj.com/`). Sure this does not have much online help for Win32 Perl, but it is *the* journal for any Perl hack. It covers all platforms, including Win32. A subscription is fairly cheap and it is well worth the price for the knowledge that comes in each issue.

- **Usenet** (`nntp://comp.lang.perl.misc`). This is about the most informative group of Perl users, addicts, and hackers that you can find. Sometimes this group can get quite ornery and flame wars are common; with a little netiquette, however, your problems can quickly find resolutions.

- **Usenet** (`nntp://comp.lang.perl.modules`). Don't be fooled, this group also covers extensions. Most posts in this group pertain only to modules and extensions. A wonderful resource.

- **DejaNews.com** (`http://www.dejanews.com/`). This one may not be so obvious, but you would be surprised how many other non–Perl related groups discuss Perl issues (possibly even problems you may have).

Appendix **A**

Win32 Perl Resources

This appendix illustrates the syntax for functions within the Win32 extensions. Each function's proper syntax is followed by a brief description of what the function does, a description of the return values.

Win32::AdminMisc

The **Win32::AdminMisc** extension provides miscellaneous administrative functions. This is a hodgepodge of functions that were either missing from other extensions or modifications of existing functions.

CreateProcessAsUser($CommandString [, $DefaultDirectory] [, %Config])

This function creates a process based on the specified parameters that will be running under the account that you are impersonating with **LogonAsUser()**. If successful, the function returns the new process's PID; otherwise, it returns a FALSE (undef) value.

DelEnvVar($Name [, $Type [, $Timeout]])

This function deletes the specified environmental variable of the specified type using the specified timeout (for applications to acknowledge the change). The effect of this function will be seen by all running (non-DOS) programs globally. If successful, the function returns TRUE; otherwise, it returns a FALSE value.

DNSCache([1|0])

This function sets the local DNS cache on (1) or off (0). If nothing is specified, it returns only the current state of the DNS cache. The function returns the new state of DNS caching (either a 1 [caching enabled] or 0 [caching disabled] value).

DNSCacheCount()

This function returns the current number of cached elements. This cannot exceed the value of **DNSCacheSize()**. **DNSCacheCount()** returns the number of cached elements in the DNS cache.

DNSCacheSize([$Size])

This function sets the local DNS cache size to the specified size. **DNSCacheSize([$Size])** returns the new (or current) DNS cache size.

ExitWindows($Flag)

This function either logs off the current user or shuts down Windows. If successful, this function returns TRUE; otherwise, it returns a FALSE value.

GetComputerName()

This function returns the name of the computer. This performs the same function as the **Win23::GetNodeName()** found in the Win32 module. If successful, this function returns the computer's network name; otherwise, it returns undef.

GetDC($Domain)

This function returns a domain controller (primary or backup) for the specified domain. If successful, this function returns a domain controller's network name; otherwise, it returns undef.

GetDriveGeometry($Drive)

This function returns an array consisting of drive information for the specified drive. If successful, this function returns an array; otherwise, it returns undef.

GetDrives([$Type])

This function returns an array of drive roots of the specified type. If successful, this function returns an array; otherwise, it returns undef.

GetDriveSpace($Drive)

This function returns an array consisting of the total drive capacity and the available space on the specified drive. If successful, this function returns an array; otherwise, it returns undef.

GetDriveType($Drive)

This function returns an integer describing the type of drive specified. If successful, this function returns an integer representing the drive type or a 1 if unable to determine the type; otherwise, it returns a FALSE value.

GetEnvVar($Name [, $Type])

This function returns the value of the specified environmental variable based on the specified type. If successful, this function returns the variables value; otherwise, it returns undef.

GetFileInfo($File, \%Info)

This function retrieves extended file information (such as copyright, original name, company name) for the specified file. If successful, this function populates the specified hash with file-related information and returns TRUE; otherwise, it returns a FALSE value.

GetGroups($Machine $GroupType, (\@List | \%List) [, $Prefix])

This function retrieves the names of all groups that match the specified type and, optionally, match the specified prefix. If successful, this function populates either a hash or an array and returns TRUE; otherwise, it returns a FALSE value.

GetHostAddress($DNSName), GetHostName($IPAddress), gethostbyname($DNSName), gethostbyaddr($IPAddress)

These four functions are the same but go by different names for backward compatibility. They return either an IP address or DNS name depending upon what is passed into the function. If successful they return an IP address or DNS name; otherwise, they return a FALSE value.

GetIdInfo()

This function returns an array containing process and thread ID information. If successful, the function returns an array; otherwise, it returns a FALSE value.

GetLogonName()

This function returns the name of the user this account is logged on as. This is not necessarily the same as the account the Perl script is running under. An account can log on as another user (known as "impersonating" another account). If successful, this function returns the current user account name; otherwise, it returns undef.

GetMachines($Machine, $MachineType, (\@List | \%List) [, $Prefix])

This function retrieves an array or a hash populated with the names of computers that are of the specified type. The list will optionally only consist of those machine names that begin with the specified prefix. The list is generated by the specified machine. If successful, this function returns TRUE; otherwise, it returns a FALSE value.

GetMemoryInfo()

This function retrieves a hash of memory-related information. If successful, this function returns a hash; otherwise, it returns undef.

GetPDC($Domain)

This function returns the primary domain controller (PDC) of the specified domain. If successful, this function returns the name of the PDC; otherwise, it returns undef.

GetProcessorInfo()
This function retrieves a hash of processor-related information. If successful, this function returns a hash; otherwise, it returns undef.

GetStdHandle($Handle)
This function retrieves the Win32 handle to the specified standard handle specified in handle. If successful, this function returns the Win32 handle; otherwise, it returns undef.

GetTOD($Machine)
This function retrieves the time of day from the specified machine. If successful, this function returns the time in Perl time format; otherwise, it returns undef.

GetUsers($Server, $Prefix, (\@List | \%List))
This function retrieves an array or a hash populated with the names of user accounts that match the specified prefix. If successful, this function returns TRUE; otherwise, it returns a FALSE value.

GetVolumeInfo($Drive)
This function retrieves a hash of drive volume information for the specified drive. If successful, this function returns a hash; otherwise, it returns undef.

GetWinVersion()
This function retrieves a hash of Windows versions. If successful, this function returns a hash; otherwise, it returns undef.

LogoffAsUser([1|0])
This function logs the current account out from an "impersonated" account. The logout may use force if specified, which forces the logoff to occur even if applications are currently open. This function always returns TRUE.

LogonAsUser($Domain, $User, $Password [, $LogonType])
This function logs the current account on under the specified user account in the specified domain using the specified password. The logon type can be specified as well. If successful, this function returns TRUE; otherwise, it returns a FALSE value.

ReadINI($File, $Section, $Key)
This function retrieves data from an INI file based on the specified file, section, and key. If successful, this function returns an array or string; otherwise, it returns undef.

RenameUser($Machine, $User, $NewUser)
This function renames the specified user account on the specified machine. If successful, this function returns TRUE; otherwise, it returns a FALSE value.

ScheduleAdd($Machine, $Time, $DOM, $DOW, $Flags, $Command)
This function schedules the specified command to execute at the specified time on the specified machine. If successful, this function returns the new scheduled job number; otherwise, it returns undef.

ScheduleDel($Machine, $JobNumber [, $MaxJobNumber])
This function removes the specified job number (or numbers) from the specified machine. If successful, this function returns TRUE; otherwise, it returns a FALSE value.

ScheduleGet($Machine, $JobNumber, \%JobInfo)
This function retrieves information about the specified scheduled job on the specified machine. If successful, this function populates the hash and returns TRUE; otherwise, it returns a FALSE value.

ScheduleList($Machine [, \%List])
This function retrieves the total number of jobs scheduled to run on the specified machine. Optionally a hash is populated with information regarding each job. If successful, this function returns the number of jobs listed; otherwise, it returns undef.

SetComputerName($Name)
This function sets the network name for the current computer. If successful, this function returns the new computer name; otherwise, it returns a FALSE value.

SetEnvVar($Name, $Value [, $Type [, $Timeout]])
This function sets the type-specified environmental variable to have the specified value. Optionally the variable will be of the specified type and will have a specified timeout value for applications to acknowledge the modification. If successful, this function returns TRUE; otherwise, it returns a FALSE value.

SetPassword(($Machine | $Domain), $User, $Password)
This function sets the password for the specified user on the specified machine. This can be performed only by an administrator. If successful, this function returns TRUE; otherwise, it returns a FALSE value.

SetVolumeLabel($Drive, $Label)
This function sets the label on the specified drive. If successful, this function returns TRUE; otherwise, it returns a FALSE value.

UserChangePassword($Domain , $User, $OldPassword, $NewPassword)
This function modifies the password for the specified user on the specified machine (or domain). If successful, this function returns TRUE; otherwise, it returns a FALSE value.

UserCheckPassword(($Machine I $Domain), $User, $Password)
This function verifies whether the specified password is indeed the password for the specified user account on the specified machine (or domain). There are many reasons for this function to fail; check the documentation. If successful (password is validated), it returns TRUE; otherwise, it returns a FALSE value.

UserGetAttributes(($Machine I $Domain), $UserName, $UserFullName, $Password, $PasswordAge, $Privilege, $HomeDir, $Comment, $Flags, $ScriptPath)
This function retrieves some properties of the specified user account information for the specified user on the specified machine (or domain). If successful, this function returns TRUE; otherwise, it returns a FALSE value.

UserGetMiscAttributes(($Machine I $Domain), $User, \%Hash)
This function retrieves a hash of account properties for the specified user account on the specified machine (or domain). If successful, this function populates a hash and returns TRUE; otherwise, it returns undef.

UserSetAttributes(($Machine I $Domain), $UserName, $UserFullName, $Password, $PasswordAge, $Privilege, $HomeDir, $Comment, $Flags, $ScriptPath)
This function sets some properties of the specified user account on the specified machine (or domain). If successful, this function returns TRUE; otherwise, it returns a FALSE value.

UserSetMiscAttributes(($Machine I $Domain), $User, $Attribute1=>$Value1[, $Attribute2=>$Value2 [, ...]])
This function sets attributes of the specified user account on the specified machine (or domain). If successful, this function returns TRUE; otherwise, it returns a FALSE value.

WriteINI($File, $Section, $Key, $Value)
This function writes data to an INI file with the specified file, section, key, and value. If successful, this function returns TRUE; otherwise, it returns undef.

Win32::ChangeNotification and Win32::ChangeNotify

Both of these extensions are the same, just with different names. It is suggested that **Win32::ChangeNotify** be used; however, the **Win32::ChangeNotification** exists for backward compatibility.

$Obj–>Close()

This function closes and terminates a change notification object. This function returns TRUE.

$Obj–>FindNext()

This function clears the current state of the **Win32::ChangeNotification** and advances the change notification queue. This must be called before calling the **Wait()** method. If successful, this function returns TRUE; otherwise, it returns undef.

$Obj–>Wait($TimeOut)

This function waits for a change to take place or until the timeout value expires. The timeout is in milliseconds. If successful, this function returns FALSE (0); otherwise, it returns a non undef and non 0 value.

FindFirst($Obj, $PathName, $WathSubTree, $Filter)

This function creates a **Win32::ChangeNotification** object looking at the specified path and (possibly) any subtrees. This is all based on the specified filter. If successful, this function sets the object variable (the first parameter) to the newly created object and returns TRUE; otherwise, it returns undef.

Win32::Console

The **Win32::Console** extension interfaces Win32 Perl with a Win32 console. This allows a script to interact with a DOS-like window.

$Obj–>Alloc()

This function creates (allocates) a new console for the application. This can be used to display the contents of a console buffer. If successful, this function returns TRUE; otherwise, it returns a FALSE (undef) value.

$Obj–>Attr([$Attributes])

This function sets and retrieves the attributes for the current console. If successful, this function returns the new attributes.

$Obj–>Cls([$Attributes])

This function clears the console buffer, optionally filling the buffer with the specified attributes. If successful, this function returns TRUE; otherwise, it returns a FALSE (undef) value.

$Obj–>Cursor([$X, $Y [, $Size, $Visible]])

This function retrieves and optionally sets the X and Y coordinates of the console buffer's cursor. It optionally sets the size and visibility of the cursor. If successful, this function returns a four-element array of location, size, and visibility of the cursor; otherwise, it returns a FALSE (undef) value.

$Obj–>Display()

This function displays the console buffer in the application's console. If successful, this function returns TRUE; otherwise, it returns a FALSE (undef) value.

$Obj–>FillAttr($Attribute, $Number, $X, $Y)

This function fills the console buffer with the specified number of attributes beginning at the specified location. If successful, this function returns the number of attributes written; otherwise, it returns a FALSE (undef) value.

$Obj–>FillChar($Character, $Number, $X, $Y)

This function fills the console buffer with the specified number of characters beginning at the specified location. If successful, this function returns the number of characters written; otherwise, it returns a FALSE (undef) value.

$Obj–>Flush()

This function flushes everything from the console input buffer. If successful, this function returns TRUE; otherwise, it returns a FALSE (undef) value.

$Obj–>GenerateCtrlEvent($Type, $ProcessPID)

This function sends a break signal of the specified type to the specified process. If successful, this function returns TRUE; otherwise, it returns a FALSE (undef) value.

$Obj–>GetEvents()

This function retrieves the number of pending events in the console input buffer. If successful, this function returns the number of pending events; otherwise, it returns a FALSE (undef) value.

$Obj–>Info()

This function retrieves an array of information related to the console buffer including its size, position, attributes, and cursor-related information. If successful, this function returns and array; otherwise, it returns a FALSE (undef) value.

$Obj–>Input()

This function retrieves an array of events from the console input buffer. If successful, this function returns an array of events; otherwise, it returns a FALSE (undef) value.

$Obj->InputChar($Number)

This function reads the specified number of characters from the console input buffer. If successful, this function returns the read characters; otherwise, it returns a FALSE (undef) value.

$Obj->InputCP([$CodePage])

This function retrieves and optionally sets the console's code page. If successful, this function returns the code page; otherwise, it returns a FALSE (undef) value.

$Obj->MaxWindow()

This function retrieves the maximum X and Y coordinates the console buffer allows. If successful, this function returns a two-element array; otherwise, it returns a FALSE (undef) value.

$Obj->Mode([$Mode])

This function retrieves and optionally sets the input and output modes of the console. If successful, this function returns the new mode; otherwise, it returns a FALSE (undef) value.

$Obj->MouseButtons()

This function retrieves the number of buttons on the computer's mouse. If successful, this function returns the number of mouse buttons; otherwise, it returns a FALSE (undef) value.

$Obj->OutputCP([$CodePage])

This function retrieves and optionally sets the output buffer code page. If successful, this function returns the new output code page; otherwise, it returns a FALSE (undef) value.

$Obj->PeekInput()

This function retrieves the list of events from the console input buffer without removing the events from the input buffer. If successful, this function returns an array of events; otherwise, it returns a FALSE (undef) value.

$Obj->ReadAttr($Number, $X, $Y)

This function retrieves the specified number of attributes from the specified location within the console buffer. If successful, this function returns the read attributes; otherwise, it returns a FALSE (undef) value.

$Obj->ReadChar($Number, $X, $Y)

This function retrieves the specified number of characters from the specified location within the console buffer. If successful, this function returns a string of character data; otherwise, it returns a FALSE (undef) value.

$Obj->ReadRect($Left, $Top, $Right, $Bottom)

This function reads data (both characters and attributes) from within the specified rectangle. The returned data is used with the **WriteRect()** method. If successful, this function returns a string of data; otherwise, it returns a FALSE (undef) value.

$Obj->Scroll($Left, $Top, $Right, $Bottom, $X, $Y, $Character, $Attribute [, $ClipLeft, $ClipTop, $ClipRight, $ClipBottom])

This function moves the data (characters and attributes) from the specified rectangle to the location specified (by $X and $Y). Any empty space left is filled with the specified character and attribute. Optionally a clipping region can be specified. If successful, this function returns TRUE; otherwise, it returns a FALSE (undef) value.

$Obj->Select($StdHandle)

This function redirects the specified standard buffer to the console buffer ($Obj). If successful, this function returns TRUE; otherwise, it returns a FALSE (undef) value.

$Obj->Size([$X, $Y])

This function retrieves and optionally sets the console buffer size. If successful, this function returns a two-element array; otherwise, it returns a FALSE (undef) value.

$Obj->Title([$Title])

This function changes the title bar's text for the application's console. If successful, this function returns the new (or current) title; otherwise, it returns a FALSE (undef) value.

$Obj->Window($Flag, $Left, $Top, $Right, $Bottom)

This function retrieves and optionally sets the application's console window size. The specified parameters are either relative to the window's current coordinates or absolute depending on the specified flag. If successful, this function returns a four-element array; otherwise, it returns a FALSE (undef) value.

$Obj->Write($Text)

This function writes the specified text string to the console buffer. If successful, this function returns the number of characters written; otherwise, it returns a FALSE (undef) value.

$Obj->WriteAttr($Attributes, $X, $Y)

This function writes the specified attributes to the specified location in the console buffer. If successful, this function returns the number of attributes written; otherwise, it returns a FALSE (undef) value.

$Obj–>WriteChars($Text, $X, $Y)

This function writes the specified text to the specified location in the console buffer. If successful, this function returns the number of characters written; otherwise, it returns a FALSE (undef) value.

$Obj–>WriteInput(@Events)

This function writes the specified list of events to the console input buffer. If successful, this function returns the number of characters written to the input buffer; otherwise, it returns a FALSE (undef) value.

$Obj–>WriteRect($Data, $Left, $Top, $Right, $Bottom)

This function writes the specified rectangle data to the specified window. The data is obtained by calling the **ReadRect**() method. If successful, this function returns a four-element array (indicating the affected window size); otherwise, it returns a FALSE (undef) value.

new Win32::Console(), new Win32::Console($StdHandle), new Win32::Console($AccessMode, $ShareMode)

The **new Win32::Console**() function creates a new default console buffer.

The **new Win32::Console($StdHandle)** function creates a new console buffer object based on the specified standard console buffer.

The **new Win32::Console($AccessMode, $ShareMode)** function creates a new console buffer in memory with the specified a access and share modes. If successful, these functions return a reference to a **Win32::Console** object; otherwise, they will return undef.

Win32::EventLog

The **Win32::EventLog** extension interacts with the Win32 event log. This works specifically on Windows NT (and also on Windows 95 and 98 if they have the domain admin programs installed).

$Obj–>Backup($File)

This function creates a backup copy of the event log by saving it to the specified file. If successful, this function returns TRUE; otherwise, it returns a FALSE value.

$Obj–>Clear($File)

This function creates a backup of the event log to the specified file, and then clears the log of all records. If successful, this function returns TRUE; otherwise, it returns a FALSE value.

$Obj->GetNumber($Record)

This function retrieves the total number of records in the event log. If successful, this function sets the value of the first parameter to the total number of records and returns TRUE; otherwise, it returns a FALSE value.

$Obj->GetOldest($Record)

This function retrieves the oldest record that exists in the event log. If successful, this function stores the record number in the first parameter and returns TRUE; otherwise, it returns a FALSE value.

$Obj->Read($Flags, $RecordOffSet, \%Event)

This function reads one entry from the event log based on the specified record offset and flags. If successful, this function returns a hash reference that is stored in the third parameter and returns TRUE; otherwise, it returns a FALSE value.

$Obj->Report(%EventRecord)

This function writes the event defined by the specified event record to the event log. If successful, this function returns TRUE; otherwise, it returns a FALSE value.

new($Source, $Machine), Open($Source, $Machine)

Both functions create a new event log object on the specified machine referencing the specified event log source. If successful, they return an event log object; otherwise, they return a FALSE value.

Win32::File

This extension provides general file attribute management. A series of constants represents the different attributes of a file.

GetAttributes($Path, $Attributes)

This function retrieves the attributes from the specified file or directory. If successful, this function assigns $Attributes with the value representing the different attributes and returns TRUE (1); otherwise, it returns a FALSE (0) value.

SetAttributes($Path, $Attributes)

This function sets the attributes for the specified file or directory. If successful, this function sets the attributes on the specified path and returns TRUE (1); otherwise, it returns a FALSE (0)value.

Win32::FileSecurity

This extension manages permissions placed on files and directories. This will work only on a Windows NT machine.

EnumerateRights($Mask, \@Rights)

This function translates a permission bitmask into an array of permission strings. If successful, this function populates the array with permission strings and returns TRUE; otherwise, it returns a FALSE value.

Get($Path, \%Permissions)

This function retrieves the permissions (DACL) from the specified file or directory. If successful, this function populates the hash with permission information and returns TRUE; otherwise, it returns a FALSE value.

MakeMask(@Permissions)

This function creates a permission bitmask from a list of permission strings (by using the extensions constants). If successful, this function returns a bitmask; otherwise, it returns a FALSE (undef) value.

Set($Path, \%Permissions)

This function sets the permissions (DACL) on the specified file or directory. If successful, the path's permissions are set and the function returns TRUE; otherwise, it returns a FALSE value.

Win32::IPC

This extension is a base extension used by **Win32::ChangeNotification** (and **Win32::ChangeNotify**), **Win32::Mutex**, **Win32::Semaphore**, and **Win32::Process**. It has no useful methods or functions that a script calls directly.

The other listed extensions inherit functions from **Win32::IPC**, which they use internally.

Win32::Message

This extension provides an interface into the Win32 NetBIOS messaging API. It enables you to register network names and send messages.

NameAdd([$Machine,] $Name)

This function adds the specified network name to the specified machine (or local host by default). If successful, this function returns TRUE; otherwise, it returns a FALSE (0) value.

NameDel([$Machine,] $Name)

This function removes the specified network name from the specified machine (or local host by default). If successful, this function returns TRUE; otherwise, it returns a FALSE (0) value.

NameEnum([$Machine])

This function returns an array of the registered network names for the specified machine (or local host by default). If successful, this function returns an array of network names; otherwise, it returns a FALSE (0) value.

Send([$Machine,] $Receiver, $Sender, $Message)

This function sends the specified message to the specified receiver from the specified sender. The specified machine will actually send the message (provided that the account executing the command has permissions to do so). If the message is successfully sent (this does not mean that it was successfully received), the function returns TRUE; otherwise, it returns a FALSE (0) value.

Win32::Mutex

This extension creates and manages Win32 MUTEX (MUTually EXclusive) objects.

Create($MutObj, $InitialOwner, $Name)

This function opens a MUTEX object that can be used by any running process. If the MUTEX does not currently exist, it is created.

The value of $InitialOwner determines whether the calling thread (because Perl does not truly support threads, yet considers this to be the calling process) owns the MUTEX. A non-zero value means the process indeed does own the MUTEX. Typically this value will be 1. If successful, this function returns TRUE and sets $MutObj to the new MUTEX; otherwise, it returns a FALSE value.

Open($MutObj,$Name)

This function opens an existing MUTEX with the specified name. If successful, this function returns TRUE and $MutObj is set to the MUTEX object; otherwise, it returns a FALSE value.

$Obj->Release();

This function releases the MUTEX object. If no other process has attached to the MUTEX, it is destroyed. If successful, this function returns TRUE; otherwise, it returns a FALSE value.

$Obj->Wait($Timeout)

This method will wait until the MUTEX becomes signaled or until the timeout value expires. If successful, this function returns TRUE; otherwise, it returns a FALSE value.

Win32::NetAdmin

The **Win32::NetAdmin** extension provides administrative, network, domain, and account management functions.

GetAnyDomainController($Server, $Domain, $Name)

This function discovers the name of any domain controller (either a PDC or a BDC). If successful, $Name will contain the name of the domain's PDC and the function returns TRUE; otherwise, it returns undef.

GetDomainController($Server, $Domain, $Name)

This function discovers the name of a Primary Domain Controller (PDC). If successful, $Name will contain the name of the domain's PDC and the function returns TRUE; otherwise, it returns undef.

GetServers($Server, $Domain, $Flags, \@ServerList)

This function retrieves the list of machine names that satisfy the specified flags. If successful, this function populates the array with computer names and returns TRUE; otherwise, it returns undef.

GetUsers($Server, $Filter, \@UserList)

This function obtains a list of user accounts on the specified server that satisfies the specified filter. If successful, this function returns TRUE and the array is populated with the names of user accounts; otherwise, it returns undef.

GroupAddUsers($Server, $Group, $User)

This function adds the specified user to the global group on the specified server. If the third parameter is an array reference all of the user accounts listed in the array are added to the global group. If successful, this function returns TRUE; otherwise, it returns undef.

GroupCreate($Server, $Group, $Comment)

This function creates a global group on the specified server giving it the specified comment. If successful, this function returns TRUE; otherwise, it returns undef.

GroupDelete($Server, $Group)

This function deletes a global group from the specified server. If successful (the global group exists and was deleted), it returns TRUE; otherwise, it returns undef.

GroupDeleteUsers($Server, $Group, $Users)

This function removes a user account from the specified global group on the specified server. If the third parameter is an array reference, all the user accounts listed in the array are removed from the global group. If successful, this function returns TRUE; otherwise, it returns undef.

GroupGetAttributes($Server, $Group, $Comment)

This function retrieves the comment from the specified global group that exists on the specified server. If successful, this function sets the third comment variable (the parameter) with the global group's comment and returns TRUE; otherwise, it returns undef.

GroupGetMembers($Server, $Group, \@UserList)

This function populates the specified array with the list of user accounts that make up the global group. If successful, the array is populated with account names and the function returns TRUE; otherwise, it returns undef.

GroupIsMember($Sserver, $Group, $User)

This function checks that the user is a member of the global group on the specified server. If the user exists in the global group, it returns TRUE; otherwise, it returns undef.

GroupSetAttributes($Server, $Group, $Comment)

This function sets the comment for the global group on the specified server. If successful, this function returns TRUE; otherwise, it returns undef.

LocalGroupAddUsers($Server, $Group, $User)

This function adds the specified user to the local group on the specified server. If the third parameter is an array reference all of the user accounts listed in the array are added to the local group. If successful, this function returns TRUE; otherwise, it returns undef.

LocalGroupCreate($Server, $Group, $Comment)

This function creates a local group on the specified server giving it the specified comment. If successful, this function returns TRUE; otherwise, it returns undef.

LocalGroupDelete($Server, $Group)

This function deletes a local group from the specified server. If successful, it returns TRUE; otherwise, it returns undef.

LocalGroupDeleteUsers($Server, $Group, $Users)

This function removes a user account from the specified local group on the specified server. If the third parameter is an array reference, all the user accounts listed in the array are removed from the local group. If successful, this function returns TRUE; otherwise, it returns undef.

LocalGroupGetAttributes($Server, $Group, $Comment)

This function retrieves the comment from the specified local group that exists on the specified server. If successful, this function sets the third comment variable (the parameter) with the local group's comment and returns TRUE; otherwise, it returns undef.

LocalGroupGetMembers($Server, $Group, \@UserList)

This function populates the specified array with the list of user accounts that make up the local group. If successful the array is populated with account names and the function returns TRUE; otherwise, it returns undef.

LocalGroupIsMember($Server, $Group, $User)

This function checks that the user is a member of the local group on the specified server. If the user exists in the local group, it returns TRUE; otherwise, it returns undef.

LocalGroupSetAttributes($Server, $Group, $Comment)

This function sets the comment for the local group on the specified server. If successful, this function returns TRUE; otherwise, it returns undef.

UserChangePassword($Domain, $Username, $OldPassword, $NewPassword)

This function changes the password of the specified user account on the specified server. This function can be run from any user. If successful, this function returns TRUE; otherwise, it returns undef.

UserCreate($Server, $UserName, $Password, $PasswordAge, $Privilege, $HomeDir, $Comment, $Flags, $ScriptPath)

This function creates a user account on the specified server. If successful, this function returns TRUE; otherwise, it returns undef.

UserDelete($Server, $User)

This function deletes a user account from the specified server. If successful, this function returns TRUE; otherwise, it returns undef.

UserGetAttributes($Server, $UserName, $Password, $PasswordAge, $Privilege, $HomeDir, $Comment, $Flags, $ScriptPath)

This function retrieves the comment, home directory, flags, password, password age, privilege, and logon script path for the specified user on the specified server. If successful, this function returns TRUE and sets each of the passed in variables with their respective values; otherwise, it returns undef.

UserSetAttributes($Server, $UserName, $Password, $PasswordAge, $Privilege, $HomeDir, $Comment, $Flags, $ScriptPath)

This function sets the comment, home directory, flags, password, password age, privilege, and logon script path for the specified user on the specified server. If successful, this function returns TRUE and modifies the specified user account; otherwise, it returns undef.

UsersExist($Server, $UserName)
This function checks to see whether the specified user account exists on the specified server. If successful (the account exists), it returns TRUE; otherwise, it returns undef.

Win32::NetResource

The **Win32::NetResource** extension provides network resource management functions.

AddConnection(\%NetResource, $Password, $UserName, $Connection)
This function connects to the specified network resource using the specified user name and password. The connection is mapped to the specified device. If successful, this function returns TRUE; otherwise, it returns a FALSE value.

CancelConnection($Device, $Connection, $Force)
This function terminates a network connection that is mapped to the specified device. This will either be a temporary or permanent termination based on the value of the connection parameter. Force can be used to terminate the connection even if open resources are using it. If successful, this function returns TRUE; otherwise, it returns a FALSE value.

GetError($ErrorCode)
This function retrieves the error code for previous calls to any **Win32::NetResource** function. If successful, this function sets $ErrorCode with the last generated error and returns TRUE; otherwise, it returns a FALSE value.

GetSharedResources(\@Resources, $Type)
This function generates a list of hashes representing all the network resources of the specified type. If successful, this function returns TRUE; otherwise, it returns a FALSE value.

GetUNCName($UNC, $Device)
This function retrieves the UNC of the shared network resource connected to the specified device. If successful, this function sets the $UNC variable with the UNC name and returns TRUE; otherwise, it returns a FALSE value.

NetShareAdd(\%Share, $ParamError [, $Machine])
This function shares the device specified by the %Share hash on the specified machine (local host is the default). The second parameter needs to be a scalar variable but should be ignored. If successful, this function returns TRUE; otherwise, it returns a FALSE value.

NetShareCheck($Device, $Type [, $Machine])

This function checks whether a particular device is shared on the specified machine (local host is the default). If successful, this function returns TRUE; otherwise, it returns a FALSE value.

NetShareDel($ShareName [, $Machine])

This function stops sharing the specified shared device on the specified machine (local host is the default). If successful, this function returns TRUE; otherwise, it returns a FALSE value.

NetShareGetInfo($ShareName, \%Share [, $Machine])

This function retrieves share information regarding the specified shared device residing on the specified machine (local host is the default). If successful, this function returns TRUE; otherwise, it returns a FALSE value.

NetShareSetInfo($ShareName, \%Share ,$ParamError [, $Machine])

This function sets attributes of the specified shared resource on the specified machine (local host is the default). The third parameter needs to be a scalar variable, but should be ignored. If successful, this function returns TRUE; otherwise, it returns a FALSE value.

WNetGetLastError($ErrorCode, $Description, $Name)

This function retrieves the "Extended Network Error" specified. This is only applicable for certain types of errors generated by certain functions. If successful, this function sets $Description and $Name with the error description and error name respectively and returns TRUE; otherwise, it returns a FALSE value.

Win32::ODBC

This extension provides an interface into the ODBC API.

$Obj–>Catalog($Qualifier, $Owner, $Name, $Type)

This function creates a data set that contains table information about the DSN based on the specified criteria. If successful, this function generates a data set and returns TRUE; otherwise, it returns a FALSE value.

$Obj–>Close()

This function closes the ODBC connection. If successful, this function returns TRUE; otherwise, it returns a FALSE value.

$Obj–>ColAttributes($Attribute [, @FieldNames])

This function returns the specified attribute on each of the specified fields in the current record set. If successful, this function returns the attribute; otherwise, it returns a undef.

$Obj–>ConfigDSN($Option, $Driver, $Attribute1 [, $Attribute2 [, $Attribute3 ...]]))

This function configures a DSN with the specified parameters. If successful, this function returns TRUE; otherwise, it returns a FALSE value.

$Obj–>Connection()

This function returns the connection number associated with the ODBC connection. If successful, this function returns TRUE; otherwise, it returns a FALSE value.

$Obj–>Data([$FieldName [, $FieldName2 ...]])

This function returns the contents of column with names $FieldName, $FieldName2, and so forth, or the current row (if nothing is specified). This method is available only for backward compatibility. The preferred method is **DataHash**(). If successful, this function returns an array of column values; otherwise, it returns undef.

$Obj–>DataHash([$Field1, $Field2, $Field3, ...])

This function returns the contents for specified fields in a hash. If no fields are specified then all fields are returned. If successful, this function returns a hash of field names and values; otherwise, it returns undef.

$Obj–>DataSources()

This function returns a hash of data sources and ODBC remarks about them. If successful, this function returns a hash of data sources and remarks; otherwise, it returns a FALSE value.

$Obj–>Drivers()

This function returns a hash of ODBC drivers and their attributes. If successful, this function returns a hash of drivers and attributes; otherwise, it returns a FALSE value.

$Obj–>DropCursor([$CloseType])

This function drops the cursor associated with the ODBC object, forcing the cursor to be de-allocated. If successful, the function returns TRUE; otherwise, it returns a FALSE value.

$Obj–>Error(), Error()

Th **Error**() function returns the last encountered error. The returned value is context dependent.

It returns a string or an array, depending on the return context containing error information.

$Obj–>FetchRow([$Row [, $Type]])

This function retrieves the next record from the current dataset, optionally specifying the number of rows to be fetched (default is 1) and the type of fetch (default is a relative fetch). If successful, this function returns TRUE; otherwise, it returns a FALSE value.

$Obj–>FieldNames()

This function retrieves all the field names in the current dataset. If successful, this function returns an array of field names; otherwise, it returns undef.

$Obj–>GetConnections()

This function returns an array of connection IDs showing which connections are currently open. If successful, this function returns an array of connection IDs; otherwise, it returns undef.

$Obj–>GetConnectOption($Option)

This function retrieves the value of the specified connection option. If successful, this function returns the option value; otherwise, it returns undef.

$Obj–>GetCursorName()

This function retrieves the name of the current cursor. If successful, this function returns the cursor's name; otherwise, it returns undef.

$Obj–>GetDSN([$DSN])

This function returns the configuration for the specified DSN. If no DSN is specified, the current connection is used. If successful, this function returns a hash of DSN configuration data; otherwise, it returns undef.

$Obj–>GetFunctions([$Function1, $Function2, [el]])

This function returns a hash of values indicating the ODBC driver's capability to support specified functions. If no functions are specified, a 100-element associative array is returned containing all possible functions and their values. If successful, this function returns a hash; otherwise, it returns undef.

$Obj–>GetInfo($Option)

This function retrieves the value of the specified option. If successful, this function returns the option value; otherwise, it returns undef.

$Obj–>GetMaxBufSize()

This function retrieves the current allocated limit for the MaxBufSize. If successful, the function returns the current buffer size.

$Obj->GetSQLState()

This function retrieves the SQL state as reported by the ODBC manager and driver. If successful, the function returns the SQL state.

$Obj->GetStmtCloseType([$Connection])

This function returns the type of closure that will be used every time the hstmt is freed. If successful, the function returns the closure type.

$Obj->GetStmtOption($Option)

This function retrieves the value of the specified statement option value. If successful, the function returns the statement option value.

$Obj->MoreResults()

This function reports whether there is data yet to be retrieved from the query. If data remains, the function returns TRUE; otherwise, it returns a FALSE value.

new(($ODBCObject | $DSN) [, ($Option1, $Value1), ($Option2, $Value2) ...])

This function creates a new ODBC connection based on the specified DSN or the specified ODBC object. All specified connection options will be set to the specified values before the physical connection occurs. If successful, the function returns a **Win32::ODBC** object; otherwise, it returns undef.

$Obj->RowCount($Connection)

For UPDATE, INSERT, and DELETE statements the returned value from this function is the number of rows affected by the request. If successful, the function returns the number of affected rows; otherwise, it returns a -1 value.

$Obj->Run($Sql)

This function executes the $Sql command and dumps to the screen info about it. *This is used primarily for debugging.* If successful, the function returns TRUE; otherwise, it returns a FALSE value.

$Obj->SetConnectOption($Option, $Value)

This function sets the value of the specified connect option to the specified value. If successful, this function returns TRUE; otherwise, it returns a FALSE value.

$Obj->SetCursorName($Name)

This function sets the name of the current cursor. If successful, this function returns TRUE; otherwise, it returns a FALSE value.

$Obj->SetMaxBufSize($Size)

This function sets the MaxBufSize for a particular connection. If successful, this function returns the new buffer size.

$Obj->SetPos($Row [, $Option, $Lock])

This function moves the cursor to the specified row within the current keyset (not the current data/result set). If successful, this function returns TRUE; otherwise, it returns a FALSE value.

$Obj->SetStmtCloseType($Type [, $Connection])

This function sets a specified connection's statement close type for the connection. If successful, this function returns the new value; otherwise, it returns undef.

$Obj->SetStmtOption($Option)

This function sets the value of the specified statement option. If successful, this function returns TRUE; otherwise, it returns a FALSE value.

$Obj->Sql($SQLString)

This function executes the specified SQL command. If successful, this function returns FALSE; otherwise, it returns a TRUE value.

$Obj->TableList($Qualifier, $Owner, $Name, $Type)

This function returns the catalog of tables available to the DSN based on the specified criteria. If successful, this function generates a data set and returns TRUE; otherwise, it returns a FALSE value.

$Obj->Transact($Type)

This function forces the ODBC connection to perform a rollback or commit transaction. If successful, this function returns TRUE; otherwise, it returns a FALSE value.

Win32::Pipe

The **Win32::Pipe** extension provides Win32-specific named pipe management.

$Obj->BufferSize()

This function retrieves the current buffer size of the named pipe. If successful, this function returns the size of the buffer; otherwise, it returns a FALSE value.

$Obj->Close()

This function closes and terminates the named pipe. If successful, this function returns TRUE; otherwise, it returns a FALSE value.

$Obj->Connect()

This function waits for a client to connect to the named pipe. If successful, this function returns TRUE; otherwise, it returns a FALSE value.

$Obj–>Disconnect()

This function disconnects from the named pipe. If successful, this function returns TRUE; otherwise, it returns a FALSE value.

$Obj–>Error()

This function retrieves the last error generated by the specified instance of the named pipe. If successful, this function returns TRUE; otherwise, it returns a FALSE value.

$Obj–>GetInfo()

This function retrieves various information regarding the named pipe such as number of instances and the user name of the client. If successful, this function returns TRUE; otherwise, it returns a FALSE value.

new Win32::Pipe($Name [, $Timeout [, $State]])

This function creates a named pipe with the specified name, timeout value, and state. If successful, this function returns a new **Win32::Pipe** object; otherwise, it returns a FALSE value.

$Obj–>Peek($Size)

This function retrieves up to the specified number of bytes from the named pipe without removing the data from the pipe. If successful, this function returns up to the specified number of bytes of data; otherwise, it returns a FALSE value.

$Obj–>Read()

This function reads data from the named pipe. If successful, this function returns the data read from the pipe; otherwise, it returns a FALSE (undef) value.

$Obj–>ResizeBuffer($Size)

This function sets the buffer size of the named pipe to the specified size. If successful, this function returns the new size of the buffer; otherwise, it returns a FALSE value.

$Obj–>Transact($SendData, $ReadData)

This function writes the specified data to the named pipe, and then reads data from the pipe. If successful, this function sets the second parameter with the data read from the pipe and returns TRUE; otherwise, it returns a FALSE value.

$Obj–>Write($Data)

This function writes the specified data to the named pipe. If successful, this function returns TRUE; otherwise, it returns a FALSE value.

Win32::Process

The **Win32::Process** extension creates and manages Win32 processes.

Create($Obj, $AppName, $CommandLine, $Inherit, $CreateFlags, $InitialDir)

This function starts a new process using the specified parameters. If successful, this function sets $Obj to point to a Win32::Process object and returns the new processes PID; otherwise, it returns a FALSE value.

$Obj–>GetExitCode($ExitCode)

This function retrieves the exit code for the process. If successful, this function returns TRUE; otherwise, it returns a FALSE value.

$Obj–>GetPriorityClass($Class)

This function retrieves the priority class for the process. If successful, this function sets the first parameter's value to the priority class and returns TRUE; otherwise, it returns a FALSE value.

$Obj–>Kill($ExitCode);

This function terminates the process and sets the process's exit code to the specified value. If successful, this function returns TRUE; otherwise, it returns a FALSE value.

$Obj–>Resume()

This function resumes the process from a suspended state. If successful, this function returns TRUE; otherwise, it returns a FALSE value.

$Obj–>SetPriorityClass($Class)

This function sets the process's priority class to the specified value. If successful, this function returns TRUE; otherwise, it returns a FALSE value.

$Obj–>Suspend()

This function suspends the process. If successful, this function returns TRUE; otherwise, it returns a FALSE value.

$Obj–>Wait($Timeout)

This function waits for the process to terminate or until the timeout has elapsed. If successful, this function returns TRUE; otherwise, it returns a FALSE value.

Win32::RasAdmin

The **Win32::RasAdmin** extension provides management functions for Remote Access Services (RAS).

ClearStats($Machine, $Port)

This function clears the statistics on the specified port on the specified machine. If successful, this function returns TRUE; otherwise, it returns a FALSE value.

Disconnect($Machine, $Port)

This function disconnects the connection on the specified port on the specified machine. If successful, this function returns TRUE; otherwise, it returns a FALSE value.

GetAccountServer($Server | $Domain)

This function retrieves the name of the RAS account server of the specified domain (or for the specified server). If successful, this function returns the RAS account server name; otherwise, it returns a FALSE value.

GetErrorString ($ErrorNum)

This function retrieves the error message for the specified error number. This is for RAS-specific errors. If successful, this function returns the error text; otherwise, it returns a FALSE value.

GetPorts($Server [, \%Ports])

This function retrieves the number of ports available on the specified server and optionally populates the hash with port information. If successful, this function returns the number of ports; otherwise, it returns a FALSE value.

PortGetInfo(($Server | $Domain), $Port, \%Hash)

This function retrieves a hash containing information about the specified server's (or domain's RAS server) ports. If successful, this function returns TRUE; otherwise, it returns a FALSE value.

ServerGetInfo($Server, \%Info)

This function retrieves a hash populated with information about the specified server. If successful, this function returns TRUE; otherwise, it returns a FALSE value.

UserGetInfo(($Machine | $Domain), $User, \%Info)

This function populates a hash regarding the specified user from the specified machine (or domain). If successful, this function returns TRUE; otherwise, it returns a FALSE value.

UserSetInfo(($Server | $Domain), $User, $Flag1=>$Value1 [, $Flag2=>$Value2 ...])

This function sets the specified flags to the specified values for the specified user in the specified server (or domain). If successful, this function returns TRUE; otherwise, it returns a FALSE value.

Win32::Registry

The **Win32::Registry** module provides an interface to manage the Win32 Registry.

$Obj–>Close()

This function closes the Registry key. If successful, this function returns TRUE; otherwise, it returns a FALSE value.

$Obj–>Create($SubKey, $Obj)

This function creates the specified subkey. If it already exists, it is opened. If successful, this function sets $Obj to point to a new Registry object and returns TRUE; otherwise, it returns a FALSE value.

$Obj–>DeleteKey($SubKey)

This function deletes the specified subkey and any values and subkeys that it may contain. If successful, this function returns TRUE; otherwise, it returns a FALSE value.

$Obj–>DeleteValue($ValueName)

This function removes the specified value and its associated data from the key. If successful, this function returns TRUE; otherwise, it returns a FALSE value.

$Obj–>GetKeys(\@Array)

This function retrieves an array of the names of the specified key's subkeys. If successful, this function returns TRUE; otherwise, it returns a FALSE value.

$Obj–>GetValues(\%Hash)

This function retrieves a hash consisting of keys representing the subkey names. The hash values are anonymous arrays consisting of the value's name, the value's data type, and the value's data (in order). If successful, this function returns TRUE; otherwise, it returns a FALSE value.

$Obj–>Load($Key, $FileName)

This function loads the hive from the specified file (on a local hard drive) into root under the specified key name. If successful, this function returns TRUE; otherwise, it returns a FALSE value.

$Obj–>Open($SubKey, $Obj)

This function opens the specified Registry subkey. If successful, this function sets $Obj to point to a new Registry object and returns TRUE; otherwise, it returns a FALSE value.

$Obj->QueryKey($Class, $NumOfSubKeys, $NumOfValues)

This function retrieves and sets the respective values for the key's class (default value), number of subkeys, and number of values. If successful, this function returns TRUE; otherwise, it returns a FALSE value.

$Obj->QueryValue($SubKey, $Data)

This function retrieves the default data value for the specified subkey. If successful, this function returns the retrieved data; otherwise, it returns a FALSE value.

$Obj->QueryValueEx($ValueName, 0, $DataType, $Data)

This function retrieves the data and data type for the specified value from the key. Both the $DataType and Data variables will be set with their respective values. The second parameter is reserved and must be set to 0. If successful, this function returns TRUE; otherwise, it returns a FALSE value.

$Obj->Save($File)

This function saves the key and all its subkeys and values to a file on a local hard drive. If successful, this function returns TRUE; otherwise, it returns a FALSE value.

$Obj->SetValue($SubKey, $Type, $Data)

This function sets the specified subkey's default value and data type. If successful, this function returns TRUE; otherwise, it returns a FALSE value.

$Obj->SetValueEx($Name, $Reserved, $Type, $Data)

This function sets the specified named value for the key to the specified data and data type. If successful, this function returns TRUE; otherwise, it returns a FALSE value.

Win32::Semaphore

The **Win32::Semaphore** extension creates and manages Win32 semaphore objects.

Create($Obj, $Initial, $Max, $Name)

This function creates a semaphore object. If successful, this function returns TRUE; otherwise, it returns a FALSE value.

$Obj->Open($SemObject, $Name)

This function opens an already created named semaphore. If successful, this function returns TRUE; otherwise, it returns a FALSE value.

$Obj–>Release($Count, $LastValue)

This function releases ownership of a semaphore object. If successful, this function returns TRUE; otherwise, it returns a FALSE value.

$Obj–>Wait($TimeOut)

This function waits for ownership of a semaphore object. If successful, this function returns TRUE; otherwise, it returns a FALSE value.

Win32::Service

The **Win32::Service** extension provides basic management functions for Windows services.

GetServices($Machine, \@List)

This function populates an array with the names of the services on the specified machine. If successful, this function returns TRUE; otherwise, it returns a FALSE value.

GetStatus($Machine, $ServiceName, $Status)

This function retrieves the current status of the specified service on the specified machine. If successful, this function sets the value of the $Status variable and returns TRUE; otherwise, it returns a FALSE value.

PauseService($Machine, $ServiceName)

This function pauses the specified service on the specified machine. If successful, this function returns TRUE; otherwise, it returns a FALSE value.

ResumeService($Machine, $ServiceName)

This function resumes the paused service on the specified machine. If successful, this function returns TRUE; otherwise, it returns a FALSE value.

StartService($Machine, $ServiceName)

This function starts the specified service on the specified machine. If successful, this function returns TRUE; otherwise, it returns a FALSE value.

StopService($Machine, $ServiceName)

This function stops the specified service on the specified machine. If successful, this function returns TRUE; otherwise, it returns a FALSE value.

Win32::Shortcut

The **Win32::Shortcut** extension interfaces the Explorer shell's capability to make and manage shortcuts.

$Obj–>Close()

This function properly closes a shortcut object. If successful, this function returns TRUE; otherwise, it returns a FALSE value.

$Obj–>Load($ShortcutFile)

This function loads the existing specified shortcut file into the shortcut object. If successful, this function returns TRUE; otherwise, it returns a FALSE (undef) value.

new Win32::Shortcut([$ShortcutFile])

This function creates a new explorer shortcut object optionally based on the existing specified shortcut file. If successful, this function returns a **Win32::Shortcut** object; otherwise, it returns a FALSE (undef) value.

$Obj–>Resolve([$Flag])

This function attempts to resolve the shortcut object optionally prompting the user for needed details if a flag is specified. If successful, this function returns TRUE; otherwise, it returns a FALSE value.

$Obj–>Save($ShortcutFile)

This function saves the shortcut object to the specified shortcut file. If successful, this function returns TRUE; otherwise, it returns a FALSE value.

$Obj–>Set($Path, $Arguments, $WorkingDirectory, $Description, $ShowCommand, $HotKey, $IconPath, $IconNumber)

This function sets the specified attributes on the shortcut object. If successful, this function returns TRUE; otherwise, it returns a FALSE (undef) value.

Win32::WinError

The **Win32::WinError** extension exports various Windows error constants. The list of exported constants is too numerous to enumerate here. Refer to the WIN-ERROR.PM file for this list.

Appendix **B**

Win32::ODBC Specific Tables

This appendix describes many of the constants that can be used for various **Win32::ODBC** functions.

This appendix appears as a general guide to the myriad of constants that ODBC uses. The 970208 version of **Win32::ODBC** supports over 650 constants that all need some explaining. This is what this appendix attempts to describe.

Microsoft has released their ODBC 3.0 binaries that contain even more constants. Sprinkled throughout this appendix are references to ODBC 3.0. Many users will not have a need for the 3.0 information because as of this writing ODBC 2.5 is still quite common on the desktop.

The information in this appendix is available from Microsoft's Developers Network (MSDN) and is reprinted here courtesy of Microsoft Corporation. Further details regarding any information found here can be found in any good book on ODBC such as Kyle Geiger's excellent work *Inside ODBC* (Microsoft Press).

GetInfo( )

The **Win32::ODBC**'s **GetInfo**() method will retrieve information pertaining to an ODBC driver. The information retrieved is read-only and cannot be set. The **GetInfo**() method can accept any of the constants listed in the first column (Function) of Table B.1. This table is a full ODBC 3.0 **SQLGetInfo**() reference so it covers many more options than many ODBC drivers are capable of understanding. Additionally not all of the constants listed are available through Win32::ODBC. This reference is provided for those needing a better understanding of how ODBC works.

Table B.1   *Constants that can be used in conjunction with GetInfo()*

Function	ODBC Version Required	Description
SQL_ACCESSIBLE_PROCEDURES	1.0	A character string: "Y" if the user can execute all procedures returned by SQLProcedures, "N" if there may be procedures returned that the user cannot execute.
SQL_ACCESSIBLE_TABLES	1.0	A character string: "Y" if the user is guaranteed SELECT privileges to all tables returned by SQLTables, "N" if there may be tables returned that the user cannot access.
SQL_ACTIVE_ENVIRONMENTS	3.0	An SQLSMALLINT value specifying the maximum number of active environments that the driver can support. If there is no specified limit or the limit is unknown, this value is set to zero.
SQL_AGGREGATE_FUNCTIONS	3.0	An SQLINTEGER bitmask enumerating support for aggregation functions: SQL_AF_ALL SQL_AF_AVG SQL_AF_COUNT SQL_AF_DISTINCT SQL_AF_MAX SQL_AF_MIN SQL_AF_SUM
SQL_ALTER_DOMAIN	3.0	An SQL-92 Entry level-conformant driver will always return all of these options as supported. An SQLUINTEGER bitmask enumerating the clauses in the ALTER DOMAIN statement, as defined in SQL-92, supported by the data source. An SQL-92 Full level-compliant driver will always return all of

the bitmasks. A return value of "0" means that the ALTER DOMAIN statement is not supported. The SQL-92 or FIPS conformance level at which this feature needs to be supported is shown in parentheses next to each bitmask. The following bitmasks are used to determine which clauses are supported: `SQL_AD_ADD_DOMAIN_CONSTRAINT` = Adding a domain constraint is supported (Full level)

`SQL_AD_ADD_DOMAIN_DEFAULT` = <alter domain> <set domain default clause> is supported (Full level). `SQL_AD_ADD_CONSTRAINT_NAME_DEFINITION` = <constraint name definition clause> is supported for naming domain constraint (Intermediate level). `SQL_AD_DROP_DOMAIN_CONSTRAINT` = <drop domain constraint clause> is supported (Full level).

`SQL_AD_DROP_DOMAIN_DEFAULT` = <alter domain> <drop domain default clause> is supported (Full level). The following bits specify the supported <constraint attributes> if <add domain constraint> is supported (the `SQL_AD_ADD_DOMAIN_CONSTRAINT` bit is set): `SQL_AD_ADD_CON-STRAINT_DEFERRABLE` (Full level)

`SQL_AD_ADD_CONSTRAINT_NON_DEFERRABLE` (Full level) `SQL_AD_ADD_CON-STRAINT_INITIALLY_DEFERRED` (Full level)

`SQL_AD_ADD_CONSTRAINT_INITIALLY_IMMEDIATE` (Full level)

SQL_ALTER_TABLE   2.0

An SQLUINTEGER bitmask enumerating the clauses in the ALTER TABLE statement supported by the data source. The SQL-92 or FIPS conformance level at which this feature needs to be supported is shown in parentheses next to each bitmask. The following bitmasks are used to determine which clauses are supported:

`SQL_AT_ADD_COLUMN_COLLATION` = <add column> clause is supported, with facility to specify column collation (Full level) (ODBC 3.0)

`SQL_AT_ADD_COLUMN_DEFAULT` = <add column> clause is supported, with facility to specify column defaults (FIPS Transitional level) (ODBC 3.0)

`SQL_AT_ADD_COLUMN_SINGLE` = <add column> is supported (FIPS Transitional level) (ODBC 3.0)

continues

Table B.1 Continued

Function	ODBC Version Required	Description
		SQL_AT_ADD_CONSTRAINT = <add column> clause is supported, with facility to specify column constraints (FIPS Transitional level) (ODBC 3.0)
		SQL_AT_ADD_TABLE_CONSTRAINT = <add table constraint> clause is supported (FIPS Transitional level) (ODBC 3.0)
		SQL_AT_CONSTRAINT_NAME_DEFINITION = <constraint name definition> is supported for naming column and table constraints (Intermediate level) (ODBC 3.0)
		SQL_AT_DROP_COLUMN_CASCADE = <drop column> CASCADE is supported (FIPS Transitional level) (ODBC 3.0)
		SQL_AT_DROP_COLUMN_DEFAULT = <alter column> <drop column default clause> is supported (Intermediate level) (ODBC 3.0)
		SQL_AT_DROP_COLUMN_RESTRICT = <drop column> RESTRICT is supported (FIPS Transitional level) (ODBC 3.0)
		SQL_AT_DROP_TABLE_CONSTRAINT_CASCADE (ODBC 3.0)
		SQL_AT_DROP_TABLE_CONSTRAINT_RESTRICT = <drop column> RESTRICT is supported (FIPS Transitional level) (ODBC 3.0)
		SQL_AT_SET_COLUMN_DEFAULT = <alter column> <set column default clause> is supported (Intermediate level) (ODBC 3.0)
		The following bits specify the support <constraint attributes> if specifying column or table constraints is supported (the SQL_AT_ADD_CONSTRAINT bit is set):
		SQL_AT_CONSTRAINT_INITIALLY_DEFERRED (Full level) (ODBC 3.0)
		SQL_AT_CONSTRAINT_INITIALLY_IMMEDIATE (Full level) (ODBC 3.0)
		SQL_AT_CONSTRAINT_DEFERRABLE (Full level) (ODBC 3.0)

SQL_ASYNC_MODE	3.0	SQL_AT_CONSTRAINT_NON_DEFERRABLE (Full level) (ODBC 3.0) An SQLUINTEGER value indicating the level of asynchronous support in the driver: SQL_AM_CONNECTION = Connection level asynchronous execution is supported. Either all statement handles associated with a given connection handle are in asynchronous mode, or all are in synchronous mode. A statement handle on a connection cannot be in asynchronous mode while another statement handle on the same connection is in synchronous mode, and vice versa. SQL_AM_STATEMENT = Statement level asynchronous execution is supported. Some statement handles associated with a connection handle can be in asynchronous mode, while other statement handles on the same connection are in synchronous mode. SQL_AM_NONE = Asynchronous mode is not supported.
SQL_BATCH_ROW_COUNT	3.0	An SQLUINTEGER bitmask enumerating the behavior of the driver with respect to the availability of row counts. The following bit masks are used in conjunction with the information type: SQL_BRC_ROLLED_UP = Row counts for consecutive INSERT, DELETE, or UPDATE statements are rolled up into one. If this bit is not set, then row counts are available for each individual statement. SQL_BRC_PROCEDURES = Row counts, if any, are available when a batch is executed in a stored procedure. If row counts are available, they may be rolled up or individually available, depending on the SQL_BRC_ROLLED_UP bit. SQL_BRC_EXPLICIT = Row counts, if any, are available when a batch is executed directly by calling SQLExecute or SQLExecDirect. If row counts are available, they may be rolled up or individually available, depending on the SQL_BRC_ROLLED_UP bit.

continues

Table B.1 Continued

Function	ODBC Version Required	Description
SQL_BATCH_SUPPORT	3.0	An SQLUINTEGER bitmask enumerating the driver's support for batches. The following bitmasks are used to determine which level is supported: SQL_BS_SELECT_EXPLICIT = The driver supports explicit batches that can have result-set generating statements. SQL_BS_ROW_COUNT_EXPLICIT = The driver supports explicit batches that can have row-count generating statements. SQL_BS_SELECT_PROC = The driver supports explicit procedures that can have result-set generating statements. SQL_BS_ROW_COUNT_PROC = The driver supports explicit procedures that can have row-count generating statements.
SQL_BOOKMARK_PERSISTENCE	2.0	An SQLUINTEGER bitmask enumerating the operations through which bookmarks persist. The following bitmasks are used in conjunction with the flag to determine through which options bookmarks persist: SQL_BP_CLOSE = Bookmarks are valid after an application calls SQLFreeStmt with the SQL_CLOSE option, or SQLCloseCursor to close the cursor associated with a statement. SQL_BP_DELETE = The bookmark for a row is valid after that row has been deleted. SQL_BP_DROP = Bookmarks are valid after an application calls SQLFreeHandle with a HandleType of SQL_HANDLE_STMT to drop a statement. SQL_BP_TRANSACTION = Bookmarks are valid after an application commits or rolls back a transaction. SQL_BP_UPDATE = The bookmark for a row is valid after any column in that row has been updated, including key columns. SQL_BP_OTHER_HSTMT = A bookmark associated with one statement can

be used with another statement. Unless SQL_BP_CLOSE or SQL_BP_DROP is specified, the cursor on the first statement must be open.

SQL_CATALOG_LOCATION	2.0	An SQLUSMALLINT value indicating the position of the catalog in a qualified table name: SQL_CL_START or SQL_CL_END. For example, an Xbase driver returns SQL_CL_START because the directory (catalog) name is at the start of the table name, as in \EMPDATA\EMP.DBF. An ORACLE Server driver returns SQL_CL_END, because the catalog is at the end of the table name, as in ADMIN.EMP@EMPDATA. An SQL-92 Full level–conformant driver will always return SQL_CL_START. A value of 0 is returned if catalogs are not supported by the data source. To find out whether catalogs are supported, an application calls SQLGetInfo with the SQL_CATALOG_NAME information type. This InfoType has been renamed for ODBC 3.0 from the ODBC 2.0 InfoType SQL_QUALIFIER_LOCATION.
SQL_CATALOG_NAME	3.0	A character string: "Y" if the server supports catalog names, or "N" if it does not. An SQL-92 Full level–conformant driver will always return "Y".
SQL_CATALOG_NAME_SEPARATOR	1.0	A character string: the character or characters that the data source defines as the separator between a catalog name and the qualified name element that follows or precedes it. An empty string is returned if catalogs are not supported by the data source. To find out whether catalogs are supported, an application calls SQLGetInfo with the SQL_CATALOG_NAME information type. An SQL-92 Full level–conformant driver will always return ".".This InfoType has been renamed for ODBC 3.0 from the ODBC 2.0 InfoType SQL_QUALIFIER_NAME_SEPARATOR.

continues

Table B.1 Continued

Function	ODBC Version Required	Description
SQL_CATALOG_TERM	1.0	A character string with the data source vendor's name for a catalog; for example, "database" or "directory." This string can be in upper, lower, or mixed case. An empty string is returned if catalogs are not supported by the data source. To find out whether catalogs are supported, an application calls SQLGetInfo with the SQL_CATALOG_NAME information type. An SQL-92 Full level-conformant driver will always return "catalog". This InfoType has been renamed for ODBC 3.0 from the ODBC 2.0 InfoType SQL_QUALIFIER_TERM.

SQL_CATALOG_USAGE	2.0	An SQLUINTEGER bitmask enumerating the statements in which catalogs can be used. The following bitmasks are used to determine where catalogs can be used:
		SQL_CU_DML_STATEMENTS = Catalogs are supported in all Data Manipulation Language statements:
		    SELECT,
		    INSERT,
		    UPDATE,
		    DELETE, and,
		    if supported, SELECT FOR UPDATE
		    and positioned update and delete statements.
		SQL_CU_PROCEDURE_INVOCATION = Catalogs are supported in the ODBC procedure invocation statement.
		SQL_CU_TABLE_DEFINITION = Catalogs are supported in all table definition statements:
		    CREATE TABLE,
		    CREATE VIEW,
		    ALTER TABLE,

	`DROP TABLE`, and `DROP VIEW`. `SQL_CU_INDEX_DEFINITION` = Catalogs are supported in all index definition statements: `CREATE INDEX` and `DROP INDEX`. `SQL_CU_PRIVILEGE_DEFINITION` = Catalogs are supported in all privilege definition statements: `GRANT` and `REVOKE`.
	A value of 0 is returned if catalogs are not supported by the data source. To find out whether catalogs are supported, an application calls `SQLGetInfo` with the `SQL_CATALOG_NAME` information type. An SQL-92 Full level-conformant driver will always return a bitmask with all of these bits set. This InfoType has been renamed for ODBC 3.0 from the ODBC 2.0 InfoType `SQL_QUALIFIER_USAGE`.
`SQL_COLLATION_SEQ`	3.0	The name of the collation sequence. This is a character string that indicates the name of the default collation for the default character set for this server (for example 'ISO 8859-1' or EBCDIC). If this is unknown, an empty string will be returned. An SQL-92 Full level-conformant driver will always return a non-empty string.
`SQL_COLUMN_ALIAS`	2.0	A character string: "Y" if the data source supports column aliases; otherwise, "N". A column alias is an alternate name that can be specified for a column in the select list by using an AS clause. An SQL-92 Entry level-conformant driver will always return "Y".
`SQL_CONCAT_NULL_BEHAVIOR`	1.0	An `SQLUSMALLINT` value indicating how the data source handles the concatenation of NULL valued character data type columns with non-NULL valued character data type columns: `SQL_CB_NULL` = Result is NULL valued. `SQL_CB_NON_NULL` = Result is concatenation of non-NULL valued column or columns.

continues

Table B.1 Continued

Function	ODBC Version Required	Description
		An SQL-92 Entry level–conformant driver will always return SQL_CB_NULL.
SQL_CONVERT_BIGINT SQL_CONVERT_BINARY SQL_CONVERT_BIT SQL_CONVERT_CHAR SQL_CONVERT_DATE SQL_CONVERT_DECIMAL SQL_CONVERT_DOUBLE SQL_CONVERT_FLOAT SQL_CONVERT_INTEGER SQL_CONVERT_INTERVAL_YEAR_MONTH SQL_CONVERT_INTERVAL_DAY_TIME SQL_CONVERT_LONGVARBINARY SQL_CONVERT_LONGVARCHAR SQL_CONVERT_NUMERIC SQL_CONVERT_REAL SQL_CONVERT_SMALLINT SQL_CONVERT_TIME SQL_CONVERT_TIMESTAMP SQL_CONVERT_TINYINT SQL_CONVERT_VARBINARY SQL_CONVERT_VARCHAR	1.0	An SQLUINTEGER bitmask. The bitmask indicates the conversions supported by the data source with the CONVERT scalar function for data of the type named in the InfoType. If the bitmask equals zero, the data source does not support any conversions from data of the named type, including conversion to the same data type. For example, to find out if a data source supports the conversion of SQL_INTEGER data to the SQL_BIGINT data type, an application calls SQLGetInfo with the InfoType of SQL_CONVERT_INTEGER. The application performs an AND operation with the returned bitmask and SQL_CVT_BIGINT. If the resulting value is nonzero, the conversion is

Function	ODBC Version Required	Description
		supported. The following bitmasks are used to determine which conversions are supported:
		SQL_CVT_BIGINT (ODBC 1.0)
		SQL_CVT_BINARY (ODBC 1.0)
		SQL_CVT_BIT (ODBC 1.0)
		SQL_CVT_CHAR (ODBC 1.0)
		SQL_CVT_DATE (ODBC 1.0)
		SQL_CVT_DECIMAL (ODBC 1.0)
		SQL_CVT_DOUBLE (ODBC 1.0)
		SQL_CVT_FLOAT (ODBC 1.0)
		SQL_CVT_INTEGER (ODBC 1.0)
		SQL_CVT_INTERVAL_YEAR_MONTH (ODBC 3.0)
		SQL_CVT_INTERVAL_DAY_TIME (ODBC 3.0)
		SQL_CVT_LONGVARBINARY (ODBC 1.0)
		SQL_CVT_LONGVARCHAR (ODBC 1.0)
		SQL_CVT_NUMERIC (ODBC 1.0)
		SQL_CVT_REAL (ODBC 1.0)
		SQL_CVT_SMALLINT (ODBC 1.0)
		SQL_CVT_TIME (ODBC 1.0)
		SQL_CVT_TIMESTAMP (ODBC 1.0)
		SQL_CVT_TINYINT (ODBC 1.0)
		SQL_CVT_VARBINARY (ODBC 1.0)
		SQL_CVT_VARCHAR (ODBC 1.0)

continues

Table B.1 Continued

Function	ODBC Version Required	Description
SQL_CONVERT_FUNCTIONS	1.0	An SQLUINTEGER bitmask enumerating the scalar conversion functions supported by the driver and associated data source. The following bitmask is used to determine which conversion functions are supported: SQL_FN_CVT_CAST SQL_FN_CVT_CONVERT
SQL_CORRELATION_NAME	1.0	An SQLUSMALLINT value indicating whether table correlation names are supported: SQL_CN_NONE = Correlation names are not supported. SQL_CN_DIFFERENT = Correlation names are supported, but must differ from the names of the tables they represent. SQL_CN_ANY = Correlation names are supported and can be any valid user-defined name. An SQL-92 Entry level-conformant driver will always return SQL_CN_ANY.
SQL_CREATE_ASSERTION	3.0	An SQLUINTEGER bitmask enumerating the clauses in the CREATE ASSERTION statement, as defined in SQL-92, supported by the data source. The following bitmasks are used to determine which clauses are supported: SQL_CA_CREATE_ASSERTION The following bits specify the supported constraint attribute if the ability to specify constraint attributes explicitly is supported (see the SQL_ALTER_TABLE and SQL_CREATE_TABLE information types): SQL_CA_CONSTRAINT_INITIALLY_DEFERRED SQL_CA_CONSTRAINT_INITIALLY_IMMEDIATE SQL_CA_CONSTRAINT_DEFERRABLE SQL_CA_CONSTRAINT_NON_DEFERRABLE

SQL_CREATE_CHARACTER_SET	3.0	An SQL-92 Full level-conformant driver will always return all of these options as supported. A return value of 0 means that the CREATE ASSERTION statement is not supported.
		An SQLINTEGER bitmask enumerating the clauses in the CREATE CHARACTER SET statement, as defined in SQL-92, supported by the data source. The following bitmasks are used to determine which clauses are supported: SQL_CCS_CREATE_CHARACTER_SET SQL_CCS_COLLATE_CLAUSE SQL_CCS_LIMITED_COLLATION
		An SQL-92 Full level-conformant driver will always return all of these options as supported. A return value of 0 means that the CREATE CHARACTER SET statement is not supported.
SQL_CREATE_COLLATION	3.0	An SQLINTEGER bitmask enumerating the clauses in the CREATE COLLATION statement, as defined in SQL-92, supported by the data source. The following bitmask is used to determine which clauses are supported: SQL_CCOL_CREATE_COLLATION
		An SQL-92 Full level-conformant driver will always return this option as supported. A return value of 0 means that the CREATE COLLATION statement is not supported.
SQL_CREATE_DOMAIN	3.0	An SQLINTEGER bitmask enumerating the clauses in the CREATE DOMAIN statement, as defined in SQL-92, supported by the data source. The following bitmasks are used to determine which clauses are supported: SQL_CDO_CREATE_DOMAIN = The CREATE DOMAIN statement is supported. (Intermediate level)

continues

Table B.1 Continued

Function	ODBC Version Required	Description
		SQL_CDO_CONSTRAINT_NAME_DEFINITION = <constraint name definition> is supported for naming domain constraints (Intermediate level).
		The following bits specify the ability to create column constraints: SQL_CDO_DEFAULT = Specifying domain constraints is supported (Intermediate level) SQL_CDO_CONSTRAINT = Specifying domain defaults is supported (Intermediate level) SQL_CDO_COLLATION = Specifying domain collation is supported (Full level)
		The following bits specify the supported constraint attributes if specifying domain constraints is supported (SQL_CDO_DEFAULT is set): SQL_CDO_CONSTRAINT_INITIALLY_DEFERRED (Full level) SQL_CDO_CONSTRAINT_INITIALLY_IMMEDIATE (Full level) SQL_CDO_CONSTRAINT_DEFERRABLE (Full level) SQL_CDO_CONSTRAINT_NON_DEFERRABLE (Full level)
		A return value of 0 means that the CREATE DOMAIN statement is not supported.
SQL_CREATE_SCHEMA	3.0	An SQLUINTEGER bitmask enumerating the clauses in the CREATE SCHEMA statement, as defined in SQL-92, supported by the data source. The following bitmasks are used to determine which clauses are supported: SQL_CS_CREATE_SCHEMA SQL_CS_AUTHORIZATION SQL_CS_DEFAULT_CHARACTER_SET

An SQL-92 Intermediate level-conformant driver will always return the SQL_CS_CREATE_SCHEMA and SQL_CS_AUTHORIZATION options as supported. These must also be supported at the SQL-92 Entry level, but not necessarily as SQL statements. An SQL-92 Full level-conformant driver will always return all of these options as supported.

SQL_CREATE_TABLE   3.0

An SQLUINTEGER bitmask enumerating the clauses in the CREATE TABLE statement, as defined in SQL-92, supported by the data source. The SQL-92 or FIPS conformance level at which this features needs to be supported is shown in parentheses next to each bitmask. The following bitmasks are used to determine which clauses are supported:

SQL_CT_CREATE_TABLE = The CREATE TABLE statement is supported. (Entry level)

SQL_CT_TABLE_CONSTRAINT = Specifying table constraints is supported (FIPS Transitional level)

SQL_CT_CONSTRAINT_NAME_DEFINITION = The <constraint name definition> clause is supported for naming column and table constraints (Intermediate level)The following bits specify the ability to create temporary tables:

SQL_CT_COMMIT_PRESERVE = Deleted rows are preserved on commit. (Full level)

SQL_CT_COMMIT_DELETE = Deleted rows are deleted on commit. (Full level)

SQL_CT_GLOBAL_TEMPORARY = Global temporary tables can be created. (Full level)

SQL_CT_LOCAL_TEMPORARY = Local temporary tables can be created. (Full level)

The following bits specify the ability to create column constraints:

SQL_CT_COLUMN_CONSTRAINT = Specifying column constraints is supported (FIPS Transitional level)

continues

Table B.1 Continued

Function	ODBC Version Required	Description
		SQL_CT_COLUMN_DEFAULT = Specifying column defaults is supported (FIPS Transitional level)
		SQL_CT_COLUMN_COLLATION = Specifying column collation is supported (Full level)
		The following bits specify the supported constraint attributes if specifying column or table constraints is supported:
		SQL_CT_CONSTRAINT_INITIALLY_DEFERRED (Full level)
		SQL_CT_CONSTRAINT_INITIALLY_IMMEDIATE (Full level)
		SQL_CT_CONSTRAINT_DEFERRABLE (Full level)
		SQL_CT_CONSTRAINT_NON_DEFERRABLE (Full level)
SQL_CREATE_TRANSLATION	3.0	An SQLUINTEGER bitmask enumerating the clauses in the CREATE TRANSLATION statement, as defined in SQL-92, supported by the data source. The following bitmask is used to determine which clauses are supported:
		SQL_CTR_CREATE_TRANSLATION
		An SQL-92 Full level–conformant driver will always return these options as supported. A return value of 0 means that the CREATE TRANSLATION statement is not supported.
SQL_CREATE_VIEW	3.0	An SQLUINTEGER bitmask enumerating the clauses in the CREATE VIEW statement, as defined in SQL-92, supported by the data source. The following bitmasks are used to determine which clauses are supported:
		SQL_CV_CREATE_VIEW
		SQL_CV_CHECK_OPTION
		SQL_CV_CASCADED
		SQL_CV_LOCAL

		A return value of 0 means that the CREATE VIEW statement is not supported. An SQL-92 Entry level–conformant driver will always return the SQL_CV_CREATE_VIEW and SQL_CV_CHECK_OPTION options as supported. An SQL-92 Full level–conformant driver will always return all of these options as supported.
SQL_CURSOR_COMMIT_BEHAVIOR	1.0	An SQLUSMALLINT value indicating how a COMMIT operation affects cursors and prepared statements in the data source: SQL_CB_DELETE = Close cursors and delete prepared statements. To use the cursor again, the application must reprepare and reexecute the statement. SQL_CB_CLOSE = Close cursors. For prepared statements, the application can call SQLExecute on the statement without calling SQLPrepare again. SQL_CB_PRESERVE = Preserve cursors in the same position as before the COMMIT operation. The application can continue to fetch data or it can close the cursor and reexecute the statement without repreparing it.
SQL_CURSOR_ROLLBACK_BEHAVIOR	1.0	An SQLUSMALLINT value indicating how a ROLLBACK operation affects cursors and prepared statements in the data source: SQL_CB_DELETE = Close cursors and delete prepared statements. To use the cursor again, the application must reprepare and reexecute the statement. SQL_CB_CLOSE = Close cursors. For prepared statements, the application can call SQLExecute on the statement without calling SQLPrepare again. SQL_CB_PRESERVE = Preserve cursors in the same position as before the ROLLBACK operation. The application can continue to fetch data or it can close the cursor and reexecute the statement without repreparing it.

continues

Table B.1   Continued

Function	ODBC Version Required	Description
SQL_CURSOR_SENSITIVITY	3.0	An SQLUINTEGER value indicating the support for cursor sensitivity: SQL_INSENSITIVE = All cursors on the statement handle show the result set without reflecting any changes made to it by any other cursor within the same transaction. SQL_UNSPECIFIED = It is unspecified whether cursors on the statement handle make visible the changes made to a result set by another cursor within the same transaction. Cursors on the statement handle may make visible none, some, or all such changes. SQL_SENSITIVE = Cursors are sensitive to changes made by other cursors within the same transaction. An SQL-92 Entry level–conformant driver will always return the SQL_UNSPECIFIED option as supported. An SQL-92 Full level–conformant driver will always return the SQL_INSENSITIVE option as supported.
SQL_DATA_SOURCE_NAME	1.0	A character string with the data source name used during connection. If the application called SQLConnect, this is the value of the szDSN argument. If the application called SQLDriverConnect or SQLBrowseConnect, this is the value of the DSN keyword in the connection string passed to the driver. If the connection string did not contain the DSN keyword (such as when it contains the DRIVER keyword), this is an empty string.
SQL_DATA_SOURCE_READ_ONLY	1.0	A character string, "Y" if the data source is set to READ ONLY mode, "N" if it is otherwise. This characteristic pertains only to the data source itself; it is not a characteristic of the driver that enables access to the data source. A driver that is read/write can be used with a data source that is read-only. If a driver is read-only, all of its data sources must be read-only, and must return SQL_DATA_SOURCE_READ_ONLY.

SQL_DATABASE_NAME

1.0

A character string with the name of the current database in use, if the data source defines a named object called "database." Note: In ODBC 3.0, the value returned for this InfoType can also be returned by calling SQLGetConnectAttr with an Attribute argument of SQL_ATTR_CURRENT_CATALOG.

SQL_DATETIME_LITERALS

3.0

An SQLUINTEGER bitmask enumerating the SQL-92 datetime literals supported by the data source. Note that these are the datetime literals listed in the SQL-92 specification and are separate from the datetime literal escape clauses defined by ODBC.

A FIPS Transitional level–conformant driver will always return the "1" value in the bitmask for the bits listed below. A value of 0 means that SQL-92 datetime literals are not supported. The following bitmasks are used to determine which literals are supported:

SQL_DL_SQL92_DATE
SQL_DL_SQL92_TIME
SQL_DL_SQL92_TIMESTAMP
SQL_DL_SQL92_INTERVAL_YEAR
SQL_DL_SQL92_INTERVAL_MONTH
SQL_DL_SQL92_INTERVAL_DAY
SQL_DL_SQL92_INTERVAL_HOUR
SQL_DL_SQL92_INTERVAL_MINUTE
SQL_DL_SQL92_INTERVAL_SECOND
SQL_DL_SQL92_INTERVAL_YEAR_TO_MONTH
SQL_DL_SQL92_INTERVAL_DAY_TO_HOUR
SQL_DL_SQL92_INTERVAL_DAY_TO_MINUTE
SQL_DL_SQL92_INTERVAL_DAY_TO_SECOND
SQL_DL_SQL92_INTERVAL_HOUR_TO_MINUTE
SQL_DL_SQL92_INTERVAL_HOUR_TO_SECOND
SQL_DL_SQL92_INTERVAL_MINUTE_TO_SECOND

continues

Table B.1 Continued

Function	ODBC Version Required	Description
SQL_DBMS_NAME	1.0	A character string with the name of the DBMS product accessed by the driver.
SQL_DBMS_VER	1.0	A character string indicating the version of the DBMS product accessed by the driver. The version is of the form ##.##.####, where the first two digits are the major version, the next two digits are the minor version, and the last four digits are the release version. The driver must render the DBMS product version in this form, but can also append the DBMS product-specific version as well. For example, "04.01.0000 Rdb 4.1".
SQL_DDL_INDEX	3.0	An SQLUINTEGER value that indicates support for creation and dropping of indexes: SQL_DI_CREATE_INDEX SQL_DI_DROP_INDEX An SQL-92 Entry level–conformant driver will always return both of these options as supported.
SQL_DEFAULT_TXN_ISOLATION	1.0	An SQLUINTEGER value that indicates the default transaction isolation level supported by the driver or data source, or zero if the data source does not support transactions. The following terms are used to define transaction isolation levels: Dirty Read: Transaction 1 changes a row. Transaction 2 reads the changed row before transaction 1 commits the change. If transaction 1 rolls back the change, transaction 2 will have read a row that is considered to have never existed. Nonrepeatable

Read: Transaction 1 reads a row. Transaction 2 updates or deletes that row and commits this change. If transaction 1 attempts to reread the row, it will receive different row values or discover that the row has been deleted.

Phantom: Transaction 1 reads a set of rows that satisfy some search criteria. Transaction 2 generates one or more rows (either through inserts or updates) that match the search criteria. If transaction 1 re-executes the statement that reads the rows, it receives a different set of rows. If the data source supports transactions, the driver returns one of the following bitmasks:

SQL_TXN_READ_UNCOMMITTED = Dirty reads, nonrepeatable reads, and phantoms are possible.

SQL_TXN_READ_COMMITTED = Dirty reads are not possible. Nonrepeatable reads and phantoms are possible.

SQL_TXN_REPEATABLE_READ = Dirty reads and nonrepeatable reads are not possible. Phantoms are possible.

SQL_TXN_SERIALIZABLE = Transactions are serializable. Serializable transactions do not allow dirty reads, nonrepeatable reads, or phantoms.

SQL_DESCRIBE_PARAMETER	3.0	A character string: "Y" if parameters can be described; "N", if not. An SQL-92 Full level–conformant driver will usually return "Y" because it will support the DESCRIBE INPUT statement. Since this does not directly specify the underlying SQL support, however, describing parameters may not be supported, even in a SQL-92 Full level–conformant driver.
SQL_DM_VER	3.0	A character string with the version of the Driver Manager. The version is of the form ##.##.####.####, where:The first set of two digits is the major ODBC version, as given by the constant SQL_SPEC_MAJOR. The second set of two digits is the minor ODBC version, as given by the constant SQL_SPEC_MINOR.The third set of four digits is the Driver Manager major build number.The last set of four digits is the Driver Manager minor build number.

continues

Table B.1 Continued

Function	ODBC Version Required	Description
SQL_DRIVER_HDBC		
SQL_DRIVER_HENV	1.0	A SQLUINTEGER value, the driver's environment handle or connection handle, determined by the argument InfoType. These information types are implemented by the Driver Manager alone.
SQL_DRIVER_HDESC	3.0	An SQLUINTEGER value, the driver's descriptor handle determined by the Driver Manager's descriptor handle, which must be passed on input in *InfoValuePtr from the application. Note that in this case, InfoValuePtr is both an input and output argument. The input descriptor handle passed in *InfoValuePtr must have been either explicitly or implicitly allocated on the ConnectionHandle. The application should make a copy of the Driver Manager's descriptor handle before calling SQLGetInfo with this information type, to ensure that the handle is not overwritten on output. This information type is implemented by the Driver Manager alone.
SQL_DRIVER_HLIB	2.0	An SQLUINTEGER value, the handle from the load library returned to the Driver Manager when it loaded the driver DLL (on a Windows platform) or equivalent on a non-Windows platform. The handle is only valid for the connection handle specified in the call to SQLGetInfo. This information type is implemented by the Driver Manager alone.
SQL_DRIVER_HSTMT	1.0	An SQLUINTEGER value, the driver's statement handle determined by the Driver Manager statement handle, which must be passed on input in *InfoValuePtr from the application. Note that in this case, InfoValuePtr is both an input and an output argument. The input statement handle passed in *InfoValuePtr must have been allocated on the argument

		ConnectionHandle. The application should make a copy of the Driver Manager's statement handle before calling SQLGetInfo with this information type, to ensure that the handle is not overwritten on output. This information type is implemented by the Driver Manager alone.
SQL_DRIVER_NAME	1.0	A character string with the file name of the driver used to access the data source.
SQL_DRIVER_ODBC_VER	2.0	A character string with the version of ODBC that the driver supports. The version is of the form ##.##, where the first two digits are the major version and the next two digits are the minor version. SQL_SPEC_MAJOR and SQL_SPEC_MINOR define the major and minor version numbers. For the version of ODBC described in this manual, these are 3 and 0, and the driver should return "03.00".
SQL_DRIVER_VER	1.0	A character string with the version of the driver and, optionally a description of the driver. At a minimum, the version is of the form ##.##.####, where the first two digits are the major version, the next two digits are the minor version, and the last four digits are the release version.
SQL_DROP_ASSERTION	3.0	An SQLUINTEGER bitmask enumerating the clauses in the DROP ASSERTION statement, as defined in SQL-92, supported by the data source. The following bitmask is used to determine which clauses are supported: SQL_DA_DROP_ASSERTION An SQL-92 Full level-conformant driver will always return this option as supported.
SQL_DROP_CHARACTER_SET	3.0	An SQLUINTEGER bitmask enumerating the clauses in the DROP CHARACTER SET statement, as defined in SQL-92, supported by the data

continues

Table B.1 Continued

Function	ODBC Version Required	Description
		source. The following bitmask is used to determine which clauses are supported: SQL_DCS_DROP_CHARACTER_SET
		An SQL-92 Full level-conformant driver will always return this option as supported.
SQL_DROP_COLLATION	3.0	An SQLINTEGER bitmask enumerating the clauses in the DROP COLLATION statement, as defined in SQL-92, supported by the data source. The following bitmask is used to determine which clauses are supported: SQL_DC_DROP_COLLATION
		An SQL-92 Full level-conformant driver will always return this option as supported.
SQL_DROP_DOMAIN	3.0	An SQLINTEGER bitmask enumerating the clauses in the DROP DOMAIN statement, as defined in SQL-92, supported by the data source. The following bitmasks are used to determine which clauses are supported: SQL_DD_DROP_DOMAIN SQL_DD_CASCADE SQL_DD_RESTRIC
		An SQL-92 Intermediate level-conformant driver will always return all of these options as supported.
SQL_DROP_SCHEMA	3.0	An SQLINTEGER bitmask enumerating the clauses in the DROP SCHEMA statement, as defined in SQL-92, supported by the data source. The following bitmasks are used to determine which clauses are supported:

SQL_DS_DROP_SCHEMA
SQL_DS_CASCADE
SQL_DS_RESTRICT

An SQL-92 Intermediate level–conformant driver will always return all of these options as supported.

SQL_DROP_TABLE   3.0

An SQLUINTEGER bitmask enumerating the clauses in the DROP TABLE statement, as defined in SQL-92, supported by the data source. The following bitmasks are used to determine which clauses are supported:

SQL_DT_DROP_TABLE
SQL_DT_CASCADE
SQL_DT_RESTRICT

A FIPS Transitional level–conformant driver will always return all of these options as supported.

SQL_DROP_TRANSLATION   3.0

An SQLUINTEGER bitmask enumerating the clauses in the DROP TRANS- LATION statement, as defined in SQL-92, supported by the data source. The following bitmask is used to determine which clauses are sup- ported:

SQL_DTR_DROP_TRANSLATION

An SQL-92 Full level–conformant driver will always return this option as supported.

SQL_DROP_VIEW   3.0

An SQLUINTEGER bitmask enumerating the clauses in the DROP VIEW statement, as defined in SQL-92, supported by the data source. The following bitmasks are used to determine which clauses are supported:

SQL_DV_DROP_VIEW
SQL_DV_CASCADE
SQL_DV_RESTRICT. A FIPS Transitional level–conformant driver will always return all of these options as supported.

continues

Table B.1 Continued

Function	ODBC Version Required	Description
SQL_DYNAMIC_CURSOR_ATTRIBUTES1	3.0	An SQLUINTEGER bitmask that describes the attributes of a dynamic cursor that are supported by the driver. This bitmask contains the first subset of attributes; for the second subset, see SQL_DYNAMIC_CURSOR_ATTRIBUTES2. The following bitmasks are used to determine which attributes are supported: SQL_CA1_NEXT = A FetchOrientation argument of SQL_FETCH_NEXT is supported in a call to SQLFetchScroll when the cursor is a dynamic cursor. SQL_CA1_ABSOLUTE = FetchOrientation arguments of SQL_FETCH_FIRST, SQL_FETCH_LAST, and SQL_FETCH_ABSOLUTE are supported in a call to SQLFetchScroll when the cursor is a dynamic cursor. (The rowset that will be fetched is independent of the current cursor position.) SQL_CA1_RELATIVE = FetchOrientation arguments of SQL_FETCH_PRIOR and SQL_FETCH_RELATIVE are supported in a call to SQLFetchScroll when the cursor is a dynamic cursor. (The rowset that will be fetched is dependent of the current cursor position. Note that this is separated from SQL_FETCH_NEXT because in a forward-only cursor, only SQL_FETCH_NEXT is supported.) SQL_CA1_BOOKMARK = A FetchOrientation argument of SQL_FETCH_BOOKMARK is supported in a call to SQLFetchScroll when the cursor is a dynamic cursor. SQL_CA1_LOCK_EXCLUSIVE = A LockType argument of SQL_LOCK_EXCLUSIVE is supported in a call to SQLSetPos when the cursor is a dynamic cursor.

SQL_CA1_LOCK_NO_CHANGE = A LockType argument of SQL_LOCK_NO_CHANGE is supported in a call to SQLSetPos when the cursor is a dynamic cursor.

SQL_CA1_LOCK_UNLOCK = A LockType argument of SQL_LOCK_UNLOCK is supported in a call to SQLSetPos when the cursor is a dynamic cursor.

SQL_CA1_POS_POSITION = An Operation argument of SQL_POSITION is supported in a call to SQLSetPos when the cursor is a dynamic cursor. SQL_CA1_POS_UPDATE = An Operation argument of SQL_UPDATE is supported in a call to SQLSetPos when the cursor is a dynamic cursor.

SQL_CA1_POS_DELETE = An Operation argument of SQL_DELETE is supported in a call to SQLSetPos when the cursor is a dynamic cursor.

SQL_CA1_POS_REFRESH = An Operation argument of SQL_REFRESH is supported in a call to SQLSetPos when the cursor is a dynamic cursor.

SQL_CA1_POSITIONED_UPDATE = An UPDATE WHERE CURRENT OF SQL statement is supported when the cursor is a dynamic cursor. (An SQL-92 Entry level–conformant driver will always return this option as supported.)

SQL_CA1_POSITIONED_DELETE = A DELETE WHERE CURRENT OF SQL statement is supported when the cursor is a dynamic cursor. (An SQL-92 Entry level–conformant driver will always return this option as supported.)

SQL_CA1_SELECT_FOR_UPDATE = A SELECT FOR UPDATE SQL statement is supported when the cursor is a dynamic cursor. (An SQL-92 Entry level–conformant driver will always return this option as supported.)

SQL_CA1_BULK_ADD = An Operation argument of SQL_ADD is supported in a call to SQLBulkOperations when the cursor is a dynamic cursor.

SQL_CA1_BULK_UPDATE_BY_BOOKMARK = An Operation argument of SQL_UPDATE_BY_BOOKMARK is supported in a call to SQLBulkOperations when the cursor is a dynamic cursor.

continues

Table B.1 Continued

Function	ODBC Version Required	Description
		SQL_CA1_BULK_DELETE_BY_BOOKMARK = An Operation argument of SQL_DELETE_BY_BOOKMARK is supported in a call to SQLBulkOperations when the cursor is a dynamic cursor.
		SQL_CA1_BULK_FETCH_BY_BOOKMARK = An Operation argument of SQL_FETCH_BY_BOOKMARK is supported in a call to SQLBulkOperations when the cursor is a dynamic cursor. An SQL-92 Intermediate level–conformant driver will usually return the SQL_CA1_NEXT, SQL_CA1_ABSOLUTE, and SQL_CA1_RELATIVE options as supported, because it supports scrollable cursors through the embedded SQL FETCH statement. Since this does not directly determine the underlying SQL support, however, scrollable cursors may not be supported, even for an SQL-92 Intermediate level–conformant driver.
SQL_DYNAMIC_CURSOR_ATTRIBUTES2	3.0	An SQLUINTEGER bitmask that describes the attributes of a dynamic cursor that are supported by the driver. This bitmask contains the second subset of attributes; for the first subset, see SQL_DYNAMIC_CURSOR_ATTRIBUTES1. The following bitmasks are used to determine which attributes are supported:
		SQL_CA2_READ_ONLY_CONCURRENCY = A read-only dynamic cursor, in which no updates are allowed, is supported. (The SQL_ATTR_CONCURRENCY statement attribute can be SQL_CONCUR_READ_ONLY for a dynamic cursor).
		SQL_CA2_LOCK_CONCURRENCY = A dynamic cursor that uses the lowest level of locking sufficient to ensure that the row can be updated is supported. (The SQL_ATTR_CONCURRENCY statement attribute can be SQL_CONCUR_LOCK for a dynamic cursor). These locks must be consistent

with the transaction isolation level set by the `SQL_ATTR_TXN_ISOLATION` connection attribute.

`SQL_CA2_OPT_ROWER_CONCURRENCY` = A dynamic cursor that uses the optimistic concurrency control comparing row versions is supported. (The `SQL_ATTR_CONCURRENCY` statement attribute can be `SQL_CONCUR_ROWER` for a dynamic cursor).

`SQL_CA2_OPT_VALUES_CONCURRENCY` = A dynamic cursor that uses the optimistic concurrency control comparing values is supported. (The `SQL_ATTR_CONCURRENCY` statement attribute can be `SQL_CONCUR_VALUES` for a dynamic cursor).

`SQL_CA2_SENSITIVITY_ADDITIONS` = Added rows are visible to a dynamic cursor; the cursor can scroll to those rows. (Where these rows are added to the cursor is driver-dependent.)

`SQL_CA2_SENSITIVITY_DELETIONS` = Deleted rows are no longer available to a dynamic cursor, and do not leave a "hole" in the result set; after the dynamic cursor scrolls from a deleted row, it cannot return to that row.

`SQL_CA2_SENSITIVITY_UPDATES` = Updates to rows are visible to a dynamic cursor; if the dynamic cursor scrolls from and returns to an updated row, the data returned by the cursor is the updated data, not the original data.

`SQL_CA2_MAX_ROWS_SELECT` = The `SQL_ATTR_MAX_ROWS` statement attribute affects SELECT statements when the cursor is a dynamic cursor.

`SQL_CA2_MAX_ROWS_INSERT` = The `SQL_ATTR_MAX_ROWS` statement attribute affects INSERT statements when the cursor is a dynamic cursor.

`SQL_CA2_MAX_ROWS_DELETE` = The `SQL_ATTR_MAX_ROWS` statement attribute affects DELETE statements when the cursor is a dynamic cursor.

`SQL_CA2_MAX_ROWS_UPDATE` = The `SQL_ATTR_MAX_ROWS` statement attribute affects UPDATE statements when the cursor is a dynamic cursor.

continues

Table B.1 Continued

Function	ODBC Version Required	Description
		SQL_CA2_MAX_ROWS_CATALOG = The SQL_ATTR_MAX_ROWS statement attribute affects CATALOG result sets when the cursor is a dynamic cursor.
		SQL_CA2_MAX_ROWS_AFFECTS_ALL = The SQL_ATTR_MAX_ROWS statement attribute affects SELECT, INSERT, DELETE, and UPDATE statements, and CATALOG result sets, when the cursor is a dynamic cursor.
		SQL_CA2_CRC_EXACT = The exact row count is available in the SQL_DIAG_CURSOR_ROW_COUNT diagnostic field when the cursor is a dynamic cursor.
		SQL_CA2_CRC_APPROXIMATE = An approximate row count is available in the SQL_DIAG_CURSOR_ROW_COUNT diagnostic field when the cursor is a dynamic cursor.
		SQL_CA2_SIMULATE_NON_UNIQUE = The driver does not guarantee that simulated positioned update or delete statements will affect only one row when the cursor is a dynamic cursor; it is the application's responsibility to guarantee this. (If a statement affects more than one row, SQLExecute or SQLExecDirect returns SQLSTATE 01001 (Cursor operation conflict).) To set this behavior, the application calls SQLSetStmtAttr with the SQL_ATTR_SIMULATE_CURSOR attribute set to SQL_SC_NON_UNIQUE.
		SQL_CA2_SIMULATE_TRY_UNIQUE = The driver attempts to guarantee that simulated positioned update or delete statements will affect only one row when the cursor is a dynamic cursor. The driver always executes such statements, even if they might affect more than one row, such as when there is no unique key. (If a statement affects more than one row,

SQLExecute or SQLExecDirect returns SQLSTATE 01001 (Cursor operation conflict).) To set this behavior, the application calls SQLSetStmtAttr with the SQL_ATTR_SIMULATE_CURSOR attribute set to SQL_SC_TRY_UNIQUE.

SQL_CA2_SIMULATE_UNIQUE = The driver guarantees that simulated positioned update or delete statements will affect only one row when the cursor is a dynamic cursor. If the driver cannot guarantee this for a given statement, SQLExecDirect or SQLPrepare return SQLSTATE 01001 (Cursor operation conflict). To set this behavior, the application calls SQLSetStmtAttr with the SQL_ATTR_SIMULATE_CURSOR attribute set to SQL_SC_UNIQUE.

SQL_EXPRESSIONS_IN_ORDERBY   1.0

A character string: "Y" if the data source supports expressions in the ORDER BY list; "N" if it does not.

SQL_FILE_USAGE   2.0

An SQLUSMALLINT value indicating how a single-tier driver directly treats files in a data source:

SQL_FILE_NOT_SUPPORTED = The driver is not a single-tier driver. For example, an ORACLE driver is a two-tier driver.

SQL_FILE_TABLE = A single-tier driver treats files in a data source as tables. For example, an Xbase driver treats each Xbase file as a table.

SQL_FILE_CATALOG = A single-tier driver treats files in a data source as a catalog. For example, a Microsoft Access driver treats each Microsoft Access file as a complete database. An application might use this to determine how users will select data. For example, Xbase users often think of data as stored in files, while ORACLE and Microsoft Access users generally think of data as stored in tables. When a user selects an Xbase data source, the application could display the Windows File Open common dialog box; when the user selects a Microsoft Access or ORACLE data source, the application could display a custom Select Table dialog box.

continues

Table B.1 *Continued*

Function	ODBC Version Required	Description
SQL_FORWARD_ONLY_CURSOR_ATTRIBUTES1	3.0	An SQLUINTEGER bitmask that describes the attributes of a forward-only cursor that are supported by the driver. This bitmask contains the first subset of attributes; for the second subset, see SQL_FOR-WARD_ONLY_CURSOR_ATTRIBUTES2. The following bitmasks are used to determine which attributes are supported: SQL_CA1_NEXT SQL_CA1_LOCK_EXCLUSIVE SQL_CA1_LOCK_NO_CHANGE SQL_CA1_LOCK_UNLOCK SQL_CA1_POS_POSITION SQL_CA1_POS_UPDATE SQL_CA1_POS_DELETE SQL_CA1_POS_REFRESH SQL_CA1_POSITIONED_UPDATE SQL_CA1_POSITIONED_DELETE SQL_CA1_SELECT_FOR_UPDATE SQL_CA1_BULK_ADD SQL_CA1_BULK_UPDATE_BY_BOOKMARK SQL_CA1_BULK_DELETE_BY_BOOKMARK SQL_CA1_BULK_FETCH_BY_BOOKMARK For descriptions of these bitmasks, see SQL_DYNAMIC_CURSOR_ATTRIBUTES1 (and substitute "forward-only cursor" for "dynamic cursor" in the descriptions).
SQL_FORWARD_ONLY_CURSOR_ATTRIBUTES2	3.0	An SQLUINTEGER bitmask that describes the attributes of a forward-only cursor that are supported by the driver. This bitmask contains the second subset of attributes; for the first subset, see

SQL_FORWARD_ONLY_CURSOR_ATTRIBUTES1. The following bitmasks are used to determine which attributes are supported:

SQL_CA2_READ_ONLY_CONCURRENCY
SQL_CA2_LOCK_CONCURRENCY
SQL_CA2_OPT_ROWVER_CONCURRENCY
SQL_CA2_OPT_VALUES_CONCURRENCY
SQL_CA2_SENSITIVITY_ADDITIONS
SQL_CA2_SENSITIVITY_DELETIONS
SQL_CA2_SENSITIVITY_UPDATES
SQL_CA2_MAX_ROWS_SELECT
SQL_CA2_MAX_ROWS_INSERT
SQL_CA2_MAX_ROWS_DELETE
SQL_CA2_MAX_ROWS_UPDATE
SQL_CA2_MAX_ROWS_CATALOG
SQL_CA2_MAX_ROWS_AFFECTS_ALL
SQL_CA2_CRC_EXACT
SQL_CA2_CRC_APPROXIMATE
SQL_CA2_SIMULATE_NON_UNIQUE
SQL_CA2_SIMULATE_TRY_UNIQUE
SQL_CA2_SIMULATE_UNIQUE

For descriptions of these bitmasks, see SQL_DYNAMIC_CURSOR_ATTRIBUTES2 (and substitute "forward-only cursor" for "dynamic cursor" in the descriptions).

SQL_GETDATA_EXTENSIONS   2.0

An SQLUINTEGER bitmask enumerating extensions to SQLGetData. The following bitmasks are used in conjunction with the flag to determine what common extensions the driver supports for SQLGetData:

SQL_GD_ANY_COLUMN = SQLGetData can be called for any unbound column, including those before the last bound column. Note that the columns must be called in order of ascending column number unless SQL_GD_ANY_ORDER is also returned.

continues

Table B.1 Continued

Function	ODBC Version Required	Description
		SQL_GD_ANY_ORDER = SQLGetData can be called for unbound columns in any order. Note that SQLGetData can only be called for columns after the last bound column unless SQL_GD_ANY_COLUMN is also returned.
		SQL_GD_BLOCK = SQLGetData can be called for an unbound column in any row in a block (where the rowset size is greater than 1) of data after positioning to that row with SQLSetPos.
		SQL_GD_BOUND = SQLGetData can be called for bound columns as well as unbound columns. A driver cannot return this value unless it also returns SQL_GD_ANY_COLUMN.
		SQLGetData is only required to return data from unbound columns that occur after the last bound column, are called in order of increasing column number, and are not in a row in a block of rows. If a driver supports bookmarks (either fixed- or variable-length), it must support calling SQLGetData on column 0. This support is required regardless of what the driver returns for a call to SQLGetInfo with the SQL_GET-DATA_EXTENSIONS InfoType.
SQL_GROUP_BY	2.0	An SQLUSMALLINT value specifying the relationship between the columns in the GROUP BY clause and the non-aggregated columns in the select list: SQL_GB_COLLATE = A COLLATE clause can be specified at the end of each grouping column. (ODBC 3.0) SQL_GB_NOT_SUPPORTED = GROUP BY clauses are not supported. (ODBC 2.0)

SQL_GB_GROUP_BY_EQUALS_SELECT = The GROUP BY clause must contain all non-aggregated columns in the select list. It cannot contain any other columns. For example, SELECT DEPT, MAX(SALARY) FROM EMPLOYEE GROUP BY DEPT. (ODBC 2.0)

SQL_GB_GROUP_BY_CONTAINS_SELECT = The GROUP BY clause must contain all non-aggregated columns in the select list. It can contain columns that are not in the select list. For example, SELECT DEPT, MAX(SALARY) FROM EMPLOYEE GROUP BY DEPT, AGE. (ODBC 2.0)

SQL_GB_NO_RELATION = The columns in the GROUP BY clause and the select list are not related. The meaning of non-grouped, non-aggregated columns in the select list is data source-dependent. For example, SELECT DEPT, SALARY FROM EMPLOYEE GROUP BY DEPT, AGE. (ODBC 2.0)

An SQL-92 Entry level–conformant driver will always return the SQL_GB_GROUP_BY_EQUALS_SELECT option as supported. An SQL-92 Full level–conformant driver will always return the SQL_GB_COLLATE option as supported. If none of the options is supported, the GROUP BY clause is not supported by the data source.

An SQLUSMALLINT value as follows:

SQL_IC_UPPER = Identifiers in SQL are not case-sensitive and are stored in uppercase in system catalog.

SQL_IC_LOWER = Identifiers in SQL are not case-sensitive and are stored in lowercase in system catalog.

SQL_IC_SENSITIVE = Identifiers in SQL are case-sensitive and are stored in mixed case in system catalog.

SQL_IC_MIXED = Identifiers in SQL are not case-sensitive and are stored in mixed case in system catalog. Since identifiers in SQL-92 are never case-sensitive, a driver that conforms strictly to SQL-92 (any level) will never return the SQL_IC_SENSITIVE option as supported.

1.0

SQL_IDENTIFIER_CASE

continues

Table B.1 Continued

Function	ODBC Version Required	Description
SQL_IDENTIFIER_QUOTE_CHAR	1.0	The character string used as the starting and ending delimiter of a quoted (delimited) identifiers in SQL statements. (Identifiers passed as arguments to ODBC functions do not need to be quoted.) If the data source does not support quoted identifiers, a blank is returned. This character string can also be used for quoting catalog function arguments when the connection attribute SQL_ATTR_METADATA_ID is set to SQL_TRUE. Since the identifier quote character in SQL-92 is the double quotation mark ("), a driver that conforms strictly to SQL-92 will always return the double quotation mark character.
SQL_INDEX_KEYWORDS	3.0	An SQLUINTEGER bitmask that enumerates keywords in the CREATE INDEX statement that are supported by the driver. SQL_IK_NONE = None of the keywords are supported. SQL_IK_ASC = ASC keyword is supported. SQL_IK_DESC = DESC keyword is supported. SQL_IK_ALL = All keywords are supported. To see if the CREATE INDEX statement is supported, an application calls SQLGetInfo with the SQL_DLL_INDEX information type.
SQL_INFO_SCHEMA_VIEWS	3.0	An SQLUINTEGER bitmask enumerating the views in the INFORMATION_SCHEMA that are supported by the driver. The views in, and the contents of, INFORMATION_SCHEMA are as defined in SQL-92. The SQL-92 or FIPS conformance level at which this feature needs to be supported is shown in parentheses next to each bitmask. The following bitmasks are used to determine which views are supported:

SQL_ISV_ASSERTIONS = Identifies the catalog's assertions that are owned by a given user. (Full level)

SQL_ISV_CHARACTER_SETS = Identifies the catalog's character sets that are accessible to a given user. (Intermediate level)

SQL_ISV_CHECK_CONSTRAINTS = Identifies the CHECK constraints that are owned by a given user. (Intermediate level)

SQL_ISV_COLLATIONS = Identifies the character collations for the catalog that are accessible to a given user. (Full level)

SQL_ISV_COLUMN_DOMAIN_USAGE = Identifies columns for the catalog that are dependent on domains defined in the catalog and are owned by a given user. (Intermediate level)

SQL_ISV_COLUMN_PRIVILEGES = Identifies the privileges on columns of persistent tables that are available to or granted by a given user. (FIPS Transitional level)

SQL_ISV_COLUMNS = Identifies the columns of persistent tables that are accessible to a given user. (FIPS Transitional level)

SQL_ISV_CONSTRAINT_COLUMN_USAGE = Similar to CONSTRAINT_TABLE_USAGE view, columns are identified for the various constraints that are owned by a given user. (Intermediate level)

SQL_ISV_CONSTRAINT_TABLE_USAGE = Identifies the tables that are used by constraints (referential, unique, and assertions), and are owned by a given user. (Intermediate level)

SQL_ISV_DOMAIN_CONSTRAINTS = Identifies the domain constraints (of the domains in the catalog) that are accessible to a given user. (Intermediate level)

SQL_ISV_DOMAINS = Identifies the domains defined in a catalog that are accessible to the user. (Intermediate level)

SQL_ISV_KEY_COLUMN_USAGE = Identifies columns defined in the catalog that are constrained as keys by a given user. (Intermediate level)

SQL_ISV_REFERENTIAL_CONSTRAINTS = Identifies the referential constraints that are owned by a given user. (Intermediate level)

continues

Table B.1 Continued

Function	ODBC Version Required	Description
		SQL_ISV_SCHEMATA = Identifies the schemas that are owned by a given user. (Intermediate level)
		SQL_ISV_SQL_LANGUAGES = Identifies the SQL conformance levels, options, and dialects supported by the SQL implementation. (Intermediate level)
		SQL_ISV_TABLE_CONSTRAINTS = Identifies the table constraints that are owned by a given user. (Intermediate level)
		SQL_ISV_TABLE_PRIVILEGES = Identifies the privileges on persistent tables that are available to or granted by a given user. (FIPS Transitional level)
		SQL_ISV_TABLES = Identifies the persistent tables defined in a catalog that are accessible to a given user. (FIPS Transitional level)
		SQL_ISV_TRANSLATIONS = Identifies character translations for the catalog that are accessible to a given user. (Full level)
		SQL_ISV_USAGE_PRIVILEGES = Identifies the USAGE privileges on catalog objects that are available to or owned by a given user. (FIPS Transitional level)
		SQL_ISV_VIEW_COLUMN_USAGE = Identifies the columns on which the catalog's views that are owned by a given user are dependent. (Intermediate level)
		SQL_ISV_VIEW_TABLE_USAGE = Identifies the tables on which the catalog's views that are owned by a given user are dependent. (Intermediate level)
		SQL_ISV_VIEWS = Identifies the viewed tables defined in this catalog that are accessible to a given user. (FIPS Transitional level)

InfoType	Version	Description

`SQL_INSERT_STATEMENT`	3.0	An SQLUINTEGER bitmask that indicates support for INSERT statements:
		`SQL_IS_INSERT_LITERALS`
		`SQL_IS_INSERT_SEARCHED`
		`SQL_IS_SELECT_INTO`
		An SQL-92 Entry level–conformant driver will always return all of these options as supported.

`SQL_INTEGRITY`	1.0	A character string: "Y" if the data source supports the Integrity Enhancement Facility; "N" if it does not. This InfoType has been renamed for ODBC 3.0 from the ODBC 2.0 InfoType `SQL_ODBC_SQL_OPT_IEF`.

`SQL_KEYSET_CURSOR_ATTRIBUTES1`	3.0	An SQLUINTEGER bitmask that describes the attributes of a keyset cursor that are supported by the driver. This bitmask contains the first subset of attributes; for the second subset, see `SQL_KEYSET_CURSOR_ATTRIBUTES2`. The following bitmasks are used to determine which attributes are supported:
		`SQL_CA1_NEXT`
		`SQL_CA1_ABSOLUTE`
		`SQL_CA1_RELATIVE`
		`SQL_CA1_BOOKMARK`
		`SQL_CA1_LOCK_EXCLUSIVE`
		`SQL_CA1_LOCK_NO_CHANGE`
		`SQL_CA1_LOCK_UNLOCK`
		`SQL_CA1_POS_POSITION`
		`SQL_CA1_POS_UPDATE`
		`SQL_CA1_POS_DELETE`
		`SQL_CA1_POS_REFRESH`
		`SQL_CA1_POSITIONED_UPDATE`
		`SQL_CA1_POSITIONED_DELETE`
		`SQL_CA1_SELECT_FOR_UPDATE`

continues

Table B.1 Continued

Function	ODBC Version Required	Description

		`SQL_CA1_BULK_ADD`
		`SQL_CA1_BULK_UPDATE_BY_BOOKMARK`
		`SQL_CA1_BULK_DELETE_BY_BOOKMARK`
		`SQL_CA1_BULK_FETCH_BY_BOOKMARK`
		
		For descriptions of these bitmasks, see `SQL_DYNAMIC_CURSOR_ATTRIBUTES1` (and substitute "keyset-driven cursor" for "dynamic cursor" in the descriptions).
		
		An SQL-92 Intermediate level–conformant driver will usually return the `SQL_CA1_NEXT`, `SQL_CA1_ABSOLUTE`, and `SQL_CA1_RELATIVE` options as supported, because it supports scrollable cursors through the embedded `SQL FETCH` statement. Since this does not directly determine the underlying SQL support, however, scrollable cursors may not be supported, even for an SQL-92 Intermediate level–conformant driver.

`SQL_KEYSET_CURSOR_ATTRIBUTES2`	3.0	An SQLUINTEGER bitmask that describes the attributes of a keyset cursor that are supported by the driver. This bitmask contains the second subset of attributes; for the first subset, see `SQL_KEYSET_CURSOR_ATTRIBUTES1`. The following bitmasks are used to determine which attributes are supported:
		`SQL_CA2_READ_ONLY_CONCURRENCY`
		`SQL_CA2_LOCK_CONCURRENCY`
		`SQL_CA2_OPT_ROWER_CONCURRENCY`
		`SQL_CA2_OPT_VALUES_CONCURRENCY`
		`SQL_CA2_SENSITIVITY_ADDITIONS`
		`SQL_CA2_SENSITIVITY_DELETIONS`
		`SQL_CA2_SENSITIVITY_UPDATES`

SQL_CA2_MAX_ROWS_SELECT
SQL_CA2_MAX_ROWS_INSERT
SQL_CA2_MAX_ROWS_DELETE
SQL_CA2_MAX_ROWS_UPDATE
SQL_CA2_MAX_ROWS_CATALOG
SQL_CA2_MAX_ROWS_AFFECTS_ALL
SQL_CA2_CRC_EXACT
SQL_CA2_CRC_APPROXIMATE
SQL_CA2_SIMULATE_NON_UNIQUE
SQL_CA2_SIMULATE_TRY_UNIQUE
SQL_CA2_SIMULATE_UNIQUE

For descriptions of these bitmasks, see SQL_DYNAMIC_CURSOR_ATTRIBUTES1 (and substitute "keyset-driven cursor" for "dynamic cursor" in the descriptions).

SQL_KEYWORDS	2.0	A character string containing a comma-separated list of all data source-specific keywords. This list does not contain keywords specific to ODBC or keywords used by both the data source and ODBC. This list represents all the reserved keywords; interoperable applications should not use these words in object names.
SQL_LIKE_ESCAPE_CLAUSE	2.0	A character string: "Y" if the data source supports an escape character for the percent character (%) and underscore character (_) in a LIKE predicate and the driver supports the ODBC syntax for defining a LIKE predicate escape character; "N" otherwise.
SQL_MAX_ASYNC_CONCURRENT_STATEMENTS	3.0	An SQLUINTEGER value specifying the maximum number of active concurrent statements in asynchronous mode that the driver can support on a given connection. If there is no specific limit or the limit is unknown, this value is zero.

continues

Table B.1 Continued

Function	ODBC Version Required	Description
SQL_MAX_BINARY_LITERAL_LEN	2.0	An SQLUINTEGER value specifying the maximum length (number of hexadecimal characters, excluding the literal prefix and suffix returned by SQLGetTypeInfo) of a binary literal in an SQL statement. For example, the binary literal 0xFFAA has a length of 4. If there is no maximum length or the length is unknown, this value is set to zero.
SQL_MAX_CATALOG_NAME_LEN	1.0	An SQLUSMALLINT value specifying the maximum length of a catalog name in the data source. If there is no maximum length or the length is unknown, this value is set to zero. An FIPS Full level–conformant driver will return at least 128. This InfoType has been renamed for ODBC 3.0 from the ODBC 2.0 InfoType SQL_MAX_QUALIFIER_NAME_LEN.
SQL_MAX_CHAR_LITERAL_LEN	2.0	An SQLUINTEGER value specifying the maximum length (number of characters, excluding the literal prefix and suffix returned by SQLGetTypeInfo) of a character literal in an SQL statement. If there is no maximum length or the length is unknown, this value is set to zero.
SQL_MAX_COLUMN_NAME_LEN	1.0	An SQLUSMALLINT value specifying the maximum length of a column name in the data source. If there is no maximum length or the length is unknown, this value is set to zero. An FIPS Entry level–conformant driver will return at least 18. An FIPS Intermediate level–conformant driver will return at least 128.
SQL_MAX_COLUMNS_IN_GROUP_BY	2.0	An SQLUSMALLINT value specifying the maximum number of columns allowed in a GROUP BY clause. If there is no specified limit or the limit is unknown, this value is set to zero. An FIPS Entry level–conformant driver will return at least 6. An FIPS Intermediate level–conformant driver will return at least 15.

SQL_MAX_COLUMNS_IN_INDEX	2.0	An SQLUSMALLINT value specifying the maximum number of columns allowed in an index. If there is no specified limit or the limit is unknown, this value is set to zero.
SQL_MAX_COLUMNS_IN_ORDER_BY	2.0	An SQLUSMALLINT value specifying the maximum number of columns allowed in an ORDER BY clause. If there is no specified limit or the limit is unknown, this value is set to zero. An FIPS Entry level–conformant driver will return at least 6. An FIPS Intermediate level–conformant driver will return at least 15.
SQL_MAX_COLUMNS_IN_SELECT	2.0	An SQLUSMALLINT value specifying the maximum number of columns allowed in a select list. If there is no specified limit or the limit is unknown, this value is set to zero. An FIPS Entry level–conformant driver will return at least 100. An FIPS Intermediate level–conformant driver will return at least 250.
SQL_MAX_COLUMNS_IN_TABLE	2.0	An SQLUSMALLINT value specifying the maximum number of columns allowed in a table. If there is no specified limit or the limit is unknown, this value is set to zero. An FIPS Entry level–conformant driver will return at least 100. An FIPS Intermediate level–conformant driver will return at least 250.
SQL_MAX_CONCURRENT_ACTIVITIES	1.0	An SQLUSMALLINT value specifying the maximum number of active statements that the driver can support for a connection. A statement is defined as active if it has results pending, with the term "results" meaning rows from a SELECT operation or rows affected by an INSERT, UPDATE, or DELETE operation (such as a row count), or if it is in a NEED_DATA state. This value can reflect a limitation imposed by either the driver or the data source. If there is no specified limit or the limit is unknown, this value is set to zero. This InfoType has been renamed for ODBC 3.0 from the ODBC 2.0 InfoType SQL_ACTIVE_STATEMENTS.

continues

Table B.1   Continued

Function	ODBC Version Required	Description
SQL_MAX_CURSOR_NAME_LEN	1.0	An SQLUSMALLINT value specifying the maximum length of a cursor name in the data source. If there is no maximum length or the length is unknown, this value is set to zero. An FIPS Entry level–conformant driver will return at least 18. An FIPS Intermediate level–conformant driver will return at least 128.
SQL_MAX_DRIVER_CONNECTIONS	1.0	An SQLUSMALLINT value specifying the maximum number of active connections that the driver can support for an environment. This value can reflect a limitation imposed by either the driver or the data source. If there is no specified limit or the limit is unknown, this value is set to zero. This InfoType has been renamed for ODBC 3.0 from the ODBC 2.0 InfoType SQL_ACTIVE_CONNECTIONS.
SQL_MAX_IDENTIFIER_LEN	3.0	An SQLUSMALLINT that indicates the maximum size in characters that the data source supports for user-defined names. An FIPS Entry level–conformant driver will return at least 18. An FIPS Intermediate level–conformant driver will return at least 128.
SQL_MAX_INDEX_SIZE	2.0	An SQLUINTEGER value specifying the maximum number of bytes allowed in the combined fields of an index. If there is no specified limit or the limit is unknown, this value is set to zero.
SQL_MAX_PROCEDURE_NAME_LEN	1.0	An SQLUSMALLINT value specifying the maximum length of a procedure name in the data source. If there is no maximum length or the length is unknown, this value is set to zero.
SQL_MAX_ROW_SIZE	2.0	An SQLUINTEGER value specifying the maximum length of a single row in a table. If there is no specified limit or the limit is unknown, this value is set to zero. An FIPS Entry level–conformant driver will return

SQL_MAX_ROW_SIZE_INCLUDES_LONG	3.0	at least 2,000. A FIPS Intermediate level–conformant driver will return at least 8,000.
		A character string: "Y" if the maximum row size returned for the SQL_MAX_ROW_SIZE information type includes the length of all SQL_LONGVARCHAR and SQL_LONGVARBINARY columns in the row; "N" otherwise.
SQL_MAX_SCHEMA_NAME_LEN	1.0	An SQLUSMALLINT value specifying the maximum length of a schema name in the data source. If there is no maximum length or the length is unknown, this value is set to zero. An FIPS Entry level-conformant driver will return at least 18. An FIPS Intermediate level–conformant driver will return at least 128.This InfoType has been renamed for ODBC 3.0 from the ODBC 2.0 InfoType SQL_MAX_OWNER_NAME_LEN.
SQL_MAX_STATEMENT_LEN	2.0	An SQLUINTEGER value specifying the maximum length (number of characters, including white space) of an SQL statement. If there is no maximum length or the length is unknown, this value is set to zero.
SQL_MAX_TABLE_NAME_LEN	1.0	An SQLUSMALLINT value specifying the maximum length of a table name in the data source. If there is no maximum length or the length is unknown, this value is set to zero. An FIPS Entry level-conformant driver will return at least 18. An FIPS Intermediate level–conformant driver will return at least 128.
SQL_MAX_TABLES_IN_SELECT	2.0	An SQLUSMALLINT value specifying the maximum number of tables allowed in the FROM clause of a SELECT statement. If there is no speci-fied limit or the limit is unknown, this value is set to zero. An FIPS Entry level-conformant driver will return at least 15. An FIPS Intermediate level–conformant driver will return at least 50.
SQL_MAX_USER_NAME_LEN	2.0	An SQLUSMALLINT value specifying the maximum length of a user name in the data source. If there is no maximum length or the length is unknown, this value is set to zero.

continues

Table B.1 Continued

Function	ODBC Version Required	Description
SQL_MULT_RESULT_SETS	1.0	A character string: "Y" if the data source supports multiple result sets, "N" if it does not.
SQL_MULTIPLE_ACTIVE_TXN	1.0	A character string: "Y" if multiple active transactions on a single connection are allowed, "N" if only one active transaction at a time is supported on a connection.
SQL_NEED_LONG_DATA_LEN	2.0	A character string: "Y" if the data source needs the length of a long data value (the data type is SQL_LONGVARCHAR, SQL_LONGVARBINARY, or a long, data source-specific data type) before that value is sent to the data source, "N" if it does not. For more information, see SQLBindParameter and SQLSetPos.
SQL_NON_NULLABLE_COLUMNS	1.0	An SQLUSMALLINT value specifying whether the data source supports NOT NULL in columns: SQL_NNC_NULL = All columns must be nullable. SQL_NNC_NON_NULL = Columns cannot be nullable (the data source supports the NOT NULL column constraint in CREATE TABLE statements). An SQL-92 Entry level–conformant driver will return SQL_NNC_NON_NULL.
SQL_NULL_COLLATION	2.0	An SQLUSMALLINT value specifying where NULLs are sorted in a result set: SQL_NC_END = NULLs are sorted at the end of the result set, regardless of the ASC or DESC keywords. SQL_NC_HIGH = NULLs are sorted at the high end of the result set, depending on the ASC or DESC keywords. SQL_NC_LOW = NULLs are sorted at the low end of the result set, depending on the ASC or DESC keywords.

SQL_NC_START = NULLs are sorted at the start of the result set, regardless of the ASC or DESC keywords.

1.0

SQL_NUMERIC_FUNCTIONS

An SQLUINTEGER bitmask enumerating the scalar numeric functions supported by the driver and associated data source. The following bitmasks are used to determine which numeric functions are supported:

SQL_FN_NUM_ABS (ODBC 1.0)
SQL_FN_NUM_ACOS (ODBC 1.0)
SQL_FN_NUM_ASIN (ODBC 1.0)
SQL_FN_NUM_ATAN (ODBC 1.0)
SQL_FN_NUM_ATAN2 (ODBC 1.0)
SQL_FN_NUM_CEILING (ODBC 1.0)
SQL_FN_NUM_COS (ODBC 1.0)
SQL_FN_NUM_COT (ODBC 1.0)
SQL_FN_NUM_DEGREES (ODBC 2.0)
SQL_FN_NUM_EXP (ODBC 1.0)
SQL_FN_NUM_FLOOR (ODBC 1.0)
SQL_FN_NUM_LOG (ODBC 1.0)
SQL_FN_NUM_LOG10 (ODBC 2.0)
SQL_FN_NUM_MOD (ODBC 1.0)
SQL_FN_NUM_PI (ODBC 1.0)
SQL_FN_NUM_POWER (ODBC 2.0)
SQL_FN_NUM_RADIANS (ODBC 2.0)
SQL_FN_NUM_RAND (ODBC 1.0)
SQL_FN_NUM_ROUND (ODBC 2.0)
SQL_FN_NUM_SIGN (ODBC 1.0)
SQL_FN_NUM_SIN (ODBC 1.0)
SQL_FN_NUM_SQRT (ODBC 1.0)
SQL_FN_NUM_TAN (ODBC 1.0)
SQL_FN_NUM_TRUNCATE (ODBC 2.0)

continues

Table B.1 Continued

Function	ODBC Version Required	Description
SQL_ODBC_INTERFACE_CONFORMANCE	3.0	An SQLUINTEGER value indicating the level of the ODBC 3.0 interface that the driver conforms to. SQL_OIC_CORE: The minimum level that all ODBC drivers are expected to conform to. This level includes basic interface elements such as connection functions; functions for preparing and executing an SQL statement; basic result set metadata functions; basic catalog functions; and so on. SQL_OIC_LEVEL1: A level including the core standards compliance level functionality, plus scrollable cursors, bookmarks, positioned updates and deletes, and so on. SQL_OIC_LEVEL2: A level including level 1 standards compliance level functionality, plus advanced features such as sensitive cursors; update, delete, and refresh by bookmarks; stored procedure support; catalog functions for primary and foreign keys; multi-catalog support; and so on.
SQL_ODBC_VER	1.0	A character string with the version of ODBC to which the Driver Manager conforms. The version is of the form ##.##.0000, where the first two digits are the major version and the next two digits are the minor version. This is implemented solely in the Driver Manager.
SQL_OJ_CAPABILITIES	2.0	An SQLUINTEGER bitmask enumerating the types of outer joins supported by the driver and data source. The following bitmasks are used to determine which types are supported: SQL_OJ_LEFT = Left outer joins are supported. SQL_OJ_RIGHT = Right outer joins are supported. SQL_OJ_FULL = Full outer joins are supported.

SQL_OJ_NESTED = Nested outer joins are supported.

SQL_OJ_NOT_ORDERED = The column names in the ON clause of the outer join do not have to be in the same order as their respective table names in the OUTER JOIN clause.

SQL_OJ_INNER = The inner table (the right table in a left outer join or the left table in a right outer join) can also be used in an inner join. This does not apply to full outer joins, which do not have an inner table.

SQL_OJ_ALL_COMPARISON_OPS = The comparison operator in the ON clause can be any of the ODBC comparison operators. If this bit is not set, only the equals (=) comparison operator can be used in outer joins. If none of these options is returned as supported, no outer join clause is supported. For information on the support of relational join operators in a SELECT statement, as defined by SQL-92, see SQL_SQL92_RELATIONAL_JOIN_OPERATORS.

| SQL_ORDER_BY_COLUMNS_IN_SELECT | 2.0 | A character string: "Y" if the columns in the ORDER BY clause must be in the select list; otherwise, "N". |
| SQL_PARAM_ARRAY_ROW_COUNTS | 3.0 | An SQLUINTEGER enumerating the driver's properties regarding the availability of row counts in a parameterized execution. Has the following values:

SQL_PARC_BATCH = Individual row counts are available for each set of parameters. This is conceptually equivalent to the driver generating a batch of SQL statements, one for each parameter set in the array. Extended error information can be retrieved by using the SQL_PARAM_STATUS_PTR descriptor field.

SQL_PARC_NO_BATCH = There is only one row count available, which is the cumulative row count resulting from the execution of the statement for the entire array of parameters. This is conceptually equivalent to treating the statement along with the entire parameter array as one atomic unit. Errors are handled the same as if one statement were executed. |

continues

Table B.1 Continued

Function	ODBC Version Required	Description
SQL_PARAM_ARRAY_SELECTS	3.0	An SQLUINTEGER enumerating the driver's properties regarding the availability of result sets in a parameterized execution. Has the following values: SQL_PAS_BATCH = There is one result set available per set of parameters. This is conceptually equivalent to the driver generating a batch of SQL statements, one for each parameter set in the array. SQL_PAS_NO_BATCH = There is only one result set available, which represents the cumulative result set resulting from the execution of the statement for the entire array of parameters. This is conceptually equivalent to treating the statement along with the entire parameter array as one atomic unit. SQL_PAS_NO_SELECT = A driver does not allow a result-set generating statement to be executed with an array of parameters.
SQL_PROCEDURE_TERM	1.0	A character string with the data source vendor's name for a procedure; for example, "database procedure," "stored procedure," "procedure," "package," or "stored query."
SQL_PROCEDURES	1.0	A character string: "Y" if the data source supports procedures and the driver supports the ODBC procedure invocation syntax; "N" otherwise.
SQL_QUOTED_IDENTIFIER_CASE	2.0	An SQLUSMALLINT value as follows: SQL_IC_UPPER = Quoted identifiers in SQL are not case-sensitive and are stored in uppercase in the system catalog. SQL_IC_LOWER = Quoted identifiers in SQL are not case-sensitive and are stored in lowercase in the system catalog.

SQL_ROW_UPDATES	1.0	SQL_IC_SENSITIVE = Quoted identifiers in SQL are case-sensitive and are stored in mixed case in the system catalog. (Note that in an SQL-92-compliant database, quoted identifiers are always case-s ensitive.)SQL_IC_MIXED = Quoted identifiers in SQL are not case-sensitive and are stored in mixed case in the system catalog. An SQL-92 Entry level–conformant driver will always return SQL_IC_SENSITIVE. A character string: "Y" if a keyset-driven or mixed cursor maintains row versions or values for all fetched rows and therefore can detect any updates made to a row by any user since the row was last fetched. (This only applies to updates, not to deletions or insertions.) The driver can return the SQL_ROW_UPDATED flag to the row status array when SQLFetchScroll is called. Otherwise, "N".
SQL_SCHEMA_TERM	1.0	A character string with the data source vendor's name for an schema; for example, "owner," "Authorization ID," or "Schema." The character string can be returned in upper, lower, or mixed case. An SQL-92 Entry level–conformant driver will always return "schema". This InfoType has been renamed for ODBC 3.0 from the ODBC 2.0 InfoType SQL_OWNER_TERM.
SQL_SCHEMA_USAGE	2.0	An SQLUINTEGER bitmask enumerating the statements in which schemas can be used: SQL_SU_DML_STATEMENTS = Schemas are supported in all Data Manipulation Language statements: SELECT, INSERT, UPDATE, DELETE, and, if supported, SELECT FOR UPDATE and positioned update and delete statements. SQL_SU_PROCEDURE_INVOCATION = Schemas are supported in the ODBC procedure invocation statement.

continues

Table B.1 Continued

Function	ODBC Version Required	Description

		SQL_SU_TABLE_DEFINITION = Schemas are supported in all table definition statements:
		
		  CREATE TABLE,
		  CREATE VIEW,
		  ALTER TABLE,
		  DROP TABLE, and
		  DROP VIEW.
		
		SQL_SU_INDEX_DEFINITION = Schemas are supported in all index definition statements:
		
		  CREATE INDEX and
		  DROP INDEX.
		
		SQL_SU_PRIVILEGE_DEFINITION = Schemas are supported in all privilege definition statements:
		
		  GRANT and
		  REVOKE.
		
		An SQL-92 Entry level–conformant driver will always return the SQL_SU_DML_STATEMENTS, SQL_SU_TABLE_DEFINITION, and SQL_SU_PRIVILEGE_DEFINITION options as supported. This InfoType has been renamed for ODBC 3.0 from the ODBC 2.0 InfoType SQL_OWNER_USAGE.

SQL_SCROLL_OPTIONS	1.0	An SQLUINTEGER bitmask enumerating the scroll options supported for scrollable cursors. The following bitmasks are used to determine which options are supported:

SQL_SO_FORWARD_ONLY = The cursor only scrolls forward. (ODBC 1.0)SQL_SO_STATIC = The data in the result set is static. (ODBC 2.0) SQL_SO_KEYSET_DRIVEN = The driver saves and uses the keys for every row in the result set. (ODBC 1.0)

SQL_SO_DYNAMIC = The driver keeps the keys for every row in the rowset (the keyset size is the same as the rowset size). (ODBC 1.0)

SQL_SO_MIXED = The driver keeps the keys for every row in the keyset, and the keyset size is greater than the rowset size. The cursor is keyset-driven inside the keyset and dynamic outside the keyset. (ODBC 1.0)

SQL_SEARCH_PATTERN_ESCAPE	1.0	A character string specifying what the driver supports as an escape character that permits the use of the pattern match metacharacters underscore (_) and percent sign (%) as valid characters in search patterns. This escape character applies only for those catalog function arguments that support search strings. If this string is empty, the driver does not support a search-pattern escape character. Since this information type does not indicate general support of the escape character in the LIKE predicate, SQL-92 does not include requirements for this character string. This InfoType is limited to catalog functions.
SQL_SERVER_NAME	1.0	A character string with the actual data source-specific server name; useful when a data source name is used during SQLConnect, SQLDriverConnect, and SQLBrowseConnect.
SQL_SPECIAL_CHARACTERS	2.0	A character string containing all special characters (that is, all characters except a through z, A through Z, 0 through 9, and underscore) that can be used in an identifier name, such as a table, column, or index name, on the data source. For example, "#$^". If an identifier contains one or more of these characters, the identifier must be a delimited identifier.

continues

Table B.1 Continued

Function	ODBC Version Required	Description
SQL_SQL_CONFORMANCE	3.0	An SQLUINTEGER value indicating the level of SQL-92 supported by the driver: SQL_SC_SQL92_ENTRY = Entry level SQL-92 compliant SQL_SC_FIPS127_2_TRANSITIONAL = FIPS 127-2 transitional level compliant SQL_SC_SQL92_FULL = Full level SQL-92 compliant SQL_SC_SQL92_INTERMEDIATE = Intermediate level SQL-92 compliant
SQL_SQL92_DATETIME_FUNCTIONS	3.0	An SQLUINTEGER bitmask enumerating the datetime scalar functions that are supported by the driver and the associated data source, as defined in SQL-92. The following bitmasks are used to determine which datetime functions are supported: SQL_SDF_CURRENT_DATE SQL_SDF_CURRENT_TIME SQL_SDF_CURRENT_TIMESTAMP
SQL_SQL92_FOREIGN_KEY_DELETE_RULE	3.0	An SQLUINTEGER bitmask enumerating the rules supported for a foreign key in a DELETE statement, as defined in SQL-92. The following bitmasks are used to determine which clauses are supported by the data source: SQL_SFKD_CASCADE SQL_SFKD_NO_ACTION SQL_SFKD_SET_DEFAULT SQL_SFKD_SET_NULL An FIPS Transitional level–conformant driver will always return all of these options as supported.
SQL_SQL92_FOREIGN_KEY_UPDATE_RULE	3.0	An SQLUINTEGER bitmask enumerating the rules supported for a foreign key in an UPDATE statement, as defined in SQL-92. The following

bitmasks are used to determine which clauses are supported by the data source:

SQL_SFKU_CASCADE
SQL_SFKU_NO_ACTION
SQL_SFKU_SET_DEFAULT
SQL_SFKU_SET_NULL

An SQL-92 Full level-conformant driver will always return all of these options as supported.

SQL_SQL92_GRANT	3.0

An SQLUINTEGER bitmask enumerating the clauses supported in the GRANT statement, as defined in SQL-92. The SQL-92 or FIPS conformance level at which this features needs to be supported is shown in parentheses next to each bitmask. The following bitmasks are used to determine which clauses are supported by the data source:

SQL_SG_DELETE_TABLE (Entry level)
SQL_SG_INSERT_COLUMN (Intermediate level)
SQL_SG_INSERT_TABLE (Entry level)
SQL_SG_REFERENCES_TABLE (Entry level)
SQL_SG_REFERENCES_COLUMN (Entry level)
SQL_SG_SELECT_TABLE (Entry level)
SQL_SG_UPDATE_COLUMN (Entry level)
SQL_SG_UPDATE_TABLE (Entry level)
SQL_SG_USAGE_ON_DOMAIN (FIPS Transitional level)
SQL_SG_USAGE_ON_CHARACTER_SET (FIPS Transitional level)
SQL_SG_USAGE_ON_COLLATION (FIPS Transitional level)
SQL_SG_USAGE_ON_TRANSLATION (FIPS Transitional level)
QL_SG_WITH_GRANT_OPTION (Entry level)

SQL_SQL92_NUMERIC_VALUE_FUNCTIONS	3.0

An SQLUINTEGER bitmask enumerating the numeric value scalar functions that are supported by the driver and the associated data source, as defined in SQL-92. The following bitmasks are used to determine which numeric functions are supported:

continues

Table B.1 Continued

Function	ODBC Version Required	Description
		SQL_SNVF_BIT_LENGTH
		SQL_SNVF_CHAR_LENGTH
		SQL_SNVF_CHARACTER_LENGTH
		SQL_SNVF_EXTRACT
		SQL_SNVF_OCTET_LENGTH
		SQL_SNVF_POSITION
SQL_SQL92_PREDICATES	3.0	An SQLUINTEGER bitmask enumerating the predicates supported in a SELECT statement, as defined in SQL-92. The SQL-92 or FIPS conformance level at which this features needs to be supported is shown in parentheses next to each bitmask. The following bitmasks are used to determine which options are supported by the data source:
		SQL_SP_BETWEEN (Entry level)
		SQL_SP_COMPARISON (Entry level)
		SQL_SP_EXISTS (Entry level)
		SQL_SP_IN (Entry level)
		SQL_SP_ISNOTNULL (Entry level)
		SQL_SP_ISNULL (Entry level)
		SQL_SP_LIKE (Entry level)
		SQL_SP_MATCH_FULL (Full level)
		SQL_SP_MATCH_PARTIAL (Full level)
		SQL_SP_MATCH_UNIQUE_FULL (Full level)
		SQL_SP_MATCH_UNIQUE_PARTIAL (Full level)
		SQL_SP_OVERLAPS (FIPS Transitional level)
		SQL_SP_QUANTIFIED_COMPARISON (Entry level)
		SQL_SP_UNIQUE (Entry level)

SQL_SQL92_RELATIONAL_JOIN_OPERATORS   3.0

An SQLUINTEGER bitmask enumerating the relational join operators supported in a SELECT statement, as defined in SQL-92. The SQL-92 or FIPS conformance level at which this features needs to be supported is shown in parentheses next to each bitmask. The following bitmasks are used to determine which options are supported by the data source:

SQL_SRJO_CORRESPONDING_CLAUSE (Intermediate level)

SQL_SRJO_CROSS_JOIN (Full level)

SQL_SRJO_EXCEPT_JOIN (Intermediate level)

SQL_SRJO_FULL_OUTER_JOIN (Intermediate level)

SQL_SRJO_INNER_JOIN (FIPS Transitional level)

SQL_SRJO_INTERSECT_JOIN (Intermediate level)

SQL_SRJO_LEFT_OUTER_JOIN (FIPS Transitional level)

SQL_SRJO_NATURAL_JOIN (FIPS Transitional level)

SQL_SRJO_RIGHT_OUTER_JOIN (FIPSTransitional level)

SQL_SRJO_UNION_JOIN (Full level)

SQL_SRJO_INNER_JOIN indicates support for the INNER JOIN syntax, not for the inner join capability. Support for the INNER JOIN syntax is FIPS TRANSITIONAL, while support for the inner join capability is ENTRY.

SQL_SQL92_REVOKE   3.0

An SQLUINTEGER bitmask enumerating the clauses supported in the REVOKE statement, as defined in SQL-92, supported by the data source. The SQL-92 or FIPS conformance level at which this features needs to be supported is shown in parentheses next to each bitmask. The following bitmasks are used to determine which clauses are supported by the data source:

SQL_SR_CASCADE (FIPS Transitional level)

SQL_SR_DELETE_TABLE (Entry level)

SQL_SR_GRANT_OPTION_FOR (Intermediate level)

SQL_SR_INSERT_COLUMN (Intermediate level)

continues

Table B.1 Continued

Function	ODBC Version Required	Description
		SQL_SR_INSERT_TABLE (Entry level)
		SQL_SR_REFERENCES_COLUMN (Entry level)
		SQL_SR_REFERENCES_TABLE (Entry level)
		SQL_SR_RESTRICT (FIPS Transitional level)
		SQL_SR_SELECT_TABLE (Entry level)
		SQL_SR_UPDATE_COLUMN (Entry level)
		SQL_SR_UPDATE_TABLE (Entry level)
		SQL_SR_USAGE_ON_DOMAIN (FIPS Transitional level)
		SQL_SR_USAGE_ON_CHARACTER_SET (FIPS Transitional level)
		SQL_SR_USAGE_ON_COLLATION (FIPS Transitional level)
		SQL_SR_USAGE_ON_TRANSLATION (FIPS Transitional level)
SQL_SQL92_ROW_VALUE_CONSTRUCTOR	3.0	An SQLUINTEGER bitmask enumerating the row value constructor expressions supported in a SELECT statement, as defined in SQL-92. The following bitmasks are used to determine which options are supported by the data source:
		SQL_SRVC_VALUE_EXPRESSION
		SQL_SRVC_NULL
		SQL_SRVC_DEFAULT
		SQL_SRVC_ROW_SUBQUERY
SQL_SQL92_STRING_FUNCTIONS	3.0	An SQLUINTEGER bitmask enumerating the string scalar functions that are supported by the driver and the associated data source, as defined in SQL-92. The following bitmasks are used to determine which string functions are supported:
		SQL_SSF_CONVERT
		SQL_SSF_LOWER
		SQL_SSF_UPPER

		SQL_SSF_SUBSTRING SQL_SSF_TRANSLATE SQL_SSF_TRIM_BOTH SQL_SSF_TRIM_LEADING SQL_SSF_TRIM_TRAILING
SQL_SQL92_VALUE_EXPRESSIONS	3.0	An SQLUINTEGER bitmask enumerating the value expressions supported, as defined in SQL-92. The SQL-92 or FIPS conformance level at which this feature needs to be supported is shown in parentheses next to each bitmask. The following bitmasks are used to determine which options are supported by the data source: SQL_SVE_CASE (Intermediate level) SQL_SVE_CAST (FIPS Transitional level) SQL_SVE_COALESCE (Intermediate level) SQL_SVE_NULLIF (Intermediate level)
SQL_STANDARD_CLI_CONFORMANCE	3.0	An SQLUINTEGER bitmask enumerating the CLI standard or standards to which the driver conforms. The following bitmasks are used to determine which levels the driver conforms to: SQL_SCC_XOPEN_CLI_VERSION1: The driver conforms to the X/Open CLI version 1. SQL_SCC_ISO92_CLI: The driver conforms to the ISO 92 CLI.
SQL_STATIC_CURSOR_ATTRIBUTES2	3.0	An SQLUINTEGER bitmask that describes the attributes of a static cursor that are supported by the driver. This bitmask contains the first subset of attributes; for the second subset, see SQL_STATIC_CURSOR_ATTRIB-UTES2. The following bitmasks are used to determine which attributes are supported: SQL_CA1_NEXT SQL_CA1_ABSOLUTE SQL_CA1_RELATIVE SQL_CA1_BOOKMARK

continues

Table B.1 Continued

Function	ODBC Version Required	Description
		SQL_CA1_LOCK_NO_CHANGE
		SQL_CA1_LOCK_EXCLUSIVE
		SQL_CA1_LOCK_UNLOCK
		SQL_CA1_POS_POSITION
		SQL_CA1_POS_UPDATE
		SQL_CA1_POS_DELETE
		SQL_CA1_POS_REFRESH
		SQL_CA1_POSITIONED_UPDATE
		SQL_CA1_POSITIONED_DELETE
		SQL_CA1_SELECT_FOR_UPDATE
		SQL_CA1_BULK_ADD
		SQL_CA1_BULK_UPDATE_BY_BOOKMARK
		SQL_CA1_BULK_DELETE_BY_BOOKMARK
		SQL_CA1_BULK_FETCH_BY_BOOKMARK
		For descriptions of these bitmasks, see SQL_DYNAMIC_CURSOR_ATTRIBUTES1 (and substitute "static cursor" for "dynamic cursor" in the descriptions). An SQL-92 Intermediate level–conformant driver will usually return the SQL_CA1_NEXT, SQL_CA1_ABSOLUTE, and SQL_CA1_RELATIVE options as supported, because it supports scrollable cursors through the embedded SQL FETCH statement. Since this does not directly determine the underlying SQL support, however, scrollable cursors may not be supported, even for an SQL-92 Intermediate level–conformant driver.
SQL_STATIC_CURSOR_ATTRIBUTES2	3.0	An SQLUINTEGER bitmask that describes the attributes of a static cursor that are supported by the driver. This bitmask contains the second

subset of attributes; for the first subset, see SQL_STATIC_CURSOR_ATTRIBUTES1. The following bitmasks are used to determine which attributes are supported:

SQL_CA2_READ_ONLY_CONCURRENCY
SQL_CA2_LOCK_CONCURRENCY
SQL_CA2_OPT_ROWVER_CONCURRENCY
SQL_CA2_OPT_VALUES_CONCURRENCY
SQL_CA2_SENSITIVITY_ADDITIONS
SQL_CA2_SENSITIVITY_DELETIONS
SQL_CA2_SENSITIVITY_UPDATES
SQL_CA2_MAX_ROWS_SELECT
SQL_CA2_MAX_ROWS_INSERT
SQL_CA2_MAX_ROWS_DELETE
SQL_CA2_MAX_ROWS_UPDATE
SQL_CA2_MAX_ROWS_CATALOG
SQL_CA2_MAX_ROWS_AFFECTS_ALL
SQL_CA2_CRC_EXACT
SQL_CA2_CRC_APPROXIMATE
SQL_CA2_SIMULATE_NON_UNIQUE
SQL_CA2_SIMULATE_TRY_UNIQUE
SQL_CA2_SIMULATE_UNIQUEF

or descriptions of these bitmasks, see SQL_DYNAMIC_CURSOR_ATTRIB-UTES2 (and substitute "static cursor" for "dynamic cursor" in the descriptions).

SQL_STRING_FUNCTIONS 1.0 An SQLUINTEGER bitmask enumerating the scalar string functions supported by the driver and associated data source. The following bitmasks are used to determine which string functions are supported:

SQL_FN_STR_ASCII (ODBC 1.0)
SQL_FN_STR_BIT_LENGTH (ODBC 3.0)
SQL_FN_STR_CHAR (ODBC 1.0)

continues

Table B.1 Continued

Function	ODBC Version Required	Description
		SQL_FN_STR_CHAR_LENGTH (ODBC 3.0)
		SQL_FN_STR_CHARACTER_LENGTH (ODBC 3.0)
		SQL_FN_STR_CONCAT (ODBC 1.0)
		SQL_FN_STR_DIFFERENCE (ODBC 2.0)
		SQL_FN_STR_INSERT (ODBC 1.0)
		SQL_FN_STR_LCASE (ODBC 1.0)
		SQL_FN_STR_LEFT (ODBC 1.0)
		SQL_FN_STR_LENGTH (ODBC 1.0)
		SQL_FN_STR_LOCATE (ODBC 1.0)
		SQL_FN_STR_LTRIM (ODBC 1.0)
		SQL_FN_STR_OCTET_LENGTH (ODBC 3.0)
		SQL_FN_STR_POSITION (ODBC 3.0)
		SQL_FN_STR_REPEAT (ODBC 1.0)
		SQL_FN_STR_REPLACE (ODBC 1.0)
		SQL_FN_STR_RIGHT (ODBC 1.0)
		SQL_FN_STR_RTRIM (ODBC 1.0)
		SQL_FN_STR_SOUNDEX (ODBC 2.0)
		SQL_FN_STR_SPACE (ODBC 2.0)
		SQL_FN_STR_SUBSTRING (ODBC 1.0)
		SQL_FN_STR_UCASE (ODBC 1.0
		If an application can call the LOCATE scalar function with the string_exp1, string_exp2, and start arguments, the driver returns the SQL_FN_STR_LOCATE bitmask. If an application can call the LOCATE scalar function with only the string_exp1 and string_exp2 arguments, the driver returns the SQL_FN_STR_LOCATE_2 bitmask. Drivers that fully support the LOCATE scalar function return both bitmasks.

SQL_SUBQUERIES	2.0	An SQLINTEGER bitmask enumerating the predicates that support sub-queries: SQL_SQ_CORRELATED_SUBQUERIES SQL_SQ_COMPARISON SQL_SQ_EXISTS SQL_SQ_IN SQL_SQ_QUANTIFIED The SQL_SQ_CORRELATED_SUBQUERIES bitmask indicates that all predicates that support subqueries support correlated subqueries. An SQL-92 Entry level–conformant driver will always return a bitmask in which all of these bits are set.
SQL_SYSTEM_FUNCTIONS	1.0	An SQLINTEGER bitmask enumerating the scalar system functions supported by the driver and associated data source. The following bitmasks are used to determine which system functions are supported: SQL_FN_SYS_DBNAME SQL_FN_SYS_IFNULL SQL_FN_SYS_USERNAME
SQL_TABLE_TERM	1.0	A character string with the data source vendor's name for a table; for example, "table" or "file". This character string can be in upper, lower, or mixed case. An SQL-92 Entry level–conformant driver will always return "table".
SQL_TIMEDATE_ADD_INTERVALS	2.0	An SQLINTEGER bitmask enumerating the timestamp intervals supported by the driver and associated data source for the TIMESTAMPADD scalar function. The following bitmasks are used to determine which intervals are supported: SQL_FN_TSI_FRAC_SECOND SQL_FN_TSI_SECOND SQL_FN_TSI_MINUTE SQL_FN_TSI_HOUR

continues

Table B.1 Continued

Function	ODBC Version Required	Description
		SQL_FN_TSI_DAY SQL_FN_TSI_WEEK SQL_FN_TSI_MONTH SQL_FN_TSI_QUARTER SQL_FN_TSI_YEAR A FIPS Transitional level–conformant driver will always return a bit-mask in which all of these bits are set.
SQL_TIMEDATE_DIFF_INTERVALS	2.0	An SQLUINTEGER bitmask enumerating the timestamp intervals supported by the driver and associated data source for the TIMESTAMPDIFF scalar function. The following bitmasks are used to determine which intervals are supported: SQL_FN_TSI_FRAC_SECOND SQL_FN_TSI_SECOND SQL_FN_TSI_MINUTE SQL_FN_TSI_HOUR SQL_FN_TSI_DAY SQL_FN_TSI_WEEK SQL_FN_TSI_MONTH SQL_FN_TSI_QUARTER SQL_FN_TSI_YEAR An FIPS Transitional level–conformant driver will always return a bit-mask in which all of these bits are set.
SQL_TIMEDATE_FUNCTIONS	1.0	An SQLUINTEGER bitmask enumerating the scalar date and time functions supported by the driver and associated data source. The

following bitmasks are used to determine which date and time functions are supported:

SQL_FN_TD_CURRENT_DATE ODBC 3.0)
SQL_FN_TD_CURRENT_TIME (ODBC 3.0)
SQL_FN_TD_CURRENT_TIMESTAMP (ODBC 3.0)
SQL_FN_TD_CURDATE (ODBC 1.0)
SQL_FN_TD_CURTIME (ODBC 1.0)
SQL_FN_TD_DAYNAME (ODBC 2.0)
SQL_FN_TD_DAYOFMONTH (ODBC 1.0)
SQL_FN_TD_DAYOFWEEK (ODBC 1.0)
SQL_FN_TD_DAYOFYEAR (ODBC 1.0)
SQL_FN_TD_EXTRACT (ODBC 3.0)
SQL_FN_TD_HOUR (ODBC 1.0)
SQL_FN_TD_MINUTE (ODBC 1.0)
SQL_FN_TD_MONTH (ODBC 1.0)
SQL_FN_TD_MONTHNAME (ODBC 2.0)
SQL_FN_TD_NOW (ODBC 1.0)
SQL_FN_TD_QUARTER (ODBC 1.0)
SQL_FN_TD_SECOND (ODBC 1.0)
SQL_FN_TD_TIMESTAMPADD (ODBC 2.0)
SQL_FN_TD_TIMESTAMPDIFF (ODBC 2.0)
SQL_FN_TD_WEEK (ODBC 1.0)
SQL_FN_TD_YEAR (ODBC 1.0)

SQL_TXN_CAPABLE   1.0

information type was introduced in ODBC 1.0; each return value is labeled with the version in which it was introduced.
An SQLUSMALLINT value describing the transaction support in the driver or data source:

SQL_TC_NONE = Transactions not supported. (ODBC 1.0)
SQL_TC_DML = Transactions can only contain Data Manipulation Language (DML) statements (SELECT, INSERT, UPDATE, DELETE). Data

continues

Table B.1 Continued

Function	ODBC Version Required	Description
		Definition Language (DDL) statements encountered in a transaction cause an error. (ODBC 1.0)
		SQL_TC_DDL_COMMIT = Transactions can only contain DML statements. DDL statements (CREATE TABLE, DROP INDEX, and so on) encountered in a transaction cause the transaction to be committed. (ODBC 2.0)
		SQL_TC_DDL_IGNORE = Transactions can only contain DML statements. DDL statements encountered in a transaction are ignored. (ODBC 2.0)
		SQL_TC_ALL = Transactions can contain DDL statements and DML statements in any order. (ODBC 1.0)
		(Since support of transactions is mandatory in SQL-92, a SQL-92 conformant driver (any level) will never return SQL_TC_NONE.)
SQL_TXN_ISOLATION_OPTION	1.0	An SQLUINTEGER bitmask enumerating the transaction isolation levels available from the driver or data source. The following bitmasks are used in conjunction with the flag to determine which options are supported:
		SQL_TXN_READ_UNCOMMITTED
		SQL_TXN_READ_COMMITTED
		SQL_TXN_REPEATABLE_READ
		SQL_TXN_SERIALIZABLE
		For descriptions of these isolation levels, see the description of SQL_DEFAULT_TXN_ISOLATION.
		To set the transaction isolation level, an application calls SQLSetConnectAttr to set the SQL_ATTR_TXN_ISOLATION attribute. For more information, see SQLSetConnectAttr. An SQL-92 Entry level-conformant driver will always return SQL_TXN_SERIALIZABLE as

		supported. A FIPS Transitional level–conformant driver will always return all of these options as supported.
SQL_UNION	2.0	An SQLUINTEGER bitmask enumerating the support for the UNION clause: SQL_U_UNION = The data source supports the UNION clause. SQL_U_UNION_ALL = The data source supports the ALL keyword in the UNION clause. (SQLGetInfo returns both SQL_U_UNION and SQL_U_UNION_ALL in this case.) An SQL-92 Entry level–conformant driver will always return both of these options as supported.
SQL_USER_NAME	1.0	A character string with the name used in a particular database, which can be different from the login name.
SQL_XOPEN_CLI_YEAR	3.0	A character string that indicates the year of publication of the X/Open specification with which the version of the ODBC Driver Manager fully complies.

GetStmtOption() / SetStmtOption()

The **GetStmtOption**() and **SetStmtOption**() functions query or set particular options that directly affect a query or other statement that is submitted to a data source. For more information refer to the "Managing ODBC Statement Options" section of Chapter 7. Table B.2 lists the possible constants that can be passed into the **GetStmtOption**() and **SetStmtOption**() functions.

Table B.2 Possible constants that can be passed into the GetStmtOption() and SetStmtOption() functions

Constant	Description
SQL_GET_BOOKMARK	A 32-bit integer value that is the bookmark for the current row. Before using this option, an application must set the SQL_USE_BOOKMARKS statement option to SQL_UB_ON, create a result set, and call SQLExtendedFetch. To return to the rowset starting with the row marked by this bookmark, an application calls SQLExtendedFetch with the SQL_FETCH_BOOKMARK fetch type and irow set to this value. Bookmarks are also returned as column 0 of the result set.
SQL_ROW_NUMBER	A 32-bit integer value that specifies the number of the current row in the entire result set. If the number of the current row cannot be determined or there is no current row, the driver returns 0.
SQL_ASYNC_ENABLE	A 32-bit integer value that specifies whether a function called with the specified hstmt is executed asynchronously: SQL_ASYNC_ENABLE_OFF = Off (the default) SQL_ASYNC_ENABLE_ON = On Once a function has been called asynchronously, no other functions can be called on the hstmt or the hdbc associated with the hstmt except for the original function, SQLAllocStmt, SQLCancel, or SQLGetFunctions, until the original function returns a code other than SQL_STILL_EXECUTING. Any other function called on the hstmt returns SQL_ERROR with an SQLSTATE of S1010 (Function sequence error). Functions can be called on other hstmts. The following functions can be executed asynchronously: SQLColAttributes SQLColumnPrivileges SQLColumns SQLDescribeCol SQLDescribeParam SQLExecDirect

continues

Table B.2 Continued

Constant	Description
	SQLExecute
	SQLExtendedFetch
	SQLFetch
	SQLForeignKeys
	SQLGetData
	SQLGetTypeInfo
	SQLMoreResults
	SQLNumParams
	SQLNumResultCols
	SQLParamData
	SQLPrepare
	SQLPrimaryKeys
	SQLProcedureColumns
	SQLProcedures
	SQLPutData
	SQLSetPos
	SQLSpecialColumns
	SQLStatistics
	SQLTablePrivileges
	SQLTables
SQL_BIND_TYPE	A 32-bit integer value that sets the binding orientation to be used when SQLExtendedFetch is called on the associated hstmt. Column-wise binding is selected by supplying the defined constant SQL_BIND_BY_COLUMN for the argument vParam. Row-wise binding is selected by supplying a value for vParam specifying the length of a structure or an instance of a buffer into which result columns will be bound. The length specified in vParam must include space for all of the bound columns and any padding of the structure or buffer to ensure that when the address of a bound column is incremented with the specified length, the result will point to the beginning of

the same column in the next row. When using the sizeof operator with structures or unions in ANSI C, this behavior is guaranteed.

Column-wise binding is the default binding orientation for SQLExtendedFetch.

SQL_CONCURRENCY

A 32-bit integer value that specifies the cursor concurrency:

SQL_CONCUR_READ_ONLY = Cursor is read-only. No updates are allowed.

SQL_CONCUR_LOCK = Cursor uses the lowest level of locking sufficient to ensure that the row can be updated.

SQL_CONCUR_ROWVER = Cursor uses optimistic concurrency control, comparing row versions, such as SQLBase ROWID or Sybase TIMESTAMP.

SQL_CONCUR_VALUES = Cursor uses optimistic concurrency control, comparing values. The default value is SQL_CONCUR_READ_ONLY. This option cannot be specified for an open cursor and can also be set through the fConcurrency argument in SQLSetScrollOptions.

If the specified concurrency is not supported by the data source, the driver substitutes a different concurrency and returns SQLSTATE 01S02 (Option value changed). For SQL_CONCUR_VALUES, the driver substitutes SQL_CONCUR_ROWVER, and vice versa. For SQL_CONCUR_LOCK, the driver substitutes, in order, SQL_CONCUR_ROWVER or SQL_CONCUR_VALUES.

SQL_CURSOR_TYPE

A 32-bit integer value that specifies the cursor type:

SQL_CURSOR_FORWARD_ONLY = The cursor only scrolls forward.

SQL_CURSOR_STATIC = The data in the result set is static.

SQL_CURSOR_KEYSET_DRIVEN = The driver saves and uses the keys for the number of rows specified in the SQL_KEYSET_SIZE statement option.

SQL_CURSOR_DYNAMIC = The driver only saves and uses the keys for the rows in the rowset.

The default value is SQL_CURSOR_FORWARD_ONLY. This option cannot be specified for an open cursor and can also be set through the crowKeyset argument in SQLSetScrollOptions.

If the specified cursor type is not supported by the data source, the driver substitutes a different cursor type and returns SQLSTATE 01S02 (Option value changed). For a

continues

Table B.2 Continued

Constant	Description
	mixed or dynamic cursor, the driver substitutes, in order, a keyset-driven or static cursor. For a keyset-driven cursor, the driver substitutes a static cursor.
SQL_KEYSET_SIZE	A 32-bit integer value that specifies the number of rows in the keyset for a keyset-driven cursor. If the keyset size is 0 (the default), the cursor is fully keyset-driven. If the keyset size is greater than 0, the cursor is mixed (keyset-driven within the keyset and dynamic outside of the keyset). The default keyset size is 0. If the specified size exceeds the maximum keyset size, the driver substitutes that size and returns SQLSTATE 01S02 (Option value changed). SQLExtendedFetch returns an error if the keyset size is greater than 0 and less than the rowset size.
SQL_MAX_LENGTH	A 32-bit integer value that specifies the maximum amount of data that the driver returns from a character or binary column. If vParam is less than the length of the available data, SQLFetch or SQLGetData truncates the data and returns SQL_SUCCESS. If vParam is 0 (the default), the driver attempts to return all available data. If the specified length is less than the minimum amount of data that the data source can return (the minimum is 254 bytes on many data sources), or greater than the maximum amount of data that the data source can return, the driver substitutes that value and returns SQLSTATE 01S02 (Option value changed). This option is intended to reduce network traffic and should only be supported when the data source (as opposed to the driver) in a multiple-tier driver can implement it. To truncate data, an application should specify the maximum buffer length in the cbValueMax argument in SQLBindCol or SQLGetData. Note In ODBC 1.0, this statement option only applied to SQL_LONGVARCHAR and SQL_LONGVARBINARY columns.
SQL_MAX_ROWS	A 32-bit integer value corresponding to the maximum number of rows to return to the application for a SELECT statement. If vParam equals 0 (the default), then the driver returns all rows.

This option is intended to reduce network traffic. Conceptually, it is applied when the result set is created and limits the result set to the first vParam rows.

If the specified number of rows exceeds the number of rows that can be returned by the data source, the driver substitutes that value and returns SQLSTATE 01S02 (Option value changed).

SQL_NOSCAN

A 32-bit integer value that specifies whether the driver does not scan SQL strings for escape clauses

SQL_NOSCAN_OFF = The driver scans SQL strings for escape clauses (the default).

SQL_NOSCAN_ON = The driver does not scan SQL strings for escape clauses instead, the driver sends the statement directly to the data source.

SQL_QUERY_TIMEOUT

A 32-bit integer value corresponding to the number of seconds to wait for an SQL statement to execute before returning to the application. If vParam equals 0 (the default), then there is no time out.

If the specified timeout exceeds the maximum timeout in the data source or is smaller than the minimum timeout, the driver substitutes that value and returns SQLSTATE 01S02 (Option value changed).

Note that the application need not call SQLFreeStmt with the SQL_CLOSE option to reuse the hstmt if a SELECT statement timed out.

SQL_RETRIEVE_DATA

A 32-bit integer value:

SQL_RD_ON = SQLExtendedFetch retrieves data after it positions the cursor to the specified location. This is the default.

SQL_RD_OFF = SQLExtendedFetch does not retrieve data after it positions the cursor. By setting SQL_RETRIEVE_DATA to SQL_RD_OFF, an application can verify if a row exists or retrieve a bookmark for the row without incurring the overhead of retrieving rows.

SQL_ROWSET_SIZE

A 32-bit integer value that specifies the number of rows in the rowset. This is the number of rows returned by each call to SQLExtendedFetch. The default value is 1. If the specified rowset size exceeds the maximum rowset size supported by the data source, the driver substitutes that value and returns SQLSTATE 01S02 (Option value changed).

continues

Table B.2 Continued

Constant	Description
SQL_SIMULATE_CURSOR	This option can be specified for an open cursor and can also be set through the crowRowset argument in SQLSetScrollOptions. A 32-bit integer value that specifies whether drivers that simulate positioned update and delete statements guarantee that such statements affect only one single row. To simulate positioned update and delete statements, most drivers construct a searched UPDATE or DELETE statement containing a WHERE clause that specifies the value of each column in the current row. Unless these columns comprise a unique key, such a statement may affect more than one row. To guarantee that such statements affect only one row, the driver determines the columns in a unique key and adds these columns to the result set. If an application guarantees that the columns in the result set comprise a unique key, the driver is not required to do so. This may reduce execution time. SQL_SC_NON_UNIQUE = The driver does not guarantee that simulated positioned update or delete statements will affect only one row; it is the application's responsibility to do so. If a statement affects more than one row, SQLExecute or SQLExecDirect returns SQLSTATE 01000 (General warning). SQL_SC_TRY_UNIQUE = The driver attempts to guarantee that simulated positioned update or delete statements affect only one row. The driver always executes such statements, even if they might affect more than one row, such as when there is no unique key. If a statement affects more than one row, SQLExecute or SQLExecDirect returns SQLSTATE 01000 (General warning). SQL_SC_UNIQUE = The driver guarantees that simulated positioned update or delete statements affect only one row. If the driver cannot guarantee this for a given statement, SQLExecDirect or SQLPrepare returns an error. If the specified cursor simulation type is not supported by the data source, the driver substitutes a different simulation type and returns SQLSTATE 01S02 (Option value changed). For SQL_SC_UNIQUE, the driver substitutes, in order, SQL_SC_TRY_UNIQUE or

	SQL_SC_NON_UNIQUE. For SQL_SC_TRY_UNIQUE, the driver substitutes SQL_SC_NON_UNIQUE. If a driver does not simulate positioned update and delete statements, it returns SQL-STATE S1C00 (Driver not capable).
SQL_USE_BOOKMARKS	A 32-bit integer value that specifies whether an application will use bookmarks with a cursor: SQL_UB_OFF = Off (the default) SQL_UB_ON = On To use bookmarks with a cursor, the application must specify this option with the SQL_UB_ON value before opening the cursor.

GetConnectOption() / SetConnectOption()

The **GetConnectOption()** and **SetConnectOption()** methods query and set particular attributes of a database connection. If you query or set any connection attribute it represents and affects not only the database connection that was queried but any cloned connection as well. For more information refer to the "Cloning ODBC Connections" section in Chapter 7.

These two methods are described in detail in the "Managing ODBC Connections" section of Chapter 7. Table B.3 lists the connection options that can be specified in the **GetConnectOption()** and **SetConnectOption()** methods.

Table B.3   Connection options that can be specified in the GetConnectOption() and SetConnectOption() methods

Constant	Description
SQLSQL_ACCESS_MODE	A 32-bit integer value. SQL_MODE_READ_ONLY is used by the driver or data source as an indicator that the connection is not required to support SQL statements that cause updates to occur. This mode can be used to optimize locking strategies, transaction management, or other areas as appropriate to the driver or data source. The driver is not required to prevent such statements from being submitted to the data source. The behavior of the driver and data source when asked to process SQL statements that are not read-only during a read-only connection is implementation defined. SQL_MODE_READ_WRITE is the default.
SQL_AUTOCOMMIT	A 32-bit integer value that specifies whether to use auto-commit or manual-commit mode: SQL_AUTOCOMMIT_OFF = The driver uses manual-commit mode, and the application must explicitly commit or roll back transactions with SQLTransact. SQL_AUTOCOMMIT_ON = The driver uses auto-commit mode. Each statement is committed immediately after it is executed. This is the default. Note that changing from manual-commit mode to auto-commit mode commits any open transactions on the connection. Some data sources delete the access plans and close the cursors for all hstmts on an hdbc each time a statement is committed; autocommit mode can cause this to happen after each statement is executed. For more information, see the SQL_CURSOR_COMMIT_BEHAVIOR and SQL_CURSOR_ROLLBACK_BEHAVIOR information types in SQLGetInfo.
SQL_CURRENT_QUALIFIER	A null-terminated character string containing the name of the qualifier to be used by the data source. For example, in SQL Server, the qualifier is a database, so the driver sends a USE database statement to the data source, where database is the database specified in vParam. For a single-tier driver, the qualifier might be a directory, so the driver changes its current directory to the directory specified in vParam.

continues

Table B.3 Continued

Constant	Description
SQL_LOGIN_TIMEOUT	A 32-bit integer value corresponding to the number of seconds to wait for a login request to complete before returning to the application. The default is driver-dependent and must be nonzero. If vParam is 0, the timeout is disabled and a connection attempt will wait indefinitely. If the specified timeout exceeds the maximum login timeout in the data source, the driver substitutes that value and returns SQLSTATE 01S02 (Option value changed).
SQL_ODBC_CURSORS	A 32-bit option specifying how the Driver Manager uses the ODBC cursor library: SQL_CUR_USE_IF_NEEDED = The Driver Manager uses the ODBC cursor library only if it is needed. If the driver supports the SQL_FETCH_PRIOR option in SQLExtendedFetch, the Driver Manager uses the scrolling capabilities of the driver. Otherwise, it uses the ODBC cursor library. SQL_CUR_USE_ODBC = The Driver Manager uses the ODBC cursor library. SQL_CUR_USE_DRIVER = The Driver Manager uses the scrolling capabilities of the driver. This is the default setting.
SQL_OPT_TRACE	A 32-bit integer value telling the Driver Manager whether to perform tracing: SQL_OPT_TRACE_OFF = Tracing off (the default) SQL_OPT_TRACE_ON = Tracing on When tracing is on, the Driver Manager writes each ODBC function call to the trace file. On Windows and WOW, the Driver Manager writes to the trace file each time any application calls a function. On Windows NT, the Driver Manager writes to the trace file only for the application that turned tracing on. Note: When tracing is on, the Driver Manager can return SQLSTATE IM013 (Trace file error) from any function. An application specifies a trace file with the SQL_OPT_TRACEFILE option. If the file already exists, the Driver Manager appends to the file. Otherwise, it creates the file. If tracing is on and no trace file has been specified, the Driver Manager writes to the file \SQL.LOG. On Windows NT, tracing should only be used for a single application or

each application should specify a different trace file. Otherwise, two or more applications will attempt to open the same trace file at the same time, causing an error.
If the Trace keyword in the [ODBC] section of the ODBC.INI file (or registry) is set to 1 when an application calls SQLAllocEnv, tracing is enabled. On Windows and WOW, it is enabled for all applications; on Windows NT it is enabled only for the application that called SQLAllocEnv.

SQL_OPT_TRACEFILE

A null-terminated character string containing the name of the trace file.
The default value of the SQL_OPT_TRACEFILE option is specified with the TraceFile keyname in the [ODBC] section of the ODBC.INI file (or registry).

SQL_PACKET_SIZE

A 32-bit integer value specifying the network packet size in bytes.
Note Many data sources either do not support this option or can only return the network packet size.
If the specified size exceeds the maximum packet size or is smaller than the minimum packet size, the driver substitutes that value and returns SQLSTATE 01S02 (Option value changed).

SQL_QUIET_MODE

A 32-bit window handle (hwnd).
If the window handle is a null pointer, the driver does not display any dialog boxes.
If the window handle is not a null pointer, it should be the parent window handle of the application. The driver uses this handle to display dialog boxes. This is the default.
If the application has not specified a parent window handle for this option, the driver uses a null parent window handle to display dialog boxes or return in SQLGetConnectOption.
Note: The SQL_QUIET_MODE connection option does not apply to dialog boxes displayed by SQLDriverConnect.

SQL_TRANSLATE_DLL

A null-terminated character string containing the name of a DLL containing the functions SQLDriverToDataSource and SQLDataSourceToDriver that the driver loads and uses to perform tasks such as character set translation. This option may only be specified if the driver has connected to the data source.

continues

Table B.3 Continued

Constant	Description
SQL_TRANSLATE_OPTION	A 32-bit flag value that is passed to the translation DLL. This option may only be specified if the driver has connected to the data source.
SQL_TXN_ISOLATION	A 32-bit bitmask that sets the transaction isolation level for the current hdbc. An application must call SQLTransact to commit or roll back all open transactions on an hdbc, before calling SQLSetConnectOption with this option. The valid values for vParam can be determined by calling SQLGetInfo with fInfoType equal to SQL_TXN_ISOLATION_OPTIONS. The following terms are used to define transaction isolation levels: Dirty Read Transaction 1 changes a row. Transaction 2 reads the changed row before transaction 1 commits the change. If transaction 1 rolls back the change, transaction 2 will have read a row that is considered to have never existed. Non-repeatable Read Transaction 1 reads a row. Transaction 2 updates or deletes that row and commits this change. If transaction 1 attempts to reread the row, it will receive different row values or discover that the row has been deleted. Phantom Transaction 1 reads a set of rows that satisfy some search criteria. Transaction 2 inserts a row that matches the search criteria. If transaction 1 re-executes the statement that read the rows, it receives a different set of rows. vParam must be one of the following values: SQL_TXN_READ_UNCOMMITTED = Dirty reads, nonrepeatable reads, and phantoms are possible. SQL_TXN_READ_COMMITTED = Dirty reads are not possible. Nonrepeatable reads and phantoms are possible. SQL_TXN_REPEATABLE_READ = Dirty reads and nonrepeatable reads are not possible. Phantoms are possible. SQL_TXN_SERIALIZABLE = Transactions are serializable. Dirty reads, nonrepeatable reads, and phantoms are not possible. SQL_TXN_VERSIONING = Transactions are serializable, but higher concurrency is possible than with SQL_TXN_SERIALIZABLE. Dirty reads are not possible. Typically,

SQL_TXN_SERIALIZABLE is implemented by using locking protocols that reduce concurrency and SQL_TXN_VERSIONING is implemented by using a non-locking protocol such as record versioning. Oracle's Read Consistency isolation level is an example of SQL_TXN_VERSIONING.

GetTypeInfo()

GetTypeInfo() returns a dataset that is a table that contains information pertaining to the particular datatype you specified.

You can request type information about the following datatypes:

```
SQL_BIGINT
SQL_BINARY
SQL_BIT
SQL_CHAR
SQL_DATE
SQL_DECIMAL
SQL_DOUBLE
SQL_FLOAT
SQL_INTEGER
SQL_LONGVARBINARY
SQL_LONGVARCHAR
SQL_NUMERIC
SQL_REAL
SQL_SMALLINT
SQL_TIME
SQL_TIMESTAMP
SQL_TINYINT
SQL_VARBINARY
SQL_VARCHAR
```

or a driver-specific data type.

SQL_ALL_TYPES specifies that information about all data types should be returned.

If successful, a dataset will return with the columns documented in Table B.4.

Table B.4 Various constants that can be used with the GetTypeInfo() method

Column Name	Description
TYPE_NAME	Data source-dependent data type name; for example, "CHAR", "VARCHAR", "MONEY", "LONG VARBINARY", or "CHAR ( ) FOR BIT DATA". Applications must use this name in CREATE TABLE and ALTER TABLE statements.
DATA_TYPE	SQL data type. This can be an ODBC SQL data type or a driver-specific SQL data type. For a list of valid ODBC SQL data types, see SQL Data Types.
PRECISION	The maximum precision of the data type on the data source. NULL is returned for data types where precision is not applicable.
LITERAL_PREFIX	Character or characters used to prefix a literal; for example, a single quote (') for character data types or 0x for binary data types; NULL is returned for data types where a literal prefix is not applicable.
LITERAL_SUFFIX	Character or characters used to terminate a literal; for example, a single quote (') for character data types; NULL is returned for data types where a literal suffix is not applicable.
CREATE_PARAMS	Parameters for a data type definition. For example, CREATE_PARAMS for DECIMAL would be "precision,scale"; CREATE_PARAMS for VARCHAR would equal "max length"; NULL is returned if the data type accepts NULL values. CREATE_PARAMS for data type definition, for example INTEGER. The driver supplies the CREATE_PARAMS text in the language of the country where it is used.
NULLABLE	Whether the data type accepts a NULL value: SQL_NO_NULLS if the data type does not accept NULL values. SQL_NULLABLE if the data type accepts NULL values. SQL_NULLABLE_UNKNOWN if it is not known if the column accepts NULL values.
CASE_SENSITIVE	Whether a character data type is case sensitive in collations and comparisons: TRUE if the data type is a character data type and is case sensitive. FALSE if the data type is not a character data type or is not case sensitive.

continues

Table B.4 Continued

Column Name	Description
SEARCHABLE	How the data type is used in a WHERE clause: SQL_UNSEARCHABLE if the data type cannot be used in a WHERE clause. SQL_LIKE_ONLY if the data type can be used in a WHERE clause only with the LIKE predicate. SQL_ALL_EXCEPT_LIKE if the data type can be used in a WHERE clause with all comparison operators except LIKE. SQL_SEARCHABLE if the data type can be used in a WHERE clause with any comparison operator.
UNSIGNED_ATTRIBUTE	Whether the data type is unsigned: TRUE if the data type is unsigned. FALSE if the data type is signed. NULL is returned if the attribute is not applicable to the data type or the data type is not numeric.
MONEY	Whether the data type is a money data type: TRUE if it is a money data type. FALSE if it is not.
AUTO_INCREMENT	Whether the data type is autoincrementing: TRUE if the data type is autoincrementing. FALSE if the data type is not autoincrementing. NULL is returned if the attribute is not applicable to the data type or the data type is not numeric. An application can insert values into a column having this attribute, but cannot update the values in the column.
LOCAL_TYPE_NAME	Localized version of the data source-dependent name of the data type. NULL is returned if a localized name is not supported by the data source. This name is intended for display only, such as in dialog boxes.

MINIMUM_SCALE

The minimum scale of the data type on the data source. If a data type has a fixed scale, the MINIMUM_SCALE and MAXIMUM_SCALE columns both contain this value. For example, an SQL_TIMESTAMP column might have a fixed scale for fractional seconds. NULL is returned where scale is not applicable.

MAXIMUM_SCALE

The maximum scale of the data type on the data source. NULL is returned where scale is not applicable. If the maximum scale is not defined separately on the data source, but is instead defined to be the same as the maximum precision, this column contains the same value as the PRECISION column.

GetFunctions()

The **GetFunctions**() function can accept any of the following statements (even though **Win32::ODBC** does not support all of functions they represent):

```
SQL_API_SQLALLOCCONNECT
SQL_API_SQLALLOCENV
SQL_API_SQLALLOCSTMT
SQL_API_SQLBINDCOL
SQL_API_SQLBINDPARAMETER
SQL_API_SQLBROWSECONNECT
SQL_API_SQLCANCEL
SQL_API_SQLCOLATTRIBUTES
SQL_API_SQLCOLUMNPRIVILEGES
SQL_API_SQLCOLUMNS
SQL_API_SQLCONNECT
SQL_API_SQLDATASOURCES
SQL_API_SQLDESCRIBECOL
SQL_API_SQLDESCRIBEPARAM
SQL_API_SQLDISCONNECT
SQL_API_SQLDRIVERCONNECT
SQL_API_SQLDRIVERS
SQL_API_SQLERROR
SQL_API_SQLEXECDIRECT
SQL_API_SQLEXECUTE
SQL_API_SQLEXTENDEDFETCH
SQL_API_SQLFETCH
SQL_API_SQLFOREIGNKEYS
SQL_API_SQLFREECONNECT
SQL_API_SQLFREEENV
SQL_API_SQLFREESTMT
SQL_API_SQLGETCONNECTOPTION
SQL_API_SQLGETCURSORNAME
SQL_API_SQLGETDATA
SQL_API_SQLGETFUNCTIONS
SQL_API_SQLGETINFO
SQL_API_SQLGETSTMTOPTION
SQL_API_SQLGETTYPEINFO
SQL_API_SQLMORERESULTS
SQL_API_SQLNATIVESQL
SQL_API_SQLNUMPARAMS
SQL_API_SQLNUMRESULTCOLS
SQL_API_SQLPARAMDATA
```

```
SQL_API_SQLPARAMOPTIONS
SQL_API_SQLPREPAR
SQL_API_SQLPRIMARYKEYS
SQL_API_SQLPROCEDURECOLUMNS
SQL_API_SQLPROCEDURES
SQL_API_SQLPUTDATA
SQL_API_SQLROWCOUNT
SQL_API_SQLSETCONNECTOPTION
SQL_API_SQLSETCURSORNAME
SQL_API_SQLSETPARAM
SQL_API_SQLSETPOS
SQL_API_SQLSETSCROLLOPTIONS
SQL_API_SQLSETSTMTOPTION
SQL_API_SQLSPECIALCOLUMNS
SQL_API_SQLSTATISTICS
SQL_API_SQLTABLEPRIVILEGES
SQL_API_SQLTABLES
SQL_API_SQLTRANSACT
```

ColAttributes()

The **ColAttributes()** method describes information about a column in a result set. This method can accept any of the constants in Table B.5. For more information refer to the section "Managing Columns" in Chapter 7.

Table B.5 Various contstants that can be used with the ColAttributes() method

Constant	Description
SQL_COLUMN_AUTO_INCREMENT	TRUE if the column is autoincrement.
	FALSE if the column is not autoincrement or is not numeric.
	Auto increment is valid for numeric data type columns only. An application can insert values into an autoincrement column, but cannot update values in the column.
SQL_COLUMN_CASE_SENSITIVE	TRUE if the column is treated as case sensitive for collations and comparisons.
	FALSE if the column is not treated as case sensitive for collations and comparisons or is noncharacter.
SQL_COLUMN_COUNT	Number of columns available in the result set. The icol argument is ignored.
SQL_COLUMN_DISPLAY_SIZE	Maximum number of characters required to display data from the column.
SQL_COLUMN_LABEL	The column label or title. For example, a column named EmpName might be labeled Employee Name.
	If a column does not have a label, the column name is returned. If the column is unlabeled and unnamed, an empty string is returned.
SQL_COLUMN_LENGTH	The length in bytes of data transferred on an SQLGetData or SQLFetch operation if SQL_C_DEFAULT is specified. For numeric data, this size may be different than the size of the data stored on the data source.
SQL_COLUMN_MONEY	TRUE if the column is money data type.
	FALSE if the column is not money data type.
SQL_COLUMN_NAME	The column name. If the column is unnamed, an empty string is returned.
SQL_COLUMN_NULLABLE	SQL_NO_NULLS if the column does not accept NULL values.
	SQL_NULLABLE if the column accepts NULL values.
	SQL_NULLABLE_UNKNOWN if it is not known if the column accepts NULL values.

SQL_COLUMN_OWNER_NAME	The owner of the table that contains the column. The returned value is implementation-defined if the column is an expression or if the column is part of a view. If the data source does not support owners or the owner name cannot be determined, an empty string is returned.
SQL_COLUMN_PRECISION	The precision of the column on the data source. For more information on precision, see Precision, Scale, Length, and Display Size.
SQL_COLUMN_QUALIFIER_NAME	The qualifier of the table that contains the column. The returned value is implementation-defined if the column is an expression or if the column is part of a view. If the data source does not support qualifiers or the qualifier name cannot be determined, an empty string is returned.
SQL_COLUMN_SCALE	The scale of the column on the data source.
SQL_COLUMN_SEARCHABLE	SQL_UNSEARCHABLE if the column cannot be used in a WHERE clause. SQL_LIKE_ONLY if the column can be used in a WHERE clause only with the LIKE predicate. SQL_ALL_EXCEPT_LIKE if the column can be used in a WHERE clause with all comparison operators except LIKE. SQL_SEARCHABLE if the column can be used in a WHERE clause with any comparison operator. Columns of type SQL_LONGVARCHAR and SQL_LONGVARBINARY usually return SQL_LIKE_ONLY.
SQL_COLUMN_TABLE_NAME	The name of the table that contains the column. The returned value is implementation-defined if the column is an expression or if the column is part of a view. If the table name cannot be determined, an empty string is returned.
SQL_COLUMN_TYPE	SQL data type. This can be an ODBC SQL data type or a driver-specific SQL data type. For a list of valid ODBC SQL data types, see SQL Data Types. For information about driver-specific SQL data types, see the driver's documentation.

continues

Table B.5   Continued

Constant	Description
SQL_COLUMN_TYPE_NAME	Data source-dependent data type name; for example, "CHAR", "VARCHAR", "MONEY", "LONG VARBINARY", or "CHAR ( ) FOR BIT DATA". If the type is unknown, an empty string is returned.
SQL_COLUMN_UNSIGNED	TRUE if the column is unsigned (or not numeric). FALSE if the column is signed.
SQL_COLUMN_UPDATABLE	Column is described by the values for the defined constants: SQL_ATTR_READONLY SQL_ATTR_WRITE SQL_ATTR_READWRITE_UNKNOWN SQL_COLUMN_UPDATABLE describes the updatability of the column in the result set. Whether a column is updatable can be based on the data type, user privileges, and the definition of the result set itself. If it is unclear whether a column is updatable, SQL_ATTR_READWRITE_UNKNOWN should be returned.

Transact()

The **Transact**() method takes one of the two following constants:

- **SQL_COMMIT**. Commits the transaction.
- **SQL_ROLLBACK**. Rolls back all the transactions since the last commit.

Before you can use **Transact**() you need to set the `SQL_AUTOCOMMIT` option to off by using the **SetConnectOption**() method.

When **Transact**() is used, it affects all cloned objects of a connection as well as the connection object itself.

SQLState Values

SQLState values as defined by X/Open Data Management: Structured Query Language (SQL), Version 2 (March 1995). SQLState values are strings that contain five characters. Table B.6 lists SQLState values that a driver can return.

The character string value returned for an SQLState consists of a two-character class value followed by a three-character subclass value. A class value of "`01`" indicates a warning and is accompanied by a return code of `SQL_SUCCESS_WITH_INFO`. Class values other than "`01`", except for the class "`IM`", indicate an error and are accompanied by a return code of `SQL_ERROR`. The class "`IM`" is specific to warnings and errors that derive from the implementation of ODBC itself. The subclass value "`000`" in any class indicates that there is no subclass for that SQLState.

The assignment of class and subclass values is defined by SQL-92.

Note

Although successful execution of a function is normally indicated by a return value of `SQL_SUCCESS`, the SQLState `00000` also indicates success.

The listings in Table B.6 are SQLStates for ODBC 2.5 drivers. ODBC 3.0 changed many of the SQLState codes. If you are using ODBC 3.0 compliant drivers you may run into SQLState code problems. In ODBC 3.0, `HYxxx` SQLSTATEs are returned instead of `S1xxx`, and `42Sxx` SQLSTATEs are returned instead of `S00XX`. This was done to align with X/Open and ISO standards. In many cases, the mapping is not one-to-one because the standards have redefined the interpretation of several SQLSTATEs.

Table B.6 ODBC 2.5 SQLStates and their descriptions

SQLState	Description
01000	General warning
01001	Cursor operation conflict
01002	Disconnect error
01003	NULL value eliminated in set function
01004	String data, right truncated
01006	Privilege not revoked
01007	Privilege not granted
01S00	Invalid connection string attribute
01S01	Error in row
01S02	Option value changed
01S06	Attempt to fetch before the result set returned the first rowset
01S07	Fractional truncation
01S08	Error saving File DSN
01S09	Invalid keyword
07002	COUNT field incorrect
07005	Prepared statement not a cursor-specification
07006	Restricted data type attribute violation
07009	Invalid descriptor index
07S01	Invalid use of default parameter

continues

Code	Description
08001	Client unable to establish connection
08002	Connection name in use
08003	Connection does not exist
08004	Server rejected the connection
08007	Connection failure during transaction
08S01	Communication link failure
21S01	Insert value list does not match column list
21S02	Degree of derived table does not match column list
22001	String data, right truncated
22002	Indicator variable required but not supplied
22003	Numeric value out of range
22007	Invalid datetime format
22008	Datetime field overflow
22012	Division by zero
22015	Interval field overflow
22018	Invalid character value for cast specification
22019	Invalid escape character
22025	Invalid escape sequence
22026	String data, length mismatch
23000	Integrity constraint violation

Table B.6 Continued

SQLState	Description
24000	Invalid cursor state
25000	Invalid transaction state
25S01	Transaction state
25S02	Transaction is still active
25S03	Transaction is rolled back
28000	Invalid authorization specification
34000	Invalid cursor name
3C000	Duplicate cursor name
3D000	Invalid catalog name
3F000	Invalid schema name
40001	Serialization failure
40003	Statement completion unknown
42000	Syntax error or access violation
42S01	Base table or view already exists
42S02	Base table or view not found
42S11	Index already exists
42S12	Index not found
42S21	Column already exists
42S22	Column not found

Code	Description
44000	WITH CHECK OPTION violation
HY000	General error
HY001	Memory allocation error
HY003	Invalid application buffer type
HY004	Invalid SQL data type
HY007	Associated statement is not prepared
HY008	Operation canceled
HY009	Invalid use of null pointer
HY010	Function sequence error
HY011	Attribute cannot be set now
HY012	Invalid transaction operation code
HY013	Memory management error
HY014	Limit on the number of handles exceeded
HY015	No cursor name available
HY016	Cannot modify an implementation row descriptor
HY017	Invalid use of an automatically allocated descriptor handle
HY018	Server declined cancel request
HY019	Non-character and non-binary data sent in pieces
HY020	Attempt to concatenate a null value
HY021	Inconsistent descriptor information

continues

Table B.6 Continued

SQLState	Description
HY024	Invalid attribute value
HY090	Invalid string or buffer length
HY091	Invalid descriptor field identifier
HY092	Invalid attribute/option identifier
HY093	Invalid parameter number
HY095	Function type out of range
HY096	Invalid information type
HY097	Column type out of range
HY098	Scope type out of range
HY099	Nullable type out of range
HY100	Uniqueness option type out of range
HY101	Accuracy option type out of range
HY103	Invalid retrieval code
HY104	Invalid precision or scale value
HY105	Invalid parameter type
HY106	Fetch type out of range
HY107	Row value out of range
HY109	Invalid cursor position
HY110	Invalid driver completion

Code	Description
HY111	Invalid bookmark value
HYC00	Optional feature not implemented
HYT00	Timeout expired
HYT01	Connection timeout expired
IM001	Driver does not support this function
IM002	Data source name not found and no default driver specified
IM003	Specified driver could not be loaded
IM004	Driver's SQLAllocHandle on SQL_HANDLE_ENV failed
IM005	Driver's SQLAllocHandle on SQL_HANDLE_DBC failed
IM006	Driver's SQLSetConnectAttr failed
IM007	No data source or driver specified; dialog prohibited
IM008	Dialog failed
IM009	Unable to load translation DLL
IM010	Data source name too long
IM011	Driver name too long
IM012	DRIVER keyword syntax error
IM013	Trace file error
IM014	Invalid name of File DSN
IM015	Corrupt file data

Scalar Functions

Tables B.7–B.10 provide the function syntax, function descriptions, and ODBC version requirements for the following scalar variables:

- Strings
- Numerics
- Time and date
- System

Table B.7 String Functions

Function	ODBC Version Required	Description
ASCII(*string_exp*)	1.0	Returns the ASCII code value of the leftmost character of string_exp as an integer.
BIT_LENGTH(*string_exp*)	3.0	Returns the length in bits of the string expression.
CHAR(*code*)	1.0	Returns the character that has the ASCII code value specified by code. The value of code should be between 0 and 255; otherwise, the return value is data source–dependent. CHAR_LENGTH(string_exp).
CHAR_LENGTH(*string_exp*)	3.0	Returns the length in characters of the string expression, if the string expression is of a character data type; otherwise, returns the length in bytes of the string expression (the smallest integer not less than the number of bits divided by 8). (This function is the same as the CHARACTER_LENGTH function.)
CHARACTER_LENGTH(*string_exp*)	3.0	Returns the length in characters of the string expression, if the string expression is of a character data type; otherwise, returns the length in bytes of the string expression (the smallest integer not less than the number of bits divided by 8). (This function is the same as the CHAR_LENGTH function.) CONCAT(string_exp1, string_exp2).
CONCAT(*string_exp1, string_exp2*)	1.0	Returns a character string that is the result of concatenating string_exp2 to string_exp1. The resulting string

continues

Table B.7 Continued

Function	ODBC Version Required	Description
		is DBMS-dependent. For example, if the column represented by string_exp1 contained a NULL value, DB2 would return NULL, but SQL Server would return the non-NULL string.
DIFFERENCE(*string_exp1*, *string_exp2*)	2.0	Returns an integer value that indicates the difference between the values returned by the SOUNDEX function for string_exp1 and string_exp2.
INSERT(*string_exp1*, *start*, *length*, *string_exp2*)	1.0	Returns a character string where length characters have been deleted from string_exp1 beginning at start and where string_exp2 has been inserted into string_exp, beginning at start.
LCASE(*string_exp*)	1.0	Returns a string equal to that in string_exp with all uppercase characters converted to lowercase.
LEFT(*string_exp*, *count*)	1.0	Returns the leftmost count characters of string_exp.
LENGTH(*string_exp*)	1.0	Returns the number of characters in string_exp, excluding trailing blanks.
LOCATE(*string_exp1*, *string_exp2[*, *start]*)	1.0	Returns the starting position of the first occurrence of string_exp1 within string_exp2. The search for the first occurrence of string_exp1 begins with the first character position in string_exp2 unless the optional argument, start, is specified. If start is specified, the search begins with the character position indicated by the value of start. The first character position in

string_exp2 is indicated by the value 1. If string_exp1 is not found within string_exp2, the value 0 is returned. If an application can call the LOCATE scalar function with the string_exp1, string_exp2, and start arguments, then the driver returns SQL_FN_STR_LOCATE when SQLGetInfo is called with an Option of SQL_STRING_FUNCTIONS. If the application can call the LOCATE scalar function with only the string_exp1 and string_exp2 arguments, then the driver returns SQL_FN_STR_LOCATE_2 when SQLGetInfo is called with an Option of SQL_STRING_FUNCTIONS. Drivers that support calling the LOCATE function with either two or three arguments return both SQL_FN_STR_LOCATE and SQL_FN_STR_LOCATE_2.

Function	Version	Description
LTRIM(string_exp)	1.0	Returns the characters of string_exp, with leading blanks removed.
OCTET_LENGTH(string_exp)	3.0	Returns the length in bytes of the string expression. The result is the smallest integer not less than the number of bits divided by 8.
POSITION(character_exp IN character_exp)	3.0	Returns the position of the first character expression in the second character expression. The result is an exact numeric with an implementation-defined precision and a scale of 0.
REPEAT(string_exp, count)	1.0	Returns a character string composed of string_exp repeated count times.
REPLACE(string_exp1, string_exp2, string_exp3)	1.0	Search string_exp1 for occurrences of string_exp2 and replace with string_exp3.

continues

Table B.7   Continued

Function	ODBC Version Required	Description
RIGHT(*string_exp*, *count*)	1.0	Returns the rightmost count characters of string_exp.
RTRIM(*string_exp*)	1.0	Returns the characters of string_exp with trailing blanks removed.
SOUNDEX(*string_exp*)	2.0	Returns a data source–dependent character string representing the sound of the words in string_exp. For example, SQL Server returns a 4-digit SOUNDEX code; Oracle returns a phonetic representation of each word.
SPACE(*count*)	2.0	Returns a character string consisting of count spaces.
SUBSTRING(*string_exp*, *start*, *length*)	1.0	Returns a character string that is derived from string_exp beginning at the character position specified by start for length characters.
UCASE(*string_exp*)	1.0	Returns a string equal to that in string_exp with all lowercase characters converted to uppercase.

Table B.8   Numeric Functions

Function	ODBC Version Required	Description
ABS(*numeric_exp*)	1.0	Returns the absolute value of numeric_exp.
ACOS(*float_exp*)	1.0	Returns the arccosine of float_exp as an angle, expressed in radians.

Function	Version	Description
`ASIN(float_exp)`	1.0	Returns the arcsine of float_exp as an angle, expressed in radians.
`ATAN(float_exp)`	1.0	Returns the arctangent of float_exp as an angle, expressed in radians.
`ATAN2(float_exp1, float_exp2)`	2.0	Returns the arctangent of the x and y coordinates, specified by float_exp1 and float_exp2, respectively, as an angle, expressed in radians.
`CEILING(numeric_exp)`	1.0	Returns the smallest integer greater than or equal to numeric_exp.
`COS(float_exp)`	1.0	Returns the cosine of float_exp, where float_exp is an angle expressed in radians.
`COT(float_exp)`	1.0	Returns the cotangent of float_exp, where float_exp is an angle expressed in radians.
`DEGREES(numeric_exp)`	2.0	Returns the number of degrees converted from numeric_exp radians.
`EXP(float_exp)`	1.0	Returns the exponential value of float_exp.
`FLOOR(numeric_exp)`	1.0	Returns the largest integer less than or equal to numeric_exp.
`LOG(float_exp)`	1.0	Returns the natural logarithm of float_exp.
`LOG10(float_exp)`	2.0	Returns the base 10 logarithm of float_exp.
`MOD(integer_exp1, integer_exp2)`	1.0	Returns the remainder (modulus) of integer_exp1 divided by integer_exp2.
`PI()`	1.0	Returns the constant value of pi as a floating point value.

continues

Table B.7   Continued

Function	ODBC Version Required	Description
POWER(*numeric_exp*, *integer_exp*)	2.0	Returns the value of numeric_exp to the power of integer_exp.
RADIANS(*numeric_exp*)	2.0	Returns the number of radians converted from numeric_exp degrees.
RAND([*integer_exp*])	1.0	Returns a random floating point value using integer_exp as the optional seed value.
ROUND(*numeric_exp*, *integer_exp*)	2.0	Returns numeric_exp rounded to integer_exp places right of the decimal point. If integer_exp is negative, numeric_exp is rounded to |integer_exp| places to the left of the decimal point.
SIGN(*numeric_exp*)	1.0	Returns an indicator of the sign of numeric_exp. If numeric_exp is less than zero, −1 is returned. If numeric_exp equals zero, 0 is returned. If numeric_exp is greater than zero, 1 is returned.
SIN(*float_exp*)	1.0	Returns the sine of float_exp, where float_exp is an angle expressed in radians.
SQRT(*float_exp*)	1.0	Returns the square root of float_exp.
TAN(*float_exp*)	1.0	Returns the tangent of float_exp, where float_exp is an angle expressed in radians.
TRUNCATE(*numeric_exp*, *integer_exp*)	2.0	Returns numeric_exp truncated to integer_exp places right of the decimal point. If integer_exp is negative, numeric_exp is truncated to |integer_exp| places to the left of the decimal point.

Table B.9   Time & Date Functions

Function	ODBC Version Required	Description
CURRENT_DATE( )	3.0	Returns the current date.
CURRENT_TIME[(*time-precision*)]	3.0	Returns the current local time. The time-precision argument determines the seconds precision of the returned value.
CURRENT_TIMESTAMP[(*timestamp-precision*)]	3.0	Returns the current local date and local time as a timestamp value. The timestamp-precision argument determines the seconds precision of the returned timestamp.
CURDATE( )	1.0	Returns the current date.
CURTIME( )	1.0	Returns the current local time.
DAYNAME(*date_exp*)	2.0	Returns a character string containing the data source-specific name of the day (for example, Sunday, through Saturday or Sun. through Sat. for a data source that uses English, or Sonntag through Samstag for a data source that uses German) for the day portion of date_exp.
DAYOFMONTH(*date_exp*)	1.0	Returns the day of the month based on the month field in date_exp as an integer value in the range of 1–31.
DAYOFWEEK(*date_exp*)	1.0	Returns the day of the week based on the week field in date_exp as an integer value in the range of 1–7, where 1 represents Sunday.
DAYOFYEAR(*date_exp*)	1.0	Returns the day of the year based on the year field in date_exp as an integer value in the range of 1–366.

continues

Table B.7 Continued

Function	ODBC Version Required	Description
EXTRACT(`extract-field` FROM `extract-source`)	3.0	Returns the extract-field portion of the extract-source. The extract-source argument is a datetime or interval expression. The extract-field argument can be one of the following keywords: YEAR MONTH DAY HOUR MINUTE SECOND The precision of the returned value is implementation-defined. The scale is 0 unless SECOND is specified, in which case the scale is not less than the fractional seconds precision of the extract-source field.
HOUR(`time_exp`)	1.0	Returns the hour based on the hour field in time_exp as an integer value in the range of 0 –23.
MINUTE(`time_exp`)	1.0	Returns the minute based on the minute field in time_exp as an integer value in the range of 0 –59.
MONTH(`date_exp`)	1.0	Returns the month based on the month field in date_exp as an integer value in the range of 1–12.
MONTHNAME(`date_exp`)	2.0	Returns a character string containing the data source-specific name of the month (for example, January through December or Jan. through Dec. for a data source that uses English, or Januar through

Dezember for a data source that uses German) for the month portion of date_exp.

Function	Version	Description
NOW( )	1.0	Returns current date and time as a timestamp value.
QUARTER(date_exp)	1.0	Returns the quarter in date_exp as an integer value in the range of 1–4, where 1 represents January 1 through March 31.
SECOND(time_exp)	1.0	Returns the second based on the second field in time_exp as an integer value in the range of 0–59.
TIMESTAMPADD(interval, integer_exp, timestamp_exp)	2.0	This is not related to SQL Server's timestampdatatypes. Returns the timestamp calculated by adding integer_exp intervals of type interval to timestamp_exp. Valid values of interval are the following keywords:

```
SQL_TSI_FRAC_SECOND
SQL_TSI_SECOND
SQL_TSI_MINUTE
SQL_TSI_HOUR
SQL_TSI_DAY
SQL_TSI_WEEK
SQL_TSI_MONTH
SQL_TSI_QUARTER
SQL_TSI_YEAR
```

where fractional seconds are expressed in billionths of a second. For example, the following SQL statement returns the name of each employee and his or her one-year anniversary date:

SELECT NAME, {fn TIMESTAMPADD(SQL_TSI_YEAR, 1, HIRE_DATE)} FROM EMPLOYEES.

If timestamp_exp is a time value and interval specifies

continues

Table B.7 Continued

Function	ODBC Version Required	Description
		days, weeks, months, quarters, or years, the date portion of timestamp_exp is set to the current date before calculating the resulting timestamp. If timestamp_exp is a date value and interval specifies fractional seconds, seconds, minutes, or hours, the time portion of timestamp_exp is set to 0 before calculating the resulting timestamp. An application determines which intervals a data source supports by calling SQLGetInfo with the SQL_TIMEDATE_ADD_INTERVALS option.
TIMESTAMPDIFF(*interval*, *timestamp_exp1*, *timestamp_exp2*)	2.0	**This is not related to SQL Server's timestamp datatypes.** Returns the integer number of intervals of type interval by which timestamp_exp2 is greater than timestamp_exp1. Valid values of interval are the following keywords: SQL_TSI_FRAC_SECOND SQL_TSI_SECOND SQL_TSI_MINUTE SQL_TSI_HOUR SQL_TSI_DAY SQL_TSI_WEEK SQL_TSI_MONTH SQL_TSI_QUARTER SQL_TSI_YEAR where fractional seconds are expressed in billionths of a

second. For example, the following SQL statement returns the name of each employee and the number of years he or she has been employed.

```
SELECT NAME, {fn TIMESTAMPDIFF(SQL_TSI_YEAR,{fn
CURDATE()}, HIRE_DATE)} FROM EMPLOYEES
```

If either timestamp expression is a time value and interval specifies days, weeks, months, quarters, or years, the date portion of that timestamp is set to the current date before calculating the difference between the timestamps. If either timestamp expression is a date value and interval specifies fractional seconds, seconds, minutes, or hours, the time portion of that timestamp is set to 0 before calculating the difference between the timestamps. An application determines which intervals a data source supports by calling SQLGetInfo with the SQL_TIMEDATE_DIFF_INTERVALS option.

WEEK(date_exp)	1.0	Returns the week of the year based on the week field in date_exp as an integer value in the range of 1–53.
YEAR(date_exp)	1.0	Returns the year based on the year field in date_exp as an integer value. The range is data-source–dependent.

Table B.10 System Functions

Function	ODBC Version Required	Description
DATABASE( )	1.0	Returns the name of the database corresponding to the connection handle. (The name of the database is also available by calling SQLGetConnectOption with the SQL_CURRENT_QUALIFIER connection option.)
IFNULL(exp, value)	1.0	If exp is null, value is returned. If exp is not null, exp is returned. The possible data type or types of value must be compatible with the data type of exp.
USER( )	1.0	Returns the user name in the DBMS. (The user name is also available by way of SQLGetInfo by specifying the information type: SQL_USER_NAME.) This may be different than the login name.

Appendix C

Win32 Network Error Numbers and Their Descriptions

Many of the Win32 Perl extensions make use of networking. However, some error numbers are not able to be resolved using the **Win32::FormatMessage()** function. Table C.1 provides a brief description for those error numbers. It is possible, but unlikely, that the error numbers will change in future versions of Windows.

All of these error codes are accessible by means of the NET.EXE command that comes standard on Win32 machines. This command takes the following format:

```
NET HELPMSG $Error
```

where $Error is an error number such as the numbers listed in Table C.1.

Table C.1   Win32 Error Numbers

Error Number	Description
2102	The workstation driver is not installed.
2103	The server could not be located.
2104	An internal error occurred. The network cannot access a shared memory segment.
2106	This operation is not supported on workstations.
2107	The device is not connected.
2114	The Server service is not started.
2115	The queue is empty.
2116	The device or directory does not exist.
2117	The operation is invalid on a redirected resource.
2118	The name has already been shared.
2119	The server is currently out of the requested resource.
2121	Requested addition of items exceeds the maximum allowed.

continues

Table C.1   Continued

Error Number	Description
2122	The Peer service supports only two simultaneous users.
2123	The API return buffer is too small.
2127	A remote API error occurred.
2131	An error occurred when opening or reading the configuration file.
2136	A general network error occurred.
2137	The Workstation service is in an inconsistent state. Restart the computer before restarting the Workstation service.
2138	The Workstation service has not been started.
2139	The requested information is not available.
2140	An internal Windows NT error occurred.
2141	The server is not configured for transactions.
2142	The requested API is not supported on the remote server.
2143	The event name is invalid.
2144	The computer name already exists on the network. Change it and restart the computer.
2146	The specified component could not be found in the configuration information.
2147	The specified parameter could not be found in the configuration information.
2149	A line in the configuration file is too long.
2150	The printer does not exist.
2151	The print job does not exist.
2152	The printer destination cannot be found.
2153	The printer destination already exists.
2154	The printer queue already exists.
2155	A network resource shortage occurred.
2155	No more printers can be added.
2156	No more print jobs can be added.
2157	No more printer destinations can be added.
2158	This printer destination is idle and cannot accept control operations.
2159	This printer destination request contains an invalid control function.
2160	The print processor is not responding.
2161	The spooler is not running.
2162	This operation cannot be performed on the print destination in its current state.

Error Number	Description
2163	This operation cannot be performed on the printer queue in its current state.
2164	This operation cannot be performed on the print job in its current state.
2165	A spooler memory allocation failure occurred.
2166	The device driver does not exist.
2167	The data type is not supported by the print processor.
2168	The print processor is not installed.
2180	The service database is locked.
2181	The service table is full.
2182	The requested service has already been started.
2183	The service does not respond to control actions.
2184	The service has not been started.
2185	The service name is invalid.
2186	The service is not responding to the control function.
2187	The service control is busy.
2188	The configuration file contains an invalid service program name.
2189	The service could not be controlled in its present state.
2190	The service ended abnormally.
2191	The requested pause or stop is not valid for this service.
2192	The service control dispatcher could not find the service name in the dispatch table.
2193	The service control dispatcher pipe read failed.
2194	A thread for the new service could not be created.
2200	This workstation is already logged on to the local area network.
2201	The workstation is not logged on to the local area network.
2202	The user name or group name parameter is invalid.
2203	The password parameter is invalid.
2204	The logon processor did not add the message alias.
2205	The logon processor did not add the message alias.
2206	The logoff processor did not delete the message alias.
2207	The logoff processor did not delete the message alias.
2209	Network logons are paused.
2210	A centralized logon-server conflict occurred.
2211	The server is configured without a valid user path.
2212	An error occurred while loading or running the logon script.
2214	The logon server was not specified. Your computer will be logged on as STANDALONE.

continues

Table C.1   Continued

Error Number	Description
2215	The logon server could not be found.
2216	There is already a logon domain for this computer.
2217	The logon server could not validate the logon.
2219	The security database could not be found.
2220	The group name could not be found.
2221	The user name could not be found.
2222	The resource name could not be found.
2223	The group already exists.
2224	The user account already exists.
2225	The resource permission list already exists.
2226	This operation is only allowed on the primary domain controller of the domain.
2227	The security database has not been started.
2228	There are too many names in the user accounts database.
2229	A disk I/O failure occurred.
2230	The limit of 64 entries per resource was exceeded.
2231	Deleting a user with a session is not allowed.
2232	The parent directory could not be located.
2233	Unable to add to the security database session cache segment.
2234	This operation is not allowed on this special group.
2235	This user is not cached in user accounts database session cache.
2236	The user already belongs to this group.
2237	The user does not belong to this group.
2238	This user account is undefined.
2239	This user account has expired.
2240	The user is not allowed to log on from this workstation.
2241	The user is not allowed to log on at this time.
2242	The password of this user has expired.
2243	The password of this user cannot change.
2244	This password cannot be used now.
2245	The password is shorter than required.
2246	The password of this user is too recent to change.
2247	The security database is corrupted.
2248	No updates are necessary to this replicant network/local security database.
2249	This replicant database is outdated; synchronization is required.

Error Number	Description
2250	The network connection could not be found.
2251	This message type is invalid.
2252	This device is currently being shared.
2270	The computer name could not be added as a message alias. The name may already exist on the network.
2271	The Messenger service is already started.
2272	The Messenger service failed to start.
2273	The message alias could not be found on the network.
2274	This message alias has already been forwarded.
2275	This message alias has been added but is still forwarded.
2276	This message alias already exists locally.
2277	The maximum number of added message aliases has been exceeded.
2278	The computer name could not be deleted.
2279	Messages cannot be forwarded back to the same workstation.
2280	An error occurred in the domain message processor.
2281	The message was sent.
2282	The message was sent but not received.
2283	The message alias is currently in use. Try again later.
2284	The Messenger service has not been started.
2285	The name is not on the local computer.
2286	The forwarded message alias could not be found on the network.
2287	The message alias table on the remote station is full.
2288	Messages for this alias are not currently being forwarded.
2289	The broadcast message was truncated.
2294	This is an invalid device name.
2295	A write fault occurred.
2297	A duplicate message alias exists on the network.
2298	This message alias will be deleted later.
2299	The message alias was not successfully deleted from all networks.
2300	This operation is not supported on computers with multiple networks.
2310	This shared resource does not exist.
2311	This device is not shared.
2312	A session does not exist with that computer name.
2314	There is not an open file with that identification number.
2315	A failure occurred when executing a remote administration

continues

Table C.1   Continued

Error Number	Description
	command.
2316	A failure occurred when opening a remote temporary file.
2317	The data returned from a remote administration command has been truncated to 64K.
2318	This device cannot be shared as both a spooled and a non-spooled resource.
2319	The information in the list of servers may be incorrect.
2320	The computer is not active in this domain.
2321	The share must be removed from the Distributed File System before it can be deleted.
2331	The operation is invalid for this device.
2332	This device cannot be shared.
2333	This device was not open.
2334	This device name list is invalid.
2335	The queue priority is invalid.
2337	There are no shared communication devices.
2338	The queue you specified does not exist.
2340	This list of devices is invalid.
2341	The requested device is invalid.
2342	This device is already in use by the spooler.
2343	This device is already in use as a communication device.
2351	This computer name is invalid.
2354	The string and prefix specified are too long.
2356	This path component is invalid.
2357	Could not determine the type of input.
2362	The buffer for types is not big enough.
2370	Profile files cannot exceed 64K.
2371	The start offset is out of range.
2372	The system cannot delete current connections to network resources.
2373	The system was unable to parse the command line in this file.
2374	An error occurred while loading the profile file.
2375	Errors occurred while saving the profile file. The profile was partially saved.
2377	Log file is full.
2378	This log file has changed between reads.
2379	Log file is corrupt.

Error Number	Description
2380	The source path cannot be a directory.
2381	The source path is illegal.
2382	The destination path is illegal.
2383	The source and destination paths are on different servers.
2385	The Run server you requested is paused.
2389	An error occurred when communicating with a Run server.
2391	An error occurred when starting a background process.
2392	The shared resource you are connected to could not be found.
2400	The LAN adapter number is invalid.
2401	There are open files on the connection.
2402	Active connections still exist.
2403	This share name or password is invalid.
2404	The device is being accessed by an active process.
2405	The drive letter is in use locally.
2430	The specified client is already registered for the specified event.
2431	The alert table is full.
2432	An invalid or nonexistent alert name was raised.
2433	The alert recipient is invalid.
2434	A user's session with this server has been deleted because the user's logon hours are no longer valid.
2440	The log file does not contain the requested record number.
2450	The user accounts database is not configured correctly.
2451	This operation is not permitted when the Netlogon service is running.
2452	This operation is not allowed on the last administrative account.
2453	Could not find domain controller for this domain.
2454	Could not set logon information for this user.
2455	The Netlogon service has not been started.
2456	Unable to add to the user accounts database.
2457	This server's clock is not synchronized with the primary domain controller's clock.
2458	A password mismatch has been detected.
2460	The server identification does not specify a valid server.
2461	The session identification does not specify a valid session.
2462	The connection identification does not specify a valid connection.
2463	There is no space for another entry in the table of available servers.

continues

Table C.1   Continued

Error Number	Description
2464	The server has reached the maximum number of sessions it supports.
2465	The server has reached the maximum number of connections it supports.
2466	The server cannot open more files because it has reached its maximum number.
2467	There are no alternate servers registered on this server.
2470	Try down-level (remote admin protocol) version of API instead.
2480	The UPS driver could not be accessed by the UPS service.
2481	The UPS service is not configured correctly.
2482	The UPS service could not access the specified Comm Port.
2483	The UPS indicated a line fail or low battery situation. Service not started.
2484	The UPS service failed to perform a system shutdown.
2500	The program below returned an MS-DOS error code:
2501	The program below needs more memory:
2502	The program below called an unsupported MS-DOS function:
2503	The workstation failed to boot.
2504	The file below is corrupt.
2505	No loader is specified in the boot-block definition file.
2506	NetBIOS returned an error: The NCB and SMB are dumped above.
2507	A disk I/O error occurred.
2508	Image parameter substitution failed.
2509	Too many image parameters cross disk sector boundaries.
2510	The image was not generated from an MS-DOS diskette formatted with /S.
2511	Remote boot will be restarted later.
2512	The call to the Remoteboot server failed.
2513	Cannot connect to the Remoteboot server.
2514	Cannot open image file on the Remoteboot server.
2515	Connecting to the Remoteboot server...
2516	Connecting to the Remoteboot server...
2517	Remote boot service was stopped; check the error log for the cause of the problem.
2518	Remote boot startup failed; check the error log for the cause of the problem.
2519	A second connection to a Remoteboot resource is not allowed.

Error Number	Description
2550	The browser service was configured with `MaintainServerList=No`.
2610	Service failed to start since none of the network adapters started with this service.
2611	Service failed to start due to bad startup information in the Registry.
2612	Service failed to start because its database is absent or corrupt.
2613	Service failed to start because `RPLFILES` share is absent.
2614	Service failed to start because `RPLUSER` group is absent.
2615	Cannot enumerate service records.
2616	Workstation record information has been corrupted.
2617	Workstation record was not found.
2618	Workstation name is in use by some other workstation.
2619	Profile record information has been corrupted.
2620	Profile record was not found.
2621	Profile name is in use by some other profile.
2622	There are workstations using this profile.
2623	Configuration record information has been corrupted.
2624	Configuration record was not found.
2625	Adapter ID record information has been corrupted.
2626	An internal service error has occurred.
2627	Vendor ID record information has been corrupted.
2628	Boot block record information has been corrupted.
2629	The user account for this workstation record is missing.
2630	The `RPLUSER` local group could not be found.
2631	Boot block record was not found.
2632	Chosen profile is incompatible with this workstation.
2633	Chosen network adapter id is in use by some other workstation.
2634	There are profiles using this configuration.
2635	There are workstations.
2636	Service failed to backup Remoteboot database.
2637	Adapter record was not found.
2638	Vendor record was not found.
2639	Vendor name is in use by some other vendor record.
2640	(boot name, vendor ID) is in use by some other boot block record.
2641	Configuration name is in use by some other configuration.
2660	The internal database maintained by the Dfs service is corrupt.

continues

Table C.1   Continued

Error Number	Description
2661	One of the records in the internal Dfs database is corrupt.
2662	There is no volume whose entry path matches the input Entry Path.
2663	A volume with the given name already exists.
2664	The server share specified is already shared in the Dfs.
2665	The indicated server share does not support the indicated Dfs volume.
2666	The operation is not valid on a non-leaf volume.
2667	The operation is not valid on a leaf volume.
2668	The operation is ambiguous because the volume has multiple servers.
2669	Unable to create a junction point.
2670	The server is not Dfs Aware.
2671	The specified rename target path is invalid.
2672	The specified Dfs volume is offline.
2673	The specified server is not a server for this volume.
2674	A cycle in the Dfs name was detected.
2675	The operation is not supported on a server-based Dfs.
2690	Dfs internal error.

Information provided courtesy of Microsoft Corporation.

Index

Symbols

$\@Users parameter,
GroupGetMembers() function, 88
%Config hash (CreateProcessAsUser()
function), values, 301-302
%Hash command, tie function, 93
%Values hash, values of, 50
%\Info hash, keys, 56
\@Array parameter, GetServers()
function, 24
/ (forward slashes), 405
0x01 value, SHARED INFO hash, 40

A

aborting system shutdowns, 348-349
ACCESS ALL constant, SHARED INFO
hash, 40
ACCESS ATRIB constant, SHARED
INFO hash, 40
ACCESS CREATE constant, SHARED
INFO hash, 40
ACCESS DELETE constant, SHARED
INFO hash, 40
ACCESS EXEC constant, SHARED
INFO hash, 40
ACCESS NONE constant, SHARED
INFO hash, 39
ACCESS PERM constant, SHARED
INFO hash, 40
ACCESS READ constant, SHARED
INFO hash, 39
ACCESS WRITE constant, SHARED
INFO hash, 40

accessing
COM objects, 166-167
persistent, 167-169
properties, 177-179
named pipes, 213, 217-218
objects from collections,
171-173, 182
shared resources, 205
stacks, 381
$Account parameter (UserDelete()
function), 78
account-based permissions, NetResource
extension, 48
accounts
group
global, 81
local, 81
managing, 80-88
machine
creating, 67-68
types of, specifying, 66
UserCreate() function, 67
UserGetMiscAttributes() function,
70-75
UserSetMiscAttributes() function,
70-75
user
changing, 68-75
creating, 62-66
disabling, 78
global, 81
local, 81
managing, 61-80
removing, 77-79
renaming, 75
testing for existence of, 61
UserCreate() function, 64-65
$AccessMode parameter (Console()
function), 311
$Action parameter (ConfigDSN()
function), 258

G

I

K

M

O

V

X—Z